THE CHARTER OF RIGHTS AND THE LEGALIZATION OF POLITICS IN CANADA

For my parents, Max and Hilda Mandel,
may they rest in peace.

The Charter of Rights and the Legalization of Politics in Canada

Michael Mandel
Associate Professor
Osgoode Hall Law School
YORK UNIVERSITY

WALL & THOMPSON
Toronto

Canadian Cataloguing in Publication Data

Mandel, Michael, 1948–

 The Charter of Rights and the legalization of politics in Canada

Bibliography: p.
Includes index.
ISBN 0–921332–13–0 (bound) ISBN 0–921332–05–X (pbk.)

1. Canada. Canadian Charter of Rights and Freedoms.
2. Canada – Constitutional law – Amendments.
3. Canada – Constitutional law – Interpretation and construction.
4. Judicial power – Canada.
5. Legislative power – Canada.
6. Separation of powers – Canada.
I. Title.

KE4381.5.M36 1989 342.71'085 C88–095306–3
KF4483.C519M36 1989

ISBN 0–921332–13–0 (hardcover)
ISBN 0–921332–05–X (paperback)
Printed in Canada.
1 2 3 4 5 93 92 91 90 89

Table of Contents

Preface

For the critic, the Charter is a lot like one of those video games that rain down invaders on you in ever increasing numbers. Just when you have cleared the screen of threats another squadron comes out of nowhere. Somewhere deep into the writing of this book, I abandoned the idea of dealing comprehensively with all of the interesting developments in the legalization of politics. The sheer mass of Charter litigation and the speed with which its influence is colonizing every corner of Canadian life have made comprehensiveness an impossible quest. There are simply too many lawyers dreaming up too many cases for too many courts. What I have done instead is to try to grasp the essentials of the general phenomenon represented by the Charter. To that end I have used whatever best illustrates those essentials or most seriously challenges my conceptions of them. I have naturally relied on the most recent and important developments, but these should in no way be regarded as the last word on any of the subjects discussed. I mean them mainly as illustrations of a general *approach* to law which neither accepts nor entirely disregards its central premises. The essence of this approach is to treat law as *politics by other means*: to find the politics in law, but also to understand what it means for politics to take on this distinctively legal form.

It is part of the argument of this book that people, judges among them, usually have reasons for the positions they take besides the ones they offer in defence of them. I try to make my arguments against the legalization of politics reflect what I believe to be my motivation for opposing it, but in case I do not succeed, let me say at the outset what it is that I have against this phenomenon *instinctively*.

If nothing else were wrong with legal politics I would still oppose it for its fundamental *dishonesty*. As dishonest politics, it is, in effect, doubly dishonest. It goes one better the ordinary expected dishonesty of conventional politics in the central pretense that it is *not politics at all*, in other words, that power has nothing to do with it. In order to accomplish this, legal politics disguises itself as *interpretation* and then takes us through a maze so complicated that we lose track of what it was we were actually talking about in the first place. The next thing we know, we start talking as if politics did not exist, as if nobody was deciding anything at all, as if the impersonal, impartial *law* was doing all of the deciding. This has always been more or less of a myth in law, but in the era of the Charter (which is really no more than a pretend law) it is just plain phony, and most lawyers know it. We should not encourage phoniness in politics. In my opinion, we should confront our political issues directly.

Then there is the authoritarian nature of the courts which makes the whole thing not only dishonest but also demeaning. *Pleading* is not a democratic form of discourse. It dates from a time when democracy was a dirty word. Expanding that form of discourse to more and more corners of life, as the Charter does, is in effect seeking to return to that time. I do not like the idea of going backwards in history. The courts try to instill in us an acceptance of arbitrary hierarchy, a one-way respect that is not based on whether it is deserved but on the (literally) elevated position of the person we are supposed to respect. The Charter exalts courts even more. I think they should be cut down to size. That is why I wrote this book. I know we can do better than this.

Having a future—or thinking you have—waters the gardens of the mind. As though one lives in two places at the same time.

Bernard Malamud, *God's Grace*

Acknowledgements

I owe so many intellectual and inspirational debts for this book that I do not know what to do with them. In one way or another I have learned something of value from all of my students, colleagues, and friends over almost twenty years of association with Osgoode Hall Law School of York University and for much briefer periods with Atkinson College of York University and with McMaster University. But I have to single out some people. For valuable advice—even if I did not always take it—and much-needed help during the writing of the book: Carl Baar, Joel Bakan, Judy Fudge, Shelley Gavigan, Reuben Hasson, James Hathaway, Peter Hogg, Daniel Latouche, Andrew Petter, Wayne Roberts, and the editorial staff at Wall & Thompson. For dedication beyond the call of a research assistant's duty: Farida Shaikh. For inspiration: Rosa Friscioni, Gina Bizzarro, and Maria Laurenza. For years of patience and hard work on this and other projects: Maggie Stockton. Two special debts: to Daniel Drache, the Canadian Left's own "idea man," whose unfailing enthusiasm and concern for the book gave me something to live up to, and to Harry Glasbeek, who is a full partner in the book's major ideas, all of which were worked out in collaboration with him in 1983 (Glasbeek and Mandel, 1984), not to mention the enormous help he has given me since.

Finally, how do you adequately thank your family without terribly embarrassing the reader? I could point out that none of the people just mentioned actually had to *live* with me while I wrote this book. But it is also a well-known fact that you learn more from the ones you love than from all the books in the world. Thank you Tulla, Max, Giulia and Lucy.

Reprinted with permission — the Toronto Star Syndicate

CHAPTER I

The Legalization of Politics in Canada

"The Kind of Democracy For Which We are All Thankful"

In May of 1985, Operation Dismantle lost the last round of its two-and-a-half year legal battle against the cruise missile. The Ottawa anti-nuclear group had won national media attention by invoking the newly entrenched *Canadian Charter of Rights and Freedoms* in an attempt to stop the Liberal government from allowing the United States to test the controversial weapon here. But the Supreme Court of Canada ruled that the case could not even go to trial (*Operation Dismantle*, 1985). In common with many other lawsuit losers, Operation Dismantle was ordered by the Court to pay the winner's (in this case the federal government's) legal costs as well as its own. But the group had won a lot of sympathy with all the attention it had received, and the government was urged from all sides in the House of Commons to be a good sport and not insist upon the costs. The Prime Minister's vague reply, while bowing to the popularity of the Charter, nevertheless showed traces of unease:

> RIGHT HON. BRIAN MULRONEY (Prime Minister): Mr. Speaker, we are involved in a policy review of the progressively litigious nature of our society as a result of the Charter, and the extent to which the government should and should not properly be involved in some of the funding dimensions. I think it is an important matter. I do not have the answer today. I think it is difficult to anticipate where we might be on these issues in four or five years, given the changes to the Charter. The courts' role will be a progressively important one. We live in the kind of a democracy for which we are all thankful (*House of Commons Debates*, May 10, 1985: 4611).

At the time of writing, not "four or five," but only three years after this statement was made, the Mulroney government, despite its huge majority in Parliament, was floundering in a sea of unpopular issues thrust upon it by the Charter. It had only just managed to pass legislation meant to overcome an enormous backlog of refugee applications which the Supreme Court of Canada had rendered it helpless to clear, and had even contributed to, by its 1985 decision that all refugees in Canada had a right to an oral hearing (*Singh*, 1985). And opponents of the law were already poised, Charter in hand, to strike again (*The Globe and Mail*, July 22, 1988: A9). The government was still trying to find a way of responding to the Supreme Court's bombshell of January 1988, which repealed Canada's abortion law and left no indication of what might replace it (*Morgentaler*, 1988). So far it had failed in two attempts at getting out from under the decision before the fall 1988 election. Trying to appear responsible and decisive and yet to avoid taking a stand on abortion, the government introduced a new concept in legislation, a "menu" of three alternatives, which it wanted MPs to vote on, free of party discipline. When Parliament refused to even discuss that, the government came back with a vaguely worded resolution "in principle." That was voted down, too. The government next claimed that it had to wait for yet another Supreme Court decision before acting.

But it had not been all bad for the government, which turned the Charter to its advantage in one of the high points of its term, the "Meech Lake Accord" of 1987.[1] This constitutional smoke and mirrors trick, which "welcomed Quebec back into the constitutional fold," consisted mainly of sharing out appointments to the Supreme Court of Canada and throwing a few new phrases into the Charter—phrases so ambiguous they could plausibly be sold in English Canada and in Quebec as accomplishing precisely opposite ends.

Is this the kind of democracy we should be thankful for? What kind of democracy is it anyway? Is it any more democratic than the one we had before the Charter? Canadian democracy used to consist of government through representative institutions such as Parliament, the Legislatures, municipal councils, and so on, elected by universal suffrage and answerable to those who elected them by those very electoral means. But these institutions and others as varied as labour unions, hockey leagues, and universities are now being pushed from centre stage and told what they can and cannot do by judges elected by and accountable to nobody. Not only accountable to nobody, but also lacking in any formal restraints, unless one wants to pretend that vague terms such as "fundamental justice" or the new "distinct society" restrain courts in any serious way.

But before we jump to conclusions about the "undemocratic" nature of the Charter, we have to remember why virtually nobody stood up for our representative institutions when they were made subject to it in the first place. Canadian representative democracy did not command great respect in the days before the Charter. While proclaiming the principle of "one-person-one-vote," in practice it was closer to the "one-dollar-one-vote" law of the marketplace. Wealth made itself felt in government in countless ways: through heavy election contributions, highly paid lobbyists, ownership of the media and, most importantly, through the sheer exercise of market power, through investment and de-investment, euphemized by the notion of "business confidence" (Panitch, 1977; Block, 1977). Government maintained an open door policy for this privileged business class, populated "our" Crown corporations, cultural agencies, and Royal Commissions with its members (Drache and Cameron, 1985; Resnick, 1984: 38), socialized with it and even married into it (Johnson, 1984; Francis, 1984), while most people experienced government as just as remote as big business itself: busy signals, long lines, and low-level bureaucrats with standard forms and unchangeable procedures. If we ever saw the

---

[1] As we go to press, the Accord is showing some signs of unravelling (see below), but there is no doubt that it was one of the government's major selling points in its successful campaign for re-election in the fall of 1988.

politicians face-to-face, it was once every four years at election time when they came seeking our vote and said they were interested in our opinion. Between elections, popular contributions to policy making consisted of letters to MPs, which would be answered by assistants using form-letter responses, staged events such as legislative hearings (where the legislators heard but hardly listened), and secret opinion polls which, statistically speaking, you could count on being involved in once in a lifetime. It is indeed appropriate that the three measly provisions under the heading "Democratic Rights" in the Charter guarantee only the right to vote or to run for Parliament once every five years except during wartime (Resnick, 1984: 51).

It was precisely this dissatisfaction with Canadian representative politics that was tapped in the enactment of the Charter. The government promised that it would "transfer power to the people" by giving them the "right to appeal to the courts" (Canada, 1982b: 12–13). It certainly delivered on the right to appeal to the courts. Nowadays it is virtually impossible to open a newspaper or turn on a television or radio without being told that this or that judge, lawyer, or law professor has decided or advised that this or that law or proposed law is or is not contrary to the Charter. From the cruise missile, abortion, and Meech Lake, to tobacco advertising, children's advertising, lawyers', dentists', and doctors' advertising, doctors' extra-billing, girls' hockey, the language of signs, the language of schooling, the funding of schooling, anti-union laws, pro-union laws—you name it and somewhere in this great country of ours some lawyer or court has said something about the application of the Charter to it. And ultimately they not only *say* something about the issues but they actually *decide* them.

Has this transferred "power to the people"? To the people in the legal profession it has. But subjecting us to their power seems an odd way of re-invigorating our democracy. The legal profession is hardly a representative sample of the general population. Law students come "disproportionately from the wealthier classes of societies" (Glasbeek and Hasson, 1987: 783n). Lawyers *are* the wealthier classes, with healthy representation in the economic and political elite (Olsen, 1980: 42–51). In law schools law students head for the business courses in droves and there are plenty to head for. In practice they generally (of course there are exceptions) put themselves at the service of the wealthiest clients they can find (Glasbeek and Hasson, 1987). Nor is it a group particularly well known for integrity.[1] As a profession, lawyers are a variation on the mercenary soldier or the professional mourner, espousing causes for pay, "affecting warmth when you have no warmth, and appearing to be clearly of one opinion when you are in reality of another opinion" (Boswell, 1791: 47). And for professionals, lawyers certainly seem to have a way of getting into trouble with the law. Reports in the press and in law society bulletins of lawyers being disbarred and convicted for misappropriation of clients' funds

---

[1] "And some of the studios I took the script to wanted the twins to be lawyers, instead of gynecologists. I think lawyers are much too sleazy. I would never make a movie about lawyers." (Director David Cronenberg talking about his new movie *Dead Ringers*: *The Globe and Mail*, September 9, 1988: C1.)

are so frequent that they have become routine. (*The Globe and Mail*, March 17, 1988: A3; July 13, 1988; *Canadian Lawyer*, November, 1987: 20; Law Society of Upper Canada, 1980–87). If any group has shown itself unworthy of standing above government as representatives of the people, this is it. Yet the Charter has puffed up lawyers and courts to the point that their values are becoming the most important ones. In a word, the Charter has *legalized* our politics. But legalized politics is the quintessential conservative politics. Not only does the legal profession not have a more democratic technique for resolving political issues—far from it—the legal technique actually *obscures* these issues by dealing with them in abstractions that are meant to disguise the political nature of the choices being made.

This is not mere theory. We have already had more than six years of concrete experience with the Charter. As the ensuing pages will show, its effect, where it has had one, has been the antithesis of democracy both in form and in content. The Charter has done much more than merely replace the formal democracy of the ballot box with the formalities of the legal system. Where the Charter has had an effect, that effect has been to strengthen the already great inequalities in Canada. It has weighed in on the side of power and, in both crude and subtle ways, has undermined popular movements as varied as the anti-nuclear movement, the labour movement, the nationalist movement in Quebec, the aboriginal peoples' movement and the women's movement. Filtering democratic opposition through the legal system has not only failed to reduce Canada's already great social inequalities but has actually strengthened them.

How did this happen?

A Brief History of the Charter

British and American Models

The legalization of politics in Canada has meant a gradual shift from a British to an American conception of the appropriate relations between the legal profession and representative institutions. Until the late 1930s, Canadian lawyers and politicians officially adhered to the traditional British idea of absolute Parliamentary sovereignty, that it was for the legislature to *make* the law and for the judiciary to *apply* it. Though this had always been regarded as the essence of British democracy, we should not forget that for most of its history, Parliament was the official representative, not of the people, but of property. Parliamentary democracy was the product of the English Revolution of the seventeenth century, a struggle against royal power by property holders who were in Parliament by virtue of their property. Until near the end of the nineteenth century only the richest five to ten percent of the English population could vote (Ogilvie, 1982: 284). Though most property qualifications were removed in 1884, only *male* householders were enfranchised. The entire female sex and those of the male sex not meeting the property requirements for householder status were left out of the picture for another 30 years (Ogilvie, 1982: 277). In Canada there was a similar pattern of development, complicated by federal-provincial differences. Property qualifications were gradually eliminated between 1885 and 1898 in federal law, but provincial restrictions remained and sometimes even governed federal elections. Women were not entitled to vote anywhere in Canada until 1917. Universal adult suffrage in federal law was attained only in 1920, when women were enfranchised on the same basis as men, with no property qualifications (Boyer, 1987: 384–388; Ogilvie, 1982: 375). Women continued to be subject to various provincial restrictions, most notably in Quebec until 1940, and various disqualifications existed for Japanese, Chinese, and East Indian Canadians until the middle of the century. Status Indians living on the reserve only became eligible to vote in federal elections in 1960 (Boyer, 1987: 384–391). So full-blown adult suffrage including both sexes and all races, at both the federal and provincial levels, is really only a post-World War II phenomenon. The doctrine of Parliamentary supremacy was a product, therefore, not of democratic ideals but of a narrow power struggle in an era when Parliament represented property, an era lasting in full force to the end of the nineteenth century and vestigially for much of the twentieth.

The doctrine of Parliamentary supremacy did not mean the judiciary was apolitical. In the first place, there were vast areas untouched by Parliament and subject to purely judge-made, so-called "common law." Property, contract, tort, and even criminal law, the essential building blocks of private, class-power relations, were created, maintained, and adapted by the judiciary alone. But even where judges were "applying" the law of Parliament, the power to "interpret" it left them plenty of room to manoeuvre. In Canada there was the added wrinkle of the judicially supervised division of powers between federal and provincial governments under the *BNA Act*. Using this jurisdictional device, the courts were able, when so minded, to defeat legislative initiatives they disagreed with. However, such action was constrained by the necessity for some plausible jurisdictional violation. The evaluation of enactments on their merits was strictly speaking beyond the power of the courts. Their job was to ascertain the meaning of the law and enforce it, on condition only that the purely jurisdictional limitations were respected. The English Judicial Committee of the Privy Council, Canada's real supreme court until 1949, decreed that the courts should adhere to British tradition and not concern themselves with the "wisdom" of legislation when judging its constitutionality:

> In assigning legislative power to the one or the other of these parliaments, it is not made a statutory condition that the exercise of such power shall be, in the opinion of a court of law, discreet. In so far as they possess legislative jurisdiction, the discretion committed to the parliaments, whether of the Dominion or of the provinces, is unfettered. It is the proper function of a court of law to determine what are the limits of the jurisdiction committed them; but, when that point has been settled, courts of law have no right whatever to inquire whether

their jurisdiction has been exercised wisely or not (Lord Watson in *Union Colliery*, 1899: 585).[1]

The American tradition was the opposite of the British one, but its history was not as pretty as one might imagine from the enthusiasm with which we would come to embrace it. It, too, was the result of a revolution in which royal power was displaced, indeed completely overthrown, but after which class power remained. In fact, the major problem for America's upper class was how to combine the popular, republican form of government that was the call to battle of the Revolution with the protection of property, "democratic government which would nevertheless provide full protection for the rights of the wealthy minority" (Galloway, 1982: 19). The solution was a Bill of Rights which gave a federally appointed judiciary a veto over state laws:

...the debate over the Constitution—both during the drafting and during the ratification process—was essentially a debate between defenders of property and defenders of the propertyless in which the latter were resoundingly defeated (Galloway, 1982: 21).

The Constitution contained explicit guarantees to protect British creditors and their wealthy American successors from the attempts of small farmers to rid themselves of their massive debt. It was a period of debtors' revolts (Shays' Rebellion of 1786) and attempts by populist state assemblies to issue paper money, to extend the time for payment of debts, and to rescind British debts entirely. But the constitution provided:

No State shall...make any Thing but gold and silver Coin a Tender in Payment of Debts; pass any...Law impairing the Obligation of Contracts...(*United States Constitution*, Article I, Section 10)

In its first century, the major function of the United States Supreme Court was to fulfil this explicit constitutional mandate by striking down state laws passed to help out debtors. Otherwise, the Court was extremely tolerant of state and federal legislation. This tolerance extended equally to the mild economic regulation measures of the state legislatures and to the racist laws of the southern states. It ended when state legislatures started seriously to regulate the economy towards the end of the nineteenth century. The years 1890–1937 saw judicial review transformed "into a defense not so much of the Constitution as of the natural law (or, more precisely, natural rights) and above all of property rights" (Wolfe, 1986: 4). In their activism on behalf of laissez faire capitalism, the courts did not rely on specific constitutional guarantees, such as those about not impairing debts and so on. They were more creative than that. For example, the procedural guarantee of "due process of law" (*United States Constitution*, Amendments V and XIV) was invoked to strike down legislation which put a limit on the maximum hours an employee could be made to

---

[1] It is worth noting that in the case itself, the Privy Council struck down a racist provincial law providing that "no Chinaman shall be employed in any mine." That they did so on purely jurisdictional grounds, however, is underlined by the fact that the racist provisions of the federal *Chinese Immigration Act 1886* were used in the case to demonstrate the exclusive federal jurisdiction over "Naturalization and Aliens."

work. The Supreme Court claimed that "due process of law" sanctified "freedom of contract" by which it meant that the legislature could not take the worker's side in dealings with the boss (*Lochner*, 1905; Galloway, 1982: 99). In the years leading to the crash of 1929, the Supreme Court paved the way for big business against all attempts at state regulation. When the Depression came and Roosevelt was elected President on the promise of a New Deal program, he was confronted with a Supreme Court thoroughly hostile to his intentions. In 1935–36 the Supreme Court nullified federal legislation providing for farm mortgage relief, industrial unemployment relief, and price supports and subsidies to farmers, as well as state minimum wage legislation, relying alternatively on the sanctity of contract and the federal division of powers. It took an enormous landslide victory for Roosevelt in the 1936 election, followed by a threat to enlarge (and "pack") the Court to persuade one of the Justices to reverse his position and tip the balance in favour of a "deferential" attitude on economic matters. After 1937, "the era of judicial nullification of social welfare laws had come to an end" (Galloway, 1982: 146). But this did not at all mean an end to judicial activism, just a shift in its focus to accommodate the new political terrain. Instead of economic freedoms, it dealt in "civil rights" such as freedom of speech, of religion, and equality before the law. Despite the confrontation with Roosevelt and in the presence of a court appointed mostly by him, the years after 1937 marked "the victory of a distinctly modern understanding of judicial power as fundamentally legislative in character" (Wolfe, 1986: 6).

Canadian Courts and the Depression

Canadian courts of the period, and their British overseers, were no more friendly to regulation of the economy than their American counterparts. They were quite aware of what the US courts were getting away with and were only slightly more inhibited by their limited powers of constitutional interpretation. In short, they held their own in the reactionary fight against regulation of the economy in the first third of this century, using only jurisdictional criteria. In 1916, the judiciary, in effect, deregulated the Canadian insurance industry by striking down federal licensing legislation as a violation of the civil rights of individuals and corporations within their provinces, and therefore an infringement of exclusive provincial jurisdiction (*Attorney General of Canada*, 1916). A few years later they dispatched two federal Acts containing strong measures to deal with postwar profiteering in scarce commodities, including the creation of a Board to investigate and restrict combines, monopolies, trusts, mergers, and the hoarding for "unfair profits" of necessities of life (*Re Board of Commerce Act*, 1923).[1] And when the Great Depression came, they acted just like their US brethren on the Bench and showed no mercy to the "Bennett New Deal" of 1935. This deathbed relief legislation was enacted by the Tories after four years of doing nothing about the Depression other than applying the "iron heel" to labour (Fudge, 1987: 10). The whole program was referred to the courts immediately after the Liberal election victory of 1935 (McNaught,

---

[1] The Judicial Committee of the Privy Council ruled against the laws after the Supreme Court of Canada had divided 3-3.

1976: 252; Pal, 1986: 88; *Attorney General of Canada*, 1936, 1937). Included in it was the *Employment and Social Insurance Act* of 1935, which set up a scheme of compulsory unemployment insurance. "Emergency" had been established in the prior decade as a constitutional exception allowing federal intervention in the marketplace (*Fort Frances Pulp and Power*, 1923). But despite thousands of western farm families on the verge of starvation, over one and a half million Canadians with no source of earned income and an unemployment rate of 23% of the labour force in 1933—compared to 3% in 1929—the Supreme Court of Canada, found "no evidence of an emergency amounting to a national peril" (Justice Rinfret in *Attorney General of Canada*, 1936: 451; McNaught, 1976: 246). No doubt they were aided by a concession to this effect by the lawyer for the unenthusiastic federal government (future Prime Minister Louis St. Laurent). It was not until 1940, with the Depression over, a war on, and people back to work, that Prime Minister Mackenzie King warmed to the idea of unemployment insurance as "a national savings instrument" (Pal, 1986: 91). A constitutional amendment was secured to give Parliament jurisdiction over unemployment insurance and the *Unemployment Insurance Act* was passed.

The judicial slaughter of 1936–37 also included farm relief legislation (the *Natural Products Marketing Act*) and three Acts in compliance with the federal government's 1935 ratification of conventions of the International Labour Organization: *The Weekly Rest in Industrial Undertakings Act*, *The Minimum Wages Act*, and *The Limitation of Hours of Work Act*. Once again the effects of the Depression were minimized:

> It is only necessary to call attention to the phrases in the various cases, "abnormal circumstances," "exceptional conditions," "standard of necessity" (*Board of Commerce* case), "some extraordinary peril to the national life of Canada," "highly exceptional," "epidemic of pestilence" (*Snider's* case), to show how far the present case is from the conditions which may override the normal distribution of powers in ss.91 and 92 (Lord Atkin in *Attorney-General of Canada*, 1937: 353).

All this was done purely within the conventions of the British tradition of Parliamentary sovereignty. However, in the late thirties the Canadian courts also began to flirt with a distinct "civil liberties" jurisdiction comparable to that of the Americans, but without the aid of an explicit Bill of Rights. An important first step was *Re Alberta Statutes* (1938) in which three judges of the Supreme Court of Canada argued that provincial legislation (though not federal legislation) might be judged on its merits alone, if it were bad enough. The legislation in question had been enacted by Alberta's Social Credit government, a government severely out of step with the rest of Canada and one that had made the serious mistake of taking on the banks. The Social Credit movement was a right wing[1] version of Depression anti-capitalism whose left wing counterpart was the Cooperative Commonwealth Federation (CCF) (Schwartz, 1949). Social Credit blamed the Depression on (Jewish) finance

---

[1] It was "right wing" in its religious fundamentalism, anti-semitism, and anti-socialism.

capital, and it came to power in a landslide 1935 election victory with a radical platform aimed at breaking Alberta out of the Depression by abolishing the debt of Alberta farmers and governments and generally increasing the purchasing power of Albertans. The main device was issuing what was in effect its own provincial money in interest-free loans based on the "unused capacity" of the economy, an action reminiscent of the American postrevolutionary assemblies. Legislation was also enacted which directly regulated the credit policies of the banks. This so irked financial circles that the federal government was moved to exercise its long dormant powers of disallowance (Mallory, 1954: 76). Social Credit came back with more carefully worded laws with the same objects. To these were added a law meant to combat its unrelentingly bad press. The law required the press, on pain of closure, to give the government the right and the space to respond to unfavourable expressions of opinion in any newspaper, and to reveal the sources of this unfavourable comment. This time the legislation was referred to the Supreme Court of Canada which unanimously held the credit measures invalid as encroaching on the federal government's exclusive jurisdiction with respect to "Currency," "Banks and Banking," and "Legal Tender." As for the Press Bill, three judges said it stood or fell with the other laws (*Re Alberta Statutes*, 1938: 160–163). But the three other judges, including the influential Chief Justice Duff, asserted the power to quash the law as interfering with Parliament's exclusive jurisdiction—asserted for the first time in this case and derived from the supposed implications of the constitution—over "the right of free public discussion of public affairs":

> Any attempt to abrogate this right of public debate or to suppress the traditional forms of the exercise of the right (in public meeting and through the press) would, in our opinion, be incompetent to the legislatures of the provinces... (*Re Alberta Statutes*, 1938: 134)

The Canadian Bill of Rights

So even before World War II judicial activism in defence of the socio-economic status quo, mostly kept within jurisdictional confines, but with emerging broader ambitions along American lines, was an important feature of Canadian politics. These ambitions were given a great boost by the War itself. From the War came the Canadian movement for an explicit bill of rights to ground judicial activism (Tarnopolsky, 1975: 3ff.). The timing and the way the issue was debated in Parliament would lead us to believe that the movement was inspired by Nazi atrocities, or Canada's own mistreatment of Canadians of Japanese origin during the War. But the heightened anti-racist sentiment provoked by all of this found expression in more traditional legal forms, such as the criminal prohibitions against discriminatory publications in Ontario's *Racial Discrimination Act* of 1944 and the more expansive rights in the *Saskatchewan Bill of Rights Act* of 1947. The latter Act was the prototype for modern provincial human rights codes. It provided specific rights to live free from racial, religious, and other specified types of discrimination in employment, housing, and other services and backed them up with fines and injunctions. However, though it bound the government as well as individuals, its main object was the private sector. It gave the courts no power to nullify laws and was specifically made subject to the law by a provision that it was not to be "construed as derogating from any right, freedom or liberty to which any person or class of persons is entitled under the law" (section 18). The Bill of Rights movement we are concerned with had to do with giving powers to the judiciary *against* the law, and its appeal to those who carried the ball had more to do with fears that emerged during the War about big government's intrusions in the private sector than about racism.

Lawyers were central to the movement. They had become uneasy about the restrictive economic measures which had been undertaken by Cabinet during the War, which by-passed Parliament, and which often cut off access to the courts. Their concerns were expressed in a series of postwar articles written by an early, distinguished advocate of entrenchment, Justice C.H. O'Halloran of the Supreme Court of British Columbia (O'Halloran, 1947). O'Halloran sounded the alarm about the possibilities of Canada becoming a dictatorship on the Nazi-Communist style—he equated the two—because of the diminishing importance of Parliament and the courts in the regulatory state. O'Halloran deplored the shift in power from Parliament to Cabinet and the Civil Service. Worse still was the establishment of regulatory tribunals which were placed by legislation beyond the control of the courts: "they adjudicate without being judges, the tribunals act as Courts without being Courts and often there is no appeal from their decisions to the Courts" (O'Halloran, 1947, No.3: 23).

What seemed to make this especially menacing for O'Halloran was postwar immigration of a non-British type, which he called

> the infiltration of European philosophies (and ways of thinking which owe their origin to those philosophies) to a degree that the peculiar and distinguishing features of the system of law and government which we have inherited may gradually become submerged in what seem to be indigenous habits of thought, of European extraction, which are finding roots particularly among the increasing percentage of the population which has not been invigorated traditionally by the well-tried and long proven principles of the common law (O'Halloran, 1947, No. 3: 21).

Mixed in with the xenophobia was a good measure of cold-warriorism. According to O'Halloran, prominent among these many dangerous foreign ideologies was "Marxian Communism" which, "in its practice which Marx did not live to see," requires that "man must make a complete abandonment of self to the will of the Marxian dictator; he must accept Communist collectivism as his God, and the Communist factory as his church" (O'Halloran, 1947, No.3: 26). It was not long after this that O'Halloran, in his judicial capacity, would rule that adherence to Marxism was outside the protection of the notion of "freedom of opinion" in upholding a British Columbia ban on Communists becoming lawyers (*Martin*, 1950).

The corollary of O'Halloran's arguments against European ideologies was his homage to the American model of government. The emergence of the United States after the War as the pre-eminent economic and military power in the world lent tremendous prestige to its institutions, including its Bill of

Rights. At the end of his four-part article, O'Halloran quoted a Canadian newspaper editorial of 1943 which described the celebration of "Bill of Rights week" in the United States. "It is one of those observances for which the American people seem to have a unique partiality," read the editorial (O'Halloran, 1947, No.3: 29). O'Halloran ended his piece with the following words:

> No Canadian can rest content unless he is convinced that his citizenship as such guarantees to him constitutionally equally full rights as are enjoyed by his friends and neighbours in the United States of America (O'Halloran, 1947, No.3: 30).

A sense of loss of control over government by the legal profession, a fear of new Canadians and collectivist ideologies, and the powerful and prestigious American example, were all elements in the argument of those lawyers anxious to make the judiciary more central to the Canadian constitutional order. To this was added the growing international human rights rhetoric of the Cold War and the ringing declarations of the United Nations Charter (1948) and other international human rights documents, as the two contending ideologies tried to outdo each other in their demonstrated commitment to respect for humanity.

O'Halloran's call for a Bill of Rights struck a chord with the legal profession (How, 1948; Scott, 1949), and the idea of an entrenched Bill of Rights on the American plan found very strong expression from lawyer-Parliamentarians. Even if it had been inspired by less democratic concerns, in Parliament it was always linked to issues of human rights. The Charter, meant by the likes of O'Halloran to *control* immigrants, was made synonymous by Parliamentarians with *enfranchising* them. A CCF member introduced a motion for a Bill of Rights in 1945 (but dropped it immediately in view of the government's promise of a new law on citizenship), and from 1946, the Conservatives' rising star, John Diefenbaker, was committed to it. Diefenbaker made a speech in its favour on April 2, 1946, on the introduction of that very law on citizenship (which abolished national origin designations—"hyphenated citizenship"—for a common Canadian citizenship). The speech was full of praise for the United States, "our friends and kinsmen across the line" (*House of Commons Debates*, April 2, 1946: 510), whose cosmopolitan features were invoked frequently ("no one thinks of Mr. Roosevelt as a Dutch-American": *House of Commons Debates*, April 2, 1946: 511–513). And he placed the Bill of Rights squarely within the ideological struggle of the Cold War:

> To-day in this world two ideologies face one another. If ever there was a time when we should assert and practice what our citizenship means, it is now (*House of Commons Debates*, April 2, 1946: 514).

The proposal appears to have been a popular one with the electorate. In 1947, Diefenbaker tabled a petition with more than half a million names.[1] A Parliamentary debate on the issue took place that year following upon

---

[1] He repeated this feat in 1949 (Romanow et al., 1984: 222–223).

Canada's adherence to the Charter of the United Nations and the Universal Declaration of Human Rights, when the Liberal government set up a committee to study the question of Canada's obligations under these documents. In the debate, the Tories expressed strong support for an entrenched bill of rights, invoking big government, the proliferation of orders-in-council, the ascendancy of boards and tribunals over courts, and the alleged abuses in the investigation of the Gouzenko spy scandal. The CCF also supported such a measure, invoking, for their part, Nazi atrocities, the treatment by the Canadian government of Canadians of Japanese descent during the war, the treatment of Jehovah's Witnesses by the government of Quebec, and the inequality of women. The Liberals were more diffident, and referred to British traditions (a bill of rights represented the "Americanization of Canada": *House of Commons Debates*, May 19, 1947: 3215) and to the existence of Soviet tyranny even though the Soviets had a fine sounding bill of rights. On the other hand, one Liberal member pointed in alarm to the rise of the welfare state in Britain and thought the American system provided better guarantees against a Canadian Parliament introducing a "complete system of Communism or socialism":

> A system of complete socialism or communism cannot be introduced in the United States without a change in the constitution of the United States, whereas in Great Britain a complete system of communism can be introduced by the will of the present parliament (*House of Commons Debates*, May 19, 1947: 3204).

However, only the ultra-conservative Union Nationale representatives from Quebec were firmly opposed in principle:

> In the province of Quebec, no one has the right to commit crimes in the name of freedom and I hope our leaders will never forget that "the word freedom may sometimes lead men into slavery." Because it cherishes freedom, the province of Quebec does not want to be fouled by trouble-makers, anarchists or advocates of revolution. Neither does she want to become a ghetto for the communist-minded Jews from the lowest strata in European countries (*House of Commons Debates*, May 19, 1947: 3228).

The major stumbling block in the view of most of those opposed was the collateral fact that such a bill would interfere with provincial jurisdiction. French-speaking Quebec Liberals, including future Premier of Quebec Jean Lesage, argued that a Bill of Rights should not even be discussed until Canada had attained "full maturity" with its own constitution capable of domestic amendment, to replace the already irksome arrangement whereby an application had to be made to the United Kingdom for all changes to Canada's constitution because it was technically a mere Act of the British Parliament (*House of Commons Debates*, May 16, 1947: 3173, 3212).

Amendment of the *BNA Act* proved to be the stumbling block three years later when a Special Senate Committee reported in favour of a constitutional Bill of Rights but recommended postponing it until there was complete provincial consent and Canada was capable of amending its own constitution. In the meantime, the Committee recommended Parliament enact a strictly federal Bill of Rights (Canada, 1950: 302–307). No agreement on constitutional amendment was forthcoming and the purely federal Bill of Rights had to await the election of a majority Conservative government under John Diefenbaker in 1958.

In the meantime, there was growing sentiment in the legal profession for an end run around the political impasse by the assertion of a broader federal constitutional jurisdiction in civil rights. Three decisions of the Supreme Court of Canada in the 1950s found it warming more and more to the idea of fashioning its own constitutional Bill of Rights, following the lead of the prewar *Alberta Statutes* case. All three decisions had to do with Quebec laws enacted by the Duplessis regime, another provincial government out of step with the rest of Canada. The cases split the Court on ethnic lines and never quite achieved a majority for the "implicit bill of rights" idea. In *Saumur* (1953), a Quebec regulation which was applied in such a way as to discriminate against Jehovah's Witnesses in the distribution of pamphlets was nullified, with four (English) judges invoking an invented federal jurisdiction on "freedom of religion." In *Birks & Sons* (1955), Quebec Sunday closing legislation was unanimously held invalid, with three (English) judges invoking freedom of religion. In *Switzman* (1957), the Court struck down Quebec's anti-communist "Padlock Law" under which houses could be padlocked if used for the "propagation of Communism or Bolshevism." Two (English) judges said only Parliament could interfere with fundamental political liberties and one (Justice Abbott) went so far as to postulate fundamental rights type limitations on *both* Parliament and the provincial legislatures.

At the same time as the Supreme Court of Canada was staking out its own constitutional claims, the United States Supreme Court was entering the most liberal activist period of its history with the appointment of Earl Warren as Chief Justice (Galloway, 1982: 155–163). The immediate post-1937 deference of the Court was followed by a "resurgence of judicial activism." A "major milestone in the growth of modern judicial power" was the desegregation case of *Brown* v. *School Board* (*Brown*, 1954) and this activist impulse was sustained into the 1960s when

> issue after issue was opened to judicial cognizance and decision. By the 1970s, it almost seemed as if it were difficult to find an issue in which some federal judge somewhere might not intervene to lay down the law (Wolfe, 1986: 7).

The influence of US institutions and culture on Canadian life is nothing new, of course. That aspect of the Free Trade debate has been a rather permanent feature of Canadian history. But the Second World War was a major turning point. It demonstrated to everyone the irrevocable decline of the United Kingdom and the ascendancy of the United States as the foremost capitalist power in the world. This had great significance for a former colony of the one situated on the northern border of the other. Common defence agreements between the US and Canada were concluded during the war (McNaught, 1976: 282), and when the nuclear age and the Cold War dawned, with Canada right smack between the US and the USSR, agreements such as NORAD in 1957 were inevitably to subordinate Canadians to the US world outlook. If that were not enough, the economic factors were overwhelming. By the end of the 1950s, seventy per cent of Canadian imports came from the US which also accounted for seventy-five per cent of direct foreign investment, sixty per cent of Canadian exports, and the ownership and control of more than half of Canadian manufacturing and resource industries (McNaught, 1976: 294; Clement, 1975: 102–105).

> The impact of American 'culture patterns' through advertising, magazines, films and television, together with what seemed an almost involuntary entanglement in the American alliance system, could be seen as irreversible signposts to the future (McNaught, 1976: 295).

Canada was not alone in the West in being on the receiving end of US cultural dominance, even if proximity, language, and other similarities made us particularly vulnerable. The division of the world into two great blocks, one dominated by the US, made itself felt in many ways. One of these was the proliferation of the institution of judicial review in the postwar constitutions of states in the American sphere of influence. In the principle Axis powers of (West) Germany and Japan, "the occupation authorities had urged the introduction of judicial review as a way of promoting the democratic way of life" (Ehrmann, 1976: 142). Similar developments occurred in Italy and throughout Latin America (Ehrmann, 1976: 145–146) and in other places where US influence was direct and substantial (United States, 1987: 39).

So, when the newly elected Progressive-Conservative government of John Diefenbaker made good on its campaign promises and introduced a *Canadian Bill of Rights* applicable only to the federal government, the main criticism levelled against it by Canada's leading legal intellectuals was that it did not go far enough.

Most interesting in retrospect is the opinion of Bora Laskin, then of the Faculty of Law of the University of Toronto, who would later, as Chief Justice of Canada, be so closely connected with the whole entrenchment project:

> ...the proposed Bill is unfortunate in its limited application to the federal level of government...It would be better that no Bill be proposed so that the common law tradition be maintained through the unifying force and position of the Supreme Court of Canada. And better too, in such case, to allow that court to continue unaided in developing constitutional doctrine which has already pointed to legal limitations on legislative encroachments on civil liberties (Laskin, 1959: 78).

Expressing the strong centralist inclinations that would characterize his judicial career, Laskin argued that the recent Supreme Court holdings gave the federal government the power to entrench a constitutional bill of rights applicable to the provinces in at least some respects, and he argued strenuously that it should have exercised it (Laskin, 1959: 130–133).

Thus, by 1950 there was strong, probably majority support, for the principle of judicial review among Canadian legal intellectuals. This support was overwhelming by 1959. And it was shared by the political community. The only real obstacles were the extraneous but delicate questions of provincial rights and an amending formula. However, some members of the practising bar

(Council of the Canadian Bar Association, 1959) and the senior judiciary were not yet ready to overthrow tradition and climb on the bandwagon. The period from the enactment of the *Canadian Bill of Rights* in 1960 to 1967 saw the growing enthusiasm dampened as claims were consistently rejected. During this period, Canadian lawyers watched with envy as the United States Supreme Court went into high gear. Though some lower courts tried to emulate their US colleagues, Canadian superior courts firmly resisted the blandishments of litigants and the occasional dissenting justice to use the Diefenbaker document to adopt a US-style posture with respect to federal law. Notable decisions of this period, especially in light of the about-face courts have recently taken on the same issues in the 1980s, were *Robertson and Rosetanni* (1963—"freedom of religion" not applicable to Sunday closing laws) and *Mc-Caud* (1964—"right to a fair hearing" not applicable to parole boards). Nor was this a good time for the "implied bill of rights" theory. In *Oil, Chemical and Atomic Workers Union* (1963), provincial legislation outlawing political contributions from union dues (the opposite of the current Charter issue discussed below in Chapter V) was upheld, by a margin of four judges to three, as within the province's exclusive jurisdiction over labour relations.

Not that questions of civil rights were ignored in this period. Anti-discrimination sentiment in Canada was strong after the War, nurtured by the War itself, postwar immigration, anti-colonialist movements around the world, the drama of the US civil rights movement and so on. Provincial human rights laws forbidding discrimination in accommodation and employment proliferated in the 1950s. In the 1960s they were being consolidated and strengthened in provincial human rights codes enforced by human rights commissions (Williams, 1986: 104–111). But it is important to distinguish between human rights codes on the one hand and the movement for a Bill of Rights on the other. Prohibitions against discrimination in human rights codes are enforced either by traditional means, such as fines or injunctions, or by means which may even *replace* the judiciary with boards composed of non-lawyers. But the movement represented by the *Canadian Bill of Rights* was for a general judicial veto power over legislation, which in its modern manifestation *even includes human rights legislation* (see Chapter VI). Though they overlap in some respects, the differences in form are fundamental. In the period we have been looking at, it was the new role for the judiciary that was encountering obstacles.

The Rise of Quebec Nationalism and the Rise of the Court

Corny as is may seem, the centennial year of 1967 was also a big one for the legalization of politics. A new *Canadian* nationalism appeared on the scene, with a new flag and a new national anthem, both signifying the demise of British influence. The world's fair in Montreal, "Expo 67," also symbolized the coming of age of Quebec and its occupation of centre stage in national politics. Forces of modernization that had been growing slowly within the confines of the intensely repressive and backward Duplessis era burst forth with his death in 1959 and produced the "Quiet Revolution" of 1960–66. During this period, Quebec began to modernize its state, economy, and educational system and to groom an indigenous elite to administer it (Milner and Milner, 1973: 167; McNaught, 1976: 305–6). One result of this was a growing "new middle class" of university or technically educated French Canadians.

> This new class confronted the reality of the social structure of Quebec, and the power of the Anglo-corporate elite. They perceived this elite as a barrier to their own mobility, for executive and management positions in the business world of Quebec had for centuries been an English prerogative (Milner and Milner, 1973: 173).

Very quickly the economic and cultural renaissance turned into a political nationalism which saw the formation of an independentist party in 1960, the Rassemblement pour L'Indépendence Nationale (RIN), and which found expression in the Lesage government's increasing demands on Ottawa for "special status," which meant increased jurisdiction in taxation, social welfare, and foreign and cultural policy, both for the wherewithal to finance the new Quebec and for the political advantages of this nationalist posture. For though it was middle class in leadership, this new nationalism resonated strongly with the overwhelmingly French working class of Quebec (Milner and Milner, 1973: 168; Latouche, 1983).

Quebec's political nationalism produced two tendencies among its intellectual elite. One was represented by René Lévesque, who, in 1964, as a Cabinet Minister in the Lesage government, had already endorsed an "associate state" with "truly special status" or outright "independence" as the only alternatives for Quebec's future (Provencher, 1975: 204–207). The other was represented by Pierre Trudeau, who entered federal politics in 1965 precisely in reaction to the independence tendency. Trudeau saw the "francophone" future in a bilingual Canada. By 1967, the battle lines were firmly drawn, with independentist parties making respectable electoral showings, the FLQ (Front de Libération du Québec) and a host of less-violent nationalist groups increasingly active, and France's President de Gaulle shouting "Vive le Québec Libre!" from a balcony at Montreal's city hall shared by Quebec Premier Daniel Johnson (Granatstein, 1986: 275, 304; McNaught, 1976: 310).

Canada's centennial was also the year Pierre Trudeau became federal Justice Minister and officially inaugurated the entrenchment project, announced in the House of Commons in July by Prime Minister Lester Pearson (*House of Commons Debates*, July 6, 1967: 2299). Trudeau's nineteen-year career in federal politics and the entrenchment project are almost exactly coextensive. He entered federal politics two years before the project was inaugurated under his auspices, and he resigned two years after the new constitution had been enacted. We might even say that the entrenchment project *made* Trudeau and that it was his distinctive contribution to Canadian political life. According to Trudeau, he entered politics "to defend federalism" against "the Lesage Government and public opinion in Quebec [which] had magnified provincial autonomy into an absolute" (Trudeau, 1968: xix). As is well known, Trudeau's essential strategy to fight the centrifugal forces of Quebec nationalism was bilingualism, both inside and outside of Quebec: "Canada must become a truly bilingual country" (Trudeau, 1968: 5). We will pursue the precise details of this strategy and its outcome in Chapter III. For now, it is enough to know that from very early on Trudeau felt that bilingualism was unattainable without the constitutional entrenchment of specific French/English minority language and language of education rights throughout the country (Trudeau, 1968: 48–50).

Naturally, the problem with such a plan was that the federal government could not unilaterally amend the constitution. Since Canada's constitution was an Act of the British Parliament with no domestic amending power, this would require the acquiescence of the British Parliament. That in itself was not the problem. The British government had always been compliant. The problem was the uniform historical practice, the "constitutional convention," that the federal government would not seek amendments to the constitution affecting provincial powers—as entrenched language rights surely would—without the unanimous consent of the provinces affected. And provincial consent to entrenched language rights would not be readily forthcoming. It was here that Trudeau offered a new tactic which capitalized on the growing popularity of the idea of a Bill of Rights. Whereas the Quebec federalists of twenty years before had thought to get constitutional renewal by refusing to discuss a Bill of Rights until *after* there was a new constitution with an acceptable amending power, Trudeau saw it the other way around. Trudeau saw the entrenchment of a general Bill of Rights, that is, one not restricted to language rights, as an *expedient*, as a means to break the bottleneck of constitutional reform, which was itself just an expedient to his goal of entrenched bilingualism. Trudeau believed that the attachment of the popular, indeed increasingly irresistible, idea of a general constitutional bill of rights to any amending proposal would immeasurably enhance its chances of success. And tucked away somewhere in the general bill of rights would be the key to the whole enterprise, entrenched minority language rights.

You do not have to read any secret diaries to find this out. Trudeau was very explicit about it at the beginning of his career. In his first speech as Justice Minister to the Canadian Bar Association in September 1967, he said:

[M]inisters and officials have been looking for the best basis on which to begin a dialogue on constitutional reform between the federal government and the provincial governments. We have reached the conclusion that the basis most likely to find a wide degree of acceptance, and one that is in itself a matter calling for urgent attention, is a constitutional Bill of Rights...

As lawyers, you will appreciate that the adoption of a constitutional Bill of Rights is intimately related to the whole question of constitutional reform...

[A]greement on a process whereby a Bill of Rights would be entrenched in the constitution will raise other basic constitutional issues. First, what procedure is to be followed in amending the constitution? How is the Bill to be entrenched? Shall we ask the Parliament at Westminster to enact the necessary changes in the British North America Act? Or will we finally agree on a formula for amending our constitution in Canada? It is inevitable that discussion of an entrenched Bill of Rights will lead to a renewed attempt to agree upon an amending formula—something we have failed to achieve after years of effort (Trudeau, 1968: 54–57).

In his speech Trudeau emphasized the importance of language to his scheme:

We all agree on the familiar basic rights...But there are rights of special importance to Canada arising, as I have said, from the fact that this country is founded on two distinct linguistic groups (Trudeau, 1968: 55).

But when it came to horse-trading fourteen years down the line, these "familiar basic rights" would place a distant constitutional second place to the others, demonstrating once again what was the means and what was the end.

In February of 1968, the entrenchment of a Charter of Rights was being advocated on television by the new Justice Minister at the proceedings of a federal-provincial constitutional conference. In April, Trudeau became leader of the Liberal Party and Prime Minister in a minority Liberal government. That June the Liberals won a majority in a federal election. The same year the Parti Québécois was formed with Lévesque its leader. The next few years saw Canadian politics dominated by the question of language, Quebec, and the Constitution: the controversial (for English Canada) *Official Languages Act* in 1969, the Quebec election of April 1970 which returned the Liberals despite a strong PQ showing, the "October crisis" of the same year, and the 1971 Victoria Conference (the fourth federal-provincial constitutional meeting in the series started in 1968), where agreement on a Charter and an amending formula were reached but never consummated because of arguments over the division of powers and second thoughts on the part of Quebec (Romanow et al., 1984: 232). We will return to these events in Chapter III.

It would be surprising if these events had left the courts untouched. They did not. A little known centennial event in the Northwest Territories that made great legal waves was the plea of guilty by Joseph Drybones to a charge of being "intoxicated off a reserve" in April 1967, contrary to a section of the *Indian Act* applicable only to Indians. The liquor laws generally applicable in the Northwest Territories were restricted to intoxication in a public place, whereas the *Indian Act* offence could theoretically take place in private, and the penalties were stiffer under the *Indian Act*. On the other hand, the inequality was purely technical in Drybones's case. He was indeed in a public place and was sentenced to the minimum fine of $10. The matter would have ended there but for the intervention of an activist Territorial Court Judge by the name of William G. Morrow, who not only advised an appeal, but actually heard it himself (Tarnopolsky, 1975: 135). Morrow found the inequality contrary to the *Canadian Bill of Rights* and declared the section "inoperative." The British Columbia Court of Appeal unanimously agreed and on a further appeal, *Drybones* (1969), a split decision of six judges to three, became the first decision of the Supreme Court of Canada to overrule federal legislation with the *Canadian Bill of Rights*. Though hailed as a milestone by the growing Charter of Rights faction, *Drybones* was a complicated, indeed curious decision. On the one hand, it advanced a pure, almost simple-minded egalitarianism against the special status Canada's aboriginal peoples were right then trying to maintain in the face of federal initiatives. A few months before, Trudeau had proposed to repeal the *Indian Act* altogether, applying his distaste for "special status" in Quebec to a quite different situation (Sanders, 1985: 538–539). This was met with massive Indian opposition and was subsequently withdrawn, but it remained a symbol to Canada's aboriginal peoples of the dangers lurking in the entrenchment project (see Chapter VI). This may partially explain the odd reversal of roles that occurred among traditional conservatives and liberals on the subject of judicial review in the Supreme Court of Canada. Those who had previously been in favour of judicial review now opposed it on the ground that the mandate was not clear enough to take such a radical step against the *Indian Act*. Chief Justice Cartwright repudiated his own activist dissent in *Robertson and Rosetanni* (1963). On the other hand, the majority threw together liberals and conservatives, including Justices Ritchie and Martland (both Diefenbaker appointees), once and future staunch opponents of judicial review in general and the Trudeau entrenchment program in particular. But *Drybones* was argued in October 1968, after the announcement of the entrenchment project and the election of Trudeau as Prime Minister with the first majority since Diefenbaker. It is just possible that with the entrenchment project now on the table, the activist judges were holding out for and hoping to encourage a stronger mandate, while the conservative judges were trying to slake the growing thirst for judicial review by reviving a document that had by then become a bad joke in legal circles. Certainly this would help explain why the decision in *Drybones*, while raising great expectations in certain quarters of the legal profession, did not usher in a new era in judicial review. Having affirmed its power, a majority of the Court consistently refrained from exercising it by resorting to its prior posture of interpreting the *Bill* so as to avoid conflicts with existing laws.

However, immediately after the decision in *Drybones*, a new dimension was added with Trudeau's appointment of Bora Laskin to the Supreme Court of Canada in March, 1970. Laskin brought to the Supreme Court his strong beliefs in American-style judicial activism (he had graduated from Harvard with a Master's Degree in 1937) as well as his dissatisfaction with the Diefenbaker Bill as a vehicle for it. In the early cases Laskin found it possible to agree with the majority while legitimizing a more American-style approach in his reasoning. However, this broke out into open dissent in *Lavell* (1973), another case involving the *Indian Act*, this time a section which disenfranchised Indian women—but not Indian men—who married non-Indians. By a margin of five to four, the law was upheld. This required a virtual repudiation of the *Drybones* decision by the very judges who had written it. The decision went down in infamy for Canadian women, but a contributing factor was the large (male) Indian presence in the case in defence of the *Indian Act* (Sanders, 1985: 540–547).

The dissent in *Lavell* included a particularly outspoken excoriation of the legislation by Judge Laskin who called it "invidious," "a statutory excommunication," and "banishment." This was obviously more to the Prime Minister's liking, because not four months later Trudeau showed his confidence in

Laskin's style of judging by breaking a long tradition to appoint him Chief Justice of Canada. Tradition had it that the low-profile appointment went to the Supreme Court Justice next in seniority, and the tradition had only been broken twice in the Court's entire history, the last time in 1924 to avoid the appointment of a judge who was a political opponent of the Prime Minister and who also had a severe drinking problem (Snell and Vaughan, 1985: 122, 224). But Trudeau passed over five senior judges to appoint Laskin in a move that simultaneously put the judge most to Trudeau's liking in the spotlight and attested to—indeed added to—the bench's growing importance in Canadian politics.

This turned out to be a very important step in the legalization of politics. After his appointment as Chief Justice, the divisions in the Court continued, but Laskin's new high profile gave far more force to his dissents than would otherwise have been the case. Media attention (and support for Laskin in the federal government) was such that in at least two cases in 1975, *Mitchell* (prisoners' rights) and *Morgentaler* (abortion), the dissents resulted in immediate announcements that the laws in question would be changed to reflect Laskin's dissenting opinions.[1] In these cases and others, such as his separate concurring opinion in *Miller and Cockriell* (1976—capital punishment), Laskin showed great enthusiasm for US-style assessment of legislation while avoiding actual radicality of decision.

By the middle of 1976, the Supreme Court was a very different institution from what it had been in 1967. In 1967, the English language press was lamenting the "weakness and timidity" of the Supreme Court in comparison to its US counterpart and urging that it be made "a stronger and more constructive force in our national life" (Snell and Vaughan, 1985: 226). By 1976, a high-profile Chief Justice was battling to increase the Court's role in politics, with the full support of the government. Besides the entrenchment project and the appointment of Laskin, the government had amended the *Supreme Court Act* in 1975 to give the Court greater control over the cases it would hear. Now the major factor would be whether, in the justices' opinion, the case involved an issue of "public importance" sufficient "to warrant decision by it" (*An Act to Amend the Supreme Court Act*, s.5). The Court effectively ceased being a court of further appeal between parties with private disputes. Henceforth, virtually all of its judgments would be, by definition, of "public importance," with a concomitant enhancement in the status and prestige of the Court. The Court itself expanded its own jurisdiction by rewriting the rules on "standing" in constitutional cases. Prior to 1975, only governments, or persons specially affected by a law, could challenge its constitutional validity. But in *Thorson* (1975), the Supreme Court of Canada decided that any taxpayer could challenge the constitutionality of any statute, reserving to itself a residual discre-

---

[1] *The Globe and Mail*, October 8, 1975: 8. In *Morgentaler*, it was not the abortion law itself that provoked the dissent but the power of a court of appeal to reverse a jury acquittal without a new trial. It was this power that was repealed within a year of the decision (*Criminal Law Amendment Act 1975*, s. 75).

tion to refuse cases it deemed unworthy of its attention.

The Election of the PQ and the Entrenchment Project

The spectacular and unexpected electoral victory of the Parti Québécois in the Quebec provincial elections of November 1976 considerably changed the pace of things. What had been a gradual strategy became a question of great urgency. The PQ government began immediately to enact its nationalist program and to plan for a referendum on "sovereignty-association." From the federal government's point of view, the timing was bad. As the recession deepened, with unemployment and inflation rates both higher than they had ever been since the War, an increasingly unpopular Liberal government faced irreconcilable demands from mostly Conservative provincial governments. The 1973 "energy crisis" gave new clout to the oil-producing provinces, especially Alberta, and pitted them against the industrial centre over the question of who should control natural resources (Romanow et al., 1984: xvii–xx). This was not a good atmosphere for urgent action on the constitution, and the federal government's attempts to convince English Canadians to put aside their material concerns and think about Quebec, through staged events like the 1977 star-studded "Task Force on Canadian Unity," simply did not work. In 1978, his hand forced by PQ government initiatives, especially the unilingualism of Bill 101 (see Chapter III), Trudeau introduced Bill C–60, the centrepiece of which was a constitutional Charter of Rights. Though initially applicable to the federal government and to provincial governments only at their option, Bill C–60 also contemplated full entrenchment according to a then unspecified amending formula (Bill C–60, 1978: s.131). The Bill was explicitly linked to the Quebec situation, as the government tried to sell it (and the Liberal Party) to the rest of Canada on the basis of "the crisis threatening the stability, unity and prosperity of the country" and "events in Quebec [which] were making the task of constitutional renewal more important and more urgent than ever" (Canada, 1978: 8, 21).

None of this could save the Liberals from electoral defeat at the hands of the Tories in May 1979. This emboldened the PQ government to hold its referendum on "a mandate to negotiate sovereignty association" which was announced in December. But the Tory interregnum was unexpectedly short, and a rejuvenated Liberal Party was back in office with a majority government in February 1980, just in the nick of time to fight the referendum (Romanow et al., 1984: 60).

The campaign was a bitter one which split the French community right down the middle, with no more than a bare majority voting "No"—the lop-sided 60–40 total split was due to the uniform negativity of the English community (*Le Devoir*, May 21, 1980: 1; *Vancouver Sun*, May 21, 1980: B4). English Canadian premiers journeyed to Quebec to threaten economic retribution if Quebec should vote "Yes" by ruling out entirely any economic association with a sovereign Quebec (Sheppard and Valpy, 1982: 33). In a last-ditch appeal at a rally in Quebec City four days before the vote, the Prime Minister made Quebeckers a "solemn commitment" to "renew the constitution" whatever the rest of Canada might think. By this time he had made up his mind to proceed unilaterally if necessary (Sheppard and Valpy, 1982: 32).

True to his word, Trudeau started his final push for a new constitution immediately after the referendum was over. He announced in the House of Commons that he had only two pre-conditions, a strong federal government and a Charter with language rights: "we consider everything else to be negotiable" (*House of Commons Debates*, May 21, 1980: 1264). Not unexpectedly, federal-provincial meetings immediately after the referendum showed most of the provinces as uninterested in "renewed federalism" for Quebec as they had been during the referendum debate. Resource ownership and regional disparity pitted most of the provinces against Ontario (Romanow et al., 1984: 64), and most had one qualm or another about the proposed Charter—Ontario, Manitoba, and Quebec specifically about language (Romanow et al., 1984: 77). But the federal government was prepared for disagreement and used the First Ministers' Conference of September 1980 primarily as a way of drumming up support for such a move. A secret memorandum set out federal strategy for the conference as follows:

> The strategy on the People's Package is really very simple. The federal positions on the issues within the package are clearly very popular with the Canadian public and should be presented on television in the most favourable light possible. The Premiers who are opposed should be put on the defensive very quickly and should be made to appear that they prefer to trust politicians rather than impartial and non-partisan courts in the protection of the basic rights of citizens in a democratic society. It is evident that the Canadian people prefer their rights protected by judges rather than by politicians (Milne, 1982: 221–2).

The conference was a predictable "resounding failure" breaking down over language (Quebec v. Ottawa) and resource ownership (Alberta, Newfoundland and Saskatchewan v. Ottawa), with the ongoing negotiations on energy pricing as a background obstacle (Romanow et al., 1984: 96). Less than a month after the conference, the federal government made public its plan for unilateral action: by resolution of Parliament, the federal government would ask the United Kingdom to "patriate" Canada's constitution with a Charter of Rights and a new amending formula. At the time of the announcement, the federal government was able to claim the support of only the federal New Democratic Party and the provincial governments of Ontario and New Brunswick. Opposed were the governments of all of the other provinces and the federal Tories.

The opponents fought on three fronts: parliamentary, diplomatic, and legal. In Parliament, they countered government attempts to speed passage of the Resolution by demanding televised public hearings (Sheppard and Valpy, 1982: 142; Romanow et al., 1984: 112–113). These hearings, before a special joint Parliamentary committee, would drag on until February of the following year and would give the opposition valuable time to pursue other tactics. But the hearings had the boomerang effect of demonstrating and drumming up support for the general idea of a Charter of Rights, if not the specific Charter originally proposed by the Liberals. The committee received 1200 submissions and letters, had 270 hours of sittings over 106 meetings and 56 days of hearings, during which it heard and televised presentations from six governments, 93 groups, and five individuals. It has been claimed that there was government "orchestration" of the testimony by a judicious selection of the witnesses to appear (Romanow et al.: 248) in order to show more support for the Charter than there actually was. A glance at the statistics on written submissions prepared by the Joint Committee does confirm that individuals were much more closely divided (though still slightly in favour) over the question of an entrenched Charter than the groups were (Canada, 1980–81, Issues No. 57: 92). Groups favoured the idea by more than two to one and their appearances outnumbered individuals by twenty to one.

Orchestration or no, by the end of the hearings, the already popular idea of an entrenched Charter had become "a motherhood issue" (Sheppard and Valpy, 1982: 138), and by March 1981, Trudeau was using the popularity of the Charter to deride Tory opposition to his unilateral resolution:

> Staring fixedly across the floor at Clark, Trudeau asked rhetorically what would be the victory cry of those attempting to derail the constitutional revision because of its divisiveness: "Praise God, we have defeated the charter of rights and freedoms?" (Sheppard and Valpy, 1982: 172)

National opinion polls conducted in May and June confirmed the popularity of the Charter. The questions were very simplistically worded ("Canadians were asked whether they supported a bill of rights which would 'provide individual Canadians with protection against unfair treatment by any level of government in Canada'"), but no more so than the issues that had been presented at the hearings and in the press. Support was substantial: 82% in favour in one poll and 72% in the other (*The Globe and Mail*, October 22, October 29, and November 10, 1981).

Nevertheless, the hearings did give the opponents of the plan breathing space to carry out the other two prongs of their strategy. The first was to lobby British Parliamentarians to oppose the Resolution when it ultimately came before them. Despite federal government posturing that the UK Parliament was bound to do its bidding and UK government assurances to that effect, the lobbying was so successful that by December 1980 Ottawa was being urged by emissaries of Prime Minister Thatcher to drop the Charter, or risk having the resolution defeated in the British House of Commons (Sheppard and Valpy, 1982: 208–213). The committee studying the issue for the UK Parliament, under the chairmanship of Sir Anthony Kershaw, reported at the end of January 1981 that Parliament was not bound by historical practice to act automatically on a request from Ottawa to amend Canada's constitution in a manner that would change its federal structure if it were opposed by the provinces. What amount of provincial consent was necessary? Kershaw first focussed on the proposed amending formula as a minimum basis (Romanow et al., 1984: 144), but in a second report, the committee preferred to leave the matter to the ongoing Canadian litigation (United Kingdom, 1981a: xxii).

The Constitutional Reference Cases of 1981

This was the third and by far most important aspect of the provincial counterattack. Three of the opposing provincial governments, Manitoba, Quebec, and Newfoundland, referred the question of the constitutionality of the federal proposal to their provincial supreme courts. But this was "constitutionality" with a difference. For in addition to the ordinary questions governments ask courts concerning matters of constitutional *legality*, each government asked a separate question about whether it was consistent with constitutional *convention* (understood as meaning, roughly, a historically recognized norm of political behaviour) for the federal government to approach the UK Parliament over such substantial provincial opposition.

Of course, everyone knew that the government's plan was *not* consistent with constitutional convention. What was extraordinary was to ask the courts to say so. Courts had sometimes ruled on conventions where doing so was necessary to resolve a question of law, but they had *never* done so where, as in this case, the supposed convention was completely detached from any legal question (Kay, 1982: 28; Hogg, 1982: 320–322). Why?

The technical distinction between conventions and laws is that conventions are *unenforceable* in the courts. This means that the courts will not authorize the use of force to obtain obedience to conventions. But they will with laws. Why is this important? Because this regulation or authorization of the use of official force, this law *enforcement*, is the not merely one of the functions of courts among many. It is their defining characteristic. Courts do not distinguish between the legal and the illegal in a vacuum or as an end in itself. Their determinations are a crucial part of the legitimate use of force in the modern state. The practical activity of the use of force by the state requires an institution capable of finally, efficiently, and authoritatively determining its legitimacy in any given case. The very idea of legality requires such an institution. That institution is the courts. Their word is law. But we do not need only one institution authorized to determine right and wrong or historical practice. Quite the contrary. We can do without "official" moralities and "official" histories. For a court to recognize a convention that by definition it will nevertheless not enforce is to do something that *anyone* has the authority to do. A court's opinion on the matter has no more formal, judicial, legal, or whatever-you-choose-to-call-it, authority than yours, mine, Pierre Trudeau's or René Lévesque's. If it is more persuasive, this is a political fact, not a legal one.

So when the courts were asked a separate question on constitutional convention, they were asked something outside of the realm of law and judging. Nevertheless, there was little reluctance on their part to answer it. Only one judge out of twenty-two refused out of a sense of judicial propriety (*Re Constitution of Canada*, 1981: 13). As for the answers to the various questions, the three appellate courts were hopelessly divided, with Manitoba and Quebec (over dissents) in favour, and Newfoundland (unanimously) opposed. Of the 13 appellate judges who heard the cases, seven found in favour of the federal government and six against it. There was no avoiding referring the whole matter to the Supreme Court of Canada.

The Supreme Court had not been standing still during the turmoil of the late seventies. No longer "weak and timid," it was confidently flexing its muscles in more and more realms. The hallmarks of the judicial institution, which limited its function to the *application* of law in the adjudication of disputes, and so limited its power, were quickly being left behind. *Stare decisis*, the doctrine that courts had to adhere to prior decisions, was being abandoned. So was the equally integral reticence of a court to express opinions on matters that were not strictly involved in the case it was deciding. In 1978, the Supreme Court of Canada revamped the rules of criminal liability out of whole cloth (*City of Sault Ste. Marie*, 1978) and threw off its prior reluctance to supervise administrative tribunals (*Nicholson*, 1978). In 1980, the Supreme Court made the extraordinarily unjudicial pronouncement that *anything* it said in a case, whether necessary to the decision or not, was binding on lower courts, thus abandoning the most fundamental limiting rule of judicial authority, a defining feature of *stare decisis* itself, the hallowed distinction between *ratio decidendi* and *obiter dicta*[1] (*Sellars*, 1980). Moreover, the Court had thrust itself into the national unity debate with some legally questionable judgments limiting the power of the Quebec government to make French the official language of Quebec and affirming Manitoba's duties to its French Canadian minority (*Blaikie*, 1979; *Forest*, 1979). On the other hand, nobody on the Supreme Court of Canada was any longer attempting to fit activism into the straightjacket of either the *Canadian Bill of Rights* (*Bliss*, 1978) or the "implied bill of rights" (officially put to rest in *Dupond*, 1978). In other words, the decks had been cleared.

The arguments before the Supreme Court of Canada by a battery of constitutional lawyers in *Re Constitution of Canada* took only five days of late April 1981, amid what court historians claim was the most concentrated public attention in its history (Snell and Vaughan, 1985: 249). However, the Court took the entire summer to prepare its decision, which was ready for release on September 28. Far from being reticent about its new role, the Court seemed eager for it, even too eager. It broke yet another tradition by allowing TV cameras into the courtroom for the first time, but the effect was ruined when one of the judges tripped a sound cable rendering the Chief Justice's reading of the judgment inaudible (Sheppard and Valpy, 1982: 241; Romanow et al.: 184). What he had to say was hardly the stuff of high television ratings anyway. It was a dry recitation of the various questions put to the Court and their technical answers, confusing even for lawyers. The Supreme Court had many lessons to learn in public relations. What the decision would mean in political terms was also unclear at first. It was interpreted differently according to

---

[1] And ensuring that future generations of law students will not get the joke about the name of the student paper at Osgoode Hall Law School, *Obiter Dicta*, which can be translated loosely as "unimportant utterings," traditionally the non-authoritative part of a judge's opinion, as contrasted with the *ratio decidendi*, "the reason for the decision," traditionally the authoritative part.

which side of the issue and which side of the Quebec border one was on. Quebec's *Le Devoir* headline was one way of looking at it: "Legal but unconstitutional,"[1] while Ontario's *Globe and Mail* headline was another: "PM's bid 'offends' but is legal" (Snell and Vaughan, 1985: 250). Both were technically correct: the legality of the plan was affirmed by a vote of seven judges to two, and its inconsistency with constitutional convention by a vote of six to three. A lot of the confusion came from the shifting alignments on the Court with some judges dissenting on one question yet joining the majority on the other. But closer examination shows the political logic of the decision. The Court voted almost perfectly along political and regional lines:

Judge	Province	Appointed by	Legal?	Conventional?
Laskin	Ont.	Trudeau	Yes	Yes
Estey	Ont.	Trudeau	Yes	Yes
MacIntyre	B.C.[2]	Trudeau	Yes	Yes
Dickson	Man.	Trudeau	Yes	No
Beetz	Que.	Trudeau	Yes	No
Lamer	Que.	Trudeau	Yes	No
Chouinard	Que.	Clark	Yes	No
Martland	Alta.	Diefenbaker	No	No
Ritchie	N.S.	Diefenbaker	No	No

This was a transparently political decision and gave us a good idea, if we were paying attention, of what Canada could expect with the Charter.

The reasoning of the judges was as revealing as their voting pattern. Of the two questions, the legality question was probably the easiest. As we have seen, for a court to hold an act of government illegal is, at least implicitly, to prohibit it. The majority argued that, however unconventional the federal government's action might be, there was nothing in the decided cases or the statutes authorizing a court actually to interfere with what was, after all, a mere request made by the Canadian Parliament to the UK Parliament. Whatever impact such a request might in fact have, it had no legal effect without a law being passed by the sovereign UK Parliament. Where could a court get the authority to *prohibit* a *request*? Furthermore, given the fact that the entire legal structure of Canada depended on a British enactment, what legal authority could a Canadian court have to refuse to recognize an amendment to the *BNA Act* by the Parliament that enacted it in the first place, however that amendment came to be proposed? The minority's answer was that the Court should, in effect, make up the authority so as to protect the fundamental federal structure of Canada. Courts had made things up before.

---

[1] "légal mais inconstitutionnel" (*Le Devoir*, September 29, 1981: 1).

[2] Ontario is generally considered to be entitled to three seats on the Supreme Court; the appointment of MacIntyre was a temporary exception to this rule (Snell & Vaughan, 1985: 234–236). Thinking of MacIntyre as a quasi-Ontario appointment makes the symmetry even more striking.

There was logic on both sides and certainly a lack of precedent had become increasingly unimportant to this court—that very day it would do a most unprecedented act. But to hold this action illegal, even if technically possible, would have been reckless on the part of the Court. What if Parliament were unable to achieve an agreement through patently unreasonable provincial intransigence? The Court would then have set up an insuperable legal obstacle to a constitutional amendment and would have found itself confronting an already popular plan (the Charter) as well as what could turn into a popular strategy (unilateralism). If, in such an event, Parliament went ahead despite the illegality, the Court would have had its *order* ignored with a consequent loss of prestige. And what then? Could it actually refuse to enforce the law once it returned? Shades of Roosevelt and 1937! Besides, it was unnecessary to go this far in light of the Court's answer on the convention question.

That there was a convention requiring more provincial consent than the federal government had obtained could not really be challenged. In fact, the historical record was that no amendments had been passed without the consent of *all* of the provinces affected, and this record strongly implied that this was indeed recognized as binding on the federal government. Indeed, the only legitimate questions concerned the requirement of unanimity and the Quebec veto. There was in fact no dissent from anyone on the Court that constitutional convention required more provincial support than had been obtained. What is intriguing about the convention question has nothing to do with the answers given to it nor the arguments offered by majority and minority for their respective conclusions. What is intriguing is the way the convention question was interpreted by each side, the way the answers of each side were presented, and, most intriguing of all, *that it was even answered.*

First, the way the question was interpreted. When it asked whether the "the consent of the provinces" was necessary, did it mean *all* of the provinces or merely *some* of them? Each side interpreted this differently, but in the way that best suited its point of view on the outcome. It was as obvious to the majority that the question did *not* mean to refer to *all* of the provinces as it was to the minority that it *did.*

Majority:
It would have been easy to insert the words "all" into the question had it been intended to narrow its meaning. But we do not think it was so intended (*Re Constitution of Canada*, 1981: 80).

Minority:
From the wording of the questions and from the course of argument it is clear that the questions meant the consent of *all* the Provinces...There is no ambiguity in the questions before the Court (*Re Constitution of Canada*, 1981: 108–109).

The only thing that was really clear, of course, was that if the majority wanted to cast doubt on the plan and the minority to approve it, interpreting the question in their respective ways made it easier for each side to achieve its respective goal. If they were only interested in the truth, each side would have given answers to each possible interpretation of the question. If this is not coincidence enough, there are the very obvious attempts by each side to give maximum impact to its respective position. The minority, which found the plan not contrary to constitutional convention, but nevertheless knew itself to have lost this issue, *minimized* the general importance of conventions:

> We cannot...agree with any suggestion that the non-observance of a convention can properly be termed unconstitutional in any strict or legal sense...In a federal State...constitutionality and legality must be synonymous, and conventional rules will be accorded less significance than they may have in a unitary State such as the United Kingdom (*Re Constitution of Canada*, 1981: 110).

> With conventions or understandings he [the lawyer and law teacher] has no direct concern. They vary from generation to generation, almost from year to year...The subject...is not one of law but of politics, and need trouble no lawyer or the class of any professor of law (*Re Constitution of Canada*, 1981: 112).

The majority, on the other hand, went to great lengths to *maximize* the significance of its holding that the federal resolution, though legal, was contrary to convention: "[W]hile they are not laws, some conventions may be more important than some laws" (*Re Constitution of Canada*, 1981: 87). Indeed, the majority went about as far as it could in this direction when it declared that conventions "form an integral part of the constitution and the constitutional system":

> That is why it is perfectly appropriate to say that to violate a convention is to do something which is unconstitutional although it entails no direct legal consequences. But the words "constitutional" and "unconstitutional" may also be used in a strict legal sense, for instance with respect to a statute which is found *ultra vires* or unconstitutional. The foregoing may perhaps be summarized in an equation: constitutional conventions plus constitutional law equal the total Constitution of the country (*Re Constitution of Canada*, 1981: 87).

But one does not have to look any further for proof of the political nature of the case than to the fact that the Court agreed to answer the convention question at all. And this is the only point upon which it was unanimous! Remember that there was no precedent for the Court ruling on a convention question divorced from any legal question. Indeed, according to the Court's own definition, conventions "are not enforced by the courts" (*Re Constitution of Canada*, 1981: 84, 111). So, answering the convention question at all was out of line with the role of courts as ordinarily conceived. In answering the convention question, the Supreme Court of Canada acted "outside its legal function and [attempted] to facilitate a political outcome" (Hogg, 1982: 314). It "intervened as another political actor, not as a court of law" (Kay, 1982: 33). What was the Court's defence of this action? The majority devoted a separate section of its reasons to the issue, but nothing it said really answered the question. We were told that the question was important (though "not confined to an issue of pure legality...it has to do with a fundamental issue of constitutionality and legitimacy": *Re Constitution of Canada* 1981: 88) and that courts should not "shrink" from answering a question "on account of the political aspects" (*Re Constitution of Canada* 1981: 89). But these are reasons for answering a *legal* question with political implications, not for answering a political question that has nothing to do with law. The minority argued that they had to answer because the majority answered, but also because the case was "unusual" and there had been extensive argument on the convention question (*Re Constitution of Canada* 1981: 107). Perhaps the judge who came the closest to the truth was the Chief Justice of Manitoba, quoted by the majority in the Supreme Court, who said that the question "calls for an answer, and I propose to answer it." (*Re Constitution of Canada* 1981: 88). Put another way, the reasons given by the various judges to justify their willingness to answer the convention question, and characterized by one commentator as "inadequate" (Kay, 1982: 28n39) as, no doubt, technically they were, amounted to no more and no less than that they were answering it because they were *expected* to answer it.

Can anyone doubt that they were right about this? Outside of scholarly criticism of the legal credentials of the decision and the dangers such political behaviour might cause the Supreme Court (Hogg, 1982: 314), not a peep of political criticism was heard of the decision to answer the question. And, while it is impossible to say what would have happened had the convention question not been answered or had it been answered differently, it is clear that with the Court decision as it was, the federal government had no political hope of going ahead without at least another round of negotiations (Romanow et al., 1984: 188). For one thing, the NDP informed the government that it would now vote against the resolution without a new conference (Romanow et al., 1984: 189). In Britain, too, the decision was regarded as decisive. The Kershaw Committee had argued for reliance on the Court before the decision: "Any judgment of the Supreme Court of Canada...is bound to weigh heavily with your Committee and with the House" (United Kingdom, 1981a: xxii). And it reiterated its position after the judgment (United Kingdom, 1981b: vi). The *Guardian* reported that even with strenuous Thatcher sponsorship, the Bill would now have a tough time.[1] Though the outcome would obviously have been impossible to predict with certainty, it is clear that there would have been a serious battle in the British Commons and House of Lords had the federal government tried to go ahead with its original plan after the judgment (Romanow et al., 1984: 153).

But most important of all was that the whole Charter enterprise depended for its success on reverence for the Court. The reason Trudeau wanted the Charter in the first place was to use it against the unilingual tendencies of provincial governments in areas beyond federal control. He needed it now to use against the popular language legislation of the PQ government of Quebec. The idea was to entrench English language rights which directly contradicted the PQ's Bill 101 so that the courts, ultimately the Supreme Court, would

---

[1] Two years later, with the constitution safely amended, Toronto's *Globe and Mail* was also ready to admit this (*The Globe and Mail*, January, 13 1983: 16).

strike down the law as violating the Charter of Rights. Trudeau was going to trump democracy by claiming a greater legitimacy for the Supreme Court of Canada than for any mere government. How could he criticize the Court for going too far today when he needed it to go all the way tomorrow?

So the Supreme Court's decision all but forced the First Ministers' conference that began on November 2, 1981. In fact, it practically determined its outcome. This was due partly to the holding on legality, because the knowledge that a unilateral federal gambit would be legal and enforceable gave the provinces an extra incentive to be conciliatory and even to break ranks to achieve individual objectives. But most important of all to the final outcome was the clear indication given by both majority and minority on the convention question that constitutional convention did not require the unanimous, or even near unanimous, assent of the provinces. Both sides let everyone know that they would approve of much less. For the minority judges, the denial of a unanimity requirement was part and parcel with their dissent, but this would have been a fragile predictor without some expression on the question by the majority judges, and express themselves they did, once again completely without judicial excuse:

> It was submitted by counsel for Manitoba, Newfoundland, Quebec, Nova Scotia, British Columbia, Prince Edward Island and Alberta that the convention does exist [and] that it requires the agreement of all the Provinces...
>
> Counsel for Saskatchewan...submitted that the convention does exist and requires a measure of provincial agreement...
>
> We wish to indicate at the outset that we find ourselves in agreement with the submissions made on this issue by counsel for Saskatchewan (*Re Constitution of Canada* 1981: 89).
> ...
> It seems clear that while the precedents taken alone point at unanimity, the unanimity principle cannot be said to have been accepted by all the actors in the precedents (*Re Constitution of Canada* 1981: 100).
> ...
> It would not be appropriate for the Court to devise in the abstract a specific formula which would indicate in positive terms what measure of provincial agreement is required...
>
> It is sufficient for the Court to decide that at least a substantial measure of provincial consent is required...Nothing more should be said about this (*Re Constitution of Canada* 1981: 103).

The Court had said more than enough already. It had introduced a completely "new element" into the equation, an element that was emphasized by the Premiers of both British Columbia and Saskatchewan (two *opposing* provinces) in their televised opening speeches to the First Ministers' conference on November 2 (Romanow et al., 1984: 188). It was this element that made possible the ultimate exclusion of Quebec, the only province with truly irreconcilable differences with Ottawa, differences over entrenched minority language rights, not only Trudeau's bottom line but actually his *raison d'être*. It is clear that these specific rights, which in their precision and prolixity read more like a tax statute than a constitution, were the only non-negotiables for Trudeau. The grand rights and freedoms of "conscience," "association," "fundamental justice," "equality," and so on, which granted a purely general supervisory jurisdiction over legislation to the courts, were expendable. Trudeau said as much after the referendum. And he proved it in the resulting constitution where none of these grand individualistic rights would be so precious as to be immune from legislative veto by use of s.33, the "notwithstanding" clause. By contrast, language rights would be immune, and at the same time, they would automatically render null and void the language of education provisions of the PQ's "Bill 101," the centrepiece of its program to make the French language *the* language of Quebec.

In other words, unanimity among provinces and the federal government was simply not achievable so long as Trudeau and Lévesque had to sign the same document. The freedom from unanimity which the Supreme Court presumed to grant made possible the only conceivable agreement, one that would exclude Quebec. Furthermore, the "deliberate vagueness" of the Court's formula (Hogg, 1982: 324) gave the other provinces more than enough incentive to jump on the federal bandwagon lest they be isolated with English Canada's anathema. This seems in fact to have been what determined Manitoba's capitulation (Sheppard and Valpy, 1982: 297). It was the only other province with a real interest in opposing entrenched language rights (because of its relatively large and linguistically mistreated French minority) and, because of this, the only other province firmly opposed to a Charter at the time of the conference (Alberta had made its deal with the federal government on energy prices in September) (Romanow et al., 1984: 189, 257). An accord excluding Quebec did not necessarily entail the sneakiness of the night of November 4–5, 1981, during which, with all parties but Quebec involved, the compromise that was to be Canada's constitution was worked out and then presented as a *fait accompli* to a shocked René Lévesque the next morning at breakfast (Sheppard and Valpy, 1982: 296). That there would be an accord, however, and that it would exclude Quebec was as about as inevitable as these things ever get.

The Court's role in the ultimate making of the deal and in its general contours was, therefore, a rather large one. Furthermore, the script required it consciously to stride outside of its judicial confines and directly into the political arena. But this, as we have tried to show, was not a random occurrence. For most of the century, everything, and more and more nearly everyone, had been grooming the Court for this part. In fact, the most obvious thing about the decision to answer the convention question was that this thoroughly non-traditional decision of the Court concerned the adoption of a law—a constitutionally entrenched Charter of Rights and Freedoms—that would invest the judiciary with essentially the same thoroughly non-traditional function, namely judging the *legitimacy* of jurisdictionally valid legislation. The Charter of Rights and Freedoms in fact transformed the Court into an institution charged with making the very sort of judgments which it made on the convention issue—though such judgments would henceforth be made under the formally satisfying umbrella of constitutional authority.[1] So if we want to know why the Court would accept such a non-traditional role in determining the outcome of a major political crisis and why its acceptance of this role would in turn be accepted by all the other actors, the answer is that it would have been strange indeed for the Court, standing on the threshold of its new era, to have been too prudish to engage in the very kind of activity that would characterize that era, or to have been criticized for doing so. The decision on the convention should be regarded as the inauguration of a new era in which the judiciary is to play a central role in the political life of this country. The triumph of the legalization of politics can be dated, then, not from the formal entrenchment of the *Charter of Rights and Freedoms* on April 17, 1982, but from the decision on the convention question in *Re Constitution of Canada* some seven months earlier.

Conclusion

What do we learn from the history of the Charter in Canada? First, Canada does not owe its Charter of Rights to the humanitarian or democratic impulses of its sponsors. However it has been sold to the public, the Charter has always been seen by its leading proponents in the political realm as an *expedient*, whether to fight the Quebec independence movement or the Cold War, or to preserve the established way of life against the immigrant hordes. Secondly, the Charter, far from being the end of a campaign for a single constitutional rearrangement, is part of an ongoing historical process, nowhere near spent and nowhere near isolated to the movement for an entrenched Charter, a process of the growing importance of judicial forms of political power. We should remember too that the legal profession, for its part, has been far from indifferent to its increasing political centrality, for feigned indifference seems to be an important strategy in the de-politicization of legal politics, via the idea of judicial neutrality. Recently Chief Justice Dickson made a speech to the Canadian Bar Association:

> The Chief Justice also told those who think the judiciary savors a power heightened under the Charter of Rights and Freedoms that it had not asked for that power. "It is a power unsought," he said. "Judges do not generate their own business" (*The Globe and Mail*, August 25, 1987: A16).

It may have been unsought in Dickson's case—the case would be harder to make for the late Judge Laskin, given his ardent advocacy of judicial review in the 1950s and his irredentism in *Re Constitution of Canada*—but Dickson certainly grabbed at the

---

[1] On the other hand, one would be mistaken to think that "conventional wisdom" from the Court is a thing of the pre-Charter past. Useful devices are not so easily abandoned. The idea of having the Supreme Court pass on the non-legal legitimacy of controversial initiatives seems to be growing in popularity. Three lawyers and two governments have recently asked the courts to pass on the propriety—apart from the legality—of the "Meech Lake Accord" (*Penikett*, 1987a; 1987b; *Sibbeston*, 1987; *The Globe and Mail*, May 3, 1988: A4; June 3, 1988: A3) and a *Globe* editorial recently argued that the propriety, "by convention" of Senate obstruction of the Free Trade deal should also be decided by the Supreme Court of Canada (*The Globe and Mail*, July 21, 1988: A6).

chance when it came his way. Anyone who signed, as he did, the intensely partisan majority opinion on the convention question in *Re Constitution of Canada*, let alone the other Dickson judgments we will have occasion to refer to later, cannot be said to have been a difficult convert to judicial power. If he did not want the power, why was he exercising it even before it was officially his? The day after Judge Dickson made this speech, the Canadian Bar Association disclosed an extraordinary communication they had received from all of the judges on the Supreme Court of Canada. The judges had given a "frosty reception" to CBA recommendations that the Court be enlarged or that new levels of courts be created to deal with judicial backlogs. The Supreme Court judges were reported to have argued that

> the structure of the Court should be entrenched in the Constitution for all time [to] preclude the possibility of a future government succumbing to the temptation to pack the Court (*The Globe and Mail*, August 24, 1987: A2).

This is not a court indifferent to its status in Canadian politics.

Finally, we have learned that the growth in judicial forms of power has been at the expense of and in direct opposition to other more popular forms of power. Herein lies its expediency. Law has been a way of getting around people. From the early days after the US revolution, when it was a means of preserving wealth from the excesses of democracy, through the Great Depression of the 1930s, when the judicial way was, politically speaking, the only way to deny relief to the newly enfranchised masses, to the period of the French renaissance in Quebec when judicial review was used to impose a vision of language rights distinctly at odds with that of the popularly elected government of Quebec—in each case, law was used to achieve an end too difficult to achieve by exclusive reliance on representative institutions or other democratic methods.

A vivid example of this can be found towards the end of the entrenchment drama itself, in the leitmotif of the referendum. One of the optional strategies up the sleeve of the federal government to legitimize unilateral action despite provincial opposition was to go directly to the people via a referendum (Sheppard and Valpy, 1982: 256). The idea was actually trotted out by Trudeau at the November conference and played a role in prying open some space between Quebec and the other provinces, as Quebec was the only province at all interested. It is generally thought that the referendum option was meant by the federal government only as a "ploy" to prod the English provinces into action. Once the agreement was made, Trudeau abandoned the idea, despite Quebec's continued interest (Sheppard and Valpy, 1982: 279, 282). The provincial opposition to a referendum was voiced in many ways: it would deprive them of the value of the Supreme Court's judgment, it was unpredictable, unparliamentary (Ontario adviser Hugh Segal gave the instinctive politician's opposition: "It will be like a free shot in a by-election"—Sheppard and Valpy, 1982: 265), and most of all it was "divisive" (Sheppard and Valpy, 1982: 256, 286, 287). But how would it be divisive? Like all referendums, it would not actually divide a united people, but rather would *reveal* the deep divisions which really existed between Quebec and the rest of the country—precisely as had the conscription referendum in 1942 where English Canada voted "yes" and Quebec voted "no." These divisions could be papered over only with Supreme Court judgments. First, they submerged Quebec in the concept of "the provinces," with the qualitative and quantitative dimensions of that concept left "deliberately vague" in *Re Constitution of Canada* (1981). Then, in the denouement decision, decided well after entrenchment, on whether or not Quebec had a "veto," the Supreme Court, predictably and unanimously, denied the province any special status for the purposes of constitutional conventions (*Attorney-General of Quebec*, 1982). In the Constitutional Reference Cases Quebec became just one of ten abstract, homogeneous, legal entities. It was not treated as if it were a special province with a special place in Canadian history, and its centrality in the constitutional process was denied by Supreme Court judges as fully cognizant of current events as anyone else in the country. The Supreme Court thus functioned as an alternative legitimator to direct democracy, as a way to legitimate the new constitutional arrangement without the dangers and inconveniences of actually going to the people. It did this by abstractly uniting a people in fact riven by concrete contradictions, that is by treating them as united when in fact they were not. Substituting the abstract for the concrete in an attempt to make the divided appear united is a tactic central to legalized politics.

So it was fitting that when the constitution came to be to be proclaimed in Canada on April 17, 1982, it was by royal and not popular decree. But even more revealing was a Macpherson cartoon that appeared in the *The Toronto Star* that day (*The Toronto Star*, April 17, 1982: B1). In it, the constitution is drawn as a large open touring car with all the premiers piled in and making merry. The car has apparently stalled and the engine trouble is Lévesque himself. But the man assigned to deal with the problem and about to resume his position *in the driver's seat* is none other than Chief Justice Laskin, all decked out in his most elaborate judicial costume.

CHAPTER II

The Charter and Democracy

Charter Democracy and the Judicial Factor

Despite the historical opposition between popular politics and judicial review, the dominant theme in the selling of the Charter has been *democracy*. The Charter, its supporters have argued, means a net gain in popular power. According to a government pamphlet issued shortly before the Charter's enactment, the constitution is "one of the most valuable possessions the people of a democratic country can have" (Canada, 1982b: 6):

Transferring Power to the People

Constitutional entrenchment of a *Charter of Rights and Freedoms* limits the power of both provincial and federal governments in favour of the rights of individual citizens. *It gives people the power to appeal to the courts* if they feel their rights have been infringed or denied. The Charter does not transfer any powers or authority from the provincial governments to the federal government—rather it transfers power to all Canadians (Canada, 1982b: 12–13; emphasis in original).

The "People's Package" strategy, too, had invoked democracy as it tried to tar the opposing premiers with preferring

to trust politicians rather than impartial and non-partisan courts in the protection of the basic rights of citizens in a democratic society. It is evident that the Canadian people prefer their rights protected by judges rather than politicians (Milne, 1982: 222).

The stress on the "impartial and non-partisan" nature of Charter adjudication was in no way incidental to the democratic thesis. It was central. Any notion of a specifically judicial factor would have complicated things enormously. So government propaganda tried to portray constitutional rights as so precise and non-controversial in their meaning that they practically enforced themselves. Opinion polls meant to show support for the Charter did not ask, "Do you support taking political decisions away from elected representatives and handing them over to unelected judges?" They asked: "Do you support a bill of rights which would provide individual Canadians with protection against unfair treatment by any level of government in Canada?" (*The Globe and Mail*, October 22, 1981: 8). The government promised Canadians a foolproof protection for our rights:

Now, these rights *will* be written into the Constitution so that you will know exactly where you stand...The courts are there as an impartial referee to correct injustices in the event that you find that your constitutional rights are being denied (Canada, 1982b: 7; emphasis in original).

Judges would correct injustices the way grade school teachers correct exercises. They would judge rights the way a referee calls an offside. Judging constitutional cases might be slightly more difficult than refereeing a game. There might be a few more hard calls. But that did not make the analogy inapt. Judges could take more time than referees. They could watch the instant replay. Like Solomon, once their decisions were understood, no one would fail to see the wisdom, indeed the necessity in them. The key thing was that judges would not take sides. The judiciary would not be a protagonist except on behalf of the constitution itself. The judiciary's duty was "to uphold the constitution," and to be its "protector and preserver" and "guarantor" (*Re Manitoba Language Rights*, 1985: 25, 26). All we needed to make sure of was that we had the right kind of constitution and standard-quality judges.[1] That done, the protection of our rights was straightforward.

This was a very widespread conception of constitutional judging at the time of the enactment of the Charter. Professor Peter Russell has written that the "popularity of the Charter was based primarily on a belief that one basic policy would flow automatically from the Charter—the better protection of fundamental rights and freedoms" and that this proceeded from "a blind, and most anachronistic view of the judicial process [which denied] the policy-making role of the judiciary" (Russell, 1983: 42–43). Before the enactment of the Charter, Professor Donald Smiley wrote of a Canadian "innocence about judicial power and a very unrealistic image of the judicial role" (Smiley, 1981: 55). Nor was this innocence restricted to the non-professionals. Political scientist Professor Reg Whitaker wrote in 1983 of the democratic character of the Charter without mentioning judges once (Whitaker, 1984a).

As we shall soon see, there is not a decision under the Charter that does not, at least partially, refute this idea of what judging is about. For now, it should be enough to recall the wide swings in approach to constitutional interpretation throughout American and Canadian history discussed in Chapter I. Canadian and American courts have repeatedly responded to political events in what can only be described as political ways, with opinions often diverging in predictable directions within the very same court. Do we need a better example than *Re Constitution of Canada* (1981) where the judges' decisions broke neatly along regional and political lines and where majorities and minorities strove to give maximum political impact to their respective positions? In legal circles it has been nothing short of conventional wisdom for the past half-century that courts are not merely interpreters of the law (McWhinney, 1983: 67). Quantitative analyses of the behaviour of the Supreme Court of Canada and other Canadian courts have shown how greatly and persistently individual

---

[1] According to the experts, the standards do not seem to be very demanding: "Common sense is, I think the most important quality a judge can have." (Judge Thomas Zuber of the Ontario Court of Appeal); "the quality of being a decent person is, I think, what is essential" (criminal lawyer Eddie Greenspan); "Among the most important qualities are an ability to listen and having an open mind" (law professor Ed Ratushny)—as quoted in *The Toronto Star*, July 18, 1987: A8.

judges differ from one another in philosophy and ideology and how this determines their decisions (Peck, 1969; Hogarth, 1971). How else to understand the persistent jockeying for judges among criminal lawyers? How else to understand the great political controversies that periodically break out in the United States over judicial appointments? How else to understand the desire of provincial governments, recently accommodated in the Meech Lake Accord, to have a say in the selection of Supreme Court of Canada judges?

Should anything different have been expected from the Charter? Quite the contrary. Most of its provisions were vague ideals with no instructions whatsoever on how they were to be achieved in reality: "freedom of conscience and religion"; "the right to life, liberty and security of the person and the right not to be deprived thereof except in accordance with the principles of fundamental justice"; "the right not to be subjected to any cruel and unusual treatment or punishment"; "the right to the equal protection and equal benefit of the law without discrimination"; and so on. Even those few rights which *seemed* fairly specific (and we shall see in Chapter III what surprises the courts had in store for us even here)—such as language rights, electoral rights, mobility rights and some of the rights of accused persons—were made subject, along with all of the other vague rights, to "such reasonable limits prescribed by law as can be demonstrably justified in a free and democratic society." Could anyone have actually thought that such things could be self-enforcing? That their application to everyday life could be discovered by looking up their meaning in a dictionary? Here is what Chief Justice Dickson wrote, with the unanimous concurrence of his colleagues, about Section 8 of the Charter in one of the earliest Supreme Court of Canada Charter judgments:

> The guarantee is vague and open...There is no specificity in the section beyond the bare guarantee of freedom from "unreasonable" search and seizure; nor is there any particular historical, political or philosophic context capable of providing an obvious gloss on the meaning of the guarantee. It is clear that the meaning of "unreasonable" cannot be determined by recourse to a dictionary, nor for that matter, by reference to rules of statutory construction (*Hunter*, 1984: 649).

If to a member of the Canadian Abortion Rights Action League the right of "everyone" to "life, liberty and security of the person" means the right of unimpeded access to safe and expeditious abortions (*Morgentaler*, 1988), but to Campaign Life it means the right of the foetus to be protected from abortion (*Borowski*, 1987), this is not because one of them is a stranger to the English language or otherwise misunderstands the meaning of any of the words. Nor is that likely to be the cause of the dispute over the meaning of "freedom of association" between a trade unionist and a corporate representative on the board of the National Citizens' Coalition (*Re Public Service Employees Relations Act (Alberta)*, 1987; *Lavigne*, 1986). These rights are what you make of them, and what you make of them depends upon your point of view. You do not have to read the thousands of pages of contradictory judicial opinions on their meaning to realize that the words of the Charter neither restrain nor guide the judges. You do not have to be a legal philosopher to realize that they were not intended to.

As for the famous legal technique of finding the "right answer" in "hard cases" (Mandel, 1979), it may work in theory, but in practice it has a hard time being reconciled with the multitude of overruled decisions, split decisions, and the decisions—almost all Charter decisions it seems—in which judges coming to the same conclusion do so for completely different reasons. The recent *Morgentaler* case (1988) is an example of all of these phenomena. A unanimous Ontario Court of Appeal, following a prior (split) decision of the Supreme Court of Canada is overruled by a (split) Supreme Court decision in which the five judges of the majority give three different opinions!

Once we admit the controversial nature of constitutional rights and the great differences in "interpretation" that can result from differing ideological points of view among judges, and between judges and the rest of us, the idea that judicial review is democratic, in the usual sense of enhancing popular power, evaporates into thin air. In fact, with judges as protagonists, who not only are not responsible to anyone for their decisions but who are empowered to nullify the laws of those who *are* responsible, we are left with the conclusion that the Charter is even less democratic than the parliamentary democracy it is meant to keep honest. And the fact that it was enacted by elected representatives is no more an answer to this than if these same elected representatives should tomorrow hand over power to the army.

Where could anyone have got the idea that judicial review was democratic? Perhaps it has to do with the notion of "the rule of law" itself which adorns the Preamble to the Charter just after "the supremacy of God." This is a profoundly ambiguous concept. It can be democratic or authoritarian. But it can only be democratic if the law that rules is really *our* law. This means it has to be made by us or by people genuinely accountable to us. And then it has to be faithfully applied and not distorted by those applying it. The democratic sense of the rule of law requires that the authorities, too, are restrained by law, with no exemptions for the judicial authorities. Leaving aside for the moment the many shortcomings of our system of representative government, at least the people who make the laws have been elected on the basis of universal adult suffrage in constituencies large and small all over the country. They must face the music of periodic re-election every so often on the record of what they or their party have done. And accepting for the sake of argument that the faithful application of the law is best achieved by an irremovable professional judiciary with unique security of tenure, any pretense that this sort of institution is democratic depends on the extent to which the laws it applies are specific and rule out personal discretion. Otherwise the laws that the judiciary apply are no longer *our* laws but *theirs*. There is no denying that Canadian laws frequently fall short of this ideal. Popular involvement is approaching nil and great discretion is increasingly vested in administrators, especially judicial administrators. But the ideal is sometimes approached, for example by some of the laws which have already been challenged under the Charter (laws governing the rights of unions, workers' compensation, the retail trade on Sundays, advertising aimed at children, protection for victims of sexual assault). Besides, the failings of democracy in the rule of law only prove the value of a democratic ideal against which existing practice can be held up and evaluated (Thompson, 1975).

But the Charter represents an entirely different side of the rule of law. The rights in the Charter depart from the democratic rule of law in every important respect. As we have noticed already, the Charter is mostly a collection of vague incantations of lofty but entirely abstract ideals, incapable of either restraining or guiding the judges in their application to everyday life. In this context, the principle that the judges are not accountable for their decisions loses all democratic justification. When this is combined with the fact that it is not only that the judges are given the power to solve questions not addressed by legislatures but actually to nullify laws that elected legislatures have made, it is clear that we are closer to the rule of *lawyers* than the rule of law. And for those of us who cringe at the words "the supremacy of God" at the head of the Preamble, while we look in vain for any mention of the people of Canada (Resnick, 1984: 54), they do serve as a useful reminder of precisely what sort of "rule of law"—authoritarian or democratic—we are dealing with here.

Even in the one instance where Charter rights appear precise and without room for judicial discretion, namely language rights,—immune by judicial fiat from even the crucible of "reasonability"—this is far from a democratic phenomenon. In its context it is quite the opposite, as we shall see in Chapter III.

The error of omitting the judicial factor from constitutional adjudication, of confounding the democratic with the anti-democratic rule of law, is not confined to laypersons. It is also made by lawyers and it does not seem to matter whether they identify themselves with the Left or with the Right. Some argue that if law itself is defensible so is judicial review (Campbell, 1984), and others contend that without judicial review politics will replace the rule of law (Brill, 1987). More frequent still is the tendency of lawyers in action to neglect entirely the judicial factor, to speak in constitutional absolutes as if only the cleverness of the legal argument determines the result, and as if they have the only clever legal argument. The accused doctors in *Morgentaler* (1985), *swore*, obviously on the advice of their lawyers, not merely that they believed they had a good case, but that the Charter "has rendered" the abortion law "of no force and effect" and that the abortion provisions were "unconstitutional on their face as they deprive women of the right to their security of the person" (*Morgentaler*, 1985: 71). Clayton Ruby, the lawyer for Energy Probe in its challenge to the *Nuclear Liability Act*, was less than tentative when he said of the law limiting liability for nuclear disasters: "It infringes Canadians' constitutional rights and freedoms" (*The Globe and Mail*, March 4, 1987: A5).[1] Law professor Gail Starr (Starr, 1984) argued for the progressive potential of the Charter by outlining all the great arguments one could make using its vague terms. He never bothered to mention that the judges were free to disagree, let alone to try and predict whether they might. Lawyer Marilou McPhedran, a

---

[1] As far as the courts were concerned, Morgentaler's lawyers were right (*Morgentaler*, 1988) and Ruby was wrong (*Energy Probe*, 1987).

prominent constitutional lobbyist for women's rights at the time of entrenchment, reported how she lectured Professor Peter Hogg for three hours one day
on the proper interpretation of section 28 of the Charter for his influential
constitutional law textbook. Lobbying legal academics is pretty extraordinary
in itself; but even more extraordinary was her genuine shock that he could
actually disagree with her argument: "and he still got it wrong!" (McPhedran,
1983).

Lawyers often seem incapable of distinguishing between the technique of
legal argument, which, for very important legitimation reasons, does not vary
much from the run-of-the-mill to the politically significant case, and the actual
ingredients of any decision. A fundamental element of this technique, also for
very important legitimation reasons, is to deny any element of choice in legal
decision making. Judges reason and lawyers argue as if there were a single
right answer to a legal issue which they are "bound" to reach (Dworkin,
1977a). They try desperately to deny personal responsibility for what they
decide. An example is the Quebec Veto Case in the Supreme Court of Canada:

> It should be borne in mind, however, that conventional rules, although quite
> distinct from legal ones, are nevertheless to be distinguished from rules of
> morality, rules of expediency and subjective rules. Like legal rules, they are
> positive rules the existence of which has to be ascertained by reference to
> objective standards. In being asked to answer the question whether the conven-
> tion did or did not exist, we are called upon to say whether or not the objective
> requirements for establishing a convention had been met. But we are in no way
> called upon to say whether it was desirable that the convention should or should
> not exist and no view is expressed on the matter (*Attorney-General of Quebec*,
> 1982: 393).

Far from retreating from this attitude since the enactment of the Charter, the
courts seem even more determined to claim that it is the disembodied law and
not the judge that determines the result in Charter cases. In *Dolphin Delivery*
(1986),[1] the entire Supreme Court of Canada subscribed to this statement from
the pen of Justice McIntyre:

> The courts are, of course, bound by the *Charter* as they are bound by all law. It
> is their duty to apply the law, but in doing so they act as neutral arbiters, not as
> contending parties involved in a dispute (*Dolphin Delivery*, 1986: 34).

And Shakespeare's line about "protesting too much" comes to mind when one
invariably reads a passage like the following in a controversial Charter case:

> I want to stress, as did the Chief Justice of Ontario in the court below, that it is
> not the role of the court to determine whether as a policy matter a publicly
> funded Roman Catholic school system is or is not desirable. That is for the
> Legislature. The sole issue before us is whether Bill 30 is consistent with the
> Constitution of Canada (Justice Wilson in *Re Education Act*, 1986: 38).

The Ontario Court of Appeal resorted to an exclamation mark to disavow responsibility for its decision about the constitutionality of the abortion law:

---

[1] Freedom of expression and the right to picket (below, Chapter V).

We wish to say again, because there appears to be some misunderstanding on the part of certain segments of the news media as to the role of the court in this case, that we have not determined whether the policy of Parliament on this issue is good or bad, right or wrong. To repeat, that is neither our jurisdiction nor our function! (*Morgentaler*, 1985: 92)

Just to be on the safe side, the Court of Appeal took a course reserved for especially controversial cases and did not identify the author of the opinion, completely de-personalizing the judgment. When a divided Supreme Court of Canada overruled the Court of Appeal, majority and minority *both* subscribed to a *tailoring* analogy and described the judicial function in the case as being "*simply* to measure the content of s.251 against the Charter" (*Morgentaler*, 1988: 458; emphasis added). According to the retiring, but certainly not shy, Justice Willard Estey, the Court in *Morgentaler* measured the law to the Charter "like a tailor measures a sleeve. It didn't fit, so we threw it back to Parliament" (*The Globe and Mail*, April 27, 1988: A5).

The minor uproar surrounding this same Judge Estey's unguarded comments to the press upon his retirement actually provides another example of the jealousy with which the legal profession tries to guard the secret of the judicial individuality. Somewhat inconsistently with his tailoring analogy, Estey is reported to have emphasized how false the conventional wisdom about courts was:

Judge Estey said it worries him that Canadians still do not realize how decisions vary according to the personality of each judge. As the misconception is gradually corrected, he said, people may lose respect and faith in the institution.

"People think a court is a court is a court," he said. "But it is elastic. It is always sliding" (*The Globe and Mail*, April 27, 1988: A5)

But when Estey said of the Charter era: "It is not a fantastic era. It's the same old era. The Charter is mostly a codification of what we have already got...," when he said that certain statements of other Supreme Court Judges "make me ill," and when he described some of them as "slow" and "plodding" and some of their judgments as "monstrosities," he had gone too far. Lawyer Morris Manning, who, as we shall see has as much a stake as anyone in the Charter's prestige, wrote in a letter to the editor of the *The Globe and Mail* that Estey's comments

demean the court as an institution and trivialize the importance of the Charter of Rights...Judge Estey's comments...are destructive and undermine the very institution we must protect (*The Globe and Mail*, May 4, 1988: A7).

Similar sentiments were expressed by other lawyers. A Quebec lawyer wrote that Estey had shown "flagrant contempt for the image of impartiality that a member of the highest court in the land must show" (*The Globe and Mail*, May 5, 1988: A3). Estey tried to undo the damage by saying he would not have been so hard on a statement quoted to him by the reporter had he known it had been made by a colleague on the Bench! (*The Globe and Mail*, May 5, 1988: A3)

Minimizing the Unrepresentative Nature of Judicial Review

Once we have dispensed with the myth of judicial non-partisanship and have recognized the specifically judicial factor in constitutional adjudication, the reconciliation of the Charter with our democratic sentiments becomes considerably more complicated. Two basic strategies are employed by Charter defenders. The oldest one is to minimize the inconsistencies between judicial review and majoritarian notions of democracy (Dahl, 1956). This starts with the uncontroversial observation that courts and legislatures rarely disagree, that courts only infrequently exercise their powers to declare laws or actions unconstitutional (Russell, 1983: 49; Hovius and Martin, 1983). The periods when courts are greatly out of step with politicians are the exception; they generally do not last long. Furthermore, this is no coincidence. There are mechanisms which more or less insure a congruence between prevailing political moods and the attitude of the courts. Foremost among these is that judges are appointed by elected politicians. In Canada that means the Cabinet (technically, the Governor General: *Constitution Act, 1867*, s. 96) and in the United States, the President "by and with the advice and consent of the Senate" (*US Constitution*, II.2). While the government cannot dismiss judges for ideological or philosophical non-conformity, when spaces come open through retirement, resignation, or death they can fill them with those who more or less share their outlook, making them more or less representative of the outlook of the electorate.

The United States historical record verifies that judicial political attitudes have swung back and forth with prevailing political forces (Galloway, 1982). The process can be dramatic as in the Roosevelt confrontation, or more gradual as with President Reagan, whose eight years of office allowed him, through attrition, to re-fashion the Supreme Court so that it now reflects his attitudes and those of his supporters to social issues and to the role of the Court. With his most recent nomination, his third conservative appointee, Reagan achieved a conservative majority on the Court for the first time since the 1950s. US constitutional lawyers are predicting an erosion, if not an outright reversal, of the liberal decisions of the sixties and seventies and a conservative bench lasting well into the next century, whatever future presidential elections might bring (Lewington, 1987). Major decisions of the Court's liberal era, for instance in the realm of racial discrimination and abortion, have now been slated for reconsideration by a Court finally composed, after years of careful selection, mostly of ideological opponents of these decisions (*The Globe and Mail*, April 26, 1988: A13; *Hartigan*, 1987).

There is plenty of evidence that Canadian courts can and do reflect both the points of view of those who appoint them and their regions of origin. One example, of course, is *Re Constitution of Canada* (1981), which we looked at in the last chapter, and there are plenty more in the remaining chapters. Naturally, Supreme Court judges have little to hope for in pleasing those who appoint them, but this does not prevent governments from appointing people who genuinely and independently share their views, even though this is never cited as a criterion for appointment.

Judges, therefore, can be relied upon to reflect the political terrain, at least over time. If we recall that one of the main appeals of judicial review was a general dissatisfaction with the representative nature of Parliament, is it not a quibble to complain about the unrepresentativeness of the judiciary? Moreover, there have been obvious moves recently to make the Supreme Court of Canada even more representative. Two of the first four appointments after the entrenchment of the Charter were women, the first two in the Court's entire history. The long-standing traditions and laws governing regional representation in the Court were to be both constitutionally entrenched and expanded as a result of the 1987 Meech Lake Accord (see below). There is no shortage of schemes to make judges more representative still:

> I would suggest a constitutional amendment replacing the present rule of retirement at 75 with a provision whereby the median age of the Court should not exceed 60 and when it did the oldest judge should be required to retire to restore this median (Smiley, 1981: 55).

But how far can representativeness go? Judges still have to be lawyers with some prominence in the profession, and the profession is still almost entirely the domain of the white and the upper class. Senior partners at large law firms, like recent Supreme Court appointment John Sopinka, are reported to have salaries averaging $250,000 per year and going as high as $700,000 (*Canadian Lawyer*, June, 1988: 6). The appointment of women merely reflects their increasing representation in the profession itself (May, 1987: 13), as the appointment of Canada's first Jewish Supreme Court Justice, let alone Chief Justice, Bora Laskin, was partly a long overdue recognition of the traditional overrepresentation of Jews among lawyers.

How does the inevitable class bias of the legal profession fit with the theory that the Charter is democratic? Some critics have argued that it completely destroys it:

> There are few public institutions in this country whose composition more poorly reflects, and whose members have less direct exposure to, the interests of the economically and socially disadvantaged...if not of wealthy origin, most became wealthy or at least achieved a degree of affluence before accepting their judicial appointments. The majority made their name in private practice where they held themselves out as business people and shared business concerns...much of their professional time was spent catering to the needs of the business community. In short there is nothing about the Canadian judiciary to suggest that they possess the experience, the training or the disposition to comprehend the social impact of claims made to them under the Charter, let alone to resolve those claims in ways that promote, or even protect, the interests of lower income Canadians (Petter, 1987a: 861).

Petter adds to this the great costs of constitutional litigation in the way of lawyers' fees. The successful challenge by Southam News to the search provisions of the *Combines Investigation Act* (*Hunter*, 1984) through three levels of court cost $200,000, and Merv Lavigne's successful challenge to the use of union dues for political purposes (*Lavigne*, 1986, 1987) cost the National Citizens' Coalition $400,000 through only *one* level:

> Costs like this represent a major obstacle to disadvantaged Canadians who wish to pursue their Charter rights in court [and] favour those who command sub-

stantial economic resources. [This] serves to shape the rights themselves [because] over time, the disproportionate attention that these interests command will shape the courts' perception of the purpose of the rights and, hence, will influence the courts' interpretation of their meaning and scope (Petter, 1987a: 860).

Concerns of this nature have even been echoed by so ardent a Charter supporter as Roy Romanow, who, as Saskatchewan's Attorney General and head negotiator at the November 1981 Charter talks, was one of the architects of the final deal (Sheppard and Valpy, 1982). He was recently reported as saying that because of their backgrounds, training, and the way they are appointed, judges are "less conscious of, and sensitive to, the disadvantaged" (*The Globe and Mail*, May 23, 1987: A5).

But the courts and their backers are not unaware of these criticisms. They have been doing their best to respond to them and to adapt to the political requirements of their new role. Of course, they are not prepared to do anything about the fact that judges are wealthy people, but this is not a major ideological problem for them. It has never been an obstacle for the credibility of senior politicians. Is the social class of judges any more removed than that of elected politicians from their constituents? Is the federal Cabinet more representative of the Canadian class structure than the Supreme Court of Canada? On the other hand, it is undeniable that the Charter is deeply "politicizing" the judiciary (Russell, 1983; Campbell, 1984). It is bringing judges into the thick of political controversies, forcing them to confront major social issues head on. Judges are starting to be scrutinized on the basis of their political and philosophical leanings, not just on issues of patronage. The recent appointment to the Manitoba Court of Appeal of former Premier Sterling Lyon, a deeply conservative Conservative and an opponent of judicial review to boot, provoked protests and calls for the revamping of the appointment process along American lines, with legislative scrutiny of the candidates before they are confirmed (*The Globe and Mail*, January 8, 1987: A5; January 30, 1987: A14). It is inevitable that we will move to this kind of system sooner or later. The pressure was already growing among the legal profession and the press for such a development even before the intense private lobbying reported to have taken place in seeking a replacement for the departing Judge Estey (*The Toronto Star*, July 18, 1987: A1). One commentator called the current system "playing Russian roulette" with our rights (Finlay, 1987). The anti-abortion lobby was especially active in trying to get someone to their liking because of the disastrous (from their point of view) *Morgentaler* decision of a few months before and the certainty that the Court would soon be deciding more abortion cases (*The Globe and Mail*, May 16, 1988: A1). But there was also reported pressure to appoint an "ethnic," which, in Canadian parlance, means someone who is neither English nor French (*The Globe and Mail*, May 17, 1988: A6). What bothered Charter enthusiasts was the secrecy of the process. They wanted the opportunities the Americans have to cross-examine and possibly reject nominees on their views (Beatty, 1988). The person selected to replace

Estey was indeed an "ethnic," high-powered civil litigation lawyer John Sopinka, whose parents came to Canada from the Ukraine (*The Globe and Mail*, June 24, 1988). But apart from this, almost nothing was known about Sopinka's political and philosophical leanings since he had spent his professional life as, in the words of one lawyer, a "hired gun" (*The Globe and Mail*, May 25, 1988: A5). The government has announced plans to have appointed committees screen nominees, but this modest step is not likely to satisfy critics of the current system (*The Globe and Mail*, April 15, 1988: A5).

All this amounts to a judiciary more sensitive, if not more responsive, to perspectives different from those of their social class or the class of their clients. This has already greatly changed the style of the Court. It now aims its decisions directly at the public. Judicial opinion writing, however inept by ordinary standards of political or philosophical writing, is extremely down to earth when compared to what obtained but a decade ago. In 1975, the majority of the Supreme Court of Canada did not feel it necessary to give any written reasons at all for its refusal to apply the *Canadian Bill of Rights* to abortion, apparently because the judges had made their feelings clear to the lawyers at the hearing (*Morgentaler*, 1975: 481, 491–503). In 1981, the Court literally tripped over itself in an attempt to reach the public by electronic means. So advanced has the process of politicization become that since 1986 the Supreme Court of Canada has taken to issuing official summaries with judgments, identical in intent to the "executive summaries" issued by politicians, so that the press, and hence the interested public, can immediately grasp the import of a judgment. The press has responded by giving ever more prominence to Supreme Court decisions. *The Globe and Mail* devoted a special page of its June 28, 1987 issue to the various decisions of the Court issued the day before, the way it would to a budget or throne speech. One of the newest members of the Court, Justice L'Heureux-Dubé, wants to go a step further and staff every appellate court in the country with a media representative (*The Globe and Mail*, August 24, 1988: A8).

And if this is not enough, access to the legal forum is already greatly expanding through government funding of legal challenges. In September 1985, the federal government, which had been funding language cases but nothing else, announced a "Court Challenges Program" promising nine million dollars over five years that would include litigation of equality and multiculturalism issues as well as language. Ontario gave one million dollars to the Women's Legal Education and Action Fund (LEAF), a group founded to use the Charter to advance women's rights (Morton, 1987: 42). Private fund-raising for legal actions on the left and the right is becoming routine. Under legalized politics, legal actions come to be carried on more and more either by specialized litigation agencies, such as LEAF or the Canadian Civil Liberties Association, or by interest groups who see litigation as an important component of their activities, such as the National Citizens' Coalition. Such groups carefully construct their cases selecting individuals and situations with the maximum emotional and political appeal. The old notion that the courts would use the Charter in the course of doing what they do best, applying the law to the resolution of concrete disputes, is being rapidly abandoned for the "test case" system. So out of line is this with the traditional role of courts, that the functions are starting to split. Judges are wondering how they can get rid of their dispute-resolution function entirely and, while they are wondering, mediators are picking up the slack caused by clogged courts. Judge L'Heureux-Dubé of the Supreme Court of Canada was recently reported as saying that she wanted more time "to determine and apply broad legal principles" uncluttered by the "many private disputes that litter court lists." According to her, such cases should be handled by mediation or arbitration (*The Globe and Mail*, August 24, 1988: A8). Before she spoke, some prominent Toronto lawyers had already announced the opening of a "rent-a-judge" firm called "Private Court" to settle business lawsuits quickly at $2,000 a day. The judges were to have included John Sopinka, but he was drafted to the less expensive leagues (*The Globe and Mail*, May 19, 1988: A17).

Because the individual situation in Charter litigation is becoming more and more just an excuse for the case, or is dispensed with altogether through the use of references, courts are opening up their doors to all interested parties. In one such reference on minority language education in Ontario (*Re Education Act*, 1984), the Ontario Court of Appeal resembled a legislative committee more than a court. It advertised in the newspapers for submissions from the public, heard from leaders of political parties, and discussed the merits of a government white paper. Access to the courts will certainly never proceed as far as the joint recommendation by the Public Interest Advocacy Centre and the National Anti-Poverty Organization. They wanted every citizen to have a summary right to apply to a judge of the Supreme Court of Canada for a hearing before the full court to challenge any law (Canada, 1980–81, Issue No. 29A: 10–11). But what seemed at the time to come from outer space now seems only to have come from left field. Clearly, access to the system is an issue on which there is much room for manoeuvre.

But there is a problem with judicial representativeness as a solution to the lack of fit between judicial power and democracy. Nobody could seriously argue that courts are *as*, let alone *more* representative than legislatures. For one thing there is the luxury of not having to face elections. Even in the nomination-hearing scenario, there is no competition with other candidates, and most importantly, no question of facing re-election. Judicial contact with the public is restricted to the stuffy atmosphere of the courtroom where judges run the show, sit on the highest chair, and wear the fanciest clothes. They do not have to go to public meetings or debate their opinions with anyone but other lawyers. Besides, if we were after more democracy than what we get from voting, we have much better ways of getting it than through judicial review. Even leaving aside the gross power imbalances of the marketplace, the so-called "private sphere" where one-dollar-one-vote rules, there is no lack of ideas for making government more democratic: proportional representation, referendums, tight restrictions on campaign spending, recall, smaller constituencies, more popular participation in government agencies, including lay judges, and the greater use of juries, all come to mind.[1] The point of placing a very crudely representative institution—the courts—in superintendence over a still crudely, *but far less crudely* representative institution—the government— cannot be its representativeness.

And what about the vaunted *impartiality* of the courts? It seems strange to justify judicial review on the basis of distinctive judicial qualities and then to defend its consistency with democracy by denying those very qualities. In fact, there has been considerable disquiet, at least among the legal profession, over the moves to make the Supreme Court of Canada more representative (Smiley, 1981: 50–55; *The Globe and Mail*, June 5, 1987: A5). While newspapers and public opinion polls supported the Meech Lake Accord for giving the provinces a say in Supreme Court appointments, or opposed it only for weakening the powers of the federal government (*The Toronto Star*, June 1, 1987: A1, A14), lawyers and Charter supporters thought it would "weaken" the Court by making it too obviously political. Canadian Bar Association President, Bryan Williams:

> Historically there have been provincial premiers who put politics ahead of anything else. Here, we are talking about the people who will be lawmakers and interpret the constitution.

And NDP justice critic Svend Robinson:

> I shudder to think what kind of judges (British Columbia Premier) Bill Vander Zalm or (Saskatchewan Premier Grant) Devine would appoint (*The Globe and Mail*, August 15, 1987: D1).

The legal profession and Charter supporters alike are embarrassed by the appointment of former politicians to the Bench, and the practice has completely ceased for the Supreme Court of Canada. Lawyers generally eschew the whole notion of "representation." They will argue that a bench that has variety in its judges creates a broader reservoir of experience or "commands more confidence" but never that it actually *represents* any constituency. Even the women lawyers who argued before the Joint Committee on the Constitution that the Supreme Court should be 52.4% women claimed only to want "a full understanding of the Canadian people" and a "court sensitive to the particular values" of their constituency:

> Law does not exist in a vacuum. It must be interpreted and applied with a full understanding of the country and its people (Canada, 1980–81, Issue No.22: 52).

When he was being sworn in as a new Supreme Court Justice, John Sopinka said:

> The purpose, as I apprehend it, of regional, sexual and multicultural representation, is to ensure continued confidence in the court by the country as a whole (*The Globe and Mail*, June 24, 1988: A4).

So the desire to reconcile the Charter to democracy through judicial representativeness runs into fundamental obstacles. Not only are there inherent

---

[1] For a well thought-out program for making Canadian government more democratic, see Resnick, 1984.

limits to judicial representativeness, but the more representative the courts, the less persuasive the whole idea of judicial review becomes. The second line of defence gets us much closer to an understanding of what the Charter is all about because it emphasizes the *distinctiveness* of courts, that is, it emphasises the fact that they are *not* representative.

Judges Make Better Decisions

The modern approach to the defence of judicial review, developed, naturally, in the United States, argues that it is precisely because of the unrepresentative nature of the judicial institution that judges can make better decisions than legislators, at least about some sorts of questions if not about all of them. In this defence, though judges may not always make *popular* decisions, they are more likely to make the *right* decisions, precisely because they are not subject to popular pressure. The Court is defended as a *deliberately* anti-majoritarian institution, the point of which is "to ensure the considered and careful protection of those principles that constitute our political inheritance" against "the momentary passions of the majority." Judges, writes a US constitutional lawyer

> are deliberately removed from the pressures to which many other governmental actors are deliberately exposed. Their relative insulation from the direct claims of special interest constituencies protects judges from the partisan views of other political actors. At the same time, the generality of their jurisdiction enables judges to discern, better than others with narrow jurisdiction and, therefore, limited vision, the enduring principles and longer range concerns that tend to be forgotten where either the interests of factions collide or the perspectives of bureaucrats prevail.

> [T]he moral ideals of the community...cannot be understood by the bureaucracy, the special pleaders, and the congressional staffers. Theirs is a tunnel vision, and the tunnel vision of one is not offset by that of the others. Nor would these ideals be given adequate voice in a simple majoritarian government where the passionate and self-interested concerns of the moment were too easily accorded sovereignty (Wellington, 1982: 493–4).

Similarly, the editor of the *Canadian Bar Review* could write that the Charter would protect our fundamental rights from being "set aside by a transient majority" (Castel, 1983: 1).

The Charter, then, is "Reason Over Passion," the reason of the judiciary, insulated from popular pressure, over the passion of the legislature, too easily the plaything of transient majorities. Who do you trust to protect your rights, especially your fundamental rights? The federal government of Pierre Trudeau was confident that "the Canadian people prefer their rights protected by judges rather than by politicians" (Milne, 1982: 222). The common belief that judges rank far ahead of politicians in occupational prestige (Smiley, 1981:49) is probably erroneous (Treiman, 1977: 239–242, 319–321, 348–349). Nevertheless, even politicians acknowledge that "politics" has become a dirty word (Rae, 1987), and the many failings of Canadian democracy to which we have already adverted more than adequately account for this phenomenon. So it seems only right that some questions, especially the fundamental ones, should not be solved "politically." Jean Chrétien, Liberal Justice Minister and one of the Charter's chief salesmen, proudly told the Joint Committee on the Constitution:

> I think we are rendering a great service to Canada by taking some of these problems away from the political debate and allowing the matter to be debated, argued, coolly before the courts with precedents and so on (Canada, 1980–81, Issue No. 48: 110).

There are narrower and broader versions of this anti-majoritarian defence of judicial review. In the narrowest version, the courts are assigned the function of policing the democratic process to ensure that the outcomes are truly democratic, for instance by ensuring that minorities are not excluded:

> The regulation of the democratic process requires an independent court...It is important...that some social institution (inevitably the courts) should have the status, integrity and power to police democratic institutions (Campbell, 1984: 38).[1]

Even this narrow version entails judicial superintendence over most of the political liberties. But in the wider versions, *all* questions of individual rights should be decided by the courts:

> A charter of rights is not...inconsistent with democratic theory or even with the principles of a parliamentary system of government. Entrenchment increases the range of issues over which legislatures and governmental administrators may be brought to account by the judiciary for ignoring values which are important for personal fulfillment and individual autonomy. In this sense it partially removes from the realm of political debate the process of mediating between claims made on behalf of individuals and claims made for the benefit of the whole community (Romanow et al., 1984: 219).

But how are we to evaluate the claim that courts make better decisions about rights? If we look at what the Charter supporters had before them at the time of the Charter, the evidence was meagre to say the least. Naturally, the Canadian courts' performance *without a Charter* could not be relied upon. It was admittedly dismal. The Charter was intended to change all that. The sole source for the claim was the United States. But the US record was far from promising. Granted, when the Charter became a serious contender in Canada, the United States courts were behaving in a way that Canadian civil libertarians could applaud and indeed envy. But the twenty-year period bounded by the path-breaking de-segregation decision in *Brown* v. *Board of Education of Topeka* (*Brown*, 1954) and the equally liberal abortion de-criminalization decision in *Roe* v. *Wade* (*Roe*, 1973) was the only such period in the US Supreme Court's entire two-hundred-year history. As we saw in Chapter I, its most active period other than that one was the period 1900–1937 when the Court fought a vigorous rear-guard action on behalf of laissez-faire capitalism

---

[1] Following the US constitutional law scholar, Ely, 1980.

against the regulation of business, striking down everything from minimum wage laws to child labour prohibitions. According to McCloskey:

> There is no way of estimating reliably the restraining effect of this cloud of negativisms on state legislators and congressmen who might otherwise have made haste more speedily along the road to the welfare state. No doubt the pace of social change was moderated; a respectable number of "excesses" were prevented; a respectable amount of money was saved for the businessman; a good many labourers were left a little hungrier than they might have been if the Court had not been there to defend economic liberty (McCloskey, 1960: 14).

In the mid-1970s the US Supreme Court entered another conservative phase in which its activism in the defence of civil liberties included such decisions as *Buckley* (1976), in which legislation limiting corporate spending in political campaigns was declared unconstitutional as an infringement on "freedom of speech" and *Bakke* (1978), in which affirmative action programmes intended to benefit historically deprived racial minorities were nullified as an infringement of "equal protection of the law." In the 1980s the decisions of the Court's liberal period have all been put on the block as the pendulum swings to a court selected mostly by ultra-conservative Presidents.

But for most of its history the Court has supported the legal status quo, no matter how contrary to contemporary civil libertarian conceptions. Famous examples include *Plessy* v. *Ferguson* (*Plessy*, 1896) in which the Court upheld legislation requiring black people to ride in separate railway cars, the genesis of the "separate but equal" doctrine that stood for sixty years until *Brown*. Another is *Korematsu* (1945) which sustained the wartime internment of Americans of Japanese descent without the necessity of any proof of anti-government activity. It is clear from this that no Charter would have saved Japanese Canadians from the parallel abuses of the Canadian government (Tarnopolsky, 1975: 327). More recently the US Supreme Court has upheld legislation withholding medicare for abortions (*Beal*, 1977), even where medically necessary (*Harris*, 1980). Indeed, it is generally agreed that the Canadian record on human rights was no worse for the absence of a Charter than the US record for the presence of one and probably somewhat better (Morton, 1987: 32). Not even government propaganda suggested that there was something seriously lacking in Canada's respect for civil rights without the Charter:

> When it comes to human rights and freedoms, Canadians are among the most fortunate people in the world...It may have come as a surprise to many Canadians during the recent constitutional discussions to learn that few of those rights were written into the Constitution (Canada, 1982b: 11).

As for "transient" majorities, Charter advocates would have been very hard pressed to point to consistent protection of minimum democratic rights by American courts in periods of upheaval. For example, during the McCarthy period, the US Bill of Rights did not prevent the Supreme Court of the United States from upholding criminal convictions against Communists for the crime of being Communists (*Dennis*, 1951). Nor did the Canadian courts distinguish themselves as more fearless defenders of democracy. When, during the same period, an otherwise qualified candidate was refused admission to the British Columbia bar on the sole ground of membership in the Communist Party, a Canadian court including none other than Judge C.H. O'Halloran (one of the earliest Canadian advocates of an entrenched Bill of Rights) approved of the action, notwithstanding the value he put on the principle (entrenched or not) of freedom of speech, thought, and opinion:

> Freedom of expression cannot be given to Communists to permit them to use it to destroy our constitutional liberties, by first poisoning the minds of the young, the impressionable, and the irresponsible...[I]n Canada the accepted and non-technical use of the term "political opinions" is not related to the philosophies underlying different systems of Government, but is directed to adherence to or acceptance of the policies of a political party that upholds the constitution and is not subversive in its programme and tendencies (*Martin*, 1950: 183, 187).

In addition to all of this, those who advocated a Charter for Canada also had before them the evidence of the difficulty of enforcement of even the most progressive of decisions:

> In 1955, the U.S. Supreme Court, in "Brown II," ordered that Topeka's schools racially desegregate "with all deliberate speed." Presently a federal district court judge is examining Topeka's schools to determine if they are in compliance with that original 1955 decision. Yet this remarkable fact should not surprise us, for in substantive areas as diverse as desegregation, school prayer, and criminal procedure, voluminous impact studies consistently informed us throughout this twenty-five-year period of the difficulties encountered in implementing judicial decisions that mandate policy reform and social change (Gambitta, 1981: 261).

Law enforcement is no more automatic than interpretation of the Charter. It depends on the alignment of real flesh and blood social forces. But these are far more likely to be in favour of the overruled legislation than vice versa, especially where a Court decision opposes the structure of social power. And this, after all, is the role assigned to judicial review by civil libertarians. Whites were able to undermine the desegregation decisions substantially by abandoning the cities, and US legislatures were able to undermine the abortion decisions by cutting off medical aid for abortions. Indeed, the abortion victories triggered a right wing backlash in the US, the effects of which are still being felt, even beyond the realm of abortion (see Chapter VI).

So this was the record as Canada entrenched its Charter. Most of the time courts could be expected to agree with legislatures. At certain periods, courts tended to differ, but not always to the liking of civil libertarians. More often, in fact, it was to the liking of conservatives. But no decision of the Court would be universally applauded. It was impossible to recommend the Charter to Canadians on the grounds that judges would make better decisions than legislatures. It was impossible to recommend it as a better form of concrete politics from a civil libertarian point of view.

The Form of Legal Argument

On what possible grounds could it be recommended? If judges were mostly going to come down on the side of the status quo, or, when they differed, were at least as likely to rule against democratic and human rights as in favour of them, what was the attraction? And what was the *defence* against the nagging sense that the whole thing was contrary to our most familiar notions of democracy?

The answer is the *form* of legalized politics, not its substance. Not what the courts do but the way they do it. "Coolly, with precedents and so on." "Reason Over Passion" as a technique, with the outcome justified, not by its independent qualities, but by the procedure used to reach it.

What is distinctive about the judicial technique? One immediately thinks of the formal atmosphere of the courtroom, the special costume of the participants, their arcane and ultra-deferential way of talking, and so on. But these are all symptoms of a deeper difference, a difference in *discourse*, not in the linguistic sense, but in the whole *structure* of judicial reasoning, in the way in which political issues are categorized and dealt with and, most importantly, the way in which political decisions are *justified*. What we are dealing with is a distinctive way of making things acceptable, a distinctive *form of legitimation*.

The structure of judicial reasoning is dictated by the delicate position of judicial review in a representative system of government. Since, when reviewing legislation, courts deal with the same issues as elected politicians, judicial reasoning has to be presented as differing from legislative reasoning in some fundamental way in order to survive the inevitable charge that they are subverting democracy. What, then, is supposed to distinguish judicial reasoning?

The best-known modern attempt to articulate the distinguishing features of judicial reasoning is that of the American legal philosopher Ronald Dworkin, whose works *Taking Rights Seriously* (1977b), *A Matter of Principle* (1985), and *Law's Empire* (1986) are much loved by Canadian Charter advocates, whether they sit on the right (Manning, 1983: 38) or left (Campbell, 1984: 41) of the political spectrum or on the Supreme Court of Canada (*Therens*, 1985: 501; *Edwards Books*, 1986: 61). According to Dworkin, the basic distinction is between arguments of "principle" and arguments of "policy." While it is proper for a legislature to take into account both types of argument, a court must restrict itself to principle. Arguments of policy are those directed to collective goals, involving the familiar cost/benefit, "utilitarian" types of analysis. An example would be to argue in favour of Free Trade on the grounds that it will encourage competition and benefit the consumer in the long run, or to argue against it on the grounds of loss of jobs or loss of control over our culture and social system. On the other hand, arguments of principle are those directed at establishing individual rights. An example would be an argument for Free Trade on the grounds that everyone has a right to engage in commerce free from government interference (that it is difficult to think of a pure rights argument *against* Free Trade says more about the nature of rights arguments than it does in favour of Free Trade). Rights are said to differ from goals in the individual nature of rights as opposed to the collective nature of goals. Rights are concerned with "distributive" justice, while goals are concerned with overall welfare. Indeed, rights are *defined* by Dworkin in terms of their power to resist collective benefits. To qualify as a right, a claim must have a "certain threshold weight against collective goals in general" (*Dworkin*, 1977b: 92).

Why must judges eschew policy and restrict themselves to principle? Here we get a refinement on the traditional "separation of powers" doctrine that in a democracy judges are supposed to apply the law and not to make it. Dworkin argues that these objections to judicial lawmaking, while applicable to questions of policy, have no force in matters of principle. While the collective welfare of the community is best left to the community to decide, through majoritarian, representative institutions, rights *against* the collective welfare are best determined by a judge who is insulated from the "demands of the political majority whose interests the right would trump" (Dworkin, 1977b: 85). To leave such decisions to the political process would be to "make the majority judge in its own cause" which would be "unjust" (Dworkin, 1977b: 142; Campbell, 1984: 41). So when judges strike down laws, they have nothing to be ashamed of if they can back up their decisions with arguments of principle. It is only when they dispute policy with the legislature that they are violating the democratic doctrine of the separation of powers.

As can be imagined, the emphasis on individual rights "trumping" collective welfare and the American sources of this doctrine of judicial review have made some people very uneasy. In belated second thoughts about the Charter, Roy Romanow has complained that it is "leading to an Americanization of the Canadian political system" in its "preoccupation" with "individual rights" which give it a "potential for trumping Canadians' major gains in collective rights" such as union rights and control of corporate concentration. This is something Romanow claims that those who negotiated the Charter never expected (*The Globe and Mail*, May 23, 1987: A5).

Historically, as the terrain covered in Chapter I indicates, it is probably more accurate to see the Charter as *part* of an Americanization of Canada than as a *cause* of it. On the other hand, once the Charter was enacted it could hardly be expected that the long US experience with this form of judging, and the oceans of American ink spilled over it, would be ignored. Anybody who has seen a Canadian law library knows how overwhelming in its sheer weight are the American legal materials within it. Only by the utmost restraint can the US law reports, statutes, periodicals, texts, and digests be kept from crowding out the Canadian content. The United States has at least twenty times as many lawyers and courts as we have. They have been dealing with all of these questions for years. It is therefore not surprising that the groundwork for most Canadian Charter decisions is laid with the US state of the art. As Justice La Forest of the Supreme Court of Canada wrote when he followed the US approach in a recent Charter case:

> This court, of course, is free to take a different path, but I think the consistent views of courts similarly placed over a period of several generations is not a negligible factor in assessing the soundness of the approach (*Edwards Books*, 1986: 70).

•

Indeed, US jurisprudence and scholarly commentary are cited in virtually every Charter decision handed down. And this integration is being institutionalized. In 1987, we saw the first "Canadian-American Legal Exchange" under the joint auspices of the Canadian and US Chief Justices, involving meetings between selected judges from all court levels, lawyers, and law reformers on areas of mutual concern, most notably the Charter (*The Toronto Star*, May 25, 1987: A8). But it is not exactly obvious what all of this means. US judgments and scholarship are far from monolithic. There are plenty of positions to choose from and it would be absurd to think Canadian courts so politically insensitive as to slavishly follow the latest pronouncements of the majority of the US Supreme Court. So far, Canadian courts have exhibited a willingness, indeed an anxiety, to do things as differently as local circumstances allow, if only to demonstrate their independence. Nevertheless, there does seem to be a broad consistency with American jurisprudence developing in Canadian Charter decisions on such questions as the rights of criminal suspects (Chapter IV), the rights of business (Chapter V), and the rights of women, for example to abortion (Chapter VI). But we must seek the causes elsewhere than in the sheer weight of the US legal system.

The "individual rights" vs. "collective rights" issue is more fundamental, but it too cannot be blamed on the Americans. It should have been clear to anyone familiar with the *Canadian* judiciary and the *Canadian* common law how the judges would approach their new task. Lawyer Stuart Rush thinks that the marginal role played by the Canadian public in the entrenchment of the Charter ensured that "rights for collectivities" were "left out" (Rush, 1984: 18), leaving the natural conservatism of the Canadian courts and the common law to interpret the document in favour of property:

> The common-law system is built upon the sanctity of property and contract. The courts historically have been reluctant to expand human rights at the expense of contractual rights. The courts are ideologically committed to the notions of individual free will and freedom of contract (Rush, 1984: 19).

The notion of "conservatism" in the context of judicial review has to be handled with care. It can refer to *political* conservatism as contrasted with political liberalism, i.e. authoritarianism and right wing positions on social and economic questions, or it can refer to a deferential attitude on the part of the courts to legislation, judicial *passivism* as contrasted with *activism*. In the 1930s political conservatism, in both Canada and the US, took the form of judicial activism, but in the 1950s judicial activism was an expression of political liberalism. Some commentators predicted a "conservative" approach to the Charter in the sense of a continuation of the deferential judicial posture towards legislation which so frustrated the critics during the era of the *Canadian Bill of Rights*. Donald Smiley, for example:

> It seems unreasonable to expect in the short-term future of a decade or so that the Court in interpreting the Charter will completely abandon its former dispositions towards a presumption of constitutionality (Smiley, 1981: 45).

Such predictions, though not unheard of (Hovius and Martin, 1983) were in a distinct minority among the legal profession (Castel, 1983; La Forest, 1983). They have been completely blasted as Canadian courts have fulfilled the greatest ambitions of judicial review advocates, time and again rejecting the approach of the *Canadian Bill of Rights* even in identical circumstances. We are dealing with a judiciary that has warmed to its new role very quickly. Its conservatism, if such it be, is not to be confused with passivism.

But why should we assume that legalized politics should be more conservative than other forms of politics? Why should it not be an empty vessel into which *any* form of politics can be poured, conservative, liberal, right wing or left wing. Just because the courts made conservative laws when they were left to their own devices in the nineteenth century does not mean they will act the same way now. This is a crucial question, because ever since the entrenchment of the Charter, there has been a trend of thought that, one way or another, through amendments or clever arguments, the Charter, if not an empty vessel, could at least be hijacked for progressive purposes:

> The fight to improve the protection of rights in the *Constitution* is important, despite the limitations which inhere in a capitalist legal system. There are enough pressure points in that system to make some victories for collective rights possible. There is room in a "bourgeois" constitution for such rights (Rush, 1984: 21).

Indeed, a left wing American constitutional lawyer has argued that it would not take too much ingenuity for a judge so inclined to decide that the US Constitution required *socialism* in order to fulfill its equality requirements (Tushnet, 1982: 34–35).

There is no lack of ingenuity among American judges, but, of course, nothing like this has yet happened, and there are important reasons why we can be sure it never will happen. Built into the very structure of legalized politics are mechanisms which insure that certain boats will not be rocked and that if any major steps are to be taken, they will be backward ones rather than forward ones. Legal politics is highly resistant to hijacking.

Not that legal discourse does not leave judges with a lot of freedom as to whether or not, when and how to intervene in political questions. For one thing, issues do not come prepackaged and brightly labelled as "principle" or "policy." Any issue can be looked at from the point of view of either of these categories. As we have seen, one can discuss Free Trade in terms of either the economic costs and benefits to various groups or the rights of the traders. One can talk about capital punishment in terms of whether it is the most efficient way of preventing murder (that is to say a better deterrent than less severe punishments) or in terms of whether murderers deserve to die or whether victims have the right to retribution. One can talk about the right to strike in terms of "freedom of association" or good labour policy, and Sunday opening can be called "freedom of religion" or the policy of having a common day off. These are just different ways of approaching the same concrete question. This means a great deal of freedom for the courts. If they are inclined to intervene, they can characterize the question as principle (*Big M*, 1985; *Morgentaler*, 1988), if not, they can call it policy (*Edwards Books*, 1986; *Re Public Service Employees Relations Act (Alberta)*, 1987). The discourse peculiar to courts imposes no greater restraints on them than the discourse peculiar to other forms of politics. We have already seen what enormous "leeway" exists within judicial reasoning in *Re Constitution of Canada*. And we will see more of it. But—and this is the main point—all of this freedom means that the courts cannot be compelled, by arguments of principle, to reach conclusions they do not want to reach.

More leeway yet comes from the *abstract* nature of principled reasoning. Remember that one of the reasons for distinguishing between principle and policy is that arguments about collective welfare are supposed to be best left to the majority. This is because of the concrete nature of policy arguments. Policy reasoning "looks to the future" and "is designed to effectuate a societal goal" which may or may not succeed. It therefore needs the discipline of electoral accountability. Principle reasoning

> looks to the past...[It] has persuasiveness because it vindicates a principle embedded in the moral ideas of the community; the justification sounds in terms of rights and obligations (Wellington, 1982: 509).

The distinction between principles and policies is fundamentally a distinction between arguments which appeal to *abstract* ideals and those which appeal to *concrete* benefits. Even though these ideals are supposed to be "embedded in the community," they cannot be derived by actual digging, but only by argument. The argument is about what *should* exist but it is entirely on the basis of what *already* exists. Obviously, the process has to be selective, because if everything that existed had to continue, judges would have very little to do, and also because there is much inconsistency "embedded" in the community. So judges have to pick among existing practices and choose those which they deem fundamental enough to constitute principles. The notion that these principles "exist" is purely a conceit. On the other hand, policy arguments appeal to the concrete needs of people. They are vindicated or refuted by observation not by argument about ideals. Free Trade either will or will not provide more jobs, but whether it falls within a right embedded in the ideals of the community derived from our settled practices is something which cannot be seen, touched, or tasted but only argued about.

But, as the notions of "embedded" principles and moral ideas "of the community" suggest, even judicial arguments of principle have limits. These come from the peculiar political position of courts, which is what compels them to characterize their interventions as principle and not policy in the first place. Dworkin, for example, insists, again on the grounds of the necessities of the electorally unrepresentative nature of the judiciary, that they only enforce *institutional* rights, that is, those which can be extracted from *existing* institutions and *accepted* practices, including prior judicial decisions under the doctrine of *stare decisis* ("coolly...with precedents and so on"). How are they to do this? They are to develop a theory which best *justifies* these institutions and practices and then they are to apply that theory to the question at hand. In the case of constitutional adjudication, the judge is to proceed as follows:

> His answer must take some form such as this. The constitution sets out a general political scheme that is sufficiently just to be taken as settled for reasons of

fairness...But [he] must then ask just what scheme of principles has been set-tled. He must construct, that is, a constitutional theory...we may suppose that he can develop a full political theory that justifies the constitution as a whole. It must be a scheme that fits the particular rules of this constitution, of course (Dworkin, 1977b: 106).

So radicality is ruled out by the very form of the argument. Theoretically, at least, in the realm of policy, *new* departures can be asked of legislatures in the interests of advancing the general welfare. A break with the past. But this is not proper where the courts are concerned. Not that it cannot be done. It just requires bending some important rules, and courts risk throwing over the whole game every time they do it. So they tend not to. Arguments of principle are forced to derive their premises from *existing* arrangements (principles must have "institutional support"). They start from, take for granted, and indeed *justify* basic social arrangements.

But in Canada, as well as in the US, existing social arrangements are also—whatever else they are—relations of unequal social power. Charter cases gen-erally concern the justification, or the lack of it, of aspects of these social relations of inequality. And even more serious implications flow from the distinctive way judicial reasoning goes about justifying inequality. Judicial justification, as we have seen, must be abstract and not concrete, and must reason without regard to questions of concrete benefits. How can social power arrangements be justified without reference to their concrete benefits? Philos-ophers have in fact derived a surprising number of ways of doing this. Rela-tions of inequality can be justified by saying that they are "deserved" or that they are "voluntary" or "freely chosen," and so on, without ever mentioning whether these relations do anyone any earthly good. But these abstract forms of justification have something else in common. Each justification requires ignoring something about the power relations in question, something that no one doubts actually exists. Therein lies the abstraction. Usually the thing ig-nored is the relation of power itself, because, in concrete terms, social power relations considerably undermine any freedom of choice and voluntariness. If they are not ignored, the whole procedure tends to evaporate.

There are many examples in law. The most obvious is from contract. How can a contract between unequals in power be justified? Think of contracts between large corporations and working people for employment, goods, or services. If we look at the facts, we see that the people involved have been more or less constrained by their material needs to enter into such contracts and that their relative economic or market power will explain what the terms are and who gets the better of the bargain. Enforcing such contracts can be justified (more or less successfully, depending on your point of view) by the policy of efficient allocation of resources according to market forces. But to justify it apart from this, on *principle*, contracts must be said to be "freely" entered into, that is all the unequal material factors that compel the bargain in the first place must be ignored. The judicial concept of freedom is strictly limited in that a bargain entered into under *normal* economic pressure (i.e. excluding fraud, duress, insanity—none of which aid the "efficient" allocation of resources) is nevertheless considered to be "free." It has to be, otherwise no contract could be enforced "on principle." The same with crimes. Punishment may be justified by the policy of deterrence which seeks to provide a material disincentive to crime, or by the principle of desert. If by desert, the crime must be "voluntary," that is freely chosen. Crimes committed under various compulsions (self-defence, necessity, duress, insanity) are excused, but the relative compulsions of class or lack of property are deemed not to affect the legal voluntariness of actions. One is judicially deemed to be "free" to withstand these pressures, and more importantly, *equally* free, no matter how rich or poor, how favourably or unfavourably located.

So it is only by ignoring the ugly facts of concrete power that judges can do their job at all. This is why Justice is always depicted with a blindfold. She is to treat the parties before her as if they were equals in power, the point being to show that Justice does not lean in favour of the strong. But all this means is that power is given *no more* than its due. Being blindfolded, Justice cannot lean in favour of the weak either. She has to ignore weakness as well as strength. As if in a prize fight the referee paid no attention to weight, but only made sure that nobody rubbed resin in the other fighter's eyes.

In the real world of politics and the Charter there are many pressures to let Justice's blindfold slip and to recognize the facts of power. But doing so risks the whole enterprise, and it is therefore fiercely resisted. It is this "constitutional" inability of judicial forms of argument to recognize the facts of social power, the false, power-serving assumption of the "equality" of individuals and the "freedom" of their choices, that makes principled reasoning conservative. It is not its concern with the individual per se. People do exist as individuals, and the enhancement of the concrete freedom of individuals should be the central goal of politics. But people also always exist in relations of social power, which, in Canada, are grossly unequal relations (see Chapter VI). The denial of this, or what amounts to the same thing, the denial of its *relevance*, merely ratifies existing inequalities. Practically, because social advantages are ignored in the distribution of rights, something like ignoring weight in prize fights. Ideologically, because political discourse is carried on as if these inequalities did not matter.

Some famous examples from US constitutional law will illustrate the point. When the US Supreme Court struck down a federal law imposing serious limitations on private campaign expenditures in the wake of the Watergate controversy, it called them an infringement of "freedom of speech" (*Buckley*, 1976), denying that limitations of class (lack of wealth) could adversely affect people's right to participate in politics. In *Regents of the University of California* v. *Bakke* (1978), the Court struck down a California medical school's affirmative action programme which gave preferential admission to members of historically disadvantaged minority groups. Holding that the program denied "equal protection of the laws" to members of groups who were *not* disadvantaged, the Supreme Court majority wrote: "There is no *principled* basis for deciding which groups would merit 'heightened judicial solicitude' and which would not" (*Bakke*, 1978: 296; emphasis added). Thus the majority ignored two obvious, concrete, historical facts: that racism in the United States was not random and that the specific clause under which it struck down the program, enacted in the aftermath of a Civil War fought over slavery, was meant to protect *black* people from discrimination, not to prevent them from overcoming it.

A New Kind of Democracy?

It seems, too, that an understanding of the distinctive form of judicial reasoning can clear up a lot of the confusion surrounding the "democratic" nature of the Charter. At the beginning of this chapter we examined the rather feeble attempts to portray the Charter as democratic by the useful omission of the crucial role of the judiciary. These arguments relied on ordinary notions of democracy, literally "rule of the many." But some Charter defenders have questioned this whole approach to democracy. Law professor Robert Sharpe (currently employed at the Supreme Court of Canada) asks: "Should we equate democracy with the raw will of the majority?" and answers: "A true democracy is surely one in which the exercise of power by the many is conditional on respect for the rights of the few." (*The Toronto Star*, April 11, 1987: B5). Others have argued that the Charter is democratic in a participatory sense: in "giving individuals direct access to some public decisions affecting their lives" (Romanow et al., 1984: 218). According to this point of view,

> the growth of government power has not been matched by a parallel growth in the sense of each individual's worth and power in the political process...Elected bodies are not truly in control of the vast bulk of governmental activity, and in any event, electors do not have immediate control of those issues which do get dealt with by the elected representatives. [The Charter is an] antidote to the frustration and alienation that this produces (Romanow et al., 1984: 218).

Similarly, Russell argues that the "opening up of the law reform process" through the ability of individuals to challenge laws independent of government law reform agendas "may be the major democratizing consequence of a constitutional charter" (Russell, 1983: 49).[1]

The plausibility of this claim of a democratizing effect through enhanced individual access to lawmaking rests on a number of subtle confusions. Naturally, the Charter does not increase access in any concrete sense. It is both simpler and cheaper to get to see your MP than to get to see a judge. If the Charter increases access, it does so in a *qualitative* and not in a quantitative sense, through a change in the *basis* of access. Under the Charter, neither one's right to be heard nor entitlement to success depends on the *representativeness* of one's claim. It rests instead, as we have seen, on its consistency, with abstract rights which take for granted and justify existing relations of social power. Because of this, a well-placed individual can succeed at the expense of everyone else. "You don't need a majority of one if you've got the

---

[1] We encounter a particularly enthusiastic version of this approach in the realm of labour relations in Chapter V.

Court on your side." But why should this be considered more egalitarian? What does it mean for one person to succeed at everyone else's expense? Majority rule can sound authoritarian, but it is merely the political expression of the profoundly egalitarian idea of "one-person-one-vote." To treat as irrelevant the unrepresentativeness of a claim is to allow some claimants to be more equal than others. This, in fact, is the "democracy" of the marketplace, where you don't need a majority of one if you've got property on your side. In fact, though defenders of the Charter always extol it as a remedy for the socially weak against majority *rule*, it is the socially strong who have more to gain by opposing the egalitarianism of the rule of the *majority*. In practice, of course, in the so-called political realm, representativeness is regularly defeated by economic power because economic power can also deliver votes one way or another. But it is also true that people without individual social power, that is to say without property, have inevitably found their interests better served by relying on the egalitarianism of one-person-one-vote and by organizing with those similarly situated in unions and political organizations than by relying on the abstract equality of individual rights. The democracy of the representative realm has to be constantly struggled for. But the principle approach supports the status quo of social power *by its very nature*. It does so both in theory and in practice, because it *justifies* ignoring the egalitarianism of representativeness as well as actually ignoring it. It legitimates both the status quo of inequality and an inegalitarian form of politics.

The Charter is admittedly a revolt against majoritarianism. But it does not substitute a new kind of democracy for it. In allowing individuals to shortcircuit representative institutions and groups, and to advance claims which "trump" more representative claims on the basis of consistency with abstract rights embedded in the status quo, it is a perversion of democracy.

One of the clearest indications of this is the fact that, legally speaking, the Charter only addresses itself to the restraint of public power and ignores private power altogether. Petter calls the Charter

> a 19th century liberal document set loose on a 20th century welfare state. The rights in the Charter are founded upon the belief that the main enemies of freedom are not disparities in wealth, not concentrations of private power, but the state. ...[M]ost judges and lawyers and...moral philosophers are drawn [from a class of people who] see their social and economic status most threatened by the regulatory and redistributive powers of the modern state. It is not surprising therefore that they regard as "fundamental" those values that afford them protection from such state powers...[T]his selective view...remove[s] from Charter scrutiny the major source of inequality in our society—the unequal distribution of property entitlements among private parties (Petter, 1987a: 857–858).

Petter finds this development "ironic" because of the extent to which the working class has had to turn to legislatures to right the wrongs of the judicially created common law. Such progress as has occurred

> has come in the democratic rather than the judicial arena...through political action aimed at displacing the common-law vision of unbridled individual au-

tonomy with a countervision of collective social responsibility. [The Charter is] predicated on the same hostility to legislative action, and the same reverence for individual autonomy, that animated the common law (Petter, 1987a: 858–859).

Russell echoes this sentiment when he writes: "It would be a pity if adoption of a constitutional charter of rights blunted our capacity to recognize that the state is not the only centre of power in our society capable of restricting freedom or equality or of abusing rights" (Russell, 1983: 50).

Indeed, the US Supreme Court showed how far the logic of the public/private distinction in judicial review can be taken when it held that a statute (enacted in the backlash against the *Roe* v. *Wade* case) which restricted medicaid funds to abortions "where the life of the mother would be endangered if the fetus were carried to term" or "for the victims of rape or incest when such rape or incest has been reported promptly to a law enforcement agency or public health service" did not interfere with "the freedom of a woman to decide whether to terminate a pregnancy":

> [A]lthough government may not place obstacles in the path of a woman's exercise of her freedom of choice, it need not remove those not of its own creation. Indigency falls into the latter category. The financial constraints that restrict an indigent woman's ability to enjoy the full range of constitutionally protected freedom of choice are the product not of government restrictions on access to abortions, but rather of her indigency (*Harris*, 1980: 316–17).

Legalized Politics Beyond the Courtroom

The Charter means that more and more political issues will be subjected to this peculiarly legal form of resolution. But it signifies an even more general ascendancy of the legal approach to politics, because the Charter's impact goes far beyond the courtroom. As Chief Justice Dickson said in a 1986 television interview:

> The coming years will undoubtedly see the Supreme Court playing a major role in shaping the legal, moral and social contours of our country ("W5," *CTV*, June 11, 1986).

Of course, politicians must now seek to fit their actions into forms that will pass muster according to judicial values, but that is not even the half of it. Earlier, we talked of the (carefully cultivated) broad public appeal of the Charter and that, too, will tend to enhance the spread of judicial ideas. But this new form of politics also has a great appeal for political actors themselves, be they professional or amateur, or on the left or the right. The beauty of the Charter from all these points of view is that it appears to *depoliticize* politics. In form, it replaces "conflicts of interest" with "matters of principle." It is easy to understand why this appeals to actors on the right, because it allows power to disguise itself in the abstraction of claims about rights. The National Citizens' Coalition's mortal struggle against all interferences in the marketplace are made, as we shall see, not on behalf of the big business interests it actually serves, but in defence of the "individual rights" of abstract, classless "citizens." And the NCC's courtroom victories under the Charter are proudly displayed to lend credibility to its claims (*The Globe and Mail*, July 15, 1987: A3). In similar fashion, the multi-billion dollar tobacco industry has tried to portray its all-out battle to protect its interests in "the most profitable consumer product ever sold legally" (Stoffman, 1987: 20) as a battle being fought on behalf of the individual rights of all Canadians. A recent full-page advertisement against government regulation of tobacco advertising began with a picture of the Parliament buildings and the flag over this caption:

> Many Canadians believe that banning advertising for a legal product is in violation of Canada's Charter of Rights and Freedoms.

In chilling terms, the ad asked:

> If the rights inherent in the Charter of Rights and Freedoms can be conveniently trampled upon in the tobacco advertising issue, whose rights will be denied next? (The Globe and Mail, July 9, 1987: A11)

The Charter's appeal for professional politicians is only slightly more difficult to understand. One might be forgiven for thinking that politicians would be as jealous of their powers and jurisdictions as they are when they come into conflict with one another. But it turns out that they are often quite relieved to have controversial and unpredictable issues transformed into "non-partisan" questions about rights and about the correct interpretation of the constitution so they can be taken off their hands and resolved by the courts. In fact, politicians are increasingly orchestrating such resolutions themselves by use of the reference procedure. In the short life of the Charter, the Ontario government has already used this device twice. In 1984, it invoked the aid of the Ontario Court of Appeal in extending French language education rights by the ingenious device of referring to the Court the question of the constitutionality of both its current law (which it wanted to change) and its proposed changes. The Court then conducted its own public hearings and obligingly declared the current law unconstitutional *and* the amendments an appropriate cure for the unconstitutionality (Re Education Act, 1984). In other words, the Court helped the government defend its amendments by saying they were not only consistent with the constitution but were actually *required* by it. Naturally, the government did not appeal this "loss."

But this case was merely a warm-up for the Catholic School Funding reference. The extension of full funding in 1984–85 to Catholic high schools, a bombshell dropped by retiring Premier William Davis, was an issue that divided Ontario right down the middle by religion and by ethnicity—but not by political party! For political reasons of their own, all three parties came out in favour of the $80 million per year enterprise that would cause mass transfers of school populations and weaken the public school system, even though the plan was opposed by slightly more than half the voters (The Globe and Mail, April 30, 1985: 1; The Toronto Star, February 19, 1986: A19; May 22, 1986: A23). Consequently, it was by mutual agreement left out of all debates during the 1985 election. Instead, it was referred to the Ontario Court of Appeal. Once again the Court acted like a legislative committee, hearing submissions from 32 groups and individuals and deciding by the narrow margin of three judges to two that the law was constitutional and not inconsistent with the equality provisions of the Charter (*Re Education Act*, 1986). The expressions of doubt did not deter the government from going ahead with its plans, but they encouraged opponents, headed by the Toronto Board of Education, to pursue the case in the Supreme Court of Canada. That Court was ultimately unanimous in its approval of full funding—not that the answer was all that obvious in legal terms (see page 242)—with a majority holding not only that the law was *consistent* with the constitution, but that it was actually *required* by it. The law, said the majority, "returns rights constitutionally guaranteed to separate schools by s.93(1) of the *Constitution Act, 1867*" (*Re Education Act*, 1987: 59). The decision put an end to the organized opposition. Immediately upon the release of the decision, the Metropolitan Toronto School Board Chairperson said the Board was giving up a fight that had cost three years and $500,000:

> While we regret the (court) decision, we acknowledge the jurisdiction and accept the decision...and we are anxious to continue our responsibility in providing a first-rate system of public education for the people of Metropolitan Toronto (*The Toronto Star*, June 26, 1987: A10).

Naturally, if the politicians were not going to debate the question before the Supreme Court decision, they were not going to debate it after. The 1987 election campaign was another one that avoided the funding issue. And it did so with relative ease. The Supreme Court decision was described as having taken "much of the wind out of the sails of full-financing opponents ... [T]here isn't something people can sink their teeth into any more" (*The Globe and Mail*, August 29, 1987: A2). And following the election, when flare-ups occurred over the mass student transfers, the Minister of Education could defend it against charges of "apartheid" by the fact that it had all been approved by the Supreme Court of Canada (*The Globe and Mail*, March 15, 1988: A1; March 9, 1988: A1).

According to Professor Morton, the reference procedure provides Canadian governments with "interesting political options in their game of Charter politics":

> ...there seems to be a growing trend of "issue avoidance" by elected political leaders...the increasing political role of the courts under the Charter may come not only because judges arrogate to themselves the policy-making function, but also because politicians abdicate this responsibility (Morton, 1987: 51).

So it is a serious error to see the threat of invalidation under the Charter as placing the government and the courts in opposition. Nor is this an entirely new development. During the Depression, the courts rescued an unenthusiastic federal government from having to bring in an unemployment insurance scheme. During the constitutional negotiations of 1981, the courts provided a means of legitimating a constitutional accord which excluded Quebec and which avoided the necessity of a "divisive" referendum. The Charter and the courts will continue to provide politicians with a means of avoiding going directly to the people when there is no political profit to be made, or when the likely results are unpalatable.

So the attraction of legalized politics for the political Right and for governments is easy to understand. But what could it be for the Left? We cannot discount entirely the personal attraction of the Charter for politically conscious lawyers. Their jobs are considerably enriched when courts are made the locus of major political confrontations. No doubt some of them genuinely, if briefly, entertain the misconception we noted earlier, that Charter concepts are open-ended enough to be hijacked for progressive purposes. Just maybe, with enough ingenuity, preparation, and so on, important political victories can be won in the courts that cannot be won in the more familiar political arenas, dominated as they are by established interests. But the most important reason is the idea that there is something to be gained by going to court even if you know you are going to lose.

Organizing political campaigns is a difficult and expensive business. Much of it is occupied with getting publicity. The press, dominated by big business, always seems reluctant to give publicity to left wing movements even when they have broad popular support, but especially when they do not. Politicians will always be counting votes. Legal action has seemed a way around these problems. You are guaranteed a day in court and the opportunity to make your case. Furthermore, the *form* of legal discourse, treating each side impartially and professing to be as blind as the Statue of Justice to political clout, appears open-ended enough to allow even the weak and unpopular to win. In court, the David and Goliath scenario always seems possible. Most lawyers can make almost any political case, no matter how weak, sound like a strong legal case and can do so in terms sufficiently removed from the predictability of everyday politics to make the press attentive. This is very hard to resist for groups on the Left. Whether they win or lose in legal terms, legalized politics affords them a platform to make their case to the world.

Operation Dismantle v. The Queen

One such group was Operation Dismantle, the Ottawa peace group that tried to stop the cruise missile with the Charter. This bizarre and ironic case is a vivid illustration of just how wrong things can go when the Left tries to appropriate legalized politics. In July 1983, the federal government announced that it would allow the American government to conduct a series of Cruise missile tests in Canada. Opinion polls indicated that most Canadians who had an opinion on the matter opposed the tests (*The Toronto Star*, August 11, 1983: A4). However, this popular opposition did not find a proportionate expression in Parliament where the two major parties combined to defeat a New Democratic Party motion against the tests 213 to 34.

Immediately following the government's announcement, Operation Dismantle commenced an action to have the tests declared unconstitutional as contrary to section 7 of the *Charter*, which guarantees

> the right to life, liberty and security of the person and the right not to be deprived thereof except in accordance with the principles of fundamental justice.

As one of the first overtly political Charter actions in English Canada on a matter of great importance and controversy, the action received an extraordinary amount of publicity. It started with the carefully staged filmclip of the footsteps of Operation Dismantle's lawyer heading into the Federal Court building to file the papers and it ended, almost two years later, with many filmclips and headlines in between, on the steps of the Supreme Court of Canada building, with a speech to reporters by Operation Dismantle's president when the action was finally lost. The publicity was encouraged by Operation Dismantle's rather surprising victory on a preliminary motion soon after the action was launched. The government had applied to have the suit thrown out before trial on legal (as opposed to factual) grounds. Indeed, Operation Dismantle's legal case was weak. It came as a surprise, therefore, when Judge Alexander Cattanach, something of a maverick (the oldest judge in the trial division and the only Diefenbaker appointment) threw the motion out and held that the case had to go to trial (*Operation Dismantle*, 1983). Cattanach's decision was very poorly reasoned—his major concern at the hearing seems to have been about the unarmed cruise missile "falling on somebody's head" during a test (*The Globe and Mail*, September 16, 1983: 2)—and despite opposition howling, the government promptly appealed.

With all the publicity, it was hardly noticed that the Charter action was only one of two initiatives spearheaded by Operation Dismantle against the cruise missile. The other was a proposal for a binding national referendum, launched right after the action, following Prime Minister Trudeau's statement that he would "reconsider" the tests if it could be demonstrated to him that a majority of Canadians were opposed to them (Mandel, 1983b).[1] Trudeau said he "could not imagine" how this could be done outside of a general election fought on the issue of membership in NATO. Operation Dismantle thought that a referendum would suffice, with the simple question: "Are you in favour of the cruise missile being tested in Canada? Yes or No," and expressed its willingness to include a separate question on NATO membership. This was not its first venture in the referendum business; Operation Dismantle had previously arranged 132 municipal referenda on general disarmament questions. In fact, the organization's main goal for its seven years of existence was to have a worldwide referendum on balanced disarmament sponsored and organized by the United Nations General Assembly.

The proposal for a referendum on the cruise tests was announced at a press conference on August 2, 1983, in Toronto, chaired by Mayor Arthur Eggleton, who announced himself in favour of the idea, saying he would vote *against* the cruise tests but *for* membership in NATO. But a curious thing happened. The media, while salivating over the court case, was supremely *un*interested in the referendum. Why? Because this was politics not law, and there was an almost complete lack of political support for the initiative. When Operation Dismantle polled all 282 Members of Parliament, only 18 replied. Of these, fifteen were opposed and only three were in favour. One MP wrote on his questionnaire: "This is pure NDP." He could not have been more wrong. One of the biggest blows to the referendum proposal was that it was opposed by NDP

---

[1] Most of the information that follows comes from my personal knowledge and documents that came into my possession as the draftsperson of the referendum initiative for Operation Dismantle.

members on the recommendation of their disarmament spokesperson, Pauline Jewett. She had written to the NDP caucus warning of the "divisiveness" of binding referenda and the dangers of putting questions like bilingualism, capital punishment, abortion, and foreign aid to the people. Where the cruise missile was concerned, the electoral process was definitely to be preferred even to a non-binding referendum:

> Canadians at the next federal election can make political choices that will reflect their views and concerns about the cruise missile...Canadians can, in fact, put a government in place, the NDP, that will refuse the cruise in Canada...Elected politicians need a good shaking up and the government of Canada should be changed for the fight (Jewett, 1983: 3).

It was obvious to everyone that the NDP had no hope of forming the next government of Canada or of stopping the cruise missile tests in a Parliamentary forum against the combined opposition of the Liberals and the Tories. As the only party to oppose cruise testing, the NDP's self-interest in making a federal election the only means of expressing opposition to the tests should also be obvious. The principled nature of its support for the electoral process is also rendered suspect by its vigorous support for Operation Dismantle's court action, even to the extent of protesting the government's appeal of the original ruling. A victory in the court case would, of course, have bound Parliament to the decision of a few judges. When challenged on this point during a speech at Osgoode Hall Law School, Jewett's feeble reply was that "judicial decisions are part of our democratic tradition" (*Obiter Dicta*, February 20, 1984: 15).[1] This sentiment appears to have been shared by the Prime Minister, who rejected outright a direct offer by the President of Operation Dismantle to drop the court action if the government would agree to the referendum. Trudeau, too, was happier to face the courts than the people.

Without institutional or press support, and embroiled in the increasingly expensive court battle,[2] Operation Dismantle lacked both the resources and enthusiasm for pursuing the referendum, which it put on the back burner, never to take it off again. As for the court action, it quickly turned sour. The Federal Court of Appeal held hearings on the government's appeal in record

---

[1] Jewett has at least been consistent in her opposition to referenda. At the Joint Committee hearings on the Charter she tried to draw representatives of the National Action Committee on the Status of Women into a condemnation of the provision in the original—but not the final—constitution plan which provided a referendum mechanism for constitutional amendment: "Now this is the referendum section and most of us, in my party anyway, feel that the referendum section should not apply to the charter and, therefore, would not apply to Section 15. One of the main purposes of entrenching rights and particularly adequately entrenching women's human right to equality, and indeed the rights of ethnic and other minorities and so on, is so they cannot be taken away by a majority vote" (Canada, 1980–81, Issue No. 9: 69). To her credit, Lynn McDonald, the NAC representative did not go along with this: "But women, of course, will be divided as men are divided on many other issues that might be brought to a referendum...So we do not want to close that off" (Canada, 1980–81, Issue No. 9: 70). Unfortunately, McDonald saw things differently when she later became an NDP MP and voted with Jewett against the cruise missile referendum (McDonald, 1983).

[2] Operation Dismantle had been denied access to the government's blatantly biased *Charter* action funding program which at the time only paid for language cases (*Ontario Lawyers Weekly*, March 16, 1984: 8), so it spent a lot of its energy looking for money.

time (less than a month after the original decision), and unanimously reversed Judge Cattanach six weeks later (*Operation Dismantle*, 1984). Each judge wrote a separate opinion, and numerous legal grounds were cited, including the lack of any alleged violation of "principles of fundamental justice" as required by the words of section 7 of the Charter, and the defence policy nature of the cruise tests which made them, as a question of "policy," a subject unfit for judicial determination.

A minor irony occurred when Operation Dismantle was granted leave by the Supreme Court to appeal the ruling of the Federal Court of Appeal in December 1983. This happened within one day of the group's announcement that its seven-year quest for a UN sponsor for the worldwide referendum had ended in success. Operation Dismantle's newspaper, *The Dismantler* (1983, Vol. 5, No. 4.), carried the large headline, "WE DID IT," to announce the event. The press completely ignored this announcement but made the Supreme Court's granting of leave to appeal front page news (*The Globe and Mail* and *The Toronto Star*, December 21, 1983).

Operation Dismantle spent the next year and a half throwing good money after bad, in and out of court, while two sets of cruise missile tests took place in Alberta. The organization put all of its eggs in one legal basket—the Supreme Court of Canada. In January 1985, when the massive protest marches against the cruise missile had dwindled from the tens of thousands to the hundreds, Operation Dismantle's President, Jim Stark, announced:

> We made our decision a year and a half ago, that protest in the streets, letter-writing campaigns, telephone campaigns were not going to stop the cruise missile tests. The only chance of stopping those tests, short of the government seeing the light, was a decision by the Supreme Court of Canada. So we have put our eggs in that basket (*The Toronto Star*, January 20, 1985: A3).

In May, when the Supreme Court of Canada put the action out of its misery and unanimously decided against Operation Dismantle, the group was reduced to trying to salvage something from its near two-year quest by proclaiming that the decision was "a victory for the strength of the Charter and the civil rights and liberties of Canadians" (*The Toronto Star*, May 9, 1985: A1). Why? Because the Supreme Court of Canada had recognized (though of course had not exercised) a judicial power to review Cabinet decisions on Charter grounds. This from a group that had alleged in its Statement of Claim that testing the cruise missile was a foot in the grave for all humanity! Similar congratulatory remarks were made by Liberal and NDP members in the House of Commons when requesting the government not to insist on its right to legal costs. A Liberal member characterized the decision as the "finest hour" of the Charter (*House of Commons Debates*, May 10, 1985: 4604). An NDP member called it "a very important court action...which established the fundamental principle that Cabinet decisions are subject to the Charter of Rights" (*House of Commons Debates*, May 14, 1985: 4721). The Prime Minister, in his response, agreed that the courts' new role made this "the kind of a democracy for which we are all thankful" (*House of Commons Debates*, May 10, 1985: 4611). Though the Government did ultimately forgive its costs, Operation Dismantle's lawyers were apparently not so generous with their fees (*The Globe and Mail*, 10 July 1985: 8).

Professor F. L. Morton recently wrote of the Operation Dismantle episode:

> While ultimately unsuccessful in stopping the testing, the litigation did achieve considerable publicity for the "peace movement." Such publicity and the legitimacy that it can confer was probably the objective of Operation Dismantle all along, and in this sense the case was a victory of sorts for the coalition (Morton, 1987: 40).

It is true that Operation Dismantle had hoped that its case, *win or lose*, would have an educative effect. And clearly Operation Dismantle got a lot of publicity from it (the peace movement hardly needed any). But what did it teach Canadians about nuclear weapons? If anything, that the cruise missile was not the catastrophe that it had been cracked up to be and that peace groups were not all that serious in their claims about the dangers of nuclear weapons. What else could Canadians learn from this newly famous anti-nuclear group that was now telling us that the power of the Supreme Court to review Cabinet decisions outweighed the threat from the cruise tests?

Certainly the Supreme Court of Canada's own reasoning did nothing to dispel this general feeling of security. A motion of the sort involved in the case, since it is meant to preempt a trial of the facts by showing it to be unnecessary, is always disposed of by accepting the plaintiff's (Operation Dismantle's) allegations of fact as true. The only question is whether, assuming the allegations are true, there is a case in law. But in *Operation Dismantle* the majority of the Supreme Court disregarded the rules and took the extraordinary step of expressing an opinion on the facts—naturally, without hearing any evidence. Speaking for five of the six judges, Chief Justice Dickson ruled that the facts alleged by Operation Dismantle, and, as several opinion polls showed, accepted by millions of Canadians, "could never be proven." (*Operation Dismantle*, 1985: 488). The unverifiability of the cruise missile, which Operation Dismantle wanted to prove would render arms control agreements unenforceable, met with this response:

> [I]t is just as plausible that lack of verification would have the effect of enhancing enforceability than of undermining it, since an inability on the part of nuclear powers to verify systems like the cruise missile could precipitate a system of enforcement based on co-operation rather than surveillance (*Operation Dismantle*, 1985: 489).

To the claim that deploying the cruise missile could lead to a "preemptive strike or an accidental firing," the majority argued:

> It would be just as plausible to argue that foreign states would improve their technology with respect to detection of missiles, thereby decreasing the likelihood of accidental firing or a preemptive strike (*Operation Dismantle*, 1985: 489).

These conclusions were reached without hearing a shred of evidence, let alone any of the experts Operation Dismantle wanted to parade in court. Nor did Justice Dickson hint at any hitherto unknown personal expertise in the art of nuclear war or politics. Instead, he seems to have decided this as a matter of *principle* flowing from the juridical sovereignty and theoretical freedom of foreign states. No matter how predictable their actions might be in fact, no matter how many livings might be earned advising governments how other governments could be expected to react, in *law* they were completely unpredictable:

> Since the foreign policy decisions of independent and sovereign nations are not capable of prediction, on the basis of evidence, to any degree of certainty approaching probability, the nature of such reactions can only be a matter of speculation...(*Operation Dismantle*, 1985: 488)

Why would the Court take such an extraordinary approach? One answer might be that any other approach to dismissing the action would have limited the authority of the Court to intervene in political questions in the future. It was better from the point of view of the Court to decide the case on the merits than on any limitations on its jurisdiction. In fact, the majority took the opportunity to stress how wide its jurisdiction was, even going beyond the self-imposed limits of the United States Supreme Court under the so-called "political questions" doctrine:

> Cabinet decisions fall under s. 32(1)(a) of the Charter and are therefore reviewable in the courts and subject to judicial scrutiny for compatibility with the Constitution. I have no doubt that the executive branch of the Canadian Government is duty bound to act in accordance with the dictates of the Charter (*Operation Dismantle*, 1985: 491).

> I have no doubt that disputes of a political or foreign policy nature may be properly cognizable by the courts (*Operation Dismantle*, 1985: 494).

Nor was there any difference between the majority and Justice Wilson in this regard. Like most of the Court of Appeal, she seems to have rested her decision on the failure of Operation Dismantle to allege the violation of some legally recognizable *principle*, such as equal treatment before the law, in their disagreement with government policy:

> I do not see how one can distinguish *in a principled way* between this particular risk and any other danger to which the government's action vis-a-vis other states might incidentally subject its citizens (*Operation Dismantle*, 1985: 518; emphasis added).

As for judicial competence in political questions, her opinion was an ardent, if unconvincing defence:

> [T]he courts should not be too eager to relinquish their judicial review function simply because they are called upon to exercise it in relation to weighty matters of State. Equally, however, it is important to realize that judicial review is not the same thing as substitution of the court's opinion on the merits for the opinion of the person or body to whom a discretionary decision-making power has been committed...

> Because the *effect* of the appellants' action is to challenge the wisdom of the government's defence policy, it is tempting to say that the court should in the same way refuse to involve itself. However, I think this would be to miss the point, to fail to focus on the question which is before us. The question before us is not whether the government's defence policy is sound but whether or not it

violates the appellants' rights under s.7 of the *Charter of Rights and Freedoms*. This is a totally different question. I do not think there can be any doubt that this is a question for the courts (*Operation Dismantle*, 1985: 503–504; emphasis in original).

Justice Wilson can call what she's doing whatever she likes, but when the constitution is as open-ended as the Charter of Rights, the difference between determining whether it has been "violated" and substituting her opinion for the government's is just words.

To summarize: a group formed to fight for popular democracy on disarmament, in search of a quick legal fix for a complex political question, is swallowed up by the legal monster and spat out two years later, not only having been denied the day in court it sought, but also having its own case turned against it with no opportunity to respond except by praising the monster for increasing its swallowing capacity. This is legalized politics *par excellence*.[1]

Operation Dismantle was not the last group to use the courts to try to short-circuit the difficulties and complexities of ordinary mass politics. We will see many more examples in the ensuing chapters. And we can expect this phenomenon to increase, if only because, as we noted earlier, the various governments, obviously less than threatened by Charter politics, have expanded the funding of Charter challenges. Nor is engaging in legalized politics always a matter of choice. As Petter points out, a lot of the money being raised by groups such as the women's action group LEAF, both privately and publicly, "is being used to defend from Charter challenge legislation that is beneficial to women" (Petter, 1987a: 859). But whether for purposes of defence or offence, the "money, time and energy devoted by such groups to the Charter are money, time and energy that will be taken away from lobbying and other forms of political action." (Petter, 1987a: 859). Russell, too, fears the "judicialization of politics":

...excessive reliance on litigation and the judicial process for settling contentious policy issues can weaken the sinews of our democracy. The danger here is not so much that non-elected judges will impose their will on a democratic majority, but that questions of social and political justice will be transformed into technical legal questions and the great bulk of the citizenry who are not judges and lawyers will abdicate their responsibility for working out reasonable and mutually acceptable resolutions of the issues which divide them (Russell, 1983: 52).

---

[1] Almost needless to say, the Americans have conducted cruise missile tests in Canada each year since March 1984. Organized protests have been invisible during the last two (*The Globe and Mail*, March 2, 1987: A8; January 21, 1988: A4). In the aftermath of the Charter action, Operation Dismantle all but folded. After laying off all of its staff and moving to cheaper offices, it says it has re-oriented itself to less ambitious projects: "We are not trying to be all things to all people anymore" (*Fundraising letter*, January 1988). The peace movement has not given up on the Charter yet, though. World Federalists of Canada are co-ordinating a "Nuclear Weapons Legal Action," that will rely partly on the interventionist reasoning of the Supreme Court in *Operation Dismantle*, to have nuclear weapons declared illegal under the Charter and international law. No longer at the top of the list of plaintiffs, but supporting it nevertheless, is Operation Dismantle itself (Nuclear Weapons Legal Action, 1987).

However harmful it is to Canadian democracy, it is clear that the legalization of politics has not "technicalized" political issues. As we have seen, the courts have taken their public relations tasks very seriously. Yet if their style has changed, the basic nature of what they have to offer has not. And if the world outside the courtroom is more receptive, it is not because of a spontaneous change in judicial style, but in the world outside the courtroom itself.

What has been missing from the discussion of technicalization and similar fears—for example, of judicial incompetence for the new tasks (Smiley, 1981: 21; *Ontario Lawyers Weekly*, June 27, 1986: 12)—is an appreciation of the extent to which the legalization of politics is not merely a phenomenon of changing *forums* but a change in the *form* of politics *whatever the forum*. What is missing is an explanation of why all this is taking place and why it is taking place now.

Understanding the Legalization of Politics

The Charter of Rights, in its substitution of judicial for representative forums and of abstract/principle for concrete/policy forms of argument for the resolution of political controversy, represents a fundamental change in the structure of Canadian political life, a "legalization of politics." In Chapter I, we reviewed the circumstances that brought us to this point: the overwhelming influence of the United States on Canadian life, and the solution the general formula provided the federalist forces for the specifically Canadian problem of Quebec independentism. But the phenomenon of legalized politics has spread far beyond the shores of North America and seems to be sweeping the Western industrialized world. It has even spread to the home of Parliamentary sovereignty, the UK, where a movement for an entrenched Charter has been gathering momentum for some time (Zander, 1985; Gwyn, 1987). So it seems reasonable to suppose that there are deeper reasons for the rise of this political form. In fact, the legalization of politics can be tied to important societal changes stretching back to the end of the last century which have picked up considerable steam since the end of the Second World War. Specifically, it is possible to understand the legalization of politics in the context of three interconnected contemporaneous phenomena: the expansion of the suffrage, the deep involvement of the state in the economy, and the increasing tendency to malfunction of Western industrial economies. Legalized politics can be seen as a defence mechanism developed to preserve the status quo of social power from the threats posed to it by these phenomena.

The Intermingling of the Public and Private Spheres

By the end of the nineteenth century, the constant and frequently revolutionary pressures of the urban working class had brought about the extension of the suffrage and, at the same time, the beginning of serious state regulation of the economy (Marx, 1867: 389–416; Resnick, 1984: 20–22). Left to their own devices ("freedom of contract") market forces tended brutally to exploit and even destroy working people. Aided by the Depression and the Second

World War, this process of state involvement in the economy has by now reached enormous proportions. When Canada entrenched its Charter, government spending in support of private enterprise and non-corporate welfare had approached fifty percent of Gross National Expenditure (Bird, 1979: 9). State sector workers accounted for perhaps one-quarter of the labour force (Bird, 1979: 97, 100). This has been a constant and increasing source of annoyance and concern to the most powerful, that is to say, the wealthiest, sectors in society, namely business, big and small, not only for the immediate interference with profit-making it poses, but for the long-term consequences of popular control of the economy. Business's response has been an unrelenting campaign against government involvement in the economy, except, naturally, where it is of direct benefit to business. The result is the wholesale privatization of government-owned enterprise (*The Globe and Mail*, August 13, 1988: B1) and, especially, the massive attempt at de-regulation that is the "Free Trade" movement, a drive to end all purely political barriers to the free movement of capital throughout the North American continent, while protecting the rights of business to receive government subsidies so long as they do not "discriminate" on merely national grounds (Drache, 1987: 77; 1988).

Central to business's case against government interference is an ideology that deems the economy a "private" sphere, despite the enormous social power that is wielded there. Increasing government involvement in the economy breaks down both the fact and ideology of the distinction between public and private spheres. According to the influential German theorist Jürgen Habermas, this "recoupling of the economic system to the political...repoliticizes the relations of production" (Habermas, 1975: 36), and it creates dangers for the very survival of private power. A genuine "substantive democracy, would bring to consciousness the contradiction between administratively socialized production and the continued private appropriation and use of surplus value" (Habermas, 1975: 36). To avoid this problem, the modern state tends to develop "a system of formal democracy" which among other things involves "a legitimation process that elicits...diffuse mass loyalty—but avoids participation [through] institutions and procedures that are democratic in form, while the citizenry...enjoy the status of passive citizens" (Habermas, 1975: 37).

The idea is that great stretches of private power and privilege cannot coexist with heavy government involvement in the economy, universal citizenship (suffrage), and genuinely popular and participatory institutions. Something's got to give. The more that people participate in a regulatory government, the less likely they are to tolerate private power. What is to stop them from *buying out*, instead of merely *bailing out*, Chrysler Corporation, Dome Petroleum, and all the other corporations that come begging for handouts? Remember that one of the popular chords struck by Charter advocates was the general dissatisfaction Canadians felt with their experience of democracy. As a solution to the failings of democracy, the Charter seems a strange device, especially when compared to the more obvious solution of democratizing popular institutions. However, if the idea is not to *enhance* real democracy, but rather to *avoid* enhancement by giving merely a *sense* of enhancement with a formal substitute, the Charter makes perfect sense. In response to our frustration at the lack of democracy in our representative institutions, we get a spectator democracy, even more removed from genuine democracy and guaranteed, because of its nature and personnel, not to rock any boats. Not only this, but the Charter is even capable, in difficult moments, of weighing in on the side of a threatened status quo—as it recently did against the threat of Quebec nationalism; as it did during the first part of this century in both Canada and the US against attempts to regulate the economy in the public interest; as it did during the early days of the US Revolution against popular demands for freedom from British debt. The general clauses of the Canadian Charter may wait patiently in the wings for many years until the big moment when they can enter the fray against radical change by a "transient majority."

Economic Stagnation and Legalized Politics

The progressive intermingling of the public and private spheres has also been accompanied by a general stagnation of the Western industrialized economies. Apart from war-related booms, there has been a general trend to declining rates of growth in material productivity. These are especially pronounced in North America where legalization is most popular, and Canada's adoption of the Charter came when we were at our lowest postwar productivity ebb (Social Planning Council of Metropolitan Toronto, 1985: 11–13). While average Canadian real-money income has risen substantially since the War, it is unclear whether this has been accompanied by a real rise in even the material standard of living. Much of it is due to the entry of women into the work force and the consequent commodification of housework (Vaillancourt, 1985: 2; Wilson, 1982: 19; Armstrong and Armstrong, 1983: 249). What is clear is that economic inequality has increased since the War and promises to continue to increase. A recent survey of Canada's top 1000 companies in *The Globe and Mail Report on Business Magazine*, was entitled "It's raining profits":

> Looking back, 1987 will be glowingly remembered as the best 12 months of the decade, the year of the profit parade for Canada's corporations...In 1987, the fifth year of recovery, Canada's vital signs were stable. Inflation held steady at 4.4%; wages rose by an average of only 2.7%; unemployment fell to 8.9% (Salter, 1988: 83).

As profits rise, the steady readjustment upwards of what are considered "normal" rates of unemployment (Social Planning Council of Metropolitan Toronto, 1985: 6) is another sign of a growing gap between our economic capabilities on the one hand and the ability of our economic system to take advantage of them on the other. An ever greater proportion of the population is being excluded from participation in the economy and relegated to dependence on one form of welfare or another. It is no coincidence that government regulation of the economy and demands for popular participation in government should be growing with all of this. The failures of the economy—to provide work and palpably rising living standards and to hold the line on material inequality—are at once a cause and an effect of the breakdown of the barriers between public and private spheres. A cause, because it was the violent dislocations of the unregulated private sphere that brought forth government intervention in the first place. An effect, because government intervention robs a capitalist economy of its dynamism and productivity (Wright, 1978). But a consequence of stagnation is that "new legitimations [have to be] essentially political in nature," as opposed to material, including, in the US, "the dangerous revival of the Cold War" and "mass dissemination of jingoistic nationalism" in an effort "to legitimate...productivity economics and more or less permanent austerity" (O'Connor, 1981: 41). One cannot fail to have noticed how recent revivals of Cold War ideology in the West have tended to emphasize abstract, classless, homogeneous "human rights" issues as opposed to the material issues which predominated in the early postwar era of booming western economies. One cannot fail to have noticed how in Canada the constitution itself, patriation, the Charter of Rights, and the plea for "*national*" unity all had a part to play in taking our minds off our drastic economic decline and in unifying a country riven by enormous disparities in material well-being and life chances. It also seems logical that ideology in a stagnating economy will emphasize distribution over production. When winning the lottery has replaced prospecting for gold and making a better mousetrap as the ideal ways to get rich, distributional rights will be increasingly emphasized at the expense of improved benefits (Mellos, 1979). Thus, the increasing substitution of abstract principles for concrete policies represented by the *Charter* seems to have its source in the legitimation problems of an economic system with a declining capacity for delivering the goods and forced to serve up rights as a cheap, but non-nutritious substitute.

The expanding jurisdiction of the legal profession over everyday life can be seen, then, as a function of the increasing need for abstract forms of legitimation of a social system less and less able to defend itself on the basis of its concrete benefits, and the increasing need for a safe and formal substitute for democracy when citizenship is universal and the state is dangerously involved in the economy. The legal profession's traditional form of argument is well suited to these legitimation problems, dealing as it does in abstractions which suppress the historical and material/class aspects of the conflicts with which they deal, treating them instead as questions of "principle" concerning the rights of free-willing legal subjects. On this hypothesis, the increasing centrality of the legal profession in the resolution of political controversy is due to the fact that lawyers' traditional form of argument is now in vogue for deep structural reasons. Legalized politics, as *simulated* politics, is better suited to the solution of the problems of power in our era (from power's point of view) than the real thing.

A Note on the Override Clause

One of the focal points for the debate on the Charter in coming years is likely to be the so called "legislative override" clause in section 33. Not in the original plan, it was conceded by the federal government to the opposing provinces as the price for agreement to the constitutional package. It provides that Parliament or a provincial legislature "may expressly declare" that any law "shall operate notwithstanding a provision included in section 2 or sections 7 to 15 of this Charter." The law will then "have such operation as it would have but for the provision of this Charter referred to in the declaration."

The provision applies to everything in the Charter but the so-called "Democratic Rights" (the citizen's right to vote and stand for election in s.3; the requirement that legislatures face elections at least every five years and meet at least once a year in ss.4 and 5) and the federal government's familiar "national unity" bottom line: "Mobility Rights," "Official Languages of Canada," and "Minority Language Education Rights." There is also a requirement that any such declaration has to be renewed at least every five years. The matters that can be legislatively overridden thus include all of the "fundamental freedoms" (conscience, religion, expression, association, etc.), the fundamental justice provision, all of the due process rights such as the right to counsel and presumption of innocence, and the equality rights (except for the ambiguous section 28 which provides that the Charter *itself* applies "equally to male and female persons"). It is generally agreed that without this clause the deal would not have been signed (Sheppard and Valpy, 1982: 144; Romanow et al., 1984: 211; Canada, 1982b: 34).

Section 33 has been much maligned for preserving the technical supremacy of the legislature. Superficially, taking the view that the Charter is a straightforward rights-guaranteeing document, the section appears to allow legislatures to deprive Canadians of their rights. It appears to invest the politicians with the power to shield themselves from answerability for their own rights abuses. Once we uncover the hidden judicial factor, however, we can see it in a much more favourable light, as reserving for elected politicians the right of keeping selected legislative programs out of the clutches of the legal profession and *its* form of politics. A government may be made to pay for or reverse an unpopular law, but what can you do about an unpopular judicial decision, lacking a section 33? Amend the constitution? Wait until the judges retire or die to appoint new ones?

But since superficiality tends to characterize discussion of the Charter, supporters of s.33 (e.g. Petter, 1987a: 11–12; Morton, 1987: 54–55) are far outnumbered by the detractors. Before the entrenchment of the Charter the clause was being denounced by prominent lawyers such as Edward Greenspan:

> The whole object of a charter is to say, you never opt out, they're inalienable rights. If you believe in liberty, if you believe in rights, the rights are not alienable (Russell, 1983: 45).

Law students were circulating petitions for

the removal of Section 33 from the Canadian Charter of Rights and Freedoms, *via prompt constitutional amendment,* so as to facilitate the true will and interests of the Canadian people, and to protect these sacred rights and freedoms by and for all Canadians, for all time to come (*Obiter Dicta,* April 5, 1982: 8; emphasis in original).

The Canadian Bar Association's official position since entrenchment has been unwavering opposition: "Fundamental rights can't be 'half-entrenched'" (*The Globe and Mail,* March 16, 1983: 9). An American lawyer recently threw in his two-cents worth in a Canadian legal magazine, and called s.33 "fundamentally sad":

[O]f what lasting legal value are the guarantees of the individual freedoms when...they can be subject to direct challenge and dilution by the politicians of the day? (Brill, 1987: 2)

Again, left-right distinctions do not apply. In light of her attitude to referenda, it is probably not surprising that the NDP's Pauline Jewett found the override clause "almost heartbreaking" (*House of Commons Debates,* November 20, 1981: 13129) and introduced a petition to delete it (*House of Commons Debates,* November 30, 1981: 13460). But she did not go as far as Svend Robinson, whose opposition to section 33 caused him not only to break ranks with his party and vote against the whole Charter Resolution (*House of Commons Debates,* December 2, 1981: 13663), but also, after it had been passed, to call on the Senate to "delete this section, which so effectively guts the provisions of the Charter of Rights and Freedoms" (*House of Commons Debates,* December 3, 1981: 13691). Left wing legal academic Gail Starr finds the only justification for s.33 to be that governments can be "thrown out" for exercising it (Starr, 1984: 14). Left wing political scientist Reg Whitaker is not even this charitable:

The one aspect of the *Constitution Act, 1982* which seems to offer a net democratic benefit is the *Charter of Rights,* and this has been deeply undercut by the infamous 'notwithstanding' clause (Whitaker, 1984a: 265).

The vituperation continues even after six years of experience with Charter politics. Panitch and Swartz, in their socialist critique of Canadian labour policy, including what the courts have done under the Charter, label section 33 "a loophole, cynically crafted by the Attorneys General of Saskatchewan, Ontario, and the Federal government in their infamous middle-of-the-night meeting in the kitchen of Ottawa's Conference Centre" (1988: 49).

Even those not opposed outright to s.33 looked forward to there being a virtual taboo on its use. Alan Borovoy, General Counsel to the Canadian Civil Liberties Association:

The "notwithstanding" clauses will be a red flag for opposition parties and the press...That will make it politically difficult for government to override the Charter. Political difficulty is a reasonable safeguard for the Charter (Canada, 1982a: 35).[1]

By now, the mere suggestion that section 33 might be used is guaranteed to bring down a torrent of righteous rhetoric. When the President of the University of British

---

[1] To the same effect were Russell, 1983: 41 and La Forest, 1983: 26.

Columbia suggested that the government consider overriding a decision on mandatory retirement with great fiscal implications for universities, he got this from the President of the British Columbia Civil Liberties Association:

> This casual invitation to constitutional vandalism would be an abomination if it originated with the enemies of the mind. That it should come from the university itself is at once astonishing and dispiriting (*The Globe and Mail*, March 23, 1988: A4).

But one cannot expect reason when even a government's *appeal* of a Charter ruling to a higher court—something it has every legal right to do—is called "flying in the face of the Constitution and the Charter of Rights" by opposition MPs (*The Globe and Mail*, June 10, 1988: A1). And this in a case where the judge himself had said that his decision should not take effect until reviewed on appeal! (*Schachter*, 1988)

Disappointment was widespread, however, when the Conservative government of Saskatchewan "treated the charter without respect" (*The Globe and Mail*, February 15, 1986: A6) and used the override to prevent judicial review of back-to-work legislation to end a government employees' strike without suffering any adverse consequences. The Saskatchewan Court of Appeal, later to be overruled by the Supreme Court of Canada, had held the right to strike to be protected by the "freedom of association" clause in an earlier case, so the government inserted a notwithstanding clause the next time out. Not only did the government suffer no adverse consequences, it was in fact solidly re-elected in a general election held nine months after the law was passed, arguably with a political assist from the override (Morton, 1987: 47). The union, with reckless disregard for the long-term consequences, went straight to court and asked that the use of section 33 be judicially rolled back. Though the subsequent decision of the Supreme Court of Canada on the right to strike rendered the union's action moot, the issue of whether courts will meddle in the use of the legislative override is very much alive.

Legal academics have been busy arguing, on the basis of some of the many ambiguities in the wording of the Charter, that contrary to all contemporary understandings, the use by a legislature of s.33 is "really," that is, should be considered to be, subject to judicial approval.[1] A form of this argument was actually accepted by the Court of Appeal for Quebec in 1985. The case involved a rather ingenious attempt by the Parti Québécois government of Quebec to neutralize the effect of the Charter as extensively and economically as legally possible, carrying through on Premier Lévesque's promise "to make it as complicated, legitimately, and as difficult as we can for some aspects of that bloody Charter to be applied to Quebec" (Gibson, 1986: 126). An Act was passed in June 1982 repealing all existing statutes of Quebec and immediately re-enacting them with the addition to each of the following clause: "This Act shall operate notwithstanding the provisions of sections 2 and 7 to 15 of the Constitution Act, 1982." The government was promptly taken to court by a

---

[1] The most determined argument is made by Slattery, 1983: 391; his argument is considered to be "plausible" by Gibson, 1986: 130, but not by Hogg, 1985: 691.

coalition of civil liberties groups, but even a judge so unsympathetic to the PQ (see Chapter III) as Quebec's Chief Justice Jules Deschênes—a federal government appointment, like all Superior Court Justices and Chief Justices— could not bring himself to interfere. Though he could not resist his habitual swipe at the PQ, he upheld the Act:

> The court is not authorized by s.33 of the Charter to declare inoperative the legislation under attack, even if it has the effect of depriving the residents of Quebec of constitutional protection which continues to be enjoyed by other Canadian citizens (*Alliance des Professeurs*, 1983: 279).

Things were different when the case reached the Court of Appeal two years later, and the PQ's popularity had dwindled to its lowest level since before 1976 (it would be trounced by the Liberals in the December general election). That court was unanimous in declaring the Act unconstitutional. Considering the importance of the issue, the reasoning of the Court of Appeal is not the easiest to follow. (Judges are the only authors in the world who do not have to submit their writings to editorial approval before they are published!) The opinion that went the farthest was that of Judge Jacques. His basic objection seems to have been that the PQ law referred only to the *numbers* of the provisions and not to their *contents*, even though in doing so it merely mimicked s.33 itself. Jacques seems to have wanted the PQ to show Quebeckers what they were missing, and though he did not exactly say so, it seems that the only safe way to have complied with his ruling would have been to re-enact the provisions of the Charter in each law of Quebec. Not an appetizing prospect for a government that was only trying to make a symbolic statement against the Charter in the first place. But there was a strong suggestion in the opinion of Judge Jacques that even so bitter a pill as this would not have sufficed, and herein lie the implications of the decision *beyond* the dispute with the PQ. Judge Jacques seems to have wanted to impose an additional requirement for the use of s.33, namely "of demonstrating the link between the legislation and the right [overridden]" (*Alliance des Professeurs*, 1985: 364). Demonstrating it to the *Court*, of course, meaning that no legislature, however determined, could ever keep the courts from pronouncing on the merits of its laws. Where did Judge Jacques get this idea? Partly from some pretty thin technical arguments, but mostly from his conception of the paramount *importance* of the rights in the Charter. Since the rights in the Charter were so important and since they were to be safeguarded by the judiciary, s.33 had to be subject to judicial review:

> The fundamental freedoms and legal guarantees which may be disregarded by statute by virtue of s.33 are so important that they should be expressly stated so as to bring into sharp focus the effect of the overriding provisions and the rights deprived.

> Section 33 permits the substitution of a purely political guarantee of fundamental rights for the new constitutional and legal guarantee...

The exercise of the s.33 power must therefore come within the basic principles which define our society (*Alliance des Professeurs*, 1983: 361–364).

The other judges on the Court of Appeal, while stressing the *formal* nature of the requirements they were imposing, also expressly aligned themselves with Judge Jacques' opinion.

The notion that Charter rights are more important than other legal rights is frequently heard in legal circles. It comes from confounding legal and social importance. In a legal sense, the Charter is the "supreme law." No law deemed by the courts to be inconsistent with it is valid. But is anyone really so silly as to believe that the rights in the Charter are uniformly of such paramount importance in any real, concrete, *social* sense? That the Charter right to be informed without unreasonable delay of the specific criminal offence with which one may be charged is of greater social importance than the law prohibiting murder? That the Charter right to have one's child educated in one's own official language anywhere in Canada at public expense is of greater social importance than the non-Charter legal right to have one's child educated at public expense, period? Or of greater social importance than the law forbidding the use of child labour so that children have the chance to go to school? That the right not to have a few dollars of union dues used for political purposes is of greater social importance than the right to strike (the former and not the latter—according to the courts—being protected by "freedom of association")?

But even this takes for granted the central conceit of legalized politics, that one can talk meaningfully about the "rights in the Charter" as if they had any independent existence, that is apart from the more or less creative meaning the judiciary might put on them. Without this conceit, section 33 is not an override of the *Charter* at all, but a refusal to let the legal profession have the final say in politics. It is not a "denial of rights" but a refusal to abide by a particular judicial conception of them, according to the particular interests or points of view the judiciary may from time to time represent. In the case of *Alliance des Professeurs*, it was a question of lawyers appointed by a federalist government judging the laws of its sworn enemy, the independentist government of Quebec. But this was only a particularly vivid case. Every confrontation over section 33 involves essentially the same scenario: different political conceptions contending with one another. That one wears the mantle of the Charter should not obscure the fact that the other wears the mantle of representative government. Logic and experience show that where the two clash, representative government is more often on the side worth being on. Even where it is not, logic and experience also show that it is better, both in the long and short run, to oppose bad government with democratic politics than with legal politics.

The debate about section 33 is a debate about the Charter itself. No doubt the legal profession will continue its campaign against the override, whittling away at it judicially or pressing for its outright repeal. Lawyers will continue to claim that it is a denial of our most important rights, not merely a guarantee that lawyers do not have the final word on important political questions. Politicians served or cowed by this, or taken in by its central conceit, will continue to heap abuse on the clause, and now and then join the call for its removal. While it survives, the override is the one remaining check on the full fury of legalized politics, because one of the legal profession's greatest fears, as we shall see, is of "trivializing" the Charter by provoking frequent or popular resort to it (*Altseimer*, 1982; La Forest, 1983: 29; *Re Public Service Employees Relations Act (Alberta)*, 1987: 236). This means that how the courts interpret a Charter with an override is a very unsure guide to what they would do if they were rid of it. But it also means that only by "debunking and demystifying" the Charter in general, can we "lay the political groundwork for the progressive use of the section 33 override" (Petter, 1987a: 12) and, indeed, make its repeal more difficult.

Postscript: Section 33 and Bill 101

As we go to press a chorus of calls for the repeal of section 33 such as has never been heard before is echoing throughout English Canada. The cause is the invocation of the override by the Liberal government of Quebec in response to a decision of the Supreme Court of Canada invalidating the provisions of Bill 101 requiring unilingual French business signs (*Ford* v. *Quebec (Attorney General)*, December 15, 1988). The Supreme Court held this to be a violation of "freedom of expression" under the Canadian and Quebec Charters. Premier Bourassa introduced a compromise law allowing English on indoor signs, but not on outdoor signs, and has insulated the law from both Charters by a "notwithstanding" clause. Though the reviews have been mixed about the specific compromise, the one thing that is clear in the whole affair is the radical difference of feelings about section 33 between English and French Canada. The only criticism of Bourassa among French speakers in Quebec is that he did not go far enough in defending the PQ language law. This French-English difference over section 33 was also revealed during the federal election of 1988 when Liberal leader John Turner was chastised by the Quebec wing of his party for statements criticizing the clause. Feelings about section 33 are coming to symbolize the political differences between Quebec and the rest of Canada.

Oddly enough, in deciding the Bill 101 case, the Supreme Court went out of its way to overrule the Quebec Court of Appeal decision in *Alliance des Professeurs* limiting the freedom to use the override. The government of Quebec had apparently tried to forestall a decision on this point by not proceeding on the section 33 appeal until it had received the Supreme Court's opinion on Bill 101. Nevertheless, there appears to have been extensive argument on the point with the province of Ontario *supporting* the Quebec Court of Appeal and asking for limits to be put on the use of section 33 (*The Globe and Mail*, November 19, 1987: A5). But, technically, the issue was not before the Court. Nor was it necessary to decide it in order to decide the Bill 101 case. Yet the Court came out four-square in favour of a literal reading of section 33 which gave complete freedom to the provinces, completely disavowing any power to supervise the substance of a use of the notwithstanding clause. The Court did not even criticize the use of numbers to refer to the provisions overridden. Since the government of Quebec had expressed itself clearly, if economically, the override was valid. Why would the Supreme Court combine an activist and politically explosive holding with a gratuitously strong affirmation of the override powers under section 33? If the Court were seeking to provoke a political debate on section 33 which might lead to its ultimate demise, this would be an excellent way of doing it. Especially since, in the context of a teetering Meech Lake Accord, the effect might well be to send constitutional reform back to the drawing board. Another explanation might just be institutional self-interest. Putting substantive limits on section 33, the way the Quebec Court of Appeal had tried to do, was so obviously contrary to the original deal that it might have been denounced as an unseemly power grab by the Court. It might have backfired. Requiring a clearer and better mandate for judicial power was a safer strategy, and one with a good track record if we consider the aftermath of judicial reticence during the era of the *Canadian Bill of Rights*.

The Meech Lake Accord

Section 33 has played something of a rhetorical role in the debate about the Meech Lake Accord, the constitutional amendment agreement announced in April 1987 and signed by all of the Premiers and the Prime Minister in June of 1987.[1] If ratified by all of the provincial legislatures before June 1990, it will become part of the Constitution (see Appendix B for the text of the Accord).

In his broadside against the Accord, which condemned it for weakening the federal government[2] and "balkanizing" Canada, former Prime Minister Pierre Trudeau chided the federal government for relinquishing federal power to the provinces without asking anything in return:

> ...be it national regulation of securities markets, be it the power to strengthen the Canadian common market, *be it even the repeal of the overriding ("notwithstanding") clause of the Charter* (Trudeau, 1987: A12; emphasis added).

In defending the accord, Prime Minister Mulroney claimed that, on the contrary, he had strengthened the Charter and made resort to section 33 less likely by increasing

---

[1] As we go to press, this role has become a rather large one. The use of section 33 by the government of Quebec to limit the effect of the Supreme Court's Charter ruling against the unilingual business sign law has been seized upon by opponents of the Accord in English Canada as a reason for scuttling the whole thing. At the time of writing, only two provinces, Manitoba and New Brunswick, have yet to ratify the Accord. The governments of both provinces have strongly criticized the action of the government of Quebec. The Premier of Manitoba invoked Quebec's action as a reason for suspending debate on ratification of the Accord. The meaning of all this is hard to determine at this point. Ratification of the Accord in Manitoba had been in great danger anyway because of the minority government situation with both opposition parties on record against it. As the text argues, the relationship between section 33 and the Accord seems to be purely symbolic, but so is the relationship between the Accord and the Charter itself. If the Meech Lake Accord should be opened up for renegotiation, it is certain that the question of whether section 33 should continue to exist will be an important element of the discussion.

[2] In an excess of genital imagery, Trudeau said the Accord would "render the Canadian state impotent [and] destine it ... to eventually be governed by eunuchs" (Trudeau, 1987: A12).

the Constitution's legitimacy in Quebec:

> We have gained the signature of Quebec on our Constitution, ending its divisive and potentially dangerous estrangement from our constitutional family. In the process, we have strengthened the Canadian Charter of Rights and Freedoms because, for the first time, Quebec has accepted its moral significance and political legitimacy. That means that all the laws of Quebec will be subjected to the Charter, and the Charter will be interpreted in light of Quebec's distinctiveness, as it is now interpreted in light of Canada's multicultural and aboriginal heritage...In 1982, Canada achieved patriation and an entrenched Charter of Rights, but only at the price—the tremendous price—of a notwithstanding clause. So, while the most fundamental rights of Canadians were guaranteed in 1982, the federal Government agreed that Parliament or provincial legislatures could override these rights by invoking the notwithstanding clause (*The Globe and Mail*, June 15, 1988: A5).[1]

On the contrary, according to the founder of Alliance Quebec, the major English rights group in Quebec:

> The distinct society clause will encourage use of section 33 by giving it constitutional legitimacy in case of a contrary judicial ruling (Maldoff, 1987).

Technically, and even logically, Meech Lake has nothing to do with the use of section 33 in Quebec. The Bourassa Liberals stopped systematically exempting Quebec laws from the Charter right after being elected in December, 1985 (*The Globe and Mail*, March 5, 1986: A8), more than one year before Meech Lake was even dreamed up. They have used it sporadically since, but nothing in the Accord itself makes it either easier or harder for them, or indeed a future PQ government, to continue using it. In fact, since all rights except language rights are subject to section 33, the concerns that the new clauses in the Meech Lake Accord will override the Charter would be hard to understand without the assumption that section 33 is taboo. Throwing section 33 into the debate is just a way of discrediting the Accord or of selling it, according to which side you are on. All it really shows is how potent a symbol of evil section 33 has become, if only outside of Quebec.

But what *is* the Meech Lake Accord?

The Meech Lake Accord is probably the most perfect example yet of something we only glimpsed in the *Operation Dismantle* affair, the capacity of legalized politics to displace all other political forms. With Meech Lake, constitutionalism has been carried to new and dizzying heights never before thought possible. Since the premiers signed it, it has hardly left the newspapers. Two provincial elections throwing signatories out of office have dramatically put its ratification in jeopardy. Hearings on its meaning and its pros and cons have been held all across the country at both the provincial and federal levels, in both the House of Commons and the Senate. Even the old lion Trudeau was roused from his political sleep to roar once again. It is as if all

---

[1] The news story continues: "There is still a notwithstanding clause," heckled New Democrat Ian Waddell, who voted against the accord in October. "Why didn't you get rid of the notwithstanding clause?"

those who were left out of the constitutional glory of 1980–82 wanted their chance to play nation-builders and to be fathers (still no mothers) of Confederation. And Confederation is in danger of growing up a very confused child.

We have even witnessed a replay of the constitutional reference cases of 1981 and 1982 as two Territorial governments and three ace constitutional lawyers have tried to get the courts to say this amendment is contrary either to constitutional convention or to the Charter of Rights itself. The Government leaders of the Yukon and Northwest Territories, which were excluded from certain provisions of the accord and prejudiced by others, argued that they had the right by constitutional convention to be heard when amendments were considered, and by constitutional law to be fairly included in the deal. They even got one trial judge to say that he thought the Charter could actually apply to amendments of the Charter itself! But he did not say how since he thought the case premature (*Penikett*, 1987a). The euphoria did not last long, though, as the cases were quickly appealed and lost. According to the appeal courts, any conventions had been abrogated by the new amending power, and the Charter could definitely not apply to its own amendment (*Penikett*, 1987b; *Sibbeston*, 1987). Leave to appeal to the Supreme Court of Canada was refused (*The Globe and Mail*, June 3, 1988: A3). These decisions did not daunt Ontario lawyers Edward Greenspan, Morris Manning, and Timothy Danson, of whom we will hear much more later. They announced in May 1988 that they would launch a "global attack" on the Accord in Federal Court (*The Globe and Mail*, May 3, 1988: A4). And there have been several calls, by Trudeau and others (*The Globe and Mail*, April 16, 1988: D7; June 30, 1988: A2; *The Toronto Star*, February 20, 1988: A16) for a reference to the Supreme Court of Canada just to say what the Accord *means*. It sounds like a novel suggestion to have the Supreme Court interpret a constitutional amendment in the abstract and before it is enacted. In *Re Constitution of Canada*, 1981, the Court decided the constitutionality of *going ahead with* an amendment but not its proper interpretation. Novel things have a way of happening, though, and the Supreme Court has already taken to saying what it thinks of aspects of the Accord in response to a mere memo from the Canadian Bar Association (*The Gazette*, August 24, 1987: A-8).[1] But the point is that none of the signatories have taken up these calls for the very good reason that they do not *want* a definitive interpretation of the Accord. For them, its ambiguity is its appeal. In fact, an opinion poll taken in April 1988 showed that, while opposition somewhat outweighs support among Canadians (it's the opposite in Quebec), those who are unsure about it form the largest group (*The Toronto Star*, April 30, 1988: A14).

The Meech Lake Accord has several major components: (1) The "distinct society" clause and related amendments to the Charter; (2) Immigration agreements between the federal government and the provinces; (3) Opting out of shared-cost programs with compensation; (4) Amendments to the constitution;

---

[1] The Court thought that the Northwest Territories and the Yukon should also have the right to submit names for Supreme Court appointments.

(5) Agenda items for future constitutional conferences; (6) Appointments to the Supreme Court of Canada and the Senate.

Distinct Society

Politically speaking, this clause is at the centre of the whole debate. Trudeau claims that it means "goodbye to the dream of one Canada." NDP leader Ed Broadbent says it is the "essence of the Accord," and that all of the members of his caucus "believe profoundly" in it, but that it does not change the division of powers "by one iota" (*The Globe and Mail*, June 15, 1988: A5; June 23, 1988: A5). Premier Bourassa of Quebec has exulted that "the whole constitution, including the Charter, will be interpreted and applied in light of the section on our distinct identity" (*The Globe and Mail*, June 15, 1988: A5), while then PQ Opposition Leader Pierre Marc Johnson said Bourassa had sold Quebec's signature "below the market price" (*The Toronto Star*, May 2, 1987: A4). If it was worthless, replied Bourassa, how come they were so upset about it in English Canada (*The Globe and Mail*, March 12, 1988: D2). The major English-speaking group in Quebec has said English speakers are endangered by it (Maldoff, 1987; *The Globe and Mail*, February 25, 1987: A10). And the major women's groups outside of Quebec (the National Action Committee on the Status of Women, the Legal Education and Action Fund, the National Association of Women and the Law, the Ad Hoc Committee on Women and the Constitution) have claimed women's rights to be in jeopardy because they were not specifically exempted from the operation of the "distinct society" clause, the way the clauses on aboriginal rights and multiculturalism were exempted (*The Globe and Mail*, August 11, 1987: A8; August 17, 1987: A3). As for women inside Quebec, the major French women's group, Fédération des femmes du Québec, found it not even a "potential threat":

> Our sisters from other provinces should not consider Quebec's recognition as a distinct society to be a threat to women, just like we do not (*The Globe and Mail*, August 29, 1987: A6).

When Meech Lake was approved by the Ontario legislature, women sang songs of protest in the gallery (*The Toronto Star*, July 2, 1987: D5).

How could there be such opposite views of the same few words? Easy. The clause says nothing so it could say anything. It provides that the Constitution "shall be interpreted in a manner consistent with the recognition" of some facts—among others—of Canadian life, namely that "the existence of French-speaking Canadians, centred in Quebec but also present elsewhere in Canada, and English-speaking Canadians concentrated outside of Quebec but also present in Quebec, constitutes a fundamental characteristic of Canada" and that "Quebec constitutes within Canada a distinct society." Does this give more legislative power to Quebec? Who can say? The presence of English speakers in Quebec is, according to the clause, no less fundamental than the centering there of French speakers. The same goes for the situation outside Quebec.

Certain other matters are "affirmed," such as the role of Parliament and the legislatures of the provinces to "preserve" these facts and of the "legislature and *Government*" of Quebec to "preserve and *promote*" the distinctiveness of Quebec, but though much has been made of the verbal differences (Cook, 1987), there is nothing to suggest any addition or subtraction of powers. That is why Professor Hogg says the clause should be regarded as "an affirmation of sociological facts with little legal significance" and "mainly hortatory or symbolic" (Hogg, 1988: 12–13). He also says that since a law with the purposes "recognized" or "affirmed" by the amendment "will give those purposes added weight" as "reasonable limits," the clause "could" indirectly expand powers via the reasonable limits clause (Hogg, 1988: 16). But then again it might not. It all depends on what the courts make of these words. Which means it depends on the courts and not on the words. The phrases are so vague and the notion of "reasonable limits" so inherently flexible that, though the new clause might give the courts new arguments for conclusions they might want, on other grounds, to reach, it can in no sense be said to limit or even to guide them. While it is undoubtedly true to say that giving the courts such wide scope is not wise, it is a little absurd to say that the danger of this latitude is to the *Charter* (Cook, 1987), because the Charter is itself the epitome of unguided judicial power.

Immigration

The same is more or less true of the rest of Meech Lake. One complicated provision provides a mechanism for putting in place agreements between the federal government and any province to give that province control over immigration. Such agreements already exist (Hogg, 1985:23). The contribution of the Meech Lake Accord is that any such agreement, if the parties so declare, is given, in effect, *constitutional* status. It operates as an exception to the federal government's exclusive jurisdiction over immigration and cannot be revoked except by agreement of both governments. But nothing requires that any such agreement be entered into or that any agreement entered into be given such status. The most it means is that if Ottawa wants, it can bind itself and successor governments not to revoke such an agreement unilaterally. And it does not even amount to that, because another provision says that any agreement "repugnant to...national standards and objectives relating to immigration or aliens" is of no effect. Of course, in the case of a dispute, this will be for the courts to decide. What this means is that what might at most have been a right reserved to the federal government in an ordinary agreement now becomes a matter subject to the modest supervision of the courts. The federal government has, in effect, made its exercise of power subject to a modest amount of judicial review, but only to the extent it might, in future, want to. It has asked the courts to guarantee the reasonableness of its actions, something they would probably have taken it upon themselves to do under the Charter anyway. It is hard to see what putting this in the constitution really accomplishes. There were binding agreements before the Charter existed, and they did not have to be put into the constitution for the parties to have faith in them. It is as if, with the Charter, nobody trusts anybody unless they get it, not only in writing, but *entrenched.*

The Spending Power

The same can be said of the so-called spending power clause. It says that the federal government shall compensate a province which chooses to opt out of any future national shared-cost program—the one example most often given is a national day-care program—"if the province carries on a program or initiative that is compatible with national objectives." Now this power has been attacked on the left (*The Toronto Star*, February 18, 1988: A8; *The Globe and Mail*, March 10, 1988: A14) as potentially weakening the federal government's ability to carry out social programs, but it has also been said on the left that it strengthens the provincial capacity to innovate (Petter, 1987b). Since the federal government has the right to set the objectives under the mandate, it all depends on the people in federal and provincial office at any given time. When the federal Tory government introduced its long-awaited national childcare program it was immediately attacked as setting *no* national standards (*The Globe and Mail*, July 26, 1988: A1). Once again, the only limit on the federal government's power to determine how national money is spent is some modest judicial supervision. Another formerly unilateral power is now shared somewhat with the courts. How can Trudeau complain about that? Whom does he trust?

Amendments to the Constitution

Some amendments to the constitution are made more difficult by the Accord. Certain matters that had been amendable by the "7/50" formula (agreement of seven provinces constituting at least fifty percent of the population) now require unanimous consent. These have to do with fundamental changes to the Senate, the House of Commons, French and English, the Supreme Court of Canada, the creation of new provinces, and the extension of old ones. The provision seems to have been an attempt to meet Quebec's claim for a constitutional veto without being too obvious about it. It should not be forgotten that Quebec was on the receiving end of Canada's first non-unanimous constitutional amendment, the Charter of Rights itself. Particular aspects of the proposed new formula have gored particular oxen, and hypothetical scenarios have been created about holdouts against the national will by Prince Edward Island on amendments that have nothing to do with it. But unanimity was the rule in practice until 1982, and it was achieved, at least temporarily, with the Meech Lake Accord itself. If the Accord passes, it will show that unanimity can be achieved even over the most controversial issues. If it does not, it should demonstrate, paradoxically, the value of unanimity requirements for dissenters to major constitutional changes.

The unanimity requirement does not apply to amendments to the division of powers. However, the right to opt out of a constitutional amendment with "reasonable compensation" that was restricted in the 1982 agreement to "education or other cultural matters" is expanded by Meech Lake to all amendments to the division of powers. Opting out without compensation from any amendment was possible under the 1982 constitution, but was made less likely by the financial penalty. Though the provision makes it easier for a province to opt out of amendments, it is hard to see this as a *de*-centralizing mechanism since it contemplates powers being transferred to the federal government. The whole thing is too hypothetical to be more than a purely symbolic reassurance.

Constitutional Conferences

The mania for temporarily entrenching the agenda items of First Ministers' conferences that started with the question of aboriginal rights is continued in the Meech Lake Accord. This time the agenda is to include Senate reform and fisheries. Also entrenched is an annual First Ministers' conference on the economy. You would think a simple promise to hold such meetings would have sufficed. Or does anybody really contemplate taking anybody else to court for wanting to change the agenda?[1] As Canada's Indians, Métis, and Inuit found out after five years of constitutionally entrenched meetings, they are no guarantee of any agreements (Chapter VI).

The Supreme Court of Canada

As if giving it so many powers was not enough, the Supreme Court of Canada is entrenched in the constitution. Of course, since it is the guarantor of the whole enterprise, it is only to be expected that it would be put beyond the reach of any of the parties. But the real point of the amendment is to put the Court beyond the reach of the *federal* government, whose preserve it had technically been before. "Technically," because tampering with the Court would never be easy even if it were legal. But also practically, in the federal exclusivity of the power to appoint the judges. Here we have one of the few concrete gains to the provinces in the Meech Lake Accord and especially to Quebec. Even the PQ had to concede this (*The Toronto Star*, May 2, 1987: A4). Under the Accord, future appointments to the Supreme Court of Canada, though still ultimately up to the federal government, have to be made by it from names submitted by the governments of the provinces and, with respect to three of the seats on the Court, from names submitted by the government of Quebec.[2] This, as we have seen above, has greatly troubled the legal profession for what it might do to the prestige of the Court. Former judge Thomas R. Berger, an impassioned participant in the 1981 debate over aboriginal rights, has even warned of the rather unlikely possibility of a PQ government trying

---

[1] After writing this I learned that one of the arguments made by the Yukon and NWT governments against the constitutionality of the Accord was that the government had violated a conference requirement! (*Sibbeston*, 1988: 44) The argument failed.

[2] A similar procedure is laid out for the appointment of Senators, but until further Senate reform, which no doubt will encompass the way Senators are chosen, the implications of this are not obvious.

to "weaken the legitimacy of the Court as a federal institution" or even trying to "make it difficult, if not impossible, for it to function" by refusing to submit *any* names! (Berger, 1988)

Silly scenarios apart, it is hard to see how giving appointment powers to the provinces can weaken the prestige of the Court when the long-standing, exclusive power of the federal government to appoint judges has not done so. It is inevitable that the appointment process will become more and more politicized under the Charter, and it is just as inevitable that governments and judges will find it in their interests to enhance and not diminish the prestige of the Court by trying to disguise its political nature.

Meech Lake and the Legalization of Politics

Meech Lake seems mainly to have been about the Charter itself. If ratified, its main achievement will be the expansion of the domain of legalized politics. First and foremost, the Charter will now have formally conquered Quebec. This is the reason most often given for the whole affair: "bringing Quebec back into Confederation" (*The Globe and Mail*, March 19, 1988: A4); "securing Quebec's signature on the constitution" (*The Globe and Mail*, March 29, 1988: A6). "Today, we welcome Quebec back to the Canadian constitutional family" (*The Globe and Mail*, June 4, 1987: A1). "Canada is whole again. The Canadian family is together again and the nation is one again" (C.B.C. broadcast of June 4, 1987). But what can all this mean? The constitution has legally applied to Quebec since 1982 and, as we shall see in the next Chapter, this has had very concrete implications. What is the difference? The difference seems to be that now it will apply *legitimately*, and since the main point of the legalized politics is to *legitimate*, this means the Charter will be stronger. Whatever it does, it will now do it better. In Quebec, the Charter's legitimacy will have been enhanced through the formal act of acceptance, through the power in connection with appointments to the Supreme Court of Canada and, of course, through the extra words "distinct society" in the Charter. And the formal acceptance of the Charter in Quebec will probably enhance its prestige in the rest of Canada as well. At least that seems to be what Accord advocates are hoping for. Naturally, the addition of more ambiguous words will also increase judicial freedom of action, if that is possible. And the legal domain will also have spread to those areas (immigration and the spending power) that were previously the exclusive preserve of the federal government.

One looks in vain for anything concrete in the Accord. Quebec received no extra powers. Nothing that was lost in the struggle over language rights, for instance, control over minority language education, was returned. Of course, the laws struck down under the Charter were Lévesque's laws not Bourassa's. Bourassa has always been a very reluctant Quebec nationalist, representing a point of view much closer to Trudeau's than to Lévesque's. He is as relieved as anyone to turn the page on the separatist interlude and to get on with the business of the full economic integration of Quebec with the rest of Canada. Indeed, since the signing of the Accord, it has been easier for the federal government to pour money into Quebec because it has been easier for the Quebec government to accept it.[1] Meech Lake seems simply to have been about the appropriate symbols with which to accomplish these mutually desirable ends and with which to put a definite end ("to put *fini*" in Ed Broadbent's terms) to Quebec independentism. For our purposes, the thing to be underlined in red ink is that the symbols had to be *constitutional* symbols. They had to be words in the Charter. All in all, it is most appropriate that closing the book on Quebec independentism should involve a further strengthening of legalized politics. As we have seen, it was to deal with the independence movement that we were given the Charter in the first place. The only problem was that it was necessary to use different symbols to close the door on that epoch than the ones necessary to ensure its successful outcome. And this seems to be what has caused so much constitutional anxiety. None of the rights groups—Trudeau Liberals apart—who wanted the Accord reopened seem to have been opposed to the "distinct society" clause in itself (*The Globe and Mail*, August 20, 1987: A4; August 29, 1987: A2). How could they have been? They just wanted to make sure that those special Quebec symbols did not interfere with the ones that count for them. But the experience of Quebec with the Charter, to which we now turn, shows that the courts are quite capable of treating Quebec as a special case when circumstances require, no matter what the wording of the relevant constitutional documents.

---

[1] In June, 1988 a joint Ottawa-Quebec economic development project worth $970 million over five years was announced with the Prime Minister emphasizing "the solidarity between our governments in Ottawa and Quebec" and reminding everyone that "when it was necessary to redress the constitutional injustice of 1982, the federal and Quebec governments found common ground." More large projects were planned for the future (*The Globe and Mail* June 10, 1988: A1–A2).

CHAPTER III

Legalizing the Politics of Language

The Politics of Language in Quebec

The genies set loose by Quebec's "Quiet Revolution" produced both a force and a counterforce. The force was a strong nationalist-independentist tendency among the French people of Quebec. They "awoke" to find themselves second-class citizens in a province where they constituted the vast majority—80%—of the population. English, however, was the language of economic and social power. As one moved up the income ladder, the percentage of English speakers increased to the point where, at the top, the roles of minority and majority were reversed. In 1961, French Quebeckers earned, on average, 60% as much as English Quebeckers, and unilingual English Quebeckers were the best paid group, even better paid than bilingual English Quebeckers (Milner, 1984: 416). French was the language of labour and English the language of capital, that is to say of management and ownership, because the commanding heights of the economy were to be found in the United States, English Canada, and English Quebec, in that order (Breton and Stasiulis, 1980: 153–155). English was thus the language of personal advancement (d'Anglejan, 1984: 34–36). Added, and by no means unrelated to this, was the proportionate decline in French identification and language use throughout the country. Across Canada, the proportion of Canadians claiming French as their ethnic origin declined two full percentage points (from 30.8 to 28.7) between 1951 and 1971. During the same period, those claiming French as a mother tongue outside Quebec declined from 7.2% of the population to 6.0%, and those claiming it within Quebec declined from 82.5% to 80.7% (Lachapelle, 1980: 28). Furthermore, there was a steady decline in the use of their mother tongue among those identifying themselves as ethnically French. Between 1961 and 1971, over 273,000 persons of French mother tongue living outside Quebec adopted English as their everyday language with only 20,000 going the other way. There were even 73,000 such transfers within Quebec, with a net loss of 25,000 (Latouche, 1986: 126–127; Mallea, 1984: 226–228). Quebeckers of British origin also experienced a relative decline due to the great postwar immigration of people of non-British origin. However, these "allophones" tended to assimilate into the English and not into the French linguistic community because of the definite economic advantages of doing so. Allophones entered the English schooling system in droves (90% of those of Italian origin in the Montreal Catholic School Commission jurisdiction in 1972 were receiving instruction in English). Declining birthrates added to the small but perceptible decline in French ethnicity within Quebec and to the fears for the future of French people in Canada as a whole (d'Anglejan, 1984: 33). The federal government of Canada was as much the preserve of the English as the rest of Canada. The experience up until the 1960s was English dominance in federal politics. French Canadians were severely underrepresented in important Cabinet portfolios such as External Affairs, Agriculture, and Transport, and had *never* been assigned to Finance or Trade and Commerce, before the Trudeau era. The bureaucracy followed similar patterns (Breton and Stasiulis, 1980: 190–193). And when English and French Canada were politically split, for example over conscription in World Wars I and II and, before that, over the Riel affair, English Canada always got its way (Whitaker, 1984b: 73).

The nationalist solution to these problems was French sovereignty within Quebec. Ideally in political terms, but at least in cultural terms. But "making Quebec French" was not at heart a linguistic issue. It was more a question of the resentments, fears, aspirations, and pride of a people over its concrete social, political and economic position in the society of which it formed the overwhelming majority. The ability and right to speak one's mother tongue was only one aspect of this. In a sense, French just happened to be the language of the people whose social, political, and economic subordination the nationalists wanted to reverse. The idea was to make Quebec French in a *national* sense. Language delineated the nation but the nation was more than its language. According to the Parti Québécois White Paper introducing the "Charter of the French Language" the aim of the law was

...first of all political. The French of Quebec have never believed that their language could be dissociated from the destiny of the entire nationality, of its economy and of its culture...In Quebec, the French language is not just a means for expression, but a medium for living as well...Because of their common language, people realize that they are part of the same group and that their feelings are similar to those of others...What the French-speaking people want has nothing to do with "translated from the English" which policies on bilingualism wish to guarantee. It is a matter of protecting the existence of an original culture and developing it to its fullness—a mode of being, thinking, writing, creating, meeting, establishing relations between groups and individuals, and even of carrying on business (Quebec, 1977: 2, 28, 32).

For the nationalists, the status of the French language was "a question of social justice," not only in the sense that English speakers were wealthier than French speakers, but also because "cultural inequality" was itself a source of injustice, felt in many ways. French speakers had to learn an extra language in order to work. They were discriminated against on the *pretext* of linguistic inability. Besides economics there were questions of ethnic pride involved (Quebec, 1977: 47–48).

There is little choice: what Quebec's French-speaking majority must do is reassume the power which is its by right, not in order to dominate, but to regain the status and latitude proper to its size and importance... During the Riel affair, or the historic battles for French schools in the Canadian West and in Ontario, or the conscription crises, whenever there has been serious political tension, French-speaking people have been the ones to entreat, to beg, to rebel or to passively resist. Never before have they had such firm political leverage to ensure that French rights are respected (Quebec, 1977: 49, 105–06).

It is true that the revolt was lead by middle-class intellectuals and technocrats, and this set strict limits on its aspirations. It was a function of the *strengthening* economic position of the French of Quebec vis-a-vis the English (Quebec, 1977: 10–13), of *heightening* aspirations that were meeting their greatest ethnic obstacles in the upper echelons of society (Milner and Milner, 1973: 173–175; Latouche, 1986: 148). But the movement resonated strongly with Quebec workers and depended upon their allegiance (Milner and Milner, 1973: 185–191).

That English Canada did not embrace Quebec nationalism is not surprising. It was the target; at least its interests and representatives in Quebec were. Nor was it particularly appealing to the non-English immigrant to be "annexed" willy-nilly to the French community. However, even within the French community of Quebec a substantial counterforce emerged, those who "chose Canada," who saw their aspirations best fulfilled within a reformed Canadian federation, one that did not discriminate on the basis of French or English nationality. The champion of this tendency was, of course, Pierre Elliott Trudeau, himself the offspring of a marriage between wealthy members of each linguistic community.

Trudeau opposed defining the issue in terms of "nation." He sought instead to define it in terms of "language rights," with the ready-made solution of bilingualism. If not one bilingual nation, then at least one nation with two languages, one nation of "Francophones" and "Anglophones." Trudeau argued that if Quebec were accepted as the nation state of the French Canadian, the logic of the situation would require the rest of Canada to be the exclusive preserve of the English Canadian. In 1965 he wrote:

> The idea of a national state is thus unacceptable both in theory and in practice to any person who does not wish to see French Canadians withdraw from the Canadian scene and limit themselves exclusively to Quebec (Trudeau, 1968: 30).

In addition to the usual economic and social arguments against independence, Trudeau advanced cultural ones. If French Canadians represented only themselves on the international scene, they would be consigned to insignificance:

> On the other hand, if Quebec were part of a Canadian federation grouping two *linguistic* communities as I am advocating, French Canadians would be supported by a country of more than eighteen million inhabitants, with the second or third highest standard of living in the world, and with a degree of industrial maturity that promises to give it the most brilliant of futures (Trudeau, 1968: 31; emphasis in original).

Canada would be "an enormous sound-box" and Ottawa "an excellent amplifier" for French Canadian voices in "the concert of nations" (Trudeau, 1968: 32). With English not only respected but actually dominant in Quebec, Trudeau's main concern was with the fortunes of French outside of Quebec. To encourage French Canadians to abandon their concept of a national state, English Canadians must do the same. We must not find Toronto or Fredericton or, above all, Ottawa exalting the *English*-Canadian nation. On the contrary, when either the federal or provincial governments intervene in the economy to protect cultural values, they must apply the same rules of equity toward the French as Quebec has always applied toward the English segment of its population (Trudeau, 1968: 32; emphasis in original).

Two issues were particularly important in Trudeau's view, minority language education and bilingualism in the government:

For the purpose of education, wherever there is a sufficient number of French-speaking people to form a school (or a university), these people must have the same rights as English Canadians in the matter of taxes, subsidies, and legislation on education...At the federal level, the two languages must have absolute equality. With regard to legislative and judicial functions, this is already theoretically the case...but the theory must be completely incorporated into actual practice...in the civil service and the armed forces, the two languages must be on a basis of absolute equality...At the provincial level, similar reciprocal rules must be applied (Trudeau, 1968: 48–49).

As early as 1965, when this was written, Trudeau had concluded that the necessary form for these arrangements was a judicially administered constitutional amendment:

The constitution must be so worded that any French-speaking community, anywhere in Canada, can fully enjoy its linguistic rights...Of course, the concepts of 'sufficient number' and 'equal rights' will often have to be defined judicially or administratively...Such reforms must certainly be incorporated into constitutional law (Trudeau, 1968: 48).

Why was the constitution necessary?

It would not be realistic to rely upon good will or purely political action (Trudeau, 1968: 49).

It turned out that political good will was indeed in short supply. Of the two expressions of Quebec nationalism, Trudeau's was clearly the least unacceptable to English Canada, but it was by no means automatically embraced. Within the jurisdiction of the federal government, the Trudeau Liberals were able to pass *The Official Languages Act* (1969) bestowing rights to deal with the federal government in either language. They were able to bilingualize the civil service and greatly increase the national profile of French Québécois in the federal government, with high visibility Cabinet and civil service appointments (Breton and Stasiulis, 1980: 193). They could deal a smashing blow to the violent independentists and sweep along some non-violent independentists with them by the use of the *War Measures Act* in 1970. But vast, important areas were simply beyond federal jurisdiction, including, of course, the language of provincial government services and the language of education. French communities outside of Quebec were tiny minorities, socially and politically powerless within the political systems of their provinces. In Quebec, the nationalist tendency gained more and more adherents. The promotion of the French language by law had started with the Union Nationale in the late 1960s (d'Anglejan, 1984: 36). The Liberal government of Robert Bourassa merely continued this trend with the *Official Language Act* (1974). That Act sought to ride the tightrope between making Quebec officially French and not offending the powerful English minority. It did this by making French mandatory in many areas of public life, but by not making it exclusive. The law also protected legal freedom of choice in education, but made entrance to the English system conditional on the student's capacity to receive instruction in English. In practice, these measures were similar to the federal government's enforced bilingualism, which is not to say that they did not cause tensions (d'Anglejan, 1984: 36).

The election in November 1976 of a majority Parti Québécois government committed to political independence for Quebec changed everything. This meant the definite ascendancy of the nationalist tendency. Democratic means were clearly of no use to the federalist forces. They had only one hope: *the courts*. The courts came through with flying colours.

The Courts Versus Bill 101

The centerpiece of the PQ's legislative program was "Bill 101" (originally "Bill 1"), the *Charter of the French Language* (1977) passed August 26, 1977. The basic idea of the Charter, as we have seen, was to reverse the subordination of the vast majority of the population of Quebec who were French. Though it was legislation about language, that this was simply a means to nationalist ends was clear from the first words of the preamble:

> WHEREAS the French language, the distinctive language of a people that is in the majority French-speaking, is the instrument by which the people has articulated its identity; Whereas the Assemblée Nationale du Québec recognizes that Quebeckers wish to see the quality and influence of the French language assured.

This was a very different thrust from the purely linguistic concerns of the Liberal language law which was prefaced by:

> WHEREAS the French language is a national heritage which the body politic is in duty bound to preserve...(*Official Language Act*, 1974).

The thrust of the PQ legislation was to make French *the* language of public life in Quebec: the language of the legislature and the courts, of government, of labour relations, of commerce and business, and of education. Unilingualism in these realms would be the principle and bilingualism the exception. Thus everyone would have to learn French, and unilingual French Quebeckers would no longer face discrimination. The stranglehold of English would be broken. It would become another minority language, like any other—except for being the language of the largest minority—and it would be respected as such. Putting English on the same legal footing as other languages had a definite political message about relations with Canada. According to one PQ official:

Bill 101 is more than a language legislation; it is an attempt by the new government to move political consciousness away from its previous content to a Québécois content. Language legislation in Quebec…is now a nation-building mechanism (P.E. Laporte quoted in d'Anglejan, 1984: 43).

Viewed in conventional terms, the law was an extremely popular one. However, it split the community ethnically, with French Quebeckers overwhelmingly in support (in excess of 80% in 1979) and English Quebeckers overwhelmingly opposed (in excess of 90%) (Taylor and Dubé-Simard, 1984: 152–153). The "allophone" group was also mostly opposed (Taylor and Dubé-Simard, 1984: 152–153; Coleman, 1984: 137–138). Feelings about the law depended on ethnicity and not linguistic ability, thus underlining its nationalist nature. Among English Quebeckers:

> Bilinguals felt as threatened as…monolinguals. Perceptions and feelings about Quebec's language legislation extend beyond language *per se* to include social and political factors as well (Taylor and Dubé-Simard, 1984: 161).

There were divisions in each community however. They were most pronounced among the French. While organized labour gave unqualified support, the French professional and small business class was divided, and the emerging French big business sector was opposed (Coleman, 1984: 138). The opposition of English business greatly accelerated an exodus of head offices from Montreal, but this had already started in the 1960s (Miller, 1984: 127; d'Anglejan, 1984: 44).

So the population was split along class and ethnic lines, but in such a way as to provide overwhelming support for the law. Those opposed were the privileged and the English, both small minorities. Nevertheless, one does not need a majority of one to go to court. So, the legal assault on the law started almost the moment it was enacted. The first major success came well before the Charter of Rights was entrenched, in *Blaikie* (1978). The Judge who decided it was Jules Deschênes, Chief Justice of the Superior Court of Quebec, a personage worth pausing over because of his centrality in the struggle over language rights in Quebec and what this reveals about the legalization of politics.

In early 1972, Trudeau appointed Deschênes directly to the Quebec Court of Appeal from an illustrious and well-connected law practice (Deslauriers, 1980: 61). Once there, Deschênes quickly proved his value in two important political cases, *Charbonneau* (1973) and *Rose* (1973). In *Charbonneau*, a court of which he was a member upheld the convictions and lengthy prison sentences imposed upon the leadership of the "Common Front" of public sector unions whose members went on strike in March of 1972 and defied a court injunction ordering them back to work. The decision was anonymously entitled "Opinion de la cour" but it bore the unmistakable stamp of Deschênes' authorship in a lengthy attack on the unions for using "brute force" and transforming themselves into an "instrument of social revolution" with the goal of "bringing down the regime" (*Charbonneau*, 1973: 44–45). In the FLQ murder case, *Rose*, Deschênes was the swing vote and principal author of the majority opinion in a 3–2 decision upholding the conviction. In August 1973, after only a year and a half on the Court of Appeal, Trudeau put Deschênes in the strategic driver's seat as Chief Justice of the Quebec Superior Court. This appointment came just four months before the appointment of Bora Laskin as Chief Justice of Canada. But while the latter position was primarily of symbolic importance, the Chief Justice of Quebec had this added practical value: as Chief Justice he could and would assign himself to all of the important language cases, those involving the federal *Official Languages Act*, and most importantly, those involving the PQ.

Deschênes and Laskin had a lot in common. Indeed Laskin wrote a foreword to Deschênes' collection of essays, *The Sword and the Scales* (Deschênes, 1979). The title comes from a poem by Deschênes dated New Year's day, 1979, which concludes, revealingly, with a direct contradiction between democracy and the rule of law:

> Governments come and fall, but you remain:
> Absolute, untouchable rule of law.
> Oh! my life-long passion, may your reign
> Bring peace on earth and freedom under law.
>
> (Deschênes, 1979: ix)

Maybe it reads better in French.

The collection itself contains many indications why Deschênes would be Trudeau's idea of the perfect Quebec Chief Justice. Deschênes was an advocate of judicial activism, aligning himself both with the activism of the Supreme Court of Canada in the 1950s and with the activist dissents of Judge Laskin under the *Canadian Bill of Rights* in the seventies (Deschênes, 1979: 6, 18, 22–3; 1974). In fact, in a speech made just two weeks before his 1978 judgment in *Blaikie,* in which he urged Toronto lawyers and judges to adopt a kind of legal bilingualism as the solution to the separation of the English and French Canadian legal professions, Deschênes actually quoted Trudeau himself:

> "Most English Canadians fail to realize that it is their attitude...which exactly determines the extent and force of Quebec nationalism" (Deschênes, 1979: 42).

Deschênes' intellectual and (for a judge) literary capabilities, his apparent commitment to the federal vision of a bilingual Canada, and his inclination towards judicial activism all made him just the man for the hot seat of Quebec Chief Justice. It would not be stretching things too far to say that in appointing Deschênes Chief Justice, Trudeau was virtually "judge in his own cause" against the PQ.

The Language of the Legislature and the Courts

The first case Deschênes decided against the PQ (*Blaikie* 1978) was launched the moment the *Charter of the French Language* (1977) was enacted. Fittingly enough, the complainants were themselves three lawyers of carefully distributed ethnicity (English, French, and Jewish).[1] The challenge was to Chapter III of the law, "The Language of the Legislature and the Courts." In this chapter, the PQ government had used a considerable amount of ingenuity to skate as closely as possible to the restrictions in section 133 of the *BNA Act 1867*, the only example of entrenched bilingualism in Canada's original constitution. Section 133 imposed certain bilingual requirements on the federal Parliament and the superior courts of Canada as well as on the Legislature and the provincial courts of Quebec—but not on the courts or legislatures of the other provinces. In Bill 101 the PQ government tried to use every millimetre of unilingual space permitted by the words of the provision without actually transgressing it. Where section 133 required that both languages be used in the Records and Journals of the legislatures concerned and that "Acts" be "printed and published in both languages," the *Charter of the French Language* provided that all legislation was to be drafted, tabled, passed, and assented to in French and that only the French version of statutes and regulations were "official." Compliance with section 133 consisted in providing that an "English version" of all bills, statutes, and regulations would be "printed and published." Similarly, with respect to the courts, section 133 provided that "either" language "may be used by any *person* or in any pleading or process in or issuing from ...all or any of the *courts* of Quebec" (as well as federally appointed courts anywhere in Canada). The PQ law provided that the language of process for *non-court* tribunals (boards, commissions, etc.) would be French. For the courts, French would be the language where "*artificial* persons" (corporations) were concerned. Otherwise, it would be the official language of judgment, again with unofficial English translations provided. Exceptions could be made by agreement of the litigating parties. The law did not attempt to contradict the unambiguous requirement that either French or English could be used in legislative debates.

Arguments on the case took place before Deschênes on December 15, 1977. He had either done all his homework before the hearing or did nothing else thereafter, because his lengthy and exhaustively researched judgment was ready for delivery on January 23, 1978, with time for a speech in Toronto on "legal separatism" in between (Deschênes, 1979: 31). The judgment was a masterwork of legal advocacy, if not impartial judgment,[2] complete with table of contents and citations of what must have been all of the available scholarly opinion, including a list of the positions of 24 authors from 1950 to 1977 on whether Quebec could unilaterally amend section 133. To attempt to refute the judgment would consume this entire chapter. It is enough to say that it thoroughly smacked of the advice of the successful American trial lawyer who said, "when the facts are against you, argue the law, when the law is against you, argue the facts and when the facts *and* the law are against you, argue

---

[1] Blaikie was a former President of the federal Conservative Party. In 1987 he was practising law with the same Montreal firm that employed Pierre Trudeau (*The Globe and Mail*, September 30, 1987: B1).

[2] Any doubts about whether Deschênes approached this case with an open mind can be resolved retrospectively by reference to his later judgment in *Quebec Protestant School Boards*, 1982, below p. 108.

motherhood, the flag and apple pie." Deschênes had to concede that the literal meaning of section 133 was against him (*Blaikie*, 1978: 262). Nothing daunted, he resorted variously to the weight of scholarly opinion (on Quebec's ability to amend section 133 unilaterally), to the historical meaning (the definition of "Records and Journals"), and even to the meaning behind the meaning—"Act" turned out to be much more than the mere statute; it was the disembodied law itself (*Blaikie*, 1978: 261–2). When scholarly opinion, history, and deep meanings were against him (the application of section 133 to regulations) or inconclusive (the language of the courts), he used anything he could get his hands on: with regulations it was the possibility that "skeletal" laws would be passed to sneak around section 133 and load everything into regulations, the "intimate relation" between statutes and regulations and the cases supporting judicial constitutional originality. With the language of the courts it was the fact that "A judicial decision is one of the most important public Acts which our society knows" (*Blaikie*, 1978: 268). Deschênes used every available vehicle to drive to his inevitable conclusion: that every provision of the carefully drafted Chapter III was unconstitutional.

Deschênes' thorough job at trial served as the basis for the unanimous agreement of the seven judges of the Quebec Court of Appeal and the nine of the Supreme Court of Canada, not to mention the decision of the Manitoba Court of Appeal in the twin case, *Forest* (1979). The Supreme Court of Canada decision in *Blaikie* came on December 13, 1979. The basic line of reasoning was Deschênes', though the style was rather loftier and less technical or argumentative—the constitutional initiative had by now been put on the table. The Supreme Court of Canada found the requirement of enactment as well as printing and publishing "implicit" in section 133 (*Blaikie*, 1979: 402). And they argued that the reference there to "Courts" "ought to be considered broadly" (*Blaikie*, 1979: 402) to include less formal tribunals, which had grown in importance since confederation. The word "Acts" was extended to include "regulations."[1] They quoted a judge of the English House of Lords who had written in 1930 that the *BNA Act* "planted a living tree capable of growth and expansion within its natural limits" and argued that when dealing with "a constitutional guarantee" the Court should not be "overly technical" (*Blaikie*, 1979: 403).[2] As the Supreme Court approached its new role as "expounder" of the constitution, it seemed totally oblivious to the fact that expanding the rights of the *Quebec* (English) minority in section 133, inevitably narrowed the rights of the *Canadian* (French) minority, as represented by the Quebec legislature. If anything, the Court seemed determined to beat back this challenge to the status quo *as such*, finding in the technically meaningless but ideologically impudent section 7 of Bill 101 (symbolically declaring French to

---

[1] The meaning of "regulations" would itself be expanded in a follow-up decision to clarify this one. It would be held to include any rules made or even approved by the government and rules of court and rules of quasi-judicial administrative tribunals (*Blaikie (No. 2)*, 1981).

[2] Deschênes, on the other hand had written: "Nothing would justify the Court to strain the text in order to extract a meaning that their draftsmen had not wanted or did not intend to give" (*Blaikie*, 1978: 282).

be "the language of the legislature and the courts in Quebec") "a more compelling answer" to the constitutionality of the Act than any of the others.

Quebec had made an alternative argument in the case which, though somewhat weak in the circumstances, is worth considering for the light it sheds on the companion Manitoba controversy. The argument was that those parts of section 133 that imposed obligations on Quebec were part of *its* "constitution." This would grant Quebec the power unilaterally to amend those parts of section 133 under s.92(1) of the *BNA Act* which gave the provinces the power to amend their own constitutions. This argument was easily handled by the Supreme Court. In the first place, the *BNA Act* had a heading for "Provincial Constitutions," and section 133 was not under it. More importantly, section 133 imposed reciprocal obligations on both Parliament and the Quebec legislature, and thus had to be regarded as "part of the Constitution of Canada and of Quebec in an indivisible sense" (*Blaikie*, 1979: 400). Now the point of all this is that neither of these points could be made against Manitoba's unilingual legislation, the constitutionality of which, by no coincidence at all, the Supreme Court of Canada decided on the very same day in the very same way in the case of *Forest* (1979).[1]

Forest was a challenge to the validity of the 89-year-old Manitoba *Official Language Act* of 1890, which made English the "exclusive" language of the courts and legislature of Manitoba. This law directly contradicted section 23 of the *Manitoba Act, 1870*, an Act of the Parliament of Canada, subsequently given equivalent status to the *BNA Act* by an Act of the British Parliament. Section 23 of the *Manitoba Act* provided for Manitoba precisely what section 133 of the *BNA Act* had provided for Quebec three years earlier, though without mentioning reciprocal obligations on Parliament. When Manitoba became the fifth province of Confederation in 1870, it was almost evenly split between French and English inhabitants, 55% French and 45% English (Banks, 1986: 467). However, immigration patterns made the French population a definite minority by the mid-1880s. In 1890, with French Manitobans accounting for less than 20% of the population (Granatstein et al., 1983: 30), the Manitoba legislature sought to end official bilingualism and passed the impugned *Official Language Act*. French leaders protested to the Lieutenant Governor of the province, but he assented to the bill anyway and sent the protest to the Governor General of Canada. The federal government, while agreeing that the constitutionality of the Act was doubtful, preferred to leave the matter to the courts and did not exercise its power of disallowance (Banks, 1986: 474).

The Act was declared unconstitutional in two separate actions—albeit by the same French St. Boniface[2] County Court Judge—in 1892 and in 1909 (Banks, 1986: 475). But the government of Manitoba simply ignored the decisions, neither appealing them nor complying with them. The French community seems to have let the matter drop in favour of more pressing concerns over discrimination in schooling (Banks, 1986: 476). Subsequent French im-

---

[1] The cases had been argued separately, *Blaikie* in June and *Forest* in October.

[2] St. Boniface, a suburb of Winnipeg, has Manitoba's largest concentration of French speakers.

migration to Manitoba was virtually nil and the pressures to assimilate were great. By 1971, the French proportion of the population of Manitoba had dwindled to about 6.1%, and it was dropping fast (5.4% in 1976) (Mallea, 1984: 228). Its political spirit was revived, however, by the ascendancy in Ottawa of the Canada-wide bilingual vision. In fact, whatever political clout it had was due to the ideological necessity, for supporters of the federal government's line on language, of establishing French minority rights outside of Quebec as a condition of the struggle against French unilingualism in Quebec (Trudeau, 1968). Once again, ordinary political means were useless to give equivalent status to a tiny minority, to "leapfrog" it ahead of other even larger minorities.[1] The legal means were all that were available, but they proved more than adequate to turn Manitoba politics upside down.

The pretext was easy enough to find, a five-dollar parking ticket issued, like all Manitoba parking tickets, in English, to French Manitoban Georges Forest in 1976. He fought the ticket on the basis of the bilingual guarantees in the *Manitoba Act 1870*. Losing in provincial court (before an English judge appointed by the provincial government), he appealed to the County Court (of St. Boniface!) in documents drawn up entirely in French. The Attorney General objected on the basis of the 1890 legislation, but the (federally appointed, French) County Court Judge allowed the appeal to proceed and held the Act invalid.[2] There followed some complicated legal wrangling which turned on whether the case was about parking or about language. The Attorney General wanted to go ahead with the parking ticket and would not appeal the County Court ruling, but Forest was only interested in challenging the *Official Language Act* and applied to have the law struck down in the Court of Queen's Bench (a higher court). That court held Forest had no standing (that is no *personal* reason) to challenge the law because he had won, after all, in County Court. He was told he should go back and fight the parking ticket in French. Forest next appealed to the Manitoba Court of Appeal, which accepted the appeal for the forthright but rather unjudicial reason that denying the plaintiff standing "could have the effect of immunizing that Act from judicial review" (*Forest*, 1978: 409). In other words, the Court of Appeal thought it should decide the issue notwithstanding that the case itself was obviously just an excuse to get the *Act* reviewed:

> But to suggest that the heart of the dispute between Mr. Forest and the Crown is the traffic ticket is to ignore the realities of the situation. The language question and nothing else is what really concerns and divides the parties here...There has never been any mystery about the plaintiff's desire and attempt to have the language question litigated in a superior court (*Forest*, 1978: 412–413).[3]

---

[1] For example Ukrainian Manitobans and German Manitobans each outnumbered French Manitobans in the 1971 census (Reitz, 1980: 347). Status and non-status Indians outnumber all ethnic groups in Manitoba except for the British (Valentine, 1980: 81).

[2] On December 14, 1976, just weeks after the PQ victory.

[3] Interestingly enough, the judgement was given by Manitoba Chief Justice Samuel Freedman, who, as we have seen, later took the same straightforward approach to whether the convention question should be answered in *Re Constitution of Canada* (1981).

Given its enthusiasm for the case, it is not surprising that the Court agreed that the Act was unconstitutional or that it relied expressly on the judgment of Deschênes in *Blaikie*.

The Supreme Court of Canada contrived to have the judgment in *Forest* released the same day as *Blaikie*. Though the provisions were similar and the intent of the legislation the same, there were important points of difference. First, where the PQ government had done all it could to comply with the *BNA Act*, there was no such attempt in Manitoba's language law. Conflict between the two Manitoba laws was conceded from the outset. Second, the arguments which had shown conclusively that section 133 could not be considered Quebec's constitution, for it alone to amend, did not apply. Section 133 was in the *BNA Act* but nowhere near the part entitled "Provincial Constitutions." The *Manitoba Act* was not in the *BNA Act* and thus had a plausible claim, as the Supreme Court conceded, to status as the province's constitution: "in a certain way, the whole *Manitoba Act, 1870* may be said to be the Constitution of the Province." (*Forest*, 1979: 389) Finally, while section 133 imposed reciprocal obligations on Quebec and the federal government, section 23 only applied to the Manitoba legislature. To deny the right to Manitoba, the Court made some rather half-hearted and completely unconvincing technical arguments. The question was, in fact, hopelessly indeterminate in technical interpretive terms. In political terms, however, the answer was inevitable. Forest just had to be given the same treatment as the plaintiffs in *Blaikie*. This indeed had been recognized by the lawyers for the plaintiffs in *Blaikie* when they had started the case back in 1977:

> If that case [*Forest*] gets to the Supreme Court with ours, there's no way the Court can stop Quebec from doing away with English while permitting Manitoba to do away with French (*Winnipeg Free Press*, December 15, 1977: 10).

The Supreme Court's own words were not very different:

> It is enough to note that on any view it certainly cannot result in Manitoba's Legislature having towards s.23 of the *Manitoba Act, 1870* an amending power which Quebec does not have towards s.133 (*Forest*, 1979: 393).

Richard Bourhis writes: "The only difference between these two cases is that the ruling on the Manitoba case came 90 years 'after the fact' whereas the Quebec ruling came two years 'after the fact'" (Bourhis, 1984: 291). In fact, it was more like 90 years to *five months* if we take the Deschênes trial ruling to be definitive. The difference speaks volumes about the relationship between law and power. The victorious Quebec minority was the large, socio-economically powerful representative of the dominant interests in North America. Not only was it historically well-treated, it actually dominated the majority. Law came to its rescue where democratic politics could not. Could it not be said that the law also came to the rescue of the weak and historically ill-treated Manitoba minority? It could, but to leave it at that would be far too generous. The law and the constitution had been deaf to the Manitoba minority until the Quebec minority and the important interests it represented were threatened. It had been deaf (or toothless, depending on how you look at it) to the claims of the weak until they could be aligned with the interests of the strong. Historically speaking, the case was not determined by either the words of the constitution or the equities of the situation (they had never prevailed before, so why should they now?) but by the federalist political strategy of fighting the Quebec nationalist-independence movement with Canada-wide bilingualism and the fact that the Court was the only device available to carry out this strategy. When linguistic minority mistreatment was directed only at an economically and socially weak group, the law afforded no protection. Only when the powerful interests aligned with the English community of Quebec came under attack did the constitution come to the rescue. Only when they became useful to the political struggles of the powerful were these formerly abandoned people swept under the wing of constitutional protection.

The Charter and the Language of Education

In a sense, *Blaikie* was only a preliminary bout between the federal government and the Parti Québécois government of Quebec. The main event was the enactment of the Charter itself, and the central issue here was the entrenchment of minority language education rights. We have seen that Trudeau had worked this clause out as early as 1965. He was thinking mainly of the situation outside Quebec, where French language education had been forcibly denied in both Ontario and Manitoba, and his model was really the freedom of choice offered English speakers in Quebec. As late as 1965 it was inconceivable that Quebec would ever deny freedom of choice in education to its English minority. The 1974 Quebec Liberal legislation did no such thing, of course. In making entry to the English school system dependent on "sufficient knowledge" of English (*Official Language Act*, 1974: s.41), it merely (and clumsily) attempted to steer non-English immigrants into the French system. The PQ legislation was a different story altogether. It shifted the focus from language to ethnicity by making capacity irrelevant. Entry into the English system would be basically restricted to those whose father or mother had been educated in English *in Quebec*. (*Charter of the French Language*, 1977: ss.72 and 73). Otherwise education would be entirely in French. The idea was to respect the rights of the indigenous English minority to its own education system—similar exceptions were made for Native peoples—while insuring that immigrants to the province, whatever their language or ethnicity, would enter the French system. The law was entirely prospective and did not require anyone to move from the English system to the French one. It preserved the rights of anyone who had already started to educate their children in English in Quebec and even of those English speakers who had moved to Quebec before the law took effect, whether or not they had yet started their children in the English system. But anyone moving to Quebec after the law took effect, from anywhere in the globe, *including the rest of Canada*, would have to enter the French system no matter what their schooling had been prior to that. In addition to the "expressive" effects these provisions shared with the rest of

Bill 101, they would have two concrete ones. First, and perhaps most important numerically, was that the children of immigrants to Quebec, whether anglophone or allophone, from Canada or abroad, would be annexed to the French rather than to the English community. Second, French Quebeckers would have a much smaller field of English-speaking imports from the rest of Canada to compete with for high-level business jobs—only those willing to have their children educated into the French community.

Despite the chagrin of English Quebeckers and the federalists at this provision, it was beyond the reach of the federal government. As part of the same deal that had resulted in section 133 of the *BNA Act 1867*, constitutional authority over education had been entrusted exclusively to the provincial governments (section 93). Furthermore, the language of education (as opposed to the language of the legislatures and the courts) was not the subject of any constitutional provision. The federal government had only one card to play: the *Canadian Charter of Rights and Freedoms*, which it laid on the table as a direct response to Bill 101.

We have already reviewed the events leading to the adoption of the Charter and how Trudeau was able to hitch his vision of a constitutionally bilingual Canada to the soaring star of a judicially enforced Charter of Rights, and to so combine the questions that opponents of his virtually unilateral gambit could be cast as opponents of the un-opposable Charter or proponents of the unthinkable separatism. The result of all this was a Charter more or less like other Charters, with one exception: some thoroughly untypical provisions on language rights, tucked in after all of the other rights, just before the enforcement section. Most of these provisions came under the heading "*Official Languages of Canada*" and consisted of a duplication of federal government commitments under section 133 of the old *BNA Act* and parts of the federal *Official Languages Act* (1970), raising to constitutional status the commitment of the federal government to provide its services in French and English. The provision was also meant to apply to the provinces on a voluntary "opt in" basis, but since the only taker was New Brunswick, we were left with the strange sight, in a Charter of Rights and Freedoms, of a guarantee valid only within the borders of one small province. However, the climactic provision of this part of the Charter was the one at the very end entitled "*Minority Language Education Rights*." This provision was unlike any other in the Charter. Instead of the vague blanks left to the courts to fill in as they went along, such as "Everyone has the following fundamental freedoms: (a) freedom of conscience and religion" etc., there was a provision that in its detail bore more resemblance to a tax statute than to a constitution:

23.(1) Citizens of Canada

(a) whose first language learned and still understood is that of the English or French linguistic minority population of the province in which they reside, or

(b) who have received their primary school instruction in Canada in English or French and reside in a province where the language in which they received that instruction is the language of the English or French linguistic minority population of the province, have the right to have their children receive primary and secondary school instruction in that language in that province.

(2) Citizens of Canada of whom any child has received or is receiving primary or secondary school instruction in English or French in Canada, have the right to have all their children receive primary and secondary school instruction in the same language.

(3) The right of citizens of Canada under subsections (1) and (2) to have their children receive primary and secondary school instruction in the language of the English or French linguistic minority population of a province

(a) applies wherever in the province the number of children of citizens who have such a right is sufficient to warrant the provision to them out of public funds of minority language instruction; and

(b) includes, where the number of those children so warrants, the right to have them receive that instruction in minority language educational facilities provided out of public funds.[1]

It is easy to see why this provision rankled so much. Given its precision, there was no disguising the fact that it intervened directly in the field of education, a field guaranteed by the constitution to the provinces. Not only that. Given its precision there was no denying that it directly overruled a provincial law already in existence, namely Quebec's *Charter of the French Language*, Bill 101. Where Bill 101 only allowed English education (with transitional exceptions) to English speakers who had received their English education in *Quebec* (the "authentically English-speaking minority of Quebec": *Quebec Protestant School Boards*, 1982: 47), section 23 guaranteed it to English speakers no matter where they came from or how long they had been studying English. The point was often made in the hearings on the Charter that section 23 was, in effect, a direct *amendment* of a provincial law already in existence:

SENATOR ASSELIN: ...through a federal law you are amending a provincial law which is already in existence, known as law 101 and you are intervening in an area which is really the exclusive domain of the provinces without even asking for the consent of that province...

MR. CHRÉTIEN: No, no. We are only enshrining in the Constitution the proposal made by Mr. Lévesque and accepted by all the provincial premiers during the St. Andrews conference in 1977 and the Montreal conference in 1978...It is exactly the same text...We are giving French-speaking Canadians outside of Quebec the same rights that the English-speaking Quebeckers are said to have presently. And during this summer's conference, how many times have I heard Quebec representatives say that they hoped the English provinces would do for francophones what they were doing for anglophones in Quebec and that is

---

[1] The only provision which approaches section 23 in uncharacteristic precision (for a Charter of Rights) is the provision on mobility rights in section 6 (see Appendix A). Like the language rights provisions, section 6 cannot be overridden by use of section 33.

exactly what we are putting in the Constitution at this point (Canada, 1980–81, Issue No. 3: 54–55).

Later, criticized for not going far enough against Bill 101 by Liberal Warren Allmand, Chrétien said:

> I think that it is one of the difficult sections of the Charter because education is a matter of provincial jurisdiction...I do think Bill 101 will be affected in relation to Canadian citizens who speak the English language, who are in Quebec. We have not wanted to intervene to the point that we will force complete freedom in Quebec...I do not think that this government is willing to intervene that much in provincial jurisdiction (Canada, 1980–81, Issue No. 4: 11).

Mr. Chrétien's statement that section 23 merely enshrined a proposal made by the Premier of Quebec and accepted by the other premiers was a very cleverly worded deception which has been repeated often enough to have become part of Canadian political lore. It is a deception that takes us to the heart of legalized politics and is worth a moment to unravel. Just what was it that Mr. Lévesque offered and the rest of the Premiers accepted?

In July 1977, when Bill 101 was getting both a rough ride through the Quebec Legislative Assembly and a bad press across Canada, Lévesque wrote to the other premiers offering to enter into bilateral agreements whereby he would exempt immigrants to Quebec from Bill 101 if the province concerned would provide French language education for emigrants from Quebec (*The Globe and Mail*, July 22, 1977:1; *Le Devoir*, July 23, 1977: 1, 6). The move was interpreted in English Canada as an attempt by Lévesque to deflect criticism of Bill 101 (*The Globe and Mail*, July 23, 1977: 7), and a great fear suddenly arose that such agreements would boost separatist aspirations by showing how a sovereign Quebec could get along with the rest of Canada without the need for a federal structure (*The Globe and Mail*, July 27, 1977: 7). Trudeau urged the Premiers to reject the offer (*The Globe and Mail*, July 27, 1977: 9), and they did so. The government of Ontario, which would be Trudeau's staunch supporter in future constitutional negotiations, responded to Lévesque by arguing that language of education rights should not be bartered about but rather constitutionally entrenched as a matter of principle (*The Globe and Mail*, July 28, 1977: 1). Nor were there any takers among the other Premiers who offered essentially the same rationale (*The Globe and Mail*, July 29, 1977: 8). However, the idea was put on the agenda for the Premiers' conference in St. Andrews, New Brunswick, to be held that August. At that conference, Lévesque detailed his offer: as Quebec's part of any bargain, immigrants to Quebec from other provinces would be allowed to enter the English education system if they or members of their immediate families had received their education in English in Canada. This was indeed *textually similar* to the future "Canada clause" of s.23 of the Trudeau Charter. However— and here was the crucial difference—Lévesque would only permit this exemption as Quebec's part of a bilateral reciprocal interprovincial agreement under which the other province or provinces would promise to provide concrete services to their French minorities which could be taken advantage of by

Quebec emigrants. The PQ government said it had no fixed notions about what such services might be. It was willing to enter into negotiations with an open mind and to negotiate different agreements with different provinces, depending upon their special circumstances (*Le Devoir*, August 19, 1977: 1, 6). Would the PQ accept constitutional amendments or provincial laws guaranteeing French-English minority education rights, in lieu of bilateral agreements? No, said Claude Morin, Quebec's intergovernmental affairs Minister, because a constitutional amendment would mean the surrender of Quebec sovereignty over education. Furthermore, laws could be ignored with impunity while agreements could not (if a province did not live up to its part of the bargain, Quebec could end the exemption) (*The Globe and Mail*, August 19, 1977: 1, 2). At the opening of the conference, Lévesque stressed that he was after "concrete proposals" instead of "high-flown principles" (*The Globe and Mail*, August 18, 1977: 8). The nine English-speaking premiers preferred high-flown principles, however, and signed a joint declaration that they would "make their best efforts to provide instruction and education in English and French wherever numbers warrant" (*The Globe and Mail*, August 20, 1977: 1; *Re Education Act*, 1984: 514). The escape clause "wherever numbers warrant" was the crucial *textual* difference between what Lévesque offered and what would become section 23. Far more important to all of the Premiers was the *form* of the arrangement. Lévesque's offer was rejected precisely because it involved concrete bilateral commitments which the individual provinces saw no reason to make. The difference became even clearer when Trudeau took the initiative just weeks later and wrote to the premiers urging adoption of a constitutionally entrenched right to minority language education "where numbers warrant." This would be the centerpiece of the Charter program in the following year and would be accepted by the premiers and imposed on Quebec in 1982 as section 23. Lévesque replied in no uncertain terms:

> Quebec will never accept that its sovereignty in such a vital matter be replaced by a limited jurisdiction subject to judicial interpretation...It would be unthinkable that the Supreme Court of Canada, a majority of whose members will always be English-speaking and non-Quebeckers, replace the Quebec National Assembly as the final authority in the area of education (*The Globe and Mail*, September 10, 1977: 1).

In light of all this, it is nothing less than an outrageous distortion to say that section 23 of the Charter was "proposed" by Quebec. What is more, it is a distortion made possible by the myths surrounding the legalization of politics. The substantive ideas were similar, but the forms were crucially and radically different. Lévesque, as Premier of the province with by far the best minority language education system in Canada, was proposing concrete reciprocal agreements, the adequacy and reciprocity of which would be judged by the governments themselves. Trudeau was proposing a judicially administered abstract right to minority education "where numbers warrant" which would only need to satisfy the judges the federal government appointed. If the courts should decide that numbers did not warrant French language education in

British Columbia, Quebec would still have to offer English language education to immigrants from that province. If the courts thought Ontario's inferior system of French language education was good enough, Quebec would still have to grant immigrants from Ontario full access to its superior English system. Naturally, the crucial factor, but the one which had to remain invisible for the federal position to be plausible, was the *judicial factor*. The federal government was counting on a general inability to distinguish between judicially administered and democratically administered rights, while nevertheless insisting on the former.

When René Lévesque died suddenly in 1987, after all this was over, it was remarkable how often the word "democrat" appeared in tributes to him. Premier Bourassa called him a "great democrat" (*The Globe and Mail*, November 4, 1987: A4). Prime Minister Mulroney went so far as to say that Lévesque was "the ultimate democrat" and "the greatest democrat this country has ever known" (*The Globe and Mail*, November 6, 1987: A3). Though neither of them were referring to the legalization of politics, Lévesque's role in this struggle confirms the fitness of their descriptions of him, especially when he is compared with his adversaries. It seems very unlikely that the word "democrat" will ever creep into any eulogies for Pierre Trudeau—and this says a great deal about our subject.

The Quebec Protestant School Boards Case

When the Charter was proclaimed, the part of section 23 guaranteeing English education to English immigrants whether or not they had learned their English in Canada (section 23(1)(a)), was suspended pending acceptance of it by the government of Quebec (that is *any* government of Quebec, present or future). The "Canada clause" (23(1)(b)) however, was proclaimed in full, along with the "mobility" clause, which guaranteed the right to take up residence without discrimination in any province; both clauses were uniquely exempted from the section 33 legislative override. A court action to take advantage of this was launched immediately by the English School Boards and other opponents of Bill 101. It was heard and crowned with success by none other than Chief Justice Jules Deschênes (*Quebec Protestant School Boards*, 1982).

Since it was obvious to everyone that section 23 of the Charter and Bill 101 conflicted, there was really only one point of contention: the relevance of the first section of the Charter, the "reasonable limits" clause. This clause had been considerably tightened as a result of the Parliamentary committee hearings of 1980–81. It had first read that the rights in the Charter were:

> subject only to such reasonable limits *as are generally accepted* in a free and democratic society *with a parliamentary system of government.*

This had been subsequently altered, so that upon enactment it read:

> subject only to such reasonable limits *prescribed by law as can be demonstrably justified* in a free and democratic society.

The point of the clause was to make explicit the balancing of interests which would otherwise have to be done under the guise of interpretation. Does yelling "fire!" in a crowded theatre come within the protection of "freedom of expression"? Without something like section 1, United States courts have had to adopt specialized meanings of terms like these. With such a clause, Canadians courts could say, yes, it is "expression," but the limit is reasonable.

Unlike the legislative override in section 33, the reasonable limits clause contains no exceptions. It appears to apply to *all* of the rights in the Charter including language rights. So it was logical for Quebec to argue that Bill 101 was merely a reasonable limit on section 23, a limit on the rights of future English-speaking immigrants to Quebec in order to promote the vital interests of Quebec residents. The plaintiffs, on the other hand, including the government of Canada, which intervened in the case, argued that section 1 was not applicable *at all* to the conflict between Bill 101 and section 23. Because of the precision of section 23, the clear conflict between the two, and the fact that, historically speaking, section 23 was designed with Bill 101 in mind, it would be absurd for the Court to call it a "reasonable" limit (*Quebec Protestant School Boards*, 1982: 50–51).

This argument posed problems for Judge Deschênes. To deny the applicability of section 1 altogether would not only contradict the words of the Charter, but it would deny him the opportunity, which he seems to have welcomed, of debating the PQ on the merits of Bill 101. His solution was to admit the theoretical applicability of section 1, but to hold that Bill 101 constituted a "denial" instead of a mere "limit" of rights in the Charter, with the distinction turning entirely on the fact that the conflict between the two provisions was so obvious (which in turn depended on the detailed nature of the Charter provision). Thus section 1 could not save it. When Quebec countered that section 23 should be considered to be a *collective* right of minority language speakers, so that the denial of some of its benefits to some individuals was a mere "limit" on the rights of the group as a whole, Deschênes took the opportunity to launch into a red-baiting anti-PQ tirade:

> The court is amazed, to use a euphemism, to hear this argument from a government which prides itself in maintaining in America the flame of French civilization with its promotion of spiritual values and its traditional respect for liberty.

> In fact, Quebec's argument is based on a totalitarian conception of society to which the court does not subscribe. Human beings are, to us, of paramount importance and nothing should be allowed to diminish the respect due to them. Other societies place the collectivity above the individual. They use the Kolkhose steamroller and see merit in the collective result even if some individuals are left by the wayside in the process.

> This concept of society has never taken root here—even if certain political initiatives seem at times to come dangerously close to it—and this court will not honour it with its approval (*Quebec Protestant School Boards*, 1982: 64).

Having got that off of his chest, Deschênes decided he would consider the merits of the legislation anyway, just to be sure. That is, assuming it was a "limit" and not a "denial" he would consider whether it was a "reasonable" limit "demonstrably justified in free and democratic society." The first step here was the absurd proposition that one had to decide whether Canada was "free and democratic," which turned out to be just an excuse for more PQ-bashing:

> Where would one find a more democratic society than in a federation which permits a political party to come to power on the basis of a programme the aim of which is the dismemberment of this federation? (*Quebec Protestant School Boards*, 1982: 65)

Deschênes then launched into an assessment of the merits of the legislation. Casting aside traditions of judicial deference to the policy-making role of legislatures[1] (see Chapter II), he entered into a tendentious debate with the government of Quebec on the expected effects of Bill 101. Acting on evidence offered by the federal government, Deschênes found that the impact of the Quebec clause on the size of the English school population would make a difference of only 3–5% over the balance of the century, an amount he decided was "negligible" (*Quebec Protestant School Boards*, 1982: 89). Of the concentrations in areas such as Ottawa and Montreal and, more importantly, of the economic and cultural devaluation of French to which Bill 101 was, if nothing else, a symbolic response, he said nothing. Finally, at the very end of his reasons, ostensibly to help himself make up his mind as to whether the PQ government was really serious about the necessity of this law, Deschênes repeated the federal government hokum about Lévesque's "offer":

> In addition, all of these facts were taken into account when Quebec offered the other provinces reciprocal agreements with respect to the language of instruction. Whatever else may be said about it, s. 23 of the Charter bears a strange resemblance to the suggested agreements and it applies to other provinces as much as and more than to Quebec. The court has a hard time in understanding why Quebec refuses to accept today what it offered to others yesterday…(*Quebec Protestant School Boards*, 1982: 89)[2]

Jean Chrétien could not have said it better himself. In an example of legalized politics at perhaps its crudest, the law was declared unconstitutional. As much as the decision was condemned by the PQ and its supporters, it was applauded by the business community and English Quebec in general. Business was particularly happy that the decision would ease the transfer of personnel to Quebec (*La Presse*, September 9, 1982: A2, A3). Jean Chrétien hoped out loud that the judgment would convince the English community to

---

[1] The very first words of his opinion were a declaration of judicial independence from traditional limits: "…if we consider the effects of an entrenched charter of rights, we cannot fail to see that it involves giving the courts a significant degree of legislative power."

[2] Deschênes was not the only judge to misrepresent what went on at St. Andrews in 1977. The Ontario Court of Appeal did the same thing in *Re Education Act* (1984: 514), when, in justifying an expansive reading of section 23 of the *Charter*, it referred to the St. Andrews declaration as emanating from "the Premiers" without hinting that Quebec had dissented from the declaration. Incidentally, this is an example of how the acceptance of Charter norms by Quebec enhances their prestige across the country, which we noted in Chapter II as a major objective of the Meech Lake Accord.

stay in Quebec "with their money" (*The Globe and Mail*, September 9, 1982: 1).

Shortly after this decision, the fiscal crisis which was panicking many Western governments into public sector cutbacks hit Quebec particularly hard. Quebec had borrowed heavily to underwrite the Quiet Revolution and was extremely vulnerable to the economic fluctuations of the early eighties. Not by any means a socialist party, the PQ found itself turning on its most important supporters, the public sector unions. The result was massive labour unrest in 1982–83, draconian legislation in response, and irreparable harm to the popularity of the government (*Canadian Dimension*, 1983, Vol. 17 No. 3: 6–9; Whitaker, 1984b). It was therefore a very unpopular government that appealed Deschênes' judgment to the Quebec Court of Appeal. This may help explain the relatively short shrift given to the appeal, compared to Deschênes' elaborate handiwork. The Court of Appeal delivered its decision right at the hearing and filed brief reasons later (*Quebec Protestant School Boards*, 1983). The merits of Bill 101 were discussed neither by the Court of Appeal nor by the Supreme Court of Canada when it unanimously upheld the decision in 1984. In effect, though not in words, the Supreme Court held that, whichever way you sliced it, section 1 of the new Charter simply could not be allowed to apply to the case:

Section 23 of the Charter is not, like other provisions in that constitutional document, of the kind generally found in such charters and declarations of fundamental rights. It is not a codification of essential, pre-existing and more or less universal rights that are being confirmed and perhaps clarified, extended or amended, and which most importantly, are being given a new primacy and inviolability by their entrenchment in the supreme law of the land. The special provisions of s.23 of the Charter make it a unique set of constitutional provisions, quite peculiar to Canada. This set of constitutional provisions was not enacted by the framers in a vacuum. When it was adopted, the framers knew, and clearly had in mind, the regimes governing the Anglophone and Francophone linguistic minorities in various provinces in Canada so far as the language of instruction was concerned... [I]n view of the period when the Charter was enacted, and especially in light of the wording of s.23 of the Charter as compared to that of ss.72 and 73 of Bill 101, it is apparent that the combined effect of the latter two sections seemed to the framers like an archetype of the regimes needing reform, or which at least had to be affected, and the remedy prescribed for all of Canada by s.23 of the Charter was in large part a response to these sections...[T]o our knowledge no other statute that was in force at the time the Charter was adopted and which dealt with the language of instruction has criteria as specific as those in s. 73 of Bill 101. These criteria are not only specific, but are also unique as a whole; it may be wondered whether the framers of the Constitution would have drafted s.23 of the Charter as they did if they had not had in view the model which s.23 was indeed in large measure meant to override (*Quebec Protestant School Boards*, 1984: 331–332, 335).

In other words, looking at the precise historical purpose of the framers in drafting section 23, namely to override Bill 101, the "reasonable limits" provision could not possibly bear an interpretation which regarded Bill 101 as a legitimate limitation. Nor, even disregarding the history, did the specificity of section 23 leave any room for coexistence between the two laws. No interpretation of either could avoid their mutual exclusivity.

Recognizing the uniqueness of section 23 saved the Supreme Court the bother of messing up its new constitutional jurisprudence with fancy arguments that attempted to de-politicize what was so obviously political. It obviously felt that "holding its nose" and getting on with it would do less damage to the general Charter enterprise than trying to dress up the exception in some ill-fitting general principle. But the decision amounted to an admission that those critics were right who had said that the federal government was in effect amending a provincial law by its Charter. And given the centrality of language to the political project of the Charter, it granted a kind of retrospective confirmation to the notion that the Charter was an expedient to the precise objective of imposing a language regime on Quebec. Had the government merely been committed to universal judicialized human rights, it would have put in a grand phrase about "freedom of linguistic expression" and let the chips fall where they might. Instead, it loaded the dice in its favour. It wrote the law and picked the judges to enforce it. In the end it seems so obvious as to render subtle theorizing a little silly.

The Manitoba Language Reference

By 1984, the political action on language had moved decisively from Quebec to Manitoba where, due entirely to the judicial process, language had become the central political issue. The judgment of the Supreme Court of Canada in the *Forest* case had left a huge question mark over the legal system of Manitoba. Quebec had been found to have been in breach of its constitutional obligations only since 1977 and, besides, had already prepared official translations for each Act in compliance with its own law. Manitoba had been violating the law since 1890, and none of its statutes had been translated. On the other hand, the Supreme Court had gone only so far as to hold the language law of 1890 unconstitutional. It had said nothing about the effect of its decision on the rest of the laws of Manitoba. That took another traffic ticket, issued once again in English only, this time for speeding, to law professor Roger Bilodeau (Bilodeau, 1986). Bilodeau's challenge was rejected in Provincial Court in August 1980, and he also lost his appeal to the Court of Appeal of Manitoba in July of the following year. Though all of the judges had held his conviction valid, one judge of the Court of Appeal was of the opinion that *all* of Manitoba's unilingual laws had been rendered invalid by the *Forest* decision. Bilodeau was given leave to appeal to the Supreme Court of Canada on November 15, 1981, while the ink from the constitutional accord was still drying. The case was set down to be heard a year later, but as the time for hearing approached, negotiations were undertaken between the government of Manitoba and the Société Franco-Manitobaine (SFM) for a compromise. In lieu of proceeding with the case, the SFM would settle for the publication of just the *current* laws in both languages and official constitutional bilingualism with services in French guaranteed along the lines of the federal government and New Brunswick under the new Charter. The SFM would then agree to a constitutional amendment to the *Manitoba Act* to validate all prior laws. In the meantime, Bilodeau agreed to adjourn the case. However, opponents of official bilingualism held plebiscites in various municipalities which showed as much as 80% of the population opposed. The government consequently abandoned the project in February 1984 (Bilodeau, 1986; Doern, 1985).

Bilodeau then proceeded with his appeal to the Supreme Court of Canada. The federal government responded by joining to this appeal a reference on the general question of the validity of Manitoba's laws. This suited the Supreme Court of Canada, indeed all of the parties, very well, because once again, it was not the traffic ticket they were interested in but the abstract constitutional question. In fact, the concrete question of the traffic ticket was quite likely to go against Bilodeau (as it had so far) and that could muddy the ideological waters considerably. As it turned out, although the general reference on Manitoba's laws and the traffic ticket that had been its pretext were argued together before the Court, the judgment in the reference case was announced well in advance of the decision on the ticket.

The Manitoba Language Rights Reference (*Re Manitoba Language Rights*, 1985) outdid even the Constitutional Reference Cases of 1981 in judicial inventiveness. As for its barely concealed politicality, you know you are in for something special when a judgment begins like this:

> This Reference combines legal and constitutional questions of the utmost subtlety and complexity with political questions of great sensitivity (*Re Manitoba Language Rights*, 1985: 7).

The sensitivity and complexity lay in this. The constitution, so the Court had already held in *Forest*, required bilingualism. In traditional constitutional terms, and in the words of Canada's new constitution, this meant the unilingual laws of Manitoba were "of no force or effect" (*Canada Act 1982*, section 52). But what did that entail for all of the laws and the actions taken under them from 1890 to 1982?[1] Were the laws really of no effect? Were the actions taken under them illegal? Did Manitoba have no law? Could everyone sue everyone else for everything done under the false authority of law for the last ninety years? Would it be a legal free-for-all until all the statutes were translated? None of the many lawyers or even the parties involved in the case wanted that (Bilodeau, 1986: 220). So the task for the Court was to fashion a politically and legally acceptable solution, to decide not so much *what* to do as *how* to do it. In July of 1981, with the debate on the constitution raging, the Manitoba Court of Appeal, by majority, had come up with the device of saying that the constitutional provision was not "mandatory," only "directory," meaning failure to observe it did not result in invalidity (*Bilodeau*, 1981). The legislature would have to

---

[1] In 1982 the NDP government started to enact legislation in both languages.

solve the problem by ordinary political means (*Bilodeau*, 1981: 235). Even the dissenter on the Court of Appeal would have excused the legislature for all the invalidity up to the Supreme Court's definitive decision in *Forest* (*Bilodeau*, 1981: 231).

Four years later, from the safe perspective of Ottawa and with the Charter entrenched, the Supreme Court of Canada lacked the reticence of both the majority and the minority of the Manitoba Court of Appeal. The distinction between mandatory and directory was rejected because of "the harm that would be done to the supremacy of Canada's Constitution if such a vague and expedient principle were used to interpret it":

> It would do great violence to our Constitution to hold that a provision on its face mandatory should be labelled directory on the ground that to hold otherwise would lead to inconvenience or even chaos (*Re Manitoba Language Rights*, 1985: 18).

So there was no alternative, said the unanimous Court, but to declare the unilingual laws—virtually *all* of the laws—of Manitoba "invalid and of no force or effect" (*Re Manitoba Language Rights*, 1985: 21). Did this mean that legal "chaos" had to reign? No, because that would

> undermine the principle of the rule of law, a fundamental principle of our Constitution [which requires] that the law is supreme over officials of the government as well as private individuals, and thereby preclusive of the influence of arbitrary power [and] the creation and maintenance of an actual order of positive laws which preserves and embodies the more general principle of normative order. Law and order are indispensable elements of civilized life (*Re Manitoba Language Rights*, 1985: 22).

The pedigree of "the principle of the rule of law" was not hard to establish. The Court could cite *Re Constitution of Canada* (1981), several legal philosophers, and naturally, the preamble to the Charter itself. How then to protect the rule of law from legal chaos? One alternative was to declare the laws invalid "and leave it at that, relying on the legislatures to work out a constitutional amendment" (*Re Manitoba Language Rights*, 1985: 25). The Court rejected this solution because

> it would rely on a future and uncertain event...For the Court to allow such a situation [a transgression of the rule of law] to arise and fail to resolve it would be an abdication of its responsibility as protector and preserver of the Constitution (*Re Manitoba Language Rights*, 1985: 25).

Similarly, to rely on the power of the Lieutenant Governor of the province to refuse assent to a unilingual law or on the long dormant power of the Governor General to disallow such a law, would be to

> make the executive branch of the federal government, rather than the courts, the guarantor of constitutionally entrenched language rights...Such a result would be entirely inconsistent with the judiciary's duty to uphold the Constitution (*Re Manitoba Language Rights*, 1985: 26).

Since nobody else could be trusted to do the job right, it was up to the Court itself "to take such steps as will ensure the rule of law in the Province of Manitoba" (*Re*

Manitoba Language Rights, 1985: 26). Once it had decided to come to the rescue, the Supreme Court had no difficulty finding "doctrines" to support its right to do so. The "*de facto* doctrine" would protect the legality of everything officially done in reliance on the unilingual acts; "*res judicata*" would prevent the reopening of cases already decided by the courts; and, most important of all because of the technical limitations of the other two doctrines, was "the doctrine of state necessity" under which, the Court in effect decided, it could do anything it wanted to do. So, although all unilingual acts "are, and always have been, invalid and of no force or effect":

> The Constitution will not suffer a province without laws. Thus the Constitution requires that a temporary validity and force and effect be given to the current Acts of the Manitoba Legislature from the date of this judgment, and that rights, obligations and other effects which have arisen under these laws and the re-pealed and spent laws of the province prior to the date of this judgment, which are not saved by the *de facto* or some other doctrine, are deemed temporarily to have been and continue to be effective and beyond challenge (*Re Manitoba Language Rights*, 1985: 36).

The temporary validity would last "from the date of this judgment to the expiry of the minimum period necessary for translation, re-enactment, printing and publishing." Any unilingual laws enacted after the judgment, the Court warned, would be really invalid.

Though the Court cited numerous cases from all over the common law world (the US, the UK, Cyprus, Pakistan) where "necessity" had been invoked to validate the technically invalid laws, it could cite none in which a court had quite matched the judicial chutzpa of the Supreme Court of Canada.[1] In every case cited it had been the *government* which had acted out of necessity with the courts merely giving retroactive validity to the government initiative. Here it was the *Court* taking the initiative. This did not strike the Court as a relevant distinction (*Re Manitoba Language Rights*, 1985: 35).

The whole thing reminds me of the scene in the movie *Superman* where the Man of Steel, too late to save Lois Lane from certain death, actually reverses the spinning of the world on its axis and *turns back time*. One could be for-given for feeling just a little manipulated. If you had known he could do *that*, would you have been so nervous when the school bus was falling off the bridge? Messy, yes, but nothing a little spin on the axis couldn't cure. But, if we have a right to expect limits even on our superheroes, what about our

---

[1] One judge of the Manitoba Court of Appeal was so exercised that he chastised the Supreme Court with the following words: "I do not understand how the Supreme Court or any other court has a power to declare judicially valid or enforceable that which is judicially invalid. I do not understand how it can be said that emergency situations justify an usurpation by a court of the royal power. If the laws of Manitoba were really judicially invalid, I think it is the Queen in right of Manitoba who has the right to proclaim measures necessary to meet the situation, not the Supreme Court. I do not know of anyone ever until this time disputing the Queen's prerogative in this respect. The Supreme Court cannot dictate to the Queen in right of Manitoba. If she or her representatives were to refuse assent to French language reenactments of her laws, I do not see what the Supreme Court could do about it" (Justice Joseph O'Sullivan quoted in *Ontario Lawyers Weekly* Vol. 5, No. 13:1, July 26, 1985).

Supreme Court judges? This little device of "necessity" makes the rest of the constitution rather superfluous. In fact, it reveals rather starkly how little constitutional documents restrain their "interpreters." Of course, the device has to be used sparingly. And you have to make sure there are no rude little boys running around yelling that the Court has no clothes on, either. Everybody has to be willing to suspend their disbelief. In *Re Manitoba Language Rights*, it was crucial that the Court had the full consent of all the parties to the action for what it was doing.[1]

What was the effect of all this legal hocus-pocus? The Court declared the laws invalid in one breath and temporarily validated them in the next. Manitoba would have to translate all its laws, old and new, or so it seemed. What if the government refused? Would the Court then declare legal chaos? But, of course, Manitoba was *anxious* to translate its current laws. That was part of the constitutional deal it could not get past the electorate. The court order merely legitimized the exercise by taking responsibility for it away from the government and placing it with "the Constitution." On the other hand, nobody wanted the old laws translated. The 50,000 or so French Manitobans could probably find better uses for the tens of millions of dollars it would cost to do that (*The Globe and Mail*, February 20, 1986: A9). The SFM really wanted the extension of French services (Brandt, 1986: 211). You could get a lot of service for thirty million dollars. But avoiding translation of the old statutes would take a constitutional amendment. This would require the support of Ottawa which, as the main financial and political backer of the SFM (*The Globe and Mail*, March 21, 1983: 9; Lockhart, 1986: 16), would hold back until the SFM got a satisfactory *quid pro quo*. When last seen, Manitoba was expected to announce, sooner or later, that such a deal had been made, with some form of "official bilingualism" the outcome (*The Toronto Star*, April 30, 1988: D4).

Thus the SFM and the Manitoba government got a large assist from the Supreme Court in their quest for a bilingual Manitoba, despite their inability to overcome the opposition of the vast majority of Manitobans. Of course, the form that the political solution took made it possible for everyone to deny responsibility for it—including the Court, which went out of its way to emphasize the disembodied nature of the authority requiring the result: "The Constitution will not suffer...," "the Constitution requires..." etc., never "The Court will not suffer..." or "the Court requires..." This was a form of politics calculated to confound the people of Manitoba, who were reduced to the status of spectators, forced even in their referendum to choose between accepting a consitutional amendment they opposed or leaving the solution to the judges (Bilodeau, 1986: 221n). Finally, whatever the eventual outcome, it is important to remember the historical conditions for the favourable response of the courts to the claims of the franco-Manitobans, namely the threat to the far

---

[1] It even left it to them to work out among themselves the period during which the Constitution would be suspended so that the laws could be translated. Until December 31, 1988 for current statutes, regulations and rules of court and December 31, 1990 for old ones: [1986] 1 W.W.R. 289.

more powerful interests represented by the English minority of Quebec.

The Court Changes its Approach

Where was Roger Bilodeau after all this? Though his traffic case was the excuse[1] for the Manitoba Language Reference and the two cases were argued at the same time, the release of his decision did not come until a year later. And the result was very different. In stark contrast to the six-year winning streak language cases had had at the Supreme Court, Bilodeau lost by the lopsided margin of six judges to one (*Bilodeau*, 1986). Once again the Manitoba case was twinned by the Court with the identical issue from Quebec, an English speaker challenging a unilingual French traffic ticket (*MacDonald*, 1986). This took a little doing on the part of the Court. Not only were the cases not argued together, the Supreme Court actually had to overrule a prior decision, of only 1980 vintage, in order to get around a procedural objection to hearing the Quebec case at all. Even the Court admitted the connection between the two cases was no accident:

> It can safely be assumed that [a reason] why leave was granted in the case at bar [was] that it had been granted in *Bilodeau* (Justice Beetz in *MacDonald*, 1986: 330).

Indeed the formula was once again employed of deciding the Quebec case and merely applying the results to the Manitoba case. Granted Manitoba's laws were all invalid, they had been temporarily rescued, so the question in the two cases was the same: was a summons issued under valid legislation nevertheless defective because it was unilingual? Once again, the answer turned on the extent to which the Court would take the constitution literally or otherwise. Section 23 of the *Manitoba Act* (and section 133 of the *BNA Act*) expressly stated that "*either* [French or English] may be used by any person, or in any pleading or process in or issuing from any Court." Literally, this meant that a summons could be in either language at the option of the Court issuing it. But Bilodeau (and MacDonald) argued that to make effective the *citizen's* right in the same section to *use* either language "implicitly" required at least a translation into the other official language. In dissent in the Quebec case, Justice Wilson put the argument this way:

> ...a right conferred by law on an individual entails a correlative obligation on the part of the State and...his or her right would be illusory if the State were not obliged to respect it...[T]he essence of language is communication and...implicit in the notion of language rights in the context of court proceedings is the ability both to understand and to be understood...[A] narrow, literal interpretation of the section can totally defeat [its true] purpose...The purpose of the provision, it seems to me, goes beyond validating the use of both languages. It validates them for a reason and that reason is that the person before the court will be dealt with in the language he or she understands. To say otherwise is to

---

[1] There is even a suggestion that Bilodeau got the speeding ticket on purpose (*The Globe and Mail*, May 2, 1986: A2), something like the fellow who drove around with his seat belt dangling out of the car door hoping to get charged so he could challenge the seat belt law in court (*The Globe and Mail*, July 6, 1987: A1). The Charter is turning out to be a major hazard to road safety!

make a mockery of the individual's language right (*MacDonald*, 1986: 362, 369, 380, 382).

What is at first surprising is not the "large and liberal" approach taken by Justice Wilson, which was well established by the three prior decisions on language in the Supreme Court, but that it attracted no support whatever from the rest of the Court. They had suddenly turned literal. To Justice Wilson's accusation of making a mockery of the purpose of the sections, they answered with the charge that her view made "a mockery of the text of this section" (*MacDonald*, 1986: 341). According to Justice Beetz, who wrote the majority opinion, respect had to be given to "the plain meaning" of the sections, which conferred rights on "litigants, counsel, witnesses, judges and other judicial officers who actually speak, not those of parties or others who are spoken to":

> This incomplete but precise scheme is a constitutional minimum which resulted from a historical compromise arrived at by the founding people who agreed upon the terms of the federal union...[I]t is not open to the courts, under the guise of interpretation, to improve upon, supplement or amend this historical constitutional compromise (*MacDonald*, 1986: 348).

A respectable attitude, no doubt, but where was it in *Blaikie*, *Forest*, and *Association of Protestant School Boards*? The same question can be asked of the unwillingness of the Court to allow MacDonald and Bilodeau to supplement their arguments from the fair trial provisions of the Charter and the strong line it drew between the "political" nature of language rights and the principled nature of the other Charter rights:

> They are based on a political compromise rather than on principle and lack the universality, generality and fluidity of basic rights resulting from the rules of natural justice. They are expressed in more precise and less flexible language. To link these two types of rights is to risk distorting both rather than reinforcing either (*MacDonald*, 1986: 352).

Whatever happened to the "living tree" the constitution was supposed to have planted in Canada? And since when did the Court pierce the juridical veil to hold the real political object of the litigant against him?

> The sole purpose of the appellant...has been from the start...to vindicate his language rights as an English-speaking Quebecker the way he understands them, not the rights to a fair hearing which he has in common with everybody else (*MacDonald*, 1986: 353).

In effect, the majority of the Court was continuing the unsentimental attitude it had taken to language rights in *Quebec Protestant School Boards* (1984), the Bill 101 case. Language rights were a category unto themselves, not to be mistaken for or supplemented by the other rights in the Charter. They were *political*. But there was an important difference. Where the result in the Bill 101 case had been to *expand* minority rights by a "purposive" or historical approach to the Charter, even if that meant disregarding some of its words, in this case, the result was to narrow minority language rights through a literal approach.

On the same day as the ticket cases, the Supreme Court took the opportunity, again by majority, to place limits on the official languages provisions of the Charter. The pretext was an absurdly complicated case involving a conflict over French immersion programmes in New Brunswick (*Société des Acadiens*, 1986). However, the issue before the Court was not the subject of the conflict itself but rather whether the French parties to the conflict had a right to a judge capable, with or without technical aids, of handling the case in both languages. In typical fashion, it was not even clear on the facts whether the judge was really unable to handle the case and, indeed, it was agreed by the whole court that the incapacity of the judge in question had not been sufficiently demonstrated. It was also agreed that whether or not the right claimed existed under the Charter, it was certainly available under the more broadly worded *Official Languages of New Brunswick Act* as well as the common law. As we shall see below, this was not the first or the last time the pronouncement of the Court bore no relation to any real factual dispute and had no impact on the case that was the excuse for the pronouncement. But pronounce they did. The question they pronounced upon was whether section 19(2) of the Charter, which guaranteed New Brunswick litigants the right to use either English or French in court, by implication guaranteed the right to be understood by the judge or judges hearing the case. The Court split five to two this time, with the majority, written once again by Justice Beetz, taking the same restrictive view of constitutional language rights seen in *MacDonald* and *Bilodeau*. Language rights were distinct from Charter or common law rights to a fair trial, were not "rooted in principle" but "founded on political compromise" and, therefore, "the courts should pause before they decide to act as instruments of change with respect to language rights." They should "approach them with more restraint than they would in construing legal rights" (*Société des Acadiens*, 1986: 425). The Court even defended its approach with an unusual bit of strategizing about judicial activism. Since the Charter (section 43(b)) contemplated provinces "opting in" the way New Brunswick had, the Court should avoid discouraging them with expansive interpretations of the language provisions:

> If, however, the provinces were told that the scheme provided by ss.16–22 of the Charter was inherently dynamic and progressive, apart from legislation and constitutional amendment, and that the speed of progress of this scheme was to be controlled mainly by the courts, they would have no means to know with relative precision what it is they were opting into. This would certainly increase their hesitation in so doing... (*Société des Acadiens*, 1986: 426)

Dissenting on the Charter point, Judge Wilson reiterated the points she had made in *Bilodeau* and *MacDonald*. This time, however, she was joined by Judge Dickson who relied on the absence of a literal obstacle he had found in the other two cases. He summed up the prior jurisprudence as showing

> for the most part a willingness to give constitutional language guarantees a liberal construction, while retaining an acceptance of certain limits on the scope of protection when required by the text of the provisions (*Société des Acadiens*, 1986: 414).

Clearly this was not the view of the majority of the Court, and the cases taken altogether were perceived, critically, in English Canada at least, as a "retreat" from the prior "hard line" on language rights (*The Globe and Mail*, May 1, 1986: A1–2; May 2, 1986: A1–2; May 7, 1986: A6). But it is more accurate to regard them as a change in the *approach to the adjudication* of language rights—from a "large and liberal" approach which gave a central role to the advancement of language rights to the judiciary, to a literalist approach which left major initiatives to the legislatures. What could account for such a change? It was certainly not the composition of the Court. The identical Court had been unanimous in the Manitoba Language Reference. Virtually the same Court had been unanimous in the *Quebec Protestant School Boards* case. And two members of the majority, including the author of its opinion, had joined with the now dissenting Judge Dickson on the unanimous courts of *Blaikie* and *Forest*. Furthermore, all of the new members of the Court, like all but one of the old members, had been appointed by Trudeau. Regions played a tiny part, in that the French judges from Quebec voted against an expansive reading of minority language rights, while the dissenters were English speakers. Furthermore, Judge Dickson, an English speaker from Manitoba, voted *against* the French of Manitoba but *for* the French of New Brunswick (stressing that what he was saying about New Brunswick did not necessarily apply to Manitoba).

But none of this explains why the majority had so radically changed its approach. For that we must look to the *context* of the decision. That had also radically changed. Most importantly, the PQ had been decisively defeated in the Quebec general elections six months prior to the decisions. Moderate forces were back in office in the form of a Liberal government committed to the full economic and political integration of Quebec and Canada, with a free flow of capital, people, goods, and services, including, so far as the political climate would allow, the encouragement of an English presence in Quebec. In March of 1986, it was formally announced that the Liberals had ended the PQ government practice of exempting all Quebec laws from the Charter, a move applauded by the federal government (*The Globe and Mail*, March 5, 1986: A8; March 21, 1986: A10). In their first year in office, the Liberals would expand English language education in the French school system (*The Globe and Mail*, October 3, 1986: A3) and English language health and social services (*The Globe and Mail*, December 19, 1986: A14). What is more, the Liberals were elected on a platform that included amendment of Bill 101 to allow bilingual signs, and though the popularity of the law (*The Globe and Mail*, October 20, 1986: A5)[1] prevented them from delivering right away, within five months of taking office it became clear that they had adopted a policy of non-prosecution of violations of the unilingual sign provisions (*The Globe and Mail*, April 4, 1986: A8). When the Quebec Court of Appeal struck them down as contrary to "freedom of expression" (*Chaussure Brown's Inc.*, 1987), to the applause of the business and English communities,[2] the Liberals would reject the demands of organized labour to resurrect the law by exempt-

---

[1] Opinion polls indicated a majority of Quebeckers in favour of unilingual signs.

[2] The anglophone lobby Alliance Quebec had "sponsored" the action.

ing it from the Charter through the use of section 33 (*The Globe and Mail*, December 23, 1986: A1, A5; *The Toronto Star*, December 23, 1986: A11). Despite appealing the decision "for technical and legal reasons" (*The Globe and Mail*, February 27, 1987: A5), it was later revealed that the government was actually paying the legal fees of the other side (*The Globe and Mail*, April 21, 1988: A8). And it would not be too long before the Meech Lake Accord would be signed, "welcoming Quebec back into the constitutional fold" and putting a definite end to the independentist interlude. Why fan the embers of linguistic nationalism by judicially extending English rights when the legislative process could be relied upon to protect them to the extent possible? As for Judge Beetz's strategic hypothesis that the road to bilingualism is actually paved with judicial restraint, this was at least to some extent borne out when the Supreme Court decided its next major language case on Saskatchewan's bilingual obligations, after the Meech Lake Accord had been signed and, indeed, after it had been ratified by Saskatchewan (*Mercure*, 1988).

This was yet another speeding ticket that the recipient wanted to fight in French. In *Mercure*, the Court continued to pursue its new "soft" line on constitutional language requirements, while gently prodding the governments concerned. As in the cases of *Blaikie* and *Forest*, the Court held that the long superseded foundation laws of both Saskatchewan and Alberta required official bilingualism. But distinctly *unlike Blaikie* and *Forest*, these obligations were held to be part of the "provincial constitutions" and so could be amended unilaterally by their governments. In justifying his narrow reading of constitutional language requirements, Justice La Forest said the "living tree" of the earlier language judgments was, at the relevant time, "a mere sapling" (*Mercure*, 1988: 95). Even this went too far for Justice Estey, who was about to take early retirement. In dissent, he complained about the "unhappy" tendency of traffic tickets to turn into constitutional references (*Mercure*, 1988: 146), and he castigated the majority for doing its own historical research:

> The courts, and particularly those at the second level of appeal, are neither qualified nor authorized to conduct a trial of historical issues (*Mercure*, 1988: 177).

He thought the modern governments of Saskatchewan and Alberta were free of even these quasi-constitutional bilingual obligations. Politically speaking, however, the majority's decision was just what the doctor ordered. Binding constitutional requirements were not necessary with Quebec safely back in the "constitutional fold." They would have provoked a political crisis and might even have threatened the Meech Lake Accord itself. But this judgment could maintain the bilingualist vision, in theory at least, while coaxing whatever there was to be coaxed out of the governments concerned. Saskatchewan responded by removing its strict bilingual obligations and introducing modest advances in French rights (*The Globe and Mail*, April 6, 1988: A1). Further encouragement from the federal government, in the amount of sixty million dollars, led Saskatchewan to start translating its laws and expanding French services with the goal of eventually becoming "officially bilingual" (*The Globe and Mail*, June 16, 1988: A5). Alberta, as well, made some modest moves in expanding French services, also with promises of federal financial help, while remaining adamant that it would not translate its statutes, even if it were paid to do so (*The Globe and Mail*, June 23, 1988: A1; June 24, 1988: A5). Still, nobody was tearing up the Meech Lake Accord over it.

All of this might lead us to the following hypothesis. When the status quo of social power—in this case represented by the federalist forces battling independentism through a strategy of bilingualism—is threatened in the democratic arena, the courts will adopt an activist and interventionist approach to support that status quo. When conservative forces are in office, the Court will become passive and deferential, with the same net effect on the status quo. In each case the determining factor seems to be the approach that best supports the status quo of social power. In the United States of the 1930s, political conservatism was represented in court by judicial activism against social democratic governments. Nowadays, as we have been reminded by the recent battles over Reagan administration appointments to the United States Supreme Court, conservative politics are best represented on the bench by deference to the conservative-dominated legislatures. In Canada, the situation has been a little more volatile, but the principle seems to be the same.

Postscript: December 1988
The Supreme Court Strikes Down the Signs Law

As we go to press, the Supreme Court of Canada has severely tested this hypothesis by making what seems at first sight a politically counterproductive decision in *Ford* v. *Attorney General (Quebec)* (December 15, 1988). The announcement of the decision that the unilingual business signs provisions of Bill 101 were contrary to the Charter guarantee of "freedom of expression" was followed rapidly (within four days) by a rather predictable and obviously well-planned invocation of the section 33 override by the government of Quebec. Section 33 was, of course, available with respect to freedom of expression the way it was not with respect to language of education. It was invoked by Premier Bourassa to protect a new compromise law which promised to allow (to an as yet unspecified extent) bilingualism on *indoor* business signs while maintaining French as the sole language of outdoor business signs. The Supreme Court judgment and its aftermath has reinflamed passions on both sides of the language question and has provided new ammunition for foes of the Meech Lake Accord. Apart altogether from the merits of the question of the language of signs, English Canada has seized on the use of the notwithstanding clause as evidence of Quebec's bad faith. The government of Quebec has in turn threatened to withdraw from participation in future constitutional discussions if Meech Lake is not ratified. Whether or not all this is serious or just posturing, it seems that the Court could have avoided the whole mess by simply sticking to its soft line on language and upholding the law. How does this square with the idea in the text above that the Court, for political reasons, had turned accommodating on language legislation now that the independentist threat had diminished?

The Court's own justification for departing from the "precise historical compromise" theory developed after the defeat of the PQ was that the theory only applied to positive constitutional obligations on the government, for example to provide services in a minority language, and not to negative constitutional limits on the government, for example, not to interfere with the "freedom" to use your own language in the marketplace. This is merely another version of the sharp ideological distinction between public and private spheres endemic to legal politics, discussed in Chapter II. Courts are typically more willing to intervene to *prevent* interferences with the status quo of social power than to *require* them. In other words, this is the everyday, garden-variety conservatism of judicial review. Of course, this does not explain the Court's about-face from its "large and liberal" interpretation of positive constitutional obligations in the PQ era to the narrow readings of those *same* types of obligations in the post-PQ era, for which the hypothesis in the text above seems to me the only plausible explanation.

Nevertheless, there are some elements in the decision on business signs which suggest that we should not take these events entirely at face value. Though there were a lot of issues in *Ford*, the central question was whether unilingual business signs were a "reasonable limit" under the federal and provincial Rights Charters (the Court conveniently interpreted them as having essentially identical meanings). But a reading of the decision discloses something rather extraordinary: if the Court is to be believed, *the lawyers for the government of Quebec made no effort whatsoever to justify unilingual signs as necessary to protect the French character of Quebec.* They lost that issue by default, as if on purpose. This, of course, was consistent with the program of the Quebec Liberals under Robert Bourassa, from their successful campaign for office against the PQ to their response to the Supreme Court ruling three years later. They had been bilingualists since 1974 and were in favour of softening the law to allow some English alongside of the obligatory French. But to have weakened Bill 101 without the aid of the Court would have been greatly to provoke the nationalists. Opinion polls taken right after the decision showed a substantial majority of Quebeckers would have preferred the PQ law to have been maintained in full force. The best thing from the government of Quebec's point of view, representing the federalist forces in Quebec, would be to have the Court strike down the law and then to have Bourassa come in to defend it, at least in part, with a bold use of section 33—especially if this would be to the loud protests of English Canada. In this way, striking down the law was, in fact, the safest thing the Court could do to help the status quo of social power in Canada and in Quebec. As with Manitoba, the Court would obligingly take the responsibility off the shoulders of the politicians.

There is one problem with this explanation: Meech Lake. The predictable use of section 33 may well be the straw that breaks its back. I have already argued that Meech Lake was intended to enhance the prestige of the Charter in various ways, but especially by getting Quebec's signature on it. On the other hand, the attachment of the legal profession to some of its specifics, as we have seen, is not great. Some lawyers are downright hostile. The new method of appointment to the Supreme Court, the messiness of the "distinct society" clause, and the political controversy may have made the Court indifferent or even worse to its fate. Am I being too Machiavellian in my analysis? Perhaps. But this case is extraordinary in many respects: two of the judges who sat on the appeal did not render judgment, which, without researching the matter, must be something of a first in Court history; one, who had expressed distaste with the Court's new approach to constitutional cases, retired early; another resigned—*after* undertaking the writing of some or all of the Bill 101 judgment—for health reasons, but these were rumored by the press to have had something to do with the strain of conscientiously deciding Charter cases with such grave implications (*The Globe and Mail*, December 1, 1988: A1); the decision, rendered by only five judges, was unanimous and anonymous. One thing is certain: the words of the Charter did not determine the outcome of this case, so something else must have.

Conclusion

Language is at once central and peripheral to the phenomenon of legalized politics in Canada. It is central because of the influence the politics of language had on the timing of the Charter and on its form. In the 1950s, it was the problem of constitutionally accommodating Quebec that prevented the Charter from coming to Canada. Then, with the Trudeau era, the Charter became the means to *solve* the problem of Quebec. On the other hand, language rights are peripheral in that they sit very uncomfortably in the scheme of legalized politics. They are cast in a different concrete form, the form of a detailed statute leaving little scope to the judiciary; they refer not to abstract universals but to two particular languages; and they are not, for the most part, subject to the legislative override. The courts have even recognized their special nature and have exempted them from the ordinary norms of Charter interpretation. They have been subject to the crudest political manoeuvres by both the professional politicians and the courts: federal and provincial Liberals at first clandestinely and then openly paying the legal bills of language claimants,[1] the appointment of Deschênes as Chief Justice of Quebec, his polemical judgments, the careful twinning of Manitoba and Quebec cases, the careful timing of the release of judgments, the doctrine of "necessity," the about-face by the Court when the political scene changed, and so on. We might well be tempted to follow the courts themselves and relegate these cases to the category of the exceptional. However, even such a category as this, which must also include the *Re Constitution of Canada* (1981), can teach us some lessons about how tissue-thin the legal system's veneer of neutrality can become *in extremis*.

Nevertheless, it is worth noting the continuities between exception and norm, between the language cases and legalized politics in general. First, of course, is the achievement by judicial means of a solution not then or perhaps ever possible by ordinary means of responsible government. Inside Quebec,

---

[1] *The Globe and Mail*, March 21, 1983: 9; May 2, 1986: A2; Lockhart, 1986.

this meant overruling a popular law enacted by a popularly elected government. In Manitoba, this meant both setting the agenda of the government and assisting it in achieving its goals over the opposition of the electorate.

A slightly more complicated but similar scenario took place in Ontario, which has, in percentage terms, the second-largest French minority in the country. As in Manitoba, the legal system was of no avail to this socially weak group[1] until it could align itself with the federal bilingualist strategy. French was not only without constitutional language protection prior to 1982, but there had also been a long stretch between 1912 and 1944 when it was actually *banned* as a language of instruction. Even the provisions in the *BNA Act* protecting the rights of denominational schools, so generously interpreted in the 1980s with the Charter, were held by the courts not to protect Catholic schools from the ban (*Mackell*, 1917). French was not to be found as a language of instruction in secondary schools until a law was passed in 1968 as a direct response to the Royal Commission on Bilingualism and Biculturalism. Ontario Tories moved very cautiously on this issue so as not to alienate their rural English-speaking supporters, gradually extending French rights and services in the province (primarily through local option methods in education), but refusing, for example, to accept constitutional amendments that would bring a form of section 133 of the *BNA Act* to Ontario. Representing the interests of English Canada, they could not avoid acceding to section 23 of the Charter as a condition of having it imposed on Quebec, but they had already accepted it in practice anyway. Section 23, in fact, provided a way to extend French language education without having to shoulder the political responsibility for it. In 1983, the Ontario government produced a White Paper proposing amendments to the *Education Act*. These amendments would expand French language rights by taking away from the often recalcitrant boards the power to decide whether "numbers warranted" that a French school be provided, and by proposing that the administration of minority language education be in the hands of minority members specially elected for the purpose. Instead of enacting the law, the government, as we have seen, referred its current law and the proposed amendment to the Ontario Court of Appeal. That Court, in an admittedly expansive reading of the language provisions, held that the current provisions were unconstitutional and that the principles of the White Paper were in line with the constitution's requirements: *Re Education Act* (1984). When the government then went ahead with the law, it played it safe again by simply adopting the Charter's definitions of who was entitled to French education (*Education Act Amendment*, 1986: section 1). In this case, the constitution allowed politicians to achieve delicate ends with unforeseeable political fallout without having to take responsibility for them.

Nor have the courts taken responsibility for what they have done to the responsibility of the politicians. Consistent with the basic premises of legal-

---

[1] 25.3% of Franco-Ontarians were living below the poverty line in 1973 compared to an estimated 17.6% of the total population. Average median income was also 7% below the Ontario average (Allaire and Toulouse, 1973).

ized politics, the courts have invoked the disembodied authority of the constitution as the determinant of their rulings (a disembodied authority which is nevertheless compliant enough to adapt quite nicely to the needs of the status quo). This aspect of legalized politics was crucial in Quebec, where the notion that what "Lévesque offered" was essentially the same as what the constitution provided played an important role. This notion was only made possible by the general assumption of legalized politics that the judicial factor is not a significant one, that there is no important difference between a deal administered by the parties and the same deal administered by the courts. It also made an appearance in the Manitoba Language Reference where the judicial suspension of the constitution in order to coax an acceptable political solution was defended as required by the constitution itself.

Another fundamental element which made possible the results in these cases was the casting of the issues in terms of conflicts of *right* as opposed to conflicts of *interest*. Where the PQ had designed the language laws quite explicitly to promote the various socio-economic-political interests of a concrete people defined more or less precisely by its language, legalization required a transformation of the issue into something quite different, the right of abstract hypothetical individuals to choose one or the other of the official languages and to have services in that language. Thus a concrete struggle between groups of unequal power was transformed into a contest of *individual* rights, that is, the rights of abstract, equivalent, free-willing subjects.

And what was the substantive result legitimated by this form of politics? Here we have the point of the whole exercise. This abstract form of legitimation was pressed into service on the side of a socially dominant minority, representing powerful outside forces, in its struggle against the dominated local majority. The legal system weighed in on the side of power by transforming a conflict of interests between a subordinate majority and a dominant minority into a conflict of abstract rights between the majority and the minority *tout court*, with the result that the dominant interests finished up where they started off—on top.

It is difficult to say at this point what the actual impact of the legalization of politics was for Quebec. It is probable that the repeated losses of the PQ government in court on issues central to its identity contributed to disillusionment with the party and its identification as a party of losers. But it is also clear that of far greater importance were other factors stemming from the limits of social democratic governments dependent on state spending in an era of fiscal restraint. Since they are not prepared to challenge private power directly, such governments must ultimately turn on their labour supporters (Whitaker, 1984b). If, indeed, there has been a decline in nationalism in Quebec (and neither the loss of the referendum nor the defeat of the PQ in 1985 are unambiguous in this regard), it would be foolish to blame this on the defeats in the courts (Latouche, 1986).

It is possible to argue that there has been a substantial enhancement of the allegiance of Quebeckers to *Canada* by reason of the patriation of the constitution from the UK, the Charter of Rights and Freedoms itself, constitutional bilingualism, the importance of Quebec on the national scene, Meech Lake, etc. This, after all, was the intended effect of all these mechanisms in the first place. Furthermore, none of this would have been possible without legalized politics in general and the defeat of the PQ language laws in particular.

But there are more than enough non-juridical factors to explain any supposed decline in nationalism. Some have even argued that rather than the failures, the very *successes* of the PQ government, the very impact of initiatives such as Bill 101 in breaking down ethnic barriers for individual French Quebeckers (not to mention in diminishing the English population by 10% between 1976 and 1981: d'Anglejan, 1984: 44) probably have a lot more to do with the state of nationalist politics in Quebec than the constitution. There is now an important French business sector in Quebec, and North American business seems to have adjusted, thanks to the PQ, to making profits in French. In short, the ethnic barriers to individual advancement, the most personally irksome elements of French-English relations to the middle-class and technocratic elements who made up the leadership of the PQ, have greatly diminished (d'Anglejan, 1984: 44–45; Whitaker, 1984b: 77–88). Add to this the general political and economic individualism of the eighties, the passing of baby boomers into middle age, etc., and we have enough explanations for any decline in Québécois nationalism, without mentioning the courts (Latouche, 1986).

But this leaves entirely out of account those deeper, collective aspects of Quebec nationalism, the "expressive" aspects of Bill 101 so undervalued by Judge Deschênes in *Quebec Protestant School Boards*. There are many indications that these did not fare quite so well as individual Quebeckers seeking advancement did. The complacency of even two or three years ago about the flourishing of French in Quebec has recently given way to serious concerns for its survival (*The Globe and Mail*, September 26, 1987: D2; October 2, 1987: A6). Language transfers from French to English in Quebec *increased* in the decade 1971–1981, with only an increase in allophone transfers to French keeping net losses down to what they had been the decade before. But English remained the preference even for allophones, diminishing only slightly over the prior decade, from 71% of transfers to 69% (Latouche, 1986: 127).

> That such a situation can still be possible, in view of the way Bill 101 restricts access to English schools, is rather surprising. It would seem that allophones are merely following the path taken before them by the francophones and are learning English in the streets. The fact that there are no language controls on access to CEGEP and universities simply favours this trend. The assimilation occurs outside the elementary schools and is only confirmed in the university (Latouche, 1986: 127–128).

Both the economic value and cultural ubiquity of English seem to have weathered the storm, and the gradual re-introduction of bilingualism by the Bourassa Liberals is likely to see a further growth in English influence. Did the courts have anything to do with this? Obviously, the persistence of English has to do with the basic facts of economics and geography, and it is an open question whether the unimpeded implementation of Bill 101 could have countered this. But it is clear that nothing else could have. In other words, the courts weakened whatever ability democratic politics had in this case to counter private power. The Charter and the courts ensured that access to the Quebec marketplace for the interests represented by English would be free from the purely political obstacles of official unilingualism, even should the PQ have remained in power. The issue was not, of course, a linguistic one in the first place. Linguistic rights were a proxy for the group and the interests represented by those rights. But freedom from government interference with linguistic choices merely leaves them to the coercion of the marketplace, the unchecked rule of economic power.

If in Quebec it can be said that the effect of legalized politics was to protect economically powerful interests from purely democratic interference, can it not be said that outside Quebec it operated in reverse? The socially and politically weak French minorities in the rest of Canada were protected from the more powerful interests confronting them, and their linguistic rights were greatly expanded. We have already pointed out how the historical record shows that the legal system responded not to the threats to these groups *per se*, but to their strategic importance for the protection of other, more important, interests. But is it still not a fact that the weak French groups benefitted from the rights decreed by the Charter?

I do not want for a moment to question the value of the French language rights that minorities outside of Quebec got out of all this activity. But it is also undeniable that what they got compared very unfavourably to what English Canadian interests got, both inside and outside of Quebec. The linguistic rights guaranteed to Franco-Manitobans, Franco-Ontarians, and the rest, do not weaken the powerful forces of assimilation that come from the economic and cultural dominance of English in the private sphere. The ability to go to school and to the post office in French will not preserve a cultural community that must go to work in English. Net language transfers from French to English outside of Quebec actually increased in the decade 1971–81 compared to 1961–71. The proportion of Canadians claiming French as their mother tongue outside of Quebec dropped from 6% to 5.3% between 1971 and 1981, with French spoken at home decreasing from 4.4% to 3.8% (Latouche, 1986: 126–127). On the other hand, what the English won went far beyond their linguistic rights. It was a guarantee of their power. The lack of such power on the part of the French communities outside of Quebec not only limits their ability to take advantage of their new linguistic rights, but also puts in doubt their very survival. To have a right is not necessarily to be more secure. The ability to take advantage of some rights, to make use of them, depends on social power. Some rights, as we have seen, reinforce social power. Take property rights, for example. It is not merely that everybody has the equal right to own a Rolls Royce but only those with the money (the social power) can exercise it. It is that the right is a an *expression* of that social power, the means by which it is protected from the claims of those without power. Certain rights are not only of little use without social power. Their very *meaning* is different. This is an important lesson to take with us into the next chapter.

CHAPTER IV

"Principles of Fundamental Justice"
The Charter's Formal Values

Procedural Rights Under the Charter

At 2:40 p.m. Train arrested the respondent for theft and possession of the stolen car and for the armed robbery of the Mac's Milk store. He read him his rights from a card which was issued to all police officers when the Charter was proclaimed. The card from which the constable read stated as follows:

CHARTER OF RIGHTS

1. NOTICE UPON ARREST
    I am arresting you for_____(briefly describe reason for arrest).

2. It is my duty to inform you that you have the right to retain and instruct counsel without delay.
    Do you understand?

    CAUTION TO CHARGED PERSON
    You (are charged, will be charged) with _____. Do you wish to say anything in answer to the charge? You are not obliged to say anything unless you wish to do so, but whatever you say may be given in evidence.
    …

The respondent made a flippant remark at the reading of the caution and the right to counsel to the effect that "*It sounds like an American T.V. programme.*" Train reread the whole card to the respondent and, at that time, the respondent said: "*Prove it. I ain't saying anything until I see my lawyer. I want to see my lawyer.*" (emphasis added).

This is an excerpt from *R. v. Manninen* (*Manninen*, 1987: 387–388) in which the Supreme Court of Canada quashed the conviction of an armed robber whose guilt had been "clearly established" at trial (*Manninen*, 1987: 394). Why? Because following the exchange just quoted, the police continued to question Manninen and he confessed. Though the confession was legally "voluntary," in the sense that it was not induced by threats or promises, according to the Supreme Court, the police had violated Manninen's Charter right "to retain and instruct counsel without delay and to be informed of that right" (s.10 (b)). They should have stopped their questioning then and there and offered him a telephone to call a lawyer. Because they did not, the Court ruled that the trial had to be done all over again, without the benefit of the statement, *even though the Judges had no doubt that the statement was true.*

We have come a long way from the well-established rule of law that evidence was admissible so long as it was relevant and reliable, no matter how it was obtained, by fair means or foul, legal or illegal (*Wray*, 1970; *Hogan*, 1974). A long way indeed from the cliché of the sixties that Canadians did not possess the constitutional rights television police reluctantly but dutifully read to criminals on American crime shows. Life imitates television, and Free Trade in crime shows no longer poses the slightest threat to our cultural sovereignty.

This chapter is about the formal values, mostly procedural in nature, which the courts, using the Charter, have superimposed on Canadian law enforcement agencies. These are not the only values represented by the Charter but they are beyond any doubt the ones which have kept the courts the busiest. They are found in sections 7 through 14 of the Charter under the heading "Legal Rights." The central concern of the Legal Rights part of the Charter is with *how* the state may do things as opposed to *what* it may do, that is, with limitations of *form* and not of *substance*. The first provision characterizes the whole part:

> 7. Everyone has the right to life, liberty and security of the person and the right not to be deprived thereof *except in accordance with the principles of fundamental justice.*

We have already encountered this provision in Chapter II in connection with the *Operation Dismantle* action. By its terms, the section does not put anything beyond the reach of the state. Instead section 7 prescribes, if vaguely, the way in which these rights *can* be interfered with. That was the basic reason for judgment given by five of the eleven judges who saw no merit in Operation Dismantle's case.[1] Even granting that the cruise missile threatened life, liberty and security, section 7 only allowed courts to intervene when a "principle of fundamental justice" had been violated. But Operation Dismantle alleged nothing wrong in the *way* the decision to test the cruise missile had been made or implemented (*Operation Dismantle*, 1983; 1985). Not that Canadian judges have universally respected these apparent limits on the scope of section 7. As we shall see, judicial disregard for them has reached all the way to the Supreme Court of Canada.[2] Nevertheless, almost all of the many decisions under section 7 of the Charter have been concerned with questions of form.

The rest of the Legal Rights part of the Charter is an elaboration of section 7 as it applies to the specific subject of criminal procedure. There are prohibitions against "unreasonable search and seizure" (s.8), "arbitrary" detention or imprisonment (s.9), and "cruel and unusual punishment and treatment" (s.12). Witnesses and parties are guaranteed the right to an interpreter and to protection against self-incrimination. Arrested or detained persons are guaranteed the right to know the reasons for arrest, the right to counsel, and to *habeas corpus* (s.10). Persons charged with offences have the right to be informed of

---

[1] The others, it will be remembered, decided the case on the facts without hearing any evidence.

[2] Judges Beetz and Estey in *Morgentaler*, 1988, discussed below in Chapter VI.

"the specific offence" charged, "to be tried within a reasonable time," to be "presumed innocent until proven guilty according to law in a fair and public hearing by an independent and impartial tribunal," to "reasonable bail," to "trial by jury where the maximum penalty is five years or more of imprisonment," and to "protection against double jeopardy and *ex post facto* laws."[1]

These rights were not pulled out of thin air by the drafters of the constitution. Some of them are as old as *Magna Carta* (1215). Most of the others were fashioned by the common law judges as they meted out the cruel criminal justice of eighteenth- and nineteenth-century England. These rights formed the basis of the modern statute law on criminal procedure found in copious detail in the *Criminal Code* and similar statutes. Yet, since 1982, more and more of these statutory rules and the practices based on them have been called into question by judges invoking the Charter. It sometimes seems as if the criminal law reports are being taken over by Charter cases on criminal procedure.[2]

We should not be surprised to find the courts so busy with the Charter's procedural rights provisions. Parking tickets aside, well over a million prosecutions are launched every year, more than 750,000 of them serious enough to be laid under the *Criminal Code* and the *Narcotic Control Act* (Statistics Canada, 1987a: Table 2; 1984: Tables 2 and 5). The Charter has provided brandnew arguments for otherwise hopeless cases. Compliance with the vague guarantees of the Charter has become a new requirement for a finding of legal guilt in all of the criminal cases being tried by hundreds of judges across the country, judges of widely varying degrees of competence and of attraction to the idea of judicial review. Judges, who previously could show their power only in handing down sentences for largely plea-bargained cases, can now flex their muscles by dramatically striking down laws and having national significance ascribed to what goes on in their little courtrooms. In the early days, some judges took the Charter as a mandate to reconsider every aspect of criminal law from scratch. This tendency was at first resisted by courts of appeal. In the year of the Charter's enactment, the Ontario Court of Appeal, referring to a Provincial Court Judge with a marked enthusiasm for the Charter, made this pronouncement:

> In view of the number of cases in the Ontario trial courts in which Charter provisions are being argued, and especially in view of some of the bizarre and colourful arguments being advanced, it may be appropriate to observe that the Charter does not intend a transformation of our legal system or the paralysis of law enforcement. Extravagant interpretations can only trivialize and diminish respect for the Charter which is part of the supreme law of this country (*Altseimer*, 1982: 13).[3]

---

[1] They are even entitled, in a most unusual constitutional provision, to the *benefit* of *ex post facto* laws: the right to the benefit of any lesser punishment enacted for an offence after it is committed.

[2] Seven out of thirteen index pages in Volume 37 of the *Canadian Criminal Cases* (Third Series).

[3] The judge in question was Ontario Provincial Court Judge Maurice Charles who declared the breathalyzer provisions of the *Criminal Code* unconstitutional not four months after the Charter was enacted. His "bizarre and colourful" judgement (with lines such as "One wonders whether our Charter of Rights is just mere political rhetoric.": *MacDonald*, 1982: 146) was widely reported and persuaded the accused, Mr. Altseimer—no doubt among others—to give the Charter a try.

However, the Supreme Court of Canada soon gave business a boost with a series of very activist judgments. In its very first criminal procedure decision, the Court struck down a thirty-year-old provision of the *Combines Investigation Act* as contrary to the prohibition against unreasonable search and seizure, holding that the officer in charge of authorizing the searches under the Act was not sufficiently independent of the investigatory authority and that the grounds for authorizing the searches were too weak (*Hunter*, 1984). Each of the three years following *Hunter* saw the Supreme Court quashing convictions to emphatically demonstrate its intention to use the new Charter powers to the fullest. In 1985, the Court underlined the seriousness with which it regarded the right to counsel by holding that evidence obtained without informing an arrested person of the right to a lawyer could not be used against that person at trial (*Therens*, 1985). In 1986, it threw out a murder confession and conviction where the accused was too intoxicated to appreciate the consequences of waiving the right to counsel—though not too intoxicated to appreciate the truth of her confession (*Clarkson*, 1986). That same year the Supreme Court held that the "presumption of innocence" ruled out a twenty-five-year-old section of the *Narcotic Control Act* that shifted the traditional burden of proof to the accused in some drug cases (*Oakes*, 1986). In 1987, as we have seen, it quashed a robbery conviction where the police did not offer the accused a telephone when he asked for counsel (*Manninen*, 1987). Also in 1987, the Supreme Court invoked the search and seizure provisions twice to exclude reliable evidence and wipe out convictions for heroin trafficking (*Collins*, 1987) and impaired driving (*Pohoretsky*, 1987). And it held that an unreasonable delay in a trial would result in an automatic stay of proceedings, forever halting tax-evasion charges in a case where the judge had inexplicably and repeatedly delayed a decision (*Rahey*, 1987). Though the Court has refused to extend the detailed protections of criminal procedure to quasi-criminal matters such as extradition (*Schmidt*, 1987; *Mellino*, 1987; *Allard and Charette*, 1987) and police discipline (*Wigglesworth*, 1987), it has affirmed that the broader "principles of fundamental justice" protections apply in all of these circumstances. This proposition was most forcefully established by the ruling in *Singh* (1985), which turned the *Immigration Act* upside down by requiring oral hearings for all refugee claimants. Though yet to pass on the applicability of the Charter to prisoners, the Supreme Court has left little doubt of its intentions by expanding traditional pre-Charter remedies to make it easier for prisoners to gain access to the courts (*Miller*, 1985; *Cardinal and Oswald*, 1985). Trial courts and courts of appeal have taken the hint and shown great solicitude for prisoners' complaints about procedural abuses by prison and parole authorities (for example *Morin*, 1985; *Hay*, 1985; *Litwack*, 1986). In the most far-reaching of these judgments, the Federal Court of Appeal has held that section 7 of the Charter gives virtually every prisoner charged with a prison disciplinary offence the right to counsel (*Howard*, 1985).

Constitutional Rights, Law Enforcement, and Social Class

There is, in fact, no question that the courts have used the Charter to expand the procedural rights of accused persons, prisoners, and immigrants. They have fulfilled the fondest hopes of Charter advocates, in a realm of extremely high visibility (remember the American crime shows). Contrary to predictions, the timidity of the *Canadian Bill of Rights* has been left behind as one by one the restrictive precedents of that era are overruled. Canadian courts have caught up to and surpassed US courts in confining the power of police and administrative authorities within strict forms. Nor has the disappointment that has set in in the realm of language rights even started to happen in criminal procedure. And contrary to the case of language rights—contrary, once again, to the predictions of skeptics—the most direct and obvious beneficiaries of these procedural rights are groups *without* social power. Why? Because people without social power are the main objects of the kinds of law to which the courts have been busy attaching procedural guarantees.

Among those charged with criminal offences we find a severe over-representation of the most marginal social classes in Canadian society, characterized by the lowest levels of occupation and the highest levels of unemployment (Bell-Rowbotham and Boydell, 1972: Table 18; Warner and Renner, 1981). Among those sentenced to prison we find a magnification of these same characteristics. The unemployment rate of prisoners at the time of arrest is two to four times that of non-prisoners (Mandel, 1985: Appendix). Native peoples are notoriously overrepresented (Mandel, 1985: n.3). Prisons swell during periods of high unemployment (Greenberg, 1977; Tepperman, 1977: 63). Refugee applicants are by definition either persecuted or forced to use the refugee process because they cannot meet the criteria for ordinary immigration (Hathaway, 1988).

These facts have been underlined by those who seek to defend the Charter from the charge that it is only there to protect powerful people, if not power itself, a point argued extensively in Chapter II. A representative of Southam News (itself a powerful recipient of Charter largess) made this point on a television show about the impact of the Charter.[1] Nor is this a case of the weak riding on the coattails of the strong as in the matter of language rights. If anything, it is the reverse. Is this, then, an exception to the argument that the legalization of politics is fundamentally conservative, that it strengthens the *status quo* of unequal social power? If it is an exception, it is a rather big one.

Debates over the procedural provisions of the Charter have not concerned the question of social power, but rather the argument, made mostly by law enforcement agencies, that these provisions seriously interfere with the prevention of crime. When they appeared before the Joint Committee on the Constitution in 1980, the Canadian Association of Chiefs of Police were almost alone in their opposition to the very idea of an entrenched Charter. Though they invoked parliamentary sovereignty as a rationale, it was clear

---

[1] Peter Calamai appearing on the CJOH television program "Insight" hosted by Doug Fisher in January 1987.

that their main argument was the possible effect of the Charter upon law enforcement. Speaking of the American "exclusionary rule" (illegally obtained evidence is inadmissible even where reliable), a version of which ultimately would be included in the Canadian Charter, Toronto Police Chief John Ackroyd warned:

> In the United States, this rule has proven to be the greatest single road block to effective and fair law enforcement. It is of great concern to law enforcement officers in that country.
>
> When murderers are set free because a police officer has made a minor mistake in the procedures he is required to follow, does society really benefit? The American experience has produced negative results (Canada, 1980–81, Issue No. 14: 8).

Both Ackroyd and Roderick McLeod, speaking on behalf of the Canadian Association of Crown Counsels, argued that it was illogical and self-defeating to control police behaviour by acquitting guilty criminals. Police misconduct, they argued, should be dealt with directly, by professional discipline or even criminal prosecution where warranted. They claimed that the US rule had been ineffective in controlling police misconduct and even passed along some alarmist rumours that frustration with the rule had led police both to "dispense some instant justice on the scene" (McLeod) and to "literally turn their backs on what they observe on the streets" (Ackroyd) (Canada, 1980–81, Issue No. 14: 23–24).

What both the police and the crown attorneys argued for was *certainty*. They claimed they were not against procedural rights for the accused, but that these could be much more efficiently provided, without unnecessary fallout for law enforcement, by being precisely spelled out in the *Criminal Code*. The empty vaguenesses of the Charter were the worst of both worlds:

> I think it would have to be as laid out in the Criminal Code, what the times are for a preliminary hearing, for example, or for a trial.
>
> But you are putting the courts in a position of trying to interpret what is a reasonable time... "reasonable" is a very vague word.
>
> So it can only work if you have a specific time frame laid down that a man should be brought before a preliminary hearing within so many months, and following that, brought to trial within so many months. But to be as vague as to use the word "reasonable" leaves a very broad interpretation for the courts.
>
> ...
>
> If you impose upon the court that degree of discretion, it is our view that you create a degree of uncertainty... Crown prosecutors do not know what evidence is going to be admissible; police officers do not know what evidence is going to be admissible (Canada, 1980–81, Issue No. 14: 14, 20).

On the other side of the issue was the Canadian Civil Liberties Association, represented at the Charter hearings by general counsel Alan Borovoy, claiming that US due process rules had not hurt law enforcement:

> ...on the basis of the research that has been done into this, there is no reason for

us to anticipate that law enforcement would suffer unduly from granting these additional protections to accused people.

As you know, some such protections were introduced into American Law by virtue of the Miranda case in the U.S. Supreme Court. Some surveys conducted shortly thereafter indicated that although the rate of confessions dropped after the Miranda rule went into effect, the rate of convictions and crime clearances, which are another way of saying crime solutions, did not drop.

So, in other words, it appeared that custodial confessions were not the indispensable element of law enforcement that many people had until then thought (Canada, 1980–81, Issue No. 7: 13).

Five years of experience with the Charter have done nothing to resolve this debate. A fifth anniversary story in the *The Globe and Mail* (April 13, 1987: A1, A12) quoted a Niagara Regional Police deputy chief as saying:

We have had some terrible, terrible decisions...I think a lot of people are now totally frustrated and disgusted with the system. And, of course, the criminals love it. If an officer is wrong, he can be held accountable. But to turn a criminal loose doesn't serve justice or the public.

The same article reported that crown attorneys were also "unhappy about the number of cases that are being thrown out on technical violations." On the other hand, Charter supporters such as law professor Donald Stuart assured everyone that any problems were—after five years—just temporary: "once the police adjust to their 'new' responsibilities few such acquittals should occur" (*The Globe and Mail*, April 13, 1987: A12). Other lawyers have argued that it is a small price to pay. Though it "may seem to benefit the guilty...the Charter was enacted to protect all Canadians. That it can also protect the guilty is a price society pays for its freedoms" (Zucker, 1985: 7).

Almost every acquittal on Charter grounds raises the same questions. In a recent case from rural Ontario (*New*, 1987), a District Court Judge, after declaring that he had found the accused guilty of the "brutal and despicable crime" of killing a police officer's horse with a crossbow, permanently stayed proceedings against him on the grounds that police had harassed witnesses during the investigation. The crown attorney complained that the Judge should have recommended charging the officers with police disciplinary offences or criminal offences rather than having "an accused person who has been found guilty of a serious crime...let go." He said that "people are, I think, confused and shocked that a person could, because he had a beef with a police officer, go and shoot the police officer's horse and proceedings are stayed." The defence lawyer replied that the Court "had to, as a judicial officer, demonstrate society's disapproval" (*New*, 1987: 28).

Though law enforcement agencies do not usually give a class content to their criticism of the Charter, it in fact has one, because crime—at least the sort of crime that is the object of police attention—turns out to be a basically *intra-class* phenomenon. Victims of crime come overwhelmingly from the same powerless social classes as their victimizers. Victims and criminals live in the same neighbourhoods. Officially reported crime, the kind that gives the

Charter almost all its business, is primarily not only a lower-class phenomenon, but a lower-class *area* phenomenon (Tepperman, 1977; United States, 1978: Tables 6, 15, 18, 21; Braithwaite, 1979: 23–32; Hagan et al., 1978: 386; Singh, et al., 1980: 78; Platt, 1981; Schwendinger and Schwendinger, 1981). A well-known example is Canada's aboriginal peoples, in terms of social power the most marginal group in the country (Valentine, 1980). Homicide statistics for 1986 show Indians, Métis, and Inuit making up 13.7% of all Canadian homicide victims and 20% of all homicide suspects, while census figures for 1981 report them as comprising only 2% of the total Canadian population (Statistics Canada, 1987b: 95).[1] In violent crime, victims and criminals are often not only members of the same class, but actually members of the same family. Between 1976 and 1985, in 38% of solved homicides,[2] victim and killer were related to each other and 23% were immediate family. In 58.9% they were either related or closely associated, and in 76.9% they were either related or had a pre-existing social relationship of some sort (Statistics Canada, 1987b: 92). One thing strikes any observer of criminal trials: despite the theoretically adversarial nature of relations between prosecution and defence and the theoretically impartial detachment of the judge, in terms of social class, crown attorney, defence counsel, and judge have far more in common with each other than they have with either the victim or the criminal and vice versa. The lawyers in the room come from the same social background, attended the same schools, and have roughly the same career earnings. Many find themselves in all three legal roles at various times during their careers. They are only slightly less likely to be close neighbours than the victim and criminal. But apart from the exceptional case, the lawyers will live in very different parts of town from those of any of the actual parties to the case.

All this means that to the extent the Charter is indeed hampering law enforcement, the price is not being paid by all Canadians equally, but primarily by working-class and poor Canadians, who happen to be the prime targets of both the criminal law and the criminals.

American Criminal Procedure: Revolution and Counterrevolution

The Canadian debate about the Charter and law enforcement has been positively subdued compared to the political fury whipped up around the landmark rulings of the US Supreme Court in the early 1960s. The major elements of the Warren Court [3]"revolution," which brought the police practices of the United States under the scrutiny of the federal constitution, were the inadmissibility of evidence obtained through illegal searches (*Mapp*, 1961); the right to appointed counsel for indigent defendants (*Gideon*, 1963); the privilege against self-incrimination (*Malloy*, 1964); and, most famous of all, the requirement,

---

[1] Some estimates put the Native population as high as 5% (Valentine, 1980: 81), which still makes for an enormous overrepresentation in violent crime.

[2] Solved homicides accounted for about 80% of all homicides.

[3] After Earl Warren, former Republican Governor of California, Chief Justice of the Supreme Court, 1953-1969.

on pain of acquittal, that the police warn accused persons of their right to remain silent and their right to counsel (*Miranda*, 1966). Coming at a time of increasing crime and civil strife, the Warren Court became a scapegoat for right wing politicians like Richard Nixon and George Wallace:

> For the first time in at least a generation, a presidential candidate had success-fully run against the Court and had appointed a Chief Justice with a mandate for substantial change...[T]he 1968 campaign was dominated by attacks on the Court, particularly in the criminal justice field...Candidate Nixon made his promise to restore law and order a centerpiece of his campaign...Candidate Nixon went through the following litany countless times before thousands of cheering supporters during the fall of 1968:

> "A cab driver had been brutally murdered and the man that confessed the crime was let off because of a Supreme Court decision. An old woman had been murdered and robbed brutally, and the man who confessed to the crime was let off because of a Supreme Court decision. And an old man had been beaten and clubbed to death, and the man who committed the crime was let off when he was on a spending spree in Las Vegas after he confessed, because of a Supreme Court decision.

> "And I say, my friends, that some of our courts and their decisions in the light of that record have gone too far in weakening the peace forces as against the criminal forces in this country" (Seidman, 1980: 438–9).

There seems to be quite a consensus that Nixon's attack on the Warren Court contributed to his 1968 election victory:

> Richard Nixon's charge that the Warren court was soft on crime contributed to his election in 1968 because it reflected the public's belief that procedural technicalities were preventing the police from stopping crime (Aranella, 1983: 192).

Baker argues that anti-crime did for Nixon in 1968 what anti-communism had done for him earlier in his career. Nixon linked crime to the liberal policies of the Court precisely to turn the tables on the attempts of American liberalism to link crime to social inequality. In his position paper of May 1968, entitled "Toward Freedom from Fear," Nixon called then-President Lyndon Johnson's War on Poverty "no substitute for a war on crime" (Baker, 1983: 211). Similar rhetoric was used by conservative George Wallace in his impressive independent presidential campaign showing in 1968 (Baker, 1983: 258).

Critics of the Warren Court rulings have always sought, like Ackroyd and MacLeod at the Canadian Charter hearings, to minimize the effects of their rulings on deterring police misbehaviour and to maximize their effects on the crime rate through the acquittal of "factually guilty" criminals on procedural technicalities. While the effects on police misbehaviour are debatable (LaF-ave, 1987: 26–29), it is fairly certain that the effects of the rules on the crime rate have been, as the Canadian Civil Liberties Association argued at the Charter hearings, minimal. Official claims that due process rules cost the jus-tice system substantial lost arrests have consistently been shown to be false. A case in point was a 1982 study of the effect of due process rules on California law enforcement, issued by the US Department of Justice, suggesting that 4.8% of all arrests and 30% of drug arrests had to be rejected for prosecution because of search and seizure problems. In an elaborate critique of this study, using its own figures, Thomas Davies of the American Bar Foundation has shown that this was a gross exaggeration, and that the effect on criminal prosecutions "was marginal at most" (Davies, 1983: 622). Losses at the prosecution stage were not 4.8% and 30% but 0.8% and 2.4% (Davies, 1983: 645–646). Davies estimated the total losses due to the search and seizure rules at all stages of the process (police releases, prosecutors refusals to file complaints, preliminary hearing dismissals, superior court dismissals, and reversals on appeal) to be, at most, 2.35% for all offences and somewhere between 2.4% and 7.1% for drug charges (Davies, 1983: 655). The California data is supported by data from all over the country (LaFave, 1987: 22n6). Furthermore, despite an emphasis by critics since Nixon on violent crime, it is now clear "that the effects of the rule are clustered in arrests for drugs, weapons possession, and other 'victimless' offences (i.e., those in which enforcement is initiated by police without victim complainants)" (Davies, 1983: 637–638), and that most of the rest of its effects are found in minor crimes (Davies, 1983: 670). Only 0.3% of non-drug prosecutions were lost in California because of due process problems. These findings are corroborated by the many studies which have shown that crime rates and conviction rates were not affected by the Warren Court reforms (Seidman, 1980: 439–441). Similarly, the introduction of due process in prison and parole, a slightly later US Supreme Court development (*Johnson*, 1969; *Morrissey*, 1972; *Wolff*, 1974), appears to have made absolutely no difference to the rate and level of prison disciplinary punishment (Smith and Fried, 1974: 90; Berkman, 1979: 149).

Given all of the furor over these due process exclusionary rules on both sides of the issue, their picayune effects on law enforcement are something of a puzzle. At least two questions emerge. First, why did the rules make so little difference? Second, how can it be that something which made so little difference caused so much fuss?

One explanation for the lack of effect of the rules has been systematic non-compliance. Findings published in the 1960s tended to show that police practices were very slow to change (Aranella, 1983: 190–192). Courts had difficulty controlling misbehaviour with the limited devices available to them, such as exclusionary rules and stays of prosecutions. They could only deal with abuses that produced disputed evidence or prosecutions. They were hopeless against the day-to-day machinery of law enforcement that relied mainly on churning out guilty pleas (Amsterdam, 1970). Similar observations were made about due process in prisons (Bronstein, 1980: 40–41).

Complaints like these are heard much less frequently nowadays. Baker claims that by the 1980s:

> *Miranda* had come to the station house...Settled policy...The word *Miranda* had become a staple of the law enforcement community's vocabulary...The Hill Street Blues read them over national television...(Baker, 1983: 403–404).

According to Davies, the rules gradually changed practices through important "educative effects ... on police policies, training, and attitudes."

> Indeed, it may be that the most important effect of the rule is simply that it tells the police that illegal searches *are illegitimate*. Comments by a number of police officials at the time of the *Mapp* decision indicate that police had often viewed illegal searches as being within the *proper* scope of police conduct simply because the courts accepted the evidence (Davies, 1983: 629; emphasis in original).

But if the rules were more or less accepted, what could account for their lack of impact on law enforcement? The only possible explanation is what the civil libertarians have always assured us: even the most rigorous enforcement of due process norms does not interfere with law enforcement. It has even been argued that *Miranda* was actually an *aid* to police effectiveness:

> *Miranda* had contributed something to the professionalization of the patrolman who could no longer rely on the quick and easy confession but now had to dig for evidence in his crime solving, a development to which the increased workloads of the crime laboratories testified (Baker, 1983: 404).

This probably attributes too much significance to the due process rules themselves, but there can be no doubt they were part of a change in police orientation towards heavier reliance on sophisticated technology and better—or at least slicker—"community-relations." Computers, video-taped confessions (Grant, 1987), and the hiring of visible minorities and women have tended, if not completely to replace the third degree, then at least to reduce the need to resort to it.

But there is a deeper reason why due process did not interfere with law enforcement. Even the most rigorously enforced due process norms could not change the basic social facts of criminal law:

> Let there be no mistake about it. To a mind-staggering extent...the entire system of criminal justice below the level of the Supreme Court of the United States is solidly massed against the criminal suspect. Only a few appellate judges can throw off the fetters of their middle-class backgrounds—the dimly remembered friendly face of the school crossing guard, their fear of a crowd of "toughs," their attitudes engendered as lawyers before their elevation to the bench, by years of service as prosecutors or as private lawyers for honest, respectable business clients—and identify with the criminal suspect instead of with the policeman or with the putative victim of the suspect's theft, mugging, rape or murder. Trial judges still more, and magistrates beyond belief, are functionally and psychologically allied with the police, their co-workers in the unending and scarifying work of bringing criminals to book (Amsterdam, 1970: 792).

The functional/psychological alliance of the courts with the police and the class division between the courts and criminal suspects are no mere coincidences.[1] They

---

[1] Was it bias or reality that led the British Columbia Court of Appeal to state recently, in a rare display of candour: "[T]here must be a recognition of the facts of life relating to crime. One is that most accused persons, including some of those who are acquitted, committed the crime charged against them" (*Dersch*, 1987: 737).

reflect the class character of crime and criminal law in a society with deep social class divisions (see Chapter VI). We noted earlier how strongly official crime and law enforcement tend to concentrate in the most economically marginal sectors of Canadian society. Inequality of social power "breeds" not only crime (Braithwaite, 1979) but also the differential treatment of it according to its social locale (Mandel, 1987). While working-class crime is repressed as "true crime," business crime is merely taxed as "regulatory offence" (Glasbeek, 1984). Is it surprising that where power is unequally divided, the powerless and the powerful will meet on different sides of the bar of justice? Neither the right to counsel nor the right to remain silent nor any other of the procedural attributes of due process can do anything about that.

So what was the point of all these rules that could have no impact on the general outcome because they could not change the balance of power? The answer most often given is that it was all a question of symbolism.

It was perhaps as a symbol that *Miranda* had the most salutary impact, less tangible than the others but nonetheless real. Placing this ritual, however incoherently mumbled, however perfunctorily read, however abused, between a policeman and a suspect served, it was generally acknowledged, a civilizing purpose, reminding the officer of the law that however miserable the one who stood before him, however savage the crime of which he was accused, he was still a man, possessed of all the attributes, including the constitutional rights, of other men.

In a historical context *Miranda* was a statement of aspiration (Baker, 1983: 407).

Perhaps the Warren Court's most significant message about criminal procedure's functions lay in its attempts to reinforce the notion that the criminal process should treat individuals with dignity and respect even if such treatment occasionally impairs the accuracy of the system's outcomes (Aranella, 1983: 247).

The reforms were a "civilization" of criminal procedure. They meant that the accused person, no matter how lowly and alien, had to be treated as an equal, or as Dworkin would have it, with "equality of concern and respect" (Dworkin, 1977b: 182). In other words, Justice's Blindfold. One American commentator, speaking specifically of prisoners' rights, has described this process as part of the "realization of mass society," a "fundamental democratization" of the system through the extension of "rights of citizenship" to "heretofore marginal groups like racial minorities, the poor, and the incarcerated" (Jacobs, 1977: 6; 1980: 82; Mandel, 1986: 79–80). But, as another "mass society" enthusiast has pointed out: "there is no claim that prisoners, the poor, and racial minorities are becoming middle class in a social economic sense" (Huff, 1980: 51). This is a democratization of a purely formal sort. Procedural rights entail no actual shift in the balance of social power. In fact they are designed to be situated within a context of grossly unequal social power. Justice only needs a blindfold *because* the parties that appear before her are so unequal.

It is this which explains better than anything the lack of a negative effect of the due process revolution on law enforcement. Criminal procedure is required to treat accused persons *as if* they were equal to each other and everyone else;

but in fact nothing else about them changes. Neither their class, nor the social locale, nor the historical determinants of their crimes. Does the presence of a lawyer change whether a crime was committed, the nature of it, the accused's criminal record, or employment status? Does it change the unemployment rate or any of the other determinants of crimes and sentences, who commits them, and who gets them? Does it change the double standard for corporate crime and street crime? Does it change poverty or unemployment? Does it stop crime itself? A fair procedure changes neither the political nature nor the political context of criminal law. Due process puts a big blindfold on Justice but it does not put her sword in the hands of those without social power.

But if due process did not hamper law enforcement, why did the Right make such a fuss about it? Why was the Warren Court revolution followed by the so-called "counterrevolution" of the Burger Court?[1] The explanation seems to lie in the *politics* of legalized politics:

> A Court's view of the type of government misconduct that evidently mandates the exclusion of reliable evidence will be shaped by the historical and political context in which challenges to governmental authority arise. In the 1960s, racial, social, and political unrest challenged the state's moral authority to punish criminal defendants who were perceived by many to be victims of racial and class injustice. The Warren Court responded to this "legitimation crisis" by creating the image, if not the reality, of a self-regulating legal order that could not use the fruits of government misconduct to prove guilt.

> The Burger Court has responded to a different crisis. It is no longer fashionable to speak of indigent criminal defendants as victims of racial and economic inequalities. Today, the public sees itself as the victim of a system that does not appear to provide a tolerable degree of protection from street crime. Excluding reliable evidence of guilt in cases where the police acted in "good faith" now may have a "delegitimizing" effect because it confirms the public's impression of a system that is all too willing to protect the victimizer instead of the victim (Aranella, 1983: 238).

The crime-poverty-race nexus was a central element of the politics of the 1960s. Nixon argued that the War on Poverty had replaced the War on Crime, and according to Lyndon Johnson, the Democrats were defeated in 1968 because "the blue collar worker felt that the Democratic Party had traded his welfare for the welfare of the black man" (Aranella, 1983: 258). The reaction to the liberalism seen in the decisions of the Warren Court helped elect Nixon the way the abortion backlash would later help to elect Ronald Reagan (see Chapter VI). Whether or not this demonstrates the folly of legalized politics, it is yet another proof that the courts are not a separate realm autonomous from everyday political developments. Legalized politics is still politics. It is deeply affected by the struggles taking place outside the courtroom. Indeed it is deeply integrated within them, an aspect of them, an object of them, and a strategic terrain on which they take place. In the 1960s, favouring or opposing legal rights for accused persons became a way of saying whose side you

---

[1] So called after Nixon-appointee Warren Burger, Chief Justice of the United States Supreme Court, 1969–1986.

were on in the ongoing struggle between white and black and rich and poor.

But we miss everything if we leave out the *legal* element of legalized politics. It is not identical to other politics. That we have legalized politics at all means that the Court comes to be the forum in which administrative practices are judged acceptable or not. But this is only because of the special attributes of judicial discourse—special attributes which impose special limits. These cannot be violated without throwing the entire game over. The Burger Court counterrevolution had to respect these limits:

> To wage such a frontal assault on Warren Court precedents and the principle of stare decisis would weaken the distinction between law and politics that any Court must maintain to sustain its own legitimacy (Aranella, 1983: 195).

But equally important was the historical necessity of safeguarding the integrity of the criminal process itself:

> Our criminal justice system's moral legitimacy rests to some degree on its willingness to replace brute force with legal rules that limit the means government may use to pursue laudable ends (Aranella, 1983: 203).

In fact, the Warren and Burger Courts could not afford to differ on such fundamentals as the importance of a civilized criminal procedure and the need not to interfere in any serious way with law enforcement. What appeared as a revolution and counterrevolution was no more than the legalization of politics and its limits, decorated by the rhetoric appropriate to both. If we want to know why the due process revolution should have been so limited, why it did not go further, we must begin again from the first principles of legalized politics, and especially from the spectre of illegitimacy that always haunts judicial politics in a representative democracy. During his 1968 election campaign, Richard Nixon said:

> We need more strict constructionists on the highest court of the United States...In my view, the duty of a Justice of the U.S. Supreme Court is to interpret the law and not to make the law, and the men I appoint will share that view (Baker, 1983: 246).

After *Miranda*, George Wallace said that the Court had been "sitting on a continual constitutional convention, changing and altering the law from day to day" (Baker, 1983: 237). Reverence turned easily to ridicule:

> Nixon: "Whenever I begin to discuss the Supreme Court, Mr. Humphrey acts like we're in church."

> Wallace: "A sorry, lousy, no-account outfit" (Baker, 1983: 245, 243).

Lacking any real political constituency, lacking the institutional competence to reallocate resources or restructure day-to-day criminal procedure except by deciding cases that someone else chose to bring before them, the only thing the courts could do to make any impact was to acquit the guilty. Even the most fearless of judges had to resort sparingly to this device if they were to avoid total public hostility in a context of constantly rising crime rates (*Aranella*, 1983: 191). And they had to do so in a manner that avoided any impression of taking sides in concrete power struggles. They had to respect the distinction between principle and policy. Judicial politics must avoid any impression of "betting on the future." It is forbidden to attempt to devise better plans for crime prevention so it must not interfere with the policies of those with the political competence to do so. It must proceed abstractly so that it does nothing to upset the balance of social power. The only thing it can do about power is to refuse to recognize it. It can require the whole criminal justice system to act as if power did not exist. But this can no more rid criminal law of the influence of social power than could the refusal of Quebec to recognize the constitution protect its language law.

The Canadian Courts and the Charter's Procedural Guarantees

It is already clear that the Canadian experience with constitutionalized criminal procedure will be strikingly similar to the US one, with necessary variations for the remaining cultural differences between the two countries.[1] In the first place, in perfect conformity with the principles of legalized politics, virtually all of the (considerable) judicial activism in the realm of repressive law has been concerned with *formal* rights, which is not to say they are mere *formalities*, but that Canadian courts, like US courts, have refrained from making decisions which could alter the balance of power in criminal justice. If anything, the necessity of re-inventing the wheel in a hurry has forced Canadian courts to be more frank than their US counterparts about the nature and limits of their enterprise.

The Exclusionary Rule

One of the most sensitive issues has been the admissibility of improperly obtained evidence. As we have seen, much was said about this at the Charter hearings. The eventual Charter provision *required* courts to exclude evidence obtained in violation of the Charter where

> it is established that, having regard to all the circumstances, the admission of it in the proceedings would bring the administration of justice into disrepute (s. 24 (2)).

In its very first attempt at elaboration of this provision, the Supreme Court has already told us more than enough to confirm that in Canada, as in the US, the constitutionalization of criminal procedure performs an essentially symbolic, legitimizing, or to put it bluntly, *public relations* function. *R. v. Collins* (*Collins*, 1987) is fairly typical of Charter procedure cases in the "air of unreality" about it (Justice McIntyre in *Smith*, 1987: 103). On a trial for possession of heroin for the purposes of trafficking, the accused sought to exclude the heroin found in her possession on

---

[1] The important ones for our purposes are the great differences in the level of official and unofficial violence. The US has four times the Canadian per capita murder rate and, notwithstanding its Bill of Rights, twice the Canadian per capita imprisonment rate. As of June 30, 1986, 37 US states authorized the death penalty, and 1772 persons were under sentence of death, 661 of them black. At last count the US had executed 98 persons since 1976, 41 of them black (Hooker, 1988). (Black people make up only 11% of the US population.) Canada's last executions took place in 1962 and the death penalty was formally abolished in 1976. The US record for international violence, for example in Vietnam in the 1960s and '70s, and in South and Central America in the 1970s and '80s, has no parallel in Canada. The United States also has more than twice the number of lawyers and judges per capita that Canada has (Canada, 1982: 85, 107, 115; American Correctional Association, 1987: xxxiv).

the ground that the search was "unreasonable." Correctly suspecting Collins had heroin, a police officer made a flying tackle and applied a choke hold on her. The trial judge admitted the evidence, and she was convicted. The air of unreality came from the fact that nobody on the Court thought that the choke hold would have been unreasonable if the police had had good grounds for believing that Collins had heroin. This was standard procedure to prevent the evidence from being swallowed. But the record of the trial did not disclose the grounds for the search. Why? Because the trial judge had incorrectly (according to the Supreme Court) excluded the substantial evidence of the grounds for the search as hearsay. So the case was decided as if there were no grounds and sent back to trial (Justice McIntyre dissenting) to see if there were any.

In other words, a hypothetical case. That did not prevent the Court from expounding on the principles of the exclusionary rule. And what it said showed how completely beside the point was the police criticism of the Charter at the Joint Parliamentary Committee hearings. The police and the crown attorneys had been foolish enough to think that the Charter was aimed at controlling police misbehaviour and argued persuasively that excluding relevant evidence and acquitting guilty criminals was a very crude means of doing so. In *Collins*, the Supreme Court held that the exclusionary rule was meant to do nothing of the sort. Section 24 was not meant to protect people from the system but to protect the *system itself* from "disrepute":

> ...s.24(2) is not a remedy for police misconduct...the purpose of s.24(2) is to prevent having the administration of justice brought into *further disrepute* by the admission of evidence in the proceedings. This further disrepute will result from the admission of evidence that would deprive the accused of a fair hearing, or from judicial condonation of unacceptable conduct by the investigatory and prosecutorial agencies (*Collins*, 1987: 16).

It was not the "unacceptable conduct," but the avoidance of *judicial condonation* of it that mattered to the Court. Not preventing police misbehaviour, period, but preventing police misbehaviour from soiling the purity of the judicial process, from damaging its *reputation.* Accurate verdicts are important, but so is the civility of the process. Where the two interests converge, the course is clear. But sometimes they do not. Collins herself was clearly guilty. Here we have a dilemma very similar to the one experienced by the US courts. Disrepute can occur from being oppressive with criminals, but it can also occur from being too soft on them. The American tendency, as revealed by the data (Davies, 1983), is for the exclusionary rule to have its greatest observable effect in less serious cases, though there is no law to this effect and it may only be due to more care being taken by police in more serious cases (LaFave, 1987: 43–44). The Supreme Court of Canada went further than this in *Collins*, and adopted the strategy of an explicit sliding scale according to the seriousness of the offence:

> In my view, the administration of justice would be brought into disrepute by the exclusion of evidence essential to substantiate the charge, and thus the acquittal of the accused, because of a trivial breach of the Charter. Such disrepute would be greater if the offence was more serious...evidence is more likely to be excluded if the offence is less serious...I hasten to add, however, that if the

admission of the evidence would result in an unfair trial, the seriousness of the offence could not render that evidence admissible. If any relevance is to be given to the seriousness of the offence in the context of the fairness of the trial, it operates in the opposite sense: the more serious the offence, the more damaging to the system's repute would be an unfair trial (Justice Lamer in *Collins*, 1987: 21).

An approach like this obviously does nothing to enhance the predictability the police and prosecutors were asking for at the Charter hearings. But the Court has too complicated a task to do here to worry about that. It must walk a tightrope, appearing to condone neither police misconduct nor crime. And for whose benefit is the high-wire act? Here, too, one has to keep up appearances. The Court has to respond to public opinion but it cannot appear to "pander" to it, because the pretense of judicial independence is central to the whole Charter enterprise:

> The concept of disrepute necessarily involves some element of community views, and the determination of disrepute thus requires the judge to refer to what he conceives to be the views of the community at large. This does not mean that evidence of the public's perception of the repute of the administration of justice...will be determinative of the issue...Members of the public generally become conscious of the importance of protecting the rights and freedoms of accused only when they are in some way brought closer to the system either personally or through the experience of friends or family...[quoting *Gibson*, 1986: 246:] "The ultimate determination must be with the courts, because they provide what is often the only effective shelter for individuals and unpopular minorities from the shifting winds of public passion." The Charter is designed to protect the accused from the majority, so the enforcement of the Charter must not be left to that majority...(*Collins*, 1987: 17)

To allow public opinion to determine the result would be to de-legitimize the Court's activities by taking them out of the realm of principle and into the realm of politics. Moreover, it would actually render the Court redundant, without a specific function. It is for representative politicians to pander to public opinion. The Court, despite all the blather about the democratic character of the Charter, cannot concede for a minute its subordination to the community. On the contrary, it must remain aloof. Instead of public opinion the Court prefers an old and useful fiction which keeps things right side up, the "reasonable person," reserving for itself a kind of presidential veto:

> The reasonable person is usually the average person in the community, but only when that community's current mood is reasonable (*Collins*, 1987: 17).

One feature of this glorified confidence game is that the Court tries to choose its spots so that its object lessons about the purity of the process pose no long-term obstacles to law enforcement. This is illustrated by another search and seizure case, with an "air of unreality" to it (*Pohoretsky*, 1987), in which the Supreme Court quashed a conviction for impaired driving because the police had procured a doctor to take a blood sample of the accused while he was unconscious. The procedure was allowed by Manitoba law, but the Court felt that a provision of the *Criminal Code* (in fact rather ambiguous) ruled it out. Admitting that the police had ample grounds to believe the accused was guilty, the Supreme Court's sense of fair play seems to have been offended. The judges could afford to be profligate with the conviction, however, since the *Criminal Code* had been amended prior to their decision to authorize just such a procedure!

Naturally, since the exclusionary rule is not meant to protect people from official harm, or to compensate them for it, but to protect the system from disrepute, it also leaves plenty of room for "good faith" exceptions, as in those cases where the Supreme Court upheld unreasonable searches made under authority of unconstitutional search powers that had not yet (at the time of the search) been called into question by any court (*Hamill*, 1987; *Sieben*, 1987).

The Presumption of Innocence

The relation between law enforcement and the Charter can be more complicated, as the case of *Oakes* (1986) illustrates. In that case the Supreme Court unanimously struck down a provision of the *Narcotic Control Act* which reversed the burden of proof and provided that on a charge of possession of a narcotic for the purposes of trafficking (maximum penalty: life imprisonment), the Crown had only to prove that the accused possessed the narcotic (maximum penalty: 7 years imprisonment), and then it was the *accused* who had to prove that he or she did not have it for the purpose of trafficking. This provision had long been condemned by liberal jurists. Fifteen years earlier it had fallen afoul of the Le Dain Commission[1] (Canada, 1972: 302). This time the Supreme Court held that it violated the "right to be presumed innocent" under s.11 (d) of the Charter. Because of the serious consequences to the accused of a finding of guilt, the presumption of innocence, held the Court, required that the state prove guilt "beyond all reasonable doubt." The evil of s.8 was that "it would be possible for a conviction to occur despite the existence of a reasonable doubt" (*Oakes*, 1986: 222).

Let's look at this a little more closely. Why should the words "presumption of innocence" be interpreted in this way? Why should they not require some lesser burden of proof than the very high standard "beyond a reasonable doubt"? Why, indeed, should it not suffice, in order to call for some explanation from the accused, for the Crown to prove that the accused was not "innocent" in the sense that he or she was guilty of possession of prohibited drugs? As in many of these cases, the Court did not strain itself with any detailed analysis of the meaning of the words or alternative options. It merely relied on a common law rule (the standard of proof beyond a reasonable doubt in criminal cases) invented and applied by judges long before the Charter was even dreamed of and raised it to the status of a constitutionally entrenched principle. But the reasonable doubt standard is not the only rational standard of proof available. It is not even the *most* rational one. In non-criminal cases (civil suits and the like) it is only required that guilt be proved to be more likely than innocence "on a balance of probabilities." In "regulatory offences"

---

[1] After the same Le Dain who was appointed to the Supreme Court in time to cast his vote against the same law in *Oakes*.

(offences regarded by the courts as less serious than "true crimes") the Supreme Court itself has placed the burden on the accused to show lack of fault ("due diligence"). The balance of probabilities standard has a lot to be said for it. Its main advantage is that it leads to more accurate verdicts overall because it asks fact finders (jury or judge) to decide according to their genuine view of the evidence. The reasonable doubt standard builds in a higher level of errors overall in order to reduce the chances of one type of error, namely convicting innocent people. "Do not convict unless you are sure" means "Acquit even if, on balance, you think the accused is guilty."

Why is it more important to acquit the innocent than to convict the guilty? This is a complicated subject which deserves more space than I can give it here, but the answer seems to have nothing to do with humanitarianism or crime prevention and everything to do with public relations. If criminal punishment were only permitted where absolutely necessary to prevent a greater evil, accurate verdicts would be crucial. As it turns out, it is impossible to justify the severe and chaotic sentences handed down by Canadian courts on the basis of their value, let alone their necessity, for the prevention of crime (Mandel, 1984). The reasonable doubt standard seems to exist in the same symbolic realm as the Charter itself. It seems aimed at resolving the doubts about the *point* of the system by ensuring that those convicted at least have nothing to complain about on the score of their guilt or innocence. In this way, the high burden of proof actually lends legitimacy to severe sentences. Convicted persons are treated as object lessons in the game of "emphatically denouncing" crime by receiving sentences which emphasize their personal guilt. This object lesson would be lost if there were real doubts about guilt. When the law seeks not to "denounce" but merely to regulate, it uses more rational standards of proof. In a sense, the many who are convicted pay for the few who are acquitted. The reasonable doubt standard, like the Charter itself, is tied up with the irrationality of criminal law, reasserting itself when the modest goal of crime prevention at the least social and human cost is being abandoned. We will return to this theme shortly.

As for *Oakes* itself, the rule in s.8 of the *Narcotic Control Act*, though clearly violating this holy legal principle, merely required that the accused offer an explanation for having the illegal drugs. If the judge or jury had the slightest faith in this explanation, they had to acquit. Only when they did not believe the explanation, or when their minds were precisely evenly balanced, were they required to convict. The difference between this and a civil burden on the Crown is almost non-existent. Even an acquittal on the charge of possession for the purpose of trafficking as a result of *Oakes* would mean a conviction for simple possession. The sentence would be in the discretion of the Court and could be as high as seven years, depending on the accused's record and the type and amount of drugs. Sentences of seven years for possession are extremely rare, but so, though less so, are such sentences for possession for the purposes of trafficking. Neither are unheard of, but the usual range is much lower and does not depend on the technical offence committed so much as on the circumstances and the record of the offender (Canada, 1986:

Table 7; Mandel, 1984). In other words, the cases in which *Oakes* would make a difference to anyone charged with possession for the purpose of trafficking would be rare, and the difference would be small.

The figures we have for drug convictions in the eighties are very ambiguous, but they are at least consistent with the assumption that *Oakes* would not hamper law enforcement in any way. Excluding cannabis (for which there was a drastic decline in prosecutions over the period), convictions for possession for the purposes of trafficking rose steadily in the post-Charter era,[1] (by 19% from 1982–86) even though convictions for trafficking rose faster (28.9%) and convictions for possession still faster (78.3%). More interesting still is the fact that the success rate for all three types of drug prosecutions improved, and that for possession for the purposes of trafficking improved faster than the others (18.6% for possession for the purposes of trafficking to 12.2% for simple possession and 9.3% for trafficking)[2] (Canada, 1987: Tables 1 and 6). If *Oakes*, or indeed the judiciary's other due process activity under the Charter, was responsible for any of this, it means that far from making possession for the purposes convictions harder to obtain, it either made the police more proficient at obtaining them, or it moved them to change their charging practices. If the latter, some of these new charges became *trafficking* charges as well as possession charges, and the police became better at making all types of charges stick. The long-run impact of *Oakes* on law enforcement is difficult to predict, but it is at least as likely to result in more rather than less punishment for drug use.

The Right to Counsel

The procedural realm of legalized politics is epitomized by the right to counsel. It did not take the Supreme Court of Canada very long to show it meant business with this right. In *R. v. Therens* (*Therens*, 1985) the Court held that evidence obtained without informing an arrested person of his or her right to a lawyer could not be used against that person at trial.

This case had the familiar "air of unreality" about it. The accused was charged with driving with a higher than allowed alcohol-to-blood ratio. He was stopped and, on reasonable grounds, asked to take a breath test which he failed. He cooperated throughout. The only problem was that he was never informed of his right to counsel as the Charter clearly requires:

10.(b) Everyone has the right on arrest or detention to retain and instruct counsel without delay and to be informed of that right.

The unreality of the case consisted in this: the accused never asked for counsel, and there was no evidence that he wanted one or that the presence of

---

[1] The Ontario Court of Appeal ruled against the provision in 1983 (*Oakes*, 1983) and the Supreme Court of Canada decision came early in 1986.

[2] That is, the success rate in possession for the purposes of trafficking went from 56.4% to 66.9% compared to a change from 70.3% to 78.9% for possession and 73.5% to 80.3% in trafficking.

counsel would have made any difference to his taking the test. Nevertheless, the Court felt that the evidence had to be excluded and the conviction quashed. Judge Estey, for the majority, called this a "flagrant" and "overt" violation (*Therens*, 1985: 488), but can one really conceive of a lesser violation, if not of the Charter, then of the right to counsel? Why was the Court so insistent?

> To do otherwise than reject this evidence on the facts and circumstances in this appeal would be to invite police officers to disregard the Charter rights of the citizen and to do so with an assurance of impunity (*Therens*, 1985: 488).

It seems that the Court was looking for an opportunity at this early stage—and a bare violation would do almost better than a serious one—to demonstrate that it was serious about the right to counsel. The two dissenting judges in the case would have admitted the evidence despite the Charter violation only because of the conflicting Supreme Court authority under the *Canadian Bill of Rights*. They wanted the ruling to be purely prospective. But they were no less adamant about the essential point:

> In my opinion, the right to counsel is of such fundamental importance that its denial in a criminal law context must *prima facie* discredit the administration of justice (Justice Le Dain in *Therens*, 1985: 512).

The Supreme Court was anxious to point out that it did not have to bother with section 1 of the Charter ("reasonable limits") because the only thing that might qualify as a limitation was the requirement that the test be taken within two hours, and this did not seem to the Court to rule out being told of one's right to counsel and being given an opportunity to exercise it. The Crown was not prepared to argue the necessity of excluding counsel ("a very incomplete file" according to Justice Lamer, *Therens*, 1985: 491), and the Court expressly refrained from talking about the case where the right to counsel might interfere with law enforcement. Such a case was not long in coming forward, however, and the answer was precisely what we would expect.

The groundwork was all done for the Supreme Court in the Ontario Court of Appeal decision in *R. v. Seo* (*Seo*, 1986). The Crown had by now caught on to the seriousness of this Charter business. Far from an "incomplete file," seven volumes of evidence were introduced to defend Ontario's roadside screening test program from being eviscerated by the Charter's guarantee of a right to counsel. The provisions at issue were subtly different from those in *Therens*. *Therens* concerned a section of the *Criminal Code* which gave a police officer the right to demand a breath sample where he or she "believes on reasonable and probable grounds" that an impaired driving offence has been committed. If the driver took the test and registered an alcohol/blood ratio of more than 80 milligrams of alcohol per 100 millilitres of blood, he or she was *ipso facto* guilty of an offence ("over 80"). *Seo* concerned a different provision of the *Code* which allowed a police officer to demand a roadside breath test where he or she "reasonably suspects" that a driver "has alcohol in his body." Technically speaking, failing this test carried no legal implications. However, the police would then have reasonable grounds to charge the suspect with an impaired driving offence or to ask for a formal breathalyzer test. As its name implies, the roadside screening test was an investigative device to help determine whether or not the virtually conclusive breathalyzer test was warranted.

In *Seo*, the accused was charged with refusing to take the roadside test. At no time prior to the charge was he offered the right to counsel. Nevertheless he was convicted, and the Ontario Court of Appeal upheld the conviction. The seven volumes of material submitted by the Crown included complicated statistical studies showing: the serious impact of drunken driving, the difficulty of detection without mechanical aids, the importance of the likelihood of detection in the deterrence of drunken driving, the increase in the likelihood of detection with a program of random stopping employing the roadside device, the increase in the incidence of drunken driving late at night when it was difficult to obtain counsel, and the urgency of testing because of the decreasing detectability of alcohol in the blood over time—in short, the importance of the program and the destructive effects of allowing counsel to intervene. The Court held that the section imposed an implicit limit on the right to counsel, demonstrably justified under section 1, and stressed that the roadside test was an investigative device only, carrying no legal consequences and in fact a "minor inconvenience." When the Supreme Court of Canada got hold of the issue in another case, it issued the briefest of judgments, merely "adopting" the judgment in *Seo (Thomsen*, 1988: 14).[1]

Though the right to counsel is limited by needs of state, Canadian courts will still go to absurd proportions to enforce it when there are no long-term deleterious consequences for law enforcement. We have already seen in *Manninen* that the failure to *offer a telephone* to a suspect will wipe out a deserved conviction for armed robbery. The Supreme Court has stopped short only of requiring the police to *encourage* the presence of counsel when the right is clearly and soberly waived (*Baig*, 1987). In the prison context, the Federal Court of Appeal used the dubious authority of section 7 of the Charter to grant prisoners charged with prison disciplinary offences the right to counsel where time off for good behaviour was at stake. In doing so, however, the Court stressed that there were many other informal and equally effective discretionary means of controlling prisoners outside of the formal disciplinary process should the need arise, and in such cases counsel could be dispensed with (*Howard*, 1985).[2]

The right to counsel holds a very exalted place in the legal system. The Chief Justice of British Columbia has called it "the most important safeguard in the legal process" (*Joplin*, 1982: 410). Why is it so prized? It is often said that counsel is necessary to explain complicated and foreign legal rules to the "layman" (*Joplin*, 1982: 410; *Seo*, 1986: 414). But this does not mean that

---

[1] In a companion case, the Supreme Court used the Crown material in *Seo*, as well as three additional volumes of evidence, to save random spot-checking authority under provincial traffic legislation against the claim that it constituted "arbitrary detention" (*Hufsky*, 1988).

[2] An appeal was taken to the Supreme Court but the Court declared the case moot for undisclosed reasons and exercised its discretion to dismiss the appeal without consideration of the merits (*Howard*, 1987).

counsel's presence is aimed at ensuring accuracy of verdicts, anymore than anything else in the Charter. This is made crystal clear by *R. v. Clarkson*[1] (*Clarkson*, 1986), where a confession obtained from an intoxicated suspect in the absence of counsel was excluded, but not because it was inaccurate. What troubled the Court was not that Clarkson was incapable of understanding *what* she was saying (that is whether it was true or not), but *whether* she should say it, that is the *legal implications* of what she was saying:

> This constitutional provision is clearly unconcerned with the probative value of any evidence obtained by the police: but rather the concern is for "fair treatment of an accused person" (Justice Wilson in *Clarkson*, 1986: 218).

According to the Court, it was unfair of the police to let Clarkson waive her right to counsel until she was sober and could appreciate the *strategic value* to her of a lawyer, guilty or not. In denying her this purely strategic choice, the police short-circuited the system. They wrecked the game. They acted too much like professionals ("winning is not the main thing but the only thing") and not enough like amateurs ("it's not whether you win or lose but how you play the game"). They wrecked the legal game by, in effect, *de-legalizing* it. This is because counsel is at the threshold of all the other legal values. The right to counsel ensures that legal values will be respected by a strategically placed guardian. The lawyer is not necessarily the accused person's best friend and ally in the criminal process. For professional and class reasons he or she usually falls far short of the ideal of fearless advocate, more often than not playing the role of the double agent in reducing accused persons to a status of dependency (Ericson and Baranek, 1982: 77–110). But by definition the lawyer is the best friend and ally of the values of the legal profession. Not only a friend and ally of them, but their actual *embodiment*. The central legal value is that accused persons are to be treated, if only in form, as equals in power, to each other, to the rest of society, and to the system they confront, even though they are anything but. Representation by counsel ensures this. Instead of unequal parties, we have roughly equal counsel: equal in training, equal in class, even equal in dress in more serious cases where individual differences are masked by identical outerwear. Though the accused has come from a system of class power and is headed back to it, at the moment of the courtroom, where the whole thing is legitimized, class ceases to exist. In court, equality is portrayed by equality of legal champions. And just as this disguises inequality of power, it also suits it very well. Some lawyers, beneath those identical black robes, are more equal than others. They are also more expensive. What good is money if you have to do everything yourself?

> It is not every man who has the ability to defend himself, on his own. He cannot bring out the points in his own favour or the weakness in the other side. He may be tongue-tied or nervous, confused or wanting in intelligence. He cannot examine or cross-examine witnesses...I should have thought, therefore, that when a man's reputation or livelihood is at stake, he not only has a right to speak by his own mouth, he has also a right to speak by counsel or solicitor (Lord Denning in *Pett*, 1968: 549).

---

[1] Another case in which the Charter was not necessary. The case could have been decided on common law grounds, but the majority of the Court preferred the Charter.

So the right to counsel not only ensures that legal values are respected, it actually carries out the central legal value represented by Justice's Blindfold.

Questions of Substance

By far the greater part of judicial activity under the Charter has concerned traditional questions of criminal procedure of the sort which have formed the bulk of US constitutional litigation: the right to counsel, the burden of proof, trial within a reasonable time, the right to a hearing, the admissibility of improperly obtained evidence. However, the Supreme Court of Canada has caused a flutter of alarm by extending the protections of the Legal Rights provisions beyond purely procedural questions to what the judges themselves have termed questions of "substance." Far from contradicting the limits of the constitutionalization of criminal law, however, these decisions merely serve to *emphasize* them.

At the Charter hearings, Assistant Deputy Minister of Justice B.L. Strayer explained the choice of the wording of section 7 as follows:

> Mr. Chairman, it was our belief that the words "fundamental justice" would cover the same thing as what is called procedural due process, that is the meaning of due process in relation to requiring fair procedure. However, it in our view does not cover the concept of what is called substantive due process, which would impose substantive requirements as to the policy of the law in question...Natural justice or fundamental justice in our view does not go beyond the procedural requirements of fairness (Canada, 1980–81, Issue No. 46: 32).

The Mental Element in Crime

It took the Supreme Court of Canada just three years to show how misguided the drafters were about the meaning of their own document, in a reference concerning a provision of the British Columbia *Motor Vehicle Act* (*Re Motor Vehicle Act (B.C.)*, 1985). In this case, the Court ruled unconstitutional a provincial law that imposed a minimum term of seven days imprisonment on anyone caught driving with a suspended licence. The grounds had nothing to do with procedure. What bothered the Court was not the harshness of the penalty, but that the legislation had removed the judge-made defence of "due diligence." This defence would provide an excuse where the offence was not due to the accused person's fault, for example where the person was not aware that his or her licence was suspended and the lack of awareness was not due to carelessness. In holding that this law was contrary to the "principles of fundamental justice," though, the judges explicitly abandoned any notion that section 7 was limited to matters of procedure:

> We should not be surprised to find that many of the principles of fundamental justice are procedural in nature. Our common law has largely been a law of remedies and procedures and as Frankfurter J. wrote in *McNabb* v. *U.S.*,...(1942): "The history of liberty has largely been the history of observance of procedural safeguards." This is not to say, however, that the principles of fundamental justice are limited solely to procedural guarantees...

Whether any given principle may be said to be a principle of fundamental justice within the meaning of s.7 will rest upon an analysis of the nature, sources, rationale and essential role of that principle within the judicial process and our legal system, as it evolves.

Consequently, those words cannot be given any exhaustive content or simple enumerative definition, but will take on concrete meaning as the courts address alleged violations of s.7 (*Re Motor Vehicle Act (B.C.)*, 1985: 557–558).

This statement was at once sufficiently clear in its intention to abandon procedure as the touchstone for fundamental principles of justice, and sufficiently ambiguous with respect to the question of how far the Court would go with this idea, to be greeted with alarm by advocates of judicial restraint. They saw it as opening the door—by its reasoning, at least—to the "substantive due process" of the US courts of the thirties, when "due process" was held to constitutionalize "freedom of contract," making social welfare legislation unconstitutional. The decision was welcomed for the same reason by lawyers making a good living from Charter litigation (*The Globe and Mail*, February 24, 1986: A1, A14).

What the decision really shows, however, is that the dichotomy of procedure/substance is not adequate to grasp the limits of legalized politics, for the decision involved neither. What it involved was the *form* of the legislation, not whether there could be an imprisonable offence of driving while one's licence was suspended, but the *way* in which such an offence could be enacted, the *principles* upon which such a policy could be carried out. And not just any form would do. It had to be a recognizably *legal* form. Where did the judges get the idea that depriving the accused of a defence of lack of fault was contrary to the principles of fundamental justice? As with the case of *Oakes* and the reasonable doubt standard, they merely had to consult the law reports. The "defence of due diligence" had been invented by the Supreme Court of Canada itself, at the urging of law reformers, less than a decade earlier, for use in everyday criminal law (*City of Sault Ste. Marie*, 1978). More or less the same words ("fundamental principles of penal liability") had been used when Chief Justice Dickson had decided, four years before the Charter, that in *interpreting* statutory offences a court should assume—unless, naturally, the law clearly indicated to the contrary—that a due diligence defence existed. It was not too great a leap for the Court to assume (without reflecting on the point at all) that interpretive principles of criminal law, invented less than a decade earlier, could serve equally well as fundamental constitutional principles. What the Court did, as in *Oakes*, was to assert its own particular logic of principle against the contrary logic of policy of the legislature, by dressing it up in constitutional clothing.

No doubt the law was very strict. Nor was the Crown prepared with any evidence showing a necessity for such strictness—typical, as we have seen, of the early Charter cases. But, though it seems very grand and humanitarian of the Court to allow accused persons to defend themselves, in fact the Court had nothing to lose and everything to gain. The number of cases where people without valid licences have no reason to suspect that their licences are suspended, or some other good excuse for driving while it is suspended, must be few indeed. The decision itself was on a reference and did not actually involve any such real person. Whether the rare genuine case will be worth all the phony ones lawyers will now be hired to argue in court is dubious. Furthermore, police and prosecutors exercise considerable discretion in driving cases, and however tough the laws appear in themselves, they are invariably softened in application on grounds which do not seem to differ much from the judicial ones (Ericson, 1982; *The Globe and Mail*, September 20, 1984: 1; *Wood*, 1982; *Kischel*, 1979). Canadian courts and governments have traditionally been very solicitous to dangerous and drunken driving, as compared to crimes that do not so often involve upstanding citizens (*Bigham*, 1982; *McVeigh*, 1985; *Vaillancourt*, 1987). The due diligence defence merely means judges have the final say. They can overrule police or prosecutorial unwillingness to accept a defence. Though the actual decision in any given case is extremely unlikely to differ no matter who makes it, the defence of due diligence in imprisonable offences ensures that nobody goes to jail unless a judge has a free hand in approving or disapproving of it. It does not prevent people from going to jail. It frees courts from being bound by police/prosecutor decisions, just like the procedural cases, but does not require them actually to see things differently. It enhances their formal independence, their *appearance* of independence. Whether or not this reduces the potential for *abuse* of power, it certainly does nothing to inhibit its *exercise*.

Similar observations can be made about the decision of the Supreme Court in *Vaillancourt* (1987), which also employed a "substantive" interpretation of "fundamental justice." The object this time was a very long-standing and frequently used provision of the *Criminal Code* which provided an extended definition of murder. The law deemed even the accidental causing of death during one of a number of specified serious crimes to be "murder" if the accused was carrying a weapon at the time. This was a very old rule, naturally of judicial origin, but it had been out of favour for at least a century, and its practical importance had been greatly diminished by the abolition of the death penalty. Justice McIntyre, in dissent, put the issue in a nutshell:

> The principle complaint in this case is not that the accused should not have been convicted of a serious crime deserving of severe punishment, but simply that Parliament should not have chosen to call that crime "murder" (*Vaillancourt*, 1987: 124).

To Justice McIntyre, this did not warrant holding the law unconstitutional. The majority completely ignored his opinion and focussed on the formal question of the appropriate mental state for murder. Again, it was not the very severe punishment for causing death while carrying a weapon during a crime that was condemned, but the formal notion of "murder" without *mens rea*. In fact, the majority had no problem with stiffer penalties for manslaughter and the use of weapons:

> It is not necessary to convict of murder persons who did not intend or foresee the death and who could not even have foreseen the death in order to deter

others from using or carrying weapons. If Parliament wishes to deter the use or carrying of weapons, it should punish the use or carrying of weapons. A good example of this is the minimum imprisonment for using a firearm in the commission of an indictable offence under s.83 of the *Criminal Code*. In any event, the conviction for manslaughter which would result instead of a conviction for murder is punishable by, from a day in jail, to confinement for life in a penitentiary. Very stiff sentences when weapons are involved in the commission of the crime of manslaughter would sufficiently deter the use or carrying of weapons in the commission of crimes. But stigmatizing the crime as murder unnecessarily impairs the Charter right (Justice Lamer for the majority in *Vaillancourt*, 1987: 139).

Justice Lamer neglected to mention that from the judiciary's point of view the main difference between murder and manslaughter is judicial discretion. The practical effect of this decision is again to loosen one of the few formal constraints on judges. Where a murder conviction binds the judge to an automatic life sentence, with release only under authority of the parole board, in manslaughter and almost all other cases, the Court is free to do what it wants. The net effect of the decision then is to increase (however slightly) the realm of judicial decision making at the expense of Parliament and prosecutorial authorities, but not necessarily to reduce imprisonment for this kind of offence. As for Vaillancourt himself, he would go back for a new trial where he would certainly be found guilty of a serious crime and where he could receive, in effect, if not in formal terms, the identical prison sentence. The federal government was so unconcerned that it did not even intervene in the case to defend its law.

Cruel and Unusual Punishment

The same goes for *R. v. Smith* (*Smith*, 1987) where the Supreme Court used the more stable footing of the provision against "cruel and unusual punishment" to strike down the minimum punishment of seven years imprisonment for importing a narcotic. Once again, the Court had nothing against severe sentences for narcotics importers:

> ...a long term of penal servitude for he or she who has imported large amounts of heroin for the purpose of trafficking would certainly not contravene s.12 of the Charter, quite the contrary. However, the seven-year minimum prison term of s.5(2) is grossly disproportionate when examined in the light of the wide net cast by s.5(1).

> ...the offence of importing...covers numerous substances of varying degrees of dangerousness and totally disregards the quantity of the drug imported. The purpose of a given importation, such as whether it is for personal consumption or for trafficking, and the existence or non-existence of previous convictions for offence of a similar nature or gravity are disregarded as irrelevant.

> ...

> The result sought could be achieved by limiting the imposition of a minimum sentence to the importing of certain quantities, to certain specific narcotics of

the schedule, to repeated offenders, or even to a combination of these factors. But the wording of the section and the schedule is much broader. I should add that, in my view, the minimum sentence also creates some problems. In particular, it inserts into the system a reluctance to convict and thus results in acquittals for picayune reasons of accused who do not deserve a seven-year sentence, and it gives the Crown an unfair advantage in plea bargaining as an accused will be more likely to plead guilty to a lesser or included offence (Justice Lamer for the majority in *Smith*, 1987: 143, 145).

The objection was, in effect, not that the law dealt too harshly with offenders but that it interfered with the discretion judges traditionally exercise to distinguish between offenders who commit the same offence. In fact, at least until the Charter came into effect, sentencing discretion provided most of the opportunities criminal court judges had to wield real power. Sentencing, as the courts admit themselves, is the "gist" of criminal law (*Gardiner*, 1982). And it is one of its most undemocratic features, as judges freely tailor the sentence not only to what the offender has done, but also to who he or she is. Criminal record and employment status figure prominently not only in the practice, but also in the *law* of sentencing. It is in sentencing, too, that the ideological distinction between "regulatory offences" (business crime) and "true crime" (working-class crime) figures most prominently. Sentencing discretion is a major mechanism by which the criminal law maintains the status quo of social power (Mandel, 1984). Yet, according to the dissenting judge in *Smith*, the decision "would, in effect, constitutionally entrench the power of judges to determine the appropriate sentence in their absolute discretion" (Justice McIntyre in *Smith*, 1987: 121). Technically speaking this was not quite accurate. The majority did leave open the possibility of a constitutionally valid statutory minimum sentence, carefully tailored in judicially acceptable terms. But practically speaking, Parliament is most reluctant to impose any restrictions whatever on judicial sentencing discretion. That is why the importing provision was not only "cruel" but also very "unusual." Recently, the Minster of Justice rejected the most modest of proposals to limit judicial sentencing discretion (*The Globe and Mail*, August 25, 1988: A1).[1]

Given this climate, then, the practical effect of *Smith* is as described by Justice McIntyre, to leave sentencing to the unfettered discretion of the judiciary. Not that the minimum importing sentence had anything to recommend it. It was a product of the US induced postwar drug hysteria, making importing any narcotic the most serious offence on the books next to murder. For years, it had been condemned by law reformers. The Le Dain Commission had proposed that it be abolished fifteen years earlier (Canada, 1972: 302), but no political party had had sufficient nerve to appear so soft on drugs as to push for the reform. It seems all they were willing to do was appoint Le Dain

---

[1] Interestingly enough, these recommendations had been made by the Canadian Sentencing Commission whose further recommendation that all minimum sentences be abolished was cited by Justice Lamer to bolster his conclusion (Canada, 1987: 190). This Commission is itself an excellent example of the legalization of politics. Made up of six judges, one lawyer, one court worker and one criminologist, its recommendation on the minimum sentence was part of a completely court-oriented approach to sentencing which included the abolition of parole altogether. In compensation for this it recommended very modest guidelines for judges.

himself to the Supreme Court of Canada and let nature take its course! Indeed the decision vindicates, partially at least, the judgment of the National Organization for the Reform of the Marijuana Laws (NORML): "Marijuana is no longer a political issue. It hasn't been since the Charter of Rights came into effect April 17, 1982" (*Canadian Press*, July 6, 1983), meaning that reform was now up to the courts. A constitutional challenge to the prohibition against cannabis use has already started its long trek through the judicial system, encouraged by the victory in *Smith* (*The Globe and Mail*, November 30, 1987: A7).

This is not the only case of the courts delivering law reform when the political process is too paralyzed to do so. A more dramatic example can be found in the *Morgentaler* decision (1988) discussed in Chapter VI. But before we congratulate the Charter for its ability to break through political logjams, let us at least raise the question of whether the Charter itself had anything to do with the necessity of having to wait for judicial action for law reform, and of what effects decisions like *Smith* might have in encouraging people to suspend other forms of politics until they have tried their luck with the courts. When NORML was disbanded in 1984, the Charter was cited again: "It gave politicians a terrific way out for things they used to be responsible for—changing the laws" (*Canadian Press*, September 13, 1984). And when the group, which appears to have its ups and downs, resurrected itself in 1985, it did so only for the purpose of launching a Charter challenge (*Canadian Press*, October 17, 1985).

We cannot let Justice Lamer's comments on plea bargaining pass without comment. According to him, abolishing the minimum sentence would allow the Court to rescue the accused from the oppressive plea-bargaining tactics of the Crown. It is true that the most powerful inducements to pleading guilty are the considerations that the Crown can offer on withdrawal and substitution of charges. It is also true that judges are deeply implicated in the coercion of pleas of guilty. A familiar sentencing principle is the discount for a timely guilty plea (*Layte*, 1983), and the judiciary has the power—but almost never exercises it—to veto virtually any bargain by the exercise of its sentencing discretion. Indeed, that is what was different about the minimum for importing. The Crown could trump judicial discretion by exercising its own. Once again the judiciary has merely used the Charter to transfer discretion from prosecutor to court. Not that they more than rarely disagree. In fact the sentence in *Smith* was actually *above* the minimum (meaning that the trial judge obviously thought that the seven-year minimum was too low in this case), though this seems to have bothered only the dissent:

> As a preliminary matter, I would point out that there is an air of unreality about this appeal...The judges who have considered the case...are unanimously of the view that a long sentence of imprisonment is appropriate and no one has suggested that the appellant has been sentenced to cruel and unusual punishment. Recognizing this fact, the appellant does not attack s.5(2)...on the ground that it violates s.12 of the Charter in general, but rather on the ground that the imposition of "a mandatory minimum sentence of seven years" on a hypothetical

"first-time importer of a single marijuana cigarette" would constitute cruel and unusual punishment. In effect, the appellant is stating that while the law is not unconstitutional in its application to him, it may be unconstitutional in its application to a third party, and, therefore, should be declared of no force or effect (Justice McIntyre dissenting in *Smith*, 1987: 103–104).

The majority was forced to admit that indeed:

No such case has actually occurred to my knowledge ...merely because the Crown has chosen to exercise favourably its prosecutorial discretion to charge such a person not with the offence that that person has really committed, but rather with a lesser offence (Justice Lamer in *Smith*, 1987: 124).

The consistent exercise of discretion in this manner probably rendered the actual impact of the case nil (*The Globe and Mail*, August 12, 1987: A13).

That the Supreme Court was not concerned with the severity of the penalty *per se* in *Smith* is clear from the decision in *Lyons* (1987), in which it upheld an at least equally harsh law—"indeterminate" that is indefinite, potentially life-lasting detention for "dangerous offenders"—which did not suffer from the perceived defects present in *Smith*. Far from interfering with the traditional judicial approach to sentencing, the impugned legislation actually gave the sentencing judge *more* power by allowing the maximum sentence for any offence to be ignored if the judge thought a life sentence was warranted in the circumstances, the circumstances having more to do with the kind of person the offender was than with what he or she had done this time. The Supreme Court was especially impressed by the overriding residual discretion left to the judge:

Finally, the court has the discretion not to designate the offender as dangerous or to impose an indeterminate sentence, even in circumstances where all of these criteria are met (Justice La Forest for the majority in *Lyons*, 1987: 29).

What we see in the "substance" cases is a systematic loosening of Parliamentary restrictions on judicial administration. This does not essentially differ from the cases on strictly procedural questions, which ensure both judicial control over the symbolic purity of the courtroom (as in the admissibility of improperly obtained evidence and the burden of proof) and extension of legal supervision over a wider range of administrative activity, through the right to counsel in police contacts and through hearing rights in such areas as parole, prison discipline, and immigration. The substance cases ensure that the final determination of important questions of criminal liability and punishment are gathered into the hands of the judiciary and not transferred to bureaucratic administration. Everything must pass through the exalted and sanctified forum of the courtroom for judicial approval unfettered by externally imposed constraints. But as far as we have been able to tell, none of this poses any obstacles to the objectives of law enforcement or shifts the balance of power in favour of the "little guy" who the procedural protections of the Charter are supposed to protect. All that has occurred is a transfer of authority over law enforcement to the courts and a consequent subordination of the bureaucratic apparatus to the values of the legal profession. Police, prosecutors, prison and parole authorities must now respect certain formal legal values in their work, but, however irksome, they do not in any way interfere with their objectives. The Charter has not placed the judiciary between the police and the citizen, it has merely perched it on the former's shoulder. If we want to understand these developments it will have to be in some other way than as a purely liberal or humanitarian limitation on official power.

Judicial Control and Democratic Control

The general appeal of the legalization of politics stems from the powerlessness most of us feel in the face of government. Access to the courts is offered up as a remedy for the failures of Canadian democracy, as an alternative to more responsive representative institutions. Criminal procedure is an important example of this. If the chance to control the government's repressive apparatus by the medium of the Charter looks like a progressive development, it is because of the slim pickings in alternative methods. They are either non-existent or virtually identical. Which means that legalized methods are the only ones on offer.

Police forces in Canada operate almost entirely independently of the public. Even if they are under the nominal supervision of provincially or municipally appointed Police Commissions and Boards, the operating ethos of these bodies is police *independence*. In fact, these bodies are generally meant to "insulate" the police from political "pressure" (Stenning, 1981: I 85). The legal profession stands on guard here, too. Membership on Commissions and Boards is heavily weighted in favour of lawyers, usually presided over by a judge, with staff mostly comprised of former police personnel (Stenning, 1981: II 13–17, 131). According to the Ontario Police Commission:

> The primary rule is that the Chief of Police is charged with the responsibility for the control of the conduct of his men, particularly as it relates to the wide discretionary power which they exercise (Stenning, 1981: III 29).

Police commissions and boards rarely issue policy instructions to the police, and when they do, it is with the concurrence or on the initiative of the Chief (Stenning, 1981: III 46, 56–57). If police operate independently of their political supervisors, their political supervisors also operate independently of the public, even though their meetings may have a public as well as a private part to their agendas (McMahon and Ericson, 1987: 56; Stenning, 1981: III 91).

How do police use their independence? Not by merely enforcing the law. That would be impossible. There are too many laws, and they are always being broken. Instead, they selectively use the law to keep "order" (Ericson, 1982). In other words, they protect the status quo of social power. For example, they ignore business crime and concentrate on working-class crime, they protect property from any unauthorized attempts at redistribution in favour of those without it, and they keep an eye on problem populations, especially the young, urban, unemployed males who make up most of the grist for the courtrooms and the prisons. This does not much bother those on the top of the heap, but it naturally causes conflicts with the rest. As we descend the social power ladder, experience with police becomes more a matter of confrontation than cooperation.

Until the late seventies, people who were abused by the police had either to complain to the police themselves or to undertake a civil suit or a criminal prosecution. The trouble with lawsuits is that whether you win or lose, you still have to pay an awful lot of money to the lawyers. The trouble with prosecutions is that crown attorneys and criminal court judges have a close working relationship with the police and are not exactly anxious to undermine it by zealous application of the full rigors of the law against them (*The Toronto Star*, November 28, 1987: A2). Furthermore, the typical complainant is, socially and criminally speaking, the kind of person the police, courts, and crown attorneys are in the business of protecting the social order *from*, and the typical complaint is that the police merely went too far in the way of protection (Mandel, 1983a). This is not a recipe for success when it comes to prosecuting the police. Recently, some jurisdictions have set up complaint mechanisms more or less independent of the police. Usually it is less. For example, in Toronto, the "Public Complaints Commission" was set up in 1981 after some explosive confrontations between police and minority groups, including police shootings of blacks and raids on gay bathhouses. The offended groups called for more community control over police policy and civilian review of police complaints (McMahon and Ericson, 1987: 40). Naturally, control over police policy was not in the slightest relinquished. Nor was there anything "civilian" about the review process. The legislation gave extensive powers to a Complaints Commissioner to intervene in the discipline of police and to appoint boards of inquiry with disciplinary powers up to and including dismissal. But these powers were totally discretionary. They were powers but not duties. Consequently, they are only rarely exercised. The primary responsibility for investigating and dealing with complaints remains with the police themselves, and the Commission mainly monitors the progress of these complaints. Of 735 official complaints resolved in 1986, the police decision was effectively final in all but five. This meant formal discipline in only 36 cases, which took the form of a reprimand in all but seven.[1] Of six inquiry decisions released in 1986, action against the officer was taken in only two (forfeiture of a few days off or a few days suspension) (Ontario, 1987).

Not surprisingly, the legal profession is much in evidence. The current Commissioner is a former Provincial Court Judge, and inquiry boards are generally staffed by lawyers who ensure that legal forms are fully respected. The subject of the investigation has the right to counsel, and the burden of proof is the traditional common law standard for criminal cases, proof beyond a reasonable doubt. Some critics argue that the system is more solicitous to police than even the old internal complaints system still in force in the rest of the province and most of the country (*The Globe and Mail*, November 30,

---

[1] Four charges were laid under the *Police Act* resulting in three convictions with punishments in each case amounting to forfeiture of a few days off. Three charges were laid under the *Criminal Code*. The results of these are not disclosed by the report except that at least two were acquittals.

1987: A18). So mild has the Commission been on police that its first order of dismissal (for brutality), when upheld by the Court of Appeal, was protested by a police work slowdown and calls for a return to the old system (*The Globe and Mail*, February 3, 1988: A14). Initial dissatisfaction with the limits of the new system on the part of police critics was great enough that a volunteer, non-governmental organization, "Citizen's Independent Review of Police Activities" (CIRPA), was set up in competition with the Complaint Commission in 1981. Dominated by criminal lawyers affiliated with the left wing Law Union of Ontario, the body seems gradually to have lost its confrontational approach to both the Complaints Commission and the Police Commission, which is the political overseer of police activities (McMahon and Ericson, 1987: 48). Lawyers originally critical of the new system have recently come to its defence against the movement to abolish it for being too hard on police (*The Globe and Mail*, February 3, 1988: A14; June 17, 1988: A18).

The Charter itself probably has contributed to the reduced enthusiasm, among lawyers at least, for more democratic control over the police. It has provided them, including those who set up CIRPA, with a way to challenge police behaviour in a manner that can be completely integrated with their service to their clients in defending criminal cases. Sometimes the challenge can even result in the charges being thrown out altogether. This naturally tends to displace the more cumbersome political remedies (e.g. publicity campaigns) and legal remedies (prosecutions and suits) available before the Charter. Of course the Charter works both ways. It has also provided protection to the police whether they are charged under the *Criminal Code*, the *Police Act*, or before inquiries called by the Complaints Commission. With constitutional protections, police are able to stall the day of reckoning or even avoid discipline altogether. So far, their attempts to have complaints tribunals rendered completely impotent have been unsuccessful (*Wigglesworth*, 1987; *The Globe and Mail*, June 25, 1987: A16). But the lawyers that sit on these boards of inquiry do not need much encouragement to give police the full protections of the Charter, and the police are certainly well-placed to take advantage of them.

What we see in the realm of conventional police work, we see in more controversial realms as well. An example is the so-called "RCMP Scandal" of the late seventies. This was a series of revelations that the Security Service of the RCMP had been involved in the investigation, disruption, and suppression of lawful political activity by groups on the left of the political spectrum: social democratic parties such as the PQ and the NDP, Marxists of all stripes, unions, Native groups, black people's groups, student groups, and left wing news agencies. This activity involved the commission of many crimes on the part of the RCMP, including breaking and entering, theft, arson, kidnapping, and mail opening. Through various more or less dubious mechanisms with heavy judicial involvement (most notably in the Inquiry headed by Mr. Justice David MacDonald of Alberta), no police were ever brought to justice for their crimes (Mandel, 1983a). However, a major reorganization of the political police took place, including the creation of the Canadian Security Intelligence Service. The interesting thing from our point of view is that despite calls (in some quarters at least) for equal enforcement of the law against the police, even greater legal restrictions on them, and more Parliamentary supervision of their policies and procedures, the system that resulted actually *expanded* the discretionary powers of the political police. It *legalized* many of the crimes they had committed and rejected Parliamentary control as too "partisan" and lacking in sufficient "confidentiality" (Canada, 1983: 32). As compensation, the judiciary was given more or less unlimited supervision over the most intrusive measures, which would now require judicial warrants (*Canadian Security Intelligence Act*, ss. 21–28). For Parliamentary supervision was substituted a Cabinet committee (the Security Intelligence Review Committee) to be appointed after consultation with Opposition leaders (s. 34). The first incarnation of this committee (four lawyers and a businessman) seems to have started out with the same anti-left prejudices as the police itself (Mandel, 1985), though it has recently come to identify them as such and has agreed that the CSIS is biased in favour of matters it should not be:

> We cannot agree that a nonviolent attack on U.S. foreign policy is necessarily a threat to the security of Canada...CSIS may too readily accept the foreign policy objectives of our allies as its own and neglect Canadian foreign policy...CSIS is expending money and effort on too many counter-subversion targets and it is intruding on the lives and activities of too many Canadians in this area (Canada, 1987a: 37).

Following this report and some other scandals in the service, the government announced a major overhaul of CSIS that would greatly reduce its counter-subversion activities (*The Globe and Mail*, December 1, 1987: A1, A2; December 5, 1987: D2). It remains to be seen whether they reappear in some other guise. Still, the Review Committee, biases and all, appears to have a better record than the judiciary in reining in CSIS initiatives. To date, of the hundreds of requests for judicial intrusion warrants made by CSIS, not one has been turned down (Canada, 1987a: 9). An attempt to challenge CSIS information gathering by invoking the Charter was recently dismissed with these words:

> In light of six years of rhetoric and jurisprudence about the *Charter*, some Canadians may shudder to realize that the security needs of a free and democratic society are, in a few basic essentials, much the same as those which totalitarian societies arrogate unto themselves. Utter secrecy, subject to certain checks, in security intelligence matters is one (Justice Muldoon in *Zanganeh*, 1988: 14).

Naturally, one of the "checks" Justice Muldoon found that distinguished free from totalitarian societies was "the right to apply to this Court for a review," even if the review was denied (*Zanganeh*, 1988: 15). All this only goes to show that even the most tenuous political supervision can be infinitely more responsive than an army of judges.

We could make similar observations about the parole system. For years it has operated in secret, completely undermining whatever egalitarianism criminal law might have and distributing prison sentences according to the social characteristics of prisoners, their attitudes to authority, and such like, reducing the relation between the severity of the actual crime committed and the length of sentence almost to insignificance. Despite periodic outcries against the release of privileged prisoners and persistent calls for the abolition of the entire system by "clients,"—victims and prisoners alike—frustrated by its arbitrary and unresponsive behaviour, parole board powers have continued to expand. Instead of abolishing or limiting parole board powers, in the late seventies the government merely *legalized* them, that is, made them subject to judicial supervision for conformity with procedural values (*Parole Regulations*, 1978). Of course, this in no way interfered with board objectives, as it entailed no change in the criteria for granting parole and no increase in the rate at which it was granted. In parole, the process of legalization was well under way before entrenchment. The Charter merely intensified this process. (Mandel, 1975; 1985; 1986; Canada, 1981; 1987c). Naturally, there have been calls for the democratization of judicial sentencing as well, but since the only "democratization" possible under legalized politics is the judicial kind, nothing whatsoever has happened here (Mandel, 1984; Canada, 1987c; *The Globe and Mail*, August 25, 1988: A1).

The Charter is not a remedy for a lack of democracy in criminal law. It may appear that way because of the vacuum it replaces:

> In the area of controls upon the police, a vast abnegation of responsibility at the level of...ordinary sources of legal rulemaking has forced the Court to construct *all* the law regulating the everyday functioning of the police (Amsterdam, 1970: 790; emphasis in original).

But the "abnegation of responsibility" is in no way accidental, and the acceptability of judicial solutions compared to democratic solutions has to do with the easier accommodation of the former than the latter to the needs of the social status quo. The Charter is part of the modern strategy of meeting demands for more popular control over government with the intercession of lawyers, whose function is limited to ensuring compliance with their formal procedural values.

Legalization and Repression

It should be clear by now that constitutionalizing criminal procedure, despite its formally "civilizing" effects, does not otherwise make for a criminal law system that is less repressive overall, though these civilizing effects might make us think of it as less *op*pressive. Charter holdings have posed no long-term obstacles to law enforcement. While police must change their form of behaviour towards suspects and the occasional conviction must be sacrificed to ensure that they do so, nothing in the decisions of the courts weakens their effectiveness once these forms are complied with. We have plenty of evidence from the US and some from Canada that even the short-term effects on conviction rates are tiny or non-existent. They are more than compensated for by changes in police tactics and increases in efficiency, some of which are probably due in part to the constitutional rules themselves.

But is this anything to complain about? Does it matter if the system is no less repressive? Is it not enough that it is less *op*pressive? Maybe it would be nicer to have more democracy, but if we cannot have that should we not be grateful that the courts have made the police a little more polite and leave it at that?

The problem is that the constitutionalization of criminal procedure has not merely not been accompanied by *less* repression. It has gone hand in hand with *greatly expanded repression* and this raises disturbing questions about the *relationship* between legalization and repression.

Along with the legalization of politics, the postwar period has seen an enormous growth in the proportion of the population subject to criminal sanctions. In terms of per capita prison populations alone, Canada's historical high-water mark of the Great Depression was already equalled by the early sixties (the time of the *Canadian Bill of Rights*). Although a lot of the slack was taken off thereafter by the growth of "alternatives to incarceration," mainly probation, by the 1980s we were back to all-time highs in prison *in addition to* a probation population never before seen in history, three times the size of the prison population. Furthermore, there has been a steady increase, since the mid-seventies—the same time the Charter was put on the agenda—in both the length of prison sentences and the intensity of probation conditions. Maximum prison terms have increased for many offences. The dangerous offender legislation approved in *Lyons* has been refurbished and expanded. The penalty for murder, despite the formal abolition of capital punishment, has been increased by lengthening minimum periods of ineligibility for parole. The National Parole Board has recently been given the power, for the first time in the history of imprisonment, to deny release to penitentiary prisoners who have earned time off for good behaviour. Probation has seen intensified supervision, the addition of compulsory labour through the "community service order," and indeed the rise of the "probation hostel," where probationers reside side by side with prisoners on parole. The result is that Canada has four times the proportion of its population under criminal sentence restrictions that it had during the Great Depression (Mandel, 1987; Statistics Canada, 1986; Reed, 1983; Chan and Ericson, 1981).

What has caused this is a matter of intense debate. No one doubts that there has been a steady increase in official crime rates. Whether this is due to actually increasing crime or just to increasing police activity is the question. There has certainly been some increase in the rate of violent crime, as witness a murder rate that doubled between 1961 and 1976 (Dominion Bureau of Statistics, 1966; Statistics Canada, 1987b). But violent crime does not account for all of the changes. There has also been a great growth in police per capita, and it is possible to attribute much of the growth in official rates of reported minor crime (property and traffic) to growth in police strength and surveillance efficiency alone (Chan and Ericson, 1981). On the other hand, it has been shown that variations in the level of punishment are not due solely or even mostly to variations in the crime rate but rather to economic conditions, and more precisely to levels of social inequality (Greenberg, 1977; Braithwaite, 1979). But whether the increase in punishment is due to increasing crime or just to increasing repression, neither alternative is anything to write home about. Whether we are more repressed because we are more criminal or more repressed without being more criminal, we are still more repressed. For reasons we have already addressed it is clear that the Charter will have no effect on this. It was not intended by any of its advocates as an antidote to this trend, and in the nature of things, it cannot operate as one. One thing the simultaneous rise of legalization and repression does do, however, is to dispel the notion put abroad by Charter advocates that the Charter is part of a general humanitarian, libertarian, or otherwise progressive trend in Canadian society.

It could simply be a coincidence that the Charter appears in history with an increasing rate of repression, but it is at least worth thinking about the possibility of a more organic link between the two.

Since the early seventies a crisis of confidence has been increasingly evident in the criminal justice system, very similar to the one observable in the economic system. Despite increasing levels of repression, increasing resources devoted to it, and increasing technological and organizational sophistication, the system does not seem capable of delivering on the goal of crime prevention. So great has been the failure to prevent crime that official and unofficial defenders of the system have ceased claiming it as a goal. Instead, philosophers, law reformers, and judges have turned away from the concrete goals of deterrence and rehabilitation as justifications for what they do, to abstract notions such as "registering social disapproval," "publicly denouncing wrongful acts," "underlining crucial social values" (Law Reform Commission of Canada, 1976a; Canada, 1977b: 198), and, most revealing of all, the current fad of "anti-impunity" (Gross, 1979: 400–401; Canada 1987c: 150–151), which holds that punishment is justified by showing law-abiding people that criminals do not get away with it—at least not always! In other words, greater official repression is increasingly legitimated or justified in abstract terms, the way the economic system is. As we have argued, when it comes to abstract legitimation the courts are the experts. This means that the courts are increasingly called upon to do the legitimating. But, in order to do this, the courts have to be there in the first place. In other words, the abstract legitimation of expanded repression needs a judiciary, fit and inclined to carry out this business of abstract legitimation. It *presupposes* the legalization of politics. It presupposes courts that see themselves not as deferential executors of legislative policy in crime prevention but as having a quite different function that does not depend for its legitimacy on its effectiveness, but on its justice. The courtroom has to be seen as an end in itself. For this it has to be detached as much as possible from its social context. Its social context has to be made irrelevant. The criminal has to be erected to the status of free-willing agent. Neither the criminal nor the crime can be socially situated lest the crime be socially explained away and nagging doubts about the point of it all be raised. The embarrassing facts that criminality—whether from the criminal's or the victim's point of view—is bound up with inequality, poverty, and the irrational swings of the economy, and that punishment can do little in these circumstances but barely keep the lid on, must somehow be suppressed. To carry this off requires a heavy blindfold on Justice. The accused criminal must be treated as an equal if he or she is to be credibly punished as an equal. The criminal must be treated with the fullest respect. He or she must be represented by counsel to disguise any singularities and given the right to remain silent to make sure the effect is not ruined. The criminal must be given every opportunity of defence, and there must be a high burden to eliminate any doubts about guilt. At its most public moment the criminal law must be "gentle" with its subject (Foucault, 1977). All possible excuses must be investigated and discounted so that punishment can be seen as fully deserved. In this way any questions about the *point* of punishment are rendered irrelevant. And when the rules are violated, the accused must, at least sometimes, be allowed to win. It is not the certainty of conviction that counts, as with deterrence, but its *quality*.

Now if these norms are complied with, the courts set their highly prized, indeed indispensable, stamp of approval on the proceedings and the resultant punishment. Since they are usually complied with (because of the importance of courts as well as the fact that compliance does not interfere with law enforcement), the courts are in the position of approving of the general trend of criminal policy, whatever it may be. In this way, the constitutionalization of criminal procedure legitimates the expanded repression of our era. It is in fact its *form*.

Though the argument is more complicated than I would have liked it to be, it is bolstered by many historical examples of repression being justified by attention to procedural niceties. By all agreement, the eighteenth century was one of the bloodiest in terms of legal repression (Foucault, 1977; Thompson, 1975; Hay, 1975). Yet it was the most punctilious when it came to criminal procedure. According to historians Douglas Hay and E.P. Thompson, this procedure was designed to legitimate both the system of criminal justice and the whole system of social power by the equal formal respect it paid to those it dispatched to the gallows for crimes against property. The English show trial of the day was in fact the origin of many of the procedural principles being reinvoked under the Charter by our own judiciary. But there are other more recent examples. When capital punishment was first restricted to only certain categories of murder in 1961, its retention for those categories was legitimated by guaranteeing appeals all the way to the Supreme Court of Canada (*An Act to amend the Criminal Code (Capital Murder)*, 1961: ss. 8–12). Attacks on the powers of the National Parole Board during the seventies were neutralized by amendments in 1978 requiring the Board to act in accordance with norms of procedural fairness (*Parole Regulations*, 1978). Once these norms were in place, the Parole Board was guaranteed a decade of peaceful expansion. When the new repressive powers given the Board in 1986 were challenged on the grounds of retroactivity, the courts turned back the challenge by invoking the copious procedural rights under the new powers (*Evans*, 1986). In *Lyons*, the Supreme Court of Canada held that the difficulty of predicting dangerousness "does not appear to undermine the utility and fairness of the [dangerous offender] scheme so much as to fortify the conclusion that the procedural protections accorded to the offender, especially on review, ought to be very rigorous" (*Lyons*, 1987: 50).

A colleague of mine thinks I am completely wrong about this relationship. He argues that it makes more sense of the relationship between due process and increased repression to see the former as a *reaction* to the latter. Expanded repression, he says, is purely political. The legal profession, through the Charter, exercises a modest, but unmistakable restraining effect. It is perverse, he thinks, though he puts it more politely than that, to blame the legal profession for expanded repression, since judges and lawyers obviously do not intend their procedural guarantees to aid it in any way. I happen to agree that the complicated relationship I am trying to establish is probably not widely experienced as such. No doubt, some judges secretly hope to legitimate severe sentences by bending over backwards procedurally for accused persons, and others secretly try to mitigate the severity of the system by bending procedural rules in their favour. Most judges probably just try to do their job and believe they are moderates in a world of extremes. However, I would not want to suggest that for this reason judges should be absolved from responsibility for the expansion of repression. They are too deeply implicated in it in other ways, for example, through their sentencing practices, to be let completely off the hook.

But since I am not here to award praise or blame but merely to identify the effects of legalized politics, it really does not matter whether judges intend or recognize their procedural contributions to expanded repression as such. Devotees of the old television series *Star Trek* may remember the episode where the Enterprise lands on a planet that has been making war with its neighbour for five hundred years or so. Why had they not made peace in all that time? After a devastating thermonuclear war, they had hit upon the idea of *simulated* war by means of large electronic game boards. When one planet scored a hit on the other, the other would, according to the rules, dispatch the appropriate number of people to painless death chambers. Thus they had devised a means of making war without destruction or pain, but otherwise every bit as deadly as the real thing. The planet leaders were convinced that they were reducing suffering, but they were in fact perpetuating it, by sanitizing it. As things stood, the war could have gone on forever, except for the meddling Captain Kirk who naturally decided to destroy the machine and force the planets to make peace by confronting the option of real war. The procedural guarantees of the Charter seem to me to have a lot in common with the game board.

Does opposition to the Charter mean opposition to fair trials or to treating people as equals? That would be a nice position to have to argue! But you do not need a Charter of Rights to give concrete rights to accused persons. The Charter is much more and much less than this. It is a whole way of approving or disapproving of punishment in which the freedom of the judiciary is central. Since the rights are merely incidental to this, they are symbolic, discretionary, and conditional. They are dispensed, as we have seen, in a carefully structured way for maximum public relations effect and minimum interference with current law enforcement objectives. They are meant to protect the system and not the public. They do nothing about the mindless, ever-expanding repression except perhaps to make us feel better about it. We are a free country, even though everyone is in jail or on probation, because we have the right to counsel! Would it be better not to have a Charter and the same level of repression? That option is purely theoretical. Without something like the Charter this level of repression would be much more difficult to get away with. To oppose the Charter is not to oppose the rights it may or may not be said to grant but to oppose its contribution to expanded repression. And if it seems awfully stubborn of me to refuse to talk about the Charter as if it existed in a vacuum, it is because of a conviction that the Charter legitimizes its context best by detaching itself from it.

Who Wins From the Charter's Formal Values?

The most obvious winner in the Charter sweepstakes is the legal profession. The winnings are by no means restricted to the realm of criminal procedure, and indeed, the criminal bar is a small portion of the profession as a whole. But what has happened in criminal procedure is repeated with variations throughout the legal system. What has happened in criminal procedure is that the prestige and indeed power of judges and lawyers has been enormously enhanced vis-a-vis all other criminal justice agents. These agents must now answer to the legal profession on the home ground of the legal profession and according to its rules and values. What is not lost on the lawyers is that the ascendancy of these values is of great *value* to the legal profession. The right to counsel, which, as we have seen, stands for all the other rights, means nothing if not plenty of work for lawyers. The decision in *Howard* (1985) may have put a strain on Legal Aid funds throughout the country by guaranteeing all prisoners the right to counsel in prison disciplinary hearings (*The Globe and Mail* March 13, 1985: M1), but it relieved a lot of financial strain for lawyers who had a captive market of tens of thousands of "clients" opened wide to their services. Similarly, the decision of the Supreme Court of Canada that all refugee claimants had a constitutional right to a hearing (*Singh*, 1985) immediately brought forth this comment in the *Ontario Lawyers Weekly*:

> And from a practical point of view, the case means more work for lawyers, now that more than 10,000 potential refugee claimants are entitled to an oral hearing at a certain stage of the refugee status application procedure (Brillinger, 1986: 10).

Around the same time as his court was delivering the *Singh* decision, Chief Justice Dickson was delivering a speech to a group of newly ordained lawyers, in which he cited the Charter as a reason for optimism about their job prospects (*Ontario Lawyers Weekly*, April 26, 1985: 18). Not three years after entrenchment, the Chief Justice of Ontario was celebrating the number of statutes the courts had already struck down as making 1984 "the year of the courts" (*The Globe and Mail* January 8, 1985: 16). The Charter is even being used in attempts by the legal profession to pry more money for itself from governments. Ontario Provincial Court Judges are invoking their new weighty responsibilities under the Charter in a bid for higher salaries (*The Globe and Mail*, April 1, 1988: A12). Their supporters in the criminal bar have used the Charter in a more complicated way, arguing that low pay has led to a shortage of qualified judges and crown attorneys, which in turn has caused delays long enough for cases to be thrown out under the "trial within a reasonable time" provision of the Charter (*The Globe and Mail*, July 26, 1988: A16). When the same argument is made by the Chief Justice of Ontario, it starts to sound like blackmail (*The Globe and Mail*, January 14, 1988: A17).

Cruder still are the Canadian Bar Association's persistent attempts to use the Charter to drum up business. It promptly declared April 17, the day the Charter was signed into law by the Queen, as "Law Day," so that an annual promotional campaign could be undertaken on behalf of the legal profession. Then, on the anniversary of the Charter's proclamation, it took out a four-page "Special Advertising Feature" in *The Globe and Mail* which, along with the many private law firm advertisements, included items such as "Know your rights: The new Charter should be studied by every Canadian" and "When you need a lawyer, where do you go?" (*The Globe and Mail,* April 18, 1983) Since then, Law Day has been marked annually by local lawyers' groups with sporting events, contests, and mock trials (*The Toronto Star*, April 17, 1984). Bar Association planning is a year-round affair (*The National*, June 1988: 19), and by 1987, ads could be found on public transit facilities (in Toronto at least) *at any time of the year*. But for crudeness, will it ever be possible to surpass this pitch to lawyers by the Chairman of the Ontario Branch of the CBA's Law Day Committee?

> ...your involvement in Law Day this year can make you feel good about yourself and at the same time increase client business...These are hard times at the Bar for many of us. With overcrowding in the profession, it is not enough to shift portions of the pie—the pie, or demand for legal services, must also expand for all those wanting a slice. It is simply good marketing to get out into your community and to bring the law to people. This is a basic way of both attracting new clients and making existing clients aware of new legal needs. Think of the business that a speech to a community group on the new *Family Law Act, 1986*, may generate (Dietrich, 1986: 4).

But, however much they might congratulate themselves on their clever marketing, it would be foolish to think that the legal profession has just pulled the wool over everybody's eyes. Lawyers have to deliver the goods if they are going to have any clients. The Charter, as we know, provides much needed legitimation services for the system of social power. But it not only serves a *system* of social power, it also serves the powerful people themselves.

Power and Procedure

Shortly before the Charter was entrenched, Ontario Attorney General and Charter protagonist, Roy McMurtry, gave a speech to a group of corporate lawyers in which he stressed the value of the Charter for big business. This raised some eyebrows at the time because it was distinctly contrary to the federal sales pitch that the Charter was for the "individual." One of the examples McMurtry gave was the Charter protection against "unreasonable search and seizure." He thought this could be a useful weapon for big business to use against the powers of investigation under the *Combines Investigation Act* (*The Globe and Mail*, February 6, 1982: 12). This prediction proved deadly accurate in the Supreme Court of Canada's very first decision on criminal procedure, *Hunter* v. *Southam* (*Hunter*, 1984).

The context of the case was some rapid-fire newspaper sales and closings in 1980 involving Canada's two largest newspaper chains, Thomson Newspapers Ltd. and Southam Inc., in circumstances highly suggestive of collusion. When the dust had cleared, Montreal, Vancouver, Winnipeg, and Ottawa were left with only one English language daily each. These were divided up between the chains in such a way that they stood to gain about 35 million dollars per year between them from the resultant lack of competition for circulation and advertising. A Royal Commission was appointed to inquire into newspaper concentration, and the Combines Investigation Department started to look into the possibility of criminal charges. The companies and some of their executives were charged in 1981. Following this, in the investigations that continued up until the trial, the Combines Branch conducted a number of searches of newspaper premises across the country. Virtually every one of these searches was met by a challenge under the Charter. Success came early in 1983 when the Alberta Court of Appeal, in a case involving the Southam-owned Edmonton Journal, ruled the special search powers unconstitutional and ordered a halt to the searches (*Winnipeg Free Press*, February 1, 1983: 15). Judicial skirmishes followed throughout the country until the charges were all thrown out in Toronto in late 1983—for lack of evidence (*The Toronto Star*, December 10, 1983: A3). The Supreme Court set its stamp of approval on the Alberta judgment in *Hunter* v. *Southam* in September 1984.

The constitutional question concerned a provision of the Act which allowed the Director of Investigation and Research, Hunter, to order searches of any premises where there "may" be evidence relevant to an inquiry. The only limitation was that he had to apply to a member of the Restrictive Trade Practices Commission for a certificate authorizing the search. The Supreme Court of Canada, like the Alberta Court of Appeal, was unanimous in its opinion that this power violated the Charter prohibition on "unreasonable search and seizure" (s. 8). The case announced many of what would be the familiar hallmarks of legalized politics. The Court said it would take "a broad perspective" in interpreting the Charter, which, like "a living tree capable of growth and expansion," should receive a "generous interpretation" (*Hunter*, 1984: 649–650). That a generous interpretation of the individual rights in the Charter meant a stingy approach to the individual and collective rights expressed by representative government seems not to have crossed the Court's unanimous mind. The powers of search failed the constitutional test because neither the Commissioners nor the Director were sufficiently independent of the investigatory duties under the *Act* to insure that authorization was given in "an entirely neutral and impartial manner." Naturally, only a judge or someone "at a minimum...capable of acting judicially" would do. That judges themselves are deeply implicated in the investigation and suppression of crime through their day-to-day activities (the same judges who try charges also issue warrants, grant and deny bail, and hand down sentences) does not seem to have troubled the Court at all. It was enough for them to invoke, once again, the common law and the *Criminal Code* rules based upon it: "At common law the power to issue a search warrant was reserved for a justice" (*Hunter*, 1984: 654). "The common law required evidence on oath which gave 'strong reason to believe'" and so did the *Criminal Code* and the American *Bill of Rights* (*Hunter*, 1984: 658). Our Charter could do no less.

So once again, to the question "What is fundamental?" the judicial answer was: "judicial authority authorized by judge-made law." In fact, this case was the first in the previously examined series of Supreme Court decisions to re-judicialize criminal procedure.[1] But there was one great difference between this case and the others. These common law and statutory rights, fashioned for legitimating the punishment of the "ordinary" criminality of economic marginality and social weakness, were to be applied by this decision to the criminality of economic and social power. The rules designed with the puny individual involved in street crime in mind were held constitutionally mandated to apply equally to the corporate power of executive suite crime. Justice was blind to Southam's assets of over one billion dollars and fifteen thousand employees (*The Globe and Mail Report on Business Magazine*, July, 1988: 94–95). As far as she was concerned, Southam needed as much protection as any kid charged with a minor theft. And how did the government respond? Canadian governments have always been less than enthusiastic about combines prosecutions (Goff and Reasons, 1978; Snider and West, 1985), and the government lawyers in this case do not seem to have put up much of a fight to save the legislation. If the Court is to be believed, the government argued for special powers (though not on the basis of the power of the criminals) but did not back their arguments up with anything. That seems to be the only way to explain these two otherwise contradictory passages:

> In their [the government's] submission combines offences require specialized techniques for their detection and suppression. They say that for such offences, as compared to most other criminal offences, there is inherently less basis for certainty and specificity, both as to the commission of an offence and as to the existence of specific physical evidence in relation to such offence (*Hunter*, 1984: 648).
>
> ...
>
> In the present case the appellants have made no submissions capable of supporting a claim that even if searches under s.10(10) and (3) are "unreasonable" within the meaning of s.8, they are nevertheless a reasonable limit, demonstrably justified in a free and democratic society, on the right as set out in s.8. It is therefore, not necessary in this case to consider the relationship between s.8 and s.1. I leave to another day the difficult question of the relationship between those two sections...(*Hunter*, 1984: 660).

---

[1] The special powers of search without judicial warrant granted by the *Narcotic Control Act* did not last long either (*Rao*, 1984, *Noble*, 1984). Once again there was no loss to law enforcement, as waiting in the wings was the telephone warrant system which was enacted by the very same law that repealed the provisions the courts had struck down: *Criminal Code*, s. 443.1; S.C. 1985, c.19, ss.70 and 200.

Taking the Court at its word, let us assume for the moment that the *Act*, the product of a century of intense debate and controversy about the limits, if any, on economic power, was of some social significance. Let us assume that the government was unprepared to defend this legislation, either because of the novelty of Charter litigation, incompetence, or lack of enthusiasm. Was it too much to ask of the Court, instead of just congratulating itself on avoiding a tough question, that it adjourn the hearing and tell the Crown to go back and do its homework? In fact, despite the enormous social costs of corporate concentration, nobody seems to have taken these powers all that seriously. The government had chickened out earlier the same year to carry out recommendations to place even mild controls on concentration in the newspaper industry (*Winnipeg Free Press*, April 3, 1984: 12). And it was happy to oblige everybody by amending the *Act* to require judicial authorization on "reasonable grounds" for the exercise of its coercive powers, including even those powers that had been held consistent with the Charter [1] (*Combines Investigation Act Amendment*, 1986, s. 24).

Hunter has had implications for the prosecution of business crime beyond the confines of the *Combines Investigation Act*. *The Income Tax Act* applies to working people as well as businesses, but the primary source of violation is businesses because of the difficulty for wage earners to cheat. Probably for this reason, Canadian governments and the courts have never taken violations that seriously. Prison sentences are rare, compared for example to *Unemployment Insurance Act* violations (Hasson, 1980; 1981). Like the *Combines Investigation Act*, the nature of income tax criminality has always been thought to require special powers. Like the *Combines Act*, these powers did not fare well under the Charter, once again for the lack of judicial supervision. And once again the government obliged with substantial amendments going even beyond what the courts had to that point required (*Income Tax Act Amendment*, 1986, s. 121; *Dzagic*, 1985; *F.K. Clayton Group Ltd.*, 1986; *Hatzinicoloau*, 1987; *Oldfield*, 1987). It was not the special powers that resulted in an $130,000 income tax evasion charge against a businessman being thrown out in the Supreme Court of Canada decision in *R. v. Rahey* (*Rahey*, 1987), but rather a failure to try him within a reasonable time. For eleven months the trial judge had inexplicably stalled his decision on a motion to dismiss the case. The Court split down the middle on the theoretical question of whether the accused's business interests should be taken into account in such a case, so it is not possible to say whether this illustrates an advantage for business under the Charter, though it is hard to imagine such a stall in an ordinary criminal case. [2]

A counterexample to the thesis I am developing here might be thought to be a respectable body of decisions below the level of the Supreme Court of Canada that have held the requirements in *Hunter* not to apply to "administra-

---

[1] Partly because of some judicial involvement in exercise of the power: *Thomson Newspapers Ltd.*, 1986; *Ziegler*, 1983.

[2] In fact, well placed accused persons seem to do exceptionally well with this provision of the Charter. A Saskatchewan medical doctor escaped a drug trafficking charge on this basis in *Misra*, 1986.

tive" searches and seizures in the context of business regulation. In *Belgoma Transportation Ltd.* (1985) and *Bertram S. Miller Ltd.* (1986), the requirements of judicial warrants were held not to apply to inspections of business premises. Decisions such as these suggest that courts are not as class blind as they seem, that they can indeed recognize the inappropriateness of applying the protections of the Charter to the socially strong as well as to the socially weak. Except that such decisions have not been based on social strength and weakness but on the *form of regulation*. And the form of regulation gives social power all it needs in the way of support from the criminal law. According to the courts, "true crimes" are subject to the full power of the Charter, while "regulatory offences" are not. But the distinction between true crimes and regulatory offences is completely ideological. It is not based on the harmfulness of the conduct but on the class of the criminals. The crimes characteristic of business (marketing, production and employment standards, occupational health and safety, pollution) are regulated with financial disincentives, even though they cost more in terms of lives and money than the "street crimes" of the working class and poor (Braithwaite, 1979; Glasbeek, 1984). Historically however, the most severe and intrusive punishments (death, imprisonment, probation supervision) have been reserved for the latter. Thus the distinction between types of crime is of great benefit to business. To recognize this distinction for constitutional purposes is only a small disadvantage, completely outweighed by the big advantage conferred by the distinction itself, indeed logically entailed by it. Furthermore, *Hunter* provides that when business crime is taken seriously by the legislature and treated as "true crime," it has to be given the same protections as other true crimes.[1] Not only does this give it the extra advantage due process confers on power, it also makes it more difficult to get serious about business crime. In order to treat business crime as it should be treated, the courts tell us that we have to give it the full protection of the Charter.

The Charter and Immigration

In *Hunter* v. *Southam* and its companion decisions, the egalitarianism of Justice's blindfold is seen to work in reverse. The Charter is invoked to share with the socially powerful the procedural guarantees that legitimate the punishment of the socially weak. It is in the nature of power and procedure that these guarantees can become major obstacles to the prosecution of upperworld crime while they are no more than a minor inconvenience in the prosecution of ordinary crime. However, there is one noteworthy example in Charter jurisprudence of procedural guarantees throwing up major obstacles to the repression of a group without social power. In *Re Singh and Minister of Employment and Immigration and 6 other appeals* (*Singh*, 1985), the Supreme Court of Canada threw the immigration system for a loop by deciding that the

---

[1] There are even cases where regulatory offences have been deemed "quasi-criminal" so as to attract for business the full protection of the *Hunter* treatment (*C.E. Jamieson & Co.*, 1987; *Ontario Chrysler*, 1987).

procedures then current for determining "Convention Refugee" status under the *Immigration Act* violated the fundamental principles of justice and section 7 of the Charter.

"Convention refugees" are so called because they are technically defined in the *Immigration Act* in accordance with the United Nations Convention Relating to the Status of Refugees (1951) as:

Any person who by reason of a well-founded fear of persecution for reasons of race, religion, nationality, membership in a particular social group or political opinion, is outside the country of his nationality [or habitual residence] and is unable or, by reason of such fear, is unwilling to avail himself of the protection of that country (*Singh*, 1985: 449; *Immigration Act, 1976*, s.2(1)).

At the time of *Singh*, the procedure for claiming refugee status was a complicated one. It started with an examination on oath before an immigration officer. The officer did not decide anything, however. Instead, the transcript of the examination was sent on to various levels of decision makers, ultimately the Immigration Appeal Board. The *Immigration Act* allowed the claim to be decided on this paper record and without telling the claimant what the government had against granting status. Though there were provisions for hearings, they were not mandatory and hearings were, in fact, rarely granted. Refugee status was treated as a "privilege" and not a "right." Even if granted, refugee status did not guarantee the right to stay in Canada, though it did mean the Minister could issue a discretionary permit to stay, and it protected the refugee from being deported to the country from which he or she had fled.

Like so many other Charter decisions, *Singh* was as much about the Charter as about refugees. The Court, though unanimous in result, split in half on the question of whether the Charter should be applied to the case at all. Three judges avoided the Charter like the plague and resuscitated the *Canadian Bill of Rights* for their decision. The other three judges were so anxious to use the Charter that they studiously avoided both the *Canadian Bill of Rights* and an easy solution on the common law duty of procedural fairness. In fact, they went out of their way to close the door on the judicial reticence of the *Canadian Bill of Rights* era, with its distinctions between rights and privileges:

It seems to me rather that the recent adoption of the Charter by Parliament and nine of the ten provinces as part of the Canadian constitutional framework has sent a clear message to the courts that the restrictive attitude which at times characterized their approach to the *Canadian Bill of Rights* ought to be reexamined (*Singh*, 1985: 462).

A key holding by the Charter judges (Justices Wilson, Dickson, and Lamer) was that the word "everyone" in s.7 of the Charter encompassed not only "every human being who is physically present in Canada" (*Singh*, 1985: 456) but also anyone "seeking admission at a port of entry" (*Singh*, 1985: 463). The *Canadian Bill of Rights* judges (Justices Beetz, Estey, and McIntyre) expressly refrained from saying whether they thought the Charter applied to refugees at all. It appears that even the applicability of the *Canadian Bill of Rights* to refugees was not actually decided by them, but rather conceded by the government (*Singh*, 1985: 430–432).

The main objection taken to the refugee process by the Charter judges was "the inadequacy of the opportunity the scheme provides for a refugee claimant to state his case and know the case he has to meet" (*Singh*, 1985: 465). But they also held that "where a serious issue of credibility is involved, fundamental justice requires that credibility be determined on the basis of an oral hearing" (*Singh*, 1985: 465). The *Canadian Bill of Rights* judges expressed themselves as strongly on this question: "nothing will pass muster short of at least one full oral hearing before adjudication on the merits" (*Singh*, 1985: 435).

For an issue that was to become a major political football of the Mulroney administration, the government's legal defence of the legislation seems to have been rather pathetic: "counsel devoted relatively little time" to the question, operating "under considerable time pressure" (*Singh*, 1985: 467). You get the impression that it was late and the cleaning staff wanted to sweep up and go home. Is this any way to make refugee policy? As with *Hunter*, the question is why the Court did not send counsel back to do his or her homework and prepare a proper brief. In fact, seven months after the hearing was over, it did occur to the judges to ask for further written submissions from counsel (*Singh*, 1985: 429), but these had nothing to do with demonstrating the justifiability of the law. They wanted to know what counsel thought about the possible applicability to the case of the *Canadian Bill of Rights*!

What the government did manage to say was that Canada's procedures were not out of line with the Commonwealth and Western Europe and that they had been approved by the United Nations. It was also submitted that the Immigration Appeal Board

> was already subjected to a considerable strain in terms of the volume of cases which it was required to hear and that a requirement of an oral hearing in every case where an application for redetermination of a refugee claim has been made would constitute an unreasonable burden on the board's resources (*Singh*, 1985: 468).

Justice Wilson, in an opinion redolent of orthodox Dworkinian judicial review theory, made a strong pitch against the idea that cost might ever be a good argument against fundamental fairness:

> I have considerable doubt that the type of utilitarian consideration brought forward by Mr. Bowie can constitute a justification for a limitation on the rights set out in the Charter. Certainly the guarantees of the Charter would be illusory if they could be ignored because it was administratively convenient to do so. No doubt considerable time and money can be saved by adopting administrative procedures which ignore the principles of fundamental justice but such an argument, in my view misses the point of the exercise under s.1. The principles of natural justice and procedural fairness which have long been espoused by our courts, and the constitutional entrenchment of the principles of fundamental justice in s.7, implicitly recognize that a balance of administrative convenience does not override the need to adhere to these principles (*Singh*, 1985: 469).

Wilson could point to a number of critics who had argued for full hearings in refugee cases but had been ignored by the government. In effect, she accepted their recommendations on behalf of the government. Hearings would have to take place in all cases. The seven cases before the Court were sent on for hearings before the Immigration Appeal Board—but because of what ensued after *Singh*, due in part to *Singh* itself, it is very unlikely that those hearings were ever held.

Naturally, the decision was praised by immigration lawyers. It "reaffirms the importance and the power of the Charter." It would greatly enhance the chances of claimants: "When you can sit there and watch the individual wringing their hands and breaking down,...these things only come through in an oral hearing." But not everyone was this enthusiastic. Some lawyers complained that it had taken a court decision to do what the government had been told for years had to be done. They said that the absence of hearings was only one of the injustices of the system. Worse yet were the detention conditions for refugees and, most importantly, the visa system whereby visitors from selected countries were not allowed to board the plane without a visa, so that refugees never even made it to Canada. Would more court action be necessary to address these issues? One lawyer claimed that the federal government had embarked on a "systematic attempt to stop all refugee flows" by imposing strict visa requirements. "Every time a country produces a flow of refugees, Canada shuts the door." He added—prophetically—that you could have "the greatest refugee system in the world, but if nobody can come to Canada, it's not really worth much" (*The Globe and Mail*, April 5, 1985: 5). This was echoed in a law journal article on *Singh*:

> Will the Immigration Department tighten its screening process of prospective visitors to Canada as well, to prevent these same visitors from taking advantage of their new found Charter rights once on Canadian territory? If so the *Singh* decision may have produced an undesired side effect—while extending the rights of applicants for refugee status who are already in Canada, it may indirectly render more difficult the possibility of entering the country in the first place! (Neudorfer, 1986: 23)

It was not long before the full implications of *Singh* began to be known. First, what Justice Wilson had contemptuously dismissed as mere "administrative inconvenience" turned out to be an immense bureaucratic knot that would take millions of dollars and years of labour to untie. There was already an accumulated backlog of 13,000 refugee claims waiting to be reviewed. Their paper reviews would now have to be oral hearings. Added to this were an estimated 7000 unexecuted deportation orders now challengeable because of *Singh*. More importantly, *every new applicant* would have to get a hearing. It was estimated that the extra work imposed by *Singh* on the backlog of 20,000 cases would alone cost $50 million and would take ten years to clear (*The Globe and Mail*, May 22, 1985: 3). But even these estimates assumed a *constant* flow of refugee claims. In fact, the flow was increasing almost exponentially. The 500 a month in 1984 became 600 after *Singh* was decided in April 1985, and 700 by September. By early 1987, this became *4000* per month (*The*

Globe and Mail, February 21, 1987: A2; February 25, 1987: A4). What was causing it all? Most of the reasons were international. International wars, civil wars, official repression, and the increasingly chaotic world economy had caused a refugee explosion that was increasing annually by leaps and bounds. World refugee totals reached 11.7 million in 1986 and rose to 13.3 million in 1987 (*The Globe and Mail*, April 5, 1988: A1). In addition to this, and because of it, Western Europe had begun closing its doors to refugees, and Canada was getting the spillover. But there is no doubt that *Singh* itself was also a contributing factor. It had so clogged the refugee system that simply by declaring oneself a refugee, with no hope of coming within the strict criteria, bought three to five years of time in Canada. Moreover, since it quickly became clear that the only way out of the mess was some sort of amnesty, this was a further inducement to what would otherwise be hopeless claims. That it was *Singh* and not merely international developments causing the new claims (if not the presence of the claimants) was attested to by the great number of claims made from within the country (*The Globe and Mail*, May 25, 1985: 1–2; April 5, 1986: A15; May 28, 1985: M1, M6; Sept 12, 1985: 1).

The expected amnesty came in May 1986. Regulations allowed most of those who had claimed refugee status to date to skip the refugee process entirely and get preferred treatment for "landed immigrant" status (the right to stay in the country). (*Regulations Respecting the Refugee Claims Backlog* SOR/86–701). This meant that about 15,000 of the 21,500 backlog applicants would be allowed to stay, regardless of the validity of their claims. The move was denounced in a *Globe and Mail* editorial of June 13, 1986 (A6):

> Some of these applicants were brought forward by immigration counsellors after the Supreme Court ruled that all refugee claimants on Canadian soil had a right to an oral hearing. By flooding a fair system, the phony applicants wagered they could avoid any system at all. And they proved substantially right...It is a scandal that, in a world awash in desperate and oppressed people, Canada's limited ability to accommodate refugees should be compromised by relatively secure foreigners and their greedy Canadian agents. Conspicuous abuse of the refugee system will eventually threaten the basis of the system itself—Canadians' faith that this country is actually helping people in special need.

But the amnesty was just an attempt to clear the decks for a series of measures designed at once to introduce due process into the refugee system, streamline it, and, most importantly, as predicted, *to limit access to it.* Bill C–55, introduced in May 1986, respected the procedural rights of claimants to the fullest and then set about trying to reduce their numbers to the bare minimum. Claimants would have to make their claims at the outset of an immigration inquiry or forever be denied eligibility to make them later. The grounds for denial were greatly expanded. Claimants were not eligible for status if they came from designated "safe countries," if they had a criminal record and had been certified by the Minister as "a danger to the public in Canada," or if they had refugee status in another country. Even if eligible, they were to be denied status unless there was "a credible basis for the claim" (as opposed to the previous more lenient rubric which excluded only claims that were "manifestly unfounded"). In considering the credibility of a claim the adjudicators were to consider the human rights record of the country and the success record of refugee applications from it.

In compensation for these new substantive limitations the claimants were given all sorts of procedural rights. It was only in March that the Immigration Appeal Board had been expanded from 18 to 50 members to handle the new requirements of *Singh*. Bill C–55 created a new "Immigration and Refugee Board" with 95 full time members, 65 of whom comprised a separate "Convention Refugee Determination Division" to deal solely with refugee hearings. Plenty of work for lawyers here. The Deputy Chair and a majority of the seven Assistant Deputy Chairs as well as a *minimum* ten percent of the permanent members had to be members of the Bar. Each refugee claimant had the right to a full hearing before a member of the Division and another adjudicator from the Immigration Department. They would determine whether the claimant was eligible for a further hearing. Before them the claimant would be entitled to a full hearing with due process, what the government took to calling a "quality oral hearing," including "a reasonable opportunity to present evidence, cross-examine witnesses and make representations" with the decision to be based "on evidence adduced at the inquiry or hearing" and the right to counsel (of one's own choice at one's own expense, or appointed counsel at the government's expense). Only one favourable vote on eligibility and credibility would be necessary to send it along for a full hearing on the merits before a minimum of two members of the Refugee Division. At that hearing, there would be the right to counsel and a decision on evidence adduced at the proceedings or within the specialized knowledge of the tribunal, so long as each side was afforded "a reasonable opportunity to make representations with respect thereto." The claimant would have a right to be present, to "present evidence, cross-examine witnesses and make representations." In the case of an even split, the tie would go to the applicant. An appeal would lie to the Federal Court of Appeal on procedural grounds, an error of law, or a "perverse or capricious finding of fact," except where the Refugee Division had found that there was "no credible basis for the claim."

Despite all the due process, a storm of protest greeted the Bill. Critics immediately objected to the pre-screening process and to the limits on appeals to the courts. Naturally these restrictions were said to be contrary to the Charter (*The Globe and Mail*, May 26, 1986: A13; Green, 1986). But tighter restrictions were yet to come. In November 1986, the US government made things very difficult for Central American refugees, and this greatly increased the flow to Canada. Again the government moved to cut off access to the system that had been judicially redesigned by *Singh*. In February 1987, citing more than 6000 new claimants in the first six weeks of 1987, half due to tightened US rules, they instituted a practice of sending claimants from the US back across the border to wait for their hearings. They imposed transit visa requirements on 98 countries (including 18 of those on the former, now abolished, B–1 list of countries to which people could not be deported, e.g. the US-installed dictatorship of Chile) to prevent claimants from getting on the plane to Canada in the first place (the airlines would be responsible if they did). Those passing through Canada would be kept in lounges and not allowed to make claims. In one incident, 106 Chileans were stranded in Argentina while their families went on a hunger strike in Montreal. Naturally these moves were protested, and added fuel to the opposition to Bill C–55, especially the "safe country" idea. Critics argued that sending Central Americans to the United States would mean their eventual deportation back to Central America (Bennet, 1987: 10–11; Pope, 1987: 9. *The Globe and Mail*, February 21, 1987: A2; February 25, 1987: A4; May 6, 1987: A13).

Anti-refugee feeling (as measured by radio phone-ins and informal polls: *The Globe and Mail* March 6, 1987: A1) had been fuelled by a number of dramatic illegal entries by manifestly false refugee claimants. In the summer of 1986, 155 Tamils from Sri Lanka were found adrift in lifeboats off the coast of Newfoundland. They claimed to have journeyed from India but in fact they had come from a refugee camp in West Germany and had been dropped off in Canadian waters by an entrepreneurial sea captain for a hefty fee. History repeated itself the following summer when, on July 12, 1987, another boatload arrived, this time of 174 East Indians. That was all the government needed. Less than a month later Parliament was called into an emergency summer session to introduce Bill C–84, the toughest *titled* legislation we have seen in a long time: the "Deterrents and Detention Act." It bristled with powers and penalties. One section empowered the Minister to turn away ships at sea by force if he or she "believes on reasonable grounds" that they are bringing in anyone in contravention of the Act. Another made it an offence to help anyone get into Canada who was not in possession of proper travel documents (whether or not they were a legitimate refugee). Maximum penalties for violations went up to $500,000 and ten years in prison. Vehicles used would be forfeited. Transportation companies were ordered to ensure passengers had valid documents or be fined up to $5,000 each. Extensive powers of (judicially authorized) entry, search and seizure were given immigration officers to enforce the Act. An only partially reviewable power was given the Minister to designate security threats and deport them, refugee or not. In defence of all this, officials argued that refugee claimants had by then reached 2,000 a month, even with the new visa restrictions, that constitutional rights of claimants had made drastic measures necessary to reduce those numbers, and that stopping ships at sea was the only way to avoid having to give the occupants full hearings (*The Globe and Mail*, August 12, 1987: A1, A5).

Opposition to this Bill, joined to the opposition to C–55, was unrelenting. The Bill was attacked as targeting good Samaritans and religious groups who vowed to continue helping those they believed to be genuine refugees whether or not they had the right documents. The safe country provisions were attacked by, among others, Amnesty International's refugee spokesman and the UN High Commissioner for Refugees, as endangering the lives of real refugees by politicizing the process. Canada might be reluctant to offend countries with which it had dealings, whatever their records, by not placing them on the list (*The Globe and Mail*, August 13, 1987: A7; *The Toronto Star*, August 15,

1987, A1). A new coalition of religious, labour, women's, and ethnic groups, the "Committee for an Alternative Refugee Determination Process," called for an expensive system of expedited hearings which would guarantee claimants a hearing within ten days to be held before two members of the Board (instead of the Bill's system of one member and one government employed adjudicator), review within 30 days if the claim was rejected, and removal from the country, pending appeal, only of "manifestly unfounded" claims (*The Globe and Mail*, Sept. 1, 1987: A3).

Naturally the Charter was an important *leitmotif* in the attack on the Bill. The law was correctly seen as an attempt to counteract *Singh* (Pope, 1987; *Montreal Gazette*, August 26, 1987: B1; *The Globe and Mail*, August 26, 1987: A5), but a game of Charter checkers then ensued. Legal experts lined up to predict the certain demise of the legislation before the courts. It would be "gutted by the courts," said one (*The Globe and Mail*, August 18, 1987: A3). The law "will surely be struck down by the Supreme Court of Canada," said another (*The Toronto Star*, October 3, 1987: A1). The Tories were said to be trying to profit from an anti-refugee backlash with a Bill they "knew" was unconstitutional and were challenged to refer it to the Supreme Court. The Minister refused, arguing that the Court might take too long and the Bill was urgent (*Montreal Gazette*, August 26, 1987: B1). Critics turned to provincial premiers for a court referral, but there were no takers (*The Globe and Mail*, August 29, 1987: A13; October 28, 1987: A11). Their last-ditch effort was the Senate, but the government argued that the Senate should not worry about Charter violations: "If this Bill is really legally inadequate, then the courts will tell us so. That is their job." (*The Globe and Mail*, January 29, 1988: A3).

The government's Charter counterattack included the public relations masterstroke of appointing Canada's highest profile human rights bureaucrat to the Chair of the new Immigration and Refugee Board. Former Tory MP Gordon Fairweather was fresh from his ten-year term as the first Canadian Human Rights Commissioner when he accepted the new post (*The Globe and Mail*, October 29, 1987: A1). His appointment was accompanied by a compromise on the question of turning back ships. This was the only major change conceded by the government: a six month sunset law on the power after the new law went into effect. To the disappointment of critics, the Senate agreed to the Bills in July 1988, and the new law was scheduled to go into effect January 1, 1989 (*The Globe and Mail*, July 13, 1988: A1). The Canadian Council of Churches immediately announced its intention to challenge the constitutionality of the law (*The Toronto Star*, July 23, 1988: A10). "This thing is going to be ensnarled in legal challenges for years," said immigration lawyer David Matas (*The Globe and Mail*, June 8, 1988: A8).

By the time the Bills were passed, the backlog had reached 52,000 and would continue to grow at thousands a month until the new law was in place (*The Toronto Star*, July 23, 1988: A10). This had been added to by a short-lived judicial wrench in the works when a Federal Court Trial Judge declared all Immigration Appeal Board members suffered from an "apprehension of bias" because their jobs would all come up for review when the new Bill C–55 came into effect (*The Globe and Mail*, March 10, 1988: A1). The IAB did not resign, but it granted adjournments to anyone claiming this bias (*The Globe and Mail*, March 11, 1988: A4). It was not long before all lawyers were making the claim, and the board was "all but paralyzed" within weeks (*The Globe and Mail*, March 31, 1988: A13). The decision was overruled, but in the meantime another three months of claimants had been added to the backlog (*The Globe and Mail*, June 22, 1988: A4). The system ground to a complete halt in September, when the Immigration Department just stopped processing claims. It had collapsed under the weight of an avalanche of false claims brought forth by the expected amnesty. The backlog had reached 59,000, and claims were coming in at a rate of 3,000 per month, with immigration "consultants" making $1,000 per claimant (*The Globe and Mail*, September 10, 1988: A1; September 15, 1988: A24).[1]

So much for Justice Wilson's "administrative inconvenience."

What have the procedural rights bestowed by *Singh* meant to would-be immigrants to Canada? Here was a decision whose immediate beneficiaries were people without social power. Genuine refugee applicants are by definition oppressed. Even so-called "false claimants"—false because they do not fall within the strict refugee definition—tend to come from the economic margins of immigrant groups. There is no dispute that most false claimants are "economic refugees." Before the Senate, Canada's Minister of State for Immigration called the refugee crisis "an assault on a worldwide scale by those desperate for a better life and greater economic opportunity," invoking "the slums of Cairo and Manila and the barrios of Mexico City and Sao Paulo" (*The Globe and Mail*, January 29, 1988: A3). But the Minister neglected to point out that poverty is only part of the reason these people are forced to claim refugee status. The other is the bias of the ordinary immigration process. From all the talk of "queue jumping" and the *Globe and Mail*'s self-righteous editorials you would think we had a first-come-first-served system limited only by our own resources. In fact, the immigration process is no more democratic than the marketplace. It is subordinated to Canada's social and economic priorities so that those who are economically advantaged, either by their education, occupation, or, even better, by surplus money to invest, get priority over "economic refugees." A "point system," which gives extra points for education, favours immigrants from developed countries, and the location of visa offices (11 in the United States, three in the United Kingdom, two in France, and one each for all of Africa and India) does the same thing (*The Globe and Mail*, August 28, 1988: A5). Most notorious of all is the "entrepreneur program," instituted in 1979, under which foreign businesspeople are given preferential admission if they prove they have $500,000 in assets and promise to invest $250,000 in Canada over three years (*The Globe and Mail*, March 25, 1988: A8). The government granted 3600 visas and 2,300 permanent residencies under this program in 1987. So anxious is the government to

---

[1] As we go to press on the eve of the new law coming into force, the official backlog is 85,000 claimants (*The Globe and Mail*, December 29, 1988: A1).

attract this kind of immigrant that it is reported to be considering guaranteeing the immigrants' investments for them. Nor, it seems, has the government been checking very closely into whether immigrants actually settle here before granting them permanent resident status. In effect, this means the government has been selling citizenship to the Hong Kong business community as insurance against the Chinese takeover in 1997 (*The Globe and Mail*, July 4, 1988: A2; July 5, 1988: A3).

Canada's immigration policy is also subordinated to our foreign policy, or more correctly, to that of our main trading partner, so that the relatively privileged escapees from socialist regimes or recent revolutions against US dependency get the red carpet, while the underprivileged escapees from the poverty and repression of the United States' allies have to go to the back of the queue (Hathaway, 1988; *The Toronto Star*, July 11, 1988: A11). The crucial difference between the two systems of entry, from the government's point of view is *control*. Ordinary immigration is within government control and can be subordinated to economic interest and foreign policy, but convention refugees are defined without reference to economic circumstances or politics:

> Many bogus claimants may turn out to be good citizens, but their abuse of the system robs the country of control over its immigration policy (*The Globe and Mail*, February 20, 1988: D6; editorial).

That is why there is no contradiction between the government's expressed desire to increase immigration and the attempts to limit access to the refugee system. The problem with *Singh* was that it tended, via the backlog, to shift entry from the ordinary (controlled) immigration process to the (uncontrolled) refugee system.

All this suggests that we should chalk one up for the Charter. To the extent, and it seems to have been considerable, that the insistence of the Supreme Court of Canada on procedural rights for applicants contributed to clogging up the system, it has undoubtedly resulted in many severely disadvantaged persons being allowed to stay who would otherwise have been deported. There is also no question that this is the quite laudable objective of at least some of those who are going to try to keep the new laws "ensnarled in legal challenges for years." Clogging up the system may not be a very sporting way to help out refugee applicants. But given the seriousness of what it means to be a refugee applicant, the only question worth worrying about is whether it works.

In the first place, the benefits of *Singh* are entirely temporary. Remember that all gains in access to Canada have come not from actually *granting* hearings but from the *inability* to grant them. Only because the Court sprang the requirement on the government when it was not ready for it was there an unambiguous gain for applicants. The hearings could not be granted, so amnesty had to be. Once the new hearing process is in place, there is no reason to believe that more generosity will prevail than did in the absence of hearings. The criminal process is full of oral hearings and that has not prevented it from producing enough guilty verdicts to fill our prisons to overflowing. It sounds plausible that some claimants can be more persuasive in person than on paper, but the opposite is also true. Other things being equal, a system of oral hearings is unlikely to be more compliant than a system of paper reviews. But other things are not equal. Along with the hearings has come a determination to limit access to the system and a tightening up of the criteria intended to make it more difficult for claimants to succeed even when they have gained access. The government expects the measures it is taking to reduce the number of claimants dramatically—the official figures suggest a reduction of about one third in the first year—and to expeditiously reject about 60% of the rest (*The Globe and Mail*, June 14, 1988: A8). This means successful refugee claimants would be reduced to about one-quarter of current levels. Critics are arguing that it will be much worse. The same Toronto lawyer who said the *Singh* case "reaffirms the power of the Charter" in 1985 (Lorne Waldman, who heads up a group called "Fair Action for Immigrants and Refugees") has said that the eligibility provisions of the new law will reduce current applications by at least ninety percent and might choke them off altogether (*The Globe and Mail*, June 10, 1987: A3; *The Toronto Star*, October 3, 1987: A16). Not only are the criteria less generous than they were prior to *Singh*, but they have also been politicized by such measures as the visa requirements and the "safe country" rule, which allow the government to mesh its refugee policy with its immigration policy. The upshot is that, in quantitative terms, the reaction to *Singh* will wipe out at least some of its benefits, and there might even be a net loss over the long run. In qualitative terms, it seems inevitable that the new restrictive rules will mean many genuine refugees will fail to get into Canada. In effect, they will be paying for the gains of *Singh*.

The problem with *Singh* is *not* that it required hearings for refugee applicants, but the fact that this requirement existed, not "in the air," but in the concrete context of a political determination to keep all forms of immigration subordinated to local and international power relations. In this social context, the purely formal right to a hearing could only *legitimate* a refugee policy that is the farthest thing from humanitarianism. In this respect, *Singh* is exactly like the decisions on criminal procedure. It looks fine when it is detached from its context. The problem is that it cannot be detached from its context. If the hearing right had come out of a political determination to do better by refugee applicants, we might have had some reason for optimism. But as an irksome requirement imposed from above, we know that it is doomed. Then it becomes merely the condition upon which the courts will put their stamp of approval on government policy. And the government has understood that if only it dresses things up in the formal requirements of due process and fundamental justice, it can get away with whatever it wants in the way of refugee policy.

The refugee crisis was certainly not caused by *Singh*. And its real contribution to it may have been small—though the smaller it was, the less it can be credited with helping people get into the country. *Singh* dictated the *form* of our response. *There shall be hearings.* But this form could in no way contradict the substance: not more but rather less generosity in granting refugees admission to the country. The right to a hearing turned out to be no more than a consolation prize for our stinginess, and even then, the only certain winners were the members of the legal profession. Thus we may look upon the entire refugee episode as another example of the inability of the formal guarantees of the Charter to tilt the balance of social power in favour of those without it and of their tendency to do just the opposite.

CHAPTER V

The Class Struggle Goes to Court: Labour, Business, and the Charter

"Asleep at the Switch"

I want to say that when completed in a just form, I would like this resolution, particularly the Charter of Rights and Freedoms, to hang on the wall of every classroom in every school in every region of Canada (*House of Commons Debates*, November 20, 1981: 13055).

This was not Pierre Trudeau or Jean Chrétien speaking. It was Ed Broadbent, Leader of the New Democratic Party, organized labour's official representative in Parliament. As the passage implies, Broadbent wanted several changes made before he thought that the Charter would be "completed in a just form." But the changes he wanted had nothing to do with labour; they were, instead, issues concerning Native peoples and women. Broadbent basically got what he wanted on these points,[1] and his party was all but unanimous in its support for the final resolution. The NDP, as we have seen, had been Trudeau's most constant ally from the start of the Charter enterprise. Of course, this meant that the NDP had to abandon the Quebec labour movement, which was solidly behind the PQ initiatives that the Charter was designed to trump. But the NDP had never been very sympathetic to Quebec nationalism no matter how strongly rooted in the Quebec working class.[2]

What is odd, however, is that the NDP did not see the Charter debate as an opportunity to advance or even to defend the interests of its most important constituency. Doubly odd, since the period of the enactment of the Charter coincided with the most concerted assault on the collective bargaining system since it had been put in place during the Second World War (Panitch and Swartz, 1988). The first general postwar wage controls and banning of strikes were passed in 1975. The right to strike in the public sector, won only in the late sixties, became virtually a dead letter in the late seventies through the increasing use of back-to-work legislation. Total ad hoc abrogations of the right to strike grew from five in the decade 1955–1964, to 26 during 1965–74, to 47 during 1975–84 (Panitch and Swartz, 1988: 31). The recession of 1981–

---

[1] No override for the women's clause and the restoration of the aboriginal rights clause. These issues are fully discussed in Chapter VI.

[2] It is true that the PQ increasingly turned on its labour supporters from mid-1982 onwards (Panitch and Swartz, 1988: 39), but the NDP's antipathy had nothing to do with that. It was hostile to the nationalist/independentist enterprise from the start (Milner and Milner, 1973: 171–173).

82 provoked wage controls and a complete ban on strikes in the federal public sector. This was followed in 1982–83 by provincial restrictions on collective bargaining rights, of both an ad hoc and permanent nature (Panitch and Swartz, 1988: 35–46). Nor, as I tried to show in Chapter II, should the convergence of the Charter and the attack on labour be regarded as accidental. It makes more sense to see them as related expressions of a social system in economic and political decline, forced to rely increasingly both on repression and on abstract forms of legitimation. We saw a special case of this in Chapter IV in the intimate relationship between expanded repression and procedural legitimation. But the whole idea of the Charter can be seen as a legitimation of the basic inequalities of Canadian society, of which the subordination of labour to business is one of the most basic.

Labour, in other words, was very much a central player in the whole Charter enterprise, but it was the mission of the Charter to disguise this fact. Looking at the attitude of organized labour and its official representatives, the Charter seems to have done a good job of it, at least at the outset. Issues of class and socialism hardly surfaced during the Charter debate. About the closest the NDP came was this rather faint plea on behalf of the "hungry" and the "ailing" by Ian Waddell:

> This is not the kind of Charter that we, as socialists, believe in, Mr. Speaker. We believe that the hungry must be fed; the ailing must be helped; the old must be looked after and the young must be allowed to go as far as possible in school. These ideals are almost universally accepted. They belong in a twentieth century constitution but what we have here is a nineteenth century charter (*House of Commons Debates*, Nov. 27, 1981: 13428–29).

Not only does this plea have as much of the ring of the nineteenth century as the Charter itself, Waddell was ready to drop it for reasons that made absolutely no sense in the context of massive opposition to the Charter in Quebec and among Canada's aboriginal peoples:

> The reason that I will vote for this package is that it embodies, not in a perfect way but in a general way, the picture that I have of Canada. I see Canada as two founding societies, the English and the French, built on the foundation of the aboriginal people (*House of Commons Debates*, November 27, 1981: 13428–29).

As we saw in Chapter II, the only NDP member ultimately to vote against the Charter (Svend Robinson), did not do so because it was not socialist enough but because it contained an override clause (*House of Commons Debates*, December 2, 1981: 13663). That labour thought there was nothing either to fear or to hope for from the Charter is underlined by the fact that, unlike business, neither the Canadian Labour Congress nor any other labour body showed up at the Joint Committee hearings on the Charter. They did not even submit a brief.[1]

Triply odd, in fact, in that labour's experience with the judiciary had been

---

[1] According to Panitch and Swartz, the CLC stayed home because it was caught between NDP support for the Charter and Quebec Federation of Labour opposition to it (Panitch and Swartz, 1988: 102).

uniformly bad. When Ontario Federation of Labour President Gord Wilson said in response to a judicial setback, "The courts have seldom been the worker's friend" (*The Globe and Mail*, July 8, 1986: A3), he was expressing the conventional wisdom of the labour movement, gained over centuries of confrontation with the courts. A popular labour cartoon has a bewigged judge popping up from home plate at a baseball game just as the umpire yells "strike!" to yell back "injunction!" As we saw in Chapter I, the federal government's worker relief legislation of the 1930s was judicially invalidated on the grounds that it infringed upon provincial jurisdiction. Then, in 1976, the Supreme Court of Canada ignored these precedents and upheld the *Anti-Inflation Act*, supported by business and opposed by unions for its tendency to hold down wages without holding down prices (*Re Anti-Inflation Act*, 1976; *The Globe and Mail*, May 18, 1979: B1). Where the thirty percent unemployment of the Depression had not qualified as an "emergency," the comparatively harmless double-digit inflation of 1975 did![1] In more distant history, when labour relations were governed substantially by judge-made common law, unions were persecuted by the courts and denied all legal legitimacy. Trade union organizing, collective bargaining, striking, and picketing, all constituted criminal and civil conspiracies, apart altogether from the repressive legislation which prevailed until the early nineteenth century. When governments were finally forced to tolerate unions at the end of the nineteenth century, these activities all required specific legislation to overcome the common law precedents (Carrothers et al., 1986: 11–30; *Bhindi*, 1986).

What all this adds up to is that labour and the NDP either accepted or were willing to take a chance on the central deceptions of the Charter project, namely that the Charter—leaving aside Quebec, which they seemed willing enough to do—had nothing to do with power, either social power or judicial power, that it was a non-partisan document unambiguously advancing human rights, and that the judicial factor was either non-existent or negligible. It took about five years for labour to get an inkling of the mistake they had made. Five years after the enactment of the Charter, the labour movement was reeling from judicial assaults against it. Union lawyers were lamenting that they had been "asleep at the switch" during the Charter debate and were issuing dire warnings: "If these cases are not taken seriously, we are going to be right back in the 1930s in terms of what rights labour has in this country" (*The Globe and Mail*, March 30, 1987: A13). How could this have happened?

The Right to Strike

Freedom of Association at the Charter Hearings

If labour was "asleep at the switch" when the Charter was enacted, it woke up in time to catch the bandwagon, with Charter challenges to the spate of

---

[1] Hogg says the earlier cases must now be considered "wrongly decided" (Hogg, 1985: 395) which is polite constitutional law talk for a situation where a court contradicts itself with no legal excuse.

anti-union legislation that followed hard on the Charter's heels. As between labour and business, labour was in fact "first off the mark" in the Charter sweepstakes (Fudge, 1988a: 3). Wage controls in the federal public sector, coupled with prohibitions on strikes, appeared in the summer of 1982, with the Queen's signature on the Charter barely dry. By 1983, all of the provinces except Manitoba and New Brunswick had them in place (Black, 1988; Panitch and Swartz, 1988: 35–40). No mass protests of the sort that had greeted the *Anti-Inflation Act* of 1976 were organized this time, however. Instead, labour went straight to court, clutching the Charter and claiming that it protected the "right to strike."

This, too, was strange, given what had transpired at the Charter hearings of 1981. Labour obviously could not have argued for a right to strike if it did not appear. But more than simple neglect had occurred—in fact, what amounted to an explicit concession by the NDP that the right to strike was *not* in the Charter. On January 21, 1981, Svend Robinson, one of the NDP's most radical members and certainly its staunchest Charter advocate, moved an amendment to the freedom of association clause so that it would read "freedom of association including the freedom to organize and bargain collectively." This is what happened next:

MR. ROBINSON:....So, Mr. Chairman, this right—this fundamental right—which I would submit is included within the concept of freedom of association, should be made explicit, because we are talking about the values of Canadian society and this must be surely recognized as one of the most fundamental values of Canadian society.

I hasten to point out that this does not go so far as to entrench in the constitution the right to strike as such.

What we are talking about is the right of working men and women to organize and come together collectively and to bargain collectively.

The question of the right to strike is quite deliberately, frankly, not dealt with in this proposed amendment, because we are dealing with the fundamental incidents of freedom of association (Canada, 1980–81, Issue No. 43: 69; emphasis added).

In the ensuing debate it was made abundantly clear that none of the members thought the Charter had anything to do with the right to strike:

MR. EPP: I would like the Minister to give us the government's position on whether or not it [the amendment] would affect the right to strike.

...

MR. KAPLAN: Our position on the suggestion that there be specific reference to freedom to organize and bargain collectively is that that is already covered in the freedom of association that is provided already in the Declaration or in the Charter; and that by singling out association for bargaining one might tend to diminish all the other forms of association which are contemplated—church associations; associations of fraternal organizations or community organizations.

...

We agree with Mr. Robinson, however, that the right to strike would not necessarily be affected by the inclusion of this new expression which is being proposed by the New Democratic Party.

...

I doubt if back to work legislation could be affected by the Charter, or that the right to strike legislation could be affected by the Charter (Canada, 1980–81, Issue No. 43: 69–77).

As for the proposed amendment itself:

> MR. McGRATH: I do not recall any group coming before the Committee advocating this particular amendment. I do not recall any labour group or any labour-oriented group.

To this, Robinson was only able to cite the presentation of the United Church of Canada, which had urged the inclusion of "the right of workers to join unions and to take collective economic action" (Canada, 1980–81, Issue No. 29: 81). The proposed amendment was defeated 20–2, with the two NDP members dissenting (Svend Robinson and Lorne Nystrom).

Nevertheless "freedom of association" was the banner under which unions from coast to coast challenged the 1982–83 restrictions on the right to strike. The courts were almost completely hostile: either "freedom of association" did not include the right to strike (*Public Service Alliance of Canada*, 1984) or the restrictions on it were "demonstrably justified" (*Broadway Manor*, 1983). In only one case was there an outright victory (*Retail, Wholesale & Department Store Union*, 1985), but it was in every sense a pyrrhic one. The Saskatchewan Court of Appeal held by a 2–1 majority that "freedom of association" included the right to strike, and it declared unconstitutional a law ordering striking Saskatchewan dairy workers back to work. But the question of whether the law might be justified as a "reasonable limit" under section 1 was never even addressed because the majority felt the evidence (newspaper clippings) not of the proper sort. Furthermore, one of the judges justified his admittedly expansive reading of the Charter on the availability of section 33. Charter rights should be interpreted not only "generously" but actually:

> without excessive concern for where this liberal construction may lead in the light of the power of the legislative branch to limit their exercise under s.1, or, for that matter, to temporarily suspend them for up to five years under s.33. These powers, often referred to in the literature of the Charter as the "double-override," afford the legislative branch extensive authority to restrict the exercise of the rights and freedoms in issue, a fact which I think has a place in determining the scope of those rights and freedoms (Justice Cameron in *Retail, Wholesale & Department Store Union*, 1985: 638–639).

The government of Saskatchewan seems to have taken this as nothing less than an invitation to invoke section 33 the next time it enacted back-to-work legislation (*Saskatchewan Government Employees Union Dispute Settlement Act*, 1986). The union inevitably raised the stakes by challenging the use of section 33 in court, but before any more damage could be done[1] the Supreme Court put the matter to rest in April of 1987, by issuing its ruling on the right to strike.

The Supreme Court and the Right to Strike

The ruling involved three separate appeals: (1) *Government of Saskatchewan* v. *Retail, Wholesale and Department Store Union* (*Retail, Wholesale & Department Store Union*, 1987), the Saskatchewan dairy workers case, (2) *Public Service Alliance of Canada* v. *The Queen* (*Public Service Alliance of Canada*, 1987), the challenge to federal public sector wage control legislation, and (3) *Re Public Service Employee Relations Act (Alberta)* (1987), a reference by the Alberta government on various restrictions on collective bargaining in the Alberta public service, substituting limited compulsory arbitration for the right to strike in the case of public service employees, fire fighters, hospital employees, and police officers. The threshold issue in each case was the constitutional status of collective bargaining in general and the right to strike in particular. Was it protected by the words "freedom of association"? On this, the Court split four judges to two *against* the right to strike, but the judgment was more complicated than that indicates. There were actually three positions and four opinions.

Of the two opinions rejecting the constitutional status of the right to strike, the one which most vindicated the distrustful attitude of unions towards courts was that of Justice McIntyre. In it we find an ideology of extreme individualism surpassing even that of Judge Deschênes in the language of education case, *Quebec Protestant School Boards* (1982). In *Quebec Protestant School Boards*, Deschênes had lashed out against the PQ for arguing that linguistic rights should be regarded as collective and that, therefore, it should be possible to curtail individual rights in the interests of the group. In the right to strike cases, Justice McIntyre held that "freedom of association" was actually an *individual* right! It protected only those activities done in association that were protected or lawful when done individually. Anything that could *only* be done in association was not protected by the Charter. McIntyre's argument was a long and rambling one, but at its heart was a general view of the Charter as a document about individual rights:

> While some provisions in the Constitution involve groups, such as s.93 of the *Constitution Act, 1867* protecting denominational schools, and s.25 of the Charter referring to existing aboriginal rights, the remaining rights and freedoms are individual rights; they are not concerned with the group as distinct from its members. The group or organization is simply a device adopted by individuals to achieve a fuller realization of individual rights and aspirations. People, by merely combining together, cannot create an entity which has greater constitutional rights and freedoms than they as individuals possess. Freedom of associa-

---

[1] One feature of Charter litigation that underlines its individualism is that you cannot prevent others from going to court on your behalf. The union "movement" has no power to stop individuals or individual unions from going to court in the name of labour. In the words of United Steelworkers of America lawyer Brian Shell: "Each of us has it within our power to screw up a whole body of law for everybody else" (*The Globe and Mail*, March 30, 1987: A13).

tion cannot therefore vest independent rights in the group (*Re Public Service Employees Relations Act (Alberta)*, 1987: 219–220).

Treating "freedom of association" as an individual right narrowed its scope but did not leave it entirely without content. According to McIntyre, the freedom was violated when the state prohibited in association that which was lawful when done individually. The idea was that in tolerating an activity as lawful when done individually, the state, in effect, conceded the legitimacy of the activity. To then prohibit it when done in association would be an indication that the state was merely imposing its will and in effect acting undemocratically. It was using arbitrary power to prevent the democratic solidarity of numbers to realize what was conceded to be a legitimate object. Thus McIntyre's minimal content of freedom of association was that it prevented lawful activity from being attacked *only* on the basis of its "associational character" (*Re Public Service Employees Relations Act (Alberta)*, 1987: 228–229).

If McIntyre was going to deny the right to strike with this definition of freedom of association, it was crucial that he establish that striking was not merely the associational aspect of a lawful individual activity. But how could he do that? Did not non-unionized workers have the legal right, after all, to withhold their labour in bargaining with employers? Were they slaves? And was not this right, in effect, an individual right to "strike"? Against this, McIntyre had several points, all about equally as wide of the mark. First, he said, it is not lawful for an employee to cease work "during the currency of his contract" (*Re Public Service Employees Relations Act (Alberta)*, 1987: 229). Good point. Nor is it lawful for unions to strike during a contract. Nor were any of the claimants in these three cases claiming the right to strike during a contract. Next point: "there is no analogy whatever between the cessation of work by a single employee and a strike conducted in accordance with modern labour legislation" (*Re Public Service Employees Relations Act (Alberta)*, 1987: 229). Why not?

> The individual has, by reason of the cessation of work, either breached or terminated his contract of employment...But this is markedly different from a lawful strike. An employee who ceases work does not contemplate a return to work, while employees on strike always contemplate a return to work.

This is a complicated statement, but it is worth trying to unravel. In one sense McIntyre is right. A non-unionized employee who ceases work does not *ordinarily* contemplate a return to work. It is very unusual for non-union contracts to be renegotiated from off the job. But there is no law against it. There is no law preventing a non-unionized worker from lawfully quitting work as a bargaining strategy and saying that he or she will not come back unless there is a better offer. Of course, only highly valuable individual workers can use this strategy, and even then the high stakes involved for both sides will mean that they rarely get past the brink without settling or without the employee moving immediately to another job. Professional sports is about the closest we get to well-known instances of individual employees bargaining from off the job, and even there it is a rare phenomenon given the complexities of sports contracts. It is, indeed, much more typical to go hat in hand for a raise while one is still working. But all of this is simply due to the weak bargaining position of individual employees in the face of their employers' economic power. If there is any lack of "analogy" between individual refusals to work and strikes, it is this question of power.

This is underlined by McIntyre's final point, which was that the fundamental difference between collective and individual refusals to work was proven by the various statutory measures which had "radically altered" the common law relationship between employer and employee where unions were concerned. Here McIntyre emphasized the rights that unions had under collective bargaining legislation that non-unionized employees lacked. But all this proves is that workers have more power to refuse to work in association than they do individually. The only difference between individual and collective action is the relative effectiveness of the latter. The union movement caused a historic shift in the balance of power between labour and capital by the sheer act of combination. This called forth first the wrath of the common law and then the compromise of collective bargaining legislation. Individual action has always been easily handled by "the silent compulsion of economic relations" (Marx, 1867: 899). If there is any "lack of analogy" involved here it is only in the effectiveness of solidarity. But this, according to liberal theory, is what "freedom of association" is supposed to protect. All McIntyre's argument amounts to is that an attack on strikes is simply an attack on the "associational character" of a refusal to work, which is precisely the point he was trying to refute. You figure it out.

Justice McIntyre's attempt to reason the right to strike out of the Charter must not even have convinced him, because he felt it necessary to supplement it with a number of essentially political arguments for why Canada should not constitutionalize the right to strike, arguments about the political nature and context of the Charter. Foremost among them was Svend Robinson's concession at the hearings of the Joint Committee:

> It is apparent from the deliberations of the committee that the right to strike was understood to be separate and distinct from the right to bargain collectively. And, while a resolution was proposed for the inclusion of a specific right to bargain collectively, no resolution was proposed for the inclusion of the right to strike. This affords strong support for the proposition that the inclusion of a right to strike was not intended (*Re Public Service Employees Relations Act (Alberta)*, 1987: 231–232).

McIntyre pointedly contrasted this with the express references to the right to strike in other constitutions, for example those of Italy and France, as if to chide the unions for thinking they could get from the Court what they were too timid to even ask for from the drafters of the Charter.

Other points were typical judicial excuses for non-intervention. That the Charter was concerned with political and not economic rights:

> [T]he overwhelming preoccupation of the Charter is with individual, political, and democratic rights with conspicuous inattention to economic and property rights (*Re Public Service Employees Relations Act (Alberta)*, 1987: 232).

That the rights were not fundamental enough:

[T]he right to strike...is of relatively recent vintage. It is truly the product of this century and, in its modern form, is in reality the product of the latter half of this century *(Re Public Service Employees Relations Act (Alberta)*, 1987: 232).

Of course the same thing could have been said of some of the rules of criminal law which the Supreme Court of Canada had already held or would soon hold to be fundamental enough to be read into the Charter. Examples are the "due diligence" defence of *Re Motor Vehicle Act (B.C.)* (1985), which the Supreme Court had only invented as recently as 1978 and the judicial sentencing discretion entrenched in *Smith* (1987)—albeit over McIntyre's dissent—essentially a post World War II development (Mandel, 1987). What McIntyre was really getting at was not the vintage but the *controversial* nature of the right:

> It cannot be said that it has become so much a part of our social and historical traditions that it has acquired the status of an immutable, fundamental right, firmly embedded in our traditions, our political and social philosophy *(Re Public Service Employees Relations Act (Alberta)*, 1987: 232).

And, most importantly, that it was a product of legislators and not judges:

> The right to strike...has always been the subject of legislative control. It has been abrogated from time to time in social circumstances *(Re Public Service Employees Relations Act (Alberta)*, 1987: 232).

Underlying all of this was the question of power as represented by the distinction between policy and principle. Courts should not meddle in difficult policy questions:

> Labour law, as we have seen, is a fundamentally important as well as an extremely sensitive subject. It is based upon a political and economic compromise between organized labour—a very powerful socio-economic force—on the one hand, and the employers of labour—an equally powerful socio-economic force—on the other. The balance between the two forces is delicate...The whole process is inherently dynamic and unstable...it is obvious that the immediate direction of labour policy is unclear...Our experience with labour relations has shown that courts, as a general rule, are not the best arbiters of disputes which arise from time to time...Problems arising in labour matters frequently involve more than legal questions. Political, social and economic questions frequently dominate in labour disputes...Judges do not have the expert knowledge always helpful and sometimes necessary in the resolution of labour problems...If the right to strike is constitutionalized, then its application, its extent and any questions of its legality, become matters of law. This would inevitably throw the courts back in the field of labour relations and much of the value of specialized labour tribunals would be lost *(Re Public Service Employees Relations Act (Alberta)*, 1987: 232–235).

Of course, since union members rather outnumber the owners of the businesses they work for, this "delicate balance" is really a delicate *imbalance* of property over people. But McIntyre was thinking mainly of the practical problems for the Court, especially in the current climate. If the right to strike were held to be protected by the Charter and legislatures continued their trend to restricting it, McIntyre foresaw that the Court would be involved in the endless assessment of the "reasonability" of these restrictions under section 1 of the Charter:

The s.1 inquiry involves the reconsideration by a court of the balance struck by the legislature in the development of labour policy...In the *PSAC* case, the court must decide whether mere postponement of collective bargaining is a reasonable limit, given the government's substantial interest in reducing inflation and the growth in government expenses...None of these issues is amenable to principled resolution. There are clearly no correct answers to these questions. They are of a nature peculiarly apposite to the functions of the legislature. However, if the right to strike is found in the Charter, it will be the courts which time and time again will have to resolve these questions, relying only on the evidence and arguments presented by the parties, despite the social implications of each decision. This is a legislative function into which the courts should not intrude. [W]here no specific right is found in the Charter and the only support for its constitutional guarantee is an implication, the courts should refrain from intrusion into the field of legislation. That is the function of the freely elected legislatures and Parliament (*Re Public Service Employees Relations Act (Alberta)*, 1987: 236–237).

McIntyre saw dangers for the Court lurking from every corner. Too radical an approach would invite use of section 33; too narrow would weaken the force of the guarantees. In either case, the result might be the dreaded "trivialization" of the Charter (*Re Public Service Employees Relations Act (Alberta)*, 1987: 236). Saying there was "no principled basis" for answering the question meant that there was no decision the Court could make without appearing to take sides in a power struggle. The only safe thing to do was to abstain and leave the field to the combatants and the status quo of social power.

Justice McIntyre voted with the majority, but it is not clear to what extent his views were shared by the others. The rest of the majority (Le Dain, Beetz and La Forest) signed an opinion authored by Justice Le Dain. Given its brevity—one and a half pages compared to 23 for McIntyre and 48 for Dickson—the fact that it represented the opinion of half of the Court and three-quarters of the majority was itself rather an insult to the unions. Le Dain echoed the institutional points made by McIntyre while staying mostly out of the realm of ideology. For him the issue was not the importance of the right but whether it should be "left to be regulated by legislative policy." The substance of the reasons seem to be in this paragraph:

The rights for which constitutional protection is sought—the modern rights to bargain collectively and to strike, involving correlative duties or obligations resting on an employer—are not fundamental rights or freedoms. They are the creation of legislation, involving a balance of competing interests in a field which has been recognized by the courts as requiring specialized expertise. It is surprising that in an area in which this court has affirmed a principle of judicial restraint in the review of administrative action we should be considering the substitution of our judgment for that of the legislature by constitutionalizing in general and abstract terms rights which the legislature has found it necessary to define and qualify in various ways according to the particular field of labour relations involved. The resulting necessity of applying s.1 of the Charter to a review of particular legislation in this field demonstrates in my respectful opinion the extent to which the Court becomes involved in a review of legislative policy for which it is really not fitted (*Re Public Service Employees Relations Act (Alberta)*, 1987: 240).

In other words, the right to strike was legislative, not judicial; policy, not principle; controversial, indeed under attack, and not fundamental; and impossible to cast in terms that avoid questions of social power. To constitutionalize the right to strike would be to upset the delicate balance—the delicate imbalance—of social power. Though this lacks the extremity of McIntyre, it amounts to the same thing. If only the individual property rights of the common law are fundamental enough to be sanctified as "principle" and everything else is transient "policy," non-intervention in policy matters and intervention in the defence of principle is just a fancy way of supporting the status quo.

Chief Justice Dickson, speaking for himself and Justice Wilson, came out strongly in favour of the right to strike. His reasoning was simple: One's work is central to one's life. Association is vital if workers are to protect themselves from the superior strength of employers. Collective bargaining is the only way to do that and without the right to strike collective bargaining is meaningless. What more could workers ask for from a Judge than passages like the following?

> Work is one of the most fundamental aspects in a person's life, providing the individual with a means of financial support and, as importantly, a contributory role in society. A person's employment is an essential component of his or her sense of identity, self-worth and emotional well-being. Accordingly, the conditions in which a person works are highly significant in shaping the whole compendium of psychological, emotional and physical elements of a person's dignity and self-respect.
>
> ...
>
> The role of association has always been vital as a means of protecting the essential needs and interests of working people. Throughout history, workers have associated to overcome their vulnerability as individuals to the strength of their employers. The capacity to bargain collectively has long been recognized as one of the integral and primary functions of associations of working people. While trade unions also fulfill other important social, political and charitable functions, collective bargaining remains vital to the capacity of individual employees to participate in ensuring fair wages, health and safety protections and equitable and humane working conditions.
>
> Closely related to collective bargaining, at least in our existing industrial relations context, is the freedom to strike...the essential ingredient in collective bargaining... "If the workers could not, in the last resort, collectively refuse to work, they could not bargain collectively" (*Re Public Service Employees Relations Act (Alberta)*, 1987: 199–201).

But in saying this, it seems that Justice Dickson was only partly serious. He always had section 1 in the back of his mind. The right to strike was not so vital that a legislature would not be justified in limiting it if the circumstances were right. And the way Dickson saw things, there would be many such occasions. The protective covering of Dickson's freedom of association was in fact full of holes.

The ideological notion of "essential services" was invoked by Justice Dickson as one type of exception where compulsory arbitration could be substituted for the right to strike. Why "ideological"? Because it is only invoked when labour refuses to sell its essential services below the asking price and never when business does so. When business refuses to lower its prices, this is called "charging what the market will bear." In the Alberta case, Dickson defined "essential services" fairly conventionally as "the interruption of which would threaten serious harm to the general public or to a part of the population" in the sense of endangering "life, personal safety or health." This included maintaining "the rule of law and national security" and excluded "mere inconvenience to members of the public" (*Re Public Service Employees Relations Act (Alberta)*, 1987: 204). In the Alberta case this meant police, fire fighters, but not everyone in a hospital and not all public employees. However, in the Saskatchewan Dairy case, "essential services" were widened to include those whose interruption would bring "serious economic harm," or which were "especially injurious to the economic interests of third parties," like the harm to dairy producers in the disruption of dairy production (*Retail, Wholesale & Department Store Union*, 1987: 288). Nor did it matter whose fault the disruption was or whether the third parties were actually third parties. In the Saskatchewan Dairy case, most of the dairy workers planned rotating strikes against their employers. The employers escalated the conflict by locking out all of the workers and cutting off production. The cost in lost profits (one estimate was $250,000 daily, divided among 800 producers) was thus due to the actions of the employers, and some of these were the same producers claiming to be injured third parties! But Justice Dickson refused to "pierce the corporate veil" (*Retail, Wholesale & Department Store Union*, 1987: 289). Nor did it matter that the damage was due to the lockout. Since the right to lockout had not been challenged, it was "presumptively valid" (*Retail, Wholesale & Department Store Union*, 1987: 292). Justice Wilson thought that stretching essential services to economic harm to third parties went a bit too far, and she dissented in the case, making it five to one. Her own test was not that much stronger, however:

> [T]he government must satisfy the court that as a minimum the damage to the dairy industry as a consequence of the work stoppage would be considerably greater than that which would flow in the ordinary course of things from a work stoppage of reasonable duration (*Retail, Wholesale & Department Store Union*, 1987: 300).

In this case she was "not convinced that the dairy farmers can properly be considered third parties for this purpose" (*Retail, Wholesale & Department Store Union*, 1987: 300). Furthermore, she was not satisfied with the government's evidence of necessity, or that some less drastic action than a total ban would not have accomplished all that was necessary.

Justice Dickson, however, was prepared to allow limits on the right to strike even when the service was not essential—even on his extended definition—as long as the government was pursuing what he considered to be a legitimate goal. And he gave plenty of scope to the government here, too. Federal wage controls in the public sector were permitted even though public sector workers were admittedly not to blame and even though the hoped-for effect was purely symbolic:

> By enacting its "6 and 5" programme, Parliament intended to send a dramatic message conveying its resolve to fight inflation. It wished to demonstrate to the nation in an unequivocal fashion that it was prepared to take tough measures within its own sphere of employer-employee relations (*Public Service Alliance of Canada*, 1987: 263).

> In my opinion, courts must exercise considerable caution when confronted with difficult questions of economic policy. It is not our judicial role to assess the effectiveness or wisdom of various government strategies for solving pressing economic problems...A high degree of deference ought properly to be accorded to the government's choice of strategy in combatting this complex problem. Due deference must be paid as well to the symbolic leadership role of government (*Public Service Alliance of Canada*, 1987: 261).

Justice Wilson once again dissented, but once again her dissent was more in the nature of a quibble. She agreed that inflation might justify restricting the right to strike; she just thought that in this case the government had not shown any necessity of using the law. According to her, it would have shown more leadership to the private sector by holding fast without the law.

It was probably a blessing in disguise that Justices Dickson and Wilson were in the minority. Constitutionalizing the right to strike would not at all have meant guaranteeing it. It would have meant only the judicial regulation of its restriction, with wide deference to the economic judgment of governments. That was the best the unions could have hoped for from the courts.

Employer groups were predictably "delighted" with the right to strike decisions, and union leaders were just as predictably "gloomy." All sides seemed to think that the decisions would encourage legislatures to go even farther in limiting the right to strike, now that the highest court had decided it was not "fundamental" enough to merit the protection of the Charter (*The Toronto Star*, April 10,1987: A4; *The Globe and Mail*, April 10, 1987: A1; Hutchinson, 1987). In our era, this was like saying it did not even *exist*. This, at a time when support for the right to strike appeared to be wide and increasing.[1] Union gloom, however, was characteristically contradictory in its expression. On the one hand, we had the cynicism of Ontario Federation of Labour President Gord Wilson, who said he was not surprised:

> The courts have seldom been the worker's friend... Nobody ever gave us the right to strike. We took it. We'll do it again if governments pass unjust laws.

On the other hand, there was the wounded faith of Shirley Carr, President of the

---

[1] *The Toronto Star* (April 23, 1987: A3) reported a Canada-wide poll taken just before the Supreme Court decisions in which 68% supported the right to strike in general and 36% in public services such as the post office, airlines, railways, and telephone. In relation to previous polls, support was increasing.

Canadian Labour Congress, who was reported to have claimed that she had actually believed the right to strike was guaranteed by the Charter. (She obviously had not consulted with Svend Robinson.)[1] Worse yet, Darryl Bean, president of the Public Service Alliance of Canada, announced that his union would "try to step up political action in pursuit of a pro-labour amendment to the Charter" (*The Toronto Star*, April 10, 1987: A4). Bean's call for an amendment was reported to have been immediately supported by the Canadian Labour Congress, the National Union of Provincial Government Employees, and Canadian Auto Workers' Union leader, Bob White (*Canadian Tribune*, April 20, 1987: 1). When the Public Service Alliance made its submissions on the Meech Lake Accord, its number one recommendation was that the Charter be amended to include "the freedom to organize, bargain collectively and strike":

> Such an amendment would not, in our view, be problematical. It would not, for example, prevent Parliament from suspending and/or curtailing the right to strike. It would, however, ensure that any prohibition was "demonstrably justified" pursuant to Section 1 of the Charter of Rights and Freedoms (Public Service Alliance of Canada, 1987: 9).

The Postal Strike of 1987

Nowhere were these contradictions more evident than in the postal strike of October 1987. The Canadian Union of Postal Workers—on *legal* strike, it is easy to forget—employed a rotating strike strategy which, because it only slightly delayed mail service, was felt only by business and government. Government reaction was no less extreme for that. The inevitable back-to-work legislation was compared by postal workers to the labour laws of Pinochet's Chile (*CUPW Perspective*, November-December 1987: 1). The legislation was the most repressive labour legislation seen in Canada since World War II. It exceeded the Liberal government's response to the postal strike of 1978 in both the extent to which it made the union executive do the government's dirty work and in the penalties it imposed for defiance. The 1978 law had not only forced the workers to go back to work on pain of being fined or fired, it had also required the CUPW executive to

> forthwith...give notice to the employees that any... direction to go on strike...has become invalid by reason of the coming into force of this Act (*Postal Services Continuation Act*, 1978: s.3).

The Tory legislation of 1987 required the executive of CUPW not only to tell the membership that the strike was over, but to tell them that

> postal operations are forthwith to be continued or resumed...and the employees, when so required, are forthwith to continue or resume, as the case may be, the duties of their employment.

---

[1] She would similarly be "shocked" by the *Lavigne* decision (*The Globe and Mail*, July 8, 1986: A3). One wonders who is giving Carr her legal advice.

That is, they had to go beyond telling them a law had been passed. They actually had to order them back to work. Not only that, they were to

take all reasonable steps to ensure that employees comply (*The Postal Services Continuation Act, 1987*: s.4).

Failure to obey the law carried crippling fines of a minimum $10,000 to a maximum $50,000 *per day* for an official (compared to a *maximum* fine of $2,500 plus $250 per day, with no minimum, in the 1978 law), and $20,000 to $100,000 per day for the union (compared to a *maximum* $10,000 plus $1,000 per day in the 1978 law). These increases were obviously not just due to inflation. And there was an additional penalty: any officer who was convicted was banned from holding union office for five years (s.11), allowing the government, in effect, to choose its own postal union leaders by a process of elimination.[1] Pretty bad stuff.

The 1978 Liberal legislation was defied, and CUPW president Jean-Claude Parrot went to jail for three months. The 1987 law was obeyed "forthwith." Instead of waving a defiant fist, the union waved a writ: "CUPW CHALLENGES BILL C–86 BEFORE THE COURT" read its press release, enumerating all the sections of the Charter allegedly violated by the law. The press release also enumerated some more traditional political methods CUPW would use to fight the Tories and their privatization plans, but these were not dramatic enough to merit a headline:

[P]ublic demonstrations, local boycotts aimed at businesses that have subpost offices and franchised post offices, political action in targeted ridings, local community activities aimed at restoring and improving postal services, advertising campaigns and other initiatives that will unite opposition to the privatization plans of this government.

What is contradictory about all this? For one thing, within days of announcing the court challenge which would take place in Quebec Superior Court, Parrot was denouncing the government mediation set up during the dispute, under none other than a Quebec Superior Court Judge, as a "right-wing government fix" (*The Globe and Mail*, November 7, 1987: A12). Even when—after a massive sales job on the judge in question—the mediation award turned out not to be as bad as expected, the union could not resist some digs at the mediator:

We could not expect a judge appointed by the Conservative government to order the Post Office to change direction...We could not hope that our presentation, no matter how reasoned would change the fundamental philosophy of a judge (*CUPW Perspective*, Summer 1988: 1, 3).

For another thing, within one issue of the CUPW newspaper, *CUPW Perspective* (November-December 1987), one could find the admonition "We must fight in the

---

[1] The Tories, who introduced this little bit of fascism to Canada, have reportedly come to regard it as a "routine" clause (Panitch and Swartz, 1988: 72). Is the word "fascism" too strong? In fact, it was the official union policy of the Italian political party that gave the world this political epithet not to abolish unions but rather to integrate them into the state system and to subordinate them to the control of the Fascist Party, partly through the right to approve the appointment of union officers (Schneider, 1936: 81; Sereni, 1943: 270, 305; Miliband, 1973: 82).

courts, and in the political arena" (p.1) with these hardly flattering descriptions of judicial behaviour during the strike:

> If and when picketers were successful in stopping scab buses or trucks, another appendage of the state came forth—the courts. Injunctions were granted at the smallest whim of the Corporation...The most amazing feat of all was the relative ease with which court injunctions were doled out on the Thanksgiving holiday weekend (p.2).

> The manner in which these injunctions were granted and the conditions imposed are a clear example of how the power of the state is used against the workers. The Corporation was able to find judges on Saturday and Sunday nights on a holiday weekend to hand down these injunctions. And the conditions contained in these injunctions are some of the most repressive we've seen (p.6).

When it announced its action in Quebec, CUPW had already lost one Charter case in the West. Canada Post had imposed new inspection rules, claiming widespread theft and substance abuse at some plants. The rules provided that "Upon request, you must submit for inspection any items carried in or out of any postal facility," and "Lockers are subject to search by personnel designated by the Plant Manager, and must be opened on demand." (*Canadian Union of Postal Workers*, 1987a: 69). No warrants here, but the result was rather different than in *Hunter* v. *Southam*:

> No one likes snooping, to be spied upon, to be subjected to search or inspections, to be required to line up, nor to comply with someone else's unilateral dictates, and particularly in circumstances where that person controls the pay cheque. These are intrusions of privacy, but the real issue here is, is it a reasonable expectation of postal employees that their carried items and lockers may only be searched under a judicial warrant? I have concluded that it is not, and that the inspection procedures proposed by CPC, in the circumstances facing CPC, will constitute a reasonable intrusion on Mr. Weale or any other employee's right to be secure from unreasonable search or seizure (*Canadian Union of Postal Workers*, 1987a: 73).

Why The Unions Go To Court

So what possibly can be the attraction of the Charter for the unions? Why, despite their deeply ingrained antipathy for the courts and the virtually unbroken record of political defeats at judicial hands, do they keep going back for more punishment? Could they have been taken in by the claims that the Charter is a completely new story, a democratic nonpartisan instrument that anybody can use? There is, in fact, no lack of lawyers doing their best to convince unions of this, to persuade them to let bygones be bygones and to give the courts another chance. One of the more extreme versions of this is a remarkable book by labour lawyer, arbitrator, and professor David M. Beatty (Beatty, 1987). Beatty must be quoted at length just to be believed:

> With respect to the skepticism of workers and their organized representatives I would add, by way of encouragement to overcome a long-standing antipathy to judicial lawmaking, that there are good reasons to be optimistic. When judges

review the constitutional validity of the legal rules we have adopted to regulate the employment relationship, they will insist that the interests of the least advantaged workers be shown the respect which is now their constitutional due.

In the first place, in theory and especially in the present political climate,[1] the process of judicial review should be more hospitable than the legislative and executive processes of government to the interests of workers who are least advantaged, simply because of the nature of the interpretive process through which courts develop the law. As a matter of institutional design, groups which historically have been poorly represented in the political process should have a comparative advantage in the forum where the force of one's principle, and not the power of one's resources, determines the quality of participation in the processes of lawmaking and the integrity of the law itself. Adjudication, not political organization, may be the most effective process by which the least powerful and most poorly organized groups in our society can ensure their interests are properly considered in the process of policy formation. Where historically working people have had to devote enormous amounts of time and energy to petition for the protection of law which others already enjoyed, the Charter of Rights and Freedoms offers a forum of principle[2] in which their relative lack of resources should not count as heavily against them (Beatty, 1987: 11–12).

...Recognizing and exploiting the institution of judicial review as a new opportunity for participating in the processes of government can lead directly to an amelioration of the worst excesses of the existing legal regime. Even when it is kept within its most narrow and conservative confines, judicial review can mean that those traditionally who have had very little influence in the formulation of labour policy will be able to participate more effectively than they generally have in the other two branches of government. Compared to the kinds of debates which take place in our legislatures, judicial review offers a much fairer and more neutral forum for citizen participation. In the courts the merits of the debate are not judged by those who are directly involved in the defence of the law under scrutiny. Equally, all participation is more equitable and effective when reason and not rhetoric, principle and not material resources, determine the outcome. The quality of the dialogue and the resolutions it generates can only be enhanced when they are the product of closely argued affidavits prepared by the experts in the field rather than the result of pleas of passion and panderings to prejudice by those whose understanding of the issue may be marginal at best...

...In a sense [judicial review] represents the most basic opportunity for individual participation in the process of democratic government. From the perspective of the participants, judicial review initiates a conversation of justification in which the majority benefiting from a particular rule is obliged to offer an adequate explanation to those who feel their constitutional entitlements have been unreasonably compromised. Judicial review offers a more structured and a more equal debate as to what laws can be legitimately included in our labour code than that which can take place in our political arenas (Beatty, 1987: 180–182).

---

[1] Beatty earlier characterized this climate as extremely anti-union.

[2] Here Beatty refers us to the work of Ronald Dworkin.

In these passages we find, in perhaps their purest (and most toxic) form anywhere, the basic errors and assumptions of legalized politics. Let's enumerate them:

1) The form of judicial discourse, "principle," because it is abstract and power-blind, is mistakenly assumed to insulate judicial decision making from the matrix of social power. The fact that principle ratifies power by assuming its absence, or when it cannot, as with the right to strike, by abandoning the field to the status quo, is not even hinted at.

2) The pretenses of the judicial institution, that courts are more neutral because they are independent, are taken absolutely at face value. Courts are not "directly involved" in the laws they review, because the judiciary is formally separated from the legislature and executive. Never mind that they are appointed by the latter, often from the ranks of failed candidates for the former. Never mind that when judges leave the courtroom they do not go to the moon, but rather to comfortable homes in the most exclusive sections of whatever city they live in, just like the other members of Canada's upper class.

3) Courts are reason over passion. This one is very hard to figure out coming from a lawyer in the era of the Charter. Has Beatty not read the judgments we have? As for pandering to prejudice, anyone who has been to court has heard plenty of that. What about the Ontario Provincial Court Judge recently reported to have told a Sri Lankan charged in a prostitution case: "You write back to Sri Lanka and get yourself a girlfriend. All she needs is a boat and she can come in." Or the judge of the same court who said during a witness's testimony in one trial "You know something, he's full of s----," who, in another case, challenged an accused man to a fist fight, and in yet another, said to a man charged with soliciting for oral sex, "I'm not asking you if your wife is a c---- -sucker, I ask you if you ever got a blow job, because you said you do not know how long it takes" (*The Toronto Star*, July 16, 1988). And where does Beatty get the idea that expertise is the province of the courts and not the legislatures? From watching "Question Period"? You will find many more experts in the average legislative committee than in the average courtroom. In courtrooms you find judges and lawyers.

4) Adjudication offers the powerless "participation," even "conversation" with their betters. But Beatty neglects to point out that this participation is always through the medium of the legal profession and that the Charter does not by any means turn farm workers into lawyers. Furthermore, though "participation," like the "mass society" theory of the last chapter, sounds democratic enough, it is guaranteed incapable of changing the undemocratic status quo of social power. This is because participation is always on the basis of "principle," the defining feature of which is to ratify social power by denying it. A court is "constitutionally" incapable of bestowing social power. It is forbidden by the notion of principle from doing so. Was this not the very argument of the majority of the Supreme Court of Canada in the Right to Strike cases? In fact, participation on the basis of principle is a *substitute* for equalizing social power. It is meant to reconcile the powerless to their lack of power by giving them a day in court. Which brings us to the final point.

5) Litigation is offered as a substitute for other forms of politics, indeed as

far superior to other forms. Don't bother organizing. It's so time-consuming, so messy. Come to court and leave the politics to us.

Beatty starts each of his chapters with quotes from Albert Einstein. The last chapter starts with this one:

> All of us who are concerned for peace and the triumph of justice must be keenly aware how small an influence reason and honest good will exert upon events in the political field.

Beatty seems to want in this quote to exempt the courtroom from the "political field," but the man who discovered relativity is not likely to have made the same error. Einstein (1879–1955) lived long enough to witness the Stalin show trials, the constitutionally approved internment of the Japanese in the US (*Korematsu*, 1945), and the anti-communist trials of the McCarthy era (for example, the Rosenbergs and *Dennis*, 1951). Be that as it may, Beatty never once in his book addresses the question of the extent to which principle actually binds judges. If there is a right answer to a question of law, what makes him think judges will give it? If reason over passion prevails to protect unions in the courtroom, how does Beatty explain the Right to Strike cases? He omitted any discussion of them in his book for the feeble reason that "they have already been argued before the court" (Beatty, 1987: 189, n.22). In a seminar at Osgoode Hall Law School on April 4, 1988, however, he awarded Dickson and Wilson an "A," while flunking McIntyre with a "D." Beatty actually thought McIntyre should be "impeached" for his judgment. But so what? McIntyre's judgment was in the majority, and a thousand Beatty judgments will not change that. And what are we to make of Beatty's point that, with only four judges in the majority, the case could technically be reversed in a new action without breaching judicial etiquette? Shall we go back and try again, maybe with better lawyers, maybe with Beatty himself?[1]

Which brings us back to the postal strike of 1987. Already much is being made of the puny dissenting judgments of Justices Dickson and Wilson, with a heavy de-emphasis on their minority status and on Dickson's willingness to limit the right to strike under section 1 of the Charter. A few days after the strike was ended by the Tory back-to-work law, political scientist Leo Panitch wrapped himself in the Charter with this convoluted denunciation over national radio:

> What exactly is going on in this country? The Charter of Rights and Freedoms establishes a constitutional guarantee for Canadians to exercise freedom of association. Yet in the past month...[etc.] [W]e have almost grown accustomed to seeing back-to-work legislation used against public employees. Some of us, including two Supreme Court Justices last spring, have long expressed real concern that Canadian governments and courts are rendering freedom of association meaningless...(Panitch, 1988).

No doubt it would have ruined the rhetorical effect to point out that the two judges were outnumbered four to two, or, as Panitch himself was writing at about the same

---

[1] See below Chapter VI page 246.

time, that "the Chief Justice's opinions sanctioned not only the regulation of the right to strike and collective bargaining of the kind that existed in the general legislation of the earlier era,[1] but, as well, much of the 'permanent exceptionalism' of the new era" (Panitch and Swartz, 1988: 63).

Whether they think they have a snowball's chance in July in court, in an atmosphere such as this it takes great determination on the part of a union to avoid using the rhetoric of the Charter. But if you are going to use Charter rhetoric, then you have to put your legal fees where your mouth is. In the era of the Charter no one who is unwilling to go to court is taken seriously.

It could be that the Charter is just an added cost of doing union politics in the modern era, that it has no effect beyond the rhetorical. Certainly, the legal outcome of the CUPW case will not be known for years, probably not until after the next postal strike. Whatever the result, it will obviously have no effect on the postal strike of 1987. But the Charter may have had a more subtle effect, just by its existence. It provided the union with a quick and politically costless[2] way of appearing not to back down. Without the Charter, the union would have had to look a lot harder at disobeying the law, at least temporarily, as it did in 1978, with a resultant three-month jail term for Parrot. Traditional political methods on their own would have lacked all "defiance." Admittedly, the law was much tougher than the law of 1978. The stakes were very high indeed, and, as my colleague Judy Fudge puts it, there was an unmistakable "make my day" air about the whole affair. But the Charter may also have played a role in the brutal nature of the legislation. Surely the government knew that the Charter gave the union a face-saving way out of disobedience which lessened the chances of it actually having to act on the penalties in the law? And if it did have to act, did the government not foresee that the Charter would come to the rescue? That the Court would test the waters for it and declare the law unconstitutional if totally indefensible or give it the boost of judicial approval as "reasonable"? In other words, can we not apply the lessons of Chapter IV here, that the Charter can legitimate more repression than would otherwise be possible?

So, if we want to know why the union hates the Court but cannot live without it, we have more answers than we know what to do with. We have hectoring lawyers and political scientists. We have pumped-up governments. We have the hard knocks of real political action. Even where the results are easily predicted, the Charter has a way of being unavoidable.

Dolphin Delivery and the Charter's Reach

It is not even as if the Right to Strike cases were the only ones that the Supreme Court had decided against unions in the short life of the Charter.

---

[1] The "earlier era" was the one before the era of "free collective bargaining" which started in 1943 and went roughly to 1974 (Panitch and Swartz, 1988: 17–27).

[2] Though clearly not economically costless. If it goes all the way to the Supreme Court of Canada as so many of them do, it will run through several weeks of fines under the Act in legal fees.

Before the Right to Strike cases, there was *Dolphin Delivery* (1986). In that case, a union tried to use the Charter to oppose not a legislative but a common law restriction on union rights, namely the prohibition against "secondary picketing." A union involved in a dispute with one courier company threatened to picket another courier company (Dolphin) that was doing business with the first. Dolphin applied for and was granted an injunction against the union. Through a quirk in the law, it was one of the rare labour relations situations in which no statute applied. The case fell to be decided by the common law. At common law, as we noted earlier, *all* picketing was unlawful. The injunction was appealed by the union on the grounds that the common law interfered with the Charter guarantees of freedom of speech and association. The British Columbia Court of Appeal rejected the appeal. It held (by majority) that picketing was not "expression" within the meaning of the Charter and (unanimously) that, even if it were, this was a reasonable limit. The majority holding that picketing was not expression was based on the insulting and fatuous proposition that picketing lacked the element of rational persuasion. The judges quoted former Chairman of the British Columbia Labour Relations Board Paul Weiler for the proposition that a picket line

> operates as a signal, telling union members not to cross. Certainly in British Columbia the response is automatic, almost Pavlovian (Weiler, 1980: 79).

The Supreme Court of Canada was unanimous in rejecting the appeal, but only one member (Justice Beetz) adopted the British Columbia Court of Appeal's approach. The rest of the Court was willing to recognize that picketing was a form of expression. However, this was as easy for the Court as was Chief Justice Dickson's recognition of the right to strike, given its holding that the prohibition on secondary picketing, ubiquitous in provincial statute law, was a "reasonable limit" under section 1 of the Charter.[1]

What really annoyed Charter supporters was that the Court preferred to rest its decision on the far broader ground that the Charter did not apply at all to private litigation unless there was some additional "element of governmental intervention." The Charter, wrote Justice McIntyre, echoing almost all judicial and academic commentators,

> was set up to regulate the relationship between the individual and the government. It was intended to restrain government action and to protect the individual (*Dolphin Delivery*, 1986: 191).

Where McIntyre differed with Charter enthusiasts was in holding that the common law itself could not provide that "element of governmental intervention." Though the common law was enforced by the state and indeed made by judges, the Court realized that to treat it as "governmental" for the purposes of the Charter was a very slippery logical slope. If the Charter applied to the common law as such, it would

---

[1] Once again the Court relied on a rather vague Weiler argument to the effect that a company not directly involved as employer is somehow innocent and anyway "does not have it within its power to make concessions that will settle the new contract" (*Dolphin Delivery*, 1986: 190). If this were ever actually the case, one would be at a loss to explain why a union would waste its time on secondary picketing.

apply to everything, because all relations were, in a sense, governed by the common law. So the Court had to reject that proposition:

> To regard a court order as an element of governmental intervention necessary to invoke the Charter would, it seems to me, widen the scope of Charter application to virtually all private litigation. All cases must end, if carried to completion, with an enforcement order and if the Charter precludes the making of the order, where a Charter right would be infringed, it would seem that all private litigation would be subject to the Charter (*Dolphin Delivery*, 1986: 196).

Consequently, the Court held that in order to invoke the Charter, either the government had to be a party or some statute or regulation had to infringe a right.

McIntyre tried to ground his practical arguments in the words of the Charter itself and in the idea that courts were too neutral to be considered "governmental."[1] This has not convinced anybody (Slattery, 1987; Manwaring, 1987; Etherington, 1987), but, despite the great disappointment of the Charter supporters, it is hard to imagine any other result at this point. It is not that the courts could not administer all of society through the Charter. Maybe they will one day. In a sense they do it already. The only things beyond their reach are those they choose to place beyond their reach. But the ideological implications of applying the Charter to the common law as such, and via the common law to everything, are great. The common law is, as we have seen, the sanction for calling a right fundamental. No right to strike at common law, no constitutional right. To say that the common law is subject to the Charter would be like saying that the Charter is subject to the Charter. Moreover, if the courts were "government," where would they get the right to overrule the other branches of government? In other words, the courts have good reason to maintain the fiction that they are merely the disembodied voice of the Charter. That they *are* the Charter. What is more, they are perfectly at home with the idea. A case in point is one decided by the British Columbia Court of Appeal before the Supreme Court of Canada decision in *Dolphin Delivery*. In that case, the Chief Justice of British Columbia took it upon himself, without benefit of a complainant, to issue an injunction against a picket line around the Vancouver courthouse, which he appears to have encountered on his way to work one day (*B.C. Government Employees Union*, 1985). The union was involved in a lawful strike with the government, and there was no suggestion that access was impeded. The union appealed but the British Columbia Court of Appeal upheld the injunction on the grounds that this was a reasonable limit on any right you cared to name. Citing the ubiquitous Paul Weiler on the Pavlovian picket line, the Court held that any picket line must be deemed to impede (by "ethic or fear"). As for the reasonability of the limit:

> In our opinion, no limit on a Charter right could be more demonstrably justified than one which preserves the public's unfettered right to access to the courts of justice. It is implicit in the very scheme of the Charter where any citizen may apply to the courts to redress infringements of the rights enumerated. Without

---

[1] See above, page 40.

preservation of the public right the shield of judicial protection offered by the Charter would become an illusion (*B.C. Government Employees Union*, 1985: 429–430).

The Court and the Charter, like "man and wife" at common law, "are one"—and that one is the Court.[1]

The most important reason for the holding in *Dolphin Delivery* though, has to do with the indispensability of the ideological distinction between public and private spheres. This distinction is difficult enough to keep in place, but it should not be forgotten that the Charter was invented to preserve it, to restrain government intervention on a one-person-one-vote basis into the one-dollar-one-vote despotism of the marketplace. This central assumption is not yet ready for the dustbin of history.

What does *Dolphin Delivery* mean for unions? One union lawyer (Shell, 1987) has said it was a great blessing, at least for private-sector unions, because it would protect them from Charter *attacks* (of which see below). That does not help public-sector unions, of course. But the significance of the decision cannot be grasped in isolation. We have seen that most of the gains of organized labour have been through the relative democracy (however attenuated) of the legislative sphere as opposed to the market logic of the common law. Whether the courts use the Charter to restore the common law against legislation—for it is the common law that generally remains when legislation is struck down—or whether arrangements are left the way they stood at common law by excluding the common law from the ambit of the Charter, it is all the same to those without market power. *Dolphin Delivery* leaves private power beyond the reach of the Charter at the same time as public power is under Charter attack. Does this mean that a decision that the Charter applies to the private sector would have been preferable? Not at all. This is clear from the fact that, all of the noble words about picketing and freedom of expression notwithstanding, the union would have lost in this case even if the Charter had been held to apply.[2] The prohibition on secondary picketing was a "reasonable limit" according to the Court, just the way the great part of the limitations on the right to strike were for Chief Justice Dickson in the Right to Strike cases. And this is just half of what the Charter would mean for unions if it applied across the board, as we shall see in the next section. The Charter itself—judicial administration—whether through action or a combination of action and omission, is the problem, not any particular decision.

We can learn a lot from the judiciary's unwillingness to allow the Charter to be used to tilt the balance of power in labour relations if we contrast it with

---

[1] As we go to press, this decision has been resoundingly and unanimously upheld by the Supreme Court of Canada (*B.C.G.E.U.* v. *British Columbia (Attorney General)*, October 20, 1988). In a companion case, a Newfoundland union was denied the power to discipline a member for crossing a courthouse picket line (*Newfoundland (Attorney General)* v. *N.A.P.E.*, October 20, 1988).

[2] *Dolphin Delivery* has lately been invoked by the Alberta government to justify a proposed law restricting picketing to members of unions involved in the dispute. Canadian Civil Liberties Association counsel Alan Borovoy said the bill was "so bad it couldn't even make a law school examination" (*The Globe and Mail*, May 21, 1988: A10).

their fearless activism in the defence of the weak when purely formal values are at stake. By definition, formal values do not interfere with the full exercise of private social power. In fact, they can enhance it, as in the case of powerful criminals receiving procedural protection. But the right to strike and secondary picketing are in no way formal questions. They are questions about the extent to which people without property will be allowed to assert their "democratic" power against the power of property. Judicial activism on the side of the unions in these cases would have made a difference. It would have *upset* the balance when the Charter was only intended to strengthen it. That there were legal and philosophical arguments for these rights at least as persuasive as those accepted by the courts against them, was as nothing against this.

Using the Courts to Fight Unions

> By "constitutionalizing" our labour code, judicial review should silence those who argue that we should dismantle our existing collective model of work relations. A constitutional labour code will have no part of that. The invalidity of that kind of a system would be plain for all to see...(Beatty, 1987: 181)

The National Citizens' Coalition Discovers the Charter

The National Citizens' Coalition is a right wing lobby group founded by the late Colin Brown, an insurance executive from London, Ontario, and now headed by his protégé, lawyer David Somerville. According to its publicity, "The Coalition is a grass-roots group of 30,000 concerned Canadians, coast-to-coast, who are committed to 'more freedom through less government'" (*The Globe and Mail*, August 27, 1985:9). But the "grass-roots group" is actually run from the top down by an advisory board "heavily dominated by wealthy business people who are, or recently have been, in key positions with large corporations [including] Goodyear, Canadian Pacific, Brascan, Canadian Imperial Bank of Commerce, Bank of Montreal, MacMillan Bloedel, Royal Trust, Power Corporation, Bell Canada, Stelco, Caron, and Abitibi Paper" (Fillmore, 1986: 8). The NCC supports all of the expected right wing causes: cuts in social spending, the abolition of medicare, extra-billing by doctors, a white-only immigration policy, traditional roles for women, lower taxes for the rich, more freedom for multinationals, "Star Wars," putting the right to property in the constitution (Fillmore, 1986), and Free Trade with the United States (*The Toronto Star*, August 28, 1988: B2). Until recently its main propaganda device was the expensive full-page advertisement in major newspapers. In February 1987, it took out an ad against Ontario's proposed pay-equity legislation in the following terms:

> It means ignoring the law of supply and demand...Bill 154 will create a new pay police...The three major parties in Ontario distrust and dislike free enterprise, the free market and business (*The Globe and Mail*, February 19, 1987: A11).

Lately, however, the NCC has come to love the Charter every bit as much as David Beatty does. In 1984, it was able to convince an Alberta judge to

follow US precedents and strike down federal restrictions on campaign spending as an interference with "freedom of expression" (*National Citizens' Coalition*, 1984). This had indeed been predicted before the entrenchment of the
Charter at the same corporate lawyers' conference where Roy McMurtry had
sung the praises of the Charter for big business (*The Globe and Mail*, February
6, 1982: 12). The election spending restrictions had been designed to limit the
disproportionate influence of wealthy groups such as the NCC, who, following
the example of the right wing "political action committees" in the US, spend
large amounts of money on election campaigns, rendering meaningless the
already weak spending limits and disclosure rules governing candidates lucky
enough to be supported by them. This is one of the most direct ways in which
the one-dollar-one-vote principle of the marketplace undermines the one-person-one-vote idea of representative democracy. The Parliamentary parties, in
rather self-centred legislation, had tried to deal with the problem by making it
an offence to spend money for or against a candidate or party without authorization. With authorization such expenditure would have to be included in
tabulating the total expenditure limited by the Act (*Canada Elections Act*,
1983). In court, the government argued that the legislation was meant to counteract the "unfair advantage to those who have access to large campaign
funds" (*National Citizens' Coalition*, 1984: 494). Far from being a limitation
on freedom of expression, this would *enhance* it by not allowing the voices of
the many to be drowned out by those of the few with money. In other words, it
was a typical Charter confrontation between the freedom of the many against
the freedom of the few. One-person-one-vote versus one-dollar-one-vote. In
typical Charter fashion it was resolved in favour of the few. Justice Medhurst
applied the US Supreme Court decision in *Buckley* (1976) and completely
ignored the question of inequality of resources. A limitation on spending one's
money was equated with a limitation on expressing one's opinion. Money and
volunteer campaign work were all the same to the Court. The provisions,
which had received unanimous support in the House of Commons, were struck
down in time for the NCC to spend "several hundreds of thousands of dollars"
in the 1984 election a few months later, arguing for the sale of Petro-Canada,
the dismantling of the national energy program, entrenching property rights in
the Constitution, balancing the budget, and eliminating indexed pensions for
MPs and civil servants. The Liberal government, already facing disaster at the
polls, did not even appeal the ruling (*The Toronto Star*, June 27, 1984: A3;
The Globe and Mail, June 27, 1984: 1–2). The Tories were no more energetic.
Four years later, the Alberta judgment was still governing Canadian elections,
and the NCC was promising to spend $500,000 in the 1988 federal election
making Canadians "scared" of Ed Broadbent (*The Toronto Star*, August 28,
1988: B2).[1]

Emboldened by this victory the NCC turned its attention to its mortal

---

[1] As it turned out, the federal election saw an unregulated spending orgy by big business in aid of the
Free Trade deal, the fortunes of which had faltered unexpectedly in mid-campaign.

enemy, the union movement. In July 1985, it unveiled a comprehensive attack on union rights that would rely entirely on the Charter. The NCC announced that it was sponsoring a group called "Freedom of Choice" and had hired lawyer Morris Manning[1] to challenge what Manning called

> compulsory unionism and the breaking up of direct dialogue between an individual employee and management, which occurs when a union is certified to represent all employees.

In other words, Manning would challenge all of the legal protections labour had won through legislation. According to Manning, the group "was formed to attack government laws and is not anti-union," which is like saying a group formed to attack laws protecting racial minorities is not racist.[2] The estimated cost "to hire Canada's top constitutional lawyer" was $500,000 (*The Globe and Mail*, July 4, 1985: M1, M6).

Union Dues and Freedom of Association: The Lavigne Case

The first success of the NCC against the unions was the case of Francis ("Merv") Lavigne (*Lavigne*, 1986), an anti-union teacher at the Haileybury School of Mines, described in full-page fund-raising ads by the NCC as "a courageous Canadian" fighting the "Big Union Movement" (*The Globe and Mail*, August 27, 1985: 9). Lavigne was one of a minority of community college teachers who did not join the Ontario Public Service Employees Union (OPSEU), which had been certified to represent academic staff at community colleges. However, under the collective agreement he was required to pay union dues. This was the famous "Rand Formula," so named because it was used by Justice Ivan Rand of the Supreme Court of Canada to settle a Windsor auto strike in 1946. In return for concessions from the union, including no strikes during a collective agreement, the union would get the right to represent all workers in a bargaining unit, whether union members or not, and to collect dues from them. The Rand formula has since become a staple of Canadian labour relations. About 1.5 million Canadian workers, or 70% of those in units of 500 or more, are said to be covered by the Rand formula or the even stronger "union shop" agreement under which all workers actually have to be members of the union. It is estimated that tens of thousands of Canadian workers are in the Lavigne situation (Slotnick, 1986).

There is evidence that Lavigne was recruited by the NCC and not vice versa (Clancy et al., 1985: 7), but it is not disputed that the NCC paid the entire cost

---

[1] For the irony of this, see the next Chapter.

[2] This is the man who, after touring South Africa, reported to Canadians that all black people really needed there was a constitutional Charter of Rights: "Without the protection of individual rights being monitored by a truly independent judiciary in accordance with constitutionally entrenched rights, practising law in South Africa will indeed remain exciting but still quite frustrating" (Manning, 1987: 15).

of the litigation,[1] and it can be assumed from this that the strategy was theirs. That strategy included not challenging the Rand formula itself, i.e, the collection of dues from non-members, but rather restricting the challenge to the use of a part of these dues for alleged non-union purposes. In Lavigne's case the amount in question was a minuscule $2 (of $338 in union dues paid by him in 1985)[2] used by OPSEU and the larger groups to which OPSEU was affiliated (the National Union of Provincial Government Employees, the Ontario Federation of Labour and the Canadian Labour Congress) for political purposes to which Lavigne, as a true-blue right-winger, could not fail to object: donations to the NDP, to groups opposing cruise missile tests in Canada, to groups opposing the domed stadium in Toronto, to the striking English miners, to aid for Nicaragua, to support recognition of the Palestine Liberation Organization, and to support the "pro-choice" position on abortion. Spending money for these and similar purposes was supported by a majority of union members and was clearly consistent with the union's constitution. But Lavigne claimed it violated his freedom of association and expression under the Charter. Because of the implications for political action on the part of organized labour, the CLC, which we remember had not bothered to show up for the Charter hearings, claimed that victory for Lavigne might "render the labour movement absolutely impotent" (*The Globe and Mail*, December 18, 1985: A21).

In the summer of 1986, Justice White of the Ontario Supreme Court ruled in Lavigne's favour on most issues. He decided that the Rand Formula did indeed violate Lavigne's freedom of association, and that though it was saved by section 1, that is to say was a "reasonable limit" in respect of money used for collective bargaining purposes, this was not the case for purposes not related to collective bargaining. Another year was required to determine what these purposes were, but they were ultimately to include most of the things to which Lavigne objected.

A threshold issue in the case was why it should violate anyone's freedom of association to be compelled to pay dues to a union if there was no compulsion to join the union or in any other way participate in its activities. Here we have the marketplace logic of the NCC's election spending case in reverse. If protecting one's right to spend (to buy someone else's expression) is as important as protecting one's own expression, then being compelled to pay for the espousal of someone else's case is as offensive as being compelled to actually espouse it:

> It is not necessary for the collective agreement to require Mr. Lavigne to join the Union for there to be a forced association; it is the compelled combining of financial resources that has the effect of forcing Mr. Lavigne to associate with the Union (*Lavigne*, 1986: 369).

---

[1] The judge in *Lavigne* ordered the union to pay most of Lavigne's legal costs despite this, on the familiar grounds that nothing should impede Charter litigation: "To the extent that the N.C.C. or any other specific interest group puts responsible Charter litigation within the reach of the individual Canadian, they should not, even indirectly, be deterred" (*Lavigne*, 1987:127).

[2] In the Ontario Court of Appeal the unions claimed it was even less: $1.36 over three years out of more than $1,000 of dues (*The Globe and Mail*, June 16, 1988: A15).

According to Judge White, dues paid to unions engaged freedom of association because unions were intrinsically "political." Fair enough, said the unions, we're proud of being political, but what about other associations that enforce payments of dues and then use them for political lobbying purposes? What about professional groups like lawyers? Wearing the blinkers of the status quo, Judge White could not see the similarity:

> Labour unions are organizations with a strong tradition of political activism behind them. I cannot see that they are analogous to a state bar association, which exists to regulate the practice of law in a given geographical area in order to maintain high professional standards and protect the public interest...[1] The word "union" in the labour context is practically synonymous with a certain ideological and indeed political perspective (*Lavigne*, 1986: 379–380).

To the Court, "political" meant, in effect, *left wing* politics, anything that challenged the status quo of social power. That which "maintained" it was in the "public interest."

The Rand Formula itself was not challenged, but it figured importantly in the decision. Compulsory dues check-off was a reasonable limit:

> Dissenting employees are protected in that they are not forced to join the union, but as Mr. Justice Rand who is credited with the introduction of the concept in Canada stated, all employees must take the burden of collective bargaining with the benefit (*Lavigne*, 1986: 385).

But it was reasonable only in the case of collective bargaining purposes:

> The collective bargaining process can be both advanced and financed by those who benefit without the use of compulsory dues for purposes beyond the immediate concerns of collective bargaining and settlement of disputes arising out of the collective agreement (*Lavigne*, 1986: 386).

The full implications of the case would not be known until a year later, but even this first round showed just how far the fantasies of Beatty are from the actualities of Charter "participation" and "conversation."[2] One example was the attempt by union lawyers to argue that, even though the government was involved, the Charter should not apply at all because the collective agreement was "private." Pretty odd for a public sector union to be arguing the "private" nature of education. But worse yet was the argument made by the government lawyer, the union's ally against Lavigne, in aid of the union case:

> Ms. Bowlby, in her argument, suggested that a collective agreement was analogous to a contract for the supply of paper clips and, therefore, could not be considered an act of government *qua* government. I do not see an analogy...A contract which establishes the terms and conditions of the employment of academic staff relates to the quality of education provided at these institutions. The

---

[1] This sentence is particularly hard to stomach for anyone who has ever been to a Law Society meeting or read any Law Society communiqués to whom it will be abundantly clear that the first duty members require of their representatives is to protect members' *living* standards. See also Chapter IV above on the activities surrounding "Law Day."

[2] In fact, Beatty's book contains an extended defence of the actual decision in *Lavigne* which will doubtless prove useful to the NCC lawyers in the appeals (Beatty, 1987: 122–132).

purpose of these colleges is to educate students; teachers are essential to achieve that purpose, in a sense that suppliers of paper clips are not (*Lavigne*, 1986: 354).

This is what "participation" and "conversation" means under the Charter. The affidavits submitted by the union (and collected under the stirring title *All for one: arguments from the labour trial of the century on the real meaning of unionism*) were at pains to stress the non-commodity nature of labour contracts. They invoked the words of Justice Rand himself that a "primary and essential error" was the idea that "the Company was buying labour as a commodity" (Clancy *et al.*, 1985: 139). But it was lawyers who got to do the talking in court on labour's behalf, and they made whatever arguments had a chance of success, even though they would make a trade unionist choke.[1]

Another irony was the small amount of money involved. In a postmortem on the case, OPSEU was asked why they just did not give Lavigne back his $2 and tell him "Now, go away" (*The Globe and Mail*, March 30, 1987: A13). OPSEU officer Wayne Roberts, one of the authors of *All for one*, conceded the possible wisdom and even propriety of such an approach, but argued that this was a question for the union to decide and not for the Court to impose upon the union (Roberts, 1987). Roberts had a point, but it was not the kind of point that would likely be made by union lawyers in court. First, because lawyers are not comfortable denying the authority of courts. Second, because it hardly lay in the mouth of the union to deny the authority of the Court to meddle in "private" labour relations, not only when it had been "first off the mark" to invoke the Charter against wage controls (OPSEU was a plaintiff in *Broadway Manor*, 1983) but when Jeffrey Sack, lawyer for one of the unions in *Broadway Manor* and for two of them in *Lavigne*, was at that very moment arguing in another Ontario courtroom on behalf of another union that the Charter permitted the Courts to meddle in university labour relations to protect professors from mandatory retirement (*The Globe and Mail*, April 26, 1986: A15).

The fact that there was such a small amount involved did not bother Judge White:

> If we try to distinguish between small breaches and more significant breaches of the Charter we risk ending up with a document of little value which can be manipulated and invoked only when it is convenient to do so (*Lavigne*, 1986: 388).

"The principle" had to be established (*Lavigne*, 1986: 388). Nor did he mind that his ruling would mean the union would have to go to an awful lot of trouble. According to *Singh*,

> A balance of administrative convenience could not override principles of fundamental justice...Thus perceived administrative hardship imposed on the union in earmarking compulsory dues used for permissible and non-permissible pur-

---

[1] "How do you stop yourself making an argument that is beneficial to the griever, but is devastating, terrible and horrible to the labour movement?" asked labour lawyer Brian Shell at the "Charter of Wrongs" conference (*The Globe and Mail*, March 30, 1987: A13). He had no answer.

poses, and in following a pattern least obtrusive to the applicant's Charter right, is no answer to the applicant's case (*Lavigne*, 1986: 387).

Nor did the amount involved matter to the NCC. It announced it had spent $400,000 on the case (*The Globe and Mail*, July 8, 1986: A3). But the NCC was not concerned with Merv Lavigne except as a test case with which to clobber the union movement as a whole. Then NCC Vice-President David Somerville hoped the decision would cut $70 million from union budgets (*The Toronto Star*, July 16, 1986: A16). A lot depended on the second part of the case, which had to do with the "remedy," that is to say the precise order Judge White would make against the union. This took another year of submissions and deliberations to determine. When the result came, the union breathed a sigh of relief. Judge White decided against the "opt-in" system proposed by the NCC, which would have ruled out political uses unless the employee specifically gave permission beforehand. The NCC was really counting on this one to "very, very substantially alter the way that left wing politics in Canada is practiced and the size and role of the major union bodies," on the assumption that "most union members do not support the NDP or other political causes championed by labour, and so would not 'opt in' to the political fund" (*The Globe and Mail*, December 18, 1985: A21). Judge White found for the union's "opt-out" plan instead, allowing political uses of all dues unless non-union employees specifically objected (*Lavigne*, 1987). His reasons included the accepted status of the Rand Formula as "among the basic postulates of collective bargaining in Canada" and "an important factor in the stabilization of industrial peace" (*Lavigne*, 1987: 99–100). It also helped that the United States Supreme Court had decided this issue in the same way, holding that in these cases "dissent is not to be presumed" (*Lavigne*, 1987: 103). Judge White was also more generous than might have been expected on the issue of what constituted collective bargaining purposes. The judge was, in fact, pretty liberal in his definition, including union solidarity as a collective bargaining purpose and thus upholding payments to the striking UK mineworkers and for the sponsorship of a tour of Nicaraguan unionists in Canada. All other political contributions, however, were deemed "improper."

But there were hidden dangers in the opt-out provision. It had its own logical requirements, once again following US precedents, to protect the would-be dissenter. The union would have to provide

a detailed accounting of funds received...Non-collective bargaining purposes will have to be identified, as will the proportion of union expenditures for such proposes...detailed accounting of disbursements...detailed breakdown of expenses made for collective bargaining, as well as non-collective bargaining purposes...at a minimum, all employees should have access to the union's accounting records which categorize and quantify expenditures, to enable the dissenting employee to follow the use of his or her dues to its ultimate disbursement...Furthermore, such an employee should have the opportunity to challenge any item of expense...it is vital that the union provide some voluntary plan by which objecting non-members would be afforded an adequate internal remedy. I regard as indispensable the need for a procedure whereby a nonmember can obtain a speedy decision from an impartial arbitrator, on the propriety of any union expenditure (*Lavigne*, 1987: 121).

Though *The Globe and Mail* wrote that the ruling "takes the sting out" of the judgment, its significance was not lost on either the NCC or the unions. David Somerville (who had by then inherited the leadership of the NCC) called it "a terrific pro-freedom judgement" with a definition of non-collective bargaining wide enough for NCC purposes and added that he was pleased that workers would "have access to more financial data from unions" (*The Globe and Mail*, July 8, 1987: A2). He said the NCC would carry on an advertising campaign on national television to exploit the decision which "would encourage hundreds of thousands of Canadian workers to revoke their union memberships and demand a good portion of their forced union dues back" (*The Globe and Mail*, July 9, 1987: A10). John Ward, a spokesman for OPSEU, said that the ruling set up "a horrendously complex and difficult procedure over an issue that involves very little money" (*The Globe and Mail*, July 8, 1987: A2).

Whether or not anyone besides Merv Lavigne "opts out," implementing and maintaining the court-ordered procedures will cost money. That money will have to come from somewhere, and that somewhere will most likely be the political account. This will tend, however slightly, to reduce unions to their assigned role of arguing about wages and to make them neglect the more fundamental questions the Court calls "political." But are there any costs besides these inevitable financial ones? Under this order, unions will have to open up all of their activities and financial dealings not only to their membership but to deadly enemies like Lavigne. This does not seem to worry the public sector unions, who claim that they already operate openly (*The Globe and Mail*, July 8, 1987: A2). It would be nice, in fact, if the same logic were applied to the government of Canada's secretive security service, to corporations, or indeed to the NCC itself. But there is little chance of that. In the last chapter we saw how jealously the courts protect the Canadian government's secrets from us (*Zanganeh*, 1988). As for corporations:

> In contrast to unions—that undertake action on the basis of majority votes at conventions—...corporations sponsor all sorts of causes without ever consulting their employees, their customers, or even their shareholders (Clancy, et al., 1985:4).

Forget about the shareholders, who have a vote (naturally on a one-dollar-one-vote basis). Imagine if unions or customers had the same right of access to corporate financial and political dealings that *Lavigne* gives the union's enemies to union dealings. Now imagine this applied to the National Citizens' Coalition.

But corporations and the NCC have too many defence mechanisms under the Charter. First among them is the fact that the Charter applies only to "government." Somerville made this point in a letter to the editor of *The Toronto Star* (July 16, 1986: A16):

> While there is clear government action involved in forcing a worker to pay dues, there is no government action involved with buying shares in, or goods and services from, corporations. The purpose of the Charter is to protect individuals and minorities from unjust government action.

It does not take much reflection to see how superficial this argument is. In reality, the government is deeply implicated in corporate power. The basic elements of the common law of property and of contract, backed up by the police, the prisons, and the courts, allow corporate power to expand and to be wielded in purely private interests. Of course, this is where *Dolphin Delivery* comes in to declare, for the purely ideological reasons we have already gone into, that the common law is not "governmental." What about government policies that support corporate power, such as tax policies that allow the deductibility of expenditures on political causes? OPSEU thought it had a good Charter argument on this one, and it actually tried to use it to get revenge against the NCC itself. In *Ontario Public Service Employees Union* v. *National Citizens' Coalition* (*OPSEU*, 1987), it challenged the tax deductibility of contributions by business to the NCC for its political activities. The claim was that this interfered with freedom of expression, freedom of association, and equality because working people were not allowed to make such deductions. The case was thrown out summarily on a combination of the precise market logic that won the day against the *Election Act* and the reliable principle/policy distinction that won in the Right to Strike cases. The Court could not "see" how giving more freedom of expression to the rich diminished freedom of expression for the rest of us:

I cannot see how different tax treatment of certain taxpayers as alleged...could affect the freedom of a taxpayer to express herself or himself. The same really holds true about the allegation of a violation of the freedom of association (*OPSEU*, 1987: 452).

Nor would it allow the Charter to be "trivialized" by delving into the nuts and bolts of tax policy:

It seems to me that it comes very close to trivializing that very important constitutional law, if it is used to get into the weighing and balancing of the nuts and bolts of taxing statutes (*OPSEU*, 1987: 452).

So the Charter logic that requires public sector unions to respect the freedoms of their dissenters cannot be readily applied to either the government, corporations, or right wing lobby groups. *Lavigne* may mean that public sector unions are the only institutions in Canada that have to respect the rules of liberal democracy! But the real negative impact of *Lavigne* is not on the openness of unions but on their willingness and ability to engage in political activity beyond the narrow economistic confines of collective bargaining:

...[T]he danger is that in so far as the unions ward off challenges by minimizing the scope and significance of their political activities, the NCC and their ilk win a substantive victory whatever the court decisions (Panitch and Swartz, 1988: 113).

The limits of the applicability of the decision to non-members is also a red herring. Realistically, a union cannot offer its non-members greater rights to opt out than it offers to its members. Any rights the courts grant to the Lavignes of this world will have to be extended by unions to their own membership, or that membership can be expected to decline. *Lavigne* effectively stigmatizes "political" activity by unions as less legitimate than collective bargaining activity, even if this was not its precise holding. It rigidifies the separation of public and private spheres and, in effect, confines the unions to the private sphere where they are no match for business. And it does this at the same time as the Charter prohibits government from making business stay out of politics by election spending laws. Quite an achievement for the NCC. But it could not have done it without the Charter.

The Lavigne case is only the first blood in the holy Charter war against unionism. Lawyer Morris Manning has been busy earning his money from "Freedom of Choice." In July 1986, he issued a notice on behalf of two anti-union Eaton's workers, challenging eleven sections of the Ontario *Labour Relations Act* as contrary to three sections of the Charter. If successful, this action would abolish all "restrictions on the rights of an employer and employee to negotiate directly the terms and conditions of employment" (*Butters and Oberlein*, 1986). Another "Freedom of Choice" case, involving first Manning (*The Globe and Mail*, October 31, 1986: A9) and then the late Chief Justice's son, John I. Laskin, challenged closed-shop agreements and province-wide construction industry bargaining. Freedom of Choice member Dorothy Foran, owner of Arlington Cranes Services, claims she wants to hire her grandson, who does not want to join the union. She has already spent more than one million dollars fighting unions and claims she is ready to go to the Supreme Court of Canada "to free everybody in this country." Laskin, however, claims

the issue in this case is not whether unions are good or bad...This case is very simply about freedom of choice (*The Globe and Mail*, June 2, 1988: A17).

The Charter is being used in similar ways all over the country. A closed-shop agreement entered into by a purely private sector union narrowly escaped scrutiny in a 3–2 decision of the British Columbia Court of Appeal (*Bhindi*, 1986), decided just two weeks before *Lavigne*. A majority held that the Charter did not apply to private contracts, and the fact that the particular contract provision was permitted by law did not make it governmental enough. Two judges, however, held that since unions had no rights at common law and their legal status (the enforceability of their collective agreements) depended entirely on statute, the Charter should apply.

In the OPSEU promotional video on the *Lavigne* case, Wayne Roberts tells a story about the elaborate iron gatework at Osgoode Hall, Toronto's main courthouse. It has a curious maze-like entrance that can only be entered one person at a time. It seems there was a large Irish working-class community living nearby, and Roberts claims the gate was constructed to prevent rushes on the courts when anti-working-class judgments were issued (though others have said it had more to do with stray cows). Roberts argues that the Charter is merely "a fancier gate for our generation," isolating workers and unions from each other by preventing united political action in cases like *Lavigne*. Nice point, but does he mean it? The same film shows OPSEU defiantly taking the NCC to court over deductions (it omits the part where it loses) and promising to fight *Lavigne* all the way to the Supreme Court of Canada (*OPSEU*, 1987; Clancy et al., 1985: 1).

At the time of writing the *Lavigne* appeal had just opened in the Ontario Court of Appeal. The main argument for the union was once again that the collective agreement was "private" (*The Globe and Mail*, June 16, 1988: A15). In fact, the realization must finally be dawning on unions that they will be far better off the more narrowly the notion of "governmental" is interpreted by the courts—the more narrow the Charter's range of applicability. But this is only because organized labour would have been better off still if the Charter had never been enacted.

Doing Business with the Charter

Collective bargaining is only one of the fronts in the war between the classes where the Charter has been a useful new weapon for business. Business has also trained the Charter at every other imaginable form of government regulation as part of an all-out assault on purely political forms of interference with the free reign of economic power. The goal seems to be to turn back the clock to the days of the so-called free market when the law of the jungle—otherwise known as the common law—prevailed. So far business has been only partially successful, but this has not been for lack of trying, and it is more than labour can say for itself.

Property in the Constitution

If labour took a holiday for the Charter hearings, the same cannot be said of business. The Business Council on National Issues, made up of the chief executive officers of 140 corporations with over 125 billion in annual sales among them, was front and centre, calling for the entrenchment of property rights in the Charter "and the right not to be deprived thereof except by due process of law and not without just compensation." Represented at the hearings by the chairman of Stelco (annual revenue: $2.5 billion), the Council naturally argued that these rights, among others in the Charter, "should extend, not just to individuals or citizens, but to all persons, including corporate persons" (Canada, 1980–81, Issue No. 33: 134–135).

Explicit protection for property rights can be found in both the United States Constitution and the *Canadian Bill of Rights*. It was in the original draft of the Charter introduced as Bill C–60 by the Liberals in 1978. At the Charter hearings the Liberals claimed that their own personal preference was for the inclusion of property rights (Canada, 1980–81, Issue No. 45: 34). But property did not make it into the final version of the Charter for at least two reasons. First, provincial governments and the NDP (more on behalf of the NDP government of Saskatchewan than on behalf of socialism) insisted that it be dropped. The provinces had the major jurisdiction over property, and they feared judicial interference, especially in the realm of natural resources (Sheppard and Valpy, 1982: 151). The Liberals said it was only because of promises made to the provinces that they had to oppose the insertion of property rights. When the Tories formally proposed a property amendment at the Joint Committee, the Liberals combined with the NDP to defeat it (Canada, 1980–81, Issue No. 44: 12; Issue No. 46: 30). The second factor was the ideology of the Charter itself, as it appeared, for example, in the brief of the Canadian Bar Association to the Joint Committee. Anticipating the Supreme Court of Canada in the Right to Strike cases, the lawyers argued that "economic rights are not appropriate for protection in a Bill of Rights, that this question, too, is fundamentally one for the legislatures" (Canada, 1980–81, Issue No. 44: 27). If this suggests that the guild interests of the lawyers in a depoliticized Charter were more important to them than their purely *gilt* interests as property holders, we should not forget how closely these two things are related in the era of the Charter.

Section 7

Despite the inability to get property explicitly protected in the Charter, entrepreneurs have been arguing strenuously from the outset that it is in there implicitly. Is not doing business an exercise of "liberty"? So far, the courts have resisted this logic and have stayed faithful to the implications of the lack of the word "property" in the catalogue of interests in section 7. Almost without exception,[1] they have rejected business arguments that section 7 protects its right to do business free from regulation. Courts have consistently held that purely economic rights are not covered by the section:

> That section deals with rights to life, liberty and security of the person and commercial or economic rights are not covered by the clear wording of that section (*Gershman Produce*, 1985: 528; holding a trucking licence not to be protected by section 7).

> The concepts of 'life, liberty and security of the person'…have to do with the bodily well-being of a natural person. As such they are not apt to describe any rights of a corporation nor are they apt to describe purely economic interests of a natural person (*Smith, Kline & French Laboratories*, 1985: 363–364; holding patent rights not to be covered by section 7).

The courts have considered and rejected the application of section 7 to such matters as: the right to market wine kits in grocery stores (*Homemade Winecrafts*, 1986); the right to do business with the government (*Home Orderly Services*, 1986); the right of the aluminum industry to compete in the soft-drink can business (*Aluminum Co. of Canada*, 1986); the right to hold a liquor licence (*R.V.P. Enterprises*, 1987); the right to be free from compensation orders made by human rights commissions (*Pasqua Hospital*, 1987); and from adminstration fees charged by government (*Snell*, 1987). A judge of the Court of Appeal for Prince Edward Island argued

---

[1] One exception was *D.& H. Holdings*, 1985 in which a British Columbia trial judge held that a pub licence revocation was subject to section 7.

persuasively that some property rights must be implicitly protected by "security of the person" which

> must include provision for an adequate standard of living [and] a right for everyone to acquire such property, including land, as becomes necessary in order for them to enjoy in full measure the guaranteed right to security of the person (*Re PEI Lands Protection Act*, 1987: 17).

But there is no telling what this might mean. It had nothing to do with the case at hand in which the Court unanimously upheld the constitutionality of legislation limiting the size of land holdings in Prince Edward Island. The other two judges took the conventional view that property rights were not protected by section 7. And such a concept was nowhere to be seen when a tenant tried to assert a right to keep his apartment, despite a demolition clause expressly permitted by legislation (*Grant*, 1986).

The Supreme Court of Canada offhandedly confirmed this interpretation of section 7 in one of the Sunday opening cases (discussed below) with the following words of Chief Justice Dickson:

> Whatever the precise contours of "liberty" in s.7, I cannot accept that it extends to an unconstrained right to transact business whenever one wishes (*Edwards Books*, 1986: 54).

Somewhat more sympathy has been shown to claims by professionals that the right to practise a profession is covered by section 7. The medical profession in particular had some early successes. In *Mia* (1985), the Chief Justice of British Columbia took a very broad view of the word "liberty":

> There are some rights enjoyed by our people including the right to work or practice a profession that are so fundamental that they must be protected even if they include an economic element...

> Rights we have enjoyed for centuries include the right to pursue a calling or profession for which we are qualified, and to move freely throughout the realm for that purpose (*Mia*, 1985: 412).

The case involved a challenge by a British Columbia doctor to geographical and other restrictions placed on the right to bill the Medical Services Plan for services to patients. The limits had been introduced in 1983 without the benefit of legislation, and because of this, Justice McEachern deemed it unnecessary to consider whether or not they were reasonable (they were not "prescribed by law"). The government introduced the requisite legislation and did not bother to appeal. A Yukon Territory court subsequently held that "the right to go on practicing one's profession after full licensure and many years of practice" comes within s.7 (*Branigan*, 1986: 278), though it went on to hold that the disciplinary procedures challenged by the doctor were a "reasonable limit" under section 1.

These decisions seem to have allowed the Charter to play a role in the Ontario doctors' strike of 1986. Facing a threatened loss of $100 million under new federal legislation if it did not act, the Ontario government proposed to ban "extra-billing" (doctors charging patients more than they would be compensated for under provincial health insurance plans) in December 1985. There followed some legal sabre-rattling by the Ontario Medical Association.

The OMA's lawyer, Aubrey Golden, pronounced that the proposed law violated the Charter and would be challenged once enacted, under both section 7, as a denial of "freedom of contract," and under the equality provisions of the Charter, newly in force since April 1985 (*The Globe and Mail*, January 30, 1986: A18). It was not long before Charter free-lancers like Morris Manning were strutting their stuff on the Charter and the doctors. In an article in *Canadian Lawyer*, Manning warned of the law's unconstitutionality in terms he had recently been using for labour relations law. The proposed law, he wrote: "interferes directly in the physician-patient relationship," "has a direct impact on the liberty of contract between the physician (or hospital) and patient," and "seeks to end free enterprise in the physician-patient relationship":

> Fortunately, the constitution does not allow for this sort of political manipulation.

> The right to regulate physicians may be nothing new. But constitutional protection from the invasion of rights *is* something quite new.

> Canadians now live in an age when we are entitled to tell the government to stay out of our lives...The Ontario government's only reasonable course of action, in light of the constitutional infirmities it faces, is to hold off, negotiate and perhaps seek a constitutional reference (Manning, 1986: 44).

But the government was not going to be bullied by lawyers over a popular Bill to which it was committed, both because of the threatened federal sanctions and because of its minority government deal with the NDP. It enacted the Bill in June, provoking a 26-day doctors' strike that saw people being turned away from closed emergency wards.

About 10 days into the unpopular strike, the Charter emerged as the face-saving solution. The OMA announced it would go to court, and the government (obviously no more intimidated by court than Trudeau had been over the cruise missile or Mulroney would be over the postal strike) said it would do everything to expedite the action (*The Globe and Mail*, June 21, 1986: A17). A *Globe and Mail* editorial urged the doctors to end the strike with the legal action:

> The relegation of such questions to the courts should leave the way clear for doctors to suspend their disruptive and potentially injurious actions (*The Globe and Mail*, June 24, 1986: A6).

It only remained to pick the lucky lawyer. Top gun Edward Greenspan hoped out loud to be hired by the doctors, deeply offending OMA lawyer Aubrey Golden, who had to admit the case was "a bell-ringer, the kind of case lawyers dream about and want to do." Morris Manning himself went on radio to describe what his strategy would be if he were handling the case (*The Globe and Mail*, June 26, 1986: A18). When the OMA finally filed its papers and, then, on the same weekend ended the strike, it was announced that the plum assignment had gone to Gordon Henderson (of the Operation Dismantle action in the Supreme Court of Canada), who was already handling the CMA action. The two would be joined (*The Globe and Mail*, July 7, 1986: A10).[1]

This seems to be another example, in a completely different social context, of what we saw with the postal workers' strike of 1987. The Charter was a face-saving device, a way of appearing not to give in without actually taking any risks. The doctors could maintain their "principled" opposition while ending a strike that had proved very unpopular. However, the result in each case was somewhat different, in conformity with the Charter's tendency to replicate differences in social power. The postal workers wound up with judicial arbitration, a pay increase of 2.1%, less than half the rate of inflation (*The Toronto Star*, July 9, 1988: D5), and a saw-off on other issues, neither gains nor losses. But the doctors negotiated directly with the government and wound up with a fee increase of 8.8%, more than twice the rate of inflation, on incomes somewhat heftier than postal workers have—incomes that could be supplemented by an increase in total billings beyond what could be accounted for by the fee increase alone (*The Toronto Star*, July 30, 1988: A3). Not only that, persistent violations of the extra-billing law over the two years of its being in force have not led to a single prosecution (*The Globe and Mail*, August 25, 1988: A17).

What will the outcome be of the court case? Despite the spirited arguments of Manning and the rest it seems unlikely that section 7 will avail the doctors against the Ontario law. They have several obstacles to overcome. The first is to get their freedom of contract interests recognized as worthy of section 7 protection. Though Canadian courts are divided on whether the practice of a profession is "liberty" or not (*Charboneau*, 1985; *Wilson*, 1987, 1988), there seems to be agreement that those aspects of a profession that are purely commercial are not covered. A Manitoba doctor who challenged reductions in hospital insurance payments (for "over-servicing") was told by the Manitoba courts that such payments were not protected by section 7 (*Isabey*, 1985; 1986). And when the British Columbia courts thwarted for a second time the provincial government's attempts to impose geographical restrictions on doctors, they stressed the difference between questions of where, and even whether, a doctor could practice at all, on the one hand, and purely economic questions, such as how much a doctor could charge, on the other (*Wilson*, 1988).

Section 7 has further drawbacks. As we saw in Chapter IV, its main concern is with formal, not substantial justice. The question of whether property rights are covered by section 7 is really about whether these formal guarantees apply to infringements of property rights the way they do to infringements of personal rights. The courts in *Isabey* held that whether or not purely economic rights were covered, they could intervene only if a principle of fundamental justice were violated (*Isabey*, 1986, 1987). In *Wilson*, the British Columbia Court of Appeal relied not only on the geographical restrictions but also on the

---

[1] A private citizen angered at the strike actually beat the doctors to the punch and went to court claiming his section 7 rights were violated by the *strike*. The case was thrown out on procedural grounds (*The Globe and Mail*, June 25, 1986: A15; June 27, 1986: A15).

"uncontrolled discretion" given to administrators of the law which left "substantial scope for arbitrary conduct," as well as the law's discrimination against new practitioners and those who came from out of province. For the Charter to apply, section 7 rights have to be denied "in an unfair manner" (*Aluminum Co. of Canada*, 1986: 592). Not that formal guarantees are without value, especially to powerful groups such as the professions and business. It takes a determined government to overcome the legal and practical obstacles posed by them. As we saw in Chapter IV, business has made effective use of its formal protections under the Charter's explicit procedural guarantees, including the protection from "unreasonable search and seizure" applied in *Hunter* v. *Southam*. But formal guarantees have their limits. It is hard, for example, to see how they could help the doctors fight the ban on extra-billing, whether or not there was recognition of purely economic interests under section 7.

Given these limits, given the already ample formal protections elsewhere in the Charter and given the expansive notion of "liberty" being developed by the courts, the continuing campaign to "put property in the constitution" should probably be regarded as an example of symbolic Charter politics, like the Meech Lake Accord. As for actual legal results, business and the professions have Charter cards up their sleeves with at least as much legal punch, and far more political appeal, than property rights in section 7.

Freedom of Religion and the Right to do Business on Sunday

Well before the enactment of the *Charter*, Canadian legislatures were easing up the restrictions on Sunday commercial activity. The federal *Lord's Day Act* had given provinces the option of opening up Sunday since 1906, but it was only in the 1950s that they began to exercise this right and permitted events of a cultural, recreational, and entertainment nature to take place on Sundays. By the early 1970s virtually all of the provinces had joined this trend. In the mid-seventies, a second wave of activity took place to allow further limited commercialization, mostly of the corner-store variety. Leading the way was Ontario's *Retail Business Holidays Act* of 1976 (Law Reform Commission of Canada, 1976b: 19–20). This was followed by similar legislation in other provinces. In 1976, the Law Reform Commission of Canada recommended the repeal of the *Lord's Day Act* in favour of provincial jurisdiction. They argued that treating Sunday as a question of morality and criminal law had become an anachronism and that it should be treated as a local and secular matter (Law Reform Commission of Canada, 1976b: 49). But the federal government was not anxious to embroil itself in unnecessary controversy. A big step was taken in 1980, when the Social Credit government of British Columbia enacted the *Holiday Shopping Regulation Act* (1980), which left the entire question to local municipal option, leading to more or less wide-open

Sunday shopping in Vancouver (*Vancouver Sun*, August 13, 1984: A3; October 16, 1984: A14).

A lot of things are contributing to the pressure for Sunday shopping. Most often cited are the entry of women into the work force and the increase in single parent families, making mid-week shopping almost impossible (*The Globe and Mail*, December 18, 1986: A7). Also cited are a decline in the proportion of the population adhering to Sunday-observing religions because of changing immigration patterns, a decline in overall religious observance, and even the rise of so-called "recreational shopping." All this makes it sound as if the goal were merely to accommodate the customer: the same amount of shopping spread more leisurely over a greater number of shopping days. But the problem of time to shop, and a lot of unemployment too, could easily be handled by a shorter individual work week. The major factor propelling wide-open Sundays is not customer satisfaction but business satisfaction. Wherever Sunday shopping has been allowed, total economic activity and total retail profits have increased (Laband and Heinbuch, 1987: 205; *The Globe and Mail*, February 19, 1987: A8; December 5, 1987: B1, B4). That is why the pro-Sunday shopping lobby is almost totally a business lobby. Not that business is unanimous. Its allegiance is divided between increased profits and religious affiliation, the major Christian religious groups being opposed. There are also some exceptions in the case of those small retailers who either benefit from the current law or who would be forced against their will by mall owners to open on Sunday if it were legal. Most of the non-religious opposition comes from organized labour, which knows that the freedom to shop on Sunday for some means the compulsion to work on Sundays for others. The Ontario NDP has taken to calling the issue "the Sunday working" issue (*The Globe and Mail*, April 6, 1988: A11). Although it is non-unionized workers who are most at risk, and retail is notoriously under-unionized, union members fear family disruption when non-unionized spouses have to work (women are over-represented in retail), and they fear having to bargain away something else at the negotiating table for Sunday holidays (*The Globe and Mail*, December 5, 1987: B1, B4). Some consumers, too, have opposed Sunday shopping because of the tendency of the freedom to shop to become the compulsion to shop (*The Globe and Mail*, December 2, 1987: A15).

With the enactment of the Charter, businesses opposed to Sunday closing laws saw an opportunity to achieve through the courts what they have had difficulty getting the legislatures to stick their necks out on. There had been a lot of litigation in the US on the subject, but the US courts had upheld the power of the states to prohibit Sunday shopping. Still, this technically unsuccessful litigation had gone hand in hand with a progressive opening of American Sundays to commercial activity (Laband and Heinbuch, 1987). And there were important legal differences between Canadian and American arrangements making success a reasonable prospect, including the fact that the Charter was still—is still—on its "honeymoon." The first target was the *Lord's*

Day Act itself, still in force in the majority of provinces at the time of the Charter.[1] And business scored a bull's-eye in *R. v. Big M Drug Mart* (*Big M*, 1985).

Big M was a corporation that operated a drug store in Calgary which stayed open on Sundays despite the federal *Lord's Day Act* (which was still in force in Alberta). When charged under the Act, the corporation pleaded the "freedom of religion" clause of the Charter. The Supreme Court was unanimous in overruling its prior decisions under *The Canadian Bill of Rights* and the law was struck down.

In strictly legal terms, the case was an easy one, or rather, the Court made it an easy one by adhering to the old *BNA Act* precedents holding that the *Lord's Day Act* was legislation with a primarily religious purpose. That was the ground upon which the provincial Sunday closing laws had been declared invalid at the turn of the century under the constitutional division of powers. So the law could only be justified as *federal* law on the anachronistic basis that its purpose was to enforce religious morality. But in enforcing religious morality, it ran afoul of the freedom-of-religion clause of the Charter. Furthermore, it could not be defended as a "reasonable limit" on any secular ground (e.g. a common "pause day"). That would deprive it of its jurisdictional validity, i.e. its validity as *federal* law. If this all sounds like a complicated shell game, it is because, by the 1980s, Sunday closing was being primarily defended on secular grounds. In fact, the major jurisdictional responsibility for the law was with the provinces, either in their own right or through the opt-out clauses of the federal law. But in the way the Supreme Court approached the issue, the secular function of these laws could not be considered. According to the precedents, the "purpose" of the law was *deemed* to be religious (the Court was not really interested in why any of the legislators voted for it). Its actual effect was therefore irrelevant:

> [E]ither an unconstitutional purpose or an unconstitutional effect can invalidate legislation (*Big M*, 1985: 350).

Big M is really a study in abstraction. The purpose of the law was abstractly determined, and its concrete function was deemed irrelevant. Even the respect in which the Act was said to violate freedom of religion was abstract:

> To the extent that it binds all to a sectarian Christian ideal, the *Lord's Day Act* works a form of coercion inimical to the spirit of the Charter and the dignity of all non-Christians. In proclaiming the standards of the Christian faith the Act creates a climate hostile to, and gives the appearance of discrimination against, non-Christian Canadians. It takes religious values rooted in Christian morality and using the force of the state, translates them into a positive law binding on believers and non-believers alike. The theological content of the legislation remains as a subtle and constant reminder to religious minorities within the country of their differences with, and alienation from, the dominant religious culture (*Big M*, 1985: 354).

---

[1] Though it was no longer the law in Ontario, Quebec, British Columbia, and Newfoundland.

Of course, the Act only did this by virtue of the *deemed* purpose ascribed to it by the precedents. There was not one shred of evidence before the Court that anybody was actually offended by the law. The accused was a corporation, an abstract entity created by the law to limit liability, entirely without human feeling. It was conceded by everyone that Big M had no religion and worshipped only the Almighty Dollar. It wanted to open to make money:

> [A] corporation, being a statutory creation, cannot be said to have a conscience or hold a religious belief (*Big M*, 1985: 335).

And what right did the corporation have to rely on freedom of religion? Again the answer was abstract. Though it admittedly had violated the law and the law admittedly had not offended its religion, nevertheless, according to the Court, Big M had the right to claim on a criminal charge that the law was unconstitutional, even though, to paraphrase Justice McIntyre's dissent in *Smith* (above, pages 156–157), this unconstitutionality was entirely with respect to a hypothetical third party. In other words, the case had the familiar Charter "air of unreality" about it, and, whatever the merits of the argument on standing, it shows us once again how far the courts have strayed from their role as *judges* with the advent of the Charter. The case becomes merely a *pretext* to review the law on grounds that have nothing to do with parties in court. And this is no mere debating point. It means that the case is decided and the law struck down in the absence of evidence from anyone concretely affected by it. There was clearly no one in court in *Big M* whose religious sentiments were offended by the law. The best the Court could do was to conjure up someone who might be *reminded* by the law that their religion was not the dominant one. And suppose this was an effect of the law. So what? It certainly was not the only reminder. And that is because it is a fact that if one is not Christian in Canada[1] one is not part of the religious majority. Census figures for 1981 show 90% of Canadians affiliated with some Christian church (Canada, 1985: 60–61). Are we supposed to hide all the churches behind camouflage?

Which brings us to the other singular fact about this case. Not only was there no one in court claiming they were offended by the law, there was no one in court to speak up for those who were offended by its *violation*, namely the believing Christians. (There must be some out there among those 90%!) Remember that we are not dealing with a law that forced anyone to renounce their religious beliefs or to profess the beliefs of the majority. The law merely required that non-Christians abstain from activities of no religious significance to them in order—even accepting the deemed purpose of the law—to avoid offence to the majority. The Supreme Court forbade this because it might offend the minority:

> If I am a Jew or a Sabbatarian or a Muslim, the practice of my religion at least implies my right to work on a Sunday if I wish. It seems to me that any law purely religious in purpose, which denies me that right, must surely infringe my religious freedom (*Big M*, 1985: 355).

---

[1] As I am not, I hasten to add.

"Purely religious" in *deemed* purpose that is, but never mind. On the balance of (presumed) offence who is to win? The minority who might be offended or the majority who might be offended? The Court found the notion that the law might be framed to accommodate the majority to be "fundamentally repugnant" (*Big M*, 1985: 366), an example of the "tyranny of the majority" (*Big M*, 1985: 354). But the alternative was the tyranny of the minority, and a "deemed" minority at that. Once again, the point is not merely that the Court made the wrong decision, but that it had no rational means of making the right one. It had no business deciding this issue in the first place.

One senses in reading this decision that the Court felt it had an opportunity for a free advertisement for the effectiveness of the Charter.[1] The provinces were already in effective control of Sundays. The *Lord's Day Act* was a jurisdictional anachronism whose repeal had been recommended a decade before by the Law Reform Commission of Canada.

But, in fact, the decision gave Sunday shopping a big boost. Provincial governments were thrown into confusion. Several provinces relied exclusively on the *Lord's Day Act*, and its invalidity meant that their governments would have to take immediate action on a controversial subject. The easiest thing to do was to hand the problem over to local municipalities the way the government of British Columbia had done. This was the course followed by Alberta itself and New Brunswick as well, each of which introduced new legislation within three months on British Columbia's model (*Municipal Government Amendment Act*, 1985, s. 31; *Days of Rest Act*, 1985). Essentially, this meant a capitulation to business, which would have little trouble toppling municipalities like "dominoes" (*The Globe and Mail*, December 5, 1986: A13).

Other provinces which had relied on the federal legislation rushed in with their own closing laws.[2] Within a year of *Big M*, the Supreme Court was dealing with the question of the validity of these provincial Sunday closing laws in a case involving the Ontario Act of 1976 (*The Globe and Mail*, March 3, 1986: A14; *Edwards Books*, 1986). As a situation of increasing chaos developed in the Toronto retail trade, the Court rushed to judgment and, in fact, announced it weeks in advance at the height of the Christmas shopping frenzy (*The Globe and Mail*, Dec. 5, 1986: A1–A2).

Chief Justice Dickson had already telegraphed the Supreme Court's view of provincial Sunday closing laws in *Big M*:

> The other more plausible argument is that everyone accepts the need and value

---

[1] This is one case in which one feels rather less uncomfortable than usual ascribing purposes to the Court that transcend its expressed reasons, because this is one case in which the Chief Justice himself, in perhaps an unguarded moment, employed this very type of analysis to the reasoning of other courts: "It is somewhat ironic the United States courts upheld the validity of Sunday observance laws, characterizing them as secular *in order not to run afoul of the religion clauses of the First Amendment*, while in contrast, in *Robertson v. Rosetanni*, ... the [Supreme Court of Canada] found in the same type of legislation, a religious purpose *to sustain its vires as criminal law*. At the same time it accorded to the legislation a secular effect *in order not to bring it into conflict with the religious freedom recognized and declared in the Canadian Bill of Rights*" (*Big M*, 1985: 349; emphasis added).

[2] E.g. Prince Edward Island (the *Day of Rest Act*, 1985) and Nova Scotia (the *Retail Business Uniform Closing Day Act*, 1985).

of a universal day of rest from all work, business and labour and it may as well be the day traditionally observed in our society. I accept the secular justification for a day of rest in a Canadian context and the reasonableness of a day of rest has been clearly enunciated by the courts of the United States of America (*Big M*, 1985: 366).

The Supreme Court stayed true to its word in *Edwards Books*, sustaining Ontario's *Retail Business Holidays Act* (1976) in its entirety. The Act made it an offence punishable by a maximum $10,000 fine to open on Sundays as well as eight other secular and religious days (New Year's Day, Good Friday, Victoria Day, Dominion Day, Labour Day, Thanksgiving Day, Christmas Day, and Boxing Day). There were some exemptions of the "corner-store" and recreational variety, as well as a limited exemption for stores closed on Saturday, if the Sunday operation was limited to no more than 5,000 square feet and seven employees. The appeals involved charges against a variety of Toronto retailers: a bookstore, grocery store, and furrier which were open seven days a week, and a food store which closed on Saturday and other Jewish religious days but whose Sunday operation was larger than that allowed for in the Act. The Ontario Court of Appeal had sustained the law and the convictions of all but the Jewish food store, holding that the exemption was not complete enough to avoid infringing freedom of religion (*Videoflicks*, 1984). The Supreme Court of Canada, on the other hand, sustained the law in its entirety, including (over Justice Wilson's dissent) the limited exemption for Saturday observers, thus restoring the conviction of the Jewish food store.

Though they mostly agreed in result, the judges went every which way in their reasons. They were only unanimous in declaring that the Act was secular and not religious in "purpose," meaning that it could be justified as providing uniform holidays to retail workers and not merely as a "surreptitious attempt to encourage religious worship" (*Edwards Books*, 1986: 407). This justification, equally applicable to the *Lord's Day Act* in fact, could now be applied in law, because the provinces had ample jurisdiction over labour relations under the division of powers. The many non-religious aspects of the law, and the fact that Sunday was the world's most common pause day, existing even in godless socialist countries such as the USSR and Yugoslavia, also helped.

Notwithstanding its secular purpose, four out of the seven judges (Justices Dickson, Chouinard, Wilson, and Le Dain) held that the *effect* of the Act was nevertheless to infringe upon freedom of religion. Justice La Forest expressed no opinion, and Justices Beetz and McIntyre disagreed. The infringement of freedom of religion was found in the competitive advantage conferred on Sunday observers over those who observed other days as holy days. They would have to close on their holy day, and the Act required them to close on Sunday as well. Given the competitive pressures of the retail trade, reasoned Justice Dickson, this might force observers of other holy days to forsake their religion in order to save their businesses. It was clear on this reasoning that only religious believers could complain, since it was competitive pressure to abandon one's beliefs that was the problem. Those who wanted to stay open seven days a week were out of luck. The most that they could say was that the law required them to act consistently with the dictates of some other religion (though not inconsistently with the dictates of any religion of their own). But this could be said of any law consistent with any religion. Was one exempt from the law against murder because it could be found in the Ten Commandments? Since the law had a good secular justification that could be recognized by the Court, it could not infringe the freedom of religion of non-believers.

Justice La Forest sat on the fence: he was ready to accept that a competitive advantage *could* amount to sufficient pressure to interfere with religious freedom, but he preferred not to decide this point in the absence of more evidence that it *did* constitute sufficient pressure. On the other side were Justices Beetz and McIntyre. They did not see any infringement on freedom of religion in all of this. They felt that, if anything, the proper complaint was that the law discriminated unfairly in favour of Sunday observers. In that case, the proper basis for the challenge was the equality provision of the Charter, but since the claim arose before the magic day of April 17, 1985, when the equality clause came into effect, it had to be ignored (*Edwards Books*, 1986: 442).

The majority went on to hold, though, that even if the Act did infringe freedom of religion, it was a reasonable limit under section 1. The "desirability of enabling parents to have regular days off from work in common with their child's day off from school, and with a day off enjoyed by most other family and community members" was for Chief Justice Dickson (as it is for everybody else, whether on the judicial bench or on the park bench) "self-evident" (*Edwards Books*, 1986: 426). This was also the obvious justification for the Act's exception for recreational activities. There was no dissent from these propositions from any of the judges. How could there be? The only difficulties arose over the nature of the Saturday exemption, whether there had to be one and what it had to look like.

Here a very interesting thing happened. In discussing the details of allowable exceptions, whether for the size of enterprise or the nature of the trade, Chief Justice Dickson came for a moment to the heart of the whole matter, not merely of Sunday opening, but of the Charter itself. As if in response to the critique from the left, Dickson actually let Justice's blindfold slip a little and advanced inequality in social power in defence of the Act. He said that restricting the prohibition to the retail trade was justified not only by the peculiar competitive pressures of the retail trade, but also by the vulnerability of the work force due to its "low level of unionization, its high proportion of women, and its generally heterogeneous composition" (*Edwards Books*, 1986: 427). Furthermore, though he insisted that some attempt had to be made to accommodate Saturday observers by an exemption, he did not fault the legislature for restricting the exemption to small retailers. This, he said, was justified as "minimizing the disruptive effect of any exemption on the scope and quality of the pause day" with special regard—and this is the important point—for the vulnerability of the employees intended to benefit:

> It is, perhaps, worth stating the obvious: a store with eight or more employees serving the public at any one time or with 5,000 square feet of retail space, indeed, constitutes a substantial retail operation. Such a store is not, by any

stretch, a mere corner store staffed by the family. *In interpreting and applying the Charter I believe the courts must be cautious to ensure that it does not simply become an instrument of better situated individuals to roll back legislation which has as its object the improvement of the condition of less advantaged persons.* When the interests of more than seven vulnerable employees in securing a Sunday holiday are weighed against the interests of their employer in transacting business on a Sunday, I cannot fault the Legislature for determining that the protection of the employees ought to prevail (*Edwards Books*, 1986: 433; emphasis added).

What shall we make of this sensitivity to differences in social power? Is it a contradiction of the legalization of politics thesis? This is a difficult point. One is tempted to interpret this passage in terms of orthodox judicial review theory. This is policy, a question of competing interests that must be brokered by the legislature. Courts should avoid getting enmeshed in controversial questions of policy and should stick to the clear answers of principle. But, as we have seen time and time again, the courts are the complete masters of these categories. The Right to Strike cases could have been treated as principle or as policy with equal success in philosophical terms. The results in those cases were dictated by other considerations. What might they be in this case? One difference between these cases and the Right to Strike cases is that the Right to Strike cases involved *organized* workers, and it was *unorganized* workers that attracted the Court's sympathy here. The organized working class is much more of a threat to the social status quo than unorganized workers. Unorganized workers are no threat at all. It bears remembering that when Charter advocates like Beatty sing its praises, it is for advancing "the interests of workers who are *least advantaged*" (Beatty, 1987: 11) not workers period. Things can be moderately equalized between unorganized workers and organized workers without threatening relations between workers in general and business. The Court can well afford to befriend the unorganized worker without threatening anyone, and it can, at the same time, enhance the prestige of the Charter. Especially since its friendship only goes so far:

> This is not to say that the legislature is constitutionally obligated to give effect to employee interests in preference to the interests of the store owner for large retail operations, but only that it may do so if it wishes (*Edwards Books*, 1986: 433).

Of course Justice Dickson was willing, in the Right to Strike cases, to uphold the right to organize and strike as a protected freedom whether or not the legislature agreed. But let us not forget that he was willing to see it overridden on almost any grounds. Furthermore, his ability to attract more support for his point of view on the Sunday opening issue than on the right to strike was obviously due to the differences in what was concretely at stake in the two cases.

Justice Dickson's willingness to defer to the legislature in its reconciliation of freedom of religion with the vulnerability of retail workers was in fact shared only by Justices Chouinard and Le Dain. Justice Wilson would not let the Blindfold slip an inch. According to her, the Saturday-observer exception was inadequate because it was incomplete. She would recognize absolutely no distinctions according to the size of enterprise. Why? Because that would sacrifice principle to policy, which was explicitly forbidden by Professor Dworkin:

> It is, in my view, a "compromised scheme of justice." It does not affirm a *principle* which is applicable to all. It reflects rather a failure on the part of the Legislature to make up its mind which scheme of justice to adopt. The result is, in my opinion what Professor Dworkin refers to as "checkerboard" legislation (*Edwards Books*, 1986: 445; emphasis in original).

Justice Wilson went so far as to argue that the legislation drove a wedge between co-religionists, some of whom could and some of whom could not open on Sundays:

> To do so is to introduce an invidious distinction into the group and sever the religious and cultural tie that binds them together (*Edwards Books*, 1986: 444–445).

As if the only distinction between large Jewish retailers and small Jewish retailers is whether they can open on Sunday or not. Does Justice Wilson think that, once they are subject to the same Sunday opening laws, the small-timers and the big-timers will suddenly start to live in the same neighbourhoods? Shop in the same stores? Go to the same synagogues? See eye to eye? In this judgment, abstraction has broken new records.

At the other extreme was Justice La Forest. He did not feel that the legislature had to grant any exception whatsoever. But he grounded his position in a philosophy of judicial restraint in complicated policy matters rather than in any concern for vulnerable workers:

> ...I am of the view that the nature of the choices and compromises that must be made in relation to Sunday closing are essentially legislative in nature. In the absence of unreasonableness or discrimination, courts are simply not in a position to substitute their judgment for that of the Legislature (*Edwards Books*, 1986: 459).

To prove his point La Forest refused to be bound by the ludicrously scanty evidence thrown up by the adversary system in the case. It consisted entirely of the one 16-year-old Ontario Law Reform Commission Report. As Justice Dickson had pointed out in his judgment, the adversary system had stymied any attempt for a more up-to-date record:

> It would have been preferable to have had more recent evidence, and, indeed, the Crown filed notice, less than a week before the hearing, of a motion to adduce additional evidence. Apparently, this evidence included attitudinal surveys or public opinion polls, and also various submissions to a provincial task force looking into Sunday closing laws. Crown counsel conceded the evidence was not essential to her s.1 submissions. Counsel for the retailers objected vigorously to the timing of the motion. The motion was denied in view of the possible prejudicial consequences of admitting it into evidence at the eleventh hour.

I am conscious of the possibility that some of the statistical evidence contained in the report has been rendered less helpful by the passage of time. Nevertheless, it is the only evidence before the court and I have considered the age of the materials in assessing its weight (*Edwards Books*, 1986: 426).

Justice Dickson had partially sidestepped the problem by deciding the case on its "self-evidence." But this was not good enough for La Forest, who defied judicial convention and went out and got his own evidence (or had his clerk do it):

> Besides, I do not accept that in dealing with broad social and economic facts such as those involved here the court is necessarily bound to rely solely on those presented by counsel. The admonition in *Oakes* and other cases to present evidence in Charter cases does not remove from the court the power, where it deems it expedient, to take judicial notice of broad social and economic facts and to take the necessary steps to inform itself about them...

> There are, of course, dangers to judicial notice, but the alternative in a case like this is to make an assumption without facts or to make a decision dependent on the evidence counsel has chosen to present...It is undesirable that an Act be found constitutional today and unconstitutional tomorrow simply on the basis of the particular evidence of broad social and economic facts that happens to have been presented by counsel (*Edwards Books*, 1986: 456–457).

La Forest's judgment is, in effect, a testimony to the inherent weaknesses of the legal system as a forum for resolving controversial political questions. Once we finish congratulating him for refusing to be bound by the evidence presented by the adversaries, we are left with the question of why such issues should ever be resolved in a forum that must violate its distinctive conventions even to approximate the fundamentals of rational judgment.[1]

So once again, the Supreme Court spoke with many different tongues and clarified nothing. But after the heads were counted, the law had prevailed in its general contours by the unanimous vote of the judges and in its tiniest detail by a healthy margin of six to one. Did this settle the matter? No way! The Sunday after *Edwards Books* was decided, one of the losers, Toronto furrier Paul Magder, was open for business, adding to his by then over 200 outstanding charges under the Act (*The Globe and Mail*, December 20, 1986: A12; *The Toronto Star*, December 20, 1986: A9). In April, he and his tenacious lawyer, Timothy Danson, were back in Provincial Court asking the judge to ignore the Supreme Court's barely four-month-old baby of a decision on the grounds that it was based on outdated material[2] (*The Globe and Mail*, April 29, 1987: A14). He was armed with new polls, American businessmen testifying to the glories of Sunday shopping, and Magder employees claiming they

---

[1] Justice La Forest's tendency to make decisions on the basis of his own research, whatever the evidence presented at the hearing, came in for a thinly veiled rebuke from the dissenting Justice Estey, on the eve of his retirement, in *Mercure*: "Since writing these reasons for judgment I have had the opportunity of reading those of my colleague, La Forest, J., who makes reference to historical material. The record before the Court does not include these historical opinions and comments...Without the admission of this material through the conventional processes of justice the reliability of such material is not demonstrated. Accordingly, I seek to confine my reasons to the record and to government census statistics and Hansard as introduced or adverted to by counsel for the several parties." (*Mercure*, 1988: 177–178).

[2] Danson was one of the "counsel for the retailers" who, according to Justice Dickson, "objected vigorously" to the admission of more up-to-date material in *Edwards Books* (1986: 391, 426).

were under no pressure to work Sundays, Magder's busiest day (*The Globe and Mail*, April 30, 1987: A17). They actually won this one, but on an equality basis. Magder claimed the legislation discriminated against him unfairly. He was unable to open despite the tourist designation of his area because of the goods he sold (*The Lawyers Weekly*, September 18, 1987: 8). In April of 1988 the acquittal was overturned, but Danson promised a return to the Supreme Court of Canada: "I'm confident this case will go back up there where it belongs" (*The Globe and Mail*, April 7, 1988: A18). At the same time, Danson was re-litigating the question of the Saturday exemption with two Jewish retailers (*The Globe and Mail*, November 18, 1987: A17; November 20, 1987: A19). He lost that one, too (*The Globe and Mail*, December 24, 1987: A14), but he has plenty of appeals left (*Canadian Jewish News*, March 10, 1988: 3), especially in light of the comments made by Justices Beetz and McIntyre in *Edwards Books* about the possible application of the equality provisions (*Edwards Books*, 1986: 442). You can bet Timothy Danson is working Sundays, even if he is not making quite as much out of it as Paul Magder is.

Most businesses decided to obey the law while simultaneously putting on the pressure to change it. Edwards Books and Art Store won a limited legislative exemption for bookstores and art galleries by the summer following the loss in the Supreme Court, after staging a "CanLit" celebrity read-in to protest against the "Philistines" in government who permitted pornographic movies to be shown on Sunday while banning the sale of good literature (*The Globe and Mail*, December 22, 1986: A17; *An Act to amend the Retail Business Holidays Act*, 1987). Apart from this exception, the law held firm. This did not satisfy the press and the major retailers, who continued to press for wide-open Sundays (*The Globe and Mail*, February 19, 1987: A8; May 26, 1987: A4; *The Toronto Star*, July 29, 1987: A20).

Before the year was up, the Ontario government announced legislation on the British Columbia—Alberta—New Brunswick model, to hand the question over to the municipalities. At the same time, Saskatchewan announced virtually the same idea (*The Globe and Mail*, December 3, 1987: A16). While the Ontario government defended handing the question over to municipalities as "democratic" (*The Globe and Mail*, April 6, 1988: A11), the municipalities responded firmly that they did not want it handed over to them. They argued that the pressure of business and competition would be irresistible. If one store opened, then another would have to. If one municipality adopted it, the others would be forced to follow suit lest their business be drawn away. They cited the "domino effect" and "border war" experience of Vancouver after 1980 and the experience of Canadian border towns that had lost Sunday business to the US (*The Globe and Mail*, December 2, 1987: A1, A2; December 5, 1987: B1, B4; December 15, 1987: A23; January 30, 1988; February 9, 1988: A17; February 10, 1988: A13; *The Toronto Star*, December 12, 1987: A21). The Mayor of Toronto said that if just one municipality in his city went for Sunday shopping, they all would be swept along. At the time of writing, the game of political hot potato between the provincial government and the municipalities was still going on (*The Globe and Mail*, August 13, 1988: A10; August 26,

1988: A8). Public opinion in Ontario was still deeply divided, though polls indicated a shift from a small majority in favour of Sunday shopping in 1986 to a small majority against in 1988. Across Canada there appeared to be an even split, but this reflected a majority in favour in the West and a majority against in Ontario (*The Toronto Star*, May 5, 1988: A1, A2; Todd, 1988).

Which leaves us with the question of what contribution, if any, the Charter has made to the Sunday opening controversy. One thing it has not done, of course, is to enlighten us about the subject. The opinions of the Court have been too abstract, too removed from the facts, and too restricted by the rules and conventions of Charter argument to do that. Indeed, they have been too diverse, given all the different opinions in the majority and the dissent on every little issue. And finally, they have not been particularly insightful. But has the Charter made a difference in any other way?

On the one hand, it is clear that you do not need a Charter to bring in Sunday shopping. The British Columbia government introduced Sunday shopping before the Charter was enacted. We have already pointed out how strong the market pressures for Sunday shopping are. In opposition, there are only political, non-market forces of the one-person-one-vote variety. On the other hand, there is no question that the decision of the Supreme Court in *Big M*, although not technically deciding the issue, gave Sunday shopping a boost. It led directly to the opening up of Sunday shopping in Alberta and, by imitation, in New Brunswick and Saskatchewan. Although it did not technically decide the issue, it wiped away the status quo and threw the ball into the court of a nearly petrified political system, increasingly unused, as we have seen, to taking positions on controversial issues, at least where such positions require contradicting market imperatives.

On still another hand, we have the spectacle in Ontario of a court decision upholding the law, followed by the government acting to repeal it and handing the question over to the municipalities and, via them, to the marketplace. Certainly the decision of the Supreme Court of Canada in *Edwards Books* cannot be said to have pushed Ontario to the brink. What can be said, however, is that the decision resolved nothing for the government. First, it left crucial questions, such as the extent of a required exemption and the applicability of the equality provisions, technically undecided. As for the other questions, its decision was to defer to the government. Some help. This meant the government had to go right back into court to defend the law against new litigation and that it had to face the lobbyists and the press all over again. The only way to abdicate was to hand the matter over to the municipalities, if only they could be made to accept it.

We might sum up the situation this way. The Charter clearly advanced the cause of Sunday shopping by the victory in *Big M*. And despite the loss in *Edwards Books*, the very existence of the Charter has given it a seemingly inexhaustible litigation platform. Looked at from the other side, the Charter proved no defence for those opposed to Sunday shopping. Although the law was upheld, the inclination of the government was to abdicate responsibility to the marketplace where, of course, the Charter cannot reach. In other words, the Charter could be a sword for business, as in *Big M,* or neutral, as in *Edwards Books,* but it could never be either a sword or a shield for labour, and labour has had to fight every inch of the way to keep it neutral.

Freedom of Expression and the Right to Advertise

The problem with freedom of religion as a weapon for business is its probable restriction to the Sunday shopping issue. The same cannot be said of freedom of expression, which is proving to be an all-purpose tool for dismantling the regulatory state. An example is the current controversy over tobacco advertising.

When the federal government introduced legislation to ban cigarette advertising in 1987, the tobacco industry pulled out all the stops. Well-connected lobbyists were hired, and dire warnings were made about the loss of jobs. But as the campaign wore on it came to rely almost entirely on the Charter:

> The major strategy of the tobacco industry in fighting the bill was to focus on the restriction on freedom of speech represented by the ban on advertising (Fraser, 1988: D1).

It would have been crass to rely on property rights to protect the right to market a lethal product. The Charter added a measure of principle to the arguments of the industry. Chief lobbyist William Neville called the "dangerous precedent" the law would set for the denial of freedom of expression in the Charter the "most important" cost of the law (Neville, 1988). Though the position was ridiculed in editorial cartoons (*The Globe and Mail,* June 2, 1988: A6), Neville could cite the Canadian Civil Liberties Association, which had been somehow persuaded to write a letter to the Commons Legislative Committee arguing that the Bill "unwarrantedly infringes freedom of expression" (Canadian Civil Liberties Association, 1987: 4). The Calgary Civil Liberties Association, a former president of the Canadian Bar Association, a law professor, and a philosophy professor all showed up at the Senate, after the Bill passed the House of Commons, to argue the same position (*The Globe and Mail,* June 22, 1988: A5; June 23, 1988: A4). The anti-tobacco side argued that 35,000 deaths per year should be enough to allow for a "reasonable limit" (*The Globe and Mail,* January 30, 1988: D1, D8; June 21, 1988: A7). More grist for the judicial mill. The law was passed in June, and two major tobacco companies had issued their writs before the summer was out.

A pronouncement by the Supreme Court on the applicability of the Charter to commercial speech is expected shortly in the litigation over the Quebec law on unilingual business signs (*Chaussure Brown's Inc.,* 1987).[1] But given the record of Canadian appeal courts so far, the claims of the tobacco industry are not at all farfetched. One of the most outrageous decisions (especially for

---

[1] As we go to press, the Supreme Court of Canada has announced its decision in the signs case holding that commercial advertising is, indeed, protected by the guarantee of "freedom of expression" under the Charter (*Ford* v. *Quebec (Attorney General),* December 15, 1988).

parents) was one by the Quebec Court of Appeal, striking down Parti Québécois legislation banning commercial television advertising "directed at persons under thirteen years of age" (*Irwin Toy*, 1986).[1] Though there was a dissent in the case, the Court was unanimous that commercial advertising was protected by the Charter, disagreeing only on how serious a violation the *Consumer Protection Act*, 1978, was and whether it was a reasonable limit. In the majority, Judge Jacques[2] refused to go along with any distinctions in forms of expression:

> It is not for the court to accord more prestige to political, artistic or cultural expression than to commercial expression, or to find that the nature and scope of one is greater than that of another since the Charter makes no such distinction. Artistic or cultural expression very often has a commercial purpose, for example, films, videos, records, etc., as do other activities of a purely commercial nature. Nor is it up to a government to decide what people should not know with respect to commerce, although a government can impose the obligation to disclose all facts pertinent to any commercial activity, *e.g.*, the consumption of foodstuffs, etc.

> The economic choices of the citizens are just as important, if not more important, than their artistic and cultural choices. These choices depend on what information is available and they cannot be enlightened choices unless such information circulates as freely as possible (*Irwin Toy*, 1986: 650–652).

Judge Kaufman sounded this alarm:

> Freedoms are fragile, and while the prohibition of "commercials" directed to children under 13 may seem innocuous, it is an inroad on the right to send—and with it, the public's right to receive—any message, commercial or otherwise, and careful scrutiny is, therefore, needed.

> To hold otherwise would, in effect, give *carte blanche* to the Legislature. Children under 13 today, so why not 14 or 15 or 16 tomorrow? Toys in this case, perhaps something else in another (*Irwin Toy*, 1986: 644).

Sure. Today, the right to advertise; tomorrow, the right to vote. Today, a law against murder; tomorrow, slavery.

What divided the Court was the scope that should be allowed a legislature in regulating advertising. The government of Quebec introduced eighteen studies to defend the law. According to the majority, they were not good enough because they did not *prove* advertising was *harmful* to children under thirteen (*Irwin Toy*, 1986: 662). The majority was more particularly interested in the fact that only Quebec, in all the non-socialist world, banned children's advertising totally and exclusively (Sweden banned all television advertising). In dissent, Judge Vallerand thought it was enough for the legislature to show

---

[1] The video prepared by OPSEU for the *Lavigne* case alleges personal connections between the owners of Irwin Toy, the toy company that challenged the advertising restrictions in this case, and the leadership of the National Citizens Coalition (OPSEU, 1987).

[2] The most extreme of the judges who decided the PQ section 33 case (*Alliance des Professeurs*, 1983), above, page 78.

"that there was sufficiently serious risk that, given the social values of the milieu, it is appropriate to intervene" (*Irwin Toy*, 1986: 674). He also felt that a ban on children's advertising was different and less serious than a ban on other advertising:

> ...advertising directed at children is not actually the expression of a commercial message addressed to the person whom the businessman wants to reach and to induce to act. It is actually a matter of hiring a messenger who will transmit commercial speech and often transmit it in a way which would be prohibited by the most liberal rules of advertising...the prohibition is a very slight impediment to the right of a businessman to incite the purchaser to buy his product, a right which is not truly affected by the prohibition (*Irwin Toy*, 1986: 675).

A result like this is more valuable to business than reading all the property rights in the world into section 7. Since almost all commercial activity can be characterized as expression, this makes all commercial regulation *prima facie* wrong and requiring legal justification. The heavy onus the majority placed on the government means any experiments in regulation by social democratic provincial governments can be kept closely in check. We are very close here to the "substantive due process" of the US Supreme Court at the beginning of the century. On the other hand, the onus set by the Quebec Court of Appeal seems rather inconsistent with the deferential approach of the Supreme Court of Canada in economic matters, displayed in both the Right to Strike cases and the Sunday opening cases.

The inclusion of commercial speech in the concept of freedom of expression is an extremely complicated question. It is not, as Judge Jacques suggests, the practical difficulty of separating political and economic expression, but the ideological and political implications of doing so. Granted the importance of some forms of economic expression, even their equivalent or superior importance to other forms of expression, nevertheless the line is not difficult to draw. A TV ad telling you to *vote for X* or to *believe in X*ism, even if economically motivated, is intelligibly different from one which tells you to *buy X*. The question is whether anything should *depend* on the distinction. Some judges have wanted to make the distinction for ideological reasons similar to those advanced by the Canadian Bar Association at the Charter hearings, namely that the Charter is concerned with loftier matters than mere commerce. This was the position taken by a majority of the Ontario Divisional Court in *Klein* (1985), in which a Law Society regulation restricting lawyers from advertising their fees was upheld, while a regulation preventing lawyers from initiating contacts with the press for non-advertising purposes was struck down. The majority held that advertising was not "expression" within the meaning of the Charter:

> In a democratic society the economic realm must be subordinate to the political realm...The Charter, to a certain extent, inferentially recognizes a separation of the realms of economic and political activity and the subordination of the former to the latter...The Charter reflects a concern with the political rights of the individual and does not, in my view, reflect a similar concern with the economic sphere nor with its incidents such as commercial speech (*Klein*, 1985: 532).

Similar sentiments were expressed by a British Columbia trial court in a dentist's advertising case:

> [F]reedom of expression...must not be used to entrench economic rights but instead, in this context, as a means of ensuring that the political process which leads to the regulation of any commercial activity is open to the widest possible debate (*Griffin*, 1987).

But if refusing to recognize commercial expression as speech is good for the ideology of the Charter, it is bad for business; it stigmatizes it as a lesser order of life and makes it more vulnerable to government regulation, because of the stigma itself and because it puts regulation beyond judicial scrutiny. Thus the dissent in *Klein*:

> ...the Charter, in my opinion, makes no distinction in principle between freedom of expression as it may relate to political expression or economic activity.

> Second, the dictates of the private enterprise economy to which this country is dedicated (despite legislative inroads on its functioning) require that the Charter, according to its plain meaning, be applied to freedom of economic expression. Freedom to advertise one's goods or services is fundamental to the private enterprise system. The freedom to "build a better mousetrap" is not only an essential part of the dynamics of the system but is made effective only in this era of mass marketing by the freedom to advertise in the mass media, both in the domestic market and abroad (*Klein*, 1985: 501).

This was the approach in *Irwin Toy*, and it seems to be gaining acceptance. The Divisional Court's upholding of the advertising ban in *Klein* was rapidly followed by the Law Society's repeal of it, as of January 1987 (*The Globe and Mail*, May 11, 1987: A11), something similar, though with a much lower profile, to the developments in Sunday shopping following the decision in *Edwards Books*. More recent judicial decisions have tended to favour advertising among the professions. The Alberta Court of Appeal held advertising to be "expression" for the purposes of the Charter and struck out optometry profession rules against price advertising in *Grier* (1987). And *Klein* itself was essentially overruled by the Ontario Court of Appeal in the dentist advertising case *Royal College of Dental Surgeons* v. *Rocket and Price,* again by a split decision on the facts, but with no actual dissent on the question of advertising and freedom of expression:

> In my view, the reasons put forward by the minority [in *Klein*] should prevail. The useful information society may obtain from commercial messages is so important and the potential benefits are so great that they must come within the protective ambit of s.2 (b) of the Charter. No doubt those messages in proper cases should be duly and reasonably regulated. This could readily be undertaken pursuant to provisions of s.1 of the Charter (*Rocket and Price*, 1988: 76).

Acting on legal advice that their advertising restrictions would suffer the same fate, the College of Physicians and Surgeons of Ontario is reported to have stopped enforcing them (*The Globe and Mail*, April 25, 1988: A4).

Tobacco industry, take heart, if you have one.

Conclusion

The main problem for the courts in dealing with business and labour under the Charter has been how to deal in a principled way—that is in a power-blind way—with something that is so obviously a struggle over social power. Principled reasoning is a difficult feat to carry off in the best of circumstances, but with all the charity in the world it could not be said that the courts have done anything like a respectable job. Far from bringing an added measure of wisdom or enlightenment to this realm of politics, they have mostly vented inexpert versions of ultra-conservative to centrist opinions, walking a thin line between promoting the Charter and not rocking the boat of the status quo. The general response of the courts to the obvious power clashes they have been asked to arbitrate has been to run the other way and leave the combatants to their own (unequal) resources in the marketplace. Because intervention is so fraught with significance for the "delicate balance" and because this is so difficult to camouflage, intervention is rare compared to the judicial ardour we saw in Chapter IV in the defence of formal values. On the other hand, it does happen. When it does, it is always on the side of business. Whether it is dismantling the rights of unions as in *Lavigne*, or commercializing Sunday as in *Big M*, or striking down consumer protection as in *Irwin Toy*, however small or precarious these victories have been, they have all gone one way. The attempts of labour to call on the Court for help in its struggle for social justice have all been in vain. The Right to Strike cases and *Dolphin Delivery* are the most obvious examples of this.

However, the temptation to invoke the Charter is great, almost unavoidable in some cases. The Canadian political terrain is very different with the Charter. Its availability encourages governments to do what they otherwise would not. And when the language of politics becomes one of rights, it is almost obligatory to go to court to be taken seriously. But the language of rights is much more suited to upholding the status quo than to attacking it. Rights are what appear to the Court to be natural and uncontroversial. They must be accepted and "pre-existing" in Dworkin's terms. They assume the basic justice of the status quo as a point of departure. Furthermore, they are individual, which only means that they can be invoked more easily by socially powerful individuals than by collectives of socially weak ones. They benefit those who benefit from the de-legitimation of the democratic morality of one-person-one-vote as a "tyranny of the majority." Despite the siren songs of the Beattys of this world and the fine words of the Dicksons, working people have nothing to gain from Charter politics and business has nothing to lose. The most that can be hoped for from the Charter is neutrality in the class struggle and that can by no means be guaranteed. It has to be fought for. Even neutrality has a different meaning in an era of governments so paralysed with the fear of doing anything controversial that they, too, abandon the field to the marketplace.

CHAPTER VI

The Charter and Inequality

There is hardly a law on the books that does not affect some people differently from others.[1]

Equal in Law, Unequal in Life

Inequality in Canada

Canada is a country of great social inequality. Statistics on income distribution give us only the barest glimpse of this. They tell us that, on average, the annual income of the top 20% of income receivers is eight times that of the bottom 20% (Vaillancourt, 1985: 11). And they tell us that despite the doubling of real income since World War II, inequality in its distribution in percentage terms has not changed (Vaillancourt, 1985: 12). From this it does not take much to deduce that the actual gaps have grown larger. But quintile averages exclude the greatest extremes. The $700,000 per year salary of a senior partner in a large Toronto law firm is over *seventy-five times* the yearly salary of anyone working at the Ontario minimum wage of $4.55 per hour (Watson, 1988: 7). And the chief executive officers of Canada's major corporations now receive salaries of over $1 million per year. The highest publicly known Canadian corporate salary for 1987 was $3.8 million (*Vancouver Sun*, April 12, 1988: D1). However, income figures exclude those factors associated with the greatest wealth such as capital gains, and those associated with the greatest poverty, such as income on Indian reserves and among Canada's increasing prison population (Vaillancourt, 1985: 58–59). And they give no indication of the way differences in income turn into much larger differences in wealth. In terms of actual wealth, estimates for 1980 show the richest 1% of Canadians owning about 19% of Canada's total personal wealth, for an average of about $900,000, the richest 10% owning 57%, an average of $270,000, while the 40% occupying the large area at the bottom had to divide less than 1% of the total wealth among themselves, for an average of $1,000 each (Osberg, 1981: 35–40). At the very top of Canada's personal wealth list are some of the richest people in the world. The Reichmann brothers of Toronto with $9 billion from real estate were recently ranked third in the world by *Forbes* magazine. K.C. Irving of Saint John, with $8 billion in oil, paper, and land, was ranked fifth, and Kenneth Thomson of *The Globe and Mail*, with $5 billion, was ranked eleventh (*The Globe and Mail*, July 8, 1988: A10). *For-*

---

[1] Justice Stewart of the United States Supreme Court in *San Antonio School District* (1973: 60) quoted by the Ontario Court of Appeal in *Blainey* (1986: 740).

tune magazine placed the same three in the top ten in 1987, though in a different order and all trailing the fifth-ranked Queen Elizabeth of England (and Canada) (*Fortune*, October 12, 1987: 120).

In a market economy, differences in wealth are not just differences in standards of living—though they are certainly that. They are *relations of power*, the power, among other things, directly or indirectly to hire other people's labour and not vice versa, and to determine what is made with that labour. In a market economy, the democratic principle of the private sphere is "one-dollar-one-vote."

These huge inequalities in social power and living standards have nothing to do with differences in natural endowment, talent and so on. We are all born into a vast and complicated hierarchy which distributes economic and social power and life chances in anything but an evenhanded fashion, according to such uncontrollable factors as one's sex, ethnicity, region, and social class of origin. The greatly rich and the greatly poor in this country almost all started out that way (Hunter, 1981: 146–150; Forcese, 1975: 80–81). As for the rest of us, the narrow band set by sex, ethnicity, and region is further circumscribed by the occupational and educational attainment of our parents (Hunter, 1981: 143–146; Forcese, 1975: 57–81).

Yet section 15 of the Charter proclaims with disarming simplicity:

> Every individual is equal before and under the law and has the right to the equal protection and benefit of the law without discrimination and, in particular, without discrimination based on race, national or ethnic origin, colour, religion, sex, age or mental or physical disability.

It is no accident that the Charter's list of the items according to which we must be equal in law are the very things according to which we are unequal in life. Can the Charter actually achieve this miracle?

Section 15 and the Status Quo

So fearsome were the implications of section 15 that it was not given immediate effect on entrenchment of the Charter. Governments were given three years (until April 17, 1985) to clean up their laws and to prepare to defend the ones they were not willing to change. Taken literally, section 15 throws everything up for grabs. "It is an all-encompassing right governing all legislative action" (*Re Education Act*, 1986: 42). Taken literally, it is capable of engulfing the entire Charter, section 1 included. In fact, one of the technical problems now plaguing the legal profession is how to reconcile section 15 and section 1, and indeed the rest of the Charter, without rendering any of them redundant:

> No one section should be regarded as paramount or as encompassing all of the other sections. That, however, may be what will become of s. 15 if it is interpreted as being violated by any distinction or unequal treatment (Justice MacLachlin of the British Columbia Court of Appeal in *Andrews*, 1986: 607).[1]

---

[1] See also *Blainey* (1986) and *McKinney* (1987) in the Ontario Court of Appeal.

Many of the issues of social power that we have already encountered are being replayed with the coming into force of section 15. The anti-nuclear movement has invoked section 15 in Charter litigation aimed at making the nuclear power industry more responsible (*Re Energy Probe*, 1987). French speakers outside of Quebec have tried to overcome the limits of the explicit language provisions of the Charter by using the equality section to expand the use of French in the courts (*Re Use of French in Criminal Proceedings in Saskatchewan*, 1987; *Paquette*, 1987; *McDonnell*, 1986) and to improve the quality of French language education (*Mahe*, 1987). Workers have tried to use it to expand collective bargaining rights (*Canadian Union of Postal Workers*, 1987b; *Hutton*, 1987). Business has tried to use it to fight union rights (*The Globe and Mail*, October 31, 1986: A9), indeed all forms of regulation (*Smith, Kline and French Laboratories*, 1986; *Aluminum Co. of Canada*, 1986), including the Sunday closing laws. As we saw at the end of the last chapter, Sunday opening has begun another weary trek through the court system, this time on equality grounds, courtesy of Toronto furrier Paul Magder and his erstwhile lawyer Timothy Danson (see above, page 231), among others (*London Drugs Ltd.*, 1987). The Ontario doctors also brandished section 15 in their fight against the ban on extra-billing (above, page 219).

It comes as no surprise that the courts have not allowed themselves to be swept away in the vast literal expanse of section 15. They have not attempted to dismantle Canada's hierarchical structure. They have not even made a dent in our basic social inequalities. Nor is there any chance that they will. Legalized politics does not allow for that sort of thing. In fact, it comes equipped with many devices meant to prevent it. Important among these is the preoccupation of the Charter with "government" power. As Professor Hogg has pointed out in his constitutional law text:

> The real threat to egalitarian civil liberties in Canada comes not from legislative and official action, but from discrimination by private persons—employers, trade unions, landlords, realtors, restaurateurs and other suppliers of goods or services. The economic liberties of freedom of property and contract, which imply a power to deal with whomever one pleases, come into direct conflict with egalitarian values...(Hogg, 1985: 786).[1]

Those who conceived and drafted the Charter did their best to ensure that this system of private power remained well beyond the reach of the Charter, and the courts have applied it accordingly. The common law rules of private property and "freedom" of contract, the basic building blocks of private power, were, as we have seen, declared out of bounds in *Dolphin Delivery*. Other courts have held that it does

---

[1] Hogg suggests that this power is adequately neutralized by provincial human rights legislation: "and in all Canadian jurisdictions the former have now been subordinated to the latter by the enactment of human rights legislation, which forbids various discriminatory practices on pain of a penalty, and establishes a commission to administer the legislation" (Hogg, 1985: 786). However, human rights legislation has its own limitations when it comes to private power. See below, page 300.

VI / THE CHARTER AND INEQUALITY

not render a body subject to the Charter merely to be the creature of statute (like all corporations) or to receive funding from the government (like most corporations, indeed all, if we take into account the biases of the tax system in favour of business vis-a-vis wage earners: McQuaig, 1987) (*Blainey*, 1986; *McKinney*, 1987).[1] This neatly avoids the embarrassment of having to reconcile the immense powers wielded in the corporate sphere with the requirements of section 15, since there is no question of these powers being in any way limited. In fact, the Charter implicitly removes questions of economic power from the scope of judicial review by consigning them to a purely hortatory part of the constitution. Part III, entitled "Equalization and Regional Disparities," claims that Canadian governments "are committed to":

(a) promoting equal opportunities for the well-being of Canadians;
(b) furthering economic development to reduce disparity in opportunities; and
(c) providing essential public services of reasonable quality to all Canadians.

But these commitments are prefaced by the disclaimer that they do not in any way alter the legislative authority or powers of any government, which ensures that no court will take any government to task for failing to live up to them.

Even in the absence of such cues the courts have had no difficulty reading into the equality provision other fundamental assumptions and political necessities of the Canadian social status quo. The most vivid example of this so far has been Ontario's Catholic school funding controversy, which we encountered in Chapter II. Opponents of the extension of full public funding to Catholic high schools argued that it contravened section 15 in singling out one religion for government largess ($80 million per year).[2] Opponents have gone so far as to call the program a form of "apartheid" (*The Globe and Mail*, March 15, 1988: A1). But the courts rejected the challenge, holding that section 15 had to take second place to what was variously called the "the basic compact of Confederation" and "the original confederation bargain." (*Re Education Act*, 1987: 43; 61). Original compromise apart, the majority of the Ontario Court of Appeal placed the separate school controversy in the *contemporary* context of Ontario-Quebec relations, for which it was originally, and to some extent is still, a proxy:

[T]he purpose of Bill 30 has to be seen as an attempt to redress a historical grievance in Ontario and to remove a continuing irritant in relations with Quebec when comparing the treatment of the beneficiaries of Section 93 with their counterparts in this province (*Re Education Act*, 1986: 57).

Section 15 could not be allowed to undo the main political goals of the Charter as a whole. It would have to take a backseat:

These educational rights, granted specifically to the Protestants in Quebec and the Roman Catholics in Ontario, make it impossible to treat all Canadians

---

[1] As with *Dolphin Delivery* itself, these Charter limits are entirely self-imposed. The courts have little difficulty in intervening in the private sphere when basic questions of social power are not at stake. See below, page 269.

[2] See Chapter II for the details and political context of the case.

equally. The country was founded upon the recognition of special or unequal educational rights for specific religious groups in Ontario and Quebec. The incorporation of the Charter into the *Constitution Act, 1982*, does not change the original Confederation bargain (*Re Education Act*, 1986: 64).

This passage was quoted with approval by the majority of the Supreme Court of Canada, which helped matters out by stretching the "original bargain" somewhat and holding that the Constitution not only permitted but actually *required* full funding. Bill 30, it decided, "returns rights constitutionally guaranteed to separate schools by s.93(1) of the *Constitution Act, 1867*" (*Re Education Act*, 1987: 59). To reach this conclusion the Court had to overrule a decision from the 1920s in which four levels of courts had upheld Ontario legislation which had deprived the French minority of rights which the Court now said had always been guaranteed (*Tiny Separate School Trustees*, 1928)—yet another example of how the constitution expands and contracts, at least in language matters, according to the political climate. Indeed, the majority recognized but minimized the inconsistency of their holding with the new conservative line on language: "it must still be open to a court to breathe life into a compromise that is clearly expressed" (*Re Education Act*, 1987: 44). For the minority, this historical revisionism went too far:

> It would be most inappropriate and indeed dangerous for this court over a half a century later to review and then reverse or revise findings of fact made at trial by Rose J., confirmed by a unanimous Court of Appeal and undisturbed by the even division of this court...it would be imprudent for an appellate court sitting almost 60 years distant from the scene to reassess a factual situation peculiarly within the experience of the members of the other courts who were called upon to make their judgement of then recent history (Justice Estey in *Re Education Act*, 1987: 22).

Nevertheless the minority found its own reasons for acquiescing in the result.[1]

The Ontario Catholic School Funding case is an illustration of the determination of the courts not to allow a free interpretation of equality rights to upset the Canadian political balance of power.[2] Another example, on a much lower judicial level, is the tax case we looked at in Chapter V in which the Ontario Public Service Employees Union challenged the right of business to deduct donations to political lobbyists, such as the National Citizens' Coalition. The union pointed out that workers were not allowed such deductions, except in limited circumstances (registered charities or registered political parties), and claimed discrimination. The judge was totally unsympathetic. Like the Supreme Court of Canada in the Right to Strike cases, he relied on a version of the principle/policy distinction to avoid doing anything so radical. The Charter, he said, would be "trivialized" if courts "get into the weighing and balancing of the nuts and bolts of taxing statutes" (*OPSEU*, 1987: 452).

---

[1] They found an implied *power*—as opposed to a duty—in the Province to expand separate school rights if it wished and said that the Charter could not destroy powers found elsewhere in the constitution.

[2] *Re Education Act* (1987) has already been applied to a slightly different issue. An Alberta court used it to uphold the right of a Catholic school to fire a woman teacher for pre-marital sex despite section 15 (*Casagrande*, 1987).

Section 15 and Judicial Power

Reading section 15 so as not to upset the fundamental aspects of the Canadian system of power is not the same thing as reading it narrowly. The courts have shown no hesitation in going even beyond the listed categories of prohibited discrimination to carry out pet law reform projects. These always seem to have the effect of expanding judicial power. For example, in criminal law, the courts have introduced the notion of "geographic discrimination." This has nothing to do with regional underdevelopment and everything to do with freeing the courts from restrictions on the applicability of the formal values we examined in Chapter IV. The Ontario Court of Appeal recently ruled it a violation of equality rights that an exception to the minimum prison term for drunken driving available in some provinces had not been made applicable to Ontario. The federal government had let the provinces decide whether they wanted the exception, and the most populous provinces, Ontario, Quebec, and British Columbia, as well as Nova Scotia, had declined. The government of Ontario argued that the exception weakened the deterrent effect. The Court of Appeal, however, held that it was unfair to Ontario residents not to have this right and, in effect, proclaimed it in force for Ontario (*Hamilton*, 1986). But the effect of the exception was not to guarantee anyone the right to be excused from prison (the alternative was probation with a treatment order), merely to give the sentencing court the *discretion* to order it in an appropriate case.[1] And what is an appropriate case will always involve a question of the status of the convict. Indeed, the characteristic tenderness of courts to drunken drivers, despite popular objection, is closely related to the fact that drunken driving cuts across class boundaries more than any other offence (Mandel, 1984).

When it is not a question of judicial rights, but only of the accused person's rights, this argument about geographic discrimination is less likely to be successful. The Ontario Court of Appeal held in a subsequent case that it was *not* a denial of equality rights that persons accused of murder in Ontario could not choose the mode of trial the way one could if one lived in Alberta. Where it was a question of the *accused's* rights and not the *judge's*, the Court was able to find plenty of justification for discrimination (*Turpin*, 1987).

Equality rights have also been seen by some lawyers as a golden opportunity to subvert legislative schemes which bypass the courts in favour of more rational forms of administration. They have employed the Charter in attempts to prevent the introduction of new schemes, such as "no fault" motor vehicle accident compensation, as well as in attempts to roll back such venerable institutions as the workers' compensation system. In the nineteenth century, common law judges devised many rules to prevent the increasing victims of industrial accidents from suing their employers. The "fellow servant" doctrine meant that if, as usual, a co-worker was responsible for an injury, the injured worker was barred from suing the company, though it made the profits and had

---

[1] In the cases raising the constitutional issue, nobody qualified for the exemption, but it has been applied at least once to save a woman from a 28-day jail sentence. She was sentenced to a two-year alcohol treatment program instead (*The Globe and Mail*, June 20, 1987: A11).

the money to pay; instead, the injured worker had to sue the co-worker and wind up with nothing. *"Volenti non fit injuria"* meant that injured workers were refused compensation when they "voluntarily" took jobs known to be dangerous (Tucker, 1984: 260). And there was the "fault" doctrine itself, which focussed on the narrow, immediate, individual cause of the accident and ignored its social, economic, or systemic cause. Litigation was a lottery with most of the prize money going to the legal profession (Glasbeek and Hasson, 1977). Workers fought for a compensation scheme to circumvent the courts, and workers' compensation schemes began to appear in Canadian provinces around the time of the First World War. Under them, workers injured on the job would be compensated with no question of fault, *volenti*, or "fellow servant" involved. The scheme would be administered by a board and not a court. It would be paid for by premiums from the companies.

Workers' compensation schemes have been in place in all provinces for a long time now. Compensation rates are far from adequate, and injured workers' groups have constantly campaigned for increases in amounts and for extensions to injuries not yet covered. In a serious accident, the amount one is likely to receive is certainly less than what a sympathetic jury might award a successful litigant. But successful litigants were rare in the common law courts, and they are rare today in those American jurisdictions that allow suits alongside the scheme (one out of a hundred according to one estimate: *The Toronto Star*, January 2, 1988: D1, D6). And the size of any award is greatly diminished by the lawyer's fee. In Canada, every scheme includes the barring of any civil suit against employers. This was the price extracted by employers for their consent to the scheme, but it also suits employees. A "two-tiered" system, such as exists in most of the United States, inevitably results in a deterioration of the no-fault scheme: "If you don't like it, sue." Naturally, lawyers feel the system is an outrage. With the advent of the Charter, they have started to hammer away at it. This is another case where assailants can be found on the left as well as the right.[1]

Success has been mixed, but at least two trial courts have found that the schemes discriminate against industrial accident victims by depriving them of their hallowed access to the courts. The case that attracted the most attention was *Piercey*,[2] in which the Chief Justice of Newfoundland granted a woman

---

[1] See the spirited exchange between my colleague Harry Glasbeek and lawyer Harry Kopyto in *The Law Union News*, Vol. 2 November, 1985: 6–8. To Glasbeek's impressive list of reasons why injured workers groups themselves oppose the re-invention of the old system, Kopyto responds with the dilemma of the individual who just possibly stands to gain at everybody else's expense: "Do we tell the present victims of the system that there are no immediate solutions to their problems except engaging in long term political activity?" Kopyto took this same approach when he challenged the collective bargaining arbitration system under section 15 of the Charter for denying access to the courts to a worker whose union would not proceed with his grievance. The court of first instance rejected the claim (*Bartello*, 1987).

[2] The other success occurred in Alberta, but the circumstances made the import of the decision much narrower. The law banned all suits against third parties whether or not they were contributors to the plan. In this case, it was a municipality. The Court did not seem to disapprove of the bar against employers under the plan or against employees, but held the bar against the municipality unreasonable (*Budge*, 1987). A similar challenge failed in Ontario (*The Toronto Star*, January 23, 1988: A15).

the right to sue for the industrial death of her husband despite the prohibition in the workers' compensation scheme. Nobody could accuse Chief Justice Hickman of having a low opinion of courts:

> Of all the institutions required to ensure the well-being of a democratic society, the Courts alone stand free and totally independent of Parliament, the Crown and any individual or group of individuals. The courts acting through their inherent jurisdiction, strengthened by the clear intention of the framers of the Charter, stand between the would-be oppressor and the intended victim...[S]tatutory tribunals, such as the Workers' Compensation Commission, created for the purpose of carrying out the will of the Legislature, do not have the same unimpaired independence or knowledge of the law and the skill to interpret same which the judiciary and courts have and must continue to enjoy. No substitute has been devised, to date, to replace the Courts as the guardian of liberty and freedom of all Canadians and to deprive a class of citizens of access to the Courts is at variance with the intent of the Charter and in particular, section 15 thereof (*Piercey*, 1986: 384).

This decision struck panic in the hearts of governments, large employers, and unions alike. Workers' Compensation Boards from across the country, the Canadian Manufacturers Association, the Canadian National Railway, and the Canadian Labour Congress, all appeared in force at the appeal in St. John's to support the legislation. Standing alone[1] for herself and the legal profession was Mrs. Piercey, ably assisted by none other than Charter enthusiast Professor David Beatty, imported from Toronto to do the necessary "conversing." But the odds were too uneven. When the legal profession opposes powerful interests, we know who is going to win. The Newfoundland Court of Appeal was unanimous in overturning the decision of the trial judge and upholding the legislation. There was no discrimination, because what workers got in exchange for their right to sue left them in no way worse off:

> The workers' compensation scheme provides a stable system of compensation free of the uncertainties that would otherwise prevail. While there may be those who would receive less under the Act than otherwise, when the structure is viewed in total, this is but a negative feature of an otherwise positive plan and does not warrant the condemnation of the legislation that makes it possible. Judicial deference to the legislative will is required here (Chief Justice Goodridge in *Re Workers' Compensation Act (Nfld.)*, 1987: 524).

> In my view any economic loss that may be sustained by taking away the "right of action" for work-related injuries is more than offset by the overall benefit of the Act and is a necessary incident to the implementation of a valid legislative scheme (Justice Morgan in *Re Workers' Compensation Act (Nfld.)*, 1987: 532).

Of course, lawyers will fight to their last breath in defence of the sacred right to litigate. They have had more success in their campaign against "no-fault" auto insurance. But here they have the insurance industry on their side. Appearing before

---

[1] Well, not quite alone. The government gave her, or rather her lawyers, $10,000 towards costs (*The Globe and Mail*, June 8, 1987: B13).

the Ontario Inquiry into Motor Vehicle Accident Compensation, the Canadian Bar Association declared any such scheme unconstitutional and vowed to fight it in the courts should the government have the temerity to try to end the car accident lottery in favour of universal compensation (Schmitz, 1987). Though the Ontario Supreme Court Judge conducting the inquiry did not buy the lawyers' Charter arguments (Ontario, 1988: 619–641), he did accept their points about the "moral values" inherent in the fault system (Ontario, 1988: 543), and recommended that the right to sue in tort remain, thus rendering a Charter test unnecessary.

Section 15 threatens to engulf not only the Charter but also this entire book, so we will have to restrict further discussion to two important and revealing examples of what the Charter has meant for those on the bottom end of Canada's structure of inequality. This is not to suggest in any way that these are the only important equality issues in Canada or under the Charter.

Aboriginal Peoples and the Charter

In the Parliamentary debate on the Charter, Ian Waddell of the NDP claimed he was voting for the Resolution because it embodied, if imperfectly, his picture of Canada "as two founding societies, the English and the French, built on the foundation of the aboriginal people" (*House of Commons Debates*, November 27, 1981: 13429). On another occasion he used the metaphor of the Charter as a layer cake with the most important layer being "the bottommost layer of the cake—recognition of the rights of Canada's original people" (Sheppard and Valpy, 1982: 122). Rights apart, Canada's aboriginal peoples[1] are certainly at the bottommost level of the social power structure. The descendants of the peoples who flourished in Canada for thousands of years before any European set foot here are by every material measure the least equal in the society declared equal by section 15. As the Charter was being entrenched, statistics for status Indians' housing showed more than twice as many persons per room as other Canadians, less than half as many households with bath and toilet, two-thirds as many households with a sewage system, and about 20 times as many households with no running water. Infant mortality rates were more than twice those of the Canadian population, and for those who survived, life expectancy was about two-thirds, meaning 22 years less on the average for men and 28 years less for women. Status Indians were about one-sixth as likely to have some post-secondary education and four to five times as likely to be unemployed as other Canadians. They were two to five times as likely to be victims of violent crime and just as overrepresented in the prison population (Valentine, 1980: 81–90). These are all relative measures, of

---

[1] Estimates have varied on the total Native population of Canada from the 1981 Census estimate of about 500,000 or 2% of the total Canadian population (Canada, 1985: 60) to 1.1 million collected from various sources by Valentine (1980: 80–81). The main discrepancy has been with respect to Métis and non-status Indians. When the Charter was enacted there were approximately 300,000 status Indians, 25,000 Inuit and between 175,000 (Canada, 1985: 60) and 800,000 (Valentine, 1980: 81) Métis and non-status Indians.

course; but Native poverty is no less "relational" than other forms of poverty. It is a product of centuries-old antagonistic relations between the aboriginal peoples and Canadian business (especially resource extraction) and government. Relentless destruction, expropriation, colonization, and exploitation of aboriginal lands and peoples, continuing to the present day, have ruined the natural bases of traditional aboriginal economies and undermined the development of anything capable of replacing them (Valentine, 1980: 71–77; Frideres, 1983; McCullum and McCullum, 1975).

What has legalized politics done about this?

The experience of the aboriginal peoples confirms the utter uselessness of legalized politics in the face of massive social inequality and, indeed, the many dangers lurking within this political form for those on the receiving end of it. In fact, the legalization of politics was one of the mechanisms with which the Canadian government tried to implement its postwar policy of ending Indian "special status," abolishing the reserves and assimilating aboriginal peoples "into the mainstream of Canadian life" (Sanders, 1985: 536). Indians were given the vote for the first time when the *Canadian Bill of Rights* was enacted, and the first law declared by the Supreme Court of Canada to be inoperative under it was a provision of the *Indian Act* which treated Indians differently from non-Indians (*Drybones*, 1969). At about the same time, the new government of Pierre Trudeau was proposing that Indian special status be done away with altogether, applying to Indians the logic of his solution to the problem of Quebec (Sanders, 1983: 319). Trudeau soon backed away from his plans in the face of massive Indian opposition, and the same thing seems to have contributed to the Supreme Court of Canada's rather clumsy about-face in *Lavell* (1973) on the relationship between the *Canadian Bill of Rights* and the *Indian Act* (Sanders, 1985: 539–547). The early seventies saw aboriginal peoples increasingly emphasising land claims, treaty rights, and self-government, all oriented towards sovereignty and away from the notions of equal juridical status, which the Charter movement was trying to establish as the guiding principle of Canadian political life.

Aboriginal Rights in the Charter

This is probably why the aboriginal peoples were barely mentioned in the first draft of the Charter (October, 1980). They figured only in the purely negative clause that is now section 26, which originally provided that the guarantees in the Charter

> shall not be construed as denying the existence of any other rights or freedoms that exist in Canada, *including any rights or freedoms that pertain to the native peoples of Canada* (Hogg, 1985: 703; emphasis added).

In other words, aboriginal peoples' issues were to be put on hold while the new constitutional arrangements were put in place. The major Native organizations were not about to let this happen. They saw the constitutional turmoil as an opportunity to advance their claims to land and self-government. They launched a massive public relations attack on the whole Charter enterprise. Like the PQ, the National Indian Brotherhood (NIB) opened an office in London, England, to lobby British MPs against passage of the federal resolution. The Native Council of Canada appeared before the Bertrand Russell Peace Foundation in Amsterdam and had Canada found guilty of "ethnocide." The Union of British Columbia Indian Chiefs chartered a train ("the Constitution Express") to take Indians from across the country to Ottawa and then on to the United Nations (Sheppard and Valpy, 1982: 167).

Only after much soul-searching did the NIB agree to appear at the Charter hearings in late 1980. There they put forward a detailed plan of constitutional amendments that would put aboriginal rights, treaties, and lands not only beyond the reach of the Charter, but beyond the reach of Parliament and the Legislatures as well, with clauses providing no diminution in aboriginal rights, even by constitutional amendment, "without the consent of those aboriginal peoples so affected" (Canada, 1980–81, Issue No. 27: 87–89). In addition, they called for explicit declarations that "within the Canadian federation, the aboriginal peoples of Canada shall have the right to their self-determination" and that the governments "are committed to negotiate with the aboriginal peoples of Canada mutually satisfactory constitutional rights and protections" including, among a long list, "rights of self-government," representation in Parliament and the Legislatures, "the right to adequate land and resource base and adequate revenues...so as to ensure distinct cultural, economic and linguistic identities of the aboriginal peoples of Canada" (Canada, 1980–81, Issue No. 27: 87). In other words, like the PQ, they were after national, not individual rights. They wanted to deal with Canada as sovereign peoples, not as equal citizens. In fact, they expressed fears—which would prove not at all unfounded—about the potential of section 15 to *interfere* with their special status, and called for amendments to provide explicit protection for aboriginal and treaty rights from its operation. In short, they refused to be submitted to the biased discipline of Justice's Blindfold.

How the aboriginal leadership was persuaded to relent from this uncompromising position, we may never know. But somehow, the representatives of the major aboriginal groups, the National Indian Brotherhood, the Inuit Tapirisat of Canada, and the Native Council of Canada, came to accept the federal government's offer of some modest amendments which were nowhere near what the NIB had called for. In a maudlin session of the Joint Committee, Jean Chrétien called the three Native leaders forward to sit beside him ("Now, they are my advisers!"), described the new amendments as representing "agreement among the aboriginal people themselves," and had portions of the amendments read out by various honourees as if it were a religious ceremony (Canada, 1980–81, Issue No. 49: 88–89). The amendments amounted to two distinct clauses. The first was what is now section 25 of the Charter, a non-derogation clause, providing that the Charter "shall not be construed so as to abrogate or derogate from any aboriginal, treaty or other rights or freedoms that pertain to the aboriginal peoples of Canada," including those "recognized" or those that "may be acquired...by way of land claims settlement." Though also purely negative, the clause was a definite advance on the previous formulation, which had provided merely that lack of mention in the Charter did not necessarily *preclude* the existence of aboriginal rights, but neither recognized nor protected them. The new provision at least protected aboriginal rights from the Charter itself. To this was added a completely new clause:

> The aboriginal and treaty rights of the aboriginal peoples of Canada are hereby recognized and affirmed.

This clause was to be situated just outside the Charter, which had the advantage of making it subject neither to the override of section 33 nor to the "reasonable limits" of section 1. Though the clause is in fact rather ambiguous, most constitutional scholars and at least one court (*Sparrow*, 1987) have taken "recognized and affirmed" to mean constitutionally guaranteed, that is to say, beyond the reach of Parliament or the Legislatures except by constitutional amendment or by voluntary extinguishment (Hogg, 1985: 566).

The agreement was immediately regarded as a betrayal by Indian leaders across the country. It was formally repudiated by the major Indian and Métis organizations within three months, with claims of a misunderstanding about whether the rights were to be subject to the amending formula (*The Globe and Mail*, April 17, 1981: 10; April 21, 1981: 8; Sheppard and Valpy, 1982: 169; Romanow et al., 1984: 122). The aboriginal groups increased their London lobbying activities and even went to the English courts claiming that the British government continued to have responsibility for protecting their rights (Sheppard and Valpy, 1982: 169). When the "kitchen deal"[1] was reached in November, between the federal government and the English Canadian provinces, the aboriginal rights clause had been dropped. Defending this in the House of Commons, Jean Chrétien blamed the Premiers and the aboriginal peoples themselves:

> The cause of the constitutional recognition of aboriginal rights was not helped by the fact that leaders of the native peoples have spent a great deal of time and energy lobbying against the section in the previous resolution which they now seem to like (*House of Commons Debates*, November 20, 1981: 13045).

The NDP, who had been crowing incessantly about their role in the original clause, but whose sincerity in the whole affair has been doubted (Sheppard and Valpy, 1982: 170), now said they would not support the Resolution without the aboriginal rights clause back in. A compromise, apparently proposed by Alberta, watered down the clause by restricting it to "*existing* rights," and it was quickly restored. Though the NDP protested the dilution and unsuccessfully tried to have "existing" deleted, they nevertheless supported the final package (Sheppard and Valpy, 1982: 170; *House of Commons Debates*, November 24, 1981: 13219 ff.). Canada's aboriginal peoples were not impressed. They pursued their vain legal and political struggles in England to the bitter end, but the most they could achieve was a few weeks post-

---

[1] So called because the original compromise was scribbled down by Roy Romanow for the government of Saskatchewan and Jean Chrétien for the federal government in a kitchen pantry at the Conference Centre in Ottawa (Sheppard and Valpy, 1982: 288).

ponement of the day when the Queen would sign the Constitution on Parliament Hill. Perhaps they can take credit for her having to do it in the midst of an April shower. The event was protested by status Indians all over the country, who flew flags at half-mast, kept their children home from school, and wore black arm bands (*The Globe and Mail*, April 3, 1982: A3; April 17, 1982: A8).

As a consolation prize for failing to entrench anything of meaning to aboriginal peoples, the federal government inaugurated a curious constitutional ritual, that of (temporarily) entrenching constitutional conferences and their agenda items. In the era of the Charter, one has to entrench *something*, and if it cannot be a right, it will have to be the right to *talk* about entrenching a right. Section 37 of the Constitution provided that a constitutional conference would be called within one year and would

> have included in its agenda an item respecting constitutional matters that directly affect the aboriginal peoples of Canada, including the identification and definition of the rights of those peoples to be included in the Constitution of Canada, and the Prime Minister of Canada shall invite representatives of those peoples to participate in the discussion on that item.

The conference was held as promised, and the results were the first amendments to Canada's new constitution: a clause clarifying the status of land-claims agreements as "treaty rights" (now section 35(3)); a clause guaranteeing aboriginal rights "equally to male and female persons" (section 35 (4)), reversing *Lavell*, by then substantially reversed in practice anyway (Sanders, 1985: 549); a (constitutional!) promise by the governments—but only "in principle"[1]—to consult aboriginal representatives before diminishing the federal constitutional jurisdiction over Indians and lands reserved for Indians (section 35.1); and finally—more conferences. At least two would be held, one before April 17, 1985, and one before April 17, 1987 (section 37.1).

In March 1987, this charade came to an end as the last of the entrenched constitutional talks closed with no agreement. At the final conference the irreconcilability of the respective positions was finally admitted. The aboriginal groups' minimum condition was the "explicit constitutional recognition of the right to self-government":

> Any amendment to the Constitution at this time must contain certain key elements. It must recognize our right to self-government, lands and resources, an historic right inherent in our unsurrendered sovereignty...Either bilaterally with the federal government or trilaterally including provincial governments, there must be an obligation to negotiate agreements or treaties at the request of each first nation or tribal group, or collectively, on jurisdictional matters, including self-government, lands, resources and fiscal relations...These agreements must be constitutionally protected...We must be guaranteed of the enforceability of our rights and jurisdictions...We intend to engage in a dynamic and living intergovernmental relationship on the same nation-to-nation basis that was recognized in the Royal Proclamation of 1763 (Erasmus, 1987a: 1–4).

The federal government was miles away from this. Their "compromise" position

---

[1] "The government of Canada and the provincial governments are committed to the principle..."

was to recognize the right to self-government "in principle," or what the Assembly of First Nations (formerly the NIB) characterized as a "contingent" right to self-government: contingent upon further agreements with the governments, not enforceable in the courts until any such agreement was reached, and then, only to the extent contemplated by the agreement (Assembly of First Nations, 1987: 2). Even this was opposed by the Western provinces and Newfoundland. And, of course, it was unacceptable to the four organizations representing the aboriginal groups. No government, federal or provincial, was willing to leave this one to the courts. The meeting broke up with the aboriginal group leaders calling the Premiers "racist," and no further meetings were scheduled (*The Toronto Star*, March 28, 1987: A1, A4). The amendment referring to aboriginal rights' conferences neatly self-destructed, leaving no trace of the issue in Canada's constitution and a distinctly Orwellian odour.[1]

When the Meech Lake Accord came, just one month later, it added insult to inaction. The sole reference to aboriginal peoples was the oblique one in Clause 16 which provided only that nothing in section 2 (the "distinct society" clause) "affects" section 25, 27, or 35 of the Constitution (aboriginal rights and multiculturalism). This was described by Georges Erasmus for the Assembly of First Nations as "the bare minimum":

> For five years we were engaged in constitutional discussions and it's this "*Bare Minimum*" attitude that prevailed throughout the process.

As far as the Assembly of First Nations was concerned, aboriginal interests were threatened by almost every clause of the Meech Lake Accord. What galled them the most, though, was the "distinct society" clause:

> It perpetuates the idea of a duality in Canada and strengthens the myth that the French and the English peoples are the foundation of Canada. It neglects the original inhabitants and distorts history. It is as if the peoples of the first nations never existed. It suggests that historically and presently as well the French peoples in Quebec form the *only* distinct society in Canada. The amendment fails to give explicit constitutional recognition to the existence of first nations as distinct societies that also form a fundamental characteristic of Canada...We were told for five years that governments are reluctant to entrench undefined self-government of aboriginal peoples in the constitution. Yet, here is an equally vague idea of a "distinct society" unanimously agreed to and allowed to be left to the courts for interpretation (Erasmus, 1987b).

The experience of Canada's aboriginal peoples is another refutation of any pretensions legalized politics might have to redressing major Canadian injustices. In effect, the aboriginal peoples tried to hijack the Charter enterprise to address their claims to the economic and political wherewithal for communal survival. But the Charter is highly resistant to hijacking. Its offer is strictly limited to formal equal citizenship, meant not to redress the balance of power but to legitimate it. Only individuals need apply. They can bring with them all the property they can muster, but no groups are allowed. Canada's aboriginal peoples are too far and too thoroughly removed from the material and cultural

---

[1] The Constitutional amendment of 1983 contained this clause: "54.1 Part IV.1 and this section are repealed on April 18, 1987" (*Constitutional Amendment Proclamation*, 1983, s.5).

presuppositions of this deal ever to be more than fleetingly attracted to it. It is something they have consistently tried to oppose. Not that opposing the legalization of politics is an easy matter. The aboriginal peoples were not allowed to opt out of the Charter any more than Quebec was—even less, because they had no section 33 to turn to. From the way the courts have been behaving under the Charter, it seems that they could have used one.

Charter Decisions on Aboriginal Rights

Section 15(2) of the Charter was inserted in light of the experience of disadvantaged groups in the United States. In the notorious *Bakke* decision of the United States Supreme Court, an affirmative action program instituted at a California medical school which gave preferential admission to certain historically disadvantaged groups, including black people, was held to violate the Fourteenth Amendment guarantee of "equal protection of the law" (*Bakke*, 1978). In other words, a post-Civil War amendment, enacted to turn the country's back on slavery, was used to cut back on the gains black people were finally achieving, after 100 years, through political means. Since *Bakke*, successive drafts of the Canadian Charter have attempted to allay fears of a Canadian version of the decision by inserting clauses more or less to the effect of the current section 15 (2):

(2) Subsection (1) does not preclude any law, program or activity that has as its object the amelioration of conditions of disadvantaged individuals or groups including those that are disadvantaged because of race, national or ethnic origin, colour, religion, sex, age or mental or physical disability.

The aboriginal groups appearing before the Joint Committee were not content to trust the courts with this and tried, as we have seen, to have added to this list, laws that had as their object "the recognition of the aboriginal and treaty rights of the aboriginal peoples of Canada" (Canada, 1980–81, Issue No. 27: 88). But even this would not have protected them from the judicial ingenuity shown by Manitoba's Justice Simonsen in the first application of this provision to aboriginal peoples. He read into the exception a limit closer to the typically legal "fault" requirement used by the majority in *Bakke* than anything in the words of section 15(2). In fact, the case is really an application of the *Bakke* principle *despite* 15(2). According to the judge, affirmative action programs had to "demonstrate a reasonable relationship between the cause of the disadvantage and the form of ameliorative action" to be permitted under the Charter (*Apsit*, 1987: 643). That is they had to address the *cause* of the disadvantage. The Manitoba government had adopted an "affirmative action" program "to encourage native people to take a leading role in the wild rice industry" and had embarked upon a program of granting new licenses[1] exclu-

---

[1] All expired licences that had not been allowed to lapse were renewed, whether or not the holders were Indians.

sively to Indians in most of the areas of the province. The government received approval from the provincial human rights commission for the scheme. But, as in *Bakke*, some non-Indians claimed discrimination. An association of wild rice growers applied to court, and the Court struck down the policy as violating the equality guarantees of the Charter. Because poverty, and not discriminatory licensing, was found to be the cause of the Indian inability to compete successfully in the industry, discriminatory licensing was not a permitted cure:

> The disadvantage of the target group did not arise from an inability to obtain wild rice licences, but rather the disadvantage lay in the target group's lack of resources to take advantage of the opportunities available in the industry...I conclude that the target group needed capital and management assistance in order to achieve its objective to have a leading role in the industry. In my view the respondent has failed to demonstrate a reasonable relationship between the cause of the disadvantage and the form of ameliorative action (*Apsit*, 1987: 643).

This is but another example of some of the key elements of Charter politics: the Charter is not self-enforcing; claims under it have to be put through the judicial filter; and the judiciary is most uncomfortable righting social wrongs at the expense of formal legal equality, even when given the clearest of mandates. It is almost fitting that it should be a judge who reminds aboriginal peoples that they have nothing to hope for from purely legal remedies. The trick is how to get "capital and management assistance" when only purely legal remedies are available on the menu.

Nor have the bare equality rights of the Charter proved of any value to Native people. Their limits are as evident here as they are elsewhere. In *Sinclair* (1986), a Manitoba status Indian convicted of murdering a prison guard claimed his equality rights were violated when the panel from which his jury was to be selected had only two Indians (out of 148), only one of whom was actually chosen. Sinclair wanted half the jury to be Indian, preferably fluent in Cree, his native language. The Court of Appeal rejected the claim, on the grounds of multiculturalism and the rights of *jurors*:

> To so interpret the Charter would run counter to Canada's multicultural and multiracial heritage and the right of every person to serve as a juror (unless otherwise disqualified). It would mean the imposition of inequality (*Sinclair*, 1986: 421).

When reminded of the new rights of English and French Canadians to a jury composed entirely of jurors who speak their language (*Criminal Code*, s.462.1), the Court reminded Sinclair of the structure of the Canadian layer cake, anticipating the approach that would be taken in *Re Education Act* (1987):

> Language, because of its special place in the constitutional history of Canada, is given a special categorization in the Charter consistent with our constitutional history. Indians are treated the same as all other races (*Sinclair*, 1986: 422).

Even in the non-formal realm of the "aboriginal rights" clause in the Charter, the fundamentals of legalized politics are fully in evidence. Once again, we have a parallel to the case of Quebec. The aboriginal claim for self-government through negotiated agreements was a claim for *self*-administration. But "aboriginal rights" in the context of a Charter of Rights—even when generously interpreted—mean *judicial* administration, a different thing entirely. The case of *Sparrow* (1987) is an example. The accused, a member of the Musqueam Indian band residing near Vancouver, was convicted of taking salmon with a net much bigger than allowed by federal regulation. This was in no sense an individual aberration but part of a century-old conflict between the Canadian government and West Coast Indians over control of the fishery (Shaffer, 1988). The British Columbia Court of Appeal took a generous view of the phrase "existing aboriginal and treaty rights" in the Charter and decided, over the Crown's objection and the trial judge's decision, that the constitution protected rights even where there were no treaties and even when they were subject to federal regulation at the time of the Charter's entrenchment. But that did not mean, as the defence claimed, that the aboriginal rights should be *self*-regulated by the right holders:

> The aboriginal right which the Musqueam had was, subject to conservation measures, the right to take fish for food and for the ceremonial purposes of the band. It was in the beginning a regulated, albeit self-regulated, right. It continued to be a regulated right, and on April 17, 1982 it was a regulated right. It has never been a fixed right, and it has always taken its form from the circumstances in which it has existed. If the interests of the Indians and other Canadians in the fishery are to be protected, then reasonable regulations to ensure the proper management and conservation of the resource must be continued...The general power to regulate the time, place and manner of all fishing, including fishing under an aboriginal right, remains (*Sparrow*, 1987: 608–609).

Sparrow was sent back for a new trial to see if the limits were reasonably related to conservation purposes. The Court had, in effect, introduced the notion of a "reasonable limit" into a section of the Charter formally immune from it.[1] And this was a *generous* reading of the aboriginal rights clause.[2]

---

[1] The Ontario Court of Appeal has recently reached the same conclusion in a case where federal regulations contradicted express treaty rights (*The Globe and Mail*, August 4, 1988: A16).

[2] As we go to press, the Lubicon Lake Cree of Alberta have demonstrated rather graphically the relative ineffectiveness of legal politics for aboriginal peoples. After a fruitless nine years in the courts trying to assert their land claims, the Lubicon walked out of a hearing during the 1988 federal election and set up barricades around their land, shutting off the lucrative oil production that they had been trying to resist, or at least control, through legal means. Though police smashed the barricades and charged twenty-two band members and supporters with contempt of court, within five weeks the charges had been dropped and a tentative deal with the Alberta government had been concluded (*The Toronto Star*, October 22, 1988: D1; *The Globe and Mail*, November 29, 1988: A11).

Women and the Charter

> The decisions of the Supreme Court and other courts, the courts
> generally, have been very bad.
> *Lynn McDonald (1980)*[1]

> Long live the Supreme Court of Canada.
> *Michelle Landsberg (1988)*[2]

The Charter Hearings

The women's groups who appeared before the Joint Parliamentary Committee in 1980–81 were not nearly as apprehensive about the Charter as the aboriginal peoples' groups, but they were definitely ambivalent. They mostly
liked the general idea of an entrenched Charter, but they were very skeptical
about the precise document they were being offered. The major independent
women's umbrella group, the National Action Committee on the Status of
Women, started its submission to the Joint Committee with this:

> Women could be worse off if the proposed charter of rights and freedoms is
> entrenched in Canada's constitution (Canada, 1980–81, Issue No. 9: 57).

The group's major fear was what unrestrained judicial power might mean for
women, and the frame of reference was the experience with the *Canadian Bill of
Rights*, under which, as NAC president Lynn McDonald said, decisions had been
"very bad." Two of the Supreme Court's *Bill of Rights* decisions were infamous
among women. The first was *Lavell* (1973), which shows just how differently things
can be viewed from different sides of the fence. The Supreme Court held that the
double standard in the *Indian Act* which deprived Indian women, but not Indian
men, of Indian status for marrying non-Indians, did not deprive them of equality
before the law. To do this, the Court had to go back on its decision in *Drybones*
(1970) and distinguish between inequality *in the law itself* and inequality in its
administration. With no particular justification, the *Bill of Rights* was held only to
prohibit the latter. Of course, the context was massive opposition by male-domi-
nated Indian organizations who saw in the litigation a threat to the *Indian Act* in
general, a piecemeal destruction of the special status they were just then trying to
assert, and non-Indian imposed definitions of band membership when they were
trying to take control over them (Sanders, 1985: 539–547). But to non-Indian
women, *Lavell* had nothing to do with that and everything to do with judicial biases
against women. The other decision was *Bliss* (1978), in which discrimination in
unemployment insurance benefits to women who were laid off because of pregnancy
was held by a unanimous Supreme Court of Canada not to discriminate on the basis
of sex because—believe it or not—not all women were pregnant:

> If section 46 treats unemployed women differently from other unemployed

---

[1] As President of the National Action Committee on the Status of Women appearing before the Joint
Parliamentary Committee on the Charter on November 20, 1980 (Canada, 1980–81, Issue No. 9: 66).

[2] Writing in *The Globe and Mail* (January 29, 1988: A2) the day after the Supreme Court of Canada
struck down the abortion law in *Morgentaler*.

persons, be they male or female, it is, it seems to me, because they are pregnant and not because they are women (*Bliss*, 1978: 191).

Then there was the divorce case *Murdoch* (1973), in which a wife's years of contribution to ranchwork were held by the Supreme Court (over the dissent of about-to-be Chief Justice Laskin) not to entitle her to any share of the ranch when the marriage broke up.

The strategy before the Joint Committee was to try to have the Charter tightened up in order to make such decisions less likely. "Given the sorry record of the courts on women's rights cases, this is not a matter to be left to judicial discretion" (Canada, 1980–81, Issue No. 9: 59). NAC's main focus was the equality rights clause. They wanted it to forbid discrimination "in the law" as well as "before" it. They wanted marital status and sexual orientation included in the prohibited grounds of discrimination. They opposed the delayed action of the equality clause. They wanted women specifically mentioned in section 15(2). They felt the original general term "disadvantaged persons" would allow judges to defeat affirmative action programs designed to help women, on the grounds that women were not "disadvantaged." They wanted the aboriginal rights clause to be applied "equally to native men and to native women" (Canada, 1980–81, Issue No. 9: 60). They wanted a representative number of women on the courts, conceding that it "would take some time for women to be appointed and to work up to that 50 per cent." (Canada, 1980–81, Issue No. 9: 71). They favoured, though the idea did not originate with them, a clause saying the Charter applied equally to men and women.[1] NAC argued for the deletion of the "reasonable limits" clause altogether (Canada, 1980–81, Issue No. 9: 58). Many of these ideas were echoed by the Canadian Advisory Council on the Status of Women ("a federal government-established organization": Sheppard and Valpy, 1982: 307) and the National Association of Women and the Law, a group composed mainly of women lawyers (Canada, 1980–81, Issue No. 9: 123ff.; Issue No. 22), though both groups, for their own reasons, were rather more sanguine about the Charter in general than NAC.

Although far from completely successful, the women's groups did not come away empty-handed. They got most of the changes they wanted to section 15(1), and sex was specifically mentioned in the "affirmative action" clause, section 15(2). The "reasonable limits" clause was considerably tightened up. The moratorium clause was left in, and there was nothing included about representation of women on the courts, but the next appointment to the Supreme Court of Canada was, in fact, a woman, and it was not long before she was joined by a second one, bringing the representation of women on the Supreme Court (slightly) above representation in the legal profession altogether.[2] The general equality clause (section 28) went in, was dropped out as

---

[1] This clause was the recommendation of the Chief Commissioner of the Canadian Human Rights Commission, Gordon Fairweather, who also recommended what was to be the ultimate specific wording of section 1 (Canada, 1980–81, Issue No.5: 5A: 3–4).

[2] It is estimated that 20% of lawyers are women (May, 1987: 13).

part of the deal of November 5, and was quickly put back in—and not made subject to the new section 33 override—after intense pressure was applied in a national lobbying campaign (Pal and Morton, 1986: 156–7; Sheppard and Valpy, 1982: 307–309). The Native women's clause only had to wait two years (*Constitutional Amendment Proclamation 1983*, s.2). All in all, pretty successful:

> [Feminist and civil liberties groups'] objectives coincided fortuitously with the nation-building agenda of then Prime Minister Trudeau and the Liberal Party...Feminist groups proved to be crucial allies in Trudeau's constitutional quest. They effectively bargained their support for a rewording of the equality rights clause that would preclude any future decisions like *Bliss*...No lobby fared better than the feminists (Pal and Morton, 1986: 153–156).

During the three-year waiting period, feminist lawyers honed their weapons. They undertook their own "legislative audits" that went far beyond anything that the governments were willing to undertake. While governments adopted "a minimalist methodology," limiting equality to the excision of sexist terms from legislation, feminists argued for an "equality of result" approach to section 15 to end "systemic" discrimination. They wrote articles and prepared arguments to use "systematic litigation" as a "vehicle for social change" (Pal and Morton, 1986: 157–158). When April 17, 1985, finally came, they were not discouraged by the lack of substantive action on the part of the governments; they celebrated a "Feminist Fantasy of the Future."[1]

Women on the Defensive

But women soon discovered that, as far as the courts were concerned, they did not have a monopoly on the equality clause. Not long into the life of section 15, organizations started sprouting up vowing to use the Charter to oppose laws giving advantages to women. A coalition called "Men and Women for a Fair Market Wage" said Ontario's proposed pay equity law violated the holy constitutional principles of supply and demand. Prominent among the group's members were the National Citizens' Coalition and the anti-feminist group REAL Women of Canada (*The Globe and Mail*, May 17, 1986: A15). Another group called "In Search of Justice" formed to oppose all forms of affirmative action (including pay equity), to win fathers a say in abortion, and more rights for those accused of sexual assault (*The Globe and Mail*, March 11, 1988: A1, A8; March 15, 1988: A6). Though NAC vice-president Marjorie Cohen expressed confidence in the Charter's ability to withstand these claims ("we have very good provisions in our Constitution calling for equality": *The Globe and Mail*, May 17, 1986: A15), all over the country men set out to prove her wrong.

Some decisions made it seem as if section 15 was going to turn out to be a Frankenstein's monster. One of these was *Howell* (1986), in which a New-

---

[1] A handbill for a "Dinner and Cabaret $20.00" in Toronto hosted by the "Charter of Rights Coalition," with "Proceeds to Legal Defense Fund, LEAF" read: "Feminist Fantasy of the Future / COME / Celebrate the complete Charter of Rights! / Celebrate Clause Fifteen! / Celebrate Our Future!"

foundland District Court Judge invoked not only section 15 but also section 28 of the Charter to strike down the *Criminal Code* prohibition against incest because it only made it a crime for men and not for women. A man who had sexual intercourse with his 11-year-old stepdaughter was thus acquitted because the section did not apply to stepmothers who had intercourse with their stepsons:

> For better or for worse [the Charter] may sweep away legislation which heretofore granted special status and protection to women...The Charter grants no special status to either males or females (*Howell*, 1986: 110).

This decision even had the *defence* lawyer (who made the argument) worrying about its effects on children's safety (*Canadian Lawyer*, June, 1986, 10.5: 26). Another decision was *Neely* (1985), in which an Ontario District Court Judge found that the offence in section 146 of the *Criminal Code* of statutory rape (sexual intercourse with a female under the age of fourteen) was of no force and effect because the prohibition only applied to men.[1] Of course, there were decisions going both ways in these and similar matters, but the outcome was very uncertain until the Courts of Appeal started to exercise a restraining effect with some reassuring rulings.

The British Columbia Court of Appeal won praise for its "feminist approach" (Noonan, 1985) to pornography in *Red Hot Video* (1985). The obscenity prohibitions of the *Criminal Code* had been challenged as interferences with freedom of expression and, in their vagueness, fundamental justice. Given the control exercised by the judges over the "community standards" test in obscenity,[2] it is not surprising that the standard was held not to be unduly vague. This is just an application of the principles we examined in Chapter IV. More important was the court's defence of the law as necessary to advance the equality of women. One of the judges even invoked section 28 of the Charter and wrote:

> If true equality between male and female persons is to be achieved it would be quite wrong in my opinion to ignore the threat to equality resulting from the exposure to male audiences of the violent and degrading material described above...The materials in question...have no literary or artistic merit and in a revolting and excessive way create an attitude of indifference to violence insofar as women are concerned and tend to dehumanize both men and women. They approve the domination of women by men as an acceptable social philosophy (Justice Anderson in *Red Hot Video*, 1985: 59–61).[3]

In *Le Gallant* (1986), the same court also came through and upheld the *Criminal Code* limitations on defences and defence strategies available in sexual assault cases. The case involved a 37-year-old man charged with sexually assaulting a 13-year-old boy. Where the victim was 13, the *Criminal Code* provided that consent

---

[1] *Neely* was reversed by the Ontario Court of Appeal on the ground that the trial judge had wrongly given section 15 retroactive effect (*Lucas*, 1986).

[2] "[T]he Judge must, in the final analysis, endeavour to apply what he, in the light of his experience, regards as contemporary standards of the Canadian community" (*Red Hot Video*, 1985: 42).

[3] *Red Hot Video* was followed in *Mood Video*, 1987 (Newfoundland Supreme Court, Trial Division).

was no defence unless the accused was less than three years older. The trial judge held this to be age discrimination, but the Court of Appeal ruled that the "distinction does not amount to discrimination" because "it is neither unreasonable nor unfair" (*Le Gallant*, 1986: 300).[1]

Another important issue in *Le Gallant* was the constitutionality of the special *Criminal Code* provisions designed to make life easier for complainants in sexual assault cases and more difficult for those who assault them. In 1983, responding to an intense lobbying campaign by women's organizations, the federal government enacted severe restrictions on the rights of defence lawyers to turn rape trials into trials of the complainant's sexual reputation. These replaced the common law rules under which (1) the complainant could be cross-examined about any prior sexual behaviour on her part, on the theory that a woman who was "unchaste" was probably a liar, too, and (2) evidence of the complainant's prior sexual conduct was admissible, on the theory that if she had consented before with someone else, she had probably consented this time with the accused, consent being a major issue in sexual assault cases. The only protection complainants had from this abuse was the trial judge's discretion to exclude irrelevant matters, but it appears that "the discretion was never resorted to" (*Seaboyer*, 1987: 60). The general effect of such questioning and such evidence, besides discouraging complaints, was to encourage juries to acquit even those they felt to be guilty should they feel that only virgins should be protected from sexual assault. The history of the law and certain principles within it (spousal immunity, the importance of penetration) show quite convincingly that its primary concern was with sexual exclusivity and not with bodily integrity. A half-hearted reform in 1976 gave trial judges the discretion to reject such evidence, but set out a procedure for doing so which, when turned to advantage by defence lawyers, actually made matters *worse* for complainants. The general sexual assault law reform of 1983 made the exclusion of such questions and evidence automatic except in very limited, very specific circumstances.[2] In no case could these be used to impugn credibility.

With the enactment of the Charter these restrictions started to be challenged. In *Le Gallant*, the trial judge agreed that the restrictions prejudiced the accused's section 7 Charter rights. The Court of Appeal, however, held the provisions achieved "a balance of fairness between the complainant and the accused" (*Le Gallant*, 1986: 304). This has not been the universal appellate approach, however. The Ontario Court of Appeal took quite a different view in *Seaboyer*, 1987. Actually, *Seaboyer* is probably a more important case for women than *Le Gallant*. Where *Le Gallant* involved a homosexual assault, *Seaboyer* involved heterosexual assaults. Where *Le Gallant* heard argument only from the parties themselves, *Seaboyer* pitted the women's Charter litigation group, LEAF, arguing in defence of the law on the side of the govern-

---

[1] This reasoning was adopted by the Newfoundland Court of Appeal in *Halleran*, 1987.

[2] Where the prosecution tried to show chastity first, where prior sexual activity might establish somebody else as the culprit, or where the activity was with the accused on the same occasion and might thereby show consent.

ment, against the Canadian Civil Liberties Association, arguing against the law on the side of those accused of sexual assault. To complicate matters further, LEAF's lawyer was a man and the Civil Liberties Association lawyer was a woman, Toronto law professor Louise Arbour, soon to be Justice Louise Arbour of the Supreme Court of Ontario. The law survived, but barely (3–2) and in a somewhat mutilated form. The minority would have just shot it down as interfering with the judge's unfettered power to ensure a fair trial (for the accused) by permitting any evidence thought relevant and not too prejudicial, essentially the position of the 1976 reforms. The majority thought the law generally worked well but that the judge should retain a discretion to admit evidence:

> In my view, while s.246.6 will be applicable in most cases, there may be occasions when conformity with s.7 of the Charter will require the court to consider the defence and the evidence proffered in support of that defence. If that defence is a legitimate one and the evidence has real probative force on a fact in issue, it will be admitted (Justice Grange in *Seaboyer*, 1987: 64).

The majority thought the instances where these defences would arise would be "rare," but the dissenting judges disagreed, which is why they dissented:

> It is quite apparent that there will be cases where this question will arise. This is certain. But, unlike my brother Grange, I doubt that such cases will be rare…Certainly there is no evidence before us which would justify saying that such cases will be rare or attempting to determine their number and frequency. Whatever the number, no one should be placed in a position that he does not have the same right to make his defence as any other person charged with a crime…In my view, the answer is simply to treat an accused charged with a sexual offence as an accused charged with any other crime, by applying the general rules with respect to the relevancy and the admissibility of the evidence, and make certain that the jury is properly instructed as to the use they can make of it…(Justice Brooke in *Seaboyer*, 1987: 74, 79)

In the end, there was not much difference between majority and minority. The judge would decide whether the defence was "legitimate" and whether the evidence had "real probative force," and the judge would instruct the jury what to do with it. The fact that that judge might be Justice Louise Arbour should not give women much comfort.[1]

The Ontario Court of Appeal generally has shown much more confidence in the exercise of judicial discretion than the *Criminal Code*. In *Canadian Newspapers* (1985), it modified the absolute right of a complainant in a sexual assault case to have her identity protected under section 442(3) (another 1983 reform) into a question for the discretion of the trial judge, invoking "freedom of the press" under the Charter:

---

[1] There is no evidence that female judges are any more likely to interpret the Charter equality clauses in a more feminist way than male judges. The trial judge whose expansive reading of the Charter lead to a sexual assault acquittal in *Halleran* and the trial judge who struck out paternity suits because they discriminated against men in *Shewchuck* were both women and they were overruled by all male appeal courts.

The administration of justice is dependent on public confidence in the judiciary. The discretion given to the trial judge...is a sufficient safeguard for the protection of the identity of the complainant (*Canadian Newspapers*, 1985: 402).

Three years later, the Supreme Court of Canada would overrule this decision on the ground that the protection of the complainant's identity justified the minimal infringement on freedom of the press. However, the Court emphasized that the case involved an application by a *newspaper*, not by someone accused of sexual assault. It sidestepped and expressly left open the question of what the result would be if an accused person's interests in a "fair trial" were in the balance (*Canadian Newspapers*, 1988). In such cases, the general tendency of the Supreme Court of Canada, too, is to rely heavily on judicial discretion to reconcile the conflicting interests (*Corbett*, 1988).

Still, notwithstanding the initial jitters, the overall success rate for attacks on the protections of the criminal law for women complainants has been fairly low.[1] On the whole, it must be said that the damage control of groups such as LEAF has been successful so far, despite the sanctity of the criminal trial and the importance of appearing to give accused persons every chance, a subject we discussed in Chapter IV. But putting out brush fires started by the Charter all over the country does not come free:

> Cases such as *Seaboyer* and *Canadian Newspapers* have increasingly demanded the attention and resources of groups like LEAF which were originally formed to use the Charter to further feminist struggles for equality. As a result of the Charter, feminist organizations are having to spend precious time, energy and money in the courts defending legislation that it took many women many years to achieve (Fudge, 1988b: 48).[2]

And the dangers of misuse of section 15 are not confined to criminal cases. Though attempts to invoke the Charter in custody battles have so far met with no success (*The Globe and Mail*, July 5, 1988: A8), women's welfare rights have been seriously threatened in other section 15 cases. A British Columbia Provincial Court Judge blocked a paternity suit by a single mother and declared all paternity suits contrary to the Charter because they were sexually exclusive in *Shewchuk* (1986). This required another intervention by LEAF as well as other feminist and anti-poverty groups on the side of the mother. The Court of Appeal found sex discrimination, but the statute in question was saved, according to the Court, by

> the broad public purpose of the legislation, namely to establish paternity and therefore provide a basis for shifting the financial responsibility for the child from the public to the private domain (*Shewchuk*, 1986: 448).

Some cases of men making use of sexual equality provisions pose no dangers to women and actually reduce sexual stereotyping. One such case was

---

[1] The Supreme Court of Canada granted leave to the government to appeal *Seaboyer* in May 1988.

[2] See also Petter (1987a).

MacVicar (1986), in which a natural father successfully challenged his exclusion from adoption proceedings concerning his daughter. In *MacVicar*, the father had a proven relationship with the child and was himself petitioning for a role. The Court reasoned that including the father in the proceedings in such circumstances would not tie its hands in looking after the best interests of the child. When, in another case, an Ontario Family Court Judge on his own motion held up adoption proceedings pending location and notification of the natural father, on the grounds of equality with natural mothers (though the father's only connection with the child was conception), the Divisional Court of Ontario jumped right down his throat. It pointed out that the mother had borne the child and given birth to it, and criticized the judge for raising the issue though nobody else had. The Charter, it said, "was not intended to transform this land from one governed by a parliamentary democracy into one governed by a judicial oligarchy" (*The Globe and Mail*, April 2, 1988: A4). Section 15 has also been used to extend to men accused of sexual assault the same identity protection that those they are accused of assaulting are granted by statute (*R.*, 1986) and to grant male prisoners the right to refuse non-emergency strip searches by female guards, where female prisoners are not subjected to such searches by male guards (*Weatherall*, 1987).

None of these men's equality claims posed any threats to women because what the men were asking for could be provided at no cost and without depriving women of anything. Of course, there were logical alternatives, but it would have been both ludicrous and pointless, indeed vindictive, to decide *Weatherall* by ordering that cross-sex searches apply to women prisoners, to decide *R.* by taking away complainants' identity protection, or to decide *MacVicar* by excluding mothers from adoption proceedings. But what happens when something more concrete is at stake?

One such instance was *Phillips* (1986). An unemployed Nova Scotia man with sole custody of a dependent child "born out of wedlock" applied for family benefits but was denied them because the wording of the statute only contemplated the "mother" applying in such a situation. He then went to court for a declaration that this infringed his equality rights. The Nova Scotia courts agreed that the provision was discriminatory and refused to accept it as either affirmative action (because the stated policy was to help families in need, not just women) or a reasonable limit (other provinces had repealed the distinction during the three-year section 15 waiting period). But while Phillips, as can be expected, wanted the benefits extended to him, the courts had another idea. They struck down the whole section, benefits to single unmarried mothers and all. Though this sounds rather drastic, it was not intended that anyone lose benefits, and nobody did. The trial judge invited the legislature to change the law and suggested "retroactive legislation, if necessary, to avoid any harm to people who are receiving benefits or may become entitled to benefits" (*Phillips*, 1986). But the government did not even bother. They were quite prepared to undertake the minimal extra costs. When the appeal judgment came down, affirming the trial judge, they merely moved to another, more general, section of the Act and passed regulations providing for gender-neutral benefits on the same terms as previous to the case (*Nova Scotia Regulation* 15/87). Nobody missed a cheque.[1]

Feminist legal groups such as LEAF have been scrambling to prevent such bizarre results from occurring elsewhere, especially when there is enough money at stake to make the legislative outcome less certain than in *Phillips*. They succeeded in the recent case of *Schachter* (1988), a challenge to the maternity benefits provisions of the *Unemployment Insurance Act*. This was a complicated case but well worth understanding for the light it sheds on the limits of legalized politics. An Ontario father, who wanted to take time off from work to help out at home with the new baby, was denied unemployment insurance benefits. The Act provided that the natural mother could get *maternity* benefits while she was recovering from the effects of birth, that is, *recovery* benefits, for up to 15 weeks, or she could get *childcare* benefits (for taking care of the baby, as opposed to recovering from birth) for up to 15 weeks, or a combination of both. But the total could never exceed 15 weeks. Schachter wanted to stay home after the mother recovered so she could go back to work. He wanted then to take over what remained of the 15 weeks of the total childcare benefits. But the law did not allow this. Only mothers could apply. However, things were different in the case of *adoptive* parents. They were given 15 weeks of childcare benefits (they obviously did not need recovery benefits) and were allowed to choose how to distribute them between father and mother. The total benefits for each type of family were the same, of course. Schachter went to court to claim for natural parents the right to choose that adoptive parents had by statute.

The government called expert evidence to show the greater needs of adoptive parents and children and their special problems of adjustment (*The Globe and Mail*, April 19, 1988: 22), but for some undisclosed reason its lawyers did not argue the applicability of the "reasonable limits" provision under section 1. After a well-publicized trial, Justice Barry Strayer[2] declared the provision unconstitutional as contrary to section 15.

LEAF had intervened in this case to ensure that the results were not detrimental to women. They supported the idea of encouraging men to help with child-rearing and of breaking down the sexual stereotypes implicit in the Act, but they did not want the result to be diminished benefits for women. There was always the *Phillips* scenario, but even giving natural parents the right to choose how to divide up the 15 weeks would tend to diminish the mother's childcare benefits and even her recovery benefits. An Ontario Federation of Labour representative had also asked the Court not to split the benefits between mother and father (*The Globe and Mail*, April 19, 1988: 22).

Justice Strayer's decision was the best of both worlds from the applicants' point of view. He agreed that the Act violated section 15 of the Charter by

---

[1] Personal communication from the Nova Scotia Ministry of Social Services.

[2] In a former life, Strayer was Assistant Deputy Minister to Justice Minister Jean Chrétien. As such, he had helped draft the Charter and steward it through the Joint Parliamentary Committee. See, for example, Canada, 1980–81, Issue No. 4.

discriminating against natural fathers in comparison with adoptive fathers. And he agreed that it was sex discrimination to stereotype men and women by assuming that women had to be the care-givers. Most importantly, his remedy was not to strike out the childcare benefits because of their discriminatory nature (the *Phillips* solution), but to order that benefits be *extended* to the father at the natural parents' option, all the while maintaining the mother's rights to recovery benefits. Notice that this was even more than Schachter had originally asked for, which was merely a sharing out of the total fifteen weeks of benefits (*The Globe and Mail*, April 12, 1988: A16).

Though LEAF and the applicants were happy, all was not perfect. For one thing, the decision left adoptive parents with lower overall benefits than natural parents. Even though this could be justified by the natural mother's recovery needs, it would be impossible in practice to separate out the childcare element of any such period, at least for most births. More important was the fact that the full benefit of the decision could only be had if the government paid out more in total benefits. If a mother claimed her full recovery benefits and a father his full childcare benefits, the total benefits would double from 15 to 30 weeks, and at the generally higher rates due to men's generally higher salaries. The evidence in the case was that the increased costs of such a ruling would run between $10 million and $50 million, depending on how many fathers took advantage of the decision. These figures were based on the assumption that no more than 5% of fathers would seek paternity benefits. If they all did, it would cost $1.1 *billion* (*The Globe and Mail*, April 14, 1988: A12; April 15, 1988: A16). The Canadian Federation of Independent Businesses, as might be expected, howled, warning of a radical disruption of the work force and a severe drain on the unemployment insurance fund (*The Lawyers Weekly*, June 24, 1988: 25). Because of the financial implications, the judge took the once unheard of, but now merely unusual, step of putting his judgment in abeyance pending appeal, which rather knocked the moral stuffing out of his ruling. It also made Liberal MP Sheila Copps's claim that a government appeal would "fly in the face of the Charter" sound a little overblown.

Assuming the judgment stands, it is not at all clear what the government will do. In fact, Strayer's order left the government with several options:

> I...leave it to Parliament to remedy the situation in accordance with the *Charter*, either by extending similar benefits to natural parents, or by eliminating the benefits given to adoptive parents, *or by some provision of more limited benefits on an equal basis to both adoptive and natural parents in respect of child-care.* I am not telling Parliament that it must follow one route or the other: all I am determining is that if it is going to provide such benefits it must provide them on a non-discriminatory basis (*Schachter*, 1988: 30; emphasis added).

Before *Schachter*, the government was contemplating allowing natural parents the option of choosing, but within the same maximum number of weeks of benefits. This would meet the equality challenge, but the government has already been publicly warned off it by a member of the executive of the National Action Committee:

International human-rights covenants (to which Canada subscribes) are adamant that equality provisions not be financed by reducing benefits already granted to one group. This has been particularly important in equal-pay legislation. Women's groups have argued for, and won, acceptance of the principle that giving women equal wages cannot be at the expense of lowering men's wages. The same principle holds with maternity benefits. If men receive them, it cannot be at the expense of what women already have. This approach would be equality with a vengeance (Cohen, 1988).

"Equality with a vengeance" it may be, but the federal government would not be the first Canadian government to respond to the Charter this way. In *Silano*, 1987, the British Columbia Public Interest Advocacy Centre successfully challenged a British Columbia welfare regulation, which gave $25 more per month to recipients over the age of 26 than to those under 26. The measure had been introduced in 1984 as a recession cutback. The government argued younger recipients had fewer dependents and more mobility and were more likely to receive support from parents than older recipients. The trial judge disagreed. He preferred 19 as a cutoff and struck the regulation down, entitling the younger recipients to the same amounts as the older ones. How did the government respond? Raising the benefits of the younger recipients to the level of the older ones would have added $4.5 million per year to the budget. Instead, the government split the difference. It raised the younger recipients' benefits $19 and *reduced* the benefits of the older group by $6 to keep the total net outlay the same. Though opponents cried foul, the Social Services Minster argued impeccably that the government action was perfectly consistent with the ruling: "The court says everybody has to be at the same rate. It doesn't say what the rate is" (*Calgary Herald*, August 12, 1987: B3). More legal action was vowed by civil liberties groups (*Vancouver Sun*, August 14, 1987: A1, A2).

Not long after this, the Social Credit government of British Columbia was being asked to help the universities out of the jam they were left in when the British Columbia Court of Appeal declared their mandatory retirement policies contrary to the Charter (*Harrison*, 1988). They had pleaded that funding restraints were responsible for their having to force out professors over 65. They had to make sure the older generation of faculty would retire so they would have the resources to offer jobs to young graduates. Mandatory retirement is, after all, a function of the increasing unattractiveness of retirement in economically volatile periods and the increasing lack of entry-level jobs. The private sector is unable or unwilling to provide enough new jobs and the public sector is restrained by the private sector through the concept of "business confidence." But the Court held that these economic reasons could not override the Charter and struck down the age exceptions to discrimination in employment under provincial human rights legislation. This, in effect, abolished mandatory retirement in the province. The British Columbia Court of Appeal differed in this from the Ontario Court of Appeal, which saw things much more from the point of view of the universities and held mandatory retirement to be a "reasonable limit":

Mandatory retirement makes it possible to plan for faculty renewal and the necessary funding which is entailed. Flexibility is very important as new resources may be needed in an entirely different field from that of the faculty member who is being retired...By giving up the right to indefinite employment, the faculty member receives a guarantee of tenure, favorable salary benefits and a pension on retirement. It also provides a dignified way of leaving employment without embarrassing assessments as to ability to perform work (*McKinney*, 1987).

This, too, will have to be resolved in the Supreme Court of Canada, but either way, somebody is going to lose—either the younger or older generation of faculty—unless there is more public-sector money. The President of the University of British Columbia publicly despaired of the university's ability to compete for young academic talent and formally requested government either to go back on its restraint program and provide more money or to use section 33 and override the decision. Given the policies of the government and the taboo on section 33, neither alternative seems likely (*The Globe and Mail*, March 23, 1988: A4).

The point is that using the Charter to improve general living standards is something like printing more money to improve incomes. If anybody wins, it is going to be at somebody else's expense. General living standards cannot be improved through purely redistributive means, unless what is redistributed is *power*. But this means contradicting the logic of the marketplace. It means the expansion of the public sector and the contraction of the private. Otherwise, growth is strictly limited by profitability, with the lion's share going to the lions who always insist on being fed first. Any "trickling down" has to wait. To go beyond the narrow confines of profitability and to generalize the benefits of this, the economy has to be politically redirected in the general interest. The Charter obviously has nothing to do with that. In fact, its mission is precisely the opposite. It interferes as little as possible with the logic of the market and profitability. Its redistributive effects are purely *lateral* ones among the limited pool of resources available to the mass of average wage-earners. It leaves the hoards of power and power itself untouched.

On a more prosaic level, no government is obliged to increase its spending to comply with the equality rulings of any court. And even if it does, spending increases have to come from somewhere. Either the printing presses or somebody else's pockets. And here is where the structure of social power comes in. The same power restraints that prevail in other situations (deregulation, tax incentives to business) to prevent these increases from coming out of business pockets, apply in situations forced by Charter rulings. Take the issue of equal pay, raised by Marjorie Cohen. She claims that the principle has been accepted that increases for women are not to come from the paychecks of their male co-workers. But how can this be? Nothing in equal-pay legislation requires employers to increase their total wage package (and reduce their total profits) in order to equalize things between men and women. That money has to come from somewhere. Employers are not going to be more easygoing at the bargaining table because of pay equity. Nor is business competition going to ease up because of it. Equal pay for work of equal value is undeniably a good thing. In fact, it is one of the preconditions of a democratic society. But it is also undeniable that—barring a fundamental realignment in the structure of social power—increases for working women will be entirely at the expense of working men.

And, in the same way, any extension of benefits to men under the *Unemployment Insurance Act* has got to come from somewhere. Somebody is going to lose benefits, if only in the form of an increase they would otherwise have received, and somewhere down the line women will be among those losing.

So far we have been talking about the substantial victories men have achieved and their direct and indirect impact on women. But women have won some victories, too, which have seemed to vindicate the entire Charter enterprise for them. We now turn to these.

Women's Charter Victories

During the waiting period between the enactment of the Charter and the coming into force of section 15, women's lawyers were busy scanning the statute books for sexism. All of the legislatures made changes to give women and others formal equality, but none of these things had major social impacts (for example, changing the word "wife" to "spouse"). The Charter must be credited with hastening the end of statutes requiring women to take their husband's surname on marriage, though even this required litigation (Fudge, 1988b: 31). Indeed, Professor Fudge has suggested that women's success in having the statute books quickly excised of such explicit sexism is a possible explanation for the "astounding number of successful challenges initiated by men":[1]

> Of the few remaining explicit uses of gender-based classification in the statute books most benefit women (Fudge, 1988b: 49).

Fudge also points out that the achievement of formal equality in these realms does nothing to change the concrete relations between men and women. The equal *legal right* to choose does not necessarily entail the equal *power* to choose:

> The success of this litigation demonstrates the courts' willingness to accept arguments advocating formal legal equality when issues of obvious symbolic, though of little material, import are raised... However, the attainment of such formal equality does nothing in itself to further substantive equality for women either within or outside of marriage (Fudge, 1988b: 31).

But not all of women's Charter victories in the realm of sex discrimination have been purely formal. Some of them have made a very great impact indeed. One of the first of these was the long drawn-out litigation undertaken on behalf of a twelve-year-old Ontario girl so she could play hockey in the boys' league (*Blainey*, 1986; 1987). Justine Blainey was an excellent hockey player who thought that the quality of play was too low in the girls' hockey league. She liked the rougher, more competitive style of play in the boys' leagues (*Blainey*, 1987: 10). There was no question that she was good enough. She repeatedly made the boys' teams only to be forbidden from playing by league

---

[1] According to Lahey, "male complainants are making *and winning* ten times as many equality claims as women" (Lahey, 1987: 82).

officials. The rules stipulated that girls were ineligible for boys' teams. The only exceptions were in areas of Ontario where there were no girls' teams at all. Justine Blainey lived in Toronto, and there were plenty. She complained of sex discrimination to the Ontario Human Rights Commission in 1985, but they declined jurisdiction because of an explicit exception in the Act. Sex discrimination was permitted "where membership in an athletic organization or participation in an athletic activity is restricted to persons of the same sex" (*Human Rights Code,* 1981: s.19(2)). Since it was 1985, Blainey and her mother went to court claiming that her rights under section 15 of the Charter had been violated. They lost at trial but won a split decision before the Ontario Court of Appeal. That decision became final when the Supreme Court of Canada declined to hear an appeal from it in June of 1986.

Blainey was one of those curious Charter decisions where everything is turned upside down by a court determined to reach a particular result. In the first place, the public/private distinction. Even though the activities of the hockey league were technically beyond the reach of the Charter because they were admittedly "private," this proved no obstacle to the Court in taking charge of the case. The majority found the discrimination in the *Human Rights Code* itself.[1] The Code discriminated on the basis of sex by not fully prohibiting sex discrimination! Was it a reasonable limit? According to the majority, it might have been, if the exception had been more narrowly defined and restricted to a legitimate purpose, such as "public decency or for the physical protection of participants." But nothing in the exception restricted it to that.[2]

According to the dissenting judge, it was a different story entirely. The whole thing seemed to him to be a staged confrontation so the Commission could rid itself of a restriction it was on record as opposing:

> The Commission appears to have bigger fish to fry and invites a confrontation in an attempt to extirpate a section of the *Code* which regulates its authority (*Blainey,* 1986: 750).

He thought the Commission could have dealt with the complaint, despite the exemption, if it had really cared about Blainey and not primarily about getting rid of the exemption. He was also disturbed that there was nobody there in court to defend the law. The lawyer for the Commission was on Blainey's side, and nobody represented the Attorney General, who was at that time calling for the law's repeal. Where the majority had felt it "anomalous" that an anti-discrimination statute should discriminate, the dissent thought it absurd to call a statute discriminatory when it was aimed at gradually ending discrimination. There were many exceptions to non-discrimination, including age, religious groups, public decency, etc.:

> The *Code* of this province clearly strives for a compromise between proponents of sweeping anti-discrimination legislation on the one hand, and the concerns of

---

[1] The Ontario Court of Appeal would use the same strategy in a mandatory retirement case the following year (*McKinney,* 1987), thus revealing the public/private distinction to be a wholly self-imposed restraint.

[2] The dissenting judge in *McKinney* (1987), where the law was upheld despite a similar lack of definition, would note the inconsistency with *Blainey.*

The *Code* of this province clearly strives for a compromise between proponents of sweeping anti-discrimination legislation on the one hand, and the concerns of *bona fide* groups concerned with developing their own social, religious, ethnic and sex-oriented groups...It is clearly a cautious first step...There are too many qualifications in the *Code* to the anti-discrimination provision in s.1 for any court to assume that the legislature would have enacted the rest of the *Code* without this and other limitations (*Blainey*, 1986: 752–753).

When the matter finally got back to the Human Rights Commission for a hearing, it turned out that this was not a clash between male and female but between the Human Rights Commission and the Blaineys on the one hand, and the men, and especially the women, responsible for amateur hockey on the other. The sports people were vehement that desegregation of amateur hockey would ruin it, not for men and boys, but for women and girls. Nobody denied that a minority of the girls could play boys'-style hockey on a level good enough to compete with the boys. That was the problem. According to Fran Rider, President of the Ontario Women's Hockey Association (OWHA), though most girls could not compete with the boys, the few top players in her league were as good as any of them. These girls would be gobbled up by the boys' teams as winning assets. The effect of that would be to deprive the girls' teams of their best players. They would lose role models, and the quality of play would deteriorate. Desegregation would "ruin" a system which had 286 teams and 4229 players in 1986–87. Rider, for six years the unpaid president of the OWHA, was described by the one-man Board of Inquiry as "at the forefront in the development of female hockey in Ontario" and one of two women deserving the credit for its success (*Blainey*, 1987: 7). She said the OWHA was "an affirmative action group" and the result of integration would be to label all girls' sports as "second rate." According to her, *that* would be real "discrimination" (*The Globe and Mail*, June 12, 1987: A12). The head of women's amateur hockey in Quebec was brought in to testify that a Quebec desegregation decision in 1978 had "ruined" girls hockey there. According to her, it no longer existed. About 300 girls were playing in boys' leagues until puberty when they were no longer able to compete. The rest of the girls just had to sit it out until they were older. And older women's hockey suffered as a result. On the other hand, it was flourishing in Ontario due to segregation under age 14 (*The Toronto Star*, August 27, 1988: A13).

But these pleas fell on deaf ears. In December 1987, Ian Springate, the one-man Board of Inquiry, rejected this evidence as an exaggeration of the likely effects of integration. He ruled that females could no longer be prohibited from playing hockey, and by implication any sport at any level, in the boys' leagues, though boys could be kept out of girls' leagues to prevent them from taking over (*The Toronto Star*, December 5, 1987: A1, A12). On January 14, 1988, fifteen-year-old Justine finally got to play in the boys' league. The headline was unintentionally suggestive: *"Team loses, Justine wins"* (*The Globe and Mail*, January 16, 1988: A15).

Was this a victory for women? On a symbolic level, perhaps. And it was certainly a victory for those few girls good enough to play with the boys.[1] But for the rest, for those who are intimately involved in women's hockey, in women's sport, it was experienced as a loss.[2] "We feel team sports are suffering because of this push for individual rights" said Fran Rider (*The Globe and Mail*, June 12, 1987: A12). It may even be thought a loss for all women.

...if not participating in male-defined sport does not mean fear or rejection of failure or success, but the creation of a new standard, of a new vision of sport ...[which] finds ritualized violence alien and dangerous as well as faintly ridiculous, every bit as much as it finds sex-scripted cheering from the sidelines demeaning and vicarious and silly. The place of women's athletics in a larger feminist analysis is that women *as women* have a survival stake in reclaiming our bodies in our physical relations with other people (MacKinnon, 1987: 123; emphasis in original).

But it is at best a case of some women winning and other women losing. In the realm of legal politics, this is inevitable. Compromises are not possible. Indeed, they are considered "repugnant" where "rights" are concerned (*Big M*, 1985). What's more, there is no way of even telling whether more women won or lost from this case. In the realm of legalized politics, it is irrelevant whether more win than lose. The decision was not taken on that basis at all. Nor was it taken by the women themselves, let alone the women most concerned with the issue. It was imposed by a Court of Appeal and a Board of Inquiry composed entirely of men.

Blainey is just one example of how the individualism of the Charter can be damaging to subordinate groups, even when the "individual" concerned is a member of the subordinate group. Another is *Tomen* (1987), though the situation was somewhat the reverse and the stakes were considerably higher. In *Tomen*, the Charter was called in aid of an attempt by the Ontario men's public school teachers union to impose integration on the much larger and richer women's union. The men's union wanted access to the women's union members, its dues, and its clout. The excuse was a section 15 challenge by one of the women teachers (a principal) to the bylaw of the Ontario Teachers Federation requiring women teachers, and women teachers only, to belong to the women's branch of the union. She claimed this was "sex discrimination," but her legal fees were completely paid for by the men's union. For years they had been trying to persuade the women's union to amalgamate, but without success. Tomen claimed the bylaw compelled her "to join a unisex union with a female ghetto mentality." With twice the membership (31,000) and twice the annual operating budget ($12 million) of the men's union, the women teachers

---

[1] Even these players may lose out in the long run when they find there is no adult women's hockey to return to later. After the boys pass through puberty, playing in the same league apparently becomes almost impossible (*Blainey*, 1987: 11–12).

[2] Though the law had been changed by the time the case got back to the Human Rights Commission, one should not underestimate the importance of the Charter action. The government used the *Blainey* case to make its case for a change and it waited until the Court of Appeal had decided in her favour and the Supreme Court of Canada had denied leave to appeal before going ahead with it (S.O. 1986, Chap. 64, section 10 (12); *The Globe and Mail*, May 8, 1986: A19). Besides, as we have tried to stress, the Charter represents a form of politics that can exist outside of, as well as inside of the courtroom.

replied, in effect: "Some ghetto." "We are the strongest, wealthiest women's group in the country," said their President. And, according to her, women teachers needed a strong group to do something about such things as the underrepresentation of women by more than 600% as school principals—despite exceptions such as Tomen herself (*The Globe and Mail*, July 9, 1986: A2). It was as if, in *Blainey*, the women's league was the better one and the men were trying to break into their game. The women's union lawyer, Charter equality authority Mary Eberts (Bayefsky and Eberts, 1985), warned the Court not to allow "nineteenth-century individualism" to destroy a women's organization engaged in a struggle against sexism. She urged the Court to reject "a spurious equality...that would turn the Charter on its head" and to consider that equality rights had "a group as well as individual dimension" (*The Globe and Mail*, June 5, 1987: A11). It is anything but clear that the Court would have gone for this argument. What saved the union was a ruling that the Charter did not apply to the union because the bylaw was not "governmental":

> It is now resolved that the Charter is not the universal panacea that legal scholars expected it to be. The Charter is not all things to all persons but has a limited reach as was intended by its drafters. The Charter was designed to restrain governments from abusing fundamental individual (and more limited group) rights and freedoms, but only those rights and freedoms particularized in the Charter. The Charter was designed to protect individuals from government tyranny. The Charter was *not* designed to permit individuals to tyrannize other private individuals or groups in the name of individual rights. The Charter was *not* designed to permit absolute individual freedom so as to result in unbridled anarchy, as opposed to ordered liberty. The Charter was primarily designed solely to protect individuals from governmental abuse (Justice Ewaschuk in *Tomen*, 1987: 271).

As we know by now, this judge's view of what the Charter was "designed to do" is not so well "resolved" as he alleges. There are alternative visions that emphasize the "repugnance" of the "tyranny of the majority." It remains to be seen which one prevails. And as *Tomen* heads for the Supreme Court (and the Ontario Human Rights Commission), there will be plenty of chances for the other points of view to have their day.

If this were the sum total of the Charter jurisprudence on women, we would be on very familiar territory. The "double-edged" character of the Charter's equality provisions means that women, like organized labour and aboriginal peoples, find themselves fighting *against* the Charter just to hold on to what they have begun to achieve through more conventional political means. And even where the Charter's guarantees of formal equality are not positively dangerous, they are incapable, for reasons we explored in Chapter IV, of changing the balance of power between men and women. Furthermore, the individualism of the Charter has been shown to have its own special application to women, providing a solution to the problems of some at the expense of the rest.

But this is not the sum total of the Charter jurisprudence on women. The Charter is a moving target. In January 1988, the Supreme Court of Canada decided the *Morgentaler* case and moved Canadian Charter politics into a whole new dimension.

Abortion and the Charter

Apart from obscure concerns about the word "everyone" in section 7, the women's groups appearing before the Joint Committee on the Charter generally steered clear of the abortion question. However, the issue was extremely well canvassed there. Three anti-abortion groups tried to get specific protection for the foetus (Canada, 1980–81, Issue 22: 27; Issue No. 29: 38; Issue No. 34: 123). Speaking on behalf of one of them, Campaign Life, lawyer Gwen Landolt launched a withering attack on the whole Charter enterprise because of the dangers it held for "the unborn":

> The most important effect of an entrenched Charter of Rights would be that it would give rise to a shift in power from Parliament, which is subject to public opinion, to the Supreme Court of Canada, which is not...

> This abortion legislation...can and will be changed as the Canadian public, as well as many of our legislators, are now becoming very aware of the tragedy of the abortion situation. Parliament will, we believe, in the foreseeable future, amend the callous legislation passed in 1969.

> However, the wishes of the public and Parliament which want to protect all members of the human family, born and unborn, may possibly be thwarted by the nine individuals who will be sitting on the Supreme Court of Canada, for there is little doubt that the right to life of the unborn child will be attacked through the courts by individuals who oppose legislation to protect the unborn child.

> The Supreme Court of Canada, under an entrenched Bill of Rights, will have the power to undermine the will of the people not only on abortion legislation, but on other legislation as well. This check on the power of the majority would appear to be both retrogressive and undemocratic (Canada, 1980–81, Issue No. 34: 119).

Oddly enough, and ironically, given what would occur in 1988, the pro-choice representatives at the hearings seemed to share the pro-lifers' fears of the Charter. The Canadian Abortion Rights Action League came with the limited objective of neutralizing the effects of the Charter on abortion. They did not seek a clause guaranteeing the right to choice but only to the effect that "nothing in this Charter is intended to extend rights to the embryo or fetus nor to restrict in any manner the rights of women to a medically safe abortion." CARAL's legal counsel J. Robert Kellerman:

> If that clause is placed in the existing Charter of Rights and Freedoms it will not provide any rights to women...[O]f course CARAL takes the position and would like to see reproductive rights entrenched in this constitution. That is not what I have been speaking about to this point. We would like to see a special section which talked about reproductive rights, including the rights of women to a medically safe abortion.

However, my main purpose, at least, today in speaking to you is to emphasize that this language is completely open to litigation and to the argument that somehow Parliament intended to create rights in the fetus or embryo, and if Parliament does not intend that then we suggest they must include a section which explicitly states that...

All we are arguing for is the status quo, that is all (Canada, 1980–81, Issue No. 24: 101, 116).

CARAL representatives also shared Campaign Life's preference that Parliament alone decide the abortion question. Eleanor Wright Pelrine, Honourary Director of CARAL:

My personal view is that I think I would rather take my chance with the parliamentarians, however much I may disagree with them on occasion, than I would with the Supreme Court which has never had a woman on the Bench, for example.

My personal view is that there are some women indeed represented in Parliament and I think that number is increasing, and certainly I am much more interested in seeing the democratic process of Parliament decide what the law should be...

I do not agree that the existing law is adequate. However, access is more adequate under the existing law than it would be if the fate of women who are unwillingly pregnant were left to the Canadian courts (Canada, 1980–81, Issue No. 24: 106, 116).

Tory MPs, notably David Crombie and Jake Epp, tried hard to keep the Charter abortion-neutral. They argued successfully against attempts to change the word "everyone" in section 7 to "every person" on the grounds that these were oblique attempts by women's groups and the NDP to help the pro-choice side (Canada, 1980–81, Issue No. 9: 145; Issue No. 43: 43; 45). They put an amendment in Committee (Canada, 1980–81, Issue 41A: 3) and in the House of Commons debate (*House of Commons Debates*, November 27, 1981: 13436ff) that would have included the clause, "Nothing in this Charter affects the authority of Parliament to legislate in respect of abortion,"[1] but it was defeated each time. Crombie was accurately reporting what had been publicly stated at the Charter hearings when he said:

None of us disagree on that: not the Liberals, not the New Democrats, not the Conservatives, not Pro-Life, not Pro-Choice, and not anyone in the middle. We all agree that Parliament must have the freedom to decide. The purpose of this amendment is simply to make sure and make clear to all that that is, indeed, our intention (*House of Commons Debates*, November 27, 1981: 13436).

The motion was defeated after Prime Minister Trudeau assured the members that:

The Charter does not say whether abortions will be easier or more difficult to practice in the future. The Charter is absolutely neutral on this matter...the

---

[1] The amendment proposed in committee included the words "and capital punishment."

House will probably have to decide in the weeks, months or years ahead, depending on the wishes of its members, whether the Criminal Code should be amended to make abortion less readily or more readily available. The onus will be on us.

Then the man who claimed the section 33 override clause had been imposed upon him by the provinces added:

However,...should a judge conclude that, on the contrary, the Charter does, to a certain extent, affect certain provisions of the Criminal Code, under the override clause we reserve the right to say: Notwithstanding this decision, notwithstanding the Charter of Rights as interpreted by this judge, the House legislates in such and such a manner on the abortion issue (*House of Commons Debates*, November 27, 1981: 13438).

What the pro-life side feared was a decision like *Roe* v. *Wade* (1973) in which the Supreme Court of the United States, by a majority of 7–2, had in one fell swoop wiped away the abortion laws of forty-nine states. In a decision harking back to the (right wing) activism of the 1930s, if only in form, the Court held that implicit in the right not to be "deprived of life, liberty, or property, without due process of law" (*United States Constitution*, Amendments V and XIV), was a substantive "right to privacy." The decision whether to continue a pregnancy fell within that right, at least until the foetus was "viable." In *Roe*, the US Supreme Court divided pregnancy up into trimesters, making criminalization during the first three months impossible and during the second three months very difficult, whereas the US norm before the decision had been to more or less restrict abortions at all stages of pregnancy. So radical was *Roe* that it is generally credited with having launched the modern US Right to Life movement, the overriding object of which has always been the destruction of *Roe* itself (Rubin, 1987).

But Canadians on the pro-choice side had already experienced a wall of resistance from the Canadian courts to bringing *Roe* or anything resembling it to bear on Canada's very restrictive abortion legislation. Abortion-rights hero Dr. Henry Morgentaler had spent ten months in jail in 1975 after the Supreme Court had unanimously rejected a claim that Canada's abortion law violated the *Canadian Bill of Rights* (*Morgentaler*, 1975). Canada's law dated from 1969 when the newly elected majority Liberal government under Pierre Trudeau relaxed the absolute prohibition which had existed until then. The government was following a trend to relaxation which had made itself felt in the 1960s in both the United Kingdom and the United States. Canada enacted its law two years after the United Kingdom had virtually left the decision to women and their doctors and one year before several American states followed suit. Still, in 1969, the regimes in most of the American states varied from strict prohibition to a committee system like the one Canada adopted that year (Watters, 1976: 115–117; Rubin, 1987: 64–68). The Canadian law was a compromise that essentially left the matter to *hospital* discretion. An abortion would not be criminal if performed in a hospital by a doctor armed with a certificate from a "therapeutic abortion committee" (TAC) stating that "in its opinion the continuation of the pregnancy...would or would be likely to endanger [the pregnant woman's] life or health" (*Criminal Code*, as amended 1968–69, c.38, s.18). The catch was that hospitals were not required to set up such committees. And even if they did, the committees were not required to grant any certificates, even where they were warranted in the interests of life or health. Matters were left in the control of individual hospitals and provincial governments, who were given the power to recognize facilities as hospitals for the purposes of performing abortions. As might be expected, this, and an exponential increase in the demand for abortions, caused severe problems of access. Women were forced to seek illegal alternatives. Henry Morgentaler, a Montreal gynecologist, offered the best of such alternatives at his clinic in Montreal. Safe and supportive abortion services without the bother of therapeutic abortion committees. Prosecutions against him started in 1970.

The problem with prosecuting Morgentaler was that he would inevitably take the witness stand and demonstrate the medical necessity for any abortion he performed. This was not too difficult to do because any delay in obtaining an abortion increased the danger to a pregnant woman, and applying to a TAC always caused delay (Canada, 1977a). So juries would repeatedly acquit him. The first time this happened, the Quebec Court of Appeal overturned the acquittal and convicted him. The Supreme Court of Canada upheld this conviction in 1975, despite arguments by a bevy of interveners that the abortion law, because of its arbitrariness and intrusiveness, violated the *Canadian Bill of Rights*. Most of the Court (including Justice Dickson, now Chief Justice) did not even bother to give reasons for dismissing these arguments. Only Justice Laskin, in dissent, addressed them and even he was completely unsympathetic.[1] The courts should not supervise the administration of the law, argued Laskin, and would not be warranted—at least in the absence of an *entrenched* Bill of Rights—in following the radical lead of the United States Supreme Court. Morgentaler went to jail and was facing more prosecutions when the PQ scored its upset electoral victory in 1976 on a platform that included freedom of choice. Since law enforcement is the prerogative of the provinces under the division of powers, Morgentaler was allowed to operate his Montreal clinic free from legal harassment despite the federal *Criminal Code*.

In 1983, women's groups in Ontario and Manitoba persuaded Morgentaler to open clinics in Toronto and Winnipeg. It did not take long for police to raid and close both operations. This time the doctors were charged with *conspiracy* to procure abortions *in general*, the idea being that a conspiracy charge would be easier to prove than a specific charge because Morgentaler would be precluded from taking the stand and showing how much the woman in question needed the abortion. However, the defence turned the charge to its advantage

---

[1] Laskin, joined by Justices Judson and Spence, dissented on other grounds. He argued that it was wrong for a court of appeal to convict someone who had been acquitted by a jury. The proper thing to do was to send the case back for a new trial. This view was vindicated by a subsequent amendment to the *Criminal Code*, now section 613 (4) (b) (ii), which Morgentaler could use to his advantage in future cases, but which could not keep him out of jail for this one. The dissenters also felt that Morgentaler had been wrongfully deprived of the common law defence of necessity.

and presented evidence of the necessity of *the clinic as a whole.* It also pounded away at the law with every imaginable provision of the Charter. Morgentaler's lawyer, Morris Manning, was, as we have already seen, an authority on the Charter. But while the trial judge turned back the Charter arguments, the jury accepted the defence of necessity. Once again the Court of Appeal came to the rescue. In an anonymous opinion punctuated with exclamation marks and hollow protestations that they were not deciding merits of the law, the five judges of the Ontario Court of Appeal deprived Morgentaler and his colleagues of their common law defence of necessity on the novel and purely political ground that one could not claim necessity if one were ideologically opposed to the law (*Morgentaler,* 1985). As for the Charter, they mainly applied the decisions under the *Canadian Bill of Rights* including *Morgentaler* (1975) and even *Bliss* (1979)—for the proposition that the law was not discriminatory because only women get pregnant—and they referred to the Parliamentary and Committee debates where everyone had agreed that the Charter was abortion-neutral.

Thanks to the amendment to the *Criminal Code* provoked by Morgentaler's first conviction, the Court of Appeal could not enter a conviction, merely send the case back for a new trial, but observers were pessimistic about the chances on the appeal to the Supreme Court of Canada. "I'm not terribly optimistic," said Professor Christine Boyle of Dalhousie on the eve of the Supreme Court hearing (*The Globe and Mail,* October 7, 1986: A1). The case had already entered legal lore as an example of the failure of the Charter to address the real problems of women. At a conference on equality rights in May 1986, Professor Kathleen Lahey said:

> On the substantive level, women are losing claims when a loss has a major and material impact on the conditions of inequality that women experience—need I even mention the *Morgentaler* case in this context? (Lahey, 1987: 82)

The situation smouldered around the clinic on Harbord Street for two years and then, completely without warning, on January 28, 1988, what an Ontario Medical Association spokesperson likened to an "earthquake" hit (*The Globe and Mail,* February 1, 1988: A1, A14). The Supreme Court had struck down the law as a violation of the Charter.

In a repeat performance of the "quick and stunning victory" in *Roe* v. *Wade* (Rubin, 1987: 4), Canada was suddenly without an abortion law. Real chaos reigned in the hospitals and in the provincial capitals. Those on the pro-choice side knew they had won and rejoiced. Those on the pro-life side knew that they had lost and mourned. But beyond that, nobody knew precisely what it was they had won or lost or what to do about it. It was not as if the Supreme Court had replaced the old law with a new one. Nor did any of the various governments have any laws prepared in case they needed one. Though this embarrassed the officials concerned and surprised the press (*The Toronto Star,* January 30, 1988: A12), one could not really blame the politicians this time. They were given no reason to suspect that the law would be struck down. More importantly, it was impossible to prepare alternatives in case the law *was* struck down because it was not possible to predict on what *grounds* it would be struck down. This would be crucial information if one were drafting a new law; without it one could not predict in advance what an acceptable replacement might look like. To top it all off, when people got around to reading the judgment, it was *still* not possible to tell what kind of law would be constitutional. Justice Minister Ray Hnatyshyn put it diplomatically: "it would have been helpful," he said, if the Supreme Court had expressed "its view of the rights of the fetus."[1] And furthermore:

> One problem with the Supreme Court decision, he said, is that there was not one majority opinion but three, with each judge reasoning a little differently.

> That has to be considered, as well as the possibility that any new law might go back before a different panel of judges, he said (*The Globe and Mail*, February 5, 1988: A8).

In fact there was nothing that could be called a decision. The panel was short two judges and, of the remaining seven, two dissented. So the three majority opinions came from only five judges. And they were not just "a little" but very different. Furthermore, each deliberately left certain crucial questions undecided. So, taking the judges at their word, it was, strictly speaking, impossible to draft a law that would be legally guaranteed to satisfy a majority of the Court that decided *Morgentaler*, let alone the Court that would, some years hence, pass on the validity of any such law. It was not even possible to say with certainty that *no law* would satisfy the judges of the Supreme Court, that is to say that they would be satisfied with the *status quo* that they themselves have created, because of their artificial reticence on the subject of the foetus. If lawmaking under the Charter is anything, it is interesting.

The Morgentaler Decision

There were two basic points of agreement among the five judges who formed the majority: (1) the law imposed serious hardships on pregnant women, and (2) that it did so was *not* enough to make it unconstitutional.

The abortion law came in for a serious and well-deserved drubbing in all of the majority opinions for its tendency to limit and delay access to abortions even where they were necessary for health reasons, and for its tendency to ensure that access would vary widely from place to place. The majority rehearsed the findings of the Badgely Report which had excoriated the law a decade earlier:

> The procedures set out for the operation of the Abortion Law are not working equitably across Canada. In almost every aspect dealing with induced abortion which was reviewed by this Committee, there was considerable confusion, unclear standards or social inequity involved with this procedure. These factors

---

[1] In July, the Court had given pro-lifer Joe Borowski leave to appeal the Saskatchewan Courts' rejection of his challenge to the *liberality* of the abortion law but the case had not even been argued yet and all of the judges in *Morgentaler* made a point of expressly refraining from comment on the foetus' alleged "right to life" *(Borowski,* 1987; *The Globe and Mail,* July 30, 1987: A8).

have led to: sharp disparities in the distribution and the accessibility of therapeutic abortion services; a continuous exodus of Canadian women to the United States to obtain this operation; and delays in women obtaining induced abortions in Canada (Canada, 1977a: 17).

More recent data showed that these findings basically still applied, though matters had improved in some parts of the country (Powell, 1987). The majority agreed with the conclusions in these reports that the law itself was responsible for limited and unequal access, because of the conditions it laid down for therapeutic abortions. The requirement that a therapeutic abortion committee (TAC) have three doctors and that they could not include the doctor performing the abortion, meant many hospitals did not have enough doctors to comply with the law. Many small hospitals were also ruled out because their size prevented them from becoming "accredited." Abortions could only be performed in either "accredited" hospitals or those "approved" by the provincial government. But no government was required by the law to "approve" any hospitals. As a result, less than half of all Canadian hospitals were eligible to perform abortions. But even eligible hospitals were not required by the law to set up committees. Only about half of those eligible did so. Finally, the law did not require committees to grant certificates even in cases where "life or health" was threatened. All of these limitations on access caused delays and delays made abortions riskier for women,[1] as well as adding considerably to the stress of an unwanted pregnancy, thereby, according to the majority in *Morgentaler*, interfering with a woman's "security of the person." Also cited, by two of the men judges, was the sheer fact of having to carry a baby to term contrary to a woman's own wishes under the threat of criminal punishment (Justices Dickson and Lamer) and, by the only woman on the Court, the interference with a profoundly intimate decision (Justice Wilson).

Only the dissenting judges (Justices McIntyre and La Forest) tried to minimize the hardships imposed on women and the responsibility of the law for them. They attributed most of the limitations on access, not to the law, but to limited medical resources and negative attitudes to abortion on the part of medical staff. This was not the main source of disagreement, though. *All* of the judges agreed that causing hardship to women was not enough to invalidate the law and *all* took the position that the state should be allowed to impose some hardship on pregnant women in the interests of protecting the foetus. Finally, *none* of them would say just what this meant in concrete terms.

Though they wrote two separate opinions, the four men in the majority took the same basic approach. They claimed it unnecessary to take a position on the ultimate issue of the proper balance to be struck between the interests of the pregnant woman and interests of the foetus (or as they put it, the interests of the *state* in the protection of the foetus). They claimed to find within the law itself a balance already struck, a value judgment already made, but one that, paradoxically, the law itself had violated. In striking down the law they

---

[1] Risk of complication, though low, increased with delay. Risk of death from a lawful abortion was virtually nil: two in the history of the law, with more than 60,000 performed annually (*Morgentaler*, 1988: 501).

claimed, in a sense, merely to be enforcing it, but enforcing it against itself. The approaches were slightly different. Chief Justice Dickson and Justice Lamer found a "particular balance" in the law which made the woman's life and health "paramount":

> [T]he Crown conceded... that the court is not called upon in this appeal to evaluate any claim to "foetal rights" or to assess the meaning of "the right to life." I expressly refrain from so doing. In my view, it is unnecessary for the purpose of deciding this appeal to evaluate or assess "foetal rights" as an independent constitutional value. Nor are we required to measure the full extent of the state's interest in establishing criteria unrelated to the pregnant woman's own priorities and aspirations. What we must do is evaluate the particular balance struck by Parliament in s.251, as it relates to the priorities and aspirations of pregnant women and the government's interests in the protection of the foetus.

> Section 251 provides that foetal interests are not to be protected where the "life or health" of the woman is threatened. Thus, Parliament itself has expressly stated in s.251 that the "life or health" of pregnant women is paramount (*Morgentaler*, 1988: 479).

Where the law went wrong was in defeating its own balance by setting up barriers which limited access even when a woman's life or health was threatened. It went wrong in creating an "illusory defence":

> It contains so many potential barriers to its own operation that the defence it creates will in many circumstances be practically unavailable to women who would *prima facie* qualify for the defence, or at least would force such women to travel great distances at substantial expense and inconvenience in order to benefit from a defence that is held out to be generally available (*Morgentaler*, 1988: 478).

> [The procedures] hold out an illusory defence to many women who would *prima facie* qualify under the exculpatory provisions...Many women whom Parliament professes not to wish to subject to criminal liability will nevertheless be forced by the practical unavailability of the supposed defence to risk liability or to suffer other harm...State protection of foetal interests may well be deserving of constitutional recognition under s.1. Still, there can be no escape from the fact that Parliament has failed to establish either a standard or a procedure whereby any such interests might prevail over those of the woman in a fair and non-arbitrary fashion (*Morgentaler*, 1988: 480–81).

The general approach of Justices Beetz and Estey was only slightly different. They claimed to discern in the law several clear purposes. The main purpose of the defence was "to decriminalize abortion in one circumstance,...when the continuation of the pregnancy of the woman would or would be likely to endanger her life or health. This is the crux of the exception" (*Morgentaler*, 1988: 489). The limits on the defence also had their purposes. The TAC requirement was "to ensure that the standard of the exception ...was met," and the requirement that abortions be performed in hospitals was to ensure that once the standard was met "the lawful abortion would be performed safely":

> These other rules are a means to an end and not an end unto themselves. As a

whole, s.251(4), (5), (6) and (7) seek to make therapeutic abortions lawful and available but also to ensure that the excuse of therapy will not be abused and that lawful abortions will be safe (*Morgentaler*, 1988: 490).

Having determined the purposes of the law, it was a relatively easy matter to decide which restrictions were consistent with it and which were not. Those consistent with the purposes of the law would be valid even if they caused hardship:

> Parliament is justified in requiring...reliable, independent and medically sound opinion in order to protect the state interest in the foetus...Parliament requires this independent opinion because it is not only the woman's interest that is at stake in a decision to authorize an abortion...By requiring an independent medical opinion...,Parliament seeks to ensure that in any given case, only therapeutic reasons will justify the decision to abort...I do not believe it to be unreasonable to seek independent medical confirmation of the threat to the woman's life or health when such an important and distinct interest hangs in the balance (*Morgentaler*, 1988: 508).

On the other hand, the in-hospital requirement was justified by neither of the deemed purposes of good faith or medical safety, so it had to go. The same went for the requirements that the committee come from the hospital at which the abortion was performed and that doctors who performed abortions be excluded from committees. Also eliminated was the power of the hospitals to increase the quorum. While an independent opinion could be required for the purpose of assuring any abortion was genuinely therapeutic, the stipulations in the law went far beyond what this called for.

The way they approached the issue made evaluation of Parliament's objectives as unnecessary for Beetz and Estey as it had been for Dickson and Lamer. But unlike their counterparts, Beetz and Estey did venture just a tiny bit out on the limb to drop a very cautious hint at what *might* be an acceptable solution, namely a staged, US-style approach, and what definitely would *not* be, namely removing all defences to abortion. This was about as relevant to their official reasons as the convention question had been to the legal question in *Re Constitution of Canada* (1981), and their pronouncement was about as judicial. Furthermore, it lacked all pretense of being linked to the wording of section 7 of the Charter. The "principles of fundamental justice" were nowhere to be seen:

> It is not necessary to decide whether there is a proportionality between the effects of s.251 and the objective of protecting the foetus, nor is it necessary to answer the question concerning the circumstances in which there is a proportionality between the effects of s.251 which limit the right of pregnant women to security of the person and the objective of the protection of the foetus. But I feel bound to observe that the objective of protecting the foetus would not justify the severity of the breach of pregnant women's right to security of the person which would result if the exculpatory provision of s.251 was *completely* removed from the *Criminal Code*. However, a rule that would require a higher degree of danger to health in the latter months of pregnancy, as opposed to the

early months, for an abortion to be lawful, could possibly achieve a proportionality which would be acceptable under s.1 of the Charter (*Morgentaler*, 1988: 486; emphasis in original).

While the reasoning of these four judges[1] seems a model of judicial restraint, restricting itself only to the question of means ("principle") and leaving the question of ends ("policy") to the legislature, it really shows just how malleable these categories can be in determined hands. In fact, the identification of the "balance struck" and of the law's "objective" was extremely wilful, ignoring both the history of the law and its very terms. The picture painted was one of a legislature committed to the unrestricted protection of women's life and health inexplicably throwing up numerous unnecessary obstacles to this very objective. In dissent Justices McIntyre and La Forest argued that this picture was in fact a distortion:

> It is patent on the face of the legislation that the defence is circumscribed and narrow. It is clear that this was the Parliamentary intent and it was expressed with precision. I am not able to accept the contention that the defence has been held to be generally available. It is, on the contrary, carefully tailored and limited to special circumstances. Therapeutic abortions may be performed only in certain hospitals and in accordance with certain specified provisions. It could only be classed as illusory or practically so if it could be found that it does not provide lawful access to abortions in circumstances described in the section. No such finding should be made upon the material before this court (*Morgentaler*, 1988: 539).

Justices Dickson and Lamer were not merely holding Parliament to the balance it itself had struck, nor were Justices Beetz and Estey merely enforcing Parliament's own objectives. They were striking their own balances and pursuing their own objectives by ignoring certain aspects of the law and emphasising others.

Strange, that in considering the "purpose" of the law, none of these judges thought it necessary to refer to the debates on its enactment in 1969. These show unmistakably that the limitations in the law were no oversights, but were deliberately considered. The freedom given to local hospitals to perform or not to perform abortions was in fact considered to be a matter of *conscience*. Then Liberal Justice Minister John Turner *defended* the law by underlining the freedom of hospitals and doctors not to perform abortions:

> Section 237 as amended imposes no duty on the board of a hospital to set up a therapeutic abortion committee; it imposes no duty on any medical practitioner to perform an abortion (*House of Commons Debates*, April 28, 1969: 8058).

And it is also clear that the debate over where abortions could be performed was about controlling the number of abortions, not ensuring their safety. One Social Credit MP defended his party's proposal to restrict abortions to large hospitals in terms that had nothing to do with the pregnant woman's safety:

> We are not questioning the skill of those hospital doctors, far from it, because it

---

[1] They differed on a number of subsidiary matters, the most important of which was whether "health" had to be defined with any precision.

was found in the United States that some doctor committees have after a certain time fallen into routine and when an abortion case came up...the foetus was killed and the papers were signed after by the committee of doctors.

This means that if we permit all the small country hospitals to make abortions, if they have qualified doctors to do so, there will be abortion committees throughout the country in every little village, and it will become routine. The abortion legislation will then be known as a farce and a butchery for the Canadian people (*House of Commons Debates*, April 30, 1969: 8190–91).

For his part, Turner defended the proposed law against such charges by saying that since "only" accredited or approved hospitals could perform abortions, "this is sound and secure protection" (*House of Commons Debates*, April 30, 1969: 8185). Nor was the lack of firm criteria inadvertent. It was an explicit attempt to compromise by passing the responsibility on to the medical profession:

As to whether any member of the committee should be a specialist in any field such as psychiatry, that, once again, ought to be left to the judgement of the board of the hospital. There might be circumstances in which no psychiatrist at all is needed...Boards of individual hospitals have been left with plenty of flexibility to designate the specialists needed on any therapeutic abortion committee. We would prefer to leave the judgment in these matters to the hospitals and to the medical profession (*House of Commons Debates*, May 5, 1969: 8321).

It is the sheerest revisionism to say that the abortion law had any single-minded purpose of guaranteeing abortions where they were necessary to preserve a woman's life or health. But revisionism was the only device available to the Court if it wanted to strike down the law without obviously breaking its own rules. For the judges to say forthrightly that they felt Parliament *should* give women such guarantees would have taken a lot more nerve.

And what about the Supreme Court's only woman? The opinion of Justice Wilson is worth special attention if we remember the value attached by women to representation on the Court. And if we consider only her rhetoric, it must be said that she delivered the goods for her constituency. In an important passage early in her judgment, Wilson staked out some ground for feminist legal theory by denying that women's claims were limited to a sex-blind Charter of the *Phillips* (1986) or *Blainey* (1986, 1987) variety:

It is probably impossible for a man to respond, even imaginatively, to such a dilemma [the abortion decision] not just because it is outside the realm of his personal experience (although this is, of course, the case) but because he can relate to it only by objectifying it, thereby eliminating the subjective elements of the female psyche which are at the heart of the dilemma. As Noreen Burrows has pointed out...the history of the struggle for human rights from the eighteenth century on has been the history of men struggling to assert their dignity and common humanity against an overbearing state apparatus. The more recent struggle for women's rights has been a struggle to eliminate discrimination, to achieve a place for women in a man's world, to develop a set of legislative reforms in order to place women in the same position as men...It has *not* been a struggle to define the rights of women in relation to their special place in the societal structure and in relation to the biological distinction between the two sexes. Thus, women's needs and aspirations are only now being translated into protected rights. The right to reproduce or not to reproduce which is in issue in this case is one such right and is properly perceived as an integral part of modern woman's struggle to assert *her* dignity and worth as a human being (*Morgentaler*, 1988: 555; emphasis in original).

As one might predict from such a passage, Wilson approached the question of abortion, not just as a matter of security of the person, but as a matter of "liberty," an issue studiously avoided by the men on the Court. Following US jurisprudence she found that in the "right to liberty" there was also a "right to privacy":

> Thus, an aspect of the respect for human dignity on which the Charter is founded is the right to make fundamental personal decisions without interference from the state. This right is a critical component of the right to liberty...[It] guarantees to every individual a degree of personal autonomy over important decisions intimately affecting their private lives (*Morgentaler*, 1988: 550, 554).

Not surprisingly, Wilson also found that a woman's decision to terminate her pregnancy fell within this category and that it was violated by the *Criminal Code*'s requirement of a therapeutic abortion committee. So far, so good. Even a man can understand this. But what about the "fundamental justice" issue in section 7 of the Charter? Naturally, Wilson could not restrict herself to merely procedural or formal issues. Nor was she content to ignore the limitation altogether, the way Beetz and Estey had. But that did not leave much. Her solution was to turn to the copious words of Chief Justice Dickson in *Big M* (1985), and from them extract the hitherto undiscovered theory according to which anything offending *other* provisions of the Charter also offended "fundamental justice." Judge Wilson found section 2(a) ("freedom of conscience") most apt to the question of abortion. Since abortion was "a matter of conscience," in forbidding it the law imposed "one conscientiously-held view at the expense of another" (*Morgentaler*, 1988: 561) and therefore violated a principle of fundamental justice.

Now, if Wilson had stopped there we really would have had something extraordinary. Important decisions intimately affecting one's private life cannot be interfered with where they involve conflicting moralities. This would have put not only s.251 of the *Criminal Code* up for grabs but every other section of the *Criminal Code* as well. Of course, she had no intention of stopping there. The question in the back of our minds all along was also in the back of her mind. *What about the foetus*? Given the impassioned plea for the personal nature of the abortion decision one might have expected something more or less definitive on the central issue in the public debate. It came as something of a shock to find that Wilson not only had not yet made up her mind about this, but had hardly, if she was to be taken at her word, devoted much thought to it:

> Miss Wein submitted on behalf of the Crown that the Court of Appeal was correct in concluding that "the situation respecting a woman's right to control her own person becomes more complex when she becomes pregnant and that some statutory control may be appropriate." I agree. I think s.1 of the Charter authorizes reasonable limits to be put upon the woman's right having regard to

the fact of the developing foetus within her body. The question is: at what point in the pregnancy does the protection of the foetus become such a pressing and substantial concern as to outweigh the fundamental right of the woman to decide whether or not to carry the foetus to term? (*Morgentaler*, 1988: 562)

After canvassing the conflicts in American judicial opinion between the majority in *Roe* (1973) and the dissenting opinion of Justice O'Connor (the only woman on the Supreme Court of the United States) in *City of Akron* (1983), the most Wilson would say was that foetal rights got stronger as time went on:

I agree with the observation of O'Connor J...that the foetus is potential life from the moment of conception...in balancing the state's interests in the protection of the foetus as potential life under s.1 of the Charter against the right of the pregnant woman under s.7 greater weight should be given to the state's interest in the later stages of pregnancy than in the earlier...In the early stages the woman's autonomy would be absolute; her decision, reached in consultation with her physician, not to carry the foetus to term would be conclusive. The state would have no business inquiring into her reasons. Her reasons for having an abortion would, however, be the proper subject of inquiry at the later stages of her pregnancy when the state's compelling interest in the protection of the foetus would justify it in prescribing conditions. The precise point in the development of the foetus at which the state's interest in its protection becomes "compelling" I leave to the informed judgment of the legislature which is in a position to receive guidance on the subject from all relevant disciplines. It seems to me, however, that it might fall somewhere in the second trimester (*Morgentaler*, 1988: 565–564).

Why "it might fall somewhere in the second trimester" we were never to learn. The closest thing to an explanation in the judgment was this:

It is a fact of human experience that a miscarriage or spontaneous abortion of the foetus at six months is attended by far greater sorrow and sense of loss than a miscarriage or spontaneous abortion at six days or even six weeks (*Morgentaler*, 1988: 563).

But it is also a fact of human experience that there is a sense of loss at any miscarriage.

In concrete terms, the only guidance Wilson was willing to give to anyone thinking of devising a new law was the virtually meaningless and completely unexplained holding that limiting the right to an abortion at "*all* stages" of the pregnancy would not be justifiable (*Morgentaler*, 1988: 564). And she left us with the same enigma that the others had:

One final word. I wish to emphasize that in these reasons I have dealt with the existence of the developing foetus merely as a factor to be considered in assessing the importance of the legislative objective under s.1 of the Charter. I have not dealt with the entirely separate question whether a foetus is covered by the word "everyone" in s.7 so as to have an independent right to life under that section. The Crown did not argue it and it is not necessary to decide it in order to dispose of the issues on this appeal (*Morgentaler*, 1988: 564).

The reticence on the subject of the foetus was, of course, related to the fact that a case on foetal rights (*Borowski*, 1987) was right then wending its way up to the Supreme Court. Whatever they thought about the question, it would not have been very sporting to decide it before the hearing had even taken place. Still, one must admit to a certain skepticism about technical obstacles to deciding what the Court wants to decide when it wants to decide it, given the wonderful orchestration of these things in the language rights cases (Chapter III). But one cannot wait forever and this goes double for judges. So we have yet another obstacle to rational policy making under legal politics: no case and no litigant will present every issue necessary to a proper resolution of a legal question considered as a social question. Hard as it is to feel sorry for politicians, one could not help but sympathize with the Tory Justice Minister Ray Hnatyshyn as he tried to figure out what kind of law would be acceptable to the Supreme Court after this judgment.

Which brings us finally to the dissent of Justices McIntyre and La Forest. It amounted to a vain plea to the majority of the Court to respect the limits of constitutional adjudication. Invoking the right wing "substantive due process" decisions of the American Supreme Court in the twenties and thirties, and the fervent desire expressed by Parliamentarians that the Charter should be abortion-neutral, as well as democracy itself, they rehearsed all of the arguments against using substantive judicial review in radical ways:

> It is not for the court to substitute its own views on the merits of a given question for those of Parliament. The court must consider not what is, in its view, the best solution to the problems posed; its role is confined to deciding whether the solution enacted by Parliament offends the Charter...It is essential that this principle be maintained in a constitutional democracy. The court must not resolve an issue such as that of abortion on the basis of how many judges may favour "pro-choice" or "pro-life." To do so would be contrary to sound principle and the rule of law affirmed in the preamble to the Charter which must mean that no discretion, including a judicial discretion, can be unlimited...What this basically means is that the court must be "constrained by the language, structure and history of the constitutional text, by constitutional tradition, and by the history, traditions, and underlying philosophies of our society" (*Morgentaler*, 1988: 529–531).

At the time of writing it was anybody's guess how the Supreme Court would handle the *Borowski* appeal now that the majority had said, in effect, that the political nature of the abortion question and the assurances given at the time of the enactment of the Charter were no longer relevant. These were heavily relied upon by the Saskatchewan Courts to deny his pro-life challenge to the abortion law:

> The Charter is neutral in relation to abortion; it remains for Parliament, reflecting the will of the Canadian people, to determine without reference to the Charter in what circumstances the termination of a pregnancy will be lawful or unlawful (*Borowski*, 1987: 752).

This argument was obviously not available after *Morgentaler*. Borowski was given leave to appeal in July of 1987 (*The Globe and Mail* July 30, 1987: A8). He said that he wanted to give up after the Supreme Court decision in *Morgentaler* but his organization persuaded him to carry on (*The Globe and Mail*, January 30, 1988:

A4). The Supreme Court judges' statements that they have not at least partially made up their minds about his case are hard to take seriously.

The idea that the Supreme Court had illegitimately invaded the policy area was immediately taken up by the pro-life lobby. Anti-abortion Tory MPs said the decision showed Pierre Trudeau "still governs Canada":

> Trudeau gave the final word to that little marble building down the street [referring to the Supreme Court building]...The law is made by Parliament, is disobeyed by individuals and is remade by the courts. We now have government by judges and they are not accountable to the people (*The Toronto Star*, January 29: A12).

Pro-lifer Anne Roche Muggeridge joined her warnings of the "brutalization of our society"[1] to an attack on the Court for adopting "the moral and judicial imperialism of the modern U.S. Supreme Court" in "a copycat decision":

> Judges, as leading members of the power elite, are even more susceptible to the reigning intellectual climate than the rest of us. Depressingly but not surprisingly, the majority on our court, unleashed in a U.S. direction by the Charter, have bought into the whole dominant feminist, individualist philosophy... (Muggeridge, 1988)

But criticism of the Court itself has yet to become generalized. Not a peep was heard in official circles. Despite Trudeau's assurances during the Charter debate that section 33 was always at hand to save the abortion law, the Charter had already reached such sacrosanct status that the very mention of the override, just as a theoretical option, was met with sanctimony from the Leader of the Opposition, John Turner:

> Whatever one thinks of any Supreme Court of Canada decision, we should not undermine, in our view, the charter of rights and freedoms (*The Globe and Mail*, January 30, 1988: A2).

Assurances immediately followed that no thought was being given to such an option.

Morgentaler and the Legalization of Politics

The *Morgentaler* decision poses the biggest challenge yet to a critique of the Charter and the legalization of politics. Flimsy reasoning aside, the repeal of the abortion law is perhaps the only unqualified good result to come from the Supreme Court of Canada yet. It clearly goes beyond decisions that merely did not disturb the status quo, such as the *Edwards Books* case. Nor is it a case of some women gaining at the expense of the rest as with the *Blainey* decision or the *Tomen* challenge. *Morgentaler* has removed a law whose only concrete effect was to make life more difficult for women in the already excruciating difficulty of an unwanted pregnancy. And not only is women's overall posi-

---

[1] She claimed that the decision would cause a drop in the birth rate, an increase in teenage pregnancies and venereal diseases, an increase in organ harvesting and medical experiments on live foetuses, infanticide, child abuse, crimes against women and "routine" euthanasia "for even mildly defective children."

tion in the social structure clearly a subordinate one—despite the smattering of women in positions of privilege and power, on the Supreme Court or elsewhere—the impact of this particular law was harder the more subordinate the women in question. According to the Badgely Report, the problems in access under the law varied directly with class, with poorer women more likely to have children and less likely to have either abortions or access to them than richer women (Canada, 1977a: 169–173).

Naturally, the repeal of the abortion law cannot on its own solve all of the problems of unwanted pregnancies. But no single action by any branch of government could do that. The fact is that laws restricting abortions have reduced neither abortions nor unwanted pregnancies. These laws have resulted only in humiliation, pain, and death for women, or in their being chained to unwanted children, with the children as well as the women paying the consequences. They have no redeeming value, and we would do well to be simply rid of them.

So if *Morgentaler* simply rid us of the abortion law, we should be grateful, and if we have the Charter to thank for this, we should probably reevaluate our position on the Charter, if only slightly. But that is a lot of "ifs" leaving a lot of tough questions to answer. The main ones are: did *Morgentaler* rid us of this law? And if it did, did it *simply* rid us of this law, or is there more to it?

The first potential problem with *Morgentaler* is the possibility of a backlash. The American experience is an eye-opener. In the United States, so great and so sustained was the backlash against the 1973 Supreme Court decision in *Roe* v. *Wade*, that its full implications are not clear even yet. The *Roe* decision of 1973 was a "quick and stunning victory" (Rubin, 1987: 4) which struck down almost every abortion statute in the United States[1] and made it absolutely impossible—legally speaking—for states to interfere with a woman's decision to have an abortion in the first trimester, and virtually impossible in the second trimester. But the people whose beliefs were represented by all those laws struck down in *Roe* did not sit still. They formed the "Right to Life" movement and joined it in droves. Not only has *Roe* been credited with the rise of the modern Right to Life movement, it seems we also have it to thank for much of the success in national politics of the entire New Right:

> The New Right…seized upon abortion as one of the emotional issues that could attract those voters frightened by the accelerating pace of social change (Rubin, 1987: 113).

Roe v. *Wade* has been called

> the worst thing that ever happened to American liberalism. Almost overnight it politicized millions of people and helped create a mass movement of social-issue conservatives that has grown into one of the most potent forces in our democracy (*New Republic*, 1985: 4).

The Right to Life movement has tried every conceivable means of destroying *Roe*, from constitutional amendment to judicial appointments to cutbacks

---

[1] The exception was New York where abortion had been recently decriminalized up to the 24th week.

in abortion funding. Though the constitutional Right to Life amendment drive failed, it dragged down the woman's Equal Rights Amendment (ERA) with it: "The ERA was defeated, in part, at least, due to the furor over abortion" (Rubin, 1987: 187). Opponents of abortion argued that ERA would prevent *Roe* v. *Wade* from being overruled and would force the funding of abortions (Berry, 1986: 83–83, 102, 104–105; Mansbridge, 1986: 127). *Roe* also helped elect Ronald Reagan in 1980 with a platform plank promising "the appointment of judges who respect traditional family values and the sanctity of innocent human life" (Rubin, 1987: 179, 188). For his entire eight years in office Reagan administrations sought relentlessly to reverse the decision by appointing political-judicial conservatives to the bench and repeatedly asking the Supreme Court to reconsider and overrule *Roe*. New abortion cases are constantly coming before the Court, as state legislatures, influenced by pro-life forces, have imposed more or less veiled restrictions on abortion, such as parental or spousal consent, counselling, waiting periods, and the like. Most, but not all, restrictions have failed to get judicial approval (Rubin, 1987: 133–7). But, at the time of writing, Reagan appointments had brought the Supreme Court to within one vote of reconsidering and overturning *Roe*. In 1986, the vote was 5–4 against a reconsideration (*Thornburgh*, 1986). In late 1987, a tie vote of 4–4 saved the day (*Hartigan*, 1987). American journalists were already talking about "a world without Roe" in anticipation of how the new Reagan appointment would cast his deciding vote (*Newsweek*, September 14, 1987: 33).

Alongside these potential successes have been real victories for the Right to Life movement in securing abortion-funding cutbacks at both the state and federal levels to restrict funding to abortions that are medically necessary or in some cases only where they are life-threatening. The very year *Roe* was decided, state legislatures began restricting medicare funding to "medically necessary" abortions. In 1976, the federal "Hyde Amendment" cut off federal funds for abortions other than those that threatened the woman's life or "severe and long-lasting physical health damage." In 1980, this was further restricted to life-threatening cases and rape or incest where the victim cooperated with police. The effect was to reduce federal funding of abortions to a trickle (Rubin, 1987: 176). Only a few of the states picked up the slack so that state medical aid for abortions was available in only 15 states in 1985. It has been estimated that, by as early as 1978, an annual 100,000 abortions, or one-third of those otherwise eligible for funding, were not being funded, with the result that over 80,000 poor women had to pay for their own abortions, another 14,000 had to carry the baby to term, and 3,000 had been forced to resort to self-induced or illegal abortions (Tietze and Henshaw, 1986: 43). This means that access to abortion in much of the United States after *Roe* was strongly determined by class, as it was in Canada before *Morgentaler*. As we saw in Chapter II, the Supreme Court sustained the constitutionality of all of these funding cutbacks by making a radical distinction between obstacles to freedom imposed by poverty and those imposed by the state (*Beal*, 1977; *Harris*, 1980). Finally, it is worth noting that the judicial de-criminalization of abortion has not made US public opinion more tolerant. Support for abortion rights was rising before the decision in *Roe*. It levelled off in 1974, remained stable until about 1980, and fell slightly through 1985 to at or below the levels of 1973. While 41% of the population supported the right to abortion for any reason in 1980, only 37% did so in 1985 (*Family Planning Perspectives*, 1985: 181).

An abortion-rights activist from the United States recently steeled a Toronto audience for what was to come by telling them that the Right to Life movement

> kept us tied up in court for years. We were in an endless defensive battle...People here think that abortion is available in the States. It's not. We're now reduced to fighting just to get Medicaid coverage for abortions for women who have been raped or who are victims of incest. There are 15 states where a teen-ager can't get an abortion without parental consent (*The Globe and Mail*, April 18, 1988: A3).

The likelihood, extent, and impact of a Canadian backlash to the *Morgentaler* decision is difficult to assess. Technically, it would be easier to return the law here than it would be in the US. You do not need a constitutional amendment or a packed Supreme Court if you have a section 33. But practically, as we have seen, section 33 is already virtually a dead letter. Even a determined pro-life government would be loath to use it. Another difference is more important. That is the "softness" of the decision in *Morgentaler* itself when compared to the American abortion decision. In *Roe*, the Court said very definitely what was prohibited. It left in place a new order. In *Morgentaler*, the Supreme Court said virtually *nothing*. It left a vacuum. But never underestimate the paralysis of Parliament on a controversial question. The Tories did not want this issue in the first place and when it was dumped in their lap, they had absolutely no idea what to do with it. They had to appear both decisive and neutral, because the preferred way of dealing with an increasing number of questions under legalized politics is to treat them as depoliticized matters of conscience. When they finally acted, they gave new meaning to the notion of "waffling," introducing, apparently for the first time in Parliamentary history, neither a law nor a principle (a device the government had used on the capital punishment issue the year before), but a "menu" of *three* principles to choose from. They ran from strongly pro-life to strongly pro-choice, but ended up with a preferred option of a "staged approach" in terms as vague as those used by the Supreme Court of Canada, wide open in the "earlier stages" but requiring an independent opinion in the "subsequent stages":

   (1) *the staged approach*: would prohibit abortions except when
      (a) "during the earlier stages of pregnancy" a qualified medical practitioner "is of the opinion that the continuation of the pregnancy would, or would be likely to, threaten [the woman's] physical or mental well-being"; or
      (b) "during the subsequent stages of pregnancy" other conditions are met "including a condition that after a certain point in time" the

termination would only be permitted where 2 doctors believed "the continuation of the pregnancy would or would be likely to, endanger the woman's life or seriously endanger her health."

(2) *the pro-life approach*: "giving pre-eminence to the protection of the foetus" would prohibit abortions except when "two independent qualified medical practitioners have, in good faith and on reasonable grounds, stated that in their opinion the continuation of the pregnancy would, or would be likely to, endanger the life of the pregnant woman or seriously and substantially endanger her health and there is no other commonly accepted medical procedure for effectively treating the health risk; but grounds for such opinion are not to include (I) the effects of stress or anxiety which may accompany an unexpected or unwanted pregnancy, or (II) social or economic considerations"

(3) *the pro-choice approach*: "giving pre-eminence to a woman's freedom to choose" would permit abortions "when the woman in consultation with a qualified medical practitioner decides to terminate her pregnancy" and when the termination "is performed by a qualified medical practitioner" (*House of Commons Order Paper and Notices*, May 25, 1988: 37–39).

The government's plan was to prohibit any other amendments and to take a free vote on each of the three options. But neither the Liberals nor the NDP were prepared to let the government pass on this hot potato to the Commons. Calling the move "undemocratic," they refused to agree to debate the resolution (*The Globe and Mail*, May 21, 1988: A4). And the government, acting like a minority rather than a majority government, backed down. It came back two months later with a motion that dropped the two extreme positions, leaving only the staged approach. This time there was a debate, a free vote on the motion, and five amendments from the floor (chosen from twenty-one submitted), ranging from leaving the matter up to the woman and her doctor (defeated 198–20) to allowing abortions only when two doctors certified pregnancy would endanger the woman's life (narrowly defeated 118–105). The main motion was defeated 147–76 (*The Globe and Mail*, July 29, 1988: A3). Since many opposition MPs were determined not to let any resolution pass for reasons unrelated to abortion, the meaning of the vote for the future of abortion law is hard to determine. After having failed to get the Supreme Court of Canada to put off hearing the pending *Borowski* case on the rights of the foetus, the government postponed any further action until after a federal election, on the rather inconsistent but technically correct grounds that it had to wait for a decision in *Borowski* before it could act responsibly. But all parties seemed to be happy to be off the hook on this issue and to be able to avoid giving the electorate a clean shot at any concrete policy (*The Globe and Mail*, September 2, 1988: A1).

It is too early to tell what political realignments might take place because of *Morgentaler*. Pro-lifers said shortly afterward that they were planning a massive lobbying campaign, claiming that they had been united by the

Morgentaler decision as they had never been before (*The Globe and Mail*, February 19, 1988: A1). The Catholic Church jumped right in as it had in the United States and called for the invocation of section 33 (*The Globe and Mail*, March 1, 1988: A1). Rocks were thrown through the window of the Morgentaler clinic in Montreal for the first time in its thirteen years of operation (*The Globe and Mail*, January 30, 1988: A4). CARAL, the major pro-choice group, claimed it was out-financed by pro-life and sent out an "urgent" appeal for money (*The Globe and Mail*, February 19, 1988: A1).

On the judicial front, pro-lifers were looking forward to the *Borowski* appeal and promising that if it were lost:

> [M]ore and more will follow...Science firmly supports the anti-abortion case. It is the law that is out of step with the facts. Madame Justice Bertha Wilson was talking scientific and philosophical nonsense when she referred to the human fetus as "potential life." It isn't *potential* life, it's *actual* life, actual *human* life, the baby some woman is expecting, and everybody knows it (Muggeridge, 1988; emphasis in original).

Apart altogether from the question of what, if anything, will replace the prohibition, is the question of abortion funding. Within a few months of the decision, every provincial government (save for Ontario and Quebec) had announced measures, under their health-care jurisdiction, to limit the funding, and in some cases, even the performance, of abortions. If successful, these moves would mean that abortion would vary from province to province and according to the size of one's pocketbook, as it does in the US and as it did in Canada before *Morgentaler*. The most dramatic action was that of British Columbia fundamentalist, pro-life, Social Credit Premier Bill Vander Zalm. His Cabinet quickly passed a regulation limiting medical insurance for abortions to "life-threatening" situations (*The Globe and Mail*, February 8, 1988: A1). This move was thwarted by a successful challenge in court, not on constitutional grounds, but on the ground that the regulation violated existing health-care legislation, which would have to be amended first. In the meantime, Vander Zalm announced that his government would pour money into an anti-abortion campaign stressing "family values" and creating shelters for unwed mothers (*Pro-Choice News*, Spring 1988: 4). Across Canada similar actions were taken. Alberta said it would only fund hospital abortions that had been approved by a second physician (*The Globe and Mail*, February 19, 1988: A3). Saskatchewan said government health insurance would cover only medically necessary abortions and would give medical staff the right to refuse to participate (*The Globe and Mail*, Feb 18, 1988: A1, A8; *Pro-Choice News*, Spring 1988: 4–6). Manitoba passed a regulation restricting medicare to abortions performed in hospital and announced that it would ask doctors to counsel women on alternatives to abortion (*The Globe and Mail*, June 28, 1988: A4). New Brunswick announced it would only cover accredited hospital abortions considered medically necessary by two doctors. Nova Scotia and Newfoundland hospitals imposed their own restrictions or withdrew the service entirely. Prince Edward Island hospitals had performed no abortions since 1982 and said they would not start now. Women from PEI would still be required to travel out of the province for lawful abortions. And the government announced it would fund only those out-of-province abortions ruled medically necessary by a committee of three doctors(*The Toronto Star*, February 6, 1988: C1). The Ontario government said it would fund all abortions, including those performed in clinics (*The Globe and Mail*, February 2, 1988: A1, A8), but in some parts of the province political battles over elections to hospital boards quickly began shaping up (*The Globe and Mail*, June 13, 1988: A1, A12). Quebec hospitals disbanded their TACs but some of them also withdrew the service altogether (*Pro-Choice News*, Spring 1988: 6).

In other words, through funding and hospital restrictions, provinces and hospitals enacted their own restrictive abortion laws to replace the one struck down in *Morgentaler*. The only difference was that the penalty was no longer imprisonment but rather a fine and the deterrent would only be effective against poor women. Not very different, in concrete terms, from what existed before *Morgentaler*. Naturally, these provincial restrictions could all be challenged in the courts, as they have been in the United States. What the courts would do with them is hard to predict. As usual, they have ample resources at hand to decide anything they deem expedient. They could make the radical distinction made by the US courts between legal and economic coercion, or they could find that the province was violating federal jurisdiction over criminal law. Nothing is guaranteed, though, and CARAL, among others, has been gearing up for more litigation. A small newspaper advertisement with Morgentaler's picture appeared within two weeks of the decision:

Victory has its price. We need money for past legal battles in Quebec, Ontario and Manitoba. We need funds to continue to fight against the vociferous anti-choice lobby. And we still must mount legal challenges against those reactionary provincial governments who would defy the Supreme Court of Canada judgment by continuing to deny women equal access to safe, medical abortions (*The Globe and Mail*, February 9, 1988: A12).

Revolting as it is to see the provincial governments exploit poverty to make their various statements against abortion, and deserving as they are of all of the condemnation they get for it, is it not also true that some of the responsibility for all of this lies with the Charter as a form of politics? Does not the fact that this decision came as a matter of judicial fiat (with nothing in its reasoning to persuade anybody of anything) have something to do with its lack of support and its instability? It is inconceivable that a legislative abortion initiative would have run into this type of provincial obstructionism. It would have had the federal government, at least, behind it, and that would have meant a demonstrable political consensus, something completely lacking in the vacuum left by the Supreme Court. Besides, the federal government would have had the power to prevent this sort of thing. It has that power now. As it did with extra-billing, it could withhold medical funds from provinces that did not fully pay for lawful abortions. But why should the federal government feel any responsibility to protect the *Morgentaler* decision, even if there was a decision to protect?

Of course, it is fairly clear that no legislative initiative would have been as radical as the nullity created by the Supreme Court. But it would have been at least as advanced as anything that is likely to replace it. At the time of writing, the betting was that something close to the resolution which the government introduced in July 1988 (the staged approach) would return in the form of a law. If that should happen, the radicality by default of the Supreme Court's decision will have meant nothing. If that should happen, it will be because the government believes that it is the compromise likely to gain the broadest support. And if it has that support now, it is because it had it before. It is clear that Canadians have been ready for a long time for changes in the abortion law. Canada's law was one of the most backward in the industrialized world, far behind not only the United States, but also the United Kingdom, Australia, New Zealand, France, Italy, West and East Germany, Scandinavia, and the USSR, all of whom essentially leave the question of abortion up to the woman and her doctor in the first 12 to 24 weeks of the pregnancy, and all of whom achieved their laws without benefit of litigation (*The Toronto Star*, February 14, 1988: B1; Tietze and Henshaw, 1986). Public opinion in Canada, unlike in the US, has moved substantially over the past decade. A survey in 1985 showed a majority of Canadians in favour of choice. The statement "Every woman who wants an abortion should be able to have one" was agreed to by 53% of the respondents, while only 41% disagreed (*The Globe and Mail*, June 15, 1985: 1, 12). This was up substantially from the approximately 32% who already in 1977 thought the law "too restrictive." They were outnumbered by those who thought the law "too liberal" (15%) or "about right" (24%) but there was a large group (30%) who had no opinion (Canada, 1977a: 456).

All this assumes that a change in the law could have been achieved without the Charter. Notice that this is a very different question from whether, *given the Charter*, a change in the law could have occurred without a decision like *Morgentaler*. Given the Charter, and the well-known disease of Parliamentary paralysis on matters of controversy that comes with it, nothing could happen, if not without *Morgentaler*, then at least before *Morgentaler*. If *Morgentaler* had gone the other way, the abortion-rights movement would have regrouped for a political assault that was bound sooner or later to produce results, and there is no reason to suppose they would have been any different from what is going to happen *with* Morgentaler. But nothing of this sort could occur until the Charter business had run its course. What if the Charter had not been available? Then all of the devotion, energy, and resources that were poured into the litigation would have been available for other forms of political action. And these other forms would have gained in urgency and effectiveness from the lack of the judicial alternative. It is very likely that if we had not had the Charter, we would have had what we will have after *Morgentaler*, only we would have had it a lot sooner, and with a lot less nonsense. As Professor Fudge points out, the decriminalization of the Morgentaler clinic in Quebec was achieved by purely political means eleven years before *Morgentaler* and six years before the Charter (Fudge, 1988b: 64). Even should we concede that, given the existence of the Charter, it is necessary, or even wise, to devote resources to it, this is not the same thing as saying that we have the Charter to thank for whatever victories are won under it. To the contrary, if I am right, we have the Charter to thank for the delay in reforming the abortion law and the uncertainty of the outcome.

But let us assume the best-case scenario. Let us assume what surely is possible, that for one reason or another (successful struggle, habituation, further litigation, paralysis) the law does not reappear and the provincial restrictions are overcome. What would we say then?

What we would say takes us to the heart of legalized politics. It has to do with situating the question of women's autonomy in relations of social power that are determined by class as well as by gender. And it has to do with the effect of legalized politics on these relations.

Let us start with access to abortion. There is little dispute that the obstacles to equal access are not purely legal. True, the dissenting judges in *Morgentaler* had no basis for arguing that the law had *nothing* to do with inequality of access. But it is also true that there were extra-legal factors operating as well. One was the scarcity and unequal distribution of medical resources. Naturally, this argued for clinical delivery of services. But clinics cost lots of money, and the Powell Report's recommendations for equipping poorer remote areas of Ontario (Powell, 1987: 37–39) quickly met with objections of a fiscal nature (*The Globe and Mail*, February 1, 1988: A14).

But Ontario is a "have" province. Its access inequalities are replicated nationally and exacerbated in regions with less economic strength, such as the Maritimes. Not only are Ontario residents 60% richer on average than Newfoundland residents, but their government spends more money per capita on health care (50%), and they have more hospital beds (35%) and physicians (20%) per capita. They also have more abortions per live births (600%—that's right, 600%—in 1981). The disproportion in medical services and abortion rates shows quite clearly that resources are not the only factors operating, but there is a striking relationship between standards of living, medical resources, and abortion rates, however it is accounted for (Mansell and Copithorne, 1986: 13, 23–24). So, if it is necessary to spend money in order to increase access to abortion, availability across the country is going to remain very uneven. This is not just a question of who pays for the abortions (patient or medicare), but whether the facilities in which to perform them will be available. And where abortion levels are already lower than resources allow, we can be sure that abortion will not top the list of medical priorities. Canada's experience, in other words, is likely to be no different from other countries where it has been found that legalizing abortion, even apart from the funding uncertainties, reduces but does not eliminate inequalities of access (Tietze and Henshaw, 1986: 69–74).

And abortion is just one aspect of reproductive choice. It is clear from both international and local evidence that other aspects are even more deeply class-based than abortion. For example, data from the United States indicate that half of the difference in abortion rates between blacks and whites is due to the much higher pregnancy rate of black women (Tietze and Henshaw, 1986: 70).

The rest of the difference has been attributed to the "miserable social conditions which dissuade [poor women of colour] from bringing new lives into the world" (Davis, 1983: 204), a subject we return to later. For now let us stay with the issue of unwanted pregnancy.

In attributing high birth rates and low abortion rates among poor women to the unavailability of abortion, the Badgely Report completely ignored the factor of high pregnancy rates (Canada, 1977a: 168–174). In fact, in Canada as in the rest of the world, pregnancy rates vary inversely with socio-economic status. A recent study of adolescent pregnancy in Ontario is instructive. It found a steady decline in adolescent pregnancy in the province, but one that varied greatly with the socioeconomic status of the community. Sharper declines in higher SES communities were associated with the more frequent presence of both adequate sexuality education and clinical birth control services. This is not surprising, since the authors attributed the overall decline to:

> extending education, declining adolescent marriage, changing patterns of pregnancy and fertility amongst all women, and increasing labour force participation of women...The trend is not only towards smaller families, but also postponement of the first birth to allow women time for education and employment skill development...In 1981 first-birth postponement by women ages 25–34 was greatest in localities of high socio-economic status...The incidence of pregnancy amongst older teens is connected with the local norm of life expectations amongst adults...Choices amongst older teens concerning the outcome of pregnancy (birth or abortion) were strongly associated with locality socio-economic status and thus local adult life expectations (Orton and Rosenblatt, 1986: 4–5).

If the availability of adequate clinics and education depends on attitudes to women and their "life expectations," these attitudes and life expectations in turn depend on the real-life opportunities that exist for women. And these vary greatly according to material conditions. That attitudes of men and women to abortion vary according to class (Canada, 1977a: 174) is also no accident. The higher the status of women, the more concrete alternatives women have to early pregnancy, the more important it becomes to both women and men that women have control over their reproductive capacities:

> The effectiveness of education to raise life expectations in turn depends upon community access to alternative opportunities for young women and men (Orton and Rosenblatt, 1986: 8).

And reproductive choice cannot be separated from other questions of women's autonomy:

> Adolescent pregnancy is a key point of intervention for prevention of social and health problems in general because the pattern of pregnancy outcomes (birth or abortion) tends to perpetuate a rapid generational cycle of disadvantaged families. Furthermore, strategies to promote more caring, responsible sexuality and prevent adolescent pregnancy should contribute particularly to the reduction of other problems concerning sexual behaviour, such as child abuse, coercive sexuality, sexual harassment, sexual assault, sexually transmitted diseases, pornography, and prostitution (Orton and Rosenblatt, 1986: 9–10).

There is by now plenty of evidence that general conditions of social and economic inequality have tremendous repercussions for women. As a rule, the higher the level of social and economic inequality *in general*, the higher the level of inequality for *women* in particular. That means more violence against women, more exploitation of women, and lower status for women. This rule seems to hold whether we consider longer or shorter stretches of history, contemporaneous societies, or even different sectors within the same society (Schwendinger and Schwendinger, 1981; Box, 1983: 150–153; Braithwaite, 1979: 202–229; Tepperman, 1977: 190; Statistics Canada, 1987b: 92, 95). On the other hand, general egalitarian social policies, even in poor countries, have been found simultaneously to lower birth rates and to raise the status of women (Hartman, 1987: 271–285; Bader, 1988). It also stands to reason that the more unequal a society, the more narrowly will women's opportunities be circumscribed and the more socially constrained, as well as consciously unwanted, will be their pregnancies.

It is only to be expected that reducing unwanted pregnancy would be a crucial pro-choice goal and that birth control would be seen as central to achieving it. Arguing against a law to replace the one struck down in *Morgentaler*, Norma Scarborough (President of the Canadian Abortion Rights Action League) wrote:

> The answer to later abortion is not another abortion law—the answer is access early in the pregnancy. Furthermore, sex education and birth-control counselling reduce the need for abortion, late or early (Scarborough, 1988).

There are many similar statements to this effect (Canada, 1980–81, Issue No. 24: 104; Watters, 1976: 226). It is also no big surprise that opposition to abortion is associated with opposition to contraception and sex education and with support for traditional roles for women (Canada, 1980–81: Issue No. 24: 105, 111; Issue No. 34: 117; *Lavigne*, above page 210). When pro-lifers make special exceptions for abortion in cases of rape and incest, the way the US Hyde Amendment of 1980 did or the way Prime Minister Mulroney did in a recent interview (*The Toronto Star*, August 21, 1988: A1), they reveal pretty clearly that it is not so much the life of the foetus that concerns them as it is (voluntary) sexual activity.

Yet, as the federal government was dithering on *Morgentaler* and provincial governments were trying to undermine it, we were being advised by those in the field that birth control education and availability were in dangerous decline due to cutbacks in both federal and provincial government funding (Bekar, 1988). Those who celebrated the *Morgentaler* victory were soon warning that without determined political action to provide funds for clinics, abortions, contraception, and sexuality education, the legal victory would be a hollow one:

> What we have won is the legal right to abortion. But to make this ruling real—to ensure every woman has equal access—both levels of government must act decisively and quickly...
>
> For women to have real choice in our lives, much more is needed. The Ontario Coalition for Abortion Clinics will continue to work for universal child care,

autonomous midwifery, parental work leave, employment equity, the right to define our sexuality and all those other changes without which women cannot control their lives.

The struggle for equality will be a long one, but the Supreme Court decision has at least taken us a significant step in the right direction (Lathrop, 1988).

But here is one of the catches: determined political action is a scarce commodity in the era of the Charter—except where it is in *support* of market imperatives, as with deregulatory activities like Free Trade or privatization. But what is needed in the area of birth control is the *expansion* of government services, and, if it is to solve the problem of inequality of access, on *non-market bases*. What is needed is to assert the logic of democracy against the logic of the market. But the current of the times, as represented by the Charter itself, is running in precisely the opposite direction. The Charter was meant to prevent that sort of thing. It was meant to keep the public sector hemmed in, not to let it out.

Not that legal challenges are likely to *prohibit* the funding of birth control or abortion services. The point is that the question of reproductive choice is much larger than the availability of such services. The question of reproductive choice is tied up with the social status of women, their real alternatives, and the magnitude of the social and economic constraints on what they can do. It includes the constraints that inhibit motherhood as well as those which compel it:

> Real reproductive choice includes the right to parent without economic or social penalty. This means social support for single mothers and working women. The availability and quality of childcare is part of the fight for real choices for women (Editorial, *Canadian Dimension*, March-April 1988: 3).

The real situation of women is clearly inseparable from the general workings of the economy, the level of unemployment, the stratification of work, the wage and occupational structure, and so on. In a stagnating economy, with structured unemployment and widening gaps between rich and poor—in other words, in an economy absolutely incapable of utilizing the available talents of either its men or its women—men and women are pitted against each other in a battle for opportunities too scarce to go around. It is an unequal battle which consigns women to job ghettoes of low pay, low skill, and high levels of underemployment, unemployment, and poverty (White, 1983; Armstrong and Armstrong, 1983; Wilson, 1982). Women participate in the economy at about two-thirds the rate men do. When they do participate, their unemployment rate is about 25% higher than men's and their jobs are about four times as likely to be part-time (White, 1983: 135; Armstrong and Armstrong, 1983: 249). Part-time workers are half as likely to be unionized as full-time workers (White, 1983: 50). Women are also half as likely (4.9% to 9.5%) as men to be managers (Armstrong and Armstrong, 1983: 252). And their average earnings are also about half (Armstrong and Armstrong, 1983: 268). Women are 25% more likely than men to be poor (National Council of Welfare, 1987: 7–11).

But when comparing working women to working men, we are liable to forget that in a stagnating economy, working men are engaged in a struggle of their own. When average income declines, as it did, for example, between 1981 and 1984, it does so for both men and women. Though 42.3% of female-headed families were poor in 1985 compared to 9.5% of male-headed families, it was also true that twice as many poor families were headed by men as by women (National Council of Welfare, 1985: 57–59). And women were members of these families, too.[1] The quest of business to keep wages low and profits high and the attempts of government to help, do not exempt women workers. Nor can women, struggling with men for equality in the workplace, be indifferent to the downward pressures on the standard they are aspiring to be equal to. In fact, as "the slaves of slaves," women are simultaneously waging a struggle for equality with men *qua* women, and a struggle alongside men for a decent standard of living and quality of working life *qua* working people.

That is, most women are. Some women are on the other side of this struggle. Which is to say that women, like men, are not abstractions detached from the system of private social power. Each and every one is situated in a class relation—as well as a racial, linguistic, regional, and age relation, to mention a few, none of which is irrelevant to the distribution of social power[2]—and they are most definitely not all on the same side.[3] Most, but not all, are either themselves working people or the wives, daughters, and mothers of working people. In fact, most women are more vulnerable to private power than most men, because most women have less of it. For this reason, too, women are more vulnerable to deregulation initiatives such as Free Trade (Cohen, 1987). Indeed, there seems no dispute that unequal access to property is the foundation—whether or not it is the historical cause—of the unequal power relations *between* men and women.

Is it not obvious by now where the Charter comes in?

The Charter is not merely helpless against private power; it actually reinforces it. We have seen it in action in Quebec, weighing in on the side of a privileged minority and the powerful interests it represents, when threatened by the attempts of the subordinate majority to assert its own vision and interests through popular means (Chapter III). We have seen it selectively legitimating the ever-expanding state repression called forth by increasingly chaotic social conditions, and doing all this in the name of crime prevention, while

---

[1] According to the 1981 census, 88.7% of all families had both a husband and wife, 9.3% had a lone female parent and 2.0% had a lone male parent (Canada, 1985: 64).

[2] A recent news story highlighted the situation of black poverty in Nova Scotia. "The 30,000 Nova Scotia blacks are the poorest people of a poor province." The central character in the story was a black grandmother who had spent her life as a domestic worker. She had nine children and feared that the prospects were worse yet for her grandchildren, with black unemployment rates as high as 80% and youth unemployment rampant in the province (Jones, 1988).

[3] A recent protracted labour struggle at this law school (Osgoode Hall Law School in Toronto) pitted three Italian immigrant women cafeteria workers against one Swiss immigrant male entrepreneur. The school was pretty well split over the dispute, but it was not split along gender lines (class lines hardly exist at Osgoode). Leading the political forces on the side of the entrepreneur against the workers was a young, Canadian born, white woman law student. Prominent in the political forces on the side of the workers was a mature, foreign born, non-white woman law student.

throwing up obstacle after obstacle to the suppression of business crime (Chapter IV). We have seen it eating away at union rights and standing mute while they are abrogated. We have seen it eroding the regulation of business and returning the norms of the "free" market (Chapter V). Most women, like most men, are on the receiving end of all of this. We forget this because of the abstract way the Charter defines the issues. However, in Quebec most women belong to the working-class French majority. They are far more likely to be supporters of Bill 101 than opponents. In any bargaining unit women are by definition more likely to be union members than Lavigne-type disrupters. Because they are much less likely than men to be managers themselves, they are even more likely than men to be on the side of the union in any labour dispute. They are nowhere near as likely to be the owners of businesses, even less likely to be the representatives of big business that sit on the board of the National Citizens' Coalition. They are more likely to be the postal workers than the business owners who want postal rates kept down and services privatized. They are more likely to be the retail workers than the corporation owners in *Big M*, and the parents of the targeted kids than the advertisers or the toy manufacturers in *Irwin Toy*.

In other words, women's stake in what the Charter is doing goes far beyond "women's" cases like *Morgentaler*. Everything about Charter politics that advances the interests of the minority with social power against the interests of the majority without it hurts women and diminishes their autonomy, even more than it does men.

So, what the Charter gives to women as women with one hand, it takes away from women as "ordinary Canadians" with the other. And it is a package deal. You cannot order à la carte at this restaurant ("sections 7 and 15, please, but hold the others"). This means that the Charter's gifts are of unambiguous benefit only to women who are not workers. Which is another way of saying that the benefits bestowed by the Charter are beneficial precisely according to class. The Charter is capable of opposing every kind of discrimination but class discrimination. The Supreme Court of the United States has recently held that poverty is not a prohibited ground of discrimination under the US constitution (*Kadrmas*, 1988),[1] and though it was a close decision, it was no fluke. It is in the very nature of a Charter. It comes primarily, but not solely, from the preoccupation of every Charter with *state* power.[2] The power of the marketplace is not its concern. The Charter promises one kind of freedom, freedom

---

[1] A poor family living 16 miles from the nearest school challenged the school-bus user fee as violating their equality rights. The Court held five to four that no constitutional rights were violated. Though Justice O'Connor, for the majority, avoided inflammatory language, the minority said the result of the case was to "sanction discrimination against the poor" (Justice Marshall in *Kadrmas*, 1988: 2491). The majority made one exception to the constitutional acceptability of economic discrimination: it was prohibited when access to the *courts* was in issue (*Kadrmas*, 1988: 2488).

[2] *Kadrmas* in the US Supreme Court concerned government action. But even human rights codes, which apply to the private sector, do not include poverty as a prohibited ground of discrimination in the provision of goods and services. See for example the *Human Rights Code 1981 (Ont.)*, sections 1 and 2, or try complaining of discrimination to your human rights commission the next time a supermarket, restaurant, car dealer, real estate agent, landlord, etc., will not reduce the price to match your income.

from the state. Since we all have relations with the state and they can all be more or less irksome, the Charter, in its opposition to the state, can unite the most disparate causes under the banner of freedom. But what is left when the state is vanquished? The unequal divided world of private power. We might call this strategy *unite and conquer*. It unites people against the state but the result is to leave them at the mercy of private power.

Take the case of Morgentaler's lawyer Morris Manning. If the name sounds familiar, it is because we met him in the last chapter acting for the National Citizens' Coalition front group, "Freedom of Choice," in its quest to obliterate all of the gains made by unions under modern labour legislation. We also saw him rushing to the defence of the "freedom of choice" of Ontario doctors to extra-bill. It was only after successfully representing Morgentaler at the trial level that Manning's anti-union activities became known. To say it angered supporters is to put it mildly. They wanted Morgentaler to fire Manning. They were particularly galled when it was learned that Manning had acted for strikebreakers against a union made up mostly of women in a first contract fight with the Canadian Imperial Bank of Commerce.[1] Not only that, but the Ontario Federation of Labour had donated thousands of dollars to the Morgentaler defence, in other words to Manning's fees, and he was acting for the same outfit that financed Merv Lavigne's challenge to the use of union dues for supporting causes such as abortion rights (*The Globe and Mail*, February 1, 1986: A14; February 5, 1986: A13). Could there be a more perfect example of the absurdity of Charter politics? Not only was one lawyer able through the Charter to alienate natural allies (the women's movement and the labour movement), Manning was able simultaneously to act for the causes of (1) women's right to abortion, (2) inequality of access to it according to class (extra-billing), and (3) class inequality in general (business's attack on unions)! But Manning was being perfectly consistent. He was acting in the best traditions of legalized politics for causes united by their opposition to the state, the fundamental unity in Charter terms.[2]

It would be false and self-serving for me to deny that there are many issues that engage men and women "as such." But I have to insist that they are not the only ones deeply affecting most women. They are, however, the only ones that can be recognized under the Charter. To be recognized under the Charter, struggles must take an abstract, classless form. Otherwise the judges will run the other way. They must take a form that does not challenge the material

---

[1] A bank with representation on the advisory board of the NCC.

[2] Manning was even more diversified than that. Around the same time as he was representing Henry Morgentaler in the Supreme Court of Canada, he was also appearing there on behalf of rapist James Robertson in a non-Charter case (*Robertson*, 1987).

basis of social power. They must leave that kind of power intact. The repeal of the abortion law, considered on its own, is that kind of issue. It moves the state out of the field, leaving it to the system of private power. That is why it could be united, through "lawyer-riage" at least, with extra-billing and the NCC. Although it may offend some powerful people—though some, like the organized medical profession, were in favour of the repeal (Powell, 1987: 15)—the repeal of the abortion law does not actually injure their interests. It simply privatizes the question. Like the Post Office.[1]

Now if you happen to be a woman doctor or a woman who owns a business, this would not concern you. In each case you are freed from your most significant obstacles. You are now "autonomous." The benefits of the Charter become less and less ambiguous as you go up the ladder of class. The Charter is an unqualified good for women near the top (at least when it delivers). Thus Michelle Landsberg, in her "Long live the Supreme Court" article:

> It's important to understand that the fight has not been about abortion, but something which runs far deeper; the right of women to be autonomous.
>
> I've never had, nor needed (thank heaven), an abortion. But ever since I've been a thinking adult, the power of a fanatic minority to control my body's most intimate functioning has been a biting gall. No woman's life is truly her own unless she has control over her reproduction—which is precisely why so many men, high and low, have invested such bitter ferocity in denying us that self-determination (Landsberg, 1988).

But as one goes back down the class ladder, as "autonomy" and "control over her reproduction" become more and more subject to the restrictions of private power, of poverty, and lack of real alternatives for women, the gifts of the Charter become more double-edged. Not only does it not bestow "autonomy," but, in eroding democratic restrictions on private power, it binds women even more. At least where women are concerned, legalized politics has a "dual impact," a term used by Cheryl Gordon McCleod to describe the effect of US constitutional employment law on women:

> The law has had a class-differentiated effect on women's employment rights. The vast majority of women are still engaged in low-paying work that is performed primarily by women. Only a minority of women have gained access to professional and entrepreneurial positions and to the skilled trades. For the majority of working women, federal employment law undermines, preempts, and invalidates state and judicial benefits and protections. For the minority, however, privilege and access grow. Many feminist theories of equality, by either ignoring class or treating all women as a single class, obscure this dual impact of sexual equality jurisprudence (McCleod, 1986: 277).

In Canada, we have already had an example of this dual impact within the

---

[1] Or prostitution. Recently several challenges have been launched, one successful, against the anti-prostitution provisions of the *Criminal Code*, claiming an infringement of freedom of expression. Such challenges are becoming more frequent now that the police have started to prosecute the customers as well as harassing the women. Interestingly enough, the one successful challenge at the appellate level (*Skinner*, 1987) involved a male customer while the failures involved women (*Jahelka*, 1987; *Re Criminal Code, ss.193 and 195.1*, 1987). But decriminalization plain and simple just returns the "free market," and that is certainly no picnic for the women.

confines of a single case, when lawyer Beth Symes challenged the restrictions on childcare deductions under the *Income Tax Act*. The maximum deductions for childcare under the law were $2,000 per child, no matter how much one actually had to spend. This is typical of the way workers' expenses are treated under the *Act* but not of the way business expenses are treated. The principle for business expenses, for example, transportation, is that they are fully deductible. This is just one example of tax discrimination between wage earners and profit makers (McQuaig, 1987). We have already had a glimpse of it in Chapter V (*OPSEU*, 1987). Symes claimed the right to deduct her full-time nanny's salary (apparently five times the limit), but her challenge had nothing to do with discrimination between business and labour. Her complaint was discrimination between businessmen and businesswomen. She claimed discrimination by *sex* because women overwhelmingly have the primary childcare responsibilities and were more likely to be the "parent/employers" burdened by the restriction. Symes' lawyer, Mary Eberts (the lawyer for the women's union in *Tomen*), argued that this was

> an invidious distinction between the parent/employer and other employers, who are allowed to deduct from business income the wages paid to employees. Why is it a public expense [i.e. deductible] to have someone working on an assembly line and not a public expense to have someone taking care of children? (*The Globe and Mail*, April 30, 1987: A1)

If it bothered Eberts that those "employees" or that "someone working on an assembly line" also did not have the right to exceed the childcare deduction, no matter how much she had to pay, it did not show in her argument. In fact, if pressed she would have been driven to argue that this was irrelevant. In effect, Eberts and Symes were asking that the same discriminatory tax treatment that existed between business*men* and working-class *men* be applied as between business*women* and working-class *women*. Why did they not claim that equality required the full deductibility of childcare expenses for *all* women, employers and employees alike? Because that would have been to complain about *class* discrimination and not just *sex* discrimination. It would have doomed their case to failure because it would have called into question the whole basis of tax. The only way to win was to align themselves with their class at the expense of their gender. And what happens should they ultimately win, either in the courts or in the legislature? The tax loss from the decision would have to be made up somewhere, which usually means "employees"—men and women—who lack the veto of "business confidence" available to "employers."

When section 15 was about to come into effect, the former President of the Canadian Union of Public Employees, Grace Hartman, gave a speech to working women about the dangers of the Charter both for collective bargaining in general and for women in particular. She had the prescience to foresee that sexual equality arguments on behalf of men for such things as paternity leave might threaten women's benefits. But even more telling was a joke she made in the speech to the effect that, if nothing else, the Charter will make a lot of lawyers rich. "Maybe the only plus in that is some of them will be feminist lawyers" (*The Globe and Mail*, May 13, 1985: M3). Hartman was right on both counts. The Charter has meant boom times for lawyers and more and more of these lawyers are women. Feminists or no, at last count, 20% of lawyers were women, increasing rapidly from 15.5% in 1981 and 5.2% in 1971. And this trend is continuing, with women accounting for 41.7% of law graduates in Ontario in 1987 compared to 27.1% in 1980 and 5.9% in 1970 (May, 1987: 13). Though there still appears to be discrimination in pay and responsibilities between men and women lawyers, the differences are minuscule compared to those between women lawyers and women workers. For example, Mary Eberts is a partner in one of those large downtown Toronto law firms reported to pay their senior partners an average of $214,000 to $298,000 per year (Watson, 1988; Bayefsky and Eberts, 1985). And the class position of women lawyers is reflected in their ideology. The National Association of Women and the Law was one of the few groups appearing before the Joint Committee on the Constitution to ask that full Charter protection be extended to corporations (Canada, 1980–81, Issue No. 22: 54).

Class divisions are starting to develop from the bottom up as well. American feminists are now talking of a "second wave" of feminism which groups women by class around class issues. Barbara Ehrenreich recently complained of "lethargy" in the "middle-class" women's movement, as well as the "post-feminism of young, educated, career-oriented women":

> Where did we go wrong?...The problem is not that we (the organized, publicly visible, largely middle-class feminist movement) failed, but that we *succeeded*, at least in one absolutely critical area: the doors to the professions are now open to women. Not all the way, and certainly not all the way to the top, but they are open. Consider the numbers. In 1970, fewer than 8 percent of the nation's physicians were female; today, 14.6 percent are female and approximately 30 percent of our medical students are women, and the gains are of the same magnitude in law and business.

> Some of us, anyway. Because the chief beneficiaries of the opening up to the professions and upper-middle management are women who were born to the middle class. This is one of the nasty little secrets of the American class system: that the people who get ahead are, by and large, the ones who start out ahead— that is, the ones who have the advantages of good schools, an encouraging home life, and the money and leisure for higher education. A 1976 study showed, for example, that the influx of women into medical school did not change the *class* composition of the medical student body. Most of the women, as well as the men, were the children of the approximately 20 percent of the population in the professions. If the recent *glasnost* in the professions has been feminism's greatest victory, it is a victory whose sweetness the majority of American women will never taste...

> ...the average working woman is still pretty much where she always was: waiting on tables, emptying wastebaskets, or pounding a key board for an hourly wage in the mid-single digit range. When she looks out—at television or the dressed-for-success-style magazines—she sees more fortunate women bounding ahead. But when she looks around her, she sees women like herself, going nowhere.

> Somewhere in this collision of rising expectations and unchanging conditions

lie the seeds of the next feminist upsurge...

There has already been an impressive start. Since 1980 about a half-dozen brand-new regional and statewide organizations representing low-income women's economic interests have emerged...The first national conference of the new, low-income women's organizations convened in California last spring, bringing together workplace organizers, welfare rights activists, and all-purpose community heroines from all ethnic groups and corners of the country. I was there, too, and I came away feeling I had seen the feminist future, and it is far more richly diverse, and perhaps even more militant and deeply aggrieved, than anything in the feminist past (Ehrenreich, 1988: 102–107).

The recent adoption by the US National Organization of Women (NOW) of the strategy of the "feminization of power" (a version of which was recently advocated by Michelle Landsberg herself on CBC TV's *The Journal*, January 13, 1988) brought forth this response:

While more and more Americans sink into poverty and political powerlessness, NOW wants to enter the inside track...

The women's movement has spent too much energy and money chasing power for a few women and then hoping for the trickle-down theory to work for other women...The power the women's movement has gained means little or nothing to the majority of poor women. When we think of the "feminization of power" we need to contrast the image of the highly visible, highly successful woman with that of the welfare mother or clerk-typist stuck in her job...Who does NOW want power for, and who will it benefit? Is a select group of women simply angling for a piece of the American pie, or are they willing to consider changing the recipe? (Malveaux, 1988: 104–105)

"Bottom is bottom," as Catharine MacKinnon says, to emphasize the fact that, whatever gains women have made, high or low, they are everywhere still subordinated to men (MacKinnon, 1982: 523). But these women are saying that, if you are stuck there, it does not make much difference to you that the person stepping on your face is a woman and not a man.

In Canada, this "second wave" is already well underway. A strong feminist consciousness is developing in the union movement (Briskin and Yanz, 1983), especially in public sector unions such as the Canadian Union of Public Employees (Hartman, 1983) and the Federation of Women Teachers' Associations of Ontario involved in the *Tomen* case discussed earlier this Chapter. One can also point to such special interest groups as *Indian Rights for Indian Women* and the *Native Women's Association of Canada* who appeared before the Joint Parliamentary Committee on the Constitution (Canada, 1980–81, Issue No. 17: 63, 83), as well as dozens of groups across the country organized by and for Native women, immigrant women, black women, working women, etc. (*Everywoman's Almanac*, 1988). There is emerging within mainstream feminism the uneasy recognition that somehow issues of class and race must be addressed as well as issues of gender (Adamson et al., 1988: 123–126; 239; 293–295; Kline, 1989). And cracks are beginning to show in the cross-class solidarity of the women's movement. Some of them are being provoked by the

Charter itself, as its "feminist fantasy of the future" turns out to be a reality only for the small minority of women for whom its gifts are unambiguous. Amidst the general rejoicing after the Supreme Court decision in *Morgentaler*, a few dissenting voices could be heard raising issues which, unlike the abortion law, neither confront women in the abstract nor unite them against the state, but rather divide them by class. One example of this was the critique levelled by "Bread and Roses," a Winnipeg "collective of socialist women," against the "abortion focus" in matters of reproductive choice:

> The abortion focus has meant that the larger issue of women's control over our reproductive abilities is not being addressed. The innate class bias and racism of how women's reproduction is controlled is not challenged. Thus, the single-issue focus of the movement for reproductive choice has isolated many women for whom abortion is not the issue at all. The movement in Manitoba has become small, unrepresentative and narrow because of the sole concentration on abortion. In turn, because of the lack of a broad base, tactics tend to focus on the legal arena, lobbying and back-room politicking with government members...We cannot expect a handful of middle-class white feminists to set the agenda for all women...As more women mobilize, the issues will broaden, a clear analysis of the problem will evolve and the movement will be more effective. Native women and other women of colour entering the movement, bringing with them a discussion of their right to mother, will broaden the issues to include forced sterilization, child welfare and genocide. Immigrant women will bring an international perspective to the discussion, including fertility and contraception experimentation, the economics of birth control and the new reproductive technology. Women dependent on social assistance will contribute to the discussion their experiences of sterilization, lack of childcare support, and poverty. Lesbian women will share issues such as custody rights, artificial insemination, and adoption. Differently-abled women will add their views on inadequate birth control, coercive sterilization and abortion, and lack of support for their decision to parent. Young women will voice their experiences of lack of access to reproductive information, birth control and abortion. It is difficult to predict all the reproductive issues that women might be facing, because up to now the movement has not been an arena in which these issues are discussed (Bread and Roses, 1988: 23).

So far these stirrings can only be heard at the political margins. And besides those issues that divide women by class, there remain plenty of issues to unite them by gender, including equal pay for work of equal value and sexual violence. Such issues are grist for the Charter even if the results are dubious and double-edged, a point I laboured earlier this Chapter.

But for the other issues, the ones that divide women by class, it is a different story altogether. Remember Justice Wilson's view of the development of rights struggles in *Morgentaler*? First there was "men" against "an overbearing state apparatus." Next came "women" trying to "achieve a place...in a man's world." Third, "woman's struggle to assert *her* dignity and worth as a human being" (*Morgentaler*, 1988: 555). What we seem to be seeing now is the emergence of a *fourth* stage, where the mass of women permanently excluded from the feminization of power and deep within or on the brink of the feminization poverty assert *their* dignity and worth, not just against state power or against male power, but against class power, even though it means making women of other classes uncomfortable. Whatever its role in other stages, legal politics is not merely useless here, it is a definite roadblock, one of the major devices for *protecting* and *extending* class power against any mere democratic impulses. And the Charter is as good as its word in one respect. It does not discriminate by sex. It has no more sympathy for democracy's claims against class power when they are made on behalf of women than when they are made on behalf of men. The success of any fourth stage—even more so of any *fifth* stage where women and men of the same class join hands across gender lines—will have to come, one way or another, *against* the Charter, *in spite of* it, maybe even over its dead body.

CHAPTER VII

What to do about the Charter?

This has been a long book with many complicated arguments, but when you come right down to it, all I have really tried to do is to reveal the dishonest nature of legalized politics and to show how what has been sold as a democratic movement is actually its opposite. Sometimes, as with the case of language, the opposition has been obvious. More or less the same can be said of business's successful deployment of the Charter in its struggle against all forms of regulation and, in particular, against organized labour. Other times, as with the attempts of democratic movements—the anti-nuclear movement, the labour movement, the aboriginal people's movement, and the women's movement—to "hijack" the Charter, the opposition has been more complicated. More complicated still has been the way the Charter's formal values have legitimated the expansion of official repression. But in every realm, and whether on its best or worst behaviour, the Charter's basic claims have been shown to be fraudulent. The Charter promised to even the odds in the confrontation between the strong and the weak, but it has made them even more uneven. And in those rare case where it has arguably helped those without wealth and power, it has unequivocally helped those with it even more. Despite all the heavenly exaltation, the Charter has merely handed over the custody of our politics to the legal profession. The defence of the status quo has followed from that as naturally as night follows day. The Charter would be a mute oracle without a legal priesthood to give it life. And the legal profession has shown itself more than willing to play the lead part in this hoax. Canadian lawyers and judges have, for the most part, gleefully and greedily undertaken a job—deciding the important political questions of the day—for which they lack all training and competence. And they have been more than willing to adopt the necessary pretexts to disguise these political, and politically conscious, interventions as *a*political interpretations of a document so vague as to be meaningless. For this they deserve a far rougher ride than the one they have been given here.

In the remaining pages I want to offer a few brief thoughts on a question that I am always asked at the end of a more or less successful exploration of this subject: "So what?" This usually means something different according to whether or not the person asking it is a lawyer. If it is a lawyer, the question is really "What possible use is all of this to me in my daily work? What do you want me to do, quit?" Like David Beatty:

> To those who question the legitimacy of the enterprise itself, I would only say that for me the compelling point is that the entrenchment of our Charter of Rights and Freedoms is a constitutional fact (Beatty, 1987: 186n4).

If it is not a lawyer, the question usually means: "What can we possibly do about the Charter?" Generally I am unable to come up with a satisfactory answer to either type of question. I am afraid that is still the case. But let me try to say something useful on the subject.

We are burdened not only with having to make our own history, but with having to make it in circumstances not of our own choosing. The Charter is a more or less permanent part of the political landscape. We have filled some hundreds of pages with criticism, but we look out of our window and it is still there. The Charter is not going to go away by mere criticism or by other acts of the will. Even the thought of getting together a movement to try to repeal it makes one blush.

Furthermore, the Charter is going to be used. Lawyers will be lawyers. And it is going to be used by the lawyers for the good guys and the lawyers for the bad guys alike. Sometimes the lawyers for the good guys will have no choice, as in *Morgentaler*. There were other ways to win that case, but the courts wanted no part of them. The only one they were going to allow was the Charter. To renounce the Charter was to renounce the only possible victory going. I do not believe in making points for its own sake. That is what the Charter is all about. Put another way, a game plan that depends on progressive causes committing suicide when they get to court is not likely to be a victorious one in either the long run or the short run. Still, there are circumstances where one can avoid using the Charter. And there are ways to use it when one has to.

The Charter has to be handled with care, something like nitroglycerine. To think of it as just another strategy, or, worse yet, a preferred strategy, can be disastrous. Not only in the short term, as with Operation Dismantle, but also in the long term, legitimating the general form and sinking us deeper into the quicksand. American feminist lawyer Catharine MacKinnon recently told a Canadian audience to "use the Charter" to fight pornography (*The Globe and Mail*, March 2, 1987: A16). Just one year earlier the Supreme Court of the United States "in a fairly unprecedented display of contempt" had given final approval to the judicial destruction of a famous Indianapolis anti-pornography ordinance that MacKinnon herself had drafted (MacKinnon, 1987: 210). But if you legitimate the Charter by using it, you cannot claim foul when it is used against you. You may be able to say, as MacKinnon does, in the company of all the progressive lawyers we talked about in Chapter II, that your interpretation of the Charter is better than the courts'. But the courts have the last word. And you cannot ask people to take judicial "contempt" seriously when it is on your side and not when it goes against you. You cannot ask people to be quiet and listen when you have hired Morris Manning to defend the right to abortion and then tell them not to pay any attention when the National Citizens' Coalition hires him to talk about how destructive unions are. They won't listen to you. Nor should they.

So what is a proper use of the Charter? Judy Fudge, while critical of the Charter's constitutional inability to deal with social/sexual power relations, sees litigation about formal values as nevertheless having a positive role to play:

Charter litigation and legislative lobbying, as well as political mobilization, may not be mutually exclusive in all cases, but rather reinforcing. Legal notions of formal equality, privacy and autonomy may very well be a necessary first step to achieve substantive reproductive freedom for women both within and without socialism. Moreover, it is exactly these types of arguments that courts are particularly susceptible to, and it is here that Charter litigation might have a valuable role to play. By calling upon the Supreme Court to recognize the force of the claims of bourgeois (liberal) legality in *Morgentaler*, feminists created the occasion whereby the issue of access to safe, legal and funded abortions moved to the centre of public and political debate (Fudge, 1988b: 97–98).

With great respect to an admired colleague, this seems a little too pat to me. It makes a virtue out of what was really a necessity. It is the *Charter* that *detaches* form from substance in the first place. It *forces* the agenda to be set in this artificial sequence. And what results is not a neat progression from one stage of discourse to the other, but endless discussions about the formal questions. Morgentaler and the people behind his clinic had no choice but to go to court. They did not use litigation as a strategy. They defied the law, were raided and charged with a crime. When in court, they had no choice but to detach the material problem of class and access from the formal problem of the right to privacy. This was the only approach capable of achieving success in court, let alone the approach most congenial to the particular lawyer handling the case. But it is an approach that renders necessary the detachment of questions that nobody would otherwise *dream* of detaching. It is a *way* of detaching them—probably the only way—so that those questions that do not threaten social power can be dealt with and those that do can be *forever postponed*. To embrace legal politics for doing that seems to me to be a big mistake.

Another thing. About socialism. I could not agree more that the question of legalized politics in general is the same whatever the type of society. The question of legalized politics is a question of the *form* of government and the acid test of any form of government is how concretely democratic it is. It is hard to imagine how a political form as undemocratic as the Charter could suddenly become democratic in a socialist society. Once again there is a tendency to mistake the form of constitutionalism for its content. Panitch and Swartz, for example, criticize opposition to the Charter this way:

> Moreover, this position tends to foreclose the question of whether freedom of association, with all it entails, needs to be constitutionally guaranteed, even in a socialist society (Panitch and Swartz, 1988: 103).

But we have seen what it means for something to be "constitutionally guaranteed." We have seen that the form makes all the difference in the world. Putting the bare phrase "freedom of association" in a document administered by an unfettered judiciary not responsible to anyone is unimaginable in any society we would call democratic. Nailing down the meaning of freedom of association by specific, concrete rights with institutional guarantees that they will be rigorously respected is a different thing altogether. In other words, we do not need "freedom of association" if we have "all it entails." Nor will we have democracy if we are not allowed to make up our own minds about what freedom of association entails, but instead must hand the question over to a few of our betters to decide the matter for us under the pretext of interpretation.

The problem is identical with all of the current schemes to use the Charter offensively—from the crackpot idea of the PSAC for a "freedom of association" amendment, to the more modest designs of the left wing lawyers to fill the Charter's empty phrases with collectivist content. They all ignore the essence of Charter politics, which is not its content, but its fundamentally dishonest, authoritarian, and above all anti-democratic *form*. Using the Charter offensively legitimates a form of politics we should be doing everything we can to *de*-legitimate.

But it is sometimes necessary, as we have already conceded, to use the Charter *defensively*. And it is frequently necessary to *defend ourselves against the Charter*. How should this be handled? Panitch and Swartz give this advice: go to court when you have to, but do not forget to lock the door behind you when you come back out. Do not get carried away and do not get your priorities confused:

> It was also inevitable that capital would use the Charter to secure judicial rulings against labour, in terms of the liberal individualist philosophy that the Charter espouses; and it was just as inevitable that the unions would attempt to defend themselves against this. The real issue is *how* they go about this: whether they allow lawyers to determine their overall strategy; whether they confuse the individualistic and defensive arguments they are forced to make in the courts with the message they deliver to their members; and whether they spend an inordinate amount of their energies and resources in this arena. To the extent they do this, they reduce their capacity to apply the most effective union response to state and employer attacks—the mobilization and political education of their own membership (Panitch and Swartz, 1988: 104).

This seems like good advice, but how can we expect anyone to take it, when, at the first sign of a fight, those who are giving it dress their arguments up in Charter language and brandish dissenting judgments over national radio—the way Leo Panitch did, with the best of intentions, during the postal strike of 1987? (See Chapter V)

Confining legal politics to the courtroom is not only a difficult trick, but an impossible one. A difficult but possible trick, and one that makes a lot more sense, is to bring democratic politics into the courtroom. To undermine legal politics at its source. To challenge the authority of the court and thereby authoritarianism in general. That is what I have been trying to do with this book. But the conditions have to be right for such a project to have half a chance of success. We have to deepen and strengthen the democracy of our politics so that we have something to bring into court, something to compete with legalized politics, to make it seem absurd and irrelevant, like the Monarchy or the Senate. Legalized politics cannot simply be abolished. It must be made to wither away.

APPENDIX A
THE CANADA ACT AND THE
CHARTER OF RIGHTS

CANADA ACT 1982
U.K., 1982, c.11
An Act to give effect to a request by the Senate and House of
Commons of Canada

Whereas Canada has requested and consented to the enactment of an Act of the Parliament of the United Kingdom to give effect to the provisions hereinafter set forth and the Senate and the House of Commons of Canada in Parliament assembled have submitted an address to Her Majesty requesting that Her Majesty may graciously be pleased to cause a Bill to be laid before the Parliament of the United Kingdom for that purpose.

Be it therefore enacted by the Queen's Most Excellent Majesty, by and with the advice and consent of the Lords Spiritual and Temporal, and Commons, in this present Parliament assembled, and by the authority of the same as follows:

Constitution Act, 1982 enacted

1. The *Constitution Act, 1982* set out in Schedule B to this Act is hereby enacted for and enacted shall have the force of law in Canada and shall come into force as provided in that Act.

Termination of power to legislate for Canada

2. No Act of the Parliament of the United Kingdom passed after the *Constitution Act, 1982* comes into force shall extend to Canada as part of its law.

French version

3. So far as it is not contained in Schedule B, the French version of this Act is set out in Schedule A to this Act and has the same authority in Canada as the English version thereof.

Short title

4. This Act may be cited as the *Canada Act 1982.*

CONSTITUTION ACT, 1982
Schedule B to Canada Act 1982 (U. K.)

PART I
CANADIAN CHARTER OF RIGHTS AND FREEDOMS

Whereas Canada is founded upon principles that recognize the supremacy of God and the rule of law:

Guarantee of Rights and Freedoms

Rights and freedoms in Canada

1. *The Canadian Charter of Rights and Freedoms* guarantees the rights and freedoms set out in it subject only to such reasonable limits prescribed by law as can be demonstrably justified in a free and democratic society.

Fundamental Freedoms

Fundamental freedoms

2. Everyone has the following fundamental freedoms:

(a) freedom of conscience and religion;

(b) freedom of thought, belief, opinion and expression, including freedom of the press and other media of communication;

(c) freedom of peaceful assembly; and

(d) freedom of association.

Democratic Rights

Democratic rights of citizens

3. Every citizen of Canada has the right to vote in an election of members of the House of Commons or of a legislative assembly and to be qualified for membership therein.

Maximum duration of legislative bodies

4. (1) No House of Commons and no legislative assembly shall continue for longer than five years from the date fixed for the return of the writs at a general election of its members.

Continuation in special circumstances

(2) In time of real or apprehended war, invasion or insurrection, a House of Commons may be continued by Parliament and a legislative assembly may be continued by the legislature beyond five years if such continuation is not opposed by the votes of more than one-third of the members of the House of Commons or the legislative assembly, as the case may be.

Annual sitting of legislative bodies

5. There shall be a sitting of Parliament and of each legislature at least once every twelve months.

Mobility Rights

Mobility of citizens

6. (1) Every citizen of Canada has the right to enter, remain in and leave Canada.

Rights to move and gain livelihood

(2) Every citizen of Canada and every person who has the status of a permanent resident of Canada has the right

(a) to move and to take up residence in any province; and

(b) to pursue the gaining of a livelihood in any province.

Limitation

(3) The rights specified in subsection (2) are subject to

(a) any laws or practices of general application in force in a province other than those that discriminate among persons primarily on the basis of province of present or previous residence; and

(b) any laws providing for reasonable residency requirements as a qualification for the receipt of publicly provided social services.

Affirmative action programs

(4) Subsections (2) and (3) do not preclude any law, program or activity that has as its object the amelioration in a province of conditions of individuals in that province who are socially or economically

disadvantaged if the rate of employment in that province is below the rate of employment in Canada.

Legal Rights

Life, liberty and security of person

7. Everyone has the right to life, liberty and security of the person and the right not to be deprived thereof except in accordance with the principles of fundamental justice.

Search or seizure

8. Everyone has the right to be secure against unreasonable search or seizure.

Detention or imprisonment

9. Everyone has the right not to be arbitrarily detained or imprisoned.

10. Everyone has the right on arrest or detention
(a) to be informed promptly of the reasons therefor;
(b) to retain and instruct counsel without delay and to be informed of that right; and
(c) to have the validity of the detention determined by way of *habeas corpus* and to be released if the detention is not lawful.

Proceedings in criminal and penal matters

11. Any person charged with an offence has the right
(a) to be informed without unreasonable delay of the specific offence;
(b) to be tried within a reasonable time;
(c) not to be compelled to be a witness in proceedings against that person in respect of the offence;
(d) to be presumed innocent until proven guilty according to law in a fair and public hearing by an independent and impartial tribunal;
(e) not to be denied reasonable bail without just cause;
(f) except in the case of an offence under military law tried before a military tribunal, to the benefit of trial by jury where the maximum punishment for the offence is imprisonment for five years or a more severe punishment;
(g) not to be found guilty on account of any act or omission unless, at the time of the act or omission, it constituted an offence under Canadian or international law or was criminal according to the general principles of law recognized by the community of nations;
(h) if finally acquitted of the offence, not to be tried for it again and, if finally found guilty and punished for the offence, not to be tried or punished for it again; and
(i) if found guilty of the offence and if the punishment for the offence has been varied between the time of commission and the time of sentencing, to the benefit of the lesser punishment.

Treatment or punishment

12. Everyone has the right not to be subjected to any cruel and unusual treatment or punishment.

Self-crimination

13. A witness who testifies in any proceedings has the right not to have any incriminating evidence so given used to incriminate that witness in any other proceedings, except in a prosecution for perjury or for the giving of contradictory evidence.

Interpreter

14. A party or witness in any proceedings who does not understand or speak the language in which the proceedings are conducted or who is deaf has the right to the assistance of an interpreter.

Equality Rights

Equality before and under law and equal protection and benefit of law

15. (1) Every individual is equal before and under the law and has the right to the equal protection and equal benefit of the law without discrimination and, in particular, without discrimination based on race, national or ethnic origin, colour, religion, sex, age or mental or physical disability.

Affirmative action programs

(2) Subsection (1) does not preclude any law, program or activity that has as its object the amelioration of conditions of disadvantaged individuals or groups including those that are disadvantaged because of race, national or ethnic origin, colour, religion, sex, age or mental or physical disability.

Official Languages of Canada

Official languages of Canada

16. (1) English and French are the official languages of Canada and have equality of status and equal rights and privileges as to their use in all institutions of the Parliament and government of Canada.

Official Languages of New Brunswick

(2) English and French are the official languages of New Brunswick and have equality of status and equal rights and privileges as to their use in all institutions of the legislature and government of New Brunswick.

Advancement of status and use

(3) Nothing in this Charter limits the authority of Parliament or a legislature to advance the equality of status or use of English and French.

Proceedings of Parliament

17. (1) Everyone has the right to use English or French in any debates and other proceedings of Parliament.

Proceedings of New Brunswick legislature

(2) Everyone has the right to use English or French in any debates and other proceedings of the legislature of New Brunswick.

Parliamentary statutes and records

18. (1) The statutes, records and journals of Parliament shall be printed and published in English and French and both language versions are equally authoritative.

New Brunswick statutes and records

(2) The statutes, records and journals of the legislature of New Brunswick shall be printed and published in English and French and both language versions are equally authoritative.

Proceedings in courts established by Parliament

19. (1) Either English or French may be used by any person in, or in any pleading in or process issuing from, any court established by Parliament.

Proceedings in New Brunswick courts

(2) Either English or French may be used by any person in, or in any pleading in or process issuing from, any court of New Brunswick.

Communications by public with federal institutions

20. (1) Any member of the public in Canada has the right to communicate with, and to receive available services from, any head or central office of an institution of the Parliament or government of Canada in English or French, and has the same right with respect to any other office of any such institution where

(a) there is a significant demand for communications with and services from that office in such language; or

(b) due to the nature of the office, it is reasonable that communications with and services from that office be available in both English and French.

Communications by public with New Brunswick institutions

(2) Any member of the public in New Brunswick has the right to communicate with, and to receive available services from, any office of an institution of the legislature or government of New Brunswick in English or French.

Continuation of existing constitutional provisions

21. Nothing in sections 16 to 20 abrogates or derogates from any right, privilege or obligation with respect to the English and French languages, or either of them, that exists or is continued by virtue of any other provision of the Constitution of Canada.

Rights and privileges preserved

22. Nothing in sections 16 to 20 abrogates or derogates from any legal or customary right or privilege acquired or enjoyed either before or after the coming into force of this Charter with respect to any language that is not English or French.

Minority Language Educational Rights

Language of instruction

23. (1) Citizens of Canada

(a) whose first language learned and still understood is that of the English or French linguistic minority population of the province in which they reside, or

(b) who have received their primary school instruction in Canada in English or French and reside in a province where the language in which they received that instruction is the language of the English or French linguistic minority population of the province,

have the right to have their children receive primary and secondary school instruction in that language in that province.

Continuity of language instruction

(2) Citizens of Canada of whom any child has received or is receiving primary or secondary school instruction in English or French in Canada, have the right to have all their children receive primary and secondary school instruction in the same language.

Application where numbers warrant

(3) The right of citizens of Canada under subsections (1) and (2) to have their children receive primary and secondary school instruction in the language of the English or French linguistic minority population of a province

(a) applies wherever in the province the number of children of citizens who have such a right is sufficient to warrant the provision to them out of public funds of minority language instruction; and

(b) includes, where the number of those children so warrants, the right to have them receive that instruction in minority language educational facilities provided out of public funds.

Enforcement

Enforcement of guaranteed rights and freedoms

24. (1) Anyone whose rights or freedoms, as guaranteed by this Charter, have been infringed or denied may apply to a court of competent jurisdiction to obtain such remedy as the court considers appropriate and just in the circumstances.

Exclusion of evidence bringing administration of justice into disrepute

(2) Where, in proceedings under subsection (1), a court concludes that evidence was obtained in a manner that infringed or denied any rights or freedoms guaranteed by this Charter, the evidence shall be excluded if it is established that, having regard to all the circumstances, the admission of it in the proceedings would bring the administration of justice into disrepute.

General

Aboriginal rights and freedoms not affected by Charter

25. The guarantee in this Charter of certain rights and freedoms shall not be construed so as to abrogate or derogate from any aboriginal, treaty or other rights or freedoms that pertain to the aboriginal peoples of Canada including

(a) any rights or freedoms that have been recognized by the Royal Proclamation of October 7, 1763; and

(b) any rights or freedoms that now exist by way of land claims agreements or may be so acquired.[1]

Other rights and freedoms not affected by Charter

26. The guarantee in this Charter of certain rights and freedoms shall not be construed as denying the existence of any other rights or freedoms that exist in Canada.

Multicultural heritage

27. This Charter shall be interpreted in a manner consistent with the preservation and enhancement of the multicultural heritage of Canadians.

Rights guaranteed equally to both sexes

28. Notwithstanding anything in this Charter, the rights and freedoms referred to in it are guaranteed equally to male and female persons.

Rights respecting certain schools preserved

29. Nothing in this Charter abrogates or derogates from any rights or privileges guaranteed by or under the Constitution of Canada in respect of denominational, separate or dissentient schools.

Application to territories and territorial authorities

30. A reference in this Charter to a province or to the legislative assembly or legislature of a province shall be deemed to include a reference to the Yukon Territory and the Northwest Territories, or to the appropriate legislative authority thereof, as the case may be.

Legislative powers not extended

31. Nothing in this Charter extends the legislative powers of any body or authority.

Application of Charter

Application of Charter

32. (1) This Charter applies

---

[1] Paragraph 25 (b) was amended by the *Constitution Amendment Proclamation, 1983*. It originally read "(b) any rights or freedoms that may be acquired by the aboriginal peoples of Canada by way of land claims settlement."

(a) to the Parliament and government of Canada in respect of all matters within the authority of Parliament including all matters relating to the Yukon Territory and Northwest Territories; and

(b) to the legislature and government of each province in respect of all matters within the authority of the legislature of each province.

Exception

(2) Notwithstanding subsection (1), section 15 shall not have effect until three years after this section comes into force.

Exception where express declaration

33. (1) Parliament or the legislature of a province may expressly declare in an Act of Parliament or of the legislature, as the case may be, that the Act or a provision thereof shall operate notwithstanding a provision included in section 2 or sections 7 to 15 of this Charter.

Operation of exception

(2) An Act or a provision of an Act in respect of which a declaration made under this section is in effect shall have such operation as it would have but for the provision of this Charter referred to in the declaration.

Five-year limitation

(3) A declaration made under subsection (1) shall cease to have effect five years after it comes into force or on such earlier date as may be specified in the declaration.

Re-enactment

(4) Parliament or the legislature of a province may re-enact a declaration made under subsection (1).

Five-year limitation

(5) Subsection (3) applies in respect of a re-enactment made under subsection (4).

Citation

Citation

34. This Part may be cited as the *Canadian Charter of Rights and Freedoms*.

PART II
RIGHTS OF THE ABORIGINAL PEOPLES OF CANADA

Recognition of existing aboriginal and treaty rights

35. (1) The existing aboriginal and treaty rights of the aboriginal peoples of Canada are hereby recognized and affirmed.

Definition of "aboriginal peoples of Canada"

(2) In this Act, "aboriginal peoples of Canada" includes the Indian, Inuit and Métis peoples of Canada.

Land claims agreements

(3) For greater certainty, in subsection (1) "treaty rights" includes rights that now exist by way of land claims agreements or may be so acquired.

Aboriginal and treaty rights are guaranteed equally to both sexes

(4) Notwithstanding any other provision of this Act, the aboriginal and treaty rights referred to in subsection (1) are guaranteed equally to male and female persons.[1]

Commitment to participation in constitutional conference

35.1 The government of Canada and the provincial governments are committed to the principle that, before any amendment is made to Class 24 of section 91 of the "*Constitution Act, 1867*," to section 25 of this Act or to this Part,

---

[1] Subsections (3) and (4) were added by the *Constitution Amendment Proclamation, 1983.*

(a) a constitutional conference that includes in its agenda an item relating to the proposed amendment, composed of the Prime Minister of Canada and the first ministers of the provinces, will be convened by the Prime Minister of Canada; and

(b) the Prime Minister of Canada will invite representatives of the aboriginal peoples of Canada to participate in the discussions on that item.[1]

PART III
EQUALIZATION AND REGIONAL DISPARITIES

Commitment to promote equal opportunities

36. (1) Without altering the legislative authority of Parliament or of the provincial legislatures, or the rights of any of them with respect to the exercise of their legislative authority, Parliament and the legislatures, together with the government of Canada and the provincial governments, are committed to

(a) promoting equal opportunities for the well-being of Canadians;

(b) furthering economic development to reduce disparity in opportunities; and

(c) providing essential public services of reasonable quality to all Canadians.

Commitment respecting public services

(2) Parliament and the government of Canada are committed to the principle of making equalization payments to ensure that provincial governments have sufficient revenues to provide reasonably comparable levels of public services at reasonably comparable levels of taxation.

PART IV
CONSTITUTIONAL CONFERENCE

Constitutional conference

37. (1) A constitutional conference composed of the Prime Minister of Canada and the first ministers of the provinces shall be convened by the Prime Minister of Canada within one year after this Part comes into force.

Participation of aboriginal peoples

(2) The conference convened under subsection (1) shall have included in its agenda an item respecting constitutional matters that directly affect the aboriginal peoples of Canada, including the identification and definition of the rights of those peoples to be included in the Constitution of Canada, and the Prime Minister of Canada shall invite representatives of those peoples to participate in the discussions on that item.

Participation of territories

(3) The Prime Minister of Canada shall invite elected representatives of the governments of the Yukon Territory and the Northwest Territories to participate in the discussions on any item on the agenda of the conference convened under subsection (1) that, in the opinion of the Prime Minister, directly affects the Yukon Territory and the Northwest Territories.[2]

---

[1] Section 35.1 was added by the *Constitution Amendment Proclamation, 1983.*

[2] This whole Part was automatically repealed on April 17, 1983, in accordance with section 54 of the *Constitution Act, 1982.*

PART IV.1
CONSTITUTIONAL CONFERENCES

Constitutional conferences

37.1 (1) In addition to the conference convened in March 1983, at least two constitutional conferences composed of the Prime Minister of Canada and the first ministers of the provinces shall be convened by the Prime Minister of Canada, the first within three years after April 17, 1982 and the second within five years after that date.

Participation of aboriginal peoples

(2) Each conference convened under subsection (1) shall have included in its agenda constitutional matters that directly affect the aboriginal peoples of Canada, and the Prime Minister of Canada shall invite representatives of those peoples to participate in the discussions on those matters.

Participation of territories

(3) The Prime Minister of Canada shall invite elected representatives of the governments of the Yukon Territory and the Northwest Territories to participate in the discussions on any item on the agenda of a conference convened under subsection (1) that, in the opinion of the Prime Minister, directly affects the Yukon Territory and the Northwest Territories.

Subsection 35(1) not affected

(4) Nothing in this section shall be construed so as to derogate from subsection 35(1).[1]

PART V
PROCEDURE FOR AMENDING THE CONSTITUTION OF CANADA

* * *

PART VII
GENERAL

Primacy of Constitution of Canada

52. (1) The Constitution of Canada is the supreme law of Canada, and any law that is inconsistent with the provisions of the Consititution is, to the extent of the inconsistency, of no force or effect.

Constitution of Canada

(2) The Constitution of Canada includes

(a) the *Canada Act 1982*, including this Act;
(b) the Acts and orders referred to in the schedule; and
(c) any amendment to any Act or order referred to in paragraph (a) or (b).

* * *

Repeal and consequential amendments

54. Part IV is repealed on the day that is one year after this Part comes into force and this section may be repealed and this Act renumbered, consequentially upon the repeal of Part IV and this section, by proclamation issued by the Governor General under the Great Seal of Canada.

---

[1] Part IV.1 was added by *Constitution Amendment Proclamation, 1983* which also added section 54.1: "**54.1** Part IV.1 and this section are repealed on April 18, 1987." By this device, Part IV.1 and section 54.1 were both repealed automatically on April 18, 1987.

* * *

Commencement of paragraph 23(1)(a) in respect of Quebec

59. (1) Paragraph 23(1)(a) shall come into force in respect of Quebec on a day to be fixed by proclamation issued by the Queen or the Governor General under the Great Seal of Canada.

Authorization of Quebec

(2) A proclamation under subsection (1) shall be issued only where authorized by the legislative assembly or government of Quebec.

Repeal of this section

(3) This section may be repealed on the day paragraph 23(1)(a) comes into force in respect of Quebec and this Act amended and renumbered, consequentially upon the repeal of this section, by proclamation issued by the Queen or the Governor General under the Great Seal of Canada.

* * *

THE MEECH LAKE ACCORD

CONSTITUTION AMENDMENT, 1987

Constitution Act, 1867

1. The *Constitution Act, 1867* is amended by adding thereto, immediately after section 1 thereof, the following section:

Interpretation

2. (1) The Constitution of Canada shall be interpreted in a manner consistent with

    (a) the recognition that the existence of French-speaking Canadians, centred in Quebec but also present elsewhere in Canada, and English-speaking Canadians, concentrated outside Quebec but also present in Quebec, constitutes a fundamental characteristic of Canada; and

    (b) the recognition that Quebec constitutes within Canada a distinct society.

Role of Parliament and legislatures

(2) The role of the Parliament of Canada and the provincial legislatures to preserve the fundamental characteristics of Canada referred to in paragraph (1)(a) is affirmed.

Role of legislature and Government of Quebec

(3) The role of the legislature and Government of Quebec to preserve and promote the distinct identity of Quebec referred to in paragraph (1)(b) is affirmed.

Rights of legislatures and governments

(4) Nothing in this section derogates from the powers, rights or privileges of Parliament or the Government of Canada, or of the legislatures or governments of the provinces, including any powers, rights or privileges relating to language.

2. The said Act is further amended by adding thereto, immediately after section 24 thereof, the following section:

Names to be submitted

25. (1) Where a vacancy occurs in the Senate, the government of the province to which the vacancy relates may, in relation to that vacancy, submit to the Queen's Privy Council for Canada the names of persons who may be summoned to the Senate.

Choice of Senators from names submitted

(2) Until an amendment to the Constitution of Canada is made in relation to the Senate pursuant to section 41 of the *Constitution Act, 1982*, the person summoned to fill a vacancy in the Senate shall be chosen from among persons whose names have been submitted under subsection (1) by the government of the province to which the vacancy relates and must be acceptable to the Queen's Privy Council for Canada.

3. The said Act is further amended by adding thereto, immediately after section 95 thereof, the following heading and sections:

Agreements on Immigration and Aliens

Commitment to negotiate

95A. The Government of Canada shall, at the request of the government of any province, negotiate with the government of that province for the purpose of concluding an agreement relating to immigration or the temporary admission of aliens into that province that is appropriate to the needs and circumstances of that province.

Agreements

95B. (1) Any agreement concluded between Canada and a province in relation to immigration or the temporary admission of aliens into that province has the force of law from the time it is declared to do so in accordance with subsection 95C(1) and shall from that time have effect notwithstanding class 25 of section 91 or section 95.

Limitation

(2) An agreement that has the force of law under subsection (1) shall have effect only so long and so far as it is not repugnant to any provision of an Act of the Parliament of Canada that sets national standards and objectives relating to immigration or aliens, including any provision that establishes general classes of immigrants or relates to levels of immigration for Canada or that prescribes classes of individuals who are inadmissible into Canada.

Application of Charter

(3) The *Canadian Charter of Rights and Freedoms* applies in respect of any agreement that has the force of law under subsection (1) and in respect of anything done by the Parliament or Government of Canada, or the legislature or government of a province, pursuant to any such agreement.

Proclamation relating to agreements

95C. (1) A declaration that an agreement referred to in subsection 95B(1) has the force of law may be made by proclamation issued by the Governor General under the Great Seal of Canada only where so authorized by resolutions of the Senate and House of Commons and of the legislative assembly of the province that is a party to the agreement.

Amendments of agreements

(2) An amendment to an agreement referred to in subsection 95B(1) may be made by proclamation issued by the Governor General under the Great Seal of Canada only where so authorized
(a) by resolutions of the Senate and House of Commons and of the legislative assembly of the province that is a party to the agreement; or
(b) in such other manner as is set out in the agreement.

Application of sections 46 to 48 of *Constitution Act, 1982*

95D. Sections 46 to 48 of the *Constitution Act, 1982* apply, with such modifications as the circumstances require, in respect of any declaration made pursuant to subsection 95C(1), any amendment to an agreement made pursuant to subsection 95C(2) or any amendment made pursuant to section 95E.

Amendments to section 95A to 95D or this section

95E. An amendment to sections 95A to 95D or this section may be made in accordance with the procedure set out in subsection 38(1) of the *Constitution Act, 1982*, but only if the amendment is authorized by resolutions of the legislative assemblies of all the provinces that are, at the time of the amendment, parties to an agreement that has the force of law under subsection 95B(1).

4. The said Act is further amended by adding thereto, immediately preceding section 96 thereof, the following heading:

General

5. The said Act is further amended by adding thereto, immediately preceding section 101 thereof, the following heading:

Courts Established by the Parliament of Canada

6. The said Act is further amended by adding thereto, immediately after section 101 thereof, the following heading and sections:

Supreme Court of Canada

Supreme Court continued

101A. (1) The court existing under the name of the Supreme Court of Canada is hereby continued as the general court of appeal for Canada, and as an additional court for the better administration of the laws of Canada, and shall continue to be a superior court of record.

Constitution of court

(2) The Supreme Court of Canada shall consist of a chief justice to be called the Chief Justice of Canada and eight other judges, who shall be appointed by the Governor General in Council by letters patent under the Great Seal.

Who may be appointed judges

101B. (1) Any person may be appointed a judge of the Supreme Court of Canada who, after having been admitted to the bar of any province or territory, has, for a total of at least ten years, been a judge of any court in Canada or a member of the bar of any province or territory.

Three judges from Quebec

(2) At least three judges of the Supreme Court of Canada shall be appointed from among persons who, after having been admitted to the bar of Quebec, have, for a total of at least ten years, been judges of any court of Quebec or of any court established by the Parliament of Canada, or members of the bar of Quebec.

Names may be submitted

101C. (1) Where a vacancy occurs in the Supreme Court of Canada, the government of each province may, in relation to that vacancy, submit to the Minister of Justice of Canada the names of any of the persons who have been admitted to the bar of that province and are qualified under section 101B for appointment to that court.

Appointment from names submitted

(2) Where an appointment is made to the Supreme Court of Canada, the Governor General in Council shall, except where the Chief Justice is appointed from among members of the Court, appoint a person whose name has been submitted under subsection (1) and who is acceptable to the Queen's Privy Council for Canada.

Appointment from Quebec

(3) Where an appointment is made in accordance with subsection (2) of any of the three judges necessary to meet the requirement set out in subsection 101B(2), the Governor General in Council shall appoint a person whose name has been submitted by the Government of Quebec.

Appointment from other provinces

(4) Where an appointment is made in accordance with subsection (2) otherwise than as required under subsection (3), the Governor General in Council shall appoint a person whose name has been submitted by the government of a province other than Quebec.

Tenure, salaries, etc., of judges

101D. Sections 99 and 100 apply in respect of the judges of the Supreme Court of Canada.

Relationship to section 101

101E. (1) Sections 101A to 101D shall not be construed as abrogating or derogating from the powers of the Parliament of Canada to make laws under section 101 except to the extent that such laws are inconsistent with those sections.

References to the Supreme Court of Canada

(2) For greater certainty, section 101A shall not be construed as abrogating or derogating from the powers of the Parliament of Canada to make laws relating to the reference of questions of law or fact, or any other matters, to the Supreme Court of Canada.

7. The said Act is further amended by adding thereto, immediately after section 106 thereof, the following section:

Shared-cost program

106A. (1) The Government of Canada shall provide reasonable compensation to the government of a province that chooses not to participate in a national shared-cost program that is established by the Government of Canada after the coming into force of this section in an area of exclusive provincial jurisdiction, if the province carries on a program or initiative that is compatible with the national objectives.

Legislative power not extended

(2) Nothing in this section extends the legislative powers of the Parliament of Canada or of the legislatures of the provinces.

8. The said Act is further amended by adding thereto the following heading and sections:

XII—CONFERENCES ON THE ECONOMY AND OTHER MATTERS

Conferences on the economy and other matters

148. A conference composed of the Prime Minister of Canada and the first ministers of the provinces shall be convened by the Prime Minister of Canada at least once each year to discuss the state of the Canadian economy and such other matters as may be appropriate.

XIII—REFERENCES

Reference includes amendments

149. A reference to this Act shall be deemed to include a reference to any amendments thereto.

Constitution Act, 1982

9. Sections 40 to 42 of the *Constitution Act, 1982* are repealed and the following substituted therefor:

Compensation

40. Where an amendment is made under subsection 38(1) that transfers legislative powers from provincial legislatures to Parliament, Canada shall provide reasonable compensation to any province to which the amendment does not apply.

Amendment by unanimous consent

41. An amendment to the Constitution of Canada in relation to the following matters may be made by proclamation issued by the Governor General under the Great Seal of Canada only where authorized by resolutions of the Senate and House of Commons and of the legislative assembly of each province:

(a) the office of the Queen, the Governor General and the Lieutenant Governor of a province;

(b) the powers of the Senate and the method of selecting Senators;

(c) the number of members by which a province is entitled to be represented in the Senate and the residence qualifications of Senators;

(d) the right of a province to a number of members in the House of Commons not less than the number of Senators by which the province was entitled to be represented on April 17, 1982;

(e) the principle of proportionate representation of the provinces in the House of Commons prescribed by the Constitution of Canada;

(f) subject to section 43, the use of the English or the French language;

(g) the Supreme Court of Canada;
(h) the extension of existing provinces into the territories;
(i) notwithstanding any other law or practice, the establishment of new provinces; and
(j) an amendment to this Part.

10. Section 44 of the said Act is repealed and the following substituted therefor:

Amendments by Parliament

44. Subject to section 41, Parliament may exclusively make laws amending the Constitution of Canada in relation to the executive government of Canada or the Senate and House of Commons.

11. Subsection 46(1) of the said Act is repealed and the following substituted therefor:

Initiation of amendment procedures

46. (1) The procedures for amendment under sections 38, 41 and 43 may be initiated either by the Senate or the House of Commons or by the legislative assembly of a province.

12. Subsection 47(1) of the said Act is repealed and the following substituted therefor:

Amendments without senate resolution

47. (1) An amendment to the Constitution of Canada made by proclamation under section 38, 41 or 43 may be made without a resolution of the Senate authorizing the issue of the proclamation if, within one hundred and eighty days after the adoption by the House of Commons of a resolution authorizing its issue, the Senate has not adopted such a resolution and if, at any time after the expiration of that period, the House of Commons again adopts the resolution.

13. Part VI of the said Act is repealed and the following substituted therefor:

PART VI
CONSTITUTIONAL CONFERENCES

Constitutional conference

50. (1) A constitutional conference composed of the Prime Minister of Canada and the first ministers of the provinces shall be convened by the Prime Minister of Canada at least once each year, commencing in 1988.

Agenda

(2) The conferences convened under subsection (1) shall have included on their agenda the following matters:
(a) Senate reform, including the role and functions of the Senate, its powers, the method of selecting Senators and representation in the Senate;
(b) roles and responsibilities in relation to fisheries; and
(c) such other matters as are agreed upon.

14. Subsection 52(2) of the said Act is amended by striking out the word "and" at the end of paragraph (b) thereof, by adding the word "and" at the end of paragraph (c) thereof and by adding thereto the following paragraph:

(d) any other amendment to the Constitution of Canada.

15. Section 61 of the said Act is repealed and the following substituted therefor:

References

61. A reference to the *Constitution Act, 1982*, or a reference to the *Constitution Acts 1867 to 1982*, shall be deemed to include a reference to any amendments thereto.

General

Multicultural heritage and aboriginal peoples

16. Nothing in section 2 of the *Constitution Act, 1867* affects section 25 or 27 of the *Canadian Charter of Rights and Freedoms*, section 35 of the *Constitution Act, 1982* or class 24 of section 91 of the *Constitution Act, 1867*.

CITATION

Citation

17. This amendment may be cited as the *Constitution Amendment, 1987*.

CASES

Allard and Charette
1987   *United States of America* v. *Allard and Charette* (1987), 33 C.C.C. (3d) 501.

Alliance des Professeurs
1983   *Alliance des Professeurs de Montreal et al.* v. *Attorney General of Quebec* (1983), 9 C.C.C. (3d) 268.
1985   *Alliance des Professeurs de Montreal et al.* v. *Attorney General of Quebec* (1985) 21 D.L.R. (4th) 354.

Altseimer
1982   *R.* v. *Altseimer* (1982), 1 C.C.C. (3d) 7.

Aluminum Co. of Canada
1986   *Re Aluminum Co. of Canada, Ltd. and The Queen in Right of Ontario; Dofasco Inc., Intervenor* (1986), 29 D.L.R. (4th) 583.

Andrews
1986   *Andrews* v. *Law Society of British Columbia et al.* (1986), 27 D.L.R. (4th) 600.

Apsit
1987   *Apsit* v. *Manitoba Human Rights Commission*, [1988] 1 W.W.R. 629.

Attorney General of Canada
1916   *Attorney General of Canada* v. *Attorney General of Alberta*, [1916] 1 A.C. 589.
1936   *Attorney General of Canada* v. *Attorney General of Ontario*, [1936] S.C.R. 363–538.
1937   *Attorney General of Canada* v. *Attorney General of Ontario*, [1937] A.C. 326–418.

Attorney General of Quebec
1982   *Re Attorney General of Quebec and Attorney General of Canada* (1982), 140 D.L.R. (3d) 385.

B. C. Government Employees Union
1985   *Re B. C. Government Employees Union*, [1985] 5 W.W.R. 421.

Baig
1987   *R.* v. *Baig* (1987), 37 C.C.C. (3d) 181.

Bakke
1978   *Regents of the University of California* v. *Bakke*, 438 U.S. 265 (1978).

Bartello
1987   *Bartello* v. *Canada Post Corp.* (1987), 46 D.L.R. (4th) 129.

Beal
1977   *Beal* v. *Doe*, 432 U.S. 438 (1977).

Belgoma
1985   *Re Belgoma Transportation Ltd. and Director of Employment Standards* (1985), 20 D.L.R. (4th) 156.

Bertram S. Miller Ltd.
1986   *Bertram S. Miller Ltd.* v. *The Queen* (1986), 31 D.L.R. (4th) 210.

Bhindi
1986   *Re Bhindi et al. and British Columbia Projectionists Local 348 of International Alliance of Picture Machine Operators of the United States & Canada; Attorney General of British Columbia et al., Intervenors* (1986), 29 D.L.R. (4th) 47.

Big M
1985   *R.* v. *Big M Drug Mart* (1985), 18 D.L.R. (4th) 321.

Bigham
1982   *R.* v. *Bigham* (1982), 69 C.C.C. (2d) 221 .

Bilodeau
1981   *Bilodeau* v. *Attorney-General of Manitoba* (1981), 61 C.C.C. (2d) 217 (Manitoba Court of Appeal).
1986   *Bilodeau* v. *Attorney-General of Manitoba* (1986), 27 D.L.R. (4th) 3 (Supreme Court of Canada).

Birks & Sons
1955   *Birks & Sons (Montreal) Ltd.* v. *City of Montreal*, [1955] S.C.R. 799.

Blaikie
1978   *Blaikie* v. *Attorney General of Quebec* (1978), 85 D.L.R. (3d) 252 (Quebec Superior Court).
1979   *Attorney General of Quebec* v. *Blaikie et al.; Attorney General of Quebec* v. *Laurier et al.* (1979), 101 D.L.R. (3d) 394 (Supreme Court of Canada).

Blaikie (No.2)
1981   *Attorney General of Quebec* v. *Blaikie et al.; Attorney General of Quebec* v. *Laurier et al. (No. 2)* (1981), 123 D.L.R. (3d) 15.

Blainey
1986   *Re Blainey and Ontario Hockey Association et al.* (1986), 26 D.L.R. (4th) 728 (Ontario Court of Appeal).
1987   *Blainey* v. *The Ontario Hockey Association* (Decision of a Board of Inquiry under the *Ontario Human Rights Code*, December 3, 1987).

Bliss
1978   *Bliss* v. *A.G. Canada*, [1979] 1 S.C.R. 183.

Borowski
1987   *Borowski* v. *Attorney-General for Canada* (1987), 39 D.L.R. (4th) 731.

Branigan
1986   *Re Branigan and Yukon Medical Council et al.* (1986), 26 D.L.R. (4th) 268.

Broadway Manor
1983   *Re Service Employees' International Union, Local 204 and Broadway Manor Nursing Home et al.* (1983), 44 O.R. (2d) 392.

Brown
1954   *Brown* v. *Board of Education of Topeka*, 347 U.S. 483 (1954); 349 U.S. 294 (1955).

Buckley
1976   *Buckley* v. *Valeo*, 424 U.S. 1 (1976).

Budge
1987   *Re Budge et al. and Workers' Compensation Board* (1987), 42 D.L.R. (4th) 649.

Butters and Oberlein
1986   *Butters and Oberlein* v. *Minister of Labour et al.*, Amended Notice of Constitutional Question, Supreme Court of Ontario, RE 223/86, July 3, 1986.

C. E. Jamieson & Co.
1987   *C. E. Jamieson & Co. (Dominion) Ltd.* v. *Attorney-General of Canada et al.* (1987), 37 C.C.C (3d) 193.

Canadian Newspapers
1985   *Canadian Newspapers Co. Ltd.* v. *A.G. Can.* (1985), 17 C.C.C (3d) 385 (Ontario Court of Appeal).
1988   *Canadian Newspapers* v. *Canada (A.G.)* (Supreme Court of Canada, September 1, 1988—unreported).

Canadian Union of Postal Workers
1987a   *Re Canadian Union of Postal Workers et al. and Canada Post Corp. et al.* (1987), 40 D.L.R. (4th) 67.
1987b   *Canadian Union of Postal Workers* v. *Attorney General of Canada and Canada Post Corporation*, Statement of Claim filed in Quebec Superior Court, November 3, 1987.

Cardinal and Oswald
1985   *Cardinal and Oswald* v. *Director of Kent Institution* (1985), 23 C.C.C. (3d) 118.

Casagrande
1987   *Re Casagrande and Hinton Roman Catholic Separate School* (1987), 38 D.L.R. (4th) 382.

Central Hudson Gas and Electric
1980   *Central Hudson Gas and Electric Corp.* v. *Public Service Commission of New York*, 447 U.S. 557 (1980).

Charboneau
1985   *Charboneau et al.* v. *College of Physicians & Surgeons of Ontario* (1985), 22 D.L.R. (4th) 303.

Charbonneau
1973   *Charbonneau, Laberge, Pepin et al.* v. *P.G. du Québec*, [1973] R.P. 10.

Chaussure Brown's Inc.
1987   *P.G. du Québec* v. *Chaussure Brown's Inc.*, [1987] R.J.Q. 80.

City of Akron
1983   *City of Akron* v. *Akron Center for Reproductive Health, Inc.*, 103 S.Ct. 2481 (1983).

City of Sault Ste. Marie
1978   *R.* v. *City of Sault Ste. Marie* (1978), 40 C.C.C. (2d) 353.

Clarkson
1986   *R.* v. *Clarkson* (1986), 25 C.C.C. (3d) 207.

Collins
1987   *Collins* v. *The Queen* (1987), 33 C.C.C. (3d) 1.

Corbett
1988   *R.* v. *Corbett*, [1988] 1 S.C.R. 670.

D. & H. Holdings
1985   *Re D. & H. Holdings Ltd. and City of Vancouver et. al.* (1985), 21 D.L.R. (4th) 230.

Dennis
1951   *Dennis* v. *U.S.*, 341 U.S. 494 (1951).

Dersch
1987   *Dersch* v. *Canada (A.G.)*, [1987] 6 W.W.R. 700.

Dolphin Delivery
1986   *Retail, Wholesale & Department Store Union, Local 580 et al.* v. *Dolphin Delivery Ltd.* (1986), 33 D.L.R. (4th) 174.

Drybones
1969   *R.* v. *Drybones*, [1970] S.C.R. 282.

Dupond
1978   *A.G. Canada et al.* v. *Dupond* (1978), 84 D.L.R. (2d) 420.

Dzagic
1985   *R.* v. *Dzagic* (1985), 19 C.C.C. (3d) 98, affirmed 27 C.C.C. (3d) 1 (Ontario Court of Appeal).

Edwards Books
1986   *Edwards Books and Art Ltd. et al.* v. *The Queen; R.* v. *Nortown Foods Ltd.* (1986), 30 C.C.C. (3d) 385.

Energy Probe
1987   *Re Energy Probe and Attorney General of Canada* (1987), 42 D.L.R. (4th) 349.

Evans
1986   *Evans and the Queen* (1986), 30 C.C.C. (3d) 313.

F. K. Clayton Group Ltd.
1986   *F. K. Clayton Group Ltd. et al.* v. *Minister of National Revenue et. al.*, [1986] 2 F.C. 105.

Forest
1978   *Attorney General of Manitoba* v. *Forest* (1978), 98 D.L.R. (3d) 405 (Manitoba Court of Appeal).
1979   *Attorney General of Manitoba* v. *Forest* (1979), 101 D.L.R. (3d) 385 (Supreme Court of Canada).

Fort Frances Pulp and Power
1923   *Fort Frances Pulp and Power Co.* v. *Manitoba Free Press*, [1923] A.C. 695.

Gardiner
1982   *R.* v. *Gardiner* (1982), 68 C.C.C. (2d) 477.

Gershman Produce
1985   *Re Gershman Produce Co. Ltd. and Motor Transport Board* (1985), 22 D.L.R. (4th).

Gideon
1963   *Gideon* v. *Wainwright* 372 U.S. 335 (1963).

Grant
1986   *Re Grant and Crane Construction Corp. et al.* (1986), 28 D.L.R. (4th) 606.

Grier
1987   *Re Grier and Alberta Optometric Association et al.* (1987), 42 D.L.R. (4th) 327.

Griffin
1987   *Griffin* v. *College of Dental Surgeons of B.C.* (*The Lawyers Weekly* January 29, 1988: 14).

Halleran
1987   R. v. *Halleran* (1987), 39 C.C.C. (3d) 177.

Hamill
1987   *Hamill* v. *The Queen* (1987), 33 C.C.C. (3d) 110.

Hamilton
1986   R. v. *Hamilton* (1986), 54 C.R. (3d) 193.

Harris
1980   *Harris* v. *McRae*, 448 U.S. 297 (1980).

Harrison
1988   *Harrison* v. *University of British Columbia*, [1988] 2 W.W.R. 688.

Hartigan
1987   *Hartigan* v. *Zbaraz*, 56 *Law Week* 4053 (1987).

Hatzinicoloau
1987   Re *Hatzinicoloau et al. and Minister of National Revenue et al.* (1987), 34
          C.C.C. (3d) 35.

Hay
1985   Re *Hay and National Parole Board et al.* (1985), 21 C.C.C. (3d) 408.

Hogan
1974   *Hogan* v. *The Queen* (1974), 18 C.C.C. (2d) 65.

Home Orderly Services
1986   *Home Orderly Services Ltd. et al.* v. *Government of Manitoba* (1986), 32 D.L.R.
          (4th) 755.

Homemade Winecrafts
1986   Re *Homemade Winecrafts (Canada) Ltd. and Attorney General of British
          Columbia at al.* (1986), 26 D.L.R. (4th) 468.

Howard
1985   Re *Howard and Presiding Officer of Inmate Disciplinary Court of Stony
          Mountain Institution* (1985), 19 C.C.C. (3d) 195 (Federal Court of Appeal).
1987   R. v. *Howard*, 41 C.C.C. (3d.) 287 (Supreme Court of Canada).

Howell
1986   R. v. *Howell* (1986), 26 C.C.C. (3d) 104.

Hufsky
1988   R. v. *Hufsky* (1988), 40 C.C.C. (3d) 398.

Hunter
1984   *Hunter et al.* v. *Southam Inc.* (1984), 11 D.L.R. (4th) 641.

Hutton
1987   *Hutton* v. *Ontario (Attorney General)* (1987), 46 D.L.R. (4th) 112.

Irwin Toy Ltd.
1986   *Irwin Toy Ltd.* v. *Attorney-General of Quebec; Moreau, Intervenant;
          Attorney-General of Canada, Mis-en-cause*, (1986), 32 D.L.R. (4th) 641
          (Quebec Court of Appeal; leave to appeal to the Supreme Court of Canada
          granted November 6, 1986).

Isabey
1985   Re *Isabey and Manitoba Health Services Commission et al.* (1985), 22 D.L.R.
          503 (Manitoba Queen's Bench).

MacDonald
1986   *MacDonald* v. *City of Montreal* (1986), 27 D.L.R. (4th) 321.

McDonnell
1986   *McDonnell* v. *Federation des Franco-Colombiens* (1986), 31 D.L.R. (4th) 296.

Mackell
1917   *Ottawa Roman Catholic Separate School Trustees* v. *Mackell*, [1917] A.C. 62.

McKinney
1987   *McKinney* v. *University of Guelph et al.* (1987), 24 O.A.C. 241.

McNabb
1942   *McNabb* v. *U.S.*, 318 U.S. 332 (1942).

McVeigh
1985   *R.* v. *McVeigh* (1985), 22 C.C.C. (3d) 145.

MacVicar
1986   *Re MacVicar and Superintendent of Family and Child Services et al.* (1986), 34
          D.L.R. (4th) 488.

Mahe
1987   *Mahe et al.* v. *The Queen in Right of Alberta* (1987), 42 D.L.R. (4th) 514.

Malloy
1964   *Malloy* v. *Hogan*, 378 U.S. 1 (1964).

Manninen
1987   *R.* v. *Manninen* (1987), 34 C.C.C. (3d) 385.

Mapp
1961   *Mapp* v. *Ohio*, 367 U.S. 643 (1961).

Martin
1950   *Martin* v. *Law Society of British Columbia*, [1950] 3 D.L.R. 173.

Mellino
1987   *The Republic of Argentina* v. *Mellino* (1987), 33 C.C.C. (3d) 334.

Mercure
1988   *Mercure* v. *Saskatchewan* (1988), 83 N.R. 81.

Mia
1985   *Re Mia and Medical Services Commission of British Columbia* (1985), 17
          D.L.R. (4th) 385.

Miller
1985   *Miller* v. *The Queen* (1985), 23 C.C.C. (3d) 97.

Miller and Cockriell
1976   *The Queen* v. *Miller and Cockriell* (1976), 70 D.L.R. (3d) 324.

Miranda
1966   *Miranda* v. *Arizona* 384 U.S. 436 (1966).

Mitchell
1975   *Mitchell* v. *The Queen* (1975), 24 C.C.C.(2d) 241.

Mood Video
1987   *R.* v. *Mood Video* (1987), 33 C.C.C. (3d) 221.

Morgentaler
1975   *Morgentaler* v. *The Queen* (1975), 20 C.C.C. (2d) 449 (Supreme Court of Canada).
1985   *R.* v. *Morgentaler, Smoling and Scott* (1985), 48 C.R. (3d) 1 (Ontario Court of Appeal).
1988   *Morgentaler, Smoling and Scott* v. *The Queen* (1988), 37 C.C.C. (3d) 449 (Supreme Court of Canada).

Morin
1985   *Re Morin and National SHU Review Committee et al.* (1985), 20 C.C.C. (3d) 123.

Morrissey
1972   *Morrissey* v. *Brewer*, 408 U.S. 471 (1972).

National Citizens' Coalition
1984   *National Citizens' Coalition Inc.—Coalition Nationale Des Citoyens Inc. et al.* v. *Attorney General for Canada* (1984), 11 D.L.R. (4th) 48.

Neely
1985   *R.* v. *Neely* (1985), 22 C.C.C. (3d) 73.

New
1987   *R.* v. *New* (*The Lawyers Weekly*, October 30, 1987: 1).

Nicholson
1978   *Nicholson* v. *Haldimand-Norfolk Regional Board of Commissioners of Police*, [1979] 1 S.C.R. 311.

Noble
1984   *R.* v. *Noble* (1984), 16 C.C.C. (3d) 146.

Oakes
1983   *R.* v. *Oakes* (1983), 2 C.C.C (3d) 339 (Ontario Court of Appeal).
1986   *R.* v. *Oakes* (1986), 26 D.L.R. (4th) 20 (Supreme Court of Canada).

Oil, Chemical and Atomic Workers International Union
1985   *Oil, Chemical and Atomic Workers International Union, Local 16–601* v. *Imperial Oil Ltd.*, [1963] S.C.R. 584.

Oldfield
1987   *R.* v. *Oldfield* (1987), 35 C.C.C. (3d) 95.

Ontario Chrysler
1987   *Re Ontario Chrysler (1977) Ltd and Rush* (1987), 39 D.L.R. (4th) 100.

Operation Dismantle
1983   *The Queen et al.* v. *Operation Dismantle et al.*, [1983] 1 F.C. 745 (Trial Division).
1984   *The Queen et al.* v. *Operation Dismantle et al.* (1984), 3 D.L.R. (4th) 193 (Federal Court of Appeal).
1985   *Operation Dismantle Inc. et al.* v. *The Queen* (1985), 18 D.L.R. (4th) 481 (Supreme Court of Canada).

OPSEU
1987   *Ontario Public Service Employees Union et al.* v. *National Citizens Coalition et al.* (1987), 39 D.L.R. (4th) 449.

Paquette
1987   *R.* v. *Paquette (No.2)* (1987), 46 D.L.R. (4th) 81.

Pasqua Hospital
1987   *Re Pasqua Hospital and Harmatiuk* (1987), 42 D.L.R. (4th) 134.

Penikett
1987a   *Penikett* v. *The Queen* (1987), 43 D.L.R. (4th) 324 (Yukon Territory Supreme Court).
1987b   *Penikett* v. *The Queen* (1987), 45 D.L.R. (4th) 108 (Yukon Territory Court of Appeal).

Pett
1968   *Pett* v. *Greyhound Racing Ass'n Ltd.*, [1968] 2 All E.R. 545.

Phillips
1986   *A.G.N.S.* v. *Phillips* (1986), 34 D.L.R. (4th) 633.

Piercey
1986   *Piercey* v. *General Bakeries Ltd.* (1986), 31 D.L.R. (4th) 373.

Plessy
1896   *Plessy* v. *Ferguson,* 163 U.S. 537 (1896).

Pohoretsky
1987   *Pohoretsky* v. *The Queen* (1987), 33 C.C.C. (3d) 398.

Public Service Alliance of Canada
1984   *Public Service Alliance of Canada* v. *The Queen* (1984), 11 D.L.R. (4th) 337 (Federal Court Trial Division); 387 (Federal Court of Appeal).
1987   *Public Service Alliance of Canada et al.* v. *The Queen in Right of Canada et al.* (1987), 38 D.L.R. (4th) 249 (Supreme Court of Canada).

Quebec Protestant School Boards
1982   *Quebec Protestant School Boards* v. *Attorney General of Quebec (No. 2)* (1982), 140 D.L.R. (3d) 33.
1983   *Attorney General of Quebec* v. *Quebec Protestant School Boards* (1983), 1 D.L.R. (4th) 573 (Quebec Court of Appeal).
1984   *Attorney General of Quebec* v. *Quebec Protestant School Boards* (1984), 10 D.L.R. (4th) 321 (Supreme Court of Canada).

R.
1986   *Regina* v. *R* (1986), 28 C.C.C. (3d) 188.

Rahey
1987   *Rahey* v. *The Queen* (1987), 33 C.C.C. (3d) 289.

Rao
1984   *R.* v. *Rao* (1984), 12 C.C.C. (3d) 97.

Re Alberta Statutes
1938   *Re Alberta Statutes,* [1938] S.C.R. 100.

Re Anti-Inflation Act
1976   *Reference Re Anti-Inflation Act* (1976), 68 D.L.R. (3d) 452.

Re Board of Commerce Act
1922.   *In re the Board of Commerce Act, 1919, and the Combines and Fair Prices Act, 1919,* [1922] 1 A.C. 191.

Re Constitution of Canada
1981   *Re Constitution of Canada* (1981), 125 D.L.R. (3d) 1.

Re Criminal Code, ss.193 and 195.1
>1987   *Reference re Sections 193 and 195.1(1)(c) of the Criminal Code* (1987), 38 C.C.C. (3d) 408.

Re Education Act
>1984   *Reference Re Education Act of Ontario and Minority Language Education Rights* (1984), 10 D.L.R. (4th) 491.
>1986   *Reference re an Act to Amend the Education Act* (1986), 25 D.L.R. (4th) 1 (Ontario Court of Appeal).
>1987   *Reference Re An Act to Amend the Education Act (Ontario)* (1987), 40 D.L.R. (4th) 18 (Supreme Court of Canada).

Re Manitoba Language Rights
>1985   *Reference re Language Rights under the Manitoba Act, 1870 (No. 1)*, (1985), 19 D.L.R. (4th) 1.

Re Motor Vehicle Act (B.C.)
>1985   *Re s. 94(2) of Motor Vehicle Act (B.C.)* (1985), 24 D.L.R. (4th) 536.

Re P. E. I. Lands Protection Act
>1987   *Reference Re Prince Edward Island Lands Protection Act* (1987), 40 D.L.R. (4th) 1.

Re Public Service Employee Relations Act (Alberta)
>1987   *Reference Re Public Service Employee Relations Act, Labour Relations Act and Police Officers Collective Bargaining Act* (1987), 38 D.L.R. (4th) 161.

Re Use of French in Criminal Proceedings in Saskatchewan
>1987   *Reference re: Use of French in Criminal Proceedings in Saskatchewan* (1987), 44 D.L.R. (4th) 16.

Re Workers' Compensation Act (Nfld.)
>1987   *Re ss. 32, 34, Workers' Compensation Act, 1983* (1987), 44 D.L.R. (4th) 501.

Red Hot Video
>1985   *R. v. Red Hot Video Ltd.* (1985), 45 C.R. (3d) 36.

Retail, Wholesale & Department Store Union
>1985   *Re Retail, Wholesale & Department Store Union, Locals 544, 496, 635 and 955 et al. and Government of Saskatchewan et al.* (1985), 19 D.L.R. (4th) 609 (Saskatchewan Court of Appeal).
>1987   *Government of Saskatchewan et al. v. Retail, Wholesale & Department Store Union, Locals 544, 635 & 955 et al.* (1987), 38 D.L.R. (4th) 277 (Supreme Court of Canada).

Robertson
>1987   *R. v. Robertson* (1987), 33 C.C.C. (3d) 481.

Robertson and Rosetanni
>1963   *Robertson and Rosetanni v. The Queen* (1963), 41 D.L.R. (2d) 485.

Rocket and Price
>1988   *Royal College of Dental Surgeons (Ont.) et al. v. Rocket and Price* (1988), 27 O.A.C. 52.

Roe
>1973   *Roe v. Wade* 410 U.S. 113 (1973).

Rose
>1973   *Rose v. R.* (1973), 22 C.R.N.S. 46.

338   CASES

R. V. P. Enterprises
   1987   *Re R. V. P. Enterprises Ltd. and Minister of Consumer & Corporate Affairs* (1987), 37 D.L.R. (4th) 148.

San Antonio School District
   1973   *San Antonio School District* v. *Rodriguez* 411 U.S. 1 (1973).

Saumur
   1953   *Saumur* v. *City of Quebec*, [1953] 2 S.C.R. 299.

Schachter
   1988   *Schachter* v. *Canada Employment and Immigration Commission* (Federal Court Trial Division, June 7, 1988—unreported).

Schmidt
   1987   *Schmidt* v. *The Queen* (1987), 33 C.C.C. (3d) 193.

Seaboyer
   1987   *Re Seaboyer and the Queen; Re Gayme and the Queen* (1987), 37 C.C.C. (3d) 53.

Sellars
   1980   *Sellars* v. *The Queen* (1980), 52 C.C.C. (2d) 345.

Seo
   1986   *R.* v. *Seo* (1986), 25 C.C.C. (3d) 385.

Shewchuk
   1986   *Re Shewchuk* v. *Ricard* (1986), 28 D.L.R. (4th) 429.

Sibbeston
   1988   *Sibbeston* v. *Attorney General of Northwest Territories*, [1988] N.W.T.R. 38 (Northwest Territories Court of Appeal).

Sieben
   1987   *Sieben* v. *The Queen* (1987), 32 C.C.C. (3d) 574.

Silano
   1987   *Silano* v. *B.C. (Govt.)*, [1987] 5 W.W.R. 739.

Sinclair
   1986   *R.* v. *Kent, Sinclair and Gode* (1986), 27 C.C.C. (3d) 405.

Singh
   1985   *Re Singh and Minister of Employment and Immigration and 6 other appeals* (1985), 17 D.L.R. (4th) 422.

Skinner
   1987   *R.* v. *Skinner* (1987), 35 C.C.C. (3d) 203.

Smith
   1987   *Smith* v. *The Queen* (1987), 34 C.C.C. (3d) 97.

Smith, Kline & French Laboratories
   1985   *Smith, Kline & French Laboratories Ltd. et al.* v. *Attorney General of Canada* (1985), 24 D.L.R. (4th) 321 (Federal Court Trial Division).
   1986   *Smith, Kline & French Laboratories Ltd. et al.* v. *Attorney General of Canada* (1986), 34 D.L.R. (4th) 584 (Federal Court of Appeal).

Snell
   1987   *Re Snell and Workers' Compensation Board of British Columbia* (1987), 42 D.L.R. (4th) 160.

Société des Acadiens
1986   *Société des Acadiens* v. *Ass' n of Parents, Etc.* (1986), 27 D.L.R. (4th) 406.

Sparrow
1987   *Sparrow* v. *R. et al.*,[1987] 2 W.W.R. 577.

Switzman
1957   *Switzman* v. *Elbing*, [1957] S.C.R. 285.

Therens
1985   *R.* v. *Therens* (1985), 18 C.C.C. (3d) 481.

Thomsen
1988   *R.* v. *Thomsen* (Supreme Court of Canada, April 28, 1988—unreported).

Thomson Newspapers Ltd.
1986   *Thomson Newspapers Ltd. et al.* v. *Director of Investigation and Research et al.* (1986), 30 C.C.C. (3d) 145.

Thornburgh
1986   *Thornburgh* v. *American College of Obstetricians*, 106 S. Ct. 2169 (1986).

Thorson
1975   *Thorson* v. *Attorney General of Canada*, [1975] 1 S.C.R. 138.

Tiny Separate School Trustees
1928   *Tiny Separate School Trustees* v. *The King*, [1928] A.C. 363.

Tomen
1987   *Re Tomen and Federation of Women Teachers' Associations of Ontario* (1987), 43 D.L.R. (4th) 255.

Toronto Electric Commissioners
1925   *Toronto Electric Commissioners* v. *Snider*, [1925] A.C. 396.

Turpin
1987   *R.* v. *Turpin, Siddiqui and Clauzel* (1987), 60 C.R. (3d) 63.

Union Colliery
1899   *Union Colliery of British Columbia Ltd.* v. *Bryden*, [1899] A.C. 580.

Vaillancourt
1987   *R.* v. *Vaillancourt* (1987), 39 C.C.C. (3d) 118.

Videoflicks
1984   *R.* v. *Videoflicks Ltd. et al.* (1984), 14 D.L.R. (4th) 10.

Virginia State Board Of Pharmacy
1976   *Virginia State Board of Pharmacy* v. *Virginia Citizens Consumer Council*, 425 U.S. 748 (1976).

Weatherall
1987   *Weatherall* v. *Attorney General of Canada*, [1988] 1 F.C. 369.

Wigglesworth
1987   *R.* v. *Wigglesworth* (1987), 37 C.C.C. (3d) 385.

Wilson
1987   *Re Wilson and Medical Services Commission* (1987), 36 D.L.R. (4th) 31 (British Columbia Supreme Court).
1988   *Wilson* v. *British Columbia (Medical Services Commission)* (British Columbia Court of Appeal, August 5, 1988—unreported).

Wolff
1974   *Wolff* v. *McDonnell*, 418 U.S. 539 (1974).

Wood
1982   *R.* v. *Wood* (1982), 31 C.R. (3d) 374 (Nova Scotia Provincial Magistrates' Court); (1983), 6 C.C.C. (3d) 478 (Nova Scotia Supreme Court—Appeal Division).

Wray
1970   *R.* v. *Wray*, [1970] 4 C.C.C. 1.

Zanganeh
1988   *Zanganeh* v. *Canadian Security Intelligence Service* (Federal Court Trial Division, April 21, 1988—unreported).

Ziegler
1983   *Ziegler et al.* v. *Hunter, Director of Investigation & Research et al.* (1983), 8 D.L.R. (4th) 648.

STATUTES

An Act to amend the Canada Elections Act, 1983 (Can.) 1980–81–82–83 Chap. 164.
An Act to amend the Criminal Code (Capital Murder), 1961 (Can.) 1960–61 Chap. 44.
An Act to amend the Criminal Code (victims of crime), 1988 (Can.) Chap. 30.
An Act to amend the Retail Business Holidays Act, 1987 (Ont.) Chap. 36.
An Act to amend the Supreme Court Act, 1975 (Can.) 1974–75–76, Chap. 18.
Anti-Inflation Act, 1976 (Can.) 1974–75–76, Chap. 75.
Bill C–55, 1987 (*An Act to amend the Immigration Act, 1976*), House of Commons, First Reading May 5, 1987.
Bill C–60, 1978 (*An Act to amend the Constitution of Canada*), House of Commons, First Reading June 20, 1978.
Bill C–84, 1987 (*An Act to amend the Immigration Act, 1976*), House of Commons, First Reading August 11, 1987.
Canadian Security Intelligence Act, 1984 (Can.) Chap. 21.
Charter of the French Language, 1977 (Que.) Chap. 5.
Combines Investigation Act Amendment, 1986 (Can.) Chap. 26.
Constitutional Amendment Proclamation, 1983 (Can.) SI/84–102.
Consumer Protection Act, 1978 (Que.) Chap. 9.
Criminal Law Amendment Act 1975 (Can.) 1974–75–76 Chap. 93.
Day of Rest Act, 1985 (N.B.) Chap. D–4.2.
Day of Rest Act, 1985 (P.E.I.) Chap. 12.
Education Act Amendment, 1986 (Ont.) Chap. 29.
Holiday Shopping Regulation Act, 1980 (B.C.) Chap. 17.
Human Rights Code, 1981 (Ont.) Chap. 53.
Immigration Act, 1976 (Can.) Chap. 52.
Income Tax Act Amendment, 1986 (Can.) Chap.6.
Labour Relations Act, 1980 (Ont.), R.S.O. Chap. 228.
Lord's Day Act, The, 1970 (Can.) R.S.C. 1970, Chap. L–13.
Municipal Government Amendment Act, 1985 (Alta.) Chap. 43.
Official Language Act, 1890 (Man.) Chap. 14.
Official Language Act, The, 1974 (Que.) Chap. 6.
Official Languages Act, The, 1969 (Can.) Chap. 54.
Parole Regulations, 1978 (Can.) SOR/78–494.
Postal Services Continuation Act, 1978 (Can.) Chap. 1.
Postal Services Continuation Act, 1987, The, (Can.) Chap. 40.
Racial Discrimination Act, The, 1944 (Ont.) Chap. 51.
Retail Business Holidays Act, 1976 (Ont.) Chap. 453.
Retail Business Uniform Closing Day Act, 1985 (N.S.) Chap. 6.
Saskatchewan Bill of Rights Act, 1947 (Sask.) Chap. 35.
Saskatchewan Government Employees Union Dispute Settlement Act, 1986 (Sask.) 1984–85–86 Chap. 111.
War Measures Act, 1970 (Can.) R.S.C. 1970 Chap. 288.

REFERENCES

Adamson, Nancy, Linda Briskin, and Margaret McPhail
1988   *Feminist Organizing for Change: The Contemporary Women's Movement in Canada.* Toronto: Oxford University Press.

Allaire, Yvan, and Jean-Marie Toulouse
1973   *Recherche sur la Situation Socio-Économique et Satisfaction des Chefs de Ménage Franco-Ontariens.* Ottawa: L'Association Canadienne-Française de l'Ontario.

American Correctional Association
1987   *Juvenile and Adult Correctional Departments, Institutions, Agencies and Paroling Authorities. United States and Canada.* College Park, Maryland: American Correctional Association.

Amsterdam, Anthony G.
1970   The Supreme Court and the Rights of Suspects in Criminal Cases. *New York University Law Review* 45: 785.

Anglejan, Alison, d'
1984   Language Planning in Quebec: An Historical Overview and Future Trends. In *Conflict and Language Planning in Quebec,* ed. by Richard Y. Bourhis, 29. Avon: Multilingual Matters Ltd.

Aranella, Peter
1983   Rethinking the Functions of Criminal Procedure: The Warren and Burger Courts' Competing Ideologies. *Georgia Law Journal* 72: 185.

Armstrong, Pat, and Hugh Armstrong
1983   *A Working Majority: What Women Must Do For Pay.* Ottawa: Canadian Advisory Council on the Status of Women.

Assembly of First Nations
1987   *Brief Analysis of Federal Constitutional Proposals,* (February 19–20). Toronto: Assembly of First Nations (National Indian Brotherhood). (In the possession of the author.)

Bader, Eleanor J.
1988   The connection between population control and women's status. *Utne Reader* 27: 89.

Baker, Liva
1983   *Miranda: Crime, Law, and Politics.* New York: Atheneum.

Banks, Margaret A.
1986   Defining "Constitution of the Province": The Crux of the Manitoba Language Controversy. *McGill Law Journal* 31: 466.

Bayefsky, Anne F., and Mary Eberts, eds.
1985   *Equality Rights and the Canadian Charter of Rights and Freedoms.* Toronto: Carswell.

Beatty, David M.
1987   *Putting the Charter to Work: Designing a Constitutional Labour Code.* Kingston: McGill-Queen's University Press.
1988   Cross-examining candidates for the Supreme Court. *The Globe and Mail* (May 27) A7.

Bekar, Lorena
1988   We can't have one without the other: Abortion control requires better birth control. *The Globe and Mail* (May 24) A7.

Bell-Rowbotham, Beverly, and Craig L. Boydell
1972   Crime in Canada: A Distributional Analysis. In *Deviant Behaviour and Societal Reaction*, ed. by Craig L. Boydell, Carl F. Grindstaff, and Paul C. Whitehead, 93. Toronto: Holt, Rinehart and Winston.

Bennet
1987   No Strangers in Paradise: Canada's Refugee Policy. *The Canadian Forum* 67 (No. 771).

Berger, Thomas R.
1988   Two crucial strikes against Meech Lake. *The Globe and Mail* (May 20) A7.

Berkman, Ronald
1979   *Opening the Gates: The Rise of the Prisoners' Movement.* Lexington: D.C. Heath.

Berry, Mary Frances
1986   *Why ERA Failed: Politics, Women's Rights, and the Amending Process of the Constitution.* Bloomington: Indiana University Press.

Bilodeau, Roger
1986   La Judiciarisation des Conflicts Linguistiques au Canada. *Les Cahiers de Droit* 27: 215.

Bird, R. M.
1979   *Financing Canadian Government: A Quantitative Overview.* Toronto: Canadian Tax Foundation.

Black, Errol
1988   The State of Canada's Unions. *Canadian Dimension* 21 (No.8): 28.

Block, Fred
1977   The Ruling Class Does Not Rule: Notes on the Marxist theory of the State. *Socialist Revolution* 33 (No. 7): 6.

Bourhis, Richard Y., ed.
1984   *Conflict and Language Planning in Quebec.* Avon: Multilingual Matters Ltd.

Boswell, James
[1791]   *The Life of Samuel Johnson, LL.D.*, Vol. 2, ed by G.B. Hill. Oxford: Clarendon Press, 1934.

Box, Stephen
1983   *Power, Crime, and Mystification.* London: Tavistock Publications.

Boyer, J. Patrick
1987   *Election Law in Canada.* Vol. 1. Toronto: Butterworths.

Braithwaite, John
1979   *Crime, Inequality and Public Policy.* London: Routledge and Kegan Paul.

Brandt, G. J.
1986   Parties and Participants in Constitutional Litigation: The Minority Language Rights Issue in Quebec and Manitoba. *University of New Brunswick Law Review* 35: 210.

Bread and Roses
1988   Reproductive Choice: Expanding the Parameters, Rejoining the Struggle. *Canadian Dimension* 22 (No. 4): 22.

Breton, Raymond and Daiva Stasiulis
1980   Linguistic Boundaries and the Cohesion of Canada. In *Cultural Boundaries and the Cohesion of Canada,* ed. by Raymond Breton, Jeffrey G. Reitz, and Victor F. Valentine. Montreal: The Institute for Research on Public Policy.

Brill, Herbert L.
1987   Letter to the Editor. *Canadian Lawyer* (March) 2.

Brillinger, Don
1985   Immigration Act s. 71 struck down. *Ontario Lawyers Weekly* (April 26) 10.

Briskin, Linda, and Lynda Yanz
1983   *Union Sisters: Women in the Labour Movement.* Toronto: The Women's Press.

Bronstein, Alvin J.
1980   Prisoners' Rights: A History. In *Legal Rights of Prisoners,* ed. by Geoffrey P. Alpert, 19. Beverley Hills: Sage Publications.

Campbell, Charles
1984   The Canadian Left and the Charter of Rights. *Socialist Studies* 2: 30.

Canada
1950   *Proceedings of the Special Committee of the Senate of Canada on Human Rights and Fundamental Freedoms. Report of the Committee.* Ottawa: King's Printer.
1972   *Cannabis: A Report of the Commission of Inquiry into the Non-Medical Use of Drugs.* Ottawa: Information Canada.
1977a   *Report of the Committee on the Operation of the Abortion Law.* Ottawa: Supply and Services Canada.
1977b   *Third Report of the Standing Committee on Justice and Legal Affairs, Sub-Committee on the Penitentiary System in Canada* Ottawa: Parliament of Canada.
1978   *A Time for Action: Toward the Renewal of the Canadian Federation.* Ottawa: Supply and Services Canada.
1980–81 *Minutes of Proceedings and Evidence of the Special Committee of the Senate and of the House of Commons on the Constitution.*
1981   *Solicitor General's Study of Conditional Release.* Ottawa: Solicitor General of Canada
1982a   *The Charter of Rights and Freedoms: A Guide for Canadians.* Ottawa: Government of Canada.
1982b   *The Constitution and You.* Ottawa: Government of Canada.
1982c   *The Criminal Law in Canadian Society.* Ottawa: Government of Canada.
1983   *Delicate Balance: A Security Intelligence Service in a Democratic Society. Report of the Special Committee of the Senate on the Canadian Security Intelligence Service.* Ottawa: Supply and Services Canada.
1985   *Canada Year Book 1985.* Ottawa: Supply and Services Canada.
1986   *Narcotic, Controlled and Restricted Drug Statistics 1985.* Ottawa: Department of National Health and Welfare, Bureau of Dangerous Drugs, Health Protection Branch.
1987a   *Annual Report of the Security Intelligence Review Committee, 1986–87.* Ottawa: Supply and Services Canada.
1987b   *Narcotic, Controlled and Restricted Drug Statistics 1986.* Ottawa: Department of National Health and Welfare, Bureau of Dangerous Drugs, Health Protection Branch.
1987c   *Sentencing Reform: A Canadian Approach. Report of the Canadian Sentencing Commission.* Ottawa: Supply and Services Canada.

Canadian Civil Liberties Association
1987   Letter to Ken James, M. P. (December 4).

Carrothers, A.W.R., E. E. Palmer and W. B. Rayner
1986   *Collective Bargaining Law in Canada.* 2nd ed. Toronto: Butterworths.

Castel, J.-G.
1983   The Canadian Charter of Rights and Freedoms. *Canadian Bar Review* 61: 1.

Chan, Janet B.L., and Richard V. Ericson
1981   *Decarceration and the Economy of Penal Reform.* Toronto: University of Toronto Centre of Criminology.

Clancy, James, Wayne Roberts, David Spencer, and John Ward
1985   *All for One: Arguments from the Labour Trial of the Century on the Real Meaning of Unionism.* Toronto: Ontario Public Service Employees Union.

Clement, Wallace
1975   *The Canadian Corporate Elite: An Analysis of Economic Power.* Toronto: McClelland and Stewart.

Cohen, Marjorie Griffin
1987   *Free Trade and the Future of Women's Work: Manufacturing and Service Industries.* Toronto: Garamond Press.
1988   Giving fathers an equal break: Paternity leave should be paid—but not out of mothers' pockets. *The Globe and Mail* (February 29) A7.

Coleman, William D.
1984   Social Class and Language Policies in Quebec. In *Conflict and Language Planning in Quebec,* ed. by Richard Y. Bourhis, 130. Avon: Multilingual Matters Ltd.

Cook, Ramsay
1987   Letter to the Editor. *The Globe and Mail* (November 28) D7.

Council of the Canadian Bar Association
1959   Resolution. *Canadian Bar Review* 37: 263.

Craven, Paul
1980   *An Impartial Umpire: Industrial Relations and the Canadian State 1900–1911.* Toronto: University of Toronto Press.

Dahl, Robert
1956   *A Preface to Democratic Theory.* Chicago: University of Chicago Press.

Davies, Thomas Y.
1983   A Hard Look at What We Know (and Still Need to Learn) About the "Costs" of the Exclusionary Rule: The NIJ Study and Other Studies of "Lost" Arrests. *American Bar Foundation Research Journal* 1982: 611.

Davis, Angela
1983   *Women, Race and Class.* New York: Vintage Books.

Deschênes, Jules
1974   Le Rôle Législatif du Pouvoir Judiciaire. *Revue de Droit Université de Sherbrooke* 5: 1.
1979   *The Sword and the Scales.* Toronto: Butterworths.

Deslauriers, Ignace-J., J.C.S.
1980   *La Cour supérieure du Québec et ses juges 1849–1er janvier 1980.* Québec: Bibliothèque National du Québec.

Dietrich, Nicholas E. J.
1986   Participating in Law Day: What's in it for Lawyers? *Ontario Lawyers Weekly* (May 7) 4.

Doern, Russell
1985   *The Battle over Bilingualism: The Manitoba Language Question, 1983–85.* Winnipeg: Cambridge Publishers.

Dominion Bureau of Statistics
1966   *Crime Statistics 1965.* Ottawa: Queen's Printer.

Drache, Daniel
1987   North American Integration. In *The Free Trade Deal*, ed. by Duncan Cameron. Toronto: James Lorimer & Co.
1988   Canada in American Empire. *Canadian Journal of Political and Social Theory* 12 (Nos. 1–2): 212.

Drache, Daniel, and Duncan Cameron, eds.
1985   *The Other MacDonald Report*. Toronto: James Lorimer.

Dworkin, Ronald
1977a   No Right Answer? *New York University Law Review* 53: 1.
1977b   *Taking Rights Seriously*. London: Duckworth.
1985   *A Matter of Principle*. Cambridge: Harvard University Press.
1986   *Law's Empire*. Cambridge: Belknap Press.

Ehrenreich, Barbara
1988   Feminism's next wave. *Utne Reader* 26: 102.

Ehrmann, H. W.
1976   *Comparative Legal Cultures*. Englewood Cliffs, New Jersey: Prentice-Hall.

Ely, John Hart
1980   *Democracy and Distrust: A Theory of Judicial Review*. Cambridge: Harvard University Press.

Erasmus, Georges
1987a   *Opening Remarks to the First Ministers Conference on Aboriginal Constitutional Affairs*, March 26, 1987. Ottawa: Assembly of First Nations (National Indian Brotherhood).
1987b   *Presentation to the Special Joint Committee on the 1987 Constitutional Accord*, August 19, 1987. Ottawa: Assembly of First Nations (National Indian Brotherhood).

Ericson, Richard V.
1982   *Reproducing Order: A Study of Police Patrol Work*. Toronto: University of Toronto Press.

Ericson, Richard V., and Patricia M. Baranek
1982   *The Ordering of Justice: A Study of Accused Persons As Dependents in the Criminal Justice Process*. Toronto: University of Toronto Press.

Etherington, Brian
1987   Note. *Canadian Bar Review* 66: 818.

Everywoman's Almanac
1988   *Everywoman's Almanac, 1988*. Toronto: The Women's Press.

Family Planning Perspectives
1985   American Adults Approval of Legal Abortion Has Remained Virtually Unchanged Since 1972. *Family Planning Perspectives* 17: 181.

Fillmore, Nick
1986   The Right Stuff: An Inside Look at the National Citizens' Coalition. *This Magazine* 20 (No.2): 4.

Finlay, Richard J.
1987   Cast off the cloak of secrecy. *The Globe and Mail* (October 22) A7.

Forcese, Dennis
1975   *The Canadian Class Structure*. 2nd ed. Toronto: McGraw-Hill Ryerson.

Foucault, Michel
1977   *Discipline and Punish: The Birth of the Prison*, trans. by Alan Sheridan. New York: Pantheon Books.

Francis, Diane
1984   Paul Desmarais started with an ailing bus business but now he steers a huge enter-
        prise that netted $63 million last year. *The Toronto Star* (October 14, 1984) B1.

Fraser, Graham
1988   Canada's tobacco backers are down to their last puff. *The Globe and Mail* (January
        30, 1988) D1.

Frideres, James S.
1983   *Native People in Canada: Contemporary Conflicts*. Toronto: Prentice-Hall Canada.

Fudge, Judy
1987   *Conciliation and Repression: Federal Labour Relations Policy during the 1930s*.
        Osgoode Hall Law Journal Faculty Seminars. Toronto: Osgoode Hall Law School
        of York University.
1988a   Labour, the New Constitution and Old Style Liberalism. *Queens Law Journal* 15:1.
1988b   The Public/Private Distinction: The Possibilities of and the Limits to the Use of
        Charter Litigation to Further Feminist Struggles. *Osgoode Hall Law Journal* 25
        (forthcoming).

Galloway, Russell
1982   *The Rich and the Poor in Supreme Court History 1790–1982*. Greenbrae, Califor-
        nia: Paradigm Press.

Gambitta, Richard A. L.
1981   Litigation, Judicial Deference, and Policy Change. In *Governing Through Courts*,
        ed. by Richard A. L. Gambitta, Marlynn L. May, and James C. Foster, 259. Beverly
        Hills: Sage Publications.

Gibson, Dale
1986   *The Law of the Charter: General Principles*. Toronto: Carswell.

Glasbeek, Harry J.
1984   Why Corporate Deviance is not treated as a Crime: The Need to Make "Profits" a
        Dirty Word. *Osgoode Hall Law Journal* 22: 393.

Glasbeek, Harry J., and R. A. Hasson
1977   Fault—The Great Hoax. In *Studies in Canadian Tort Law*, ed. by Lewis Klar.
        Toronto: Butterworths.
1987   Some Reflections on Canadian Legal Education. *Modern Law Review* 50: 777.

Glasbeek, Harry J., and Michael Mandel
1984   The Legalization of Politics in Advanced Capitalism: The Canadian Charter of
        Rights and Freedoms. *Socialist Studies* 2: 84.

Goff, Colin H., and Charles E. Reasons
1978   *Corporate Crime in Canada: A Critical Analysis of Anti-Combines Legislation*.
        Scarborough: Prentice-Hall of Canada.

Granatstein, J. L.
1986   *Canada 1957–1967. The Years of Uncertainty and Innovation*. Toronto: McC-
        lelland and Stewart.

**Granatstein, J. L., Irving M. Abella, David J. Bercuson, R. Craig Brown, and H. Blair
Neatby**
1983   *Twentieth Century Canada*. 2nd ed. Toronto: McGraw-Hill Ryerson.

Grant, Alan
1987   *The Audio-Visual Taping of Police Interviews with Suspects and Accused Persons
        by Halton Regional Police Force Ontario, Canada. An Evaluation. Final Report*.
        Ottawa: Law Reform Commission of Canada.

Green, Mendel M.
1986   Just What *is* the Procedure for New Refugee Claims? *The Lawyers Weekly* (June 27) 4.

Greenberg, David F.
1977   The Dynamics of Oscillatory Punishment Processes. *The Journal of Criminal Law and Criminology* 68: 643.

Grenier, Gilles
1985   Health Care Costs in Canada: Past and Future Trends. In *Income Distribution and Economic Security in Canada*, 251. Vol. 1 of studies commissioned as part of the research program of the Royal Commission on the Economic Union and Development Prospects for Canada (Francois Vaillancourt, Research Coordinator). Toronto: University of Toronto Press.

Gross, Hyman
1979   *A Theory of Criminal Justice*. New York: Oxford University Press.

Gwyn, Richard
1987   Britain considers its own charter of rights. *The Toronto Star* (February 6) A21.

Habermas, Jürgen
1975   *Legitimation Crisis*, trans. by Thomas McCarthy. Boston: Beacon Press.

Hagan, John, A.R. Gillis, and Janet Chan
1978   Explaining Official Delinquency: A Spatial Study of Class, Conflict and Control. *The Sociological Quarterly* 19: 386.

Hartman, Betsy
1987   *Reproductive Rights and Wrongs*. New York: Harper and Row.

Hartman, Grace
1983   Labour unions: What can they contribute to economic recovery. *Canadian Dimension* (May) 10.

Hasson, Reuben
1980   Tax Evasion and Social Security Abuse—Some Tentative Observations. *Canadian Taxation* 2 (No. 2): 98.
1981   The Cruel War: Social Security Abuse in Canada. *Canadian Taxation* 3 (No. 3): 114.

Hathaway, James C.
1988   Refugee Law in Canada. In *Refugee and Asylum Law Today*, ed. by G. S. Goodwin-Gill. Oxford: Oxford University Press.

Hay, Douglas
1975   Property, Authority and the Criminal Law. In *Albion's Fatal Tree: Crime and Society in Eighteenth Century England* ed. by Douglas Hay et al. London: Allen Lane.

Hogarth, John
1971   *Sentencing as a Human Process*. Toronto: University of Toronto Press.

Hogg, Peter W.
1982   Comment. *Canadian Bar Review* 60: 307
1985   *Constitutional Law of Canada*. 2nd ed. Toronto: Carswell.
1988   *Meech Lake Constitutional Accord Annotated*. Toronto: Carswell.

Hooker, Stephen
1988   It's still a question of black and white. *The Globe and Mail* (May 9, 1988) A7.

Hovius, Berend, and Robert Martin
1983   The Canadian Charter of Rights and Freedoms in the Supreme Court of Canada. *Canadian Bar Review* 61: 354.

How, W. G.
1948   The Case for a Canadian Bill of Rights. *Canadian Bar Review* 26: 759.

Huff, C. Ronald
1980   The Discovery of Prisoners' Rights: A Sociological Analysis. In *Legal Rights of Prisoners*, ed. by Geoffrey P. Alpert, 47. Beverley Hills: Sage Publications.

Hunter, Alfred A.
1981   *Class Tells. On Social Inequality in Canada.* Toronto: Butterworths.

Hutchinson, Allan
1987   Unions Have to Go Political After Letdown of the Charter. *The Globe and Mail* (April 16) A7.

Jacobs, James B.
1977   *Stateville: The Penitentiary in Mass Society.* Chicago: University of Chicago Press.
1980   The Prisoners' Rights Movement and Its Impacts, 1960–1980. In *Crime and Justice: An Annual Review of Research,* ed by N. Morris and M. Tonry. 2: 429.

Jewett, Pauline
1983   Letter to all members of the NDP Caucus, August 11, 1983. (In the possession of the author.)

Johnson, Arthur
1984   Old Friends: Business Connections overshadow Tory leader's humble heritage. *The Globe and Mail* (August 20) A1.

Jones, Deborah
1988   N.S. Blacks: A heritage of poverty. *The Globe and Mail* (July 2) D1.

Kay, R. S.
1982   Courts as Constitution-Makers in Canada and the United States. *Supreme Court Law Review* 4: 23.

Kline, Marlee
1989   Race, Racism, and Feminist Legal Theory. *Harvard Women's Law Journal*, forthcoming.

Laband, David, and Deborah Hendry Heinbuch
1987   *Blue Laws: The History, Economics, and Politics of Sunday-Closing Laws.* Lexington: D.C. Heath.

Lachapelle, Rejean
1980   Evolution of Ethnic and Linguistic Composition. In *Cultural Boundaries and the Cohesion of Canada,* ed. by Raymond Breton, Jeffrey G. Reitz, and Victor F. Valentine. Montreal: The Institute for Research on Public Policy.

LaFave, Wayne R.
1987   *Search and Seizure: A Treatise on the Fourth Amendment.* Vol. 1. 2nd ed. St. Paul, Minn.: West Publishing.

La Forest, Gerard V.
1983   The Canadian Charter of Rights and Freedoms: An Overview. *Canadian Bar Review* 61: 20.

Lahey, Kathleen A.
1987   Feminist Theories of (In)Equality. In *Equality and Judicial Neutrality,* ed. by Sheilah L. Martin and Kathleen E. Mahoney, 71. Toronto: Carswell.

Landsberg, Michelle
1988   Jubilation: The shabby abortion law has been struck down. *The Globe and Mail* (January 30) A2.

Laskin, Bora
1959   An Inquiry into the Diefenbaker Bill of Rights. *Canadian Bar Review* 37: 77.

350 REFERENCES

Lathrop, Lynn
1988   The Morgentaler decision: The biggest step since women won the right to vote. *The Globe and Mail* (February 2) A7.

Latouche, Daniel
1983   The Constitutional Misfire of 1982. In *And No One Cheered: Federalism, Democracy and The Constitution Act,* ed. by Keith Banting and Richard Simeon, 96. Toronto: Methuen.
1986   *Canada and Quebec, Past and Future: An Essay.* Vol. 70 in the series of studies commissioned as part of the research program of the Royal Commission on the Economic Union and Development Prospects for Canada. Toronto: University of Toronto Press.

Law Reform Commission of Canada
1976a   *Report: Our Criminal Law.* Ottawa: Information Canada.
1976b   *Report: Sunday Observance.* Ottawa: Supply and Services Canada.

Law Society of Upper Canada
1980–87   *Communique. A brief informal report from the Benchers of the Law Society of Upper Canada* Nos. 95–177. Toronto: Law Society of Upper Canada.

Lewington, Jennifer
1983   At the Crossroads: The Court According to Reagan. *The Globe and Mail* (July 4, 1987) D3.

Lockhart, Kim
1986   War and Peace in Winnipeg. *Canadian Lawyer* 10 (No.2): 16.

McCloskey, Robert Green
1960   *The American Supreme Court.* Chicago: University of Chicago Press.

McCullum, Hugh, and Karmel McCullum
1975   *This Land is Not for Sale: Canada's Original People and Their Land: A Saga of Neglect, Exploitation and Conflict.* Toronto: Anglican Book Centre.

McDonald, Lynn
1983   Letter to Operation Dismantle, September 16, 1983. (In the possession of the author.)

MacKinnon, Catharine A.
1982   Feminism, Marxism, Method, and the State: An Agenda for Theory. *Signs* 7: 515
1987   *Feminism Unmodified: Discourse on Life and Law.* Cambridge: Harvard University Press.

McLeod, Cheryl Gordon
1986   Feminism's Idealist Error. *New York University Review of Law and Social Change* 14: 277.

McMahon, Maeve W., and Richard V. Ericson
1987   Reforming the Police and Policing Reform. In *State Control: Criminal Justice Politics in Canada,* ed. by R. S. Ratner and John L. McMullan, 38. Vancouver: University of British Columbia Press.

McNaught, Kenneth
1976   *The Pelican History of Canada.* Rev. ed. Harmondsworth: Penguin Books.

McPhedran, Marilou
1983   Address to the Conference "Critical Perspectives on the Constitution." University of Western Ontario, March 1983.

McQuaig, Linda
1987   *Behind Closed Doors: How The Rich Won Control of Canada's Tax System...And Ended Up Richer.* Toronto: Penguin Books Canada.

McWhinney, Edward
1983   The Canadian Charter of Rights and Freedoms: The Lessons of Comparative Jurisprudence. *Canadian Bar Review* 61: 55.

Maldoff, Eric
1987   Meech pact a threat to individual rights. *The Globe and Mail* (August 20, 1987) A7.

Mallea, John R.
1984   Minority Language Education in Quebec and Anglophone Canada. In *Conflict and Language Planning in Quebec,* ed. by Richard Y. Bourhis, 221. Avon: Multilingual Matters Ltd.

Mallory, J. R.
1954   *Social Credit and the Federal Power in Canada.* Toronto: University of Toronto Press.

Malveaux, Julianne
1988   Will the feminization of power help most women? *Utne Reader* 26: 104.

Mandel, Michael
1975   Rethinking Parole. *Osgoode Hall Law Journal* 13: 501.
1979   Dworkin, Hart and the Problem of Theoretical Perspective. *Law and Society Review* 14: 57.
1983a   McDonald and the R.C.M.P. In *Law and Social Order,* by Michael Mandel, R. V. Ericson and Beth Savan. Toronto: CBC Transcripts.
1983b   *A National Referendum on the Cruise Missile.* Ottawa: Operation Dismantle Inc.
1984   Democracy, Class and Canadian Sentencing Law. *Crime and Social Justice* 21–22: 163.
1985   Democracy, Class and the National Parole Board. *Criminal Law Quarterly* 27: 159.
1986   The Legalization of Prison Discipline in Canada. *Crime and Social Justice* 26: 79.
1987   Decarceration: The Rise and Fall of Prison Populations. In *Readings in Criminology 1987,* ed. by Michael Mandel. Toronto: Osgoode Hall Law School.

Manning, Morris
1983   *Rights, Freedoms and the Courts.* Toronto: Emond-Montgomery Limited.
1986   Constitutional heartbeats and the extra-billing dispute. *Canadian Lawyer* (May 1986) 43.
1987   Practising Law in South Africa. *Canadian Lawyer* (September 1987) 10.

Mansbridge, Jane J.
1986   *Why We Lost the ERA.* Chicago: University of Chicago Press.

Mansell, Robert L., and Lawrence Copithorne
1986   Canadian Regional Economic Disparities: A Survey. In *Disparities and Interregional Adjustment,* Vol. 64 of studies commissioned as part of the research program of the Royal Commission on the Economic Union and Development Prospects for Canada, (Kenneth Norrie, Research Coordinator). Toronto: University of Toronto Press.

Manwaring, J.A.
1987   Bringing the Common Law to the Bar of Justice: A Comment on the Decision in the Case of *Dolphin Delivery Ltd.. Ottawa Law Review* 19: 413.

Marx, Karl
[1867] *Capital: A Critique of Political Economy.* Vol. 1, trans. by B. Fowkes. Harmondsworth: Penguin Books, 1976.

May, Casey
1987   Still a Boys' Club. *Canadian Lawyer* (November) 13.

Mellos, Koula
1979   Regressive Tax and Liberal Ideology. *Canadian Taxation* 1 (No.1): 16.

Miliband, Ralph
1973   *The State in Capitalist Society*. London: Quartet Books.

Miller, Roger
1984   The Response of Business Firms to the Francization Process. In *Conflict and Language Planning in Quebec,* ed. by Richard Y. Bourhis, 114. Avon: Multilingual Matters Ltd.

Milne, David
1982   *The New Canadian Constitution*. Toronto: James Lorimer.

Milner, Henry
1984   Quebec Educational Reform and the Protestant School Establishment. In *Quebec: State and Society,* ed. by Alain G. Gagnon. Toronto: Methuen.

Milner, Henry, and Sheilagh Hodgins Milner
1973   *The Decolonization of Quebec: An Analysis of Left-Wing Nationalism*. Toronto: McClelland and Stewart.

Morton, F. L.
1987   The Political Impact of the Canadian Charter of Rights and Freedoms. *Canadian Journal of Political Science* 20: 31.

Muggeridge, Anne Roche
1988   Its moral results are certain to be horrendous. *The Globe and Mail* (February 2) A7.

National Council of Welfare
1985   *Poverty Profile 1985*. Ottawa: National Council of Welfare.
1987   *Progress Against Poverty 1987*. Ottawa: National Council of Welfare.

Neudorfer, Asher
1986   Immigration—The Supreme Court Decision *vs.* Singh. *Administrative Law Journal* 2: 17.

Neville, William H.
1988   Extinguishing tobacco ads: is it a purely symbolic act? *The Globe and Mail* (June 28) A7.

New Republic
1985   TRB from Washington: Abortion Time Bomb. *New Republic* (February 25) 4.

Noonan, Sheila
1985   Pornography: Preferring the Feminist Approach of the British Columbia Court of Appeal to that of the Fraser Committee. *Criminal Reports* 45 (3d): 61.

Note
1967   Interrogations in New Haven: The Impact of Miranda. *Yale Law Journal* 76: 1519.

Nuclear Weapons Legal Action
1987   *There ought to be a law*. Ottawa: World Federalists of Canada.

O'Connor, James
1981   The Fiscal Crisis of the State Revisited: A Look at Economic Crises and Reagan's Budget Policy. *Kapitalistate* 9: 41.

Ogilvie, M. H.
1982   *Historical Introduction to Legal Studies*. Toronto: Carswell.

O'Halloran, C. H.
1947   Inherent Rights. *Obiter Dicta*, 22 (No.1): 35; (No.2): 24; (No.3): 21.

Olsen, Dennis
1980   *The State Elite*. Toronto: McClelland and Stewart.

Ontario
1987   *Fifth Annual Report of the Office of the Public Complaints Commissioner*. Toronto: Public Complaints Commissioner.

1988   *Report of the Inquiry into Motor Vehicle Accident Compensation in Ontario.* Vol. 1. Toronto: Queen's Printer for Ontario.

OPSEU
1987   *Buddy can you spare a dime?* Video tape. Toronto: Ontario Public Service Employees Union.

Orton, Maureen Jessop, and Ellen Rosenblatt
1986   *Adolescent Preganancy in Ontario: Progress in Prevention Report 2.* Hamilton: Planned Parenthood Ontario.

Osberg, Lars
1981   *Economic Inequality in Canada.* Toronto: Butterworths.

Pal, Leslie A.
1986   Relative Autonomy Revisited: The Origins of Canadian Unemployment Insurance. *Canadian Journal of Political Science* 19: 71.

Pal, Leslie A., and F. L. Morton
1986   *Bliss v. Attorney General of Canada*: From legal Defeat to Political Victory. *Osgoode Hall Law Journal* 24: 141.

Panitch, Leo
1977   *The Canadian State: Political Economy and Political Power.* Toronto: University of Toronto Press.
1988   What Does Free *Really* Mean? *Canadian Dimension* 21 (No. 8, January): 32.

Panitch, Leo, and Donald Swartz
1988   *The Assault on Trade Union Freedoms: From Consent to Coercion Revisited.* Toronto: Garamond Press.

Peck, Sidney R.
1969   A Scalogram Analysis of the Supreme Court of Canada, 1958–1967. In *Comparative Judicial Behavior; Cross-cultural Studies of Political Decision-making in the East and West,* ed. by Glendon A. Schubert and David J. Danelski. New York: Oxford University Press.

Petter, Andrew
1986   Charter loophole imperils basic right. *The Globe and Mail* (February 20) A7.
1987a   Immaculate Deception: The Charter's Hidden Agenda. *The Advocate* 45 (Pt. 6): 857.
1987b   Meech won't stall social reform in the provinces. *The Globe and Mail* (June 30) A7.

Platt, Tony
1981   Street Crime: A View from the Left. In *Crime and Social Justice,* ed. by Tony Platt and Paul Takagi. London: Macmillan.

Pope, Lori
1987   Refugees Turfed from Canada. *Obiter Dicta* (March 9) 9.

Powell, Marion
1987   *Report on Therapeutic Abortion Services in Ontario.* Toronto: Ontario Ministry of Health.

Provencher, Jean
1975   *René Lévesque: Portrait of a Québecois,* trans. by David Ellis. Toronto: Gage.

Public Service Alliance of Canada
1987   *Submission to the Special Joint Committee on the 1987 Consitutional Accord.* Ottawa: Public Service Alliance of Canada.

Quebec. Minister of State for Cultural Development
1977   *Quebec's Policy on the French Language.* Quebec: Government of Quebec.

354   REFERENCES

Rae, Bob
1987   Laws needed fast to ensure politics is kept clean. *The Globe and Mail* (March 26) A7.

Reed, Paul
1983   Justice. In *Historical Statistics of Canada*. 2nd ed. Ed. by F. H. Leacy. Ottawa: Statistics Canada.

Reitz, Jeffrey G.
1980   Immigrants, Their Descendants, and the Cohesion of Canada. In *Cultural Boundaries and the Cohesion of Canada*, ed. by Raymond Breton, Jeffrey G. Reitz, and Victor F. Valentine, 329. Montreal: The Institute for Research on Public Policy.

Resnick, Philip
1984   *Parliament vs. People: An Essay on Democracy and Canadian Political Culture.* Vancouver: New Star Books.

Roberts, Wayne
1987   Address to the Conference "The Charter of Wrongs." Faculty of Law, University of Western Ontario, March 1987.

Romanow, Roy, John Whyte and Howard Leeson
1984   *Canada...Notwithstanding: The Making of the Constitution 1976–1982.* Toronto: Carswell/Methuen.

Rubin, Eva R.
1987   *Abortion, Politics and the Courts: Roe v. Wade and Its Aftermath.* Rev. ed. New York: Greenwood Press.

Rush, Stuart
1984   Collective Rights and Collective Process: Missing Ingredients in the Canadian Constitution. *Socialist Studies* 2: 18.

Russell, Peter H.
1982.   *Leading Constitutional Decisions.* 3rd. ed. Ottawa: Carleton University Press.
1983   The Political Purposes of the Canadian Charter of Rights and Freedoms. *Canadian Bar Review* 61: 30.

Salter, Michael
1988   It's raining profits. *The Globe and Mail Report on Business Magazine* (July) 83.

Sanders, Douglas
1983   The Rights of the Aboriginal Peoples of Canada. *Canadian Bar Review* 61: 314.
1985   The Renewal of Indian Special Status. In *Equality Rights and the Canadian Charter of Rights and Freedoms*, ed. by Anne F. Bayefsky and Mary Eberts. Toronto: Carswell.

Scarborough, Norma
1988   Canadians don't need another abortion law. *The Globe and Mail* (May 17) A7.

Schmitz, Cristin
1987   No-fault insurance offends Charter: CBAO. *The Lawyers Weekly* (March 27) 1

Schneider, Herbert W.
1936   *The Fascist Government of Italy.* New York: Van Nostrand.

Schwartz, Charles
1949   Social Credit Theory and Legislation in Alberta. M. A. Thesis, Department of Political Economy, University of Manitoba.

Schwendinger, Julia, and Herman Schwendinger
1981   Rape, Sexual Inequality and Levels of Violence. *Crime and Social Justice* (Winter) 3.

Scott, F. R.
1949   Dominion Jurisdiction Over Human Rights and Fundamental Freedoms. *Canadian Bar Review* 27: 497.

Segers, M. C.
1981   Governing Abortion Policy. In *Governing Through Courts*, ed. by Richard A. L. Gambitta, Marlynn L. May and James C. Foster, 283. Beverly Hills: Sage Publications.

Seidman, Louis Michael
1980   Factual Guilt and the Burger Court: An Examination of Continuity and Change in Criminal Procedure. *Columbia Law Review* 80: 436.

Sereni, Angelo Piero
1943   *The Italian Conception of International Law.* New York: Columbia University Press.

Shaffer, Marvin
1988   It's time to make advances on Indians' fishing rights. *The Globe and Mail* (August 19) A7.

Shell, Brian
1987   Speech to the Conference "The Charter of Wrongs." Faculty of Law, University of Western Ontario, March 1987.

Sheppard, Robert, and Michael Valpy
1982   *The National Deal: The Fight for a Canadian Constitution.* Toronto: Fleet Books.

Singh, Avtar, Halena Celinski and Chas Jayewardene
1980   Ecological Correlates of Crime in Ottawa. *Canadian Journal of Criminology* 22: 78.

Slattery, Brian
1983   Override Clauses under Section 33. *Canadian Bar Review* 61: 391.
1987   The *Charter*'s Relevance to Private Litigation: Does *Dolphin* Deliver? *McGill Law Journal* 32: 905.

Slotnick, Lorne
1986   Union dues case: just how far does it reach? *The Globe and Mail* (July 14) A7.

Smiley, Donald
1981   *The Canadian Charter of Rights and Freedoms.* Toronto: Ontario Economic Council.

Smith, Joan, and William Fried
1974   *The Uses of the American Prison: Political Theory in Penal Practice.* Toronto: D.C. Heath.

Snell, James G., and Frederick Vaughan
1985   *The Supreme Court of Canada: History of the Institution.* Toronto: University of Toronto Press.

Snider, D. Laureen, and W. Gordon West
1985   A Critical Perspective on Law in the Canadian State: Delinquency and Corporate Crime. In *The New Criminologies in Canada: Crime, State and Control*, ed. by Thomas Fleming, 138. Toronto: Oxford University Press.

Social Planning Council of Metropolitan Toronto
1985   Economic Decline in Canada. In *The Other MacDonald Report*, ed. by Daniel Drache and Duncan Cameron. Toronto: James Lorimer.

Speirs, Rosemary
1987   Sorting out Sunday shopping. *The Toronto Star* (December 5) D5.

Starr, Gail
1984   Popular Rights In (and Out Of) The Constitution. *Socialist Studies* 2: 8.

Statistics Canada
1984   *Crime and Traffic Enforcement Statistics 1982.* Ottawa: Statistics Canada Centre for Justice Statistics.
1986   *Adult Correctional Services in Canada 1985–86.* Ottawa: Statistics Canada Centre for Justice Statistics.
1987a   *Canadian Crime Statistics 1986.* Ottawa: Statistics Canada Centre for Justice Statistics.
1987b   *Homicide in Canada 1986 A Statistical Perspective.* Ottawa: Statistics Canada Centre for Justice Statistics.

Stenning, Philip C.
1981   *Police Commissions and Boards in Canada.* Toronto: University of Toronto Centre of Criminology.

Stoffman, Daniel
1987   Where There's Smoke. *The Globe and Mail Report on Business Magazine* (September) 20.

Tarnopolsky, Walter Surma
1975   *The Canadian Bill of Rights.* 2nd. rev. ed. Toronto: McClelland and Stewart.

Taylor, Donald M., and Lise Dubé-Simard
1984   Language Planning and Intergroup Relations: Anglophone and Francophone Attitudes Toward the Charter of the French Language. In *Conflict and Language Planning in Quebec,* ed. by Richard Y. Bourhis, 148. Avon: Multilingual Matters Ltd.

Tepperman, Lorne
1977   *Crime Control: The Urge Toward Authority.* Toronto: McGraw-Hill Ryerson.

Thompson, Edward P.
1975   *Whigs and Hunters: The Origins of the Black Act.* Harmondsworth: Penguin Books.

Tietze, Christopher, and Stanley K. Henshaw
1986   *Induced Abortion: A World Review 1986.* 6th ed. New York: The Alan Guttmacher Institute.

Todd, Rosemary
1988   Sometimes on Sunday? *The Globe and Mail* (April 30) D2.

Treiman, Donald J.
1977   *Occupational Prestige in Comparative Perspective.* New York: Academic Press.

Trudeau, Pierre Elliott
1968   *Federalism and the French Canadians.* Toronto: Macmillan of Canada.
1987   Say goodbye to the dream of one Canada. *The Toronto Star* (May 27) A1.

Tucker, Eric
1984   The Determination of Occupational Health and Safety Standards in Ontario, 1867–1982: From the Market to Politics to…? *McGill Law Journal* 29: 260.

Tushnet, Mark
1982   Red, White and Blue: A Critical Analysis of Constitutional Law. Unpublished paper delivered at the Legal Theory Workshop Series, Faculty of Law, University of Toronto, February 12, 1982.

United Kingdom. House of Commons Foreign Affairs Committee
1981a   *Supplementary Report of the House of Commons Foreign Affairs Committee on the British North America Acts: The Role of Parliament.* London: Her Majesty's Stationery Office.

1981b   *Third Report of the House of Commons Foreign Affairs Committee on the British North America Acts: The Role of Parliament.* London: Her Majesty's Stationery Office.

United States
1978   *Criminal Victimization in the United States, 1978.* Washington: Department of Justice Bureau of Justice Statistics.
1987   *The American Constitution: Its Global Heritage.* Essays by the Staff of the Law Library of Congress on the Occasion of the Bicentennial of the Constitution of the United States. Washington: Library of Congress.

Vaillancourt, François
1985   Income Distribution and Economic Security in Canada: An Overview. In *Income Distribution and Economic Security in Canada.* Vol. 1 of studies commissioned as part of the research program of the Royal Commission on the Economic Union and Development Prospects for Canada (François Vaillancourt, Research Coordinator). Toronto: University of Toronto Press.

Valentine, Victor F.
1980   Native Peoples and Canadian Society: A Profile of Issues and Trends. In *Cultural Boundaries and the Cohesion of Canada*, ed. by Raymond Breton, Jeffrey G. Reitz, and Victor F. Valentine, 45. Montreal: The Institute for Reasearch on Public Policy.

Wade, E.C.S.
1959   Introduction. In *Introduction to the Study of the Law of the Constitution.* 10th ed. By A.V. Dicey, London: Macmillan.

Warner, A., and K. Renner
1981   The Standard of Social Justice Applied to an Evaluation of Annual Cases Appearing Before the Halifax Courts. *Windsor Yearbook of Access to Justice* 1: 62.

Watson, Debbie
1988   1988 National Compensation Survey. *Canadian Lawyer* 12 (No. 5, June): 6.

Watters, Wendell W.
1976   *Compulsory Parenthood: The Truth About Abortion.* Toronto: McClelland and Stewart.

Weiler, Paul
1980   *Reconcilable Differences.* Toronto: Carswell.

Weisberg, Robert
1985   Criminal Procedure Doctrine: Some Versions of the Skeptical. *The Journal of Criminal Law and Criminology* 76: 832.

Wellington, Harry H.
1982   The Nature of Judicial Review. *Yale Law Journal* 91: 486.

Whitaker, Reginald A.
1984a   Democracy, Federalism and the National Political Communities in Canada. *Socialist Studies* 2: 255.
1984b   The Quebec Cauldron: A Recent Account. In *Quebec: State and Society*, ed. by Alain G. Gagnon, 70. Toronto: Methuen.

White, Julie
1983   *Women and Part-time Work.* Ottawa: The Canadian Advisory Council on the Status of Women.

Williams, Cynthia
1986   The Changing Nature of Citizen Rights. In *Constitutionalism, Citizenship and Society in Canada*. Volume 33 of studies commissioned as part of the research program of the Royal Commission on the Economic Union and Development Prospects for Canada (Alan Cairns and Cynthia Williams, Research Coordinators), 99. Toronto: University of Toronto Press.

Wilson, S. J.
1982   *Women, the Family and the Economy*. Toronto: McGraw-Hill Ryerson.

Wolfe, Christopher
1986   *The Rise of Modern Judicial Review: From Constitutional Interpretation to Judge-Made Law*. New York: Basic Books.

Wright, Eric Olin
1978   *Class Crisis and the State*. London: New Left Books.

Zander, Michael
1985   *A Bill of Rights?* 3rd. ed. London: Sweet & Maxwell.

Zucker, Symon
1985   Charter Includes Freedom's Price. *The Globe and Mail* (June 3) 7.

INDEX